VOLUME 5

OUT OF EGYPT

Biblical Theology and Biblical Interpretation

The Scripture and Hermeneutics Series

Series Editors
Craig Bartholomew
Anthony Thiselton

Consultant Editors
Ann Holt
Karl Möller

Editorial Advisory Board
James Catford
Fred Hughes
Tremper Longman III
Francis Martin
Gordon McConville
Christopher Seitz
Janet Martin Soskice
Nick Wolterstorff

SCRIPTURE AND HERMENEUTICS SERIES

VOLUME 5

OUT OF EGYPT

Biblical Theology and Biblical Interpretation

editors

CRAIG BARTHOLOMEW • MARY HEALY
KARL MÖLLER • ROBIN PARRY

UNIVERSITY OF
GLOUCESTERSHIRE

PATERNOSTER PRESS

bible society

REDEEMER
University College

BAYLOR
UNIVERSITY

ZONDERVAN®

First published 2004 jointly
in the UK by Paternoster Press, an imprint of Authentic Media,
9 Holdom Avenue, Bletchley, Milton Keynes, MK1 1QR, UK
Website: www.authenticmedia.co.uk
and in the United States of America by Zondervan
5300 Patterson Ave SE, Grand Rapids, Michigan 49530
www.zondervan.com

British Library Cataloguing in Publication Data
A catalogue record for this book is available from the British Library
ISBN 1-84227-069-9

Library of Congress Cataloging-in-Publication Data
Out of Egypt : biblical theology and biblical interpretation / edited by
Craig Bartholomew ... [et al.].— 1st ed.
     p. cm. — (Scripture and hermeneutics series ; v. 5)
     Includes bibliographical references and indexes.
     ISBN 978-0-310-23415-9 (U.S.)   ISBN 1-84227-069-9 (U.K.)
     1. Bible—Theology. 2. Bible—Hermeneutics.
I. Bartholomew, Craig G., 1961- II. Series.
     BS543.O86 2004
     230'.041—dc22
2004013843

Cover Design by Gert Swart and Zak Benjamin, South Africa
Typeset by WestKey Ltd, Falmouth, Cornwall
Printed in the United States of America
Printed on acid free paper

Dr Elaine Botha

Contents

Great Themes of the Bible

Preface

The past year has been a time of change for the Scripture and Hermeneutics Seminar. Colin Greene moved from the British and Foreign Bible Society to take up the position of Dean of the School of Theology and Professor of Systematic Theology at Seattle Pacific University. We wish him well in his role there. I myself have moved from Cheltenham to take up the H. Evan Runner Chair at Redeemer University College in Ancaster, Ontario, Canada. Amidst these changes the work of the Seminar has forged ahead and we are delighted to see this volume making its appearance – there can be few more important subjects than biblical theology and biblical interpretation if we are concerned to see a renewal of interpretation of the Bible as Scripture. Our hope and prayer is that *Out of Egypt* will complement other efforts in renewing interest in biblical theology.

Several new additions to the Scripture and Hermeneutics 'team' need to be mentioned. We are delighted that Anthony Thiselton has agreed to become a Series Editor for the project. He needs no introduction – suffice it to note that his support and expertise is a great blessing. Ann Holt replaces Colin Greene as Consultant Editor – Ann joined the management team at Bible Society this past year and we welcome her expertise and positive input in the Seminar. Karl Möller, now teaching at St Martin's College, Lancaster, has also been made a Consultant Editor. Our Editorial Advisory Board has been expanded to include James Catford, Chief Executive of the British and Foreign Bible Society, Father Francis Martin who holds the Joel E. Smilow Chair for the Study of Catholic-Jewish Relations at the Intercultural Forum of the John Paul II Cultural Center, Washington, DC and Tremper Longman III, the Robert H. Gundry Professor of Biblical Studies at Westmont College, Santa Barbara, California.

We are also glad to welcome Redeemer University College as our Canadian partner in the Scripture and Hermeneutics Seminar. The four partners in the project are the University of Gloucestershire, British and Foreign Bible Society, Baylor University and now Redeemer.

Rosemary Hales, on secondment from Bible Society to the project, continues to do sterling work and her administration has been indispensable during this year of change in ensuring the timely production of this volume.

Preface

It is a pleasure to dedicate this volume to *Dr. Elaine Botha* on her retirement from Redeemer University College. Elaine was involved in the discussions about the Seminar from its inception. She played an important role in bringing several major academics into the project, and has participated in several of the consultations. While she was Vice President Academic at Redeemer, Redeemer hosted our consultation on language and biblical interpretation, the proceedings of which are now published in the Scripture and Hermeneutics Series as *After Pentecost*. Elaine is herself a distinguished philosopher and has worked tirelessly to show that faith seeking understanding is the path to pursue in Christian scholarship. Elaine is engaged at present in a research project on metaphor, and we wish her well in her retirement and her ongoing research.

Craig Bartholomew,
Ancaster, Canada,
May 2004

Contributors

Craig Bartholomew is the H. Evan Runner Professor of Philosophy and Professor of Theology and Religion at Redeemer University College, Ancaster, Canada as well as Visiting Professor in Biblical Hermeneutics at Chester University College. He is the author of *Reading Ecclesiastes* and co-author of *The Drama of Scripture*. Craig heads up the Scripture and Hermeneutics Seminar.

Stephen Barton is Reader in New Testament in the Department of Theology, University of Durham, and Assistant Curate at St John's Neville Cross, Durham. His publications include *The Spirituality of the Gospels*; *Discipleship and Family Ties in Mark and Matthew*; *Invitation to the Bible* and *Life Together: Family, Sexuality and Community in the New Testament and Today*. He has also edited *Holiness Past and Present*.

Richard Bauckham is Professor of New Testament Studies and Bishop Wardlaw Professor at the University of St Andrews, Scotland. He has published widely in the fields of theology and biblical studies. Recent books include *God Crucified: Monotheism and Christology in the New Testament*; *James: Wisdom of James, Disciple of Jesus the Sage*; *Gospel Women: Studies of the Named Women in the Gospels*; *God and the Crisis of Freedom: Biblical and Contemporary Perspectives* and *Bible and Mission: Christian Witness in a Postmodern World*.

Gerald Bray is Anglican Professor of Divinity at Samford University in Birmingham, Alabama. He is the editor of the Anglican journal Churchman and has written several books, including *The Doctrine of God*; *Creeds, Councils, and Christ* and *Biblical Interpretation: Past and Present*. He has also contributed three volumes to the Ancient Christian Commentary on Scripture.

Nuria Calduch-Benages is Professor of Wisdom Literature and Biblical Anthropology at the Pontifical Gregoriana University in Rome. She is General Assistant of her congregation 'Missionary Daughters of the Holy Family of Nazareth'. She is the author of *Otro gallo le cantara: Refranes, dichos y expresiones de origen bíblico*. She has also co-edited *Bibliographie zu Ben Sira* and *Treasures of Wisdom: Studies in Ben Sira and the Book of Wisdom*, and is the book review editor of *Biblica* and a member of the International Advisory Panel of the International Society for the Study of Deuterocanonical and Cognate Literature.

Stephen Chapman is Assistant Professor of Old Testament at Duke Divinity School, where he also serves on the board of directors for the Baptist House of Studies. He is the author of *The Law and the Prophets: A Study in Old Testament Canon Formation* and co-editor of *Biblischer Text und theologische Theoriebildung*. An ordained minister in the American Baptist Churches, USA, he is an active participant in the Baptist World Alliance.

William Dumbrell is a former Vice-Principal of Moore Theological College, Sydney. He has been a frequent contributor to scholarly journals and is the author of several books, including *Covenant and Creation: A Theology of the Old Testament Covenants*; *The Faith of Israel: Its Expression in the Books of the Old Testament* and *The Search for Order: Biblical Eschatology in Focus*. He is at present engaged in an independent ministry of teaching and writing in Sydney, Australia.

James Dunn is Emeritus Lightfoot Professor of Divinity at the University of Durham. Among his many books are *Jesus and the Spirit*; *Unity and Diversity in the New Testament*; *Christology in the Making*; *Jesus, Paul and the Law*; *The Partings of the Ways between Christianity and Judaism*; *The Theology of Paul the Apostle* and *Christianity in the Making* as well as commentaries on Acts, Romans, Galatians, Colossians and Philemon.

Michael Goheen is Associate Professor of Worldview Studies and Missiology in the Religion and Theology Department of Redeemer University College, Canada. He is the author of *'As the Father Has Sent Me, I Am Sending You': J.E. Lesslie Newbigin's Missionary Ecclesiology*, and co-author of *The Drama of Scripture*. He has also published a range of articles on mission in Western culture, worldview, and gospel and culture.

Trevor Hart is Head of the School of Divinity and Principal of St Mary's College in the University of St Andrews. His books include *The Waiting Father: Thomas Erskine of Linlathen*; *Justice the True and Only Mercy: Essays on the Life and Theology of Peter Taylor Forsyth*; *Faith Thinking: The Dynamics of Christian Theology*; *Hope Against Hope: Christian Eschatology in Contemporary Context* (with Richard Bauckham); and *Regarding Karl Barth: Toward a Reading of His Theology*. He is general editor of the *Dictionary of Historical Theology* and director of the Institute for Theology, Imagination and the Arts in the University of St Andrews.

Mary Healy is Council Chair of the Mother of God Community, a lay Catholic community in Gaithersburg, MD, and Adjunct Professor of Scripture at the Institute of Pastoral Theology in Ypsilanti, Michigan. She has also recently joined the faculty of Campion College, a new Catholic college opening in Washington, DC. She is a co-editor of *'Behind' the Text: History and Biblical Interpretation* and the author of several articles.

Andrew Lincoln is Portland Professor of New Testament at the University of Gloucestershire. He was previously Lord and Lady Coggan Professor at Wycliffe College, University of Toronto. His publications include *Paradise Now and Not Yet*; *Ephesians*; *The Theology of the Later Pauline Letters*; *Colossians* and *Truth on Trial*.

Father Francis Martin holds the Joel E. Smilow Chair for the Study of Catholic-Jewish Relations at the Intercultural Forum of the John Paul II Cultural Center in Washington, DC. His books include *Narrative Parallels to the New Testament*; *The Feminist Question: Feminist Theology in the Light of Christian Tradition* and *Fire in the Cloud*. He is consulting editor of *Communio* and chaplain of the Mother of God Community.

Karl Möller is Lecturer in Theology and Religious Studies at St Martin's College, Lancaster, and Senior Tutor at the Carlisle and Blackburn Diocesan Training Institute. He is the author of *A Prophet in Debate: The Rhetoric of Persuasion in the Book of Amos*. He has also co-edited *Renewing Biblical Interpretation* and *After Pentecost: Language and Biblical Interpretation*.

Robin Parry is Commissioning Editor for Paternoster Press. His books include *Old Testament Story and Christian Ethics: The Rape of Dinah as a Case Study* and *Worshipping Trinity: Coming Back to the Heart of Worship*. He has also co-edited *Universal Salvation?*; *The Futures of Evangelicalism* and *The Bible and Epistemology*.

Rusty Reno is Associate Professor of Theology at Creighton University in Omaha, Nebraska. His books include *Redemptive Change: Atonement and the Christian Cure of the Soul* and *In the Ruins of the Church: Sustaining Faith in an Age of Diminished Christianity*. He is the general editor for a forty-volume series of theological commentaries on the Bible, scheduled to begin publication in 2006.

Charles Scobie taught at McGill University, Montreal, and was Head of the Department of Religious Studies and Cowan Professor of Religious Studies at Mount Allison University, Canada, until his retirement in 1998. He is a past president of the Canadian Society of Biblical Studies. His most recent book is *The Ways of Our God: An Approach to Biblical Theology*.

John Webster is Professor of Systematic Theology at the University of Aberdeen. Prior to that, he was Lady Margaret Professor of Divinity at the University of Oxford. He has published widely in the area of contemporary and doctrinal theology. His recent books include *Barth's Moral Theology*; *Word and Church*; *Holiness* and *Holy Scripture*.

Al Wolters is Professor of Religion and Theology/Classical Languages at Redeemer University College, Canada. His publications include *Plotinus 'On Eros': A Detailed Exegetical Commentary on Enneads III, 5*; *Creation Regained: Biblical Basics of a Reformational Worldview* and *The Song of the Valiant Woman: Studies in the Interpretation of Proverbs 31:10–31*.

Christopher Wright is the International Ministries Director of the Langham Partnership International. Prior to that, he taught Old Testament in India from 1983–88 and then returned to the faculty of All Nations Christian College, where he was Principal from 1993–2001. He has written several books, including commentaries on Deuteronomy and Ezekiel, and *Old Testament Ethics for the People of God*.

Abbreviations

AB	Anchor Bible
ACCS	Ancient Christian Commentary on Scripture
Anton	*Antonianum*
ARG	*Archiv für Reformationsgeschichte*
AUSS	*Andrews University Seminary Studies*
Bib	*Biblica*
BTM	Biblical Theology Movement
CBQ	*Catholic Biblical Quarterly*
CC	*Cross Currents*
CSEL	Corpus scriptorum ecclesiasticorum latinorum
ChrCent	*Christian Century*
CJT	*Canadian Journal of Theology*
Comm	*Communio*
CRJ	*Christian Research Journal*
CurTM	*Currents in Theology and Mission*
CSCO	Corpus scriptorum christianorum orientalium
CCSL	Corpus Christianorum: Series latina
CSEL	Corpus scriptorum ecclesiasticorum latinorum
CT	*Christianity Today*
EgT	*Église et Théologie*
ERT	*Evangelical Review of Theology*
ExpTim	*Expository Times*
FRLANT	Forschungen zur Religion und Literatur des Alten und Neuen Testaments
GO	*Göttinger Orientforschungen*
HBT	*Horizons in Biblical Theology*
HR	*History of Religions*
IBC	Interpretation: A Bible Commentary for Teaching and Preaching
Int	*Interpretation*
IDB	*The Interpreter's Dictionary of the Bible*
IJFM	*International Journal of Frontier Missions*
ITQ	*Irish Theological Quarterly*
JAAR	*Journal of the American Academy of Religion*
JBL	*Journal of Biblical Literature*
JETS	*Journal of the Evangelical Theological Society*

JR	*Journal of Religion*
JSNTSup	Journal for the Study of the New Testament: Supplement Series
JSOT	*Journal for the Study of the Old Testament*
JSOTSup	Journal for the Study of the Old Testament: Supplement Series
JTS	*Journal of Theological Studies*
KD	*Kerygma und Dogma*
K&D	Keil, C.F., and F. Delitzsch *Biblical Commentary on the Old Testament*
LD	Lectio divina
LQ	*Lutheran Quarterly*
MTh	*Modern Theology*
NCB	New Century Bible
NEchtB	*Neue Echter Bibel*
NIGTC	New International Greek Testament Commentary
NovTSup	*Supplements to Novum Testamentum*
NTS	*New Testament Studies*
NZST	*Neue Zeitschrift für Systematische Theologie*
OBT	Overtures to Biblical Theology
OTE	*Old Testament Essays*
PG	Patrologia graeca
PL	Patrologia latina
POut	De Prediking van het Oude Testament
ProEccl	*Pro ecclesia*
RB	*Revue biblique*
RSR	*Recherches de science religieuse*
SC	Sources chrétiennes
SHS	Scripture and Hermeneutics Series
SJT	*Scottish Journal of Theology*
TDNT	*Theological Dictionary of the New Testament*
TDOT	*Theological Dictionary of the Old Testament*
TGl	*Theologie und Glaube*
Theol	*Theology*
ThTo	*Theology Today*
TJ	*Trinity Journal*
TRev	*Theologische Revue*
TRu	*Theologische Rundschau*
TS	*Theological Studies*
TynBul	*Tyndale Bulletin*
UTB	Uni-Taschenbücher
VE	*Vox evangelica*
VTSup	Supplements to Vetus Testamentum
WUNT	Wissenschaftliche Untersuchungen zum Neuen Testament
ZAW	*Zeitschrift für die alttestamentliche Wissenschaft*

The Artists

Zak Benjamin, Painter and Printmaker

Calvin Seerveld has thus characterized Zak Benjamin's style: '... bright gaiety and humour combined with ethereal seriousness. Like the unusual world of *One Hundred Years of Solitude* (Gabriel García Márquez), the paintings hold together, as natural, the most outlandish realities. Bold naiveté of forms and colours, stories of mysteries and conflict, trouble and healing – with a difference: friendly, zany, readable, provoking the viewer to look again ... a wholesome pleasure in the grit of life.'

Benjamin's friendship with sculptor Gert Swart is grounded in their mutual struggle to discover what it means to make contemporary art as Christians in post-apartheid South Africa.

His work is represented in collections internationally. He is married and lives in Vereeniging, South Africa, and has two daughters and two granddaughters.

http://zakbenjaminartist.homestead.com/index.html

Gert Swart

Gert Swart was born in Durban, South Africa, where he qualified and worked as a public health inspector before studying fine art for two years at the Natal Technikon. He now resides in Pietermaritzburg, South Africa, and works as a sculptor. He is married to Istine Rodseth.

Gert's most important solo exhibition of this period was staged at the Tatham Art Gallery in 1997. This exhibition, titled 'Contemplation: A body of work by Gert Swart', expressed the redemption of an individual as a metamorphosis from the curse of death to the hope of resurrection and how this transition affects the individual's relationship to society, nature and God.

One of Swart's most significant commissions of the past decade was a monument erected on the battlefield at Isandlwana in 1999. Although the battle of Isandlwana is known for its stunning defeat of a colonial army by an unconventional army, only monuments to fallen British soldiers had been erected on it in the past. It was a privilege to be involved in redressing this injustice and a challenge to design a monument that honours the fallen Zulu warriors but does not glorify war.

Recently Gert was commissioned by the Evangelical Seminary of Southern Africa (ESSA) to make a cross that would reflect the violence and suffering experienced in Southern Africa, particularly in the province of KwaZulu – Natal, RSA. While being a stark depiction of the cross as a brutal means of execution, the ESSA Cross is primarily a powerful symbol of hope: of the saving grace of God.

Gert met Zak Benjamin at a Christian Arts Festival over a decade ago. He and Benjamin were among the founder members of the Christian Worldview Network initiated by Craig Bartholomew. They enjoy a rich friendship that is currently finding expression in the joint design of book covers for this series in collaboration with Craig. This design project is the fruit of Craig's concern for Christian artists and his friendship with Gert and Zak.

http://gertswartsculptor.homestead.com/index.html

Flight into Egypt by Pranas Domsaitis
is used by permission of IZIKO Museums of Cape Town.

Out of Egypt by Gert Swart and Zak Benjamin

Out of Egypt

Out of Egypt alludes to Matthew 2:15. Matthew tells the story of Mary, Joseph and Jesus' escape from Egypt and then says, 'And so was fulfilled what the Lord had said through the prophet: "Out of Egypt I called my son."' The prophet Matthew is referring to Hosea – in Hosea 11:1 'out of Egypt' evokes the exodus and how in his great love God brought the Israelites out of slavery and to himself.

On the surface it is of course not at all obvious how Hosea 11:1 is fulfilled in Jesus escaping from Egypt. But as one reflects more deeply on Jesus relationship to Israel one starts to see how profound the sense might be in which Jesus, fulfils God's call of his people out of Egypt. *Out of Egypt* is thus useful shorthand for evoking the challenges *and* the richness of biblical theology.

The covers for the American edition and the British edition depict in different ways the theme of Jesus' escape from Egypt. The Swart–Benjamin version introduces a large church into the picture, the multiple doors and pathways symbolising the varieties of entrances one can take into biblical theology. Biblical theology can, legitimately, be done in a variety of styles. Is there, then, no main entrance into the edifice of biblical theology? The painting does not solve this controversial issue but – note the orange, glowing front door and its resonance with the orange halo of the Christ child – it does suggest that Christ will be/should be the centre of any *biblical* theology.

Biblical Theology and Biblical Interpretation

Introduction

Craig G. Bartholomew

'The real question is not whether to do Biblical Theology or not, but rather what kind of Biblical Theology does one have.'[1]

It is hard, in my opinion, to overestimate the importance of biblical theology for the Christian church. Week after week congregations confess in response to the readings from the Bible that 'This is the Word of the LORD', and we reply 'Thanks be to God.'[2] However it is difficult, some would say impossible, to translate that thankfulness into hard work on the Bible in the academy. For built into that confession is a strong sense of the Bible as a unified, coherent word from God,[3] and in large swathes of the academy we have in practice, if not in theory, given up on our attempts to articulate the unity of the Bible on its own terms. And that, after all, is what the discipline of biblical theology is all about. Biblical theology is, in my opinion, the attempt to grasp Scripture in its totality according to its own, rather than imposed, categories.[4]

---

[1] Childs, *Biblical Theology in Crisis*, 95.

[2] Or some such response.

[3] As Childs, *Biblical Theology in Crisis*, 8, rightly asserts, 'The Christian Church responded to this literature as the authoritative word of God, and it remains existentially committed to an inquiry into its inner unity because of its confession of the one gospel of Jesus Christ which it proclaims to the world.'

[4] For a discussion of the definition of biblical theology see Barr, *Concept*, ch. 1. My definition is akin to what Barr calls 'pan-biblical theology' because it insists on relating biblical theology to the whole of the Bible. This is not to deny the value of theologies of parts of the Bible but to argue that biblical theology should always be oriented towards the whole. In this volume we have not insisted on a particular definition of biblical theology.

The origin of biblical theology is commonly traced back to Johann Gabler's inaugural address, 'On the proper distinction between biblical and dogmatic theology and the specific objectives of each', given on 30 March 1787. Gabler commences his inaugural with his concern about the variety of views among Christians. One of the reasons he discerns for this variety is the failure to distinguish biblical theology from dogmatic theology. Gabler contrasts religion with theology:

> Religion then, is every-day, transparently clear knowledge; but theology is subtle, learned knowledge, surrounded by a retinue of many disciplines, and by the same token derived not only from the sacred Scripture but also from elsewhere, especially from the domain of philosophy and history.[5]

Gabler associates the Bible with religion in this contrast. He argues that, 'There is truly a biblical theology, of historical origin, conveying what the holy writers felt about divine matters; on the other hand there is a dogmatic theology of didactic origin ...'[6] Biblical theology remains the same, whereas dogmatics changes all the time.

Gabler's understanding of biblical theology is deeply rationalistic. There is much in the Bible that is culturally conditioned, and he argues that we need to separate the things in the Bible which refer to their own times from the 'pure notions which divine providence wished to be characteristic of all times and places'.[7] Thus we firstly need to collect the sacred ideas of the authors and then classify them, after which we should compare them with the universal ideas of reason. From this process biblical theology will appear.

Gabler was not original in making the distinction between biblical theology and dogmatics; rather he sought methodological clarity on the relationship between them.[8] Gabler's whole approach is so coloured by rationalism that one is tempted to dismiss him out of court, but this would be a mistake. His distinguishing of biblical theology from theology is helpful and, I suggest, an important step in the differentiation of biblical theology in the 'theological encyclopaedia'. For biblical theology to flourish as an entity in its own right such a distinction is important, provided we can distinguish it from Gabler's rationalism.

Does this originating moment of biblical theology mean that it never existed before 1787? Barr argues that it is anachronistic to see Calvin and others as doing 'biblical theology',[9] while Childs argues that biblical theology has a history going back to the early church fathers. Certainly the church fathers

---

[5] Gabler, 'An Oration', 495.
[6] Gabler, 'An Oration', 495.
[7] Gabler, 'An Oration', 496.
[8] Childs, *Biblical Theology*, 4.
[9] *Concept*, 3.

were drenched in Scripture. Wilken tells of how in his research into the church fathers he has been impressed by

> the omnipresence of the Bible in early Christian writings. Early Christian thought is biblical, and one of the lasting accomplishments of the patristic period was to forge a way of thinking, scriptural in language and inspiration, that gave to the church and to Western civilization a unified and coherent interpretation of the Bible as a whole.[10]

Wilken notes that 'when they [the first Christian thinkers] took the Bible in hand they were overwhelmed. It came upon them like a torrent leaping down the side of a mountain'.[11] Clement's writings embody a 'conceptual framework drawn from the Bible'.[12] And in his struggle with Marcion and the Gnostics over the unity of the Bible, Irenaeus articulates the unity of the Bible as a single story:

> Two histories converge in the biblical account, the history of Israel and the life of Christ, but because they are also the history of God's actions in and for the world, they are part of a larger narrative that begins at creation and ends in a vision of a new, more splendid city in which the 'Lord God will be their light.' The Bible begins, as it were, with the beginning and ends with an end that is no end, life with God, in Irenaeus's charming expression, a life in which one is 'always conversing with God in new ways.' Nothing falls outside of its scope.[13]

With Irenaeus's narrative approach to the Bible we certainly have an incipient biblical theology. The unity of the Testaments is affirmed – there is one God who called Abraham, spoke with Moses, sent the prophets and is also the father of our Lord Jesus Christ[14] – and is articulated in terms of the story shape of the Bible as a whole. Furthermore, the story is explained in terms of the theme of renewal, or re-creation.[15]

---

[10] Wilken, *The Spirit*, xvii.

[11] Wilken, *The Spirit*, 53.

[12] Wilken, *The Spirit*, 60.

[13] Wilken, *The Spirit*, 63.

[14] The issues Irenaeus wrestled with remain highly relevant today. The relationship between the Old Testament and New Testament is perhaps the major issue in any biblical theology. See Reventlow, *Problems of Biblical Theology*, who devotes almost the entirety of his book to this issue. And Irenaeus's fight to affirm the identity of the LORD with the God and Father of our Lord Jesus Christ remains foundational for the practice of a Christian biblical theology. In response to salvation historical readings of the Bible, Reventlow (*Problems*, 14) asserts that by itself the Christ event should not be regarded as a continuation of the Old Testament event; only faith sees it thus. Such an (faith) assumption seems to me to be an indispensable starting point for a Christian biblical theology.

[15] Reventlow, *Problems*, 66. See Bartholomew and Goheen in this volume, as well as Gunton, *Christ and Creation*, for the importance of Irenaeus in discerning the shape of the Bible as a whole.

Nevertheless, for all the common ground one finds with biblical theology in the church fathers, Aquinas and the Reformers, it remains true that prior to Gabler's time theology and biblical theology were undifferentiated.[16] It is this differentiation that Gabler is associated with, and provided it can be carefully distinguished from his rationalism and the endless fragmentation of the Bible that historical criticism led to, it is a helpful and legitimate distinction because it allows biblical theology as distinct from systematic theology to come into focus in its own right.

The story of biblical theology since Gabler has often been told and I will not repeat it here.[17] Bauer was the first to distinguish Old Testament and New Testament theology, and soon the view arose that the discontinuities between the Testaments were so strong as to defy attempts to articulate their unity. The related stress on the diversity of Scripture that has been central to most historical criticism has haunted biblical theology to this day.

The more immediate context for contemporary efforts in biblical theology is the rise and demise of the so-called Biblical Theology Movement (BTM). Dates for this movement can be set with precision, namely from around the end of World War II to 1961, when publications by Gilkey and Barr are said to have sunk the BTM. The BTM was strongly Protestant, particularly American and consciously oriented towards reading the Bible for the church, while acknowledging the legitimacy of historical criticism. The BTM was connected with the emergence of the neo-orthodoxy of Barth, although it tended to be suspicious of Barth's supposed rejection of historical criticism. Indeed, Brunner rather than Barth was the greater influence on the BTM.

The BTM in the United States represented a major attempt to break out of the impasse of the modernist/fundamentalist debate about the Bible that had plagued American churches, through a vibrant recovery of biblical theology. Its major emphases were:[18]

A recovery of the Bible as a *theological* book. Historical criticism has a legitimate role to play, but it represents the start, and not the end; it must lead us to hear God address us through his word, and biblical theology is a major ingredient in this respect. G. Ernest Wright, one of the major representatives of the BTM, lamented the neglect of biblical theology and noted that it was difficult to find a leading graduate school where one could specialize in it.[19]

---

[16] On the church fathers and biblical theology see the chapter by Gerald Bray in this volume.

[17] See, e.g., Hasel, *Old Testament Theology*, ch. 1. This is not to say that it does not need to be retold. An urgent need of our time is the retelling of the story of biblical studies and biblical theology, so that we can truly discern what is at stake in the story – such consciousness is a vital ingredient in any renewal of biblical interpretation.

[18] I am leaning heavily here on Childs's classic *Biblical Theology in Crisis*, which tells the story of the BTM.

[19] Childs, *Biblical Theology in Crisis*, 36, 37.

The BTM stressed the *unity of the Bible* as a whole and regarded it as vital that we overcome the chasm that had opened up between Old Testament and New Testament. Wright noted that 'The scholarly study of the Old Testament has been separated from that of the New and from its moorings in the proclamation of the Church.'[20] He diagnoses the condition of biblical interpretation in his day as a revival of Marcionism and argues strongly against this:

> Surely, if the New Testament is not proclaimed as the fulfillment of the Old, if the Gospel as proclaimed by Jesus and by Paul is not the completion of the faith of Israel, then it must inevitably be a completion and fulfillment of something which we ourselves substitute – and that most certainly means a perversion of the Christian faith.[21]

Wright himself articulates the unity of the Bible through a recitation of the great acts of God, finding their fulfilment in Jesus of Nazareth.

The BTM, as is evident from Wright's approach described in point two, above, made *God's revelation of himself in history* central to biblical theology. The pagan religions of the ancient Near East had no concept of history; in this respect Israel was regarded as utterly unique, and God reveals his being and will through his great acts, and particularly in the Old Testament through his redemption of the Israelites from Egypt.

Fourthly, the BTM laid great stress on *the distinctiveness of the biblical perspective*. In this respect it reacted strongly to the tendency among scholars to explain Israel's faith as part of an evolving history of religion. Israel's view of God and the world was quite unique in its ancient Near Eastern context and this stemmed from God's revelation of himself to Israel.[22]

By 1961 the BTM, which manifested such energy and hope for a recovery of the Bible, was verging on collapse. What were the structural deficiencies that facilitated the demise of this great edifice? Childs argues that there were a host of unresolved problems in the BTM that eroded it from within and made it vulnerable to the sort of attack from Barr and Gilkey from without.

According to Childs, the BTM never resolved the issue of the Bible and its authority. Fundamentalism was rejected, but so too was Barth's use of the Bible, which was regarded as not taking historical criticism sufficiently seriously. Problematically, no clear alternative emerged to either of these views. For all of its emphasis on the Bible, the BTM failed to produce great commentaries and generally seemed to confine its use of the Bible to a few favourite books.

Secondly, the emphases of the BTM were seldom translated into educational and curriculum policy in the seminaries. 'Very infrequently did Biblical Theology become an integrating factor that provided a focus for the other

---

[20] Wright, *God Who Acts*, 15.
[21] Wright, *God Who Acts*, 17. Cf. Bright, *Authority*.
[22] See, e.g., Wright, *Old Testament*.

disciplines.'[23] This meant inter alia that changes in systematic theology and hermeneutics left biblical theology vulnerable and with little defence.

In the late 1950s and in the 1960s the church was feeling the need to respond to the modern world and the great diversity of challenges it represented, challenges which extended way beyond the institutional church. The BTM appeared to be sorely lacking in this respect – it had not given rise to a new style of preaching and theological ethics seemed to be getting along quite well without it.

The BTM's emphasis on God's acts *in history* appeared to solve many problems, but this apparent success concealed some major cracks in its edifice, cracks which James Barr and Langdon Gilkey exploited ruthlessly. The distinctiveness of Israel's perspective was also being questioned as scholars such as Frank Moore Cross demonstrated that Israel's neighbours were much closer to her views in all sorts of ways than the BTM proponents had allowed. We will explore Barr's and Gilkey's critiques in more detail below – suffice it here to note that their publications in 1961 were perceived as dealing a mortal blow to the BTM. Childs says of Barr's *The Semantics of Biblical Language*, 'Seldom has one book brought down so much superstructure with such effectiveness.'[24]

The consequent thrust of Childs's *Biblical Theology in Crisis* is that biblical theology is in crisis and a new paradigm is required. In *Biblical Theology in Crisis*, and in his subsequent writings, Childs goes on to propose a *canonical* paradigm for biblical theology as the answer to this crisis. Barr argues, by contrast, that Childs overestimates the extent of the problem in order to set the stage for his new paradigm. Indeed, Barr denies that there really was/is a crisis of biblical theology, and biblical theology has continued to flourish in all sorts of ways.[25] What happened, rather, was that biblical theology lost its power to assert itself over against other aspects of the 'theological encyclopaedia'.

Either way, the arguments that facilitated the demise of the BTM bear close scrutiny. It is fascinating to look back now on the arguments that were perceived as fatally damaging for the BTM. Gilkey's 1961 article is entitled 'Cosmology, Ontology, and the Travail of Biblical Language'. He argues that the BTM got caught between being half liberal and modern and half biblical and orthodox: 'its world view or cosmology is modern, while its theological language is biblical and orthodox'.[26] In opposition to liberalism, the BTM asserted its belief in revelation through God's mighty acts, thereby understanding God's speech and acts literally and univocally. At the same time it held on to the modern belief in the causal continuum. As Gilkey notes,

---

[23]   Childs, *Biblical Theology in Crisis*, 56.
[24]   Childs, *Biblical Theology in Crisis*, 72.
[25]   Barr, 'Theological Case', 3, 4.
[26]   Gilkey, 'Cosmology', 194.

this assumption of a causal order among phenomenal events, and therefore of the authority of the scientific interpretation of observable events, makes a great difference to the validity one assigns to biblical narratives and so to the way one understands their meaning.[27]

A modern understanding of causality means that most of the biblical events did not in fact happen; they become symbols instead: '*we* believe that the biblical people lived in the same causal continuum of space and time in which we live, and so one in which no divine wonders transpired and no divine voices were heard'.[28] Gilkey probes the writings of the BTM in this respect and finds them riddled with contradictions. He argues that the implication of this tension for the BTM is that the Bible is really a book of great acts the Hebrews believed God to have done but which we know he in fact did not do. The result is that the mighty acts of God are reduced to God's 'inward incitement of a religious response to an ordinary event within the space-time continuum',[29] akin to Schleiermacher's emphasis on religious experience.

Gilkey argues that the BTM needs a more sophisticated view of language and a theological ontology. Hebrew recital must be distinguished from our recital; the biblical writers use language *univocally* whereas we know that we can only speak of God *analogically*. Furthermore, we need to relate the biblical message to our understanding of the world:

> For this reason, while the dependence of systematic and philosophical theology on biblical theology has long been recognized and is obvious, the dependence of an intelligible theology that is biblical on the cosmological and ontological inquiries of believing men, while now less universally accepted, is nonetheless real.[30]

Living as we do in the light of 'postmodernism's' undermining of many aspects of modernity, it is remarkable to think how effective was Gilkey's argument. As with Bultmann and Barr and so much modern thought, there is an implicit assumption of the modern myth of progress. The contemporary perspective is simply assumed and absolutized without ever being argued for. It is now more apparent, however, that Gilkey is assuming the particular perspective of modernity,[31] as well as misrepresenting the biblical and Christian tradition.

---

[27] Gilkey, 'Cosmology', 195.

[28] Gilkey, 'Cosmology', 196.

[29] Gilkey, 'Cosmology', 201.

[30] Gilkey, 'Cosmology', 205.

[31] Berger, *Rumour*, 46, 47, helpfully alerts us to the fact that, 'it may be conceded that there is in the modern world a certain type of consciousness that has difficulties with the supernatural. The statement remains, however, on the level of socio-historical diagnosis. The diagnosed condition is not thereupon elevated to the status of an absolute criterion: the contemporary situation is not immune to relativizing analysis.

Even within the Bible there is awareness that its language of God is not univocal, and certainly the Christian tradition[32] is well aware of the complexity of its language for and of God.[33]

Barr's critique of the BTM relates to two main areas: the concept of revelation and history central to the BTM;[34] and its misuse of word studies and the so-called Greek/Hebrew contrast in views of the world.[35] Barr's critique of the historical emphasis of the BTM is similar to that of Gilkey. He focuses on the antinomy or 'double talk'[36] between the confession of God's acts in history and history as the result of critical examination of data. Barr furthermore finds that substantial parts of the Bible do not fit with an historical emphasis.

Barr's better known critique is of the BTM's persistent failure to take modern semantics into account – thus it is guilty time and again of 'illegitimate totality transfer' and thereby wrongly reads meanings into words. Barr is critical of the tendency of the BTM to find the distinctive theological content of the Bible in its vocabulary, as exemplified for example in the Kittel-Friedrich dictionary. Barr devotes an entire book to the BTM's handling of the biblical words dealing with time.[37] According to Barr, Cullman's theology of time in the Bible is illegitimate because:

> The whole case being argued is that the Bible has, and normally and constantly displays, a particular conception of time, which can be traced in its lexical stock and which forms an essential background or presupposition for the understanding of its theology. It is therefore naturally impossible to except any example of usage from full consideration on the grounds that it is 'merely temporal' and not of theological significance.[38]

There was undoubtedly a need for Barr's critique of the understanding of how language worked in the BTM. Indeed Barr mediated modern semantics à la

---

We may say that contemporary consciousness is such and such; we are left with the question of whether we will assent to it.'

[32] Already in Aquinas we find a careful distinction between univocal, equivocal and analogical language.

[33] See, e.g., Horton, *Covenant and Eschatology*, especially ch. 2. Alston and others have developed sustained critiques of Gilkey's view of God (not) acting in our world. Alston, 'Divine and Human Action', 258, argues that language of God may be partly univocal. Alston's excellent 'How to Think About Divine Action' is devoted entirely to a rebuttal of Gilkey's view of God's action as articulated in Gilkey's 1961 article. Alston also notes that, contra Gilkey, we need to distinguish univocal from literal language.

[34] See Barr, 'The Concepts of History and Revelation', in *Old and New*, 65–102.

[35] See Barr, *Semantics*.

[36] See Barr, 'Trends and Prospects', 267, for the language of double-talk.

[37] *Biblical Words*.

[38] *Biblical Words*, 49.

Saussure into biblical studies, and his contribution in this respect has been of lasting importance. However, Francis Watson has recently and rightly argued that Barr's critique of the BTM in this respect is not as devastating as is often suggested, and not least by Barr himself.[39] According to Watson, Barr builds his sweeping criticism on a narrow foundation and wrongly suggests that the errors are foundational to the entire project of the BTM. Watson re-examines Cullmann's work on time, a particular object of Barr's critique, and demonstrates how Cullmann is aware of the diverse ways in which the New Testament words for time are used, but consciously chooses to focus on those occasions which are theologically poignant. For Watson such an approach is quite legitimate. Barr also criticizes Cullmann for his contrast between Hebrew and Greek thought. Cullmann contrasts the New Testament view of the resurrection with the 'Greek' concept of immortality and, as Watson shows, Cullmann is quite right in this respect.

Watson concludes from his analysis of Barr's critique of the BTM that 'there is little basis for his claim that "biblical theology" as once practised was fundamentally and irretrievably flawed. If biblical theology collapsed, it did not do so because of the overwhelming force of its critics' arguments.'[40] Indeed, for Watson, 'There is, then, little or nothing in this piece of modern theological history to deter one from attempting to renew and to redefine biblical theology.'[41]

What is clear from both Gilkey's and Barr's critiques of the BTM is that they stem from particular theological outlooks. The demise of the BTM is related to the radicalization of modern theology at the time, and Barr appeals regularly to this 'progress' as part of his critique. Indeed a common element in Barr's armoury is the appeal to progress. Thus, in his 1974 article on 'Trends and Prospects in Biblical Theology', he argues contra the BTM's concern to see the Bible as a whole that '*the tendency now* is to say that there is no one theology, either of the Old Testament or of the New, and still less of the entire Bible: rather, the Bible, and each Testament contains a number of quite different theologies, the theologies of different strata, different writers, and different periods'.[42] Likewise in his *The Bible in the Modern World*, Barr stresses that *nowadays* there is less enthusiasm for reading the Bible as a whole.[43]

This style of argument is found regularly in Barr's critique of the BTM,[44] and it is a style of argument which lays great weight on the theological trends of

---

[39] Watson, *Text and Truth*, 18–28.

[40] Watson, *Text and Truth*, 24.

[41] Watson, *Text and Truth*, 26.

[42] Barr, 'Trends and Prospects', 270 (italics mine).

[43] Barr, *Bible*, 6.

[44] Watson, *Text and Truth*, 23, 24, also notes this tendency of Barr to work out of a particular theological style which privileges the more radical spectrum in theology.

one's immediate context, thereby suggesting that theology has progressed towards this point. What is lacking in Barr's and Gilkey's approach is a healthy sense of plurality in theology and the way in which different theological perspectives might relate to something like the BTM. Barr's approach is very much that of liberal theology, whereas Childs's is that of a scholar working in the Reformed, Barthian tradition, and these contexts orient them towards biblical theology and the BTM in quite different ways. Theological context makes a huge difference when it comes to (the very possibility of) biblical theology, and it helps to be aware of all the elements in the often vitriolic debates around the subject.

Barr suggests, as noted above, that there never really was a crisis in biblical theology, but that Childs needed there to be one to justify his new canonical approach to the subject. This seems to me somewhat ingenious in the light of the successful attacks by Barr on the BTM, but it does alert us to the fact that biblical theology was always more than the BTM. There were real problems with the BTM, as Childs indicates. Although these were not as serious as Barr and Gilkey suggest, it is important to note that the well-being of biblical theology does not stand or fall with the BTM. Within the evangelical tradition, for example, biblical theology continued to thrive despite the so-called death knell of the BTM in 1961. Scholars such as Herman Ridderbos, O. Palmer Robertson, George Eldon Ladd, Meredith Kline, Graeme Goldsworthy, Bill Dumbrell[45] and others continued to take biblical theology seriously in the years following the demise of the BTM, with the result that a corpus of ongoing work in biblical theology is available from the evangelical stable.[46] And, since 1960, multiple works in Old Testament and New Testament theology, plus studies of the theology of parts of the Bible, have been published.[47] What is noticeably lacking, however, are a plethora of attempts at a theology of the Bible as a whole.[48] Recent decades have witnessed the appearance of only two major biblical theologies, namely those by Childs and Scobie. If biblical theology is concerned with the Bible as a whole, then this may be more significant than the multitude of publications Barr refers to, and may well indicate that biblical theology remains in something of a crisis.

---

[45] Goldsworthy and Dumbrell both worked for many years at Moore College in Sydney, Australia, where biblical theology has been a core part of the curriculum for many years, stemming from (Archbishop) Donald Robinson's innovative leadership.

[46] See, e.g., Alexander and Rosner (eds.), *New Dictionary of Biblical Theology: Exploring the Unity and Diversity of Scripture*.

[47] Consider, e.g., Brueggemann's works on Old Testament theology.

[48] Writing in 1973, Harrington, *Path*, 260, noted that for all the work on biblical theology, 'there are practically no theologies of the whole Bible'. A similar lack exists today.

Quo Vadis?

Childs discerns the following eight models for biblical theology nowadays:[49]

1. Biblical theology organized according to the categories of dogmatics
2. Allegorical or typological approaches
3. A great ideas or themes approach
4. A history of redemption approach
5. Literary approaches
6. The cultural–linguistic method
7. Sociological perspectives
8. Jewish biblical theology

Childs interacts critically with each of these approaches and then makes a new proposal for a canonical biblical theology.[50] He remains as committed as ever to his earlier view that 'There is a need for a discipline that will attempt to retain and develop a picture of the whole, and that will have a responsibility to synthesize as well as analyze.'[51] The canon is the proper context within which such biblical theology is to be done. 'The Scriptures of the church are not archives of the past but a channel of life for the continuing church, through which God instructs and admonishes his people.'[52] Biblical theology must take the different extent of the canon in Catholic compared with Protestant circles seriously and it must 'participate in the search for the Christian Bible'.[53] Utterly central to biblical theology must be the question of the Old Testament–New Testament relationship, and this needs to be carefully nuanced:

> At the heart of the problem of Biblical Theology lies the issue of doing full justice to the subtle canonical relationship of the two testaments within the one Christian Bible. On the one hand, the Christian canon asserts the continuing integrity of the OT witness. It must be heard on its own terms … On the other hand, the NT makes its own witness … the challenge of Biblical Theology is to engage in the continual activity of theological reflection which studies the canonical text in detailed exegesis, and seeks to do justice to the witness of both testaments in the light of its subject matter who is Jesus Christ.[54]

In *Biblical Theology in Crisis*, Childs used the citations of the Old Testament in the New Testament as a major route into the biblical theology of both

---

[49] *Biblical Theology of the Old and New Testaments*, 11–29.
[50] This is an extension of his earlier proposal in *Biblical Theology in Crisis*.
[51] Childs, *Biblical Theology in Crisis*, 92.
[52] Childs, *Biblical Theology in Crisis*, 99.
[53] Childs, *Biblical Theology of the Old and New Testaments*, 67.
[54] Childs, *Biblical Theologyof the Old and New Testaments*, 78, 79.

Testaments. But by the time of his *Biblical Theology of the Old and New Testaments* Childs is more wary of this approach, lest it undermine the discrete witness of the Old Testament.[55] The way in which the New Testament uses the Old need not exhaust the witness of the Old, and it is vital that we attend to the discrete witness of each Testament in its own right. Consequently, Childs organizes his *Biblical Theology of the Old and New Testaments* according to the following sections:

- Discrete witness of the Old Testament
- Discrete witness of the New Testament
- Theological reflection on the Christian Bible

Childs's extensive work on biblical theology positions him as the leading authority in this area today. Barr has been his great nemesis, but without producing a comparable corpus in constructive biblical theology.[56] What can we learn from Childs's work about the way forward for biblical theology and biblical interpretation?

1. Childs never lost sight of the vital importance of biblical theology for the church, and nor should we.

In *Biblical Theology in Crisis* Childs observed that, 'It is highly significant that many of the leading Biblical scholars of the present generation, while at times critical of the older theological positions, still identify with the long-range goals of the movement and share in gratitude a strong sense of solidarity with this generation of church-oriented scholars.'[57] Childs recognized the legitimacy of many of the criticisms of the BTM, but this did not lead him to abandon biblical theology but to a concerted attempt to establish it on better, more rigorous, foundations. A critique of the BTM was that it lacked academic rigour. Such a criticism could never be levelled against Childs's wide-ranging work on biblical theology, and our continued attempts to reinvigorate biblical theology must learn from this. 'The challenge of the Christian interpreter in our day is to hear the full range of notes within all of Scripture, to wrestle with the theological interpretation of this Biblical witness, and above all, to come to grips with the agony of our age before a living God who still speaks through the prophets and apostles.'[58]

---

[55] *Biblical Theology of the Old and New Testaments*, 76.

[56] This is not to say that Barr's position does not hold real potential for doing biblical theology. In our chapter in this volume, Mike Goheen and I find Barr's view of story most helpful in this respect.

[57] Childs, *Biblical Theology in Crisis*, 92.

[58] Childs, *Biblical Theology in Crisis*, 163.

As we have noted above, the critique of the BTM was not nearly as devastating as many thought at the time, and there is a significant legacy to be salvaged from the BTM. We need *inter alia* to revisit the BTM's vast corpus of literature and to separate off the chaff from the wheat. I suspect there is a lot of wheat there that we can distil into contemporary work on biblical theology.

2. Childs recognizes that biblical theology will flourish or decay in relation to certain theological perspectives, and so should we.

In Childs's opinion we need a strong sense of the Bible as canon for the Christian church as *the* context in which biblical theology should be done. Childs upholds the valuable contribution of historical criticism but insists on linking the historical and the theological. Biblical theology will be descriptive but always oriented towards the Christian church.

It seems to me that Childs here puts his finger on issues that are central to the flourishing of biblical theology. As I mentioned at the outset of this introduction, the impetus towards biblical theology is a sense of the Bible as God's word as a whole, *tota Scriptura*. Liberal theologies which privilege diversity over ultimate unity will be far less predisposed towards the project of biblical theology in this sense. Thus Childs's Barthianism is demonstrably a far more fecund soil for a constructive biblical theology directed towards the Bible as a whole, compared with Barr's liberalism. This is not for a moment to deny those working in different theological traditions the right to work on biblical theology. The point rather is that there is much to be gained from acknowledging the confessional plurality in theology and making room for different theological approaches to flower in biblical theology, so that real comparisons can be made between divergent approaches.[59]

3. Childs recognizes the distinction between biblical theology and systematic theology, and so should we.

Childs is right, in my opinion, to insist on the descriptive nature of biblical theology, albeit descriptive in the context of a canonical hermeneutic. In this he honours Gabler's differentiation of biblical theology and theology. Childs does not see the relationship between biblical theology and theology as one way – indeed he argues that a good theology will enable us to read Scripture better; this, after all, was the aim of Calvin's *Institutes*. Childs's acknowledgement of

---

[59] Of course, for this to happen we need a genuine pluralism in the academy. Too often a reigning ideology such as 'the discourse of the academy' is asserted so that an overtly theological approach is ruled out of court. See the dialogue between Bartholomew and Plantinga in Bartholomew et al. (eds.), *'Behind' the Text*.

the descriptive nature of biblical theology is significant in terms of the minority renewal of theological interpretation today. As is evident from this volume, the renewal draws heavily on patristic exegesis and often collapses theology and biblical theology back into a single category. Childs does not do this, and personally I think he is right in this respect.

4. Childs makes the relationship between the Old Testament and New Testament central to biblical theology, and so must we.

The Old Testament–New Testament relationship is utterly central to any biblical theology, and we mentioned above Childs's stress on doing justice to the discrete witness of each Testament. Watson, however, argues that Childs's 'treatment of "the discrete witness of the Old Testament" is in practice characterized by the absence of a single, Christological centre as the object of this discrete witness'.[60] Watson finds a healthier paradigm for Old Testament interpretation as a Christian theological enterprise in von Rad and seeks to develop this for biblical theology today.[61] There are complex issues at stake here, but clearly any biblical theology will have to attend closely to how to articulate the relationship between the Testaments. This debate needs to be a priority among biblical theologians.

5. Childs discerns a close connection between biblical theology and theological interpretation, and so should we.

For Childs, biblical theology and theological interpretation of the Bible are distinct but altogether complementary. As we noted above, not all who support the renewal of theological interpretation agree with this.[62] In my opinion it is important to distinguish the two, and to see that biblical theology is an important ingredient in theological interpretation.

In Volume 3 of the Scripture and Hermeneutics Series, *A Royal Priesthood*, we dialogue with Oliver O'Donovan about how to read the Bible ethically and politically. In the introduction to that volume I noted the role of biblical theology in O'Donovan's extraordinarily creative theological interpretation of the Bible.[63] In *Resurrection and Moral Order*, O'Donovan appropriates the Bible

---

[60] Watson, *Text and Truth*, 216.

[61] See Seitz's 'Christological Interpretation', a review of Watson's *Text and Truth*. Commenting on the issue of a discrete witness, Seitz, 'Christological Interpretation', 218, 219, asserts that 'the solution is to be found in a true trinitarian reading, based upon a *regula fidei* with exegetical parameters, not in a christological interpretation whose worry is a discrete voice of the Old Testament'.

[62] Stephen Fowl, *Engaging Scripture*, is an obvious example.

[63] Bartholomew, 'Introduction'.

through the Pauline understanding of resurrection as the reaffirmation of creation. In *The Desire of the Nations*, O'Donovan draws more on a salvation historical approach to God's work with Israel, culminating in Jesus of Nazareth. In both cases biblical theology is the means for appropriating the unity of the Bible and developing theological concepts that can do the work that theology requires.

In my opinion O'Donovan's work is an excellent example of the capacity for biblical theology to fund theological interpretation of the Bible. Childs notes that, 'Whatever shape a new Biblical Theology will take, surely it must be one that will aid in the process of making the knotty ethical decisions that daily confront the Christian.'[64] In *Biblical Theology in Crisis*, Childs laments the paucity of work from the BTM which addressed the cultural issues of the day. Not much has changed since then. There are examples of works relating biblical theology to education, and series such as the 'Overtures to Biblical Theology' have produced some fine examples of this genre. But a great deal of work remains to be done. Works of the calibre of O'Donovan are rare. We need a spate of new works in this genre, drawing deeply upon the best contemporary biblical theology.

6. Childs's work in biblical theology is ecumenical, and so should ours be.

Childs's attempt to renew biblical theology is overtly ecumenical, and it is vital that attempts to renew and reinvigorate biblical theology and biblical interpretation should be so too. One of the most exciting developments in the Scripture and Hermeneutics Seminar is the growing Catholic participation, as is evident in the essays making up this volume. Many of us have been refreshed to find in our Catholic brothers and sisters an equivalent concern to recover and promote biblical theology, and this has been a great source of encouragement. We have learned that it is still the case in Catholic as well as Protestant circles that biblical theology courses are rare in theological curricula, and that there is considerable work needed to get biblical theology firmly on our agendas.[65]

---

[64] *Biblical Theology in Crisis*, 124.

[65] An encouraging example of renewal of interest in biblical theology in Catholic circles is the academic and popular church-oriented work of Scott Hahn. His PhD, *Kinship by Covenant*, is a fascinating examination of the biblical theology of covenant in the Bible, ranging across the Testaments. Scott is also founder and president of the St Paul Center for Biblical Theology, whose website is well worth exploration: www.salvationhistory.com.

Out of Egypt: The Content of this Volume

There is no shortage of work to do if we are to see a healthy renewal of biblical theology and biblical interpretation. Childs and others have provided us with a significant corpus of literature, upon which we need to build. From its inception, the Scripture and Hermeneutics Seminar identified biblical theology as a vital topic in any agenda for renewing biblical interpretation. In September 2003 the Seminar met at St Andrews University to focus intensively on biblical theology and biblical interpretation. We had three stimulating days together in a great environment, and the chapters that make up this volume stem from that consultation. We have divided the essays into four sections.

Section One deals with *Approaches to Biblical Theology*. Gerald Bray examines the relevance of the church fathers for biblical theology. Karl Möller's chapter interacts with the most recent biblical theology, namely that of Charles Scobie, looking in dialogue with Scobie at appropriate methodologies for biblical theology. Chapters 3 and 4, by Father Francis Martin and Nuria Calduch-Benages, respectively, explore contemporary Catholic works in biblical theology thereby bring into the discussion works in languages other than English which are little known in the English world. Chris Wright argues for the fecundity of a missional biblical theology, and in a complementary way Bartholomew and Goheen seek to reinvigorate the possibilities of a narrative biblical theology. James Dunn explores the challenge to the production of biblical theology of the fact that the Old Testament is also the Hebrew Bible.

Section Two includes two *Great Themes of the Bible*. Richard Bauckham explores the theme of monotheism, while Stephen Barton unpacks that of the unity of humankind.

Section Three is concerned with the interpretation of *Parts of the Bible and Biblical Theology*. Al Wolters examines the interface between the interpretation of Zechariah 14 and biblical theology. Bill Dumbrell focuses on the relevance of biblical theology for the difficult challenge of how we read Romans 9:30 – 10:4. Andrew Lincoln explores the significance of the Epistle to the Hebrews for contemporary biblical theology.

Section Four brings together five essays that all deal in one way or another with the relationship between *Theological Interpretation and Biblical Theology*. Trevor Hart discusses the relationship between these two areas through a focus on Moltmann and Barth. John Webster unpacks the contemporary significance of the clarity of Scripture for theology and biblical interpretation. Rusty Reno examines the interface of theological interpretation and biblical theology. Stephen Chapman investigates the role of imagination in biblical theology and theological interpretation. Finally, Charles Scobie assesses the significance of biblical theology for preaching.

We do not for a moment suggest that this volume solves all the pressing challenges facing biblical theology. However, the contributions to this volume do create an agenda for a renewal of biblical theology and suggest a variety of ways forward in this vital area. Much work remains to be done.

Bibliography

Alexander, T.D., and B. Rosner (eds.), *New Dictionary of Biblical Theology: Exploring the Unity and Diversity of Scripture* (Leicester and Downers Grove, IL: IVP, 2000).

Alston, W.P., 'Divine and Human Action', in *Divine and Human Action: Essays in the Metaphysics of Theism* (ed. T.V. Morris; Ithaca and London: Cornell University Press, 1988), 257–80

—, 'How to Think About Divine Action: Twenty-Five Years of Travail for Biblical Language', in *Divine Action: Studies Inspired by the Philosophical Theology of Austin Farrar* (ed. B. Hebblethwaite and E. Henderson; Edinburgh: T. & T. Clark, 1990), 51–70

Barr, J., *Old and New in Interpretation: A Study of the Two Testaments* (London: SCM Press, 1966)

—, *The Bible in the Modern World* (London: SCM Press; Philadelphia: Trinity Press International, 1973)

—, 'Trends and Prospects in Biblical Theology', *JTS* 24 (1974), 265–82

—, 'The Theological Case Against Biblical Theology', in *Canon, Theology and Old Testament Interpretation* (ed. G.M. Tucker, D.L. Petersen and R.R. Wilson; Philadelphia: Fortress Press, 1988), 3–19

—, *The Concept of Biblical Theology: An Old Testament Perspective* (Minneapolis: Fortress Press, 1999)

—, *Biblical Words for Time* (London: SCM Press, 1962)

—, *The Semantics of Biblical Language* (London: Oxford University Press, 1961)

Bartholomew, C.G., 'Introduction', in *A Royal Priesthood? The Use of the Bible Ethically and Politically* (ed. C.G. Bartholomew, J. Chaplin, R. Song and A. Wolters; SHS 3; Carlisle: Paternoster; Grand Rapids: Zondervan, 2002), 1–45

Bartholomew, C., C.S. Evans, M. Healy and M. Rae (eds.), *'Behind' the Text: History and Biblical Interpretation* (SHS 4; Carlisle: Paternoster; Grand Rapids: Zondervan, 2003)

Berger, P., *A Rumour of Angels: Modern Society and the Rediscovery of the Supernatural* (New York: Doubleday, 1990)

Bright, J., *The Authority of the Old Testament* (Nashville: Abingdon Press, 1967)

Childs, B.S., *Biblical Theology in Crisis* (Philadelphia: Westminster Press, 1970)

—, *Biblical Theology of the Old and New Testaments: Theological Reflection on the Christian Bible* (Minneapolis: Fortress Press, 1992)

Fowl, S.E., *Engaging Scripture: A Model for Theological Interpretation* (Oxford: Basil Blackwell, 1998)

Gabler, J.P., 'An Oration on the Proper Distinction between Biblical and Dogmatic Theology and the Specific Objectives of Each', in *The Flowering of Old Testament Theology: A Reader in Twentieth-Century Old Testament Theology,*

1930–1990 (ed. B.C. Ollenburger, E.A. Martens and G.F. Hasel; Winona Lake: Eisenbrauns, 1992), 493–502

Gilkey, L., 'Cosmology, Ontology, and the Travail of Biblical Language', *JR* 41 (July 1961), 194–205

Gunton, C., *Christ and Creation* (Paternoster: Carlisle; Grand Rapids: Eerdmans, 1992)

Hahn, S., *Kinship by Covenant: A Biblical Theological Analysis of Covenant Types and Texts in the Old and New Testaments* (Edinburgh: T. & T. Clark, 2004, forthcoming)

Harrington, W.J., *The Path of Biblical Theology* (London and Dublin: Gill and Macmillan, 1973)

Hasel, G., *Old Testament Theology: Basic Issues in the Current Debate* (Grand Rapids: Eerdmans, 4th edn, 1991)

Hebblethwaite, B., and E. Henderson (eds.), *Divine Action: Studies Inspired by the Philosophical Theology of Austin Farrar* (Edinburgh: T. & T. Clark, 1990)

Horton, M.S., *Covenant and Eschatology: The Divine Drama* (Louisville and London: Westminster John Knox Press, 2002)

Reventlow, H. Graf, *Problems of Biblical Theology in the Twentieth Century* (London: SCM Press, 1986)

Seitz, C., 'Christological Interpretation of Texts and Trinitarian Claims to Truth: An Engagement with Francis Watson's *Text and Truth*', *SJT* 52 (1999), 209–26

Watson, F., *Text and Truth: Redefining Biblical Theology* (Edinburgh: T. & T. Clark, 1997)

Wilken, R.L., *The Spirit of Early Christian Thought: Seeking the Face of God* (New Haven and London: Yale University Press, 2003)

Wright, G.E., *God Who Acts: Biblical Theology as Recital* (London: SCM Press, 1952)

—, *The Old Testament against Its Environment* (London: SCM Press, 1950)

Approaches to Biblical Theology

1

The Church Fathers and Biblical Theology
Gerald Bray

Defining our Terms

Where do the church fathers stand in relation to biblical theology? In one sense, this is an extremely easy question to answer, because if we define the 'church fathers' as those Christian writers who expounded the faith in the centuries when the dominant Greco-Roman culture was still pagan, then it is clear that they all believed that the Judeo-Christian Scriptures were the only acceptable source of Christian theology, and in that sense they could all be called 'biblical theologians' virtually without exception. The difficulty comes when we turn to consider the meaning of the term 'biblical theology'. If we believe that 'biblical theology' is the attempt to grasp Scripture in its totality, according to its own categories and inner dynamic, can the claim of the Fathers to have been 'biblical theologians' be allowed to stand, even if we have to make some reservations when it comes to the phrase 'according to its own categories'.

Problems with the assertion that patristic theology was simply 'biblical theology' inevitably arise when we try to impose modern understandings of what biblical theology is (or ought to be) on the ancient texts. Even allowing for the fact that modern interpreters are by no means always agreed about how the term 'biblical theology' ought to be defined,[1] it is clear that there are some things which are now included in it which would not have occurred to the Fathers. Likewise, there are other things, including some of the basic

---

[1] See J. Barr, *The Concept of Biblical Theology*, for a recent discussion of this problem. Barr does not discuss the church fathers as such, but it is clear that he would not recognize them as 'biblical theologians' because their methods of reading Scripture were very different from what modern biblical scholars would accept as justifiable forms of interpretation. At the risk of oversimplifying Barr's approach, it can be said that his basic objection to the Fathers' reading of Scripture would be that they did not read the Bible 'according to its own categories', but rather according to a scheme which they imported from elsewhere – mainly from different types of late Hellenistic philosophy.

presuppositions of modern theological thought, which make establishing a genuine relationship between what the Fathers thought of as 'biblical theology' and what we now understand by that term somewhat problematic.

Modern scholars think of 'biblical theology' primarily in analytical terms. They start with what they regard as the theology of Paul, or of the wisdom literature (or whatever), and then they try to situate this in relation to the rest of the canonical scriptural tradition. To take only the most familiar instance, modern scholars all believe that it is possible to discern peculiarly Pauline themes in his writings and to present a generally coherent picture of them, though by no means all of them would claim that Paul's theology is either comprehensive or entirely consistent. They may assert that he developed his ideas over time, and even that he tailored his arguments to fit his different audiences, with the result that discrepancies can be detected when one compares different writings. Furthermore, many of them divide the Pauline corpus into 'authentic' and 'deutero-Pauline' writings, using theological content as one of the criteria for deciding which is which. What is true of Paul is even more true when his writings are set alongside the rest of the Bible. Broadly speaking, most modern students of biblical theology are prepared to believe that it developed over time, and that the later a document was written, the more sophisticated the theology it contains is likely to be. Loose ends and contradictions are an almost inevitable consequence of this pattern of development, so that we must not expect 'biblical theology' to offer us the kind of coherent picture that systematic theology demands.

The analytical principles and practices associated with this modern form of biblical theology are certainly not beyond questioning, and even when they are accepted they can lead to some surprisingly varied conclusions, but it can safely be said that the Fathers would have found them alien and unacceptable. They approached the Bible as pagans who had been converted to the Christian gospel, and Scripture presented them with a mental and spiritual universe that struck them as entirely different from what they had grown up with. Some of them were prepared to grant that certain pagan philosophers, like Plato, had discovered elements of the truth – but this was either because those philosophers had read the Old Testament and adapted it to their own purposes or because they had stumbled upon some aspect of reality, rather like blind men in the dark, and had correctly guessed what it was they had encountered.[2] What we now call 'natural' and 'philosophical' theology was acceptable to the Fathers only in so far as it was validated by Scripture itself. Passages like Psalm 19, for example ('The heavens declare the glory of God'), provided a basis on

---

[2] This was the opinion advanced by Justin Martyr (d. 165) in his *Hortatory Address to the Greeks* 25–36, and much the same thing can be found nearly three centuries later in Augustine, *City of God* VIII, 11.

which they could recognize the validity of some pagan insights. The Apostle Paul's appeal to the philosophers of Athens in Acts 17 showed that it was sometimes possible to quote pagan authors in support of Christian beliefs. But, for the Fathers, the true locus of authority was never in doubt. Pagan testimonies were valid only to the extent that they agreed with the biblical witness, and such agreement was likely to be haphazard and partial at best.

As far as the influence of Hellenistic philosophy was concerned, the notion that a coherent, Christian theological system could be built up using only the evidence of nature and reason was anathema to the Fathers. It is not that they were unaware of the possibility of doing this – they knew only too well that someone could take a philosophical idea, find it in some biblical text, and erect an entire system on that slender basis. This was actually being done in the late first and early second century by a number of teachers whom we collectively refer to as 'gnostics'. The first person to attempt a refutation of their methods was Irenaeus of Lyon (d. 202), who attacked their heresies (as he understood them) by claiming that the Bible was the only source of truth, that it spoke primarily of the Christian God and that it could be read and interpreted only according to a 'rule of faith' which outlined its fundamental teachings.[3]

It is not too much to say that it was Scripture, even Scripture alone, which set their theological agenda, and it is noticeable that their apologetic was often strongest precisely at those points where Scripture clashed with what the average pagan believed.[4] For example, almost all of the major church fathers wrote commentaries on the creation narrative in Genesis, because they understood that the Christian doctrine of creation was antithetical to what most ancient philosophers taught about the origin and nature of matter.[5] It must be admitted that this sometimes led them to make assertions which most modern theologians, including very conservative ones, prefer to avoid or reject. Augustine, for instance, was quite prepared to argue that the world had been created relatively recently, and in the space of six days – particularly in the face of the standard pagan belief that matter was eternal. Almost no one would now follow him in this but it ought to be recognized that, however much it was stated and believed, it was not really fundamental to the Fathers' doctrine of creation.

---

[3] See Childs, *Biblical Theology*, 30–39, followed more recently by Wilken, *Spirit*, 50–79.

[4] The phrase 'Scripture alone' must be understood in the context of the clash with pagan philosophy, and not (as in the sixteenth century) as the contrasting alternative to unwritten tradition(s), many of which the Fathers knew and recognized. At the same time, however, it should be said that most of these traditions had to do with matters of church worship and government; they were never points of (later) orthodox doctrine, which could only be derived from the biblical texts.

[5] For a sampling of these see Louth (ed.), *Genesis 1–11*.

Much more important was their belief that created matter was good, not evil (as the majority of pagans believed), and here – where it really matters – the modern reader is more inclined to go along with them.[6] On a different level, the Fathers were forced by the evidence of Scripture to work out a theology in which traditional Jewish monotheism could be held in tandem – and in tension – with the assertion that the Father, the Son and the Holy Spirit were all equally God. The Trinitarian theology which resulted flew in the face of everything that the Fathers had inherited from their Jewish and pagan backgrounds, and its emergence can only be explained as the result of accepting that the New Testament texts are the uniquely authoritative source of truth. The so-called Athanasian Creed, written sometime in the early sixth century, sums up their position quite succinctly:

> Just as we are compelled by the Christian Verity (i.e., the New Testament) to affirm that the Father, the Son and the Holy Spirit are all fully God and Lord, so are we forbidden by the Catholic Religion (i.e., the Hebrew and the Christian Verity – the two Testaments – taken together) to say that they are three gods or three lords.[7]

In these few words, we have what may be the earliest conscious statement of what might be called a form of biblical theology – as long as that term is understood to mean the systematic exposition of the teaching of the canonical Scriptures. What the Fathers did not do, and (in fairness to them) could hardly have been expected to do, was to differentiate between the study of the Bible as a historical document and the systematic reflection on its contents which we now think of as 'theology'. Of course, the Fathers were aware that the Bible had been written by a number of different people over a long period of time, and it was a fundamental part of their belief that the New Testament was a fuller revelation of God than the Old. But they did not understand these things in the same way that most modern interpreters do. Without in any way rejecting the truth of the historical narrative, the Fathers believed that it was necessary to see in it the eternal purpose of God at work, a purpose which was unchanging because it was rooted in his own eternal being.[8] The main difference between ancient and modern approaches to 'biblical theology' is that the ancients

---

[6] See Watson, *Text and Truth*, 305–29, for an extended discussion of these issues. Watson shows how Justin Martyr, in his *Dialogue with Trypho*, could declare his solidarity with Jews in matters of creation, and even of prophecy. Where Jews and Christians parted company was over the Christian belief that the prophecies had been fulfilled in Jesus of Nazareth, though it is important to note that Justin believed that Trypho would not, and could not, come to that understanding unless God should choose to reveal it to him.

[7] Text adapted from the *Book of Common Prayer 1662*.

[8] See, e.g., Fredricksen, 'Augustine and Israel'.

thought that the Bible was an objective *revelation* from (and of) the eternal, unchanging God. Most modern commentators, on the other hand, think more in terms of an essentially subjective spiritual *insight* or *inspiration* occurring to the authors of Scripture and so deriving authority from their experience, not from the God of whom they speak.

To the ancients, the God who spoke to Abraham was the same being who later spoke to Moses, David and the Christian apostles. They saw themselves in direct continuity with pre-Christian Israel, and they criticized the Jews of their own time for having rejected their heritage, which pointed to Christ. Nevertheless, the all-but-unanimous testimony of the Fathers is that God still has a purpose for his ancient chosen people, who will one day return to the faith and confess Christ. Thus Theodoret of Cyrrhus, who represents the Antiochene (more literal) tradition of ancient biblical interpretation says, when commenting on Romans 11:25:

> Paul insists that only a part of Israel has been hardened, for in fact many of them believe. He thus encourages them not to despair that others will be saved as well. After the Gentiles accepted the gospel, the Jews would believe, when the great Elijah would come to them and bring them the doctrine of faith. The Lord himself said as much: 'Elijah will come and restore all things' (Mt. 17:11; Mk. 9:12).[9]

Commenting on the same text, from the rival Alexandrian (or more allegorical) school of thought, Cyril of Alexandria had this to say:

> Although it was rejected, Israel will also be saved eventually, a hope which Paul confirms by quoting this text of Scripture. For indeed, Israel will be saved in its own time and will be called at the end, after the calling of the Gentiles.[10]

God may have said somewhat different things to the Old Testament prophets than he did to the New Testament apostles, but they both belonged to the same community of faith, which would be reunited at the end of time. What really mattered was that, in both cases, it was the same God speaking about the same basic reality – himself. Anomalies and paradoxes which might be observed by comparing one biblical text with another were therefore not to be understood as contradictions, or as errors on the part of the human authors, but as different facets of the one unchanging being of God. Augustine even went so far as to say that difficulties of harmonization between different parts of Scripture were put there by God himself, in order to keep us on our toes and make us probe more deeply into the divine reality.[11] Over time, this divine (self-) revelation grew in

---

[9] Quoted in Bray (ed.), *Romans*, 298.
[10] Bray (ed.), *Romans*, 298–99.
[11] *De doctrina christiana*, 2.15.

quantity but it did not change in quality – nor could it, since the being who is revealed does not change. For this reason, a term like 'Pauline theology' could have had no real meaning to a church father. Either Paul had an objective knowledge of God that anyone could have had, or he did not. If we accept that he had such knowledge, then it could not be essentially different from the knowledge of God possessed by Luke, John, Peter or even Abraham. 'Paulinism' would be reduced to a matter of style and vocabulary, which might be determined by the subject matter and circumstances of any particular epistle, but which would not affect the fundamental vision of God himself.

The Fathers admitted that the Old Testament spoke in types and shadows of things which were to come in the future and would be fully revealed in the New Testament, but the things themselves were (and had to be) identical. Perhaps the Fathers could have assented to H. Graf Reventlow's statement in *Problems of Biblical Theology*: 'It was only faith, in the light of the experience of Christ, that discovered the historical dimension of God's address in the Old Testament witnesses, which is necessarily extended in time.'[12] But they would have disagreed completely with Reventlow's reasoning, on the basis of a statement he quotes from P. Pokorny, to the effect that of itself, 'the Christ event attested in the New Testament is not a direct continuation or development of the Old Testament event'.[13] On the contrary, the New Testament was the unveiling (the literal meaning of 'revelation') of the Old Testament and therefore stood in complete agreement and continuity with it. If Abraham or Moses did not see exactly what Paul or John saw, this was because the Old Testament patriarchs had a veil over their faces, which prevented them from discerning the mystery of God in its exact fullness – not because they belonged to an earlier stage of religious development. Even typically New Testament themes like Trinitarian theology or Christology could be found in the Old Testament once the clues to their existence were recognized and interpreted accordingly. Because of this, the church fathers regarded the Bible as a theological unity in a way that is largely foreign to modern thought.

It must also be said that, for the Fathers of the church, 'theology' meant what we would now call the 'doctrine of God'; it did not include things like ecclesiology or anthropology. Even a concept like 'covenant theology' would have sounded strange to patristic ears, despite the fact that they were fully aware of the covenant(s) and made considerable use of them (and of the differences between them) in their writings. Because they concentrated on who and what God is in himself, the church fathers scoured the Bible for evidence of the various divine attributes (e.g., omniscience, immutability, etc.). But they had relatively little to say about grace, or even about the atonement, because these

---

[12] Reventlow, *Problems of Biblical Theology*, 14.
[13] Reventlow, *Problems of Biblical Theology*, 14.

seemed to them to be more about what God *did* than about what he *was*. To them, the death of Christ was more about the paradoxical suffering of an impassible God than it was about things like penal substitution or the extent of election, though we must not assume that such questions never occurred to them. For instance, Gregory of Nazianzus' famous statement that 'what has not been assumed [by the incarnate Christ] has not been healed [by his death and resurrection]'[14] may fairly be regarded as his way of expressing what a modern theologian would call 'penal substitutionary atonement'. Gregory's perspective on this, however, and his presuppositions, were naturally different from what one would expect from a post-Reformation Lutheran theologian.

The church fathers were concerned primarily with *ontological* issues, which led them to concentrate on questions relating directly to the being and nature of God (including the incarnation of God's Son in Jesus Christ). They were only secondarily concerned with what we know of as *functional* matters, often described in terms of the 'work' of Christ, the 'work' of the Holy Spirit and so on. Modern theology tends to place a much higher value on these 'functional' questions and to downgrade ontological matters, even to the point of regarding ontology as irrelevant.[15] Because of this, many modern theologians are liable to misread the Fathers, and to discount their theology as basically incompatible with what we are used to today. Biblical interpreters are especially prone to disregard anything premodern, and if they quote the Fathers at all, it may well be only in order to poke fun at what looks like their ignorance or naïvety.[16] Is this attitude really justified? Or do the Fathers of the church have something to say to us about biblical theology that we ought to listen to and apply to our hermeneutical practice today?

The Relevance of the Fathers for Biblical Theology Today

In our overview of the Fathers thus far, we have said that they adhered to a firm and well-defined concept of 'biblical theology', but that they interpreted this in

---

[14] *Epistle* 101.

[15] The distinction between ontology and function seems to lie at the heart of Gabler's famous distinction between 'biblical theology', which is concerned mainly with the functional or narrative aspect, and 'systematics', which extends this into the ontological realm. Gabler regarded this ontological dimension as secondary and sought to exclude it from the notion of 'biblical theology' altogether. See Childs, *Biblical Theology*, 4–5.

[16] See Watson, *Text and Truth*, 305, who does his best to demonstrate that, in spite of everything, an alternative and more serious reading of the Fathers is still possible.

ways which usually seem outdated or irrelevant to modern concerns. It is
sometimes possible, of course, to find individual Fathers, like Origen or Theodore of Mopsuestia, whose comments (or at least some of them) appear to be
very 'modern'. But, on closer inspection, the limitations of their 'modernity'
quickly become apparent. For example, Origen was clearly aware of the need
to examine the biblical text in the original languages and to discover the historical contexts in which the texts were written. He also understood that the
clearer parts of Scripture should be used as a guide for interpreting the more
obscure parts. He was also particularly conscious of the fact that any given text
could have multiple layers of meaning which would not be immediately obvious to the untrained reader, but which must be understood if the text is to be
read correctly. When these principles are stated like this, most modern interpreters might be willing to admit that they stand in the same hermeneutical tradition of 'biblical theology' as the third-century Alexandrian did.

But closer examination of the facts will soon dispel this notion. Origen's use
of textual critical methods did not lead him to accept the primacy of the
Hebrew Old Testament text. Like most of his contemporaries, he believed that
the Greek Septuagint translation was divinely inspired, and that where it dif-
fered from the Hebrew it was to be preferred to the original version! His interest in history was real, but it was also circumscribed by his inability to assess the
past in a scientifically critical way. This was not because he was unable to distinguish fact from legend (the Fathers were often much better at this than one
might suppose). On the one hand, the sophisticated palaeographical and
archaeological tools available to us today did not exist in ancient times, and so
there was no way of verifying the accuracy of many ancient accounts, which
tended to be accepted at face value as long as they appeared to be generally factual. Many errors and misunderstandings were canonized as a result. This can
be seen most clearly in the field of etymology, where the supposed origins of
names (in particular) or apparent connections between words in different languages are taken on board more or less uncritically. Admittedly this tendency
seldom makes any real difference to interpretation, but it leaves the modern
reader wondering how far he can really trust the soundness of the ancients'
judgement. Much the same phenomenon can be seen in the patristic understanding of biblical chronology, which often seems disconcertingly 'funda-
mentalist' to a modern observer. We may agree that the Fathers were right to
reject pagan notions of the eternity of matter, but how many of us would
replace these notions with the theory that the world was created about 4000
BC, as a literalistic reading of the biblical chronology would suggest? That the
Fathers did this may not have been entirely their fault, since they had no
knowledge of such things as fossils or carbon dating. But, although we cannot
condemn them for their ignorance, we can hardly embrace their conclusions
either. Indeed, the more we see where their interpretations led them, the less

inclined we are to follow along, and the easier it becomes to dismiss them altogether.

More seriously, neither Origen nor any of his contemporaries had any sense of what we now call 'historical development'. The idea that human knowledge and understanding could (and would) evolve over time seemed strange to them, and they were much less aware than we are that people in past ages lived and thought in ways very different from ours. If they thought about such things at all, it was probably in the opposite sense – past ages were *more*, not less, advanced than the present. A third-century Alexandrian like Origen would have known about the pyramids of ancient Egypt, but he would not have seen anything of comparable magnificence being built in his own day, and he would probably have sensed that the skills needed for pyramid building had been lost over the course of time. The Bible, after all, told him that in ancient times people lived far longer than they do now – something which pointed to historical decline rather than to progress. We forget it now, but it was not until about 1800 that people began to think of modern civilization as superior to that of the ancients and stopped looking up to them as models to imitate. The Fathers' deference to the past is perhaps the thing about their writings which is most alien to the modern mind, and which creates a barrier to our acceptance of them which is all the harder to surmount in that it so often goes unrecognized.

But, important as these differences undoubtedly are, they pale into insignificance when we look at the way in which the church fathers dealt with the question of different layers of meaning in Scripture. They worked these out in the context of an allegorical kind of interpretation which has more in common with something like astrology than with any form of modern hermeneutics. Like astrology, allegory tends to move from a base of factual information to a kind of speculation about it which has no inherent connection to the data provided, and which ultimately depends almost entirely on the interpreter's own creative imagination. This does not mean that it is purely arbitrary, since there is usually an agreed set of symbols and signs to guide the interpreter, but as these are not grounded in any objective criteria, they must be regarded as highly subjective, even to the point of being purely fanciful. It is true that the Antiochene school of biblical interpretation distinguished itself from the Alexandrian one by its more sceptical attitude towards allegory and by its tendency to emphasize the human and historical side of biblical texts. While these things have made it seem more appealing to most modern interpreters, the differences between the two schools of interpretation are smaller than this perception of them might suggest.[17] Furthermore, the fact that many of the leading Antiochene exegetes (like Theodore of Mopsuestia) were later condemned by the church reminds us that theirs was not the dominant view among the Fathers. Needless to say,

---

[17] On this subject, see Young, 'Alexandrian and Antiochene Exegesis', 334–54.

this realization merely adds to our sense of alienation from the ancient world, which often seems to us to have been unable (or unwilling) to give common sense its due.

In response to this, it is possible to argue, along with Henri de Lubac, that the Scriptures contain many different levels of meaning, and that to privilege the literal sense of the text over others may sometimes do a grave injustice to its true range of signification, which the original author or authors may have intended, and which the canonical status of the text(s) must now imply.[18] Ancient allegory was seldom purely arbitrary but was based, rather, on the principle that the harder parts of the biblical text were to be interpreted in the light of the clearer ones. What we find is that the narrative of Christ's saving incarnation, death and resurrection tends to be applied to passages whose literal meaning is either unclear or else makes it hard to understand why they are part of sacred Scripture at all. The classic example of this technique is found in the numerous commentaries which were written on the Song of Songs, a book which was invariably spiritualized and made to refer either to Christ's love for the church, or to his love for the individual soul, or both. De Lubac and others have argued that this reading is fundamentally sound because it is based on the sacralization of erotic love, which is part of the overall redemption of creation. Far from being a concession to Greek philosophy, it is the very opposite – a complete repudiation of Platonism (in particular) at the most fundamental level. If modern exegetes have failed to see this, it is their blindness, not that of the Fathers, which is at fault. De Lubac's work is an important corrective to the exclusive emphasis on the so-called 'literal meaning' of the text that has been so prevalent in modern historical-critical research, although it cannot be embraced without reservation.[19]

The hermeneutical failings of the church fathers, when measured against modern standards, are numerous and obvious, and this fact ought to be enough to prevent the growth of anything approaching 'patristic fundamentalism' in our midst. But if we can lay that danger aside, we cannot so easily escape the Fathers' own claims that their theology is a true expression of the biblical message, and that it therefore has a legitimate claim to be considered 'biblical'. It is certainly true that their whole approach to the question of 'biblical theology' was so different from most of what goes by that name today that many people wonder whether anything they said can be integrated into a modern approach

---

[18] De Lubac, *Histoire et Esprit*, is the classic expression of this point of view, developed further by the same author in his monumental *Exégèse Médiévale*. Both works were reprinted (Paris: Cerf, 1993–94), and the second is currently being translated into English (Grand Rapids: Eerdmans, 1997–).

[19] For a good summary of the arguments for and against de Lubac, see Theobald, 'Origène'.

without serious distortion on both sides. If we are forced to treat Augustine, for instance, in the way that he and his Christian contemporaries treated Plato – as a blind man who accidentally stumbled on truth here and there, without having a properly coherent understanding of what it was that they were perceiving – is it possible for us to regard him as a valid dialogue partner in the modern hermeneutical quest?

Ontology and Biblical Theology

The heart of the issue here is the significance of ontology for biblical interpretation. For the church fathers this went without saying, and the essence of their hermeneutic is rooted in ontological considerations of one kind or another. Who and what is God? How does God stand in relation to the universe that we call creation? What is wrong with this creation, and how must it be put right? The answers given to these and related questions form the heart and substance of patristic theology. Those answers came from the Bible – indeed, from the Bible alone. But modern interpreters might ask – was the Bible designed to provide them? Can the Fathers be accused of having distorted Scripture's principal intention(s) by making it supply answers to questions raised within a hermeneutical grid that is fundamentally alien to the text itself? The short answer to these questions is that if ontology has a legitimate place in biblical theology, then the Fathers of the church can be integrated into that tradition of biblical interpretation and regarded as legitimate dialogue partners even today. But if it does not, then the church fathers are out of place in the modern context, and whether we choose to reject them or to reject modern biblical theology, we shall have to decide one way or the other, because it will ultimately prove impossible to reconcile the two in a coherent whole.

Fundamental to any discussion of the place of ontological questions in patristic biblical interpretation is the often overlooked fact that the Fathers were writing in the context of a civilization which had no significant Jewish or Christian input to guide its basic assumptions. Myths and speculations jostled one another to provide 'explanations' of different aspects of reality – explanations that were frequently mutually contradictory and quite incoherent as an overall system of thought. It is true that Platonism provided a certain framework that attracted a number of intellectuals, and much the same could be said for Stoicism. But Platonism (which idealized the non-material) and Stoicism (which was thoroughly materialistic) were opposites in many respects, and the adherents of one school of thought were frequently bitter opponents of partisans of the other. Nor is this all – when we add in Epicureans, Aristotelians, Pythagoreans and so on, we find that we are dealing with a plethora of mutually antagonistic philosophical schools, all of them claiming to base their findings on reason. In principle, they should all have come up with the same answers to every question, but in practice the answers turned out to be very different. They could not all be right, but who was to decide which group or groups had the greater share of the truth?

Beyond the philosophical schools, which never attracted more than a tiny minority, there lay the vast mass of the population, mired in polytheism and generally despised by the intellectual elite, but nevertheless in touch with the emotional side of human spirituality which was so necessary at the great tragic points in life. People could (and many people did) pick and choose their own spiritual menu according to taste, but the honest seeker after objective truth was at a loss where to turn.

It was in this condition that the gospel of Jesus Christ found the world to which it was first addressed. Paul's missionary journey to Athens (Acts 17) expresses it perfectly. His task was to reveal the Unknown God which the Athenians, in the logic of their eclectic ignorance, had decided must be propitiated – just in case! In such a world, Christianity's greatest selling point was its claim to have access to the unique source of all truth. In the pagan universe both creation and redemption were recognized divine activities, but each of them took place within a wider context. Creator gods and goddesses were responsible for individual acts of creation, but not for creating the entire universe, and redeemers, both divine and semi-divine, had to contend with forces which were equal, or superior, to themselves. The Christians cut through such limitations by saying that there was only One Creator, who is also the One and only Redeemer – the absolute sovereign of the universe; nothing greater than him could (or did) exist. Logically, he had to be the Supreme Being, a belief that was supported by the divine name Yahweh, which was understood to mean 'He who is'.

The ontological agenda which resulted from these assertions was intrinsic to the success of the Christian mission. One might almost say that if they had not been in the Bible, they would have had to be invented for the message of the Bible to have taken hold in a pagan world. But if the theology of the Bible lacked an ontological dimension, would any ancient pagan have been converted to Christianity? What attraction would a Jewish sect have had to people for whom its entire mental universe was fundamentally alien? Without a doctrine of creation, it is hard to see how the biblical message could have claimed any kind of credible superiority over its various pagan rivals, and a doctrine of creation implies an ontology. The Bible has a doctrine of creation, and therefore it contains ontological assumptions that are intrinsic to its message. Here, if nowhere else, we are on solid ground if we say that if the modern mind fails to appreciate this, then it is our generation, and not the Fathers of the church, who are mistaken in their interpretation of Scripture. The great contribution which patristic biblical hermeneutics can make to modern debates lies at the ontological level – a fundamental dimension of our understanding which we neglect at our peril and which much modern scholarship has mistakenly decreed to be irrelevant (or inappropriate) to biblical interpretation.

As we have already hinted, the proper place to begin is as the Bible itself does – with its particular doctrine of creation. Pre-Christian paganism generally lacked such a concept. Despite the great variety and general incoherence of paganism, it may be said that in this respect it can be regarded as one. Pagans recognized the existence of what we call the universe, but they generally believed that it contained both material and non-material elements, both of which were eternal in themselves. (Stoicism was an exception to this, in that the Stoics believed that spirits were highly refined forms of matter, but this does not detract from the basic point that they believed the invisible world to be just as eternal as the visible one.) Among pagans, there were two quite different ways of understanding how the material and the non-material are related. Either they were not clearly distinguished from each other at all, or else they were regarded as polar opposites, which were radically incompatible with each other. The first type of paganism – by far the most common – led naturally to idolatry, because pagans found it easy to believe that spiritual power could be accessed in and through material objects. In the second type, represented by dualistic philosophies like Platonism, one part of the universe was pitted in opposition to the other. Purely spiritual (good) and purely material (evil) beings could be clearly differentiated from each other, but human beings caused a problem, because they were in effect a combination of both. As spirits who were imprisoned in material bodies, human beings had only one hope of salvation – escape from the body. In practice, this was a call to death (as the only escape), not to life, and it never appealed to any but an intellectual minority.

The biblical doctrine of creation challenged paganism by presenting a different cosmology, which was in turn based on a different understanding of ontology. In Christian teaching, absolute Being has to be identified with the God of Israel, a personal deity who enters into relationship with his people, rather than with a philosophical abstraction with which human beings cannot communicate directly. Everything which exists apart from this God, whether spiritual, material or both, is a creature – and therefore radically different from God himself. But although God is supremely good, it does not follow that his creatures are evil because of their radical difference from him. On the contrary, creation is both different in kind from the Creator, and yet good in its own terms. For this reason, evil cannot be equated with matter, or with creation. Some Christians, including the great Augustine, believed that evil was the absence, or privation, of good. But the biblical account is clear – evil is the fruit of rebellion against God, a point which even Augustine had to admit when

dealing with the biblical texts.[20] Because of this, evil can inhere only in responsible beings (humans and/or angels) and not in things – or in the absence of
things.

This redefinition of creation and of evil was such a radical reconstruction of
the universe that virtually all of the more significant church fathers found
themselves having to write detailed expositions of Genesis 1 – 3 in an attempt
to explain it. Augustine wrote no fewer than four such expositions – three
commentaries on Genesis (one of them incomplete) and the last three books of
his famous Confessions. On top of that, he also dealt with the subject at great
length in his magisterial work, *The City of God*. For him, as for most of his contemporaries, it was simply not possible to embark on any kind of biblical theology without first restructuring their inherited notions of the universe – in other
words, without adopting the fundamental principles of biblical ontology.

Defining creation and evil also forced the early Christians to redefine God –
as the Uncreated One. The root inspiration for this came from the biblical
attacks on idolatry, which was rejected in Scripture precisely because it
appeared as the worship of the creature instead of the Creator. God could not
be worshipped in or through material objects, not because these objects were
unconnected with him – they were creatures, after all, which he had made –
but because he himself lives above and beyond them. Not even the (apparently
limitless) heavens can contain God – a theme that constantly recurs in the Old
Testament, and that is taken for granted in the New. The church fathers understood that if they were to remain faithful to the biblical witness, God must be
recognized as an objectively existing meta-being, which they somewhat confusingly called 'non-being'. Of course, God was not 'non-being' in the way
that evil could be understood as 'non-being', but the opposite. He was not the
absence of being, but something above and beyond mere being, which now
finds itself correspondingly relativized. To call God the absolute or Supreme
Being is therefore inadequate – not because he is not absolute and supreme, but
because he cannot be limited to the dimensions of 'being' as these were generally understood by ancient philosophers.

The most telling aspect of this is not the long catalogue of negative attributes (e.g., invisible, immortal, impassible) associated with so-called 'classical
theism'. The patristic insistence that the One God is also a Trinity of three persons went completely against both ancient pagan and Jewish notions of the
Supreme Being, which by definition had to be singular. The impulse for
making this assertion was purely biblical – so much so that the church fathers
came to see the doctrine of the Trinity as the unique and essential distinguishing mark of Christian theology. What struck the Fathers so forcibly is that the

---

[20] Compare Augustine, *City of God* XII, 7 where he develops the first point, with *City
of God* XIII, 13–15, where he expounds the fall of Adam.

Trinity made it possible for them to regard both the creation and redemption not merely as *external* acts of the One God, but also – and more importantly – as acts dependent upon and realized in the *internal* relationships of the three persons.

The biblical basis of Trinitarian theology is too vast a subject to be discussed in detail within the scope of this chapter, but its significance for the church fathers' hermeneutic of Scripture must not be underestimated. To them, the core of the biblical message was that the One God has three internal relations which define both his creative and his redemptive activity. This is clearly revealed in the New Testament, especially in the Fourth Gospel and in the Epistle to the Hebrews, which were key texts for their understanding of biblical theology, but it could also be found, in types and shadows, in the Old Testament.[21] The coming of Christ was nothing less than the incarnation of the Son of God, one of the eternal persons in the divine being. Furthermore, this coming was the result of a decision taken by the Father and the Son in eternity, which is now established in our hearts by the Third Person, whom we know as the Holy Spirit. The governing principle in this decision was love – the love of the Father for the Son, the love of the Son for the Father, and the love of both poured out on us in the Holy Spirit. Because of this, our redemption belongs at the very heart of the divine reality, and we are bound to him by the power of his Trinitarian love. Those who do not share in that love are alienated from ultimate being, and the various religions and philosophies of the non-Christian world bear witness to myriad failed attempts to overcome that alienation. As Christians, however, we know that we are not marooned in an inexplicable universe but united to the source of all life. This gives us a connectedness with ultimate reality that enables us to feel secure in his everlasting care.

The Bible is the record of how God set out to seek and to save those who were lost, by choosing for himself a people who would bear faithful witness to his everlasting name and purpose. Everything God has done and continues to do finds its explanation in this context, which is alone true to reality. To study the Bible, therefore, is not to read the opinions of past sages and prophets, but to discover objective truth – which those sages and prophets were privileged to receive and reveal to us. Sin is not really a catalogue of disobedient acts, some of which are bound to be more (or less) serious than others. Rather, sin is about death, which affects the entire human race. Because of this, redemption is also not really about meritorious works of righteousness, whether Christ's or ours, but about resurrection from the dead – to a new and perfect life in God's eternity. On both sides, the functional gives way to the ontological, and who can deny that this is fundamentally biblical? If we have died with Christ, says the Apostle Paul, why do we continue to walk in our previous sinful ways? Should

---

[21] For a good discussion of this, see Wainwright, *Trinity.*

we not walk in newness of life, now that we are born again (Rom. 6:1–14)? Who we are, and what we have become in Christ, ought to determine what we do – just as who and what Christ himself was determined what he could, and did, do on our behalf. Wherever we look in Scripture, the conclusion is the same – ontological realities determine how we and every other being will function.

Modern theology, and not least modern biblical theology, has done its best to escape from the ontological, and even to deny that it is present at all in the Scriptures. But the Fathers of the church, whatever their other limitations may have been, saw more clearly than many moderns on this point. At a time when the ancient foundations of our culture are being increasingly questioned, and issues involving ultimate reality are increasingly evaded, Christian interpreters of the Bible need to hear the Fathers' voice more than ever before. It is a voice which will point them towards ontology, the end of which is the supreme Being of God, the Father, Son and Holy Spirit.

Bibliography

Barr, J., *The Concept of Biblical Theology: An Old Testament Perspective* (London: SCM Press, 1999)

Bonnardière, A.M., *Saint Augustine and the Bible* (Notre Dame: Notre Dame University Press, 1997)

Bray, G. (ed.), *Romans* (ACCS [NT] VI; Downers Grove, IL: InterVarsity Press, 1998)

Childs, B.S., *Biblical Theology of the Old and New Testaments: Theological Reflection on the Christian Bible* (London: SCM Press; Minneapolis: Fortress Press, 1992)

Daniélou, J., *From Shadows to Reality: Studies in the Biblical Typology of the Fathers* (London: Burns and Oates, 1960)

Dockery, D.S., *Biblical Interpretation Then and Now: Contemporary Hermeneutics in the Light of the Early Church* (Grand Rapids: Baker, 1992)

Edwards, M.J., *Origen against Plato* (Aldershot: Ashgate, 2002)

Fredricksen, P., 'Augustine and Israel: *Interpretatio ad litteram*, Jews and Judaism', in *Engaging Augustine on Romans: Self, Context and Theology in Interpretation* (ed. D. Patte and E. TeSelle; Harrisburg, PA: Trinity Press International, 2002), 91–110

Froehlich, K., *Biblical Interpretation in the Early Church* (Philadelphia: Fortress Press, 1984)

Green, R.P.H., *Augustine: De doctrina Christiana* (Oxford: Clarendon Press, 1995)

Greer, R.A., *The Captain of our Salvation: A Study in the Patristic Exegesis of Hebrews* (Tübingen: Mohr, 1973)

—, *Theodore of Mopsuestia: Exegete and Theologian* (Westminster: Faith Press, 1961)

Hanson, R.P.C., *Allegory and Event: A Study of the Sources and Significance of Origen's Interpretation of Scripture* (Louisville, KY: Westminster / John Knox Press, 2nd edn, 2002)

Hauser, A.J., and D.F. Watson (eds.), *A History of Biblical Interpretation I: The Ancient Period* (Grand Rapids: Eerdmans, 2003)

Louth, A. (ed.), *Genesis 1–11* (ACCS [OT] I; Downers Grove, IL: InterVarsity Press, 2001)

Lubac, H. de, *Histoire et Esprit: L'Intelligence de l'Ecriture d'après Origène* (Paris: Aubier, 1950)

—, *Exégèse Médiévale* (4 vols.; Paris: Aubier, 1959–64)

Oden, T.C. (ed.), *Ancient Christian Commentary on Scripture* (28 vols.; Downers Grove, IL: InterVarsity Press, 1998–)

Patte, D., and E. TeSelle (eds.), *Engaging Augustine on Romans: Self, Context and Theology in Interpretation* (Harrisburg, PA: Trinity Press International, 2002)

Reventlow, H. Graf, *Problems of Biblical Theology* (London: SCM Press, 1986)

Simonetti, M., *Biblical Interpretation in the Early Church: An Historical Introduction to Patristic Exegesis* (Edinburgh: T. & T. Clark, 1994)

Theobald, C., 'Origène et le Débat Herméneutique Contemporain', in *Origeniana Sexta: Origène et la Bible* (ed. G. Dorival and A. Le Boulluec; Leuven: University Press, 1995), 785–97

Trigg, J.W., *Origen: The Bible and Philosophy in the Third-century Church* (London: SCM Press, 1985)

Wainwright, A.W., *The Trinity in the New Testament* (London: SPCK, 2nd edn, 1969)

Watson, F., *Text and Truth: Redefining Biblical Theology* (Grand Rapids: Eerdmans, 1997)

Wilken, R.L., *The Spirit of Early Christian Thought* (New Haven: Yale University Press, 2002)

Young, F., 'Alexandrian and Antiochene Exegesis', in *A History of Biblical Interpretation I: The Ancient Period* (ed. A.J. Hauser and D.F. Watson; Grand Rapids: Eerdmans, 2003), 334–54

2

The Nature and Genre of Biblical Theology

Some Reflections in the Light of Charles H.H. Scobie's
'Prolegomena to a Biblical Theology'

Karl Möller

Charles Scobie's massive work *The Ways of Our God: An Approach to Biblical Theology*, published in 2003, is a significant and welcome contribution to the rejuvenated discipline of biblical theology. Resisting the current compartmentalization of biblical studies, Scobie offers an impressive and non-technical sketch of a unified and truly integrated biblical theology of the Old and New Testaments. This 'sketch', which runs to some eight hundred pages, is preceded by the author's 'prolegomena to a biblical theology', which include a discussion of the history of the discipline, important considerations concerning its method and nature and, perhaps most importantly, extensive reflections on its structure.

The present chapter is not a review of Scobie's work. Nor does it focus on his 800-page sketch of biblical theology, valuable though that would have been. My aims rather are: 1) to introduce Scobie's conceptualization of biblical theology as laid out in his prolegomena, Part I of *The Ways of Our God* (hereafter *WOG*); 2) to reflect on the limitations imposed on biblical theology by its own genre, understood as descriptive and analytical second-level discourse; and 3) to consider the role of biblical theology in the light of these limitations.

Scobie's Approach to Biblical Theology

The definition of biblical theology

Scobie begins by pointing out that theology, the *logos* of *theos*, is not to be construed as leading to a 'rigid, systematized, doctrinal, and propositional'

conception of theology, for such a conception would not sit well with the biblical material, which contains very little 'theology' in that sense of the term.[1]
Instead, biblical theology 'ought to mean ... the ordered study of what the
Bible has to say about God and his relation to the world and to humankind'.[2]
Noting Ebeling's widely accepted distinction between a 'theology that accords
with the Bible' and 'the theology of the Bible itself ',[3] Scobie is adamant that a
clear distinction between the teaching of the Bible and the application of that
teaching for today, in the sense of Stendahl's 'what it meant' and 'what it
means',[4] cannot be maintained.[5]

Indeed, Scobie stresses that prior to the eighteenth century and Gabler's
famous 1787 address 'On the Proper Distinction Between Biblical and Dogmatic Theology and the Specific Objectives of Each' no such distinction was
made.[6] For this reason, Scobie calls this 'a period of *integrated biblical theology*'.[7] It
was the dominance of historical criticism and the increased awareness of Scripture's diversity that have led to the aforementioned distinction and to what
Scobie terms an *independent biblical theology*, where biblical theology is pursued
in total independence from the church. In contrast to these two positions,
Scobie opts for a post-critical *intermediate biblical theology*, which functions as a
'bridge' between 'the historical study of the Bible and the use of the Bible as
authoritative Scripture by the church'.[8]

The history of biblical theology

As regards the history of biblical theology, Scobie maintains that the rejection
of Marcion's reduced canon and Irenaeus' advocacy of the fourfold Gospel (in
Haer. 3.2.8) indicate that the early church resisted the temptation to dispose of
Scripture's richness and diversity. Yet, unity of interpretation was achieved by
subjecting biblical interpretation to the *regula fidei* and by the use of
allegorization. Subsequently, the concept of the fourfold sense of Scripture,
with its distinction between Scripture's literal, allegorical, moral and anagogical meanings, similarly allowed the church to hold on to the unity of Scripture.

Contrary to those who consider Gabler's oft-quoted address on biblical and
dogmatic theology as the origin of an 'independent biblical theology', Scobie

---

[1] *WOG*, 4.
[2] *WOG*, 4–5.
[3] See Ebeling, *Word and Faith*, 79.
[4] See Stendahl, 'Biblical Theology', 419.
[5] *WOG*, 5.
[6] A translation of and a commentary on Gabler's address can be found in Sandys-
Wunsch and Eldredge, 'J.P. Gabler'.
[7] *WOG*, 7.
[8] *WOG*, 8.

points to Simon, Spinoza and Semler as the true pioneers of such an approach.[9] The advocates of the new historical-critical or grammatico-critical exegesis, which studied the biblical books in their original historical contexts, sought 'to throw off the shackles of centuries of church dogma and penetrate back to the true teaching of the Christian faith'.[10] The very title of Gabler's lecture led to another important development, for it was used to promote a rigorous separation between dogmatic theology and biblical theology, with the latter being understood as a purely historical and descriptive discipline.[11]

Scobie then traces the development of biblical theologies by rationalist scholars in the late eighteenth and early nineteenth centuries, the ceasing of the writing of full biblical theologies from around 1870, the concurrent development of separate Old and New Testament theologies, and the eventual eclipse of biblical theology by the descriptive and supposedly objective History of Religions approach.[12]

However, following a striking U-turn after World War I, the 1930s saw the beginning of the 'golden age' of Old Testament theology, which is associated in particular with Walther Eichrodt and Gerhard von Rad. The concurrent revival of NT theology, on the other hand, is exemplified by the existentialist approach of Rudolf Bultmann and his pupil Hans Conzelmann, by Oscar Cullmann's focus on salvation history and by the work of Joachim Jeremias and Werner Georg Kümmel, who took the historical Jesus as their starting point.[13]

Perceiving a development from theology to theologies, Scobie maintains that the period following the 1960s is characterized by 'a renewed emphasis on diversity and development within the Bible to the point where the writing not only of BT [biblical theology] but even of OT or NT theology is radically called in question'.[14] This stress on diversity is apparent not least in von Rad's work. For in distinguishing sharply between Israel's historical traditions (the focus of volume 1 of his *Theology of the Old Testament*), the prophetic traditions (volume 2 of *Theology*) and the wisdom traditions (in *Wisdom in Israel*), von Rad has in fact given us not one, but three, Old Testament theologies.[15]

---

[9] See *WOG*, 13–15.

[10] *WOG*, 15.

[11] It is here that the roots of the History of Religions school lie (see *WOG*, 16).

[12] *WOG*, 16–22.

[13] *WOG*, 23–24.

[14] *WOG*, 26.

[15] See *WOG*, 27. Terrien, *Elusive Presence*, 36, has similarly pointed out that 'von Rad's achievement … cannot justify the title *Old Testament Theology*, for the dichotomy between the theologies of the confessional reinterpretations, on the one hand, and the theologies of the responses of the psalmists, the prophets, and the wisemen, on the other, has not been successfully overcome, nor has a principle of theological homogeneity capable of accounting for the growth of the Hebrew Bible been convincingly elucidated'.

New directions in biblical theology

Turning to current trends in biblical studies, Scobie welcomes the accentuation of the Bible's literary unity by recent literary-critical approaches as well as Childs's canonical approach, as this has reversed historical criticism's propensity to increase the diversity within Scripture.[16] Similarly, reader-response criticism's 'emphasis on the role of the reader can be salutary for BT [biblical theology]' in providing 'a renewed recognition of the church as the true "interpretive community" of Scripture', which recognizes the Bible as its canonical authority.[17] Another welcome development is a post-critical openness to the claims of tradition and to transcendence.[18]

All of these trends have facilitated the revival of biblical theology, which Scobie sees exemplified in Gese and Stuhlmacher's history of traditions approach with its focus on the biblical writings understood as 'a unified process of tradition'.[19] Scobie also points to the renewed study of biblical themes in monograph series like Fortress Press's Overtures to Biblical Theology as well as dedicated journals, such as *Biblical Theology Bulletin*, *Horizons in Biblical Theology* and *Jahrbuch für Biblische Theologie*. And he perceives cautious attempts to write biblical theologies, most significant of which are Terrien's *The Elusive Presence* and Childs's *Biblical Theology of the Old and New Testaments*.[20]

The method of biblical theology

As noted earlier, Scobie argues for an *intermediate* biblical theology rather than an *integrated* or an *independent* one. This intermediate biblical theology is expected to function 'as a bridge discipline, situated between the historical study of Scripture … and its use by the church in its faith and life'.[21] As such, it must ensure that the historical location of the biblical texts is taken seriously. Yet, rather than attempting neutrality, it will quite legitimately adopt the presuppositions of the interpretative community (i.e., that the Bible conveys a divine revelation, etc.). Most crucially, an intermediate biblical theology needs to move from analysis to synthesis, attempting to present a coherent picture of biblical thought without forgoing its diversity. And it cannot be purely descriptive but, being theology, it needs to be normative, seeking to correlate the scriptural norms with the church's contemporary situation.[22]

---

[16] *WOG*, 34–39.
[17] Thus *WOG*, 29, 41, borrowing some of the phraseology from Fish, *Text*, 171–72.
[18] See *WOG*, 30–34.
[19] Thus Gese, *Essays*, 15, as quoted in *WOG*, 42.
[20] See *WOG*, 42–45.
[21] *WOG*, 46.
[22] See *WOG*, 46–49.

Scobie strongly underlines that his is a canonical theology.[23] Scripture for him provides both a standard, or norm, and a fixed list of writings, but he also maintains that 'the continuing revelation of God's truth ... consists in interpreting and applying the canonical norm to succeeding situations and circumstances'.[24] He then offers short discussions of the canonization of both the Tanak/Old Testament (which *theologically* is closed for Christians by the Christ event) and the New Testament (which contains 'apostolic teaching' written within the shadow of that Christ event),[25] before proposing the following theses:

Biblical theology is limited to the canon of Christian Scripture
That is to say, biblical theology deals only with those books that the Christian community recognizes as normative.[26]

Biblical theology is based on both Old and New Testaments
Against what he regards as a strain of 'neo-Marcionism' in the work of scholars like Schleiermacher, von Harnack and Bultmann, Scobie stresses that biblical theology must attempt to do full justice to the Old Testament. And contra Hübner's claim that New Testament theology should limit its attention to the Old Testament to *Vetus Testamentum in novo receptum*, he contends that biblical theology must deal with *Vetus Testamentum per se*. While biblical theology must resist the temptation to mute the Old Testament's authentic voice by 'Christianizing' it, a truly canonical biblical theology cannot but view the Old Testament 'from the perspective of the Christian canon as a whole'. Biblical theology thus is 'more than the sum of Old Testament theology and New Testament theology'.[27]

Biblical theology is based on the content of the Christian canon
Scobie's claim that biblical theology 'must be based on all the books that constitute the canon of the Old and New Testaments'[28] leads him into a discussion of the different OT canons provided by the Masoretic Text, the Septuagint and the Vulgate. In this context, he documents the Septuagint's importance in the early Christian centuries, the influence in the East of Jerome's identification of the additions to the Jewish canon, Luther's eventual downgrading of the Apocrypha, the Roman Catholic counter-reaction at the Council of Trent (1546), the position of the Orthodox churches, and the radicalization of the Protestant position in response to Trent.

---

[23] *WOG*, 49–76.
[24] *WOG*, 49–51; the quote is from p. 51.
[25] See *WOG*, 51–57.
[26] *WOG*, 58.
[27] See *WOG*, 58–60; the last phrase is a quote from Watson, *Text and Truth*, 8.
[28] *WOG*, 60.

Arguing that the NT writers used the Apocrypha but never cited them *as Scripture*, Scobie finally concurs with the position adopted by Jerome, Luther and the Church of England, among others. Thus, he concludes that while the apocryphal/deuterocanonical books shed light on the period leading up to the Christ event, they should not be used to support doctrines that cannot be substantiated elsewhere in the canonical Scriptures of the Old and New Testaments.[29]

Biblical theology is based on the structure of the Christian canon

Beginning with an analysis of the order of the Tanak (i.e., Torah–Prophets–Writings), Scobie underlines the emphasis accorded in this scheme primarily to the Torah but also to 'the ongoing life and worship of the Jewish community', which is at the heart of the Writings. The Christian canon, by contrast, shifts the focus to the Christ event, which the entire Old Testament is now seen as pointing to. This is evident not least in the placing of the Prophets at the end of the Old Testament, which stresses the elements of promise and of future expectation.

The New Testament order, on the other hand, emphasizes the four Gospels' witness to the Christ event. It places Acts as a bridge between Gospels and Epistles, for which it provides a context. It accords priority to the Pauline Epistles due to their theological importance. And, like the Old Testament, it ends on an eschatological note, with the book of Revelation pointing to the future consummation of all things.[30]

Biblical theology is based on the text of the Christian canon

Here the question is whether biblical theology should be based on the Hebrew text of the Old Testament or on the Greek version provided by the Septuagint. While, for instance, the Reformers and historical-critical scholarship demand the study of the original Hebrew text, approximately eighty per cent of the Old Testament quotations in the New appear to come from the Septuagint. Biblical theology therefore needs to recognize the Septuagint as part of the scriptural tradition acknowledged by the New Testament.[31]

Biblical theology is based primarily on the final canonical form of the text

Scobie stresses that biblical theology presupposes and builds upon historical-critical scholarship, seeking to listen to the distinctive authorial or textual voices of the biblical canon. Yet, as the biblical books have been placed into their new canonical contexts by the community of faith, they need to be read

---

[29] See *WOG*, 60–65.
[30] See *WOG*, 65–71.
[31] *WOG*, 71–72.

not only against their original historical contexts but also in the context of the canon.[32]

Biblical theology will reject a 'canon within the canon'
Finally, Scobie is insistent that biblical theology must do justice to the canon in its totality. It needs to resist the temptation to opt for a 'canon within the canon' along the lines of Marcion, Luther, Bultmann (with his focus on Paul and John) and much liberal scholarship, which emphasized the teaching of the reconstructed historical Jesus to the detriment of the rest of the New Testament.[33]

Yet, Scobie's intermediate biblical theology is not only canonical. It also is cooperative, by which he means that it seeks to break out of the ingrained habits of scholarly over-specialization. In order to be true to its function as a bridge discipline, it needs to overcome the chasms between Old and New Testament studies as well as biblical studies and dogmatic or systematic theology. Quoting Jodock, Scobie maintains that 'the relationship between theological reflection and the Scriptures ought to be understood as reciprocal'.[34] And biblical theology needs to be ecumenical, for the aim must be for scholars 'to encompass the full range of the biblical revelation unencumbered by the blinkers of their own particular tradition'.[35]

Some have argued that biblical theology ought to be understood as a dimension of exegesis. Yet Scobie claims that, for biblical theology to be able to mediate the results of biblical scholarship to a community of faith that looks to the Bible as a norm for its faith and life, it needs to provide an overall structure for making sense of the complexity of the biblical material.[36]

The structure of biblical theology

Turning his attention to this structure, Scobie asserts that 'the danger to be avoided at all costs is that of imposing an alien pattern upon the biblical material; so far as is humanly possible, the structure employed should be the one that arises out of the biblical material itself'.[37] For this reason, Scobie rejects the systematic approach exemplified by the compilations of prooftexts prevalent within Protestant orthodoxy, the biblical theology of Ewald as well as quite a few nineteenth- and twentieth-century Old and New Testament theologies (e.g., those of Köhler and Schelkle).

---

[32] *WOG*, 73–75.
[33] *WOG*, 75–76.
[34] Jodock, 'Reciprocity', 378, as quoted in *WOG*, 77.
[35] *WOG*, 77–78.
[36] *WOG*, 79–80.
[37] *WOG*, 81.

Indeed, noting that Childs's theological reflection on the Christian Bible in his *Biblical Theology of the Old and New Testaments* largely follows traditional systematic categories, Scobie regards the failure to develop an appropriate structure for his biblical theology as one of the disappointments of Childs's *magnum opus*. More generally, Scobie maintains that, while dogmatic theology largely derived its system from the biblical material, it nevertheless tends to superimpose categories that are foreign to biblical thought.[38]

Scobie also rejects the historical approach advocated by de Wette, von Cölln and most nineteenth- and twentieth-century Old and New Testament theologies, which are based on changing scholarly reconstructions of the historical development of biblical thought. While the historical approach is adept at handling the biblical material's diversity and demonstrating the development of biblical thought, biblical theology needs to go beyond a merely historical approach if it is to be distinct from the History of Religions approach.[39]

A thematic approach, in turn, 'seeks to structure its treatment around themes or topics that arise from the biblical material itself '.[40] An important feature of the works that have taken this line of approach has been the search for a 'centre' or 'focal point' for the Old or New Testament. Numerous proposals have been made, and a long debate ensued, but no satisfactory solution has been found for either the Old or New Testament, not to mention the biblical canon as a whole. Scobie therefore concludes that the quest for a single centre has failed and that a multi-thematic approach is needed, which identifies major themes around which related minor themes can then be arranged.[41]

Considering the relationship between the two Testaments, Scobie contends that a biblical theology that seeks to do justice to the biblical canon in its entirety must avoid an overemphasis on either Testament. He especially insists, quoting Childs, that biblical theology is 'not to Christianize the Old Testament by identifying it with the New Testament witness', but that it must allow the Old Testament's 'own theological testimony to the God of Israel whom the Church confesses also to worship' to be heard.[42]

Seeking to define the relationship between the Testaments, Scobie discusses *allegorization*, which he rejects; *typology*, whose rehabilitation by the canonical approach has led to a deeper appreciation of the continuity inherent in Scripture; and *promise and fulfilment*, in connection with which a narrow proof-texting approach is to be resisted. He also looks at *salvation history*, which aptly recognizes the storyline running through Scripture but fails to deal

---

[38] See *WOG*, 81–83.

[39] *WOG*, 83–85.

[40] *WOG*, 85.

[41] *WOG*, 85–87.

[42] *WOG*, 89; the quotes are from Childs, *Old Testament Theology*, 9.

adequately with the biblical 'history of disobedience' and of judgement. And he examines *progressive revelation*, which appreciates that the divine revelation was given in stages but could be misleading if it suggested 'that advance to a new level of revelation abrogates what went before',[43] and the category of *continuity*, which draws attention to the fact that the New Testament assumes and accepts large parts of the Old Testament witness.[44]

In his own approach to biblical theology, Scobie proposes to correlate the major themes of the two Testaments with each other. He stresses that, although the Old Testament material 'is discussed with an eye to the way the theme is developed in the NT, ... every effort is made to listen to what the OT says on its own terms'.[45] Beginning with the Old Testament, Scobie finds in it a dual emphasis of *proclamation and promise*. The Old Testament 'proclaims what God has done, both in nature and in history', but 'Israel lives between past and future, between the already and the not yet, between memory and hope, between proclamation and promise'.[46] In its canonical context, the New Testament proclamation of the Christ event is seen as a *fulfilment* of the Old Testament promise, but the New Testament too knows of the tension between the already and the not yet; it too looks forward to what Scobie terms the *final consummation*.

Scobie's biblical theology thus is an eschatological theology, for he regards eschatology as 'a key dimension of every biblical theme';[47] and the eschatological pattern of 'proclamation/promise: fulfilment/consummation' provides him with the structure for his sketch of biblical theology, a structure that reveals Scripture's 'inner canonical and theological dynamic rather than [its] ... tradition-historical development'.[48]

Having established this structure, Scobie turns to the identification of the major biblical themes, which he says 'were arrived at very largely through an extensive study of the numerous proposals that have been made by biblical scholars, especially for a so-called center or focal point of BT [biblical theology]'.[49] The themes suggested by Scobie are 'God's order', 'God's servant', 'God's people' and 'God's way'.

The first, 'God's order', attempts to be sensitive to the dialectic between creation and redemption, to God's activities in nature as well as in history, to his relation to all humankind as well as to Israel. The term 'God's order' also

---

[43] *WOG*, 91.
[44] See *WOG*, 88–91.
[45] *WOG*, 91–92.
[46] *WOG*, 92.
[47] *WOG*, 93 (emphasis removed).
[48] *WOG*, 93.
[49] *WOG*, 93.

seeks 'to express the biblical distinction between the present order and the expected new order'.[50] Secondly, rather than adopting a narrow messianic proof-text approach, such as the one underlying Vischer's formula 'the Old Testament tells us *what* the Christ is; the New *who* he is',[51] Scobie suggests 'God's servant' as a more inclusive theme. This allows him to do justice to the fact that the New Testament 'does not portray Jesus as fulfilling any one concept of the Messiah [but] ... links him in some way with virtually every form of expectation and with a variety of OT types', at the same time portraying 'him as transcending all types and expectations'.[52]

The third major theme, 'God's people', comprises notions such as election, communion between God and humankind, and the covenant,[53] while, fourthly, themes like piety, spirituality and ethics are subsumed under the biblical image of the 'way' (or 'God's way'), which expresses human conduct or behaviour. Scobie notes the frequent separation of biblical ethics from biblical theology but contends, with Childs, that 'the Old Testament portrayal of ethical behaviour is inseparable from its total message respecting Israel, that is to say, from its theological content'.[54]

For each of these four main themes Scobie identifies five associated subthemes, and the discussion of both the main themes and their associated subthemes follows the 'proclamation/promise: fulfilment/consummation' pattern.[55] The table on the next page displays the broad contours of Scobie's biblical theology.

Having subjected all sub-themes (twenty in total) to the 'proclamation/ promise: fulfilment/consummation' pattern, Scobie then offers some theological reflections on each of them. It is also worth mentioning in this context that *each* of the sub-themes is once again divided up into five sections, which are also subjected to the pattern of 'proclamation/promise: fulfilment/consummation'.[56] The first sub-theme, 'The Living God', whose outline is displayed in the table overleaf (p. 52), may serve as an illustration of this procedure.

---

[50] *WOG*, 94.

[51] Vischer, *Witness*, 7, as quoted in *WOG*, 95.

[52] *WOG*, 96.

[53] *WOG*, 97.

[54] Childs, *Biblical Theology*, 676, as quoted in *WOG*, 97.

[55] See *WOG*, Part II, 103–927.

[56] However, the structure breaks down in chapters 9 ('The Servant's Suffering'), 10 ('The Servant's Vindication'), 13 ('Land and City') and 15 ('Ministry'), where some sub-themes do not carry through into the 'final consummation' section (in addition, chapter 10 also features a shorter 'Old Testament promise' section). For a convenient outline of Scobie's biblical theology see *WOG*, 928-48.

	Proclamation	Promise	Fulfilment	Consummation
	God's Order	A New Order	The New Order	The Final Consummation
The Living God	In the beginning God	A God who hides himself	In the fullness of time	The beginning and the end
The Lord of Creation	God created the heavens and the earth	New heavens and a new earth	A new creation	New heavens and a new earth
The Lord of History	I will call to mind the deeds of the Lord	I will restore the fortunes of my people	We are witnesses to all that he did	The end will not follow immediately
The Adversary	Our adversaries	Wrath to his adversaries	Our adversary, the devil	The antichrist
The Spirit	The Spirit of the Lord	I will pour out my Spirit	All filled with the Holy Spirit	His Spirit as a guarantee
	God's Servant	A New Servant	The New Servant	The Final Consummation
The Messiah	The Lord's Messiah	The coming of a Messiah	You are the Messiah	The kingdom of his Messiah
The Son of Man	Son of man, I send you	One like a son of man	Behold, the son of man	One like a son of man
Glory, Word, Wisdom, Son	By your word and by your wisdom	The Lord will come	The word became flesh	With great power and glory
The Servant's Suffering	Despised and rejected	Many shall be astonished	He humbled himself	The lamb who was slain
The Servant's Vindication	They shall not prevail against you	A portion with the great	God has highly exalted him	Our Lord, come!
	God's People	A New People	The New People	The Final Consummation
The Covenant Community	My people Israel	The Israel of God	The new Israel	The twelve tribes of Israel
The Nations	Among the nations	All the nations shall come	Make disciples of all nations	A great multitude from every nation
Land and City	The land that I will show you	A land of delight	To the end of the earth	The holy city, new Jerusalem
Worship	O come, let us worship	All people shall come to worship	Worship in spirit and in truth	They fall down and worship
Ministry	The ministry of the Lord	They shall minister to me	Ministers of Christ	The twelve apostles and the lamb
	God's Way	A New Way	The New Way	The Final Consummation
The Human Condition	What are human beings?	There is none that does good	All are under the power of sin	The coming judgement
Faith and Hope	Trust in the Lord	A new heart I will give you	Repent and believe	Press on toward the goal
God's Commandments	Love me and keep my commandments	I will put my law within them	A new commandment	Those who keep the commandments
Love your Neighbour	You shall love your neighbour	Everyone will invite his neighbour	You shall love your neighbour	Nothing unclean shall enter
Life	The land of the living	Your dead shall live	From death to life	You will live also

Old Testament		New Testament	
Proclamation	Promise	Fulfilment	Consummation
God's Order: In the beginning God	A New Order: A God who hides himself	The New Order: In the fullness of time	The Final Consummation: The beginning and the end
The Lord is king	An everlasting kingdom	The kingdom of God has drawn near	Your kingdom come
The name of God	The name of God	The name of God	The name of God
The one God	The one God	The one God	The one God
The personal God	The personal God	The personal God	We will see him
Moses wrote all the words of the Lord	Bind up the testimony	For so it is written	The Scriptures

Following our look at the structure of Scobie's biblical theology, as explained in the prolegomena (Part I) and executed in his 'sketch of biblical theology' (Part II), we need to return once more to the prolegomena, which are concluded by some reflections on the issue of unity and diversity. Scobie is troubled by the anticipated charge that

> any proposal for a BT [biblical theology] that adopts a canonical, thematic, and structured approach faces the inevitable criticism that it will in effect impose a false unity on the biblical material, and will thereby undervalue the rich diversity of the biblical witness.[57]

Yet he maintains 'that it is precisely a canonical BT that will seek to do justice to the whole sweep of biblical thought', while at the same time providing 'ample scope for the recognition of diversity, tensions, and even paradox in biblical thought'.[58] Scobie illustrates his sensitivity to the dialectical nature of the biblical material with the help of two examples: creation and history, and the individual and the community.

With regard to the former, Scobie criticizes the Biblical Theology Movement for its overemphasis of *Heilsgeschichte* and God's dealings with his people in history, arguing that biblical theology needs to give sufficient attention to the scriptural dialectic of history and creation as the two spheres of God's activity.[59] Concerning the second example (that of the individual and the community), Scobie notes that, although the group (family, clan/tribe, Israel, humankind) is often regarded as a unity, with the individual being almost inseparable from that group, the group can also be represented by and in the person of an individual (e.g., Adam, Jacob/Israel). Scobie in this context criticizes the historical approach, which hypothesized a move from 'primitive'

---

[57] *WOG*, 99.
[58] *WOG*, 99.
[59] *WOG*, 100.

collective thinking to the individualized religion of the later 'major prophets', maintaining that the scriptural canon from beginning to end presents us with a dialectic between individual and community.[60]

Reflections on the Nature and Genre of Biblical Theology

Having thus outlined the thrust of Scobie's proposals for a biblical theology, I first wish to make some general evaluative comments on his prolegomena before moving on to reflect on the limitations and the role of descriptive analytical biblical theologies.

Scobie's 'Prolegomena to a Biblical Theology' revisited

Let me begin by pointing out that I fully endorse Scobie's conception of biblical theology as a 'bridge' between academia and the church, Scripture's 'true interpretive community'. Levenson once aptly lamented that historical criticism has shifted 'the locus of truth from the practising community to the nonpractising and unaffiliated individual',[61] even though historical critics, ironically, depend for their livelihood 'upon the vitality of traditional religious communities, Jewish and Christian'.[62] To redress this balance, Scobie is right to develop a dialectical approach that builds upon historical-critical scholarship (and its insistence upon historical readings), while at the same time adopting presuppositions shared by faith communities, such as the conception of Scripture as divine revelation. Scobie's further insistence that biblical theology needs to be ecumenical is also to be welcomed as an important attempt to prevent the blinkers of particular traditions from encumbering the task of biblical theology.

Another valuable feature of Scobie's biblical theology is the demand for an overemphasis on either Testament to be avoided and for biblical theology not to limit its attention to *Vetus Testamentum in novo receptum*. Scobie rightly stresses that biblical theology must deal with *Vetus Testamentum per se*, making every attempt to listen to what the Old Testament has to say on its own terms. Scobie's intention to base his biblical theology on the structure of the Christian canon and the canonical text in its final form and his rejection of a 'canon within the canon' are laudable too. Similarly, his decision to abandon the search for a centre for biblical theology and settle instead on a quartet of key themes with an attending multitude of sub-themes and sub-sub-themes is

---

[60] *WOG*, 101–102.

[61] Levenson, *Hebrew Bible*, 116.

[62] Levenson, *Hebrew Bible*, 110.

more than just one step in the right direction, as it allows him to do more justice to Scripture's diversity than many of his predecessors.

To be sure, many of the issues discussed in Scobie's prolegomena are controversial, and questions could be raised at several points. To give but one example, one might want to probe, for instance, just how successful Scobie is in his attempt not to superimpose any structure that is foreign to the biblical material. For he opens his sketch of biblical theology with a chapter entitled 'The Living God', in which he discusses issues such as God's kingship, the name of God, the one God (monotheism/monolatry) and the personal God (anthropomorphism). This is followed, in Chapters 2 and 3, by discussions of 'The Lord of Creation' and 'The Lord of History'. In other words, Scobie begins with theology proper, with a *logos* about *theos*, seeking to justify this approach by labelling the first sub-heading of Chapter 1 'In the Beginning God',[63] thus suggesting that he starts where the Bible also starts.

Yet, is this really where the Bible begins? After all, the opening words of the Old Testament are *bᵉrēʾšit bārāʾ ʾᵉlōhîm ʾēt haššāmayim wᵉʾēt hāʾ āreṣ* ('in the beginning God created the heavens and the earth'). The account of Genesis 1, that is to say, does not begin with a *logos* about *theos*; it rather takes God for granted, as it were, stressing instead that 'in the beginning God *created the heavens and the earth*'. For this reason, Hasel's criticism of the systematic approach to biblical theology, quoted affirmatively by Scobie in his prolegomena, at this point appears to apply to Scobie's own presentation, for indeed 'the Bible does not order its material and its theology in such a way'.[64]

This is not to suggest that a biblical theology ought to follow the canonical presentation slavishly, for if that were the case, all we could do would be to reproduce Scripture's actual words.[65] Yet, in this particular instance, the canonical presentation and order are surely highly significant and thus worthy of attention, especially since Scobie insists that 'biblical theology is based on the structure of the Christian canon'.[66] To be sure, Scobie is well aware that, as he puts it, 'the created order ... constitutes a grand "envelope structure" for the whole of Scripture with the theme of creation/new creation enclosing everything else'.[67] Regrettably, however, this insight is not reflected adequately in

---

[63] *WOG*, 105.

[64] Hasel, 'Biblical Theology', 78, as quoted in *WOG*, 83.

[65] See Chapter 5, Chris Wright's 'Mission as a Matrix for Hermeneutics and Biblical Theology'. Wright also notes that any framework for doing biblical theology to some extent distorts the original reality of the text. However, in a helpful analogy, Wright compares the function of a hermeneutical framework for reading the Bible (in his case that of mission) to the function of a map, which, while in some sense distorting the reality it portrays, makes it possible for us to navigate that reality.

[66] *WOG*, 65–71.

[67] *WOG*, 149.

the structure of his biblical theology, which, at this point at least, follows the conventions of traditional systematic theology[68] rather than the contours of the biblical canon.

Biblical theology and the 'Alien Idiom of Didactic Exposition'

Having thus pointed to some strengths and possible weaknesses of Scobie's study, we now turn to the genre of his biblical theology. Like other biblical theologies, it is of a descriptive didactic nature, in that it employs a descriptive mode (what Austin would call 'constatives')[69] in order to present a coherent picture of biblical thought or teaching, a synthesis of 'what the Bible has to say about God and his relation to the world and to humankind'.[70]

Terrien once complained that the systematic approach to biblical theology, being influenced in part by 'Platonic conceptual thinking and Aristotelian logic', was 'bound to translate the *sui generis* thrust of biblical faith into the alien idiom of didactic exposition'.[71] Scobie quotes this criticism in his discussion of the systematic approach, concluding that it demands the rejection of a 'dogmatic structure'.[72] Regrettably, however, he fails to address the question pertaining to the genre of biblical theology writing more generally. Thus, while Scobie – in line with Terrien's argument – apparently regards the danger of translating 'the *sui generis* thrust of biblical faith into the alien idiom of didactic exposition' as a weakness of an overtly systematic or dogmatic approach to biblical theology, my contention is that Scobie's own thematic (or multi-thematic) approach does not escape the problem pointed out by Terrien either.

One might want to probe, of course, whether it is in fact true to say that the idiom of didactic exposition is alien to the biblical material. And if it is, would we then have to conclude that it is inherently distorting and unsuitable? Concerning the first question, it may be helpful to note that academic discourse is sometimes referred to as 'second-level discourse' – that is, discourse that is not directly about the world but about 'first-level discourse', represented in our case by the biblical material. As regards a descriptive analytical biblical theology, even if we reject the claim that it is alien to the biblical material, there is no getting away from the fact that it differs significantly from the first-level

---

[68] See, e.g., Part III of McGrath's *Christian Theology*, which begins with the doctrine of God before moving on in turn to the doctrines of the Trinity, the person of Christ, etc.

[69] See Austin, *How to Do Things with Words*, 1–11.

[70] *WOG*, 5.

[71] Terrien, *Elusive Presence*, 34.

[72] See *WOG*, 83

discourse upon which it is based, because, as Goldingay notes, it seeks to 're-flect on [its object] analytically, critically and constructively'.[73]

Yet, why might this be problematic? In order to answer this question, it seems to me to be important to note that some of the opposition the discipline of biblical theology has faced ever since the rise of historical criticism is due to the fact that the biblical material is seen not to survive its encounter with bibli-cal theology's second-level discourse unscathed. Usually, this problem is con-ceptualized in terms of the unity-diversity debate – that is, biblical theology has been found guilty of reducing or obscuring the diversity of the biblical material in its quest for the Bible's unity.

There is no denying the fact that this has been, and is likely to continue to be, a controversial issue. However, recent criticisms of the discipline of biblical theology suggest that the unity-diversity question is only one problem among others. There also appears to be an implicit uneasiness with the way in which biblical theology's very genre requires a presentation of the biblical material which in and of itself is problematic and thus in need of critical reflection. Of course, the advantages of critical and analytical engagement with the biblical material afforded by biblical theology are hardly in doubt. I am concerned, though, that the discipline might suffer further (unnecessary) setbacks at the hands of its critics if it does not engage more openly with the limitations posed by its own descriptive and analytical approach. So it is to these limitations that we now turn.

The limitations of descriptive analytical biblical theologies

The problem of categorization

Scobie's desire to present an ordered account 'of what the Bible has to say about God and his relation to the world and to humankind' requires him to cat-egorize the biblical material and fit it into a structure created specifically for this purpose. To be sure, Scobie is adamant that his themes arise from within the biblical material and that his structure is based on that of the scriptural canon. Yet, these claims notwithstanding, the very issue of categorization presents its own problems and thus bears further reflection.

The problem of categorization is well illustrated by the difficulties faced by universal language enthusiasts who sought to categorize the universe and express these categories through some kind of linguistic system. Critics like Jorge Luis Borges have countered these attempts, arguing that 'there is no clas-sification of the universe that is not arbitrary and conjectural'.[74] As regards the classification of the biblical material undertaken in the attempt to present 'an

---

[73] Thus Goldingay, *Old Testament Theology*, 17.

[74] Borges, 'Analytical Language', 104.

ordered account' of the biblical teaching, one does not need to subscribe to the postmodern notion of total arbitrariness in order to recognize that such classifications, whether systematic, dogmatic, thematic or even multi-thematic, can hardly escape the problem of being to some degree arbitrary and conjectural.

Of course, some structures fit the biblical material better than others, but the point here is that we need to be aware of the provisional and conjectural nature of all schemes. This strikes me as important, because there sometimes seems to be the expectation that, if only we can find the right structuring principle, we can come up with *the* definitive biblical theology. The attempt to produce such a definitive solution reminds one of the quest for a correct exegetical method which has been criticized by Barton, who noting that

> much harm has been done in biblical studies by insisting that there is, somewhere, a 'correct' method which, if only we could find it, would unlock the mysteries of the text. From the quest for this method flow many evils: for example, the tendency of each newly-discovered method to excommunicate its predecessors ...[75]

This is not to say that any structure will do, or that none will. Some structures clearly do more justice to the biblical canon than others, but we cannot avoid and would do well to acknowledge the provisional and subjective nature of our schemes and conclusions. Indeed, if there is any mileage at all in the stress of much of recent hermeneutical theory on the reader's contribution to the task of interpretation, it is evident that our quest for an appropriately outlined biblical theology will not escape this element of subjectivity either.

The problem of coherence

A related problem concerns the fact that the attempt to master the wealth of the biblical material (or the universe) frequently leads to the construal of systems and concepts that are too rigid because they endeavour to be too orderly and coherent. On a purely formal level, this desire for orderliness is illustrated by the structure of Scobie's sketch of biblical theology in which each major theme is subdivided into five sub-themes, each of which is yet again broken up into five sub-sub-themes. More important for our present purposes, however, is the observation that biblical theology strives for order where the biblical material itself resists it.

I do not wish to dispute that such order can aid our understanding of the Bible, but it is imperative to note that in the very attempt to present a coherent, orderly account of the biblical material inhere limitations and the potential for misrepresentation. Goldingay, among others, has drawn our attention to this problem. Commenting on Scripture's overall narrative character, which, as he

---

[75] Barton, *Reading*, 5.

rightly points out, is not accidental but corresponds to the very nature of the biblical faith, he notes that biblical narrative is 'open-ended, allusive, and capable of embracing questions and ambiguity'.[76] Given these qualities, biblical narrative might therefore be better suited to expressing and addressing the complexities of life than a systematic, dogmatic or multi-thematic theology. Indeed, Goldingay even suggests that in being more univocal than Scripture, our theological statements also tend to be less true.[77]

Goldingay's reflections were of course made vis-à-vis the systematic approach to the biblical material, but much of what he has to say is relevant also in connection with a thematic approach like Scobie's. Most importantly, Goldingay points out that the translation of the biblical material into a system (or new structure) has leaned towards the unequivocal, replacing stories with concepts and categories and eclipsing the mysterious and the equivocal.[78] This is unfortunate, for narrative's ability to embrace complexity, ambiguity and mystery[79] is an expedient skill, given the nature of the Christian faith, which, as the apostle Paul says, obliges us to 'see in a mirror, dimly', and to 'know only in part' (1 Cor. 13:12). As McGrath so aptly notes:

> Recognition of the narrative character of Scripture allows us to appreciate how Scripture effectively conveys the tension between the limited knowledge on the part of the human characters in the story, and the omniscience of God.[80]

There is, of course, more to Scripture than narrative, even though much of the biblical material exists in narrative form. I therefore concur with McGrath's contention that 'to approach theology from a narrative point of view is, potentially, to be much more faithful to Scripture itself than to take a more theoretical approach'.[81] If this is true for theology, how much more does it apply to *biblical* theology? Yet, the biblical writings also witness to some non-negotiable core beliefs, just as they contain some binding imperatives; and both of these, one might say, are perhaps better suited to a biblical theology project such as Scobie's. However, the complexity, ambiguity and mystery so importantly brought to our attention by Goldingay are not just the domain of biblical narrative but are also very much to the fore in texts such as the book of Job or the

---

[76] Goldingay, 'Biblical Narrative', 132.

[77] Goldingay, *Old Testament Theology*, 40–41.

[78] Goldingay, 'Biblical Narrative', 132–33, in this context criticizes Childs and Watson for importing a framework of thinking that is foreign to the biblical writings.

[79] See Goldingay, 'Biblical Narrative', 135.

[80] McGrath, *Christian Theology*, 170. Of course, the concept of God's omniscience itself might not always be the most expedient notion in relation to, for instance, OT narrative, but that is a matter which need not detain us here.

[81] McGrath, *Christian Theology*, 169.

Psalms, to mention only two examples. What all these texts have in common is their potential to challenge our urge to be too coherent or, in Goldingay's terms, to 'be too straight and narrow, to be rationalist'.[82]

The problem of reductionism

Not only are biblical theologies in danger of eclipsing the mysterious and the equivocal, they are also reductionistic in the sense that a great diversity of biblical genres is here replaced by or conflated into one single genre, that of didactic exposition, to revert to Terrien's phraseology. Or, from a speech-act-theoretical perspective, one might say that the variety of biblical 'performatives' (statements that 'get something done'), such as laws, narratives, laments, psalms of praise[83] and so on, are replaced by 'constatives' (statements that describe certain states of affairs).[84]

The effect of this is that the multifaceted multi-genre performative form of the biblical material is turned into a streamlined single-genre descriptive account. Again, I do not doubt that that genre has its merits. My point here simply is that in gaining one thing, something else is being lost. In particular, there is a danger that, in comparison with the biblical material itself, descriptive biblical theologies may seem somewhat impoverished, timid, arid, bloodless and lacking in life, to use the adjectives employed by the Italian poet, scholar and philosopher Giacomo Leopardi (1798–1837) in an invective against various universal language schemes.[85]

To come back briefly to the perspective afforded to us by speech-act theory, it is highly instructive to note that the penchant for a descriptive construal of language has been associated by Selden and Widdowson with 'the old logical-positivist view of language which assume[s] that *the only meaningful statements are those which describe a state of affairs in the world*'.[86] This raises the interesting question of whether, or to what extent, some such notions might underlie our attempts to construct descriptive biblical theologies.[87]

---

[82] Goldingay, 'Biblical Narrative', 135.

[83] On the significance of lament and praise as human responses to the *Deus absconditus atque praesens*; see Terrien, *Elusive Presence*; see also Westermann, 'Role'.

[84] On speech-act theory, see especially Austin, *How to Do Things With Words*; Searle, *Speech Acts* and *Expression*; Grice, 'Logic' and 'Utterance-Meaning'.

[85] See Eco, *Search*, 303.

[86] Selden and Widdowson, *Reader's Guide*, 148 (emphasis mine).

[87] In this connection, the work of Oswald Bayer deserves special mention. Bayer's aim in many of the studies collected in *Gott als Autor* is to explore the possibility of a 'poietological theology' that takes its cue from the primary sources of the Christian faith, eschewing a total reliance on descriptive discourse as the only form of truth communication.

The Role of Descriptive Analytical Biblical Theologies

Earlier on I referred to Borges' conviction that human categorizations of the universe are bound to be arbitrary and conjectural. What I did not mention is that Borges goes on to stress that 'the impossibility of penetrating the divine scheme of the universe *cannot* dissuade us from outlining human schemes, even though we are aware that they are provisional'.[88] By the same token, I do not wish to suggest that we abandon all attempts to present an 'ordered account of what the Bible has to say about God and his relation to the world and to humankind'. I do believe, however, that in order for the discipline of biblical theology to make any headway into the future, it is important to reflect critically on its genre-related limitations, which I have begun to do in the previous section, as well as on its precise role, which is the subject of the following considerations.

A crucial question in this connection is what we are hoping, and can reasonably be expecting, to achieve in constructing descriptive analytical biblical theologies. According to Scobie, the aim is to 'provide [the Christian community with] some kind of overall structure for understanding the complex and diverse mass of biblical material'.[89] Quoting the English poet George Herbert's desire to understand 'the constellation of the storie [sic!]', Scobie stresses that biblical theology needs to help the church 'achieve an overall understanding of the biblical revelation and ... comprehend how the parts [relate] to the whole'.[90]

Both Herbert's desire and Scobie's willingness to fulfil it are laudable. Yet, in the light of the preceding discussion, it seems to me to be of central importance for the discipline of biblical theology to articulate more openly the limitations it inevitably faces as a second-level discourse. Without intending to rehearse these again, I would like to reiterate one particular benefit of the first-level discourse upon which biblical theology is based. As again Goldingay has noted, biblical narrative's discursiveness, as opposed to biblical theology's orderliness, 'reflects the fact that God takes humanity with great seriousness':[91]

> in portraying the specificity of human beings living with God ... [biblical] stories about people facing the challenges, potentials, questions, achievements, ambiguities, puzzles, disappointments, demands and failures that are intrinsic to life with God ... invite their hearers to reflect on the equivalent specificities of their own lives in light

---

[88] Borges, 'Analytical Language', 104 (emphasis mine).

[89] *WOG*, 79–80.

[90] *WOG*, 80.

[91] Goldingay, *Old Testament Theology*, 36. See also McGrath, *Christian Theology*, 169, who notes that 'narrative theology affirms that God meets us in history, and speaks to us as one who has been involved in history'.

of the stories' implicit convictions about who God is and what human life is. Such reflection needs the help of narrative with its concreteness and specificity.[92]

Given its limitations as a second-level discourse, biblical theology also needs to articulate more carefully just what kind of role it is hoping to play as the bridge discipline between academia and the Christian community that Scobie would like it to be. Sometimes, one gets the impression that an all-encompassing biblical theology like Scobie's is regarded as the pinnacle of biblical scholarship, something that biblical scholarship eventually ought to result in. It is to notions such as these that Barr appears to be reacting when he maintains that it may 'be mistaken to take the large and comprehensive Theologies of the Old Testament (or of the New, or of the Bible) as being the prime example of biblical theology or as the ideal to which all work in biblical theology should strive'.[93]

Barr's commendation of other, less sweeping, forms of biblical theology is criticized by Scobie, who insists that biblical theology cannot be content with 'such a fragmented approach'.[94] I would clearly want to side with Scobie, if Barr is implying that there is no place at all for comprehensive biblical theologies. However, in the light of the problems of categorization and coherence discussed earlier, Barr's claim that 'the production of large and comprehensive volumes of [biblical theology] *is not necessarily the highest goal* within the discipline'[95] does not appear to me to be misconceived; nor does it seem to be overly unconstructive.

The limitations imposed on biblical theology by its very genre and nature as a second-level discourse also require an unambiguous articulation of the fact that it can always only hope to star in a supportive role. This may well be implied in Scobie's aspiration to help the Christian community understand the 'constellation of the storie'. And, of course, there is nothing wrong with the desire to enable the church to come to terms with the complex and diverse mass of biblical material, especially if biblical theology aims to lead the church back to the complexity and performative force of the Bible's first-level discourse.

The ordered account, in other words, must never 'replace' that complex and diverse mass or give the impression that the Bible's complexity has been, or could ever be, mastered. For even if biblical theology succeeds in opening the eyes of the church to the complexity of the biblical material, the ordered account, which can only ever be provisional, could never hope to escape the danger of mis- or under-representing the first-level discourse's fascinating

---

[92] Goldingay, *Old Testament Theology*, 36–37.

[93] Barr, *Concept*, 52.

[94] *WOG*, 79.

[95] Barr, *Concept*, 52 (emphasis mine).

complexity and performative force. Moreover, if there is any truth to the claim that our classification of the biblical material, which an ordered account inevitably requires, is bound to be to some degree arbitrary, we must also conclude that in providing the church with a framework for understanding the biblical material as a whole, biblical theology must live with the ever-present risk of actually skewing the church's perception of the Bible. To be sure, this is a risk worth taking, but it is important to be realistic about what biblical theology can and cannot hope to achieve.

Concerning the precise role of biblical theology, Wright's suggestion to conceptualize it in terms of a map[96] might be a helpful way forward. Maps, Wright notes, inevitably distort the reality they depict, because a three-dimensional reality cannot be reproduced on a two-dimensional plane without distortion. Maps also represent reality selectively and symbolically, two further ways of distorting the original data, but they do so in order to make it possible for us to navigate the very reality they seek to depict.

This seems to me to be a valuable analogy in drawing out both the assets and the limitations of an analytical biblical theology. It illustrates that the aim of our ordered accounts must always be to lead the reader back to the biblical material itself, to the reality which the ordered account is meant to help readers navigate. Of course, as we all know, some maps are more useful than others. Some employ colours and symbols to good effect in order to point us to scenic features in the landscape or help us find the way to the next service station. But maps can also be amazingly useless. They can very easily lead us astray, if vital bits of information are missing or misleadingly presented. Biblical theologies are no different in that respect, which is precisely why Scobie is at pains to stress that any structure must arise out of the biblical material itself.[97]

The analogy of the map also points to the limitations of biblical theologies. No one who has studied even the largest-scale maps of the English Lake District will have the slightest clue of its breathtaking beauty. In order to appreciate the magnificence of the lakes and fells and face the vagaries of the weather (which is very much part of the experience), one has to go there for oneself. A map can never replace the reality it depicts just like a biblical theology can never replace the complexity of the biblical material. Nor can a map adequately convey what that reality is like; all it can do is to help us navigate that reality. Similarly, given the limitations discussed above, a biblical theology can never hope to do full justice to the biblical witness in all its performative force and multi-genre diversity. At best, what a biblical theology can hope to achieve is to enable readers to navigate the biblical landscape in all its stunning beauty and surprising (and perhaps even frustrating) jaggedness. But to accomplish this would be no mean feat.

---

[96] See Wright, 'Mission', in the present volume.
[97] See *WOG*, 81.

Bibliography

Austin, J.L., *How to Do Things With Words* (Oxford: Clarendon Press, 2nd edn, 1975)

Barr, J., *The Concept of Biblical Theology: An Old Testament Perspective* (Minneapolis: Fortress Press, 1999)

Barton, J., *Reading the Old Testament: Method in Biblical Study* (London: Darton, Longman & Todd, 2nd edn, 1996)

Bayer, O., *Gott als Autor: Zu einer poietologischen Theologie* (Tübingen: J.C.B. Mohr [Paul Siebeck], 1999)

Borges, J.L., 'The Analytical Language of John Wilkins', in *Other Inquisitions, 1937–1952* (trans. R.L.C. Simms; intro. J.E. Irby; Austin: University of Texas Press, 1964), 101–105

Childs, B.S., *Old Testament Theology in a Canonical Context* (London: SCM Press, 1985; Philadelphia: Fortress Press, 1986)

——, *Biblical Theology of the Old and New Testaments: Theological Reflection on the Christian Bible* (London: SCM Press; Minneapolis: Fortress Press, 1992)

Ebeling, G., *Word and Faith* (trans. J.W. Leitch; London: SCM Press, 1963)

Eco, U., *The Search for the Perfect Language* (trans. J. Fentress; London: Fontana Press, 1997)

Fish, S., *Is There a Text in This Class? The Authority of Interpretive Communities* (Cambridge, MA: Harvard University Press, 1980)

Gese, H., *Essays on Biblical Theology* (trans. K. Crim; Minneapolis: Augsburg, 1981)

Goldingay, J., 'Biblical Narrative and Systematic Theology', in *Between Two Horizons: Spanning New Testament Studies and Systematic Theology* (ed. J.B. Green and M. Turner; Grand Rapids: Eerdmans, 2000), 123–42

——, *Old Testament Theology*, I: *Israel's Gospel* (Downers Grove, IL: InterVarsity Press, 2003)

Grice, H.P., 'Utterance-Meaning, Sentence-Meaning, and Word-Meaning', in *The Philosophy of Language* (ed. J.R. Searle; London: Oxford University Press, 1971), 54–70

——, 'Logic and Conversation', in *Syntax and Semantics*, III: *Speech-Acts* (ed. P. Cole and J.L. Morgan; New York: Academic Press, 1975), 41–58

Hasel, G.F., 'Biblical Theology: Then, Now, and Tomorrow', *HBT* 4 (1982), 61–93

Jodock, D., 'The Reciprocity between Scripture and Theology: The Role of Scripture in Contemporary Theological Reflection', *Int* 44 (1990), 369–82

Levenson, J.D., *The Hebrew Bible, the Old Testament, and Historical Criticism: Jews and Christians in Biblical Studies* (Louisville, KY: Westminster John Knox Press, 1993)

McGrath, A.E., *Christian Theology: An Introduction* (Oxford: Basil Blackwell, 3rd edn, 2001)

Rad, G. von, *Old Testament Theology* (trans. D.M.G. Stalker; 2 vols.; Edinburgh: Oliver & Boyd, 1962–65)

——, *Wisdom in Israel* (trans. J.D. Martin; London: SCM Press, 1972)

Sandys-Wunsch, J., and L. Eldredge, 'J.P. Gabler and the Distinction between Biblical and Dogmatic Theology: Translation, Commentary, and Discussion of His Originality', *SJT* 33 (1980), 133–58

Scobie, C.H.H., *The Ways of Our God: An Approach to Biblical Theology* (Grand Rapids: Eerdmans, 2003)

Searle, J.R., *Speech Acts: An Essay in the Philosophy of Language* (Cambridge: Cambridge University Press, 1969)

——, *Expression and Meaning: Studies in the Theory of Speech Acts* (Cambridge: Cambridge University Press, 1979)

Selden, R., and P. Widdowson, *A Reader's Guide to Contemporary Literary Theory* (New York: Harvester Wheatsheaf, 3rd edn, 1993)

Stendahl, K., 'Biblical Theology, Contemporary', in *IDB* 1 (ed. G.A. Buttrick; Nashville: Abingdon Press, 1962), 418–32

Terrien, S.L., *The Elusive Presence: Toward a New Biblical Theology* (San Francisco: Harper & Row, 1978)

Vischer, W., *The Witness of the Old Testament to Christ* (London: Lutterworth Press, 1949)

Watson, F., *Text and Truth: Redefining Biblical Theology* (Grand Rapids: Eerdmans, 1997)

Westermann, C., 'The Role of Lament in the Theology of the Old Testament', *Int* 28 (1974), 20–39

3

Some Directions in Catholic Biblical Theology

Francis Martin

I will take for granted that the story of Catholic exegesis in the last two centuries is well enough known not to need a protracted history here in order to introduce my subject.[1] I will instead reflect on two aspects of the Vatican II document on divine revelation, *Dei Verbum*, and then consider how the challenge left to Catholic scholars by this document is being met. The challenge, as will be seen, is to avail ourselves of all the modern disciplines of history, linguistics, literature and cultural anthropology, while at the same time transcending the atheistic presuppositions and implications of these disciplines in order to read the Scriptures 'in the Spirit in which they were written'. Serious advances in this integration must take place through reflection on the nature of history and of communication through language. I will concentrate on these two areas, showing how both are brought to bear in a revived understanding of the 'spiritual sense'. I will conclude with some brief reflections on the important work being done in implementing the Vatican II document *Nostra Aetate*, particularly the call for Christian and Jewish scholars to reflect mutually and more profoundly on their common heritage.

In the forty years since the Second Vatican Council scholars have taken a variety of directions in biblical studies, not all of them successful. Among the more positive achievements in biblical theology has been the publication of various types of commentaries covering the whole Bible.[2] Despite the efforts of the 1993 document of the Pontifical Biblical Commission judiciously to establish a unique place for the historical-critical method, which it called 'the indispensable method for the scientific study of the meaning of ancient texts'

---

[1] One may consult Williamson, 'Place of History'; Fitzmyer, 'Interpretation of the Bible'.

[2] For example, Brown, Fitzmyer and Murphy (eds.), *The Jerome Biblical Commentary*; Navarre University Theology Faculty (ed.), *The Navarre Bible*; Farmer (ed.), *The International Bible Commentary*; Harrington (ed.), *Sacra Pagina*.

(I,A,1), the mood in both the Catholic world and that of biblical exegesis in general could be described as 'restless'. Efforts to find other approaches were described by the same document as 'in competition' with the 'diachronic' approach of the historical-critical method. The former methods were described as insisting upon 'a *synchronic* understanding of texts – that is, one which has to do with their language, composition, narrative structure and capacity for persuasion'.[3]

The larger issue, however, is not the various approaches to the text, but the philosophical presuppositions that underlie them. Sometimes a scholar manages, in the strength of a faith intuition, to go beyond what the historical methods allow, and there are scholars who have effectively forged a synthesis between faith and these methods despite their anti-transcendent bias. Yet it is only in recent years that scholars have sought to elaborate a reflective and philosophical basis for such a synthesis. Many of those doing so in the Protestant and evangelical worlds are represented in the volumes of this series. I wish here to point to Catholic efforts in the same direction. I will necessarily be brief, but these indications may serve to point to ways in which the two complementary aspects of *Dei Verbum* §12, one insisting on historical work and the other on an older theological approach, can be integrated.

Dei Verbum

Most significant for our topic of Catholic biblical theology, particularly from the point of view of the relation between the Testaments, are the directives given in *Dei Verbum* §12 regarding modern historical and cultural studies and the more traditional approaches to the Scriptures. I will give the text and then offer some comments.[4] The section picks up from the latter part of §11, where one of the primary purposes had been to rescue the discussion about inerrancy from its previously fruitless debates by introducing the concept of 'the truth which God, for the sake of our salvation (*nostrae salutis causa*), wanted put into the sacred writings'. Paragraph §12 then proceeds:

> However, since God speaks in Sacred Scripture through men in human fashion, the interpreter of Sacred Scripture, in order to see clearly what God wanted to communicate to us, should carefully investigate what meaning the sacred writers really intended, and what God wanted to manifest by means of their words.[5]

---

[3] See Introduction, above. See Williamson, 'Place of History', 209–13.

[4] Some of what follows in this section is a modified form of a study soon to be published.

[5] My translation. Usually English translations of the Vatican II documents are taken from Abbott (ed.), *Documents of Vatican II*. All other translations, unless otherwise noted, are mine.

These opening lines of §12 place the accent on grasping what 'the sacred writers really intended'. This introduces a cardinal principle already enunciated by St Athanasius and quoted by Pius XII in his encyclical *Divino Afflante Spiritu*:

> Here, as indeed is expedient in all other passages of Sacred Scripture, it should be noted on what occasion the Apostle spoke; we should carefully and faithfully observe to whom and why he wrote, lest, being ignorant of these points, or confounding one with another, we miss the real meaning of the author.[6]

Our text continues:

> To search out the intention of the sacred writers, attention should be given, among other things, to 'literary forms'. For truth is set forth and expressed differently in texts which are variously historical, prophetic, poetic, or of other forms of discourse. The interpreter must investigate what meaning the sacred writer intended to express and actually expressed in particular circumstances by using contemporary literary forms in accordance with the situation of his own time and culture. For the correct understanding of what the sacred author wanted to assert, due attention must be paid to the customary and characteristic styles of feeling, speaking and narrating which prevailed at the time of the sacred writer, and to the patterns men normally employed at that period in their everyday dealings with one another.

Allow me to call attention to the number of times the notion of the intention of the author is invoked here: 'To search out the intention of the sacred writers', attention must be paid to literary forms; the interpreter must investigate 'what meaning the sacred writer intended to express and actually expressed'; finally, due attention must be paid to common styles of speech in order to attain a correct understanding of what the sacred author 'wanted to assert in writing'.

Undoubtedly the correct application of the methods described in this paragraph has been extremely valuable to the study of the sacred page and thus to the Church. We must bear in mind, however, the earlier statement of this document which speaks of the 'economy of revelation' taking place 'by events and words intrinsically bound to each other' (*gestis verbisque intrinsice inter se connexis*, §2). That is, revelation takes place through events that have God as their origin in a unique way, and which reach us in words that are inspired by God and which thus have a unique capacity to mediate the true reality of the events.[7] In this context we may say that in order to participate more fully in the

---

[6] Athanasius, *Contra Arianos* I, 54 (PG 26, col. 123); *Divino Afflante Spiritu*, §34.

[7] This teaching is admirably summed up by von Balthasar, 'Il Senso Spirituale della Scrittura', 7: 'The gradual clothing of the events within the folds of Scripture is not only an inevitable drawback (because the people of the Orient of that time did not know, in fact, an historiography in the modern understanding of the term), but assuredly also this corresponds unqualifiedly to a positive intention of the Spirit'.

reality mediated by the words – intention understood metaphysically – it is of great importance that we grasp what, in terms of his own context, the author 'wants to say' – intention understood psychologically.[8] I will return to this.

The second part of §12 begins with a long sentence whose opening phrase changes the direction of thought, and which points successively to the canon of Scripture, the tradition of the Church and the 'analogy of faith'. This sentence is then followed by remarks about the magisterium and the way biblical interpretation both serves and is subject to it.

> But, since Holy Scripture must be read and interpreted in the same Spirit in which it was written, in order rightly to draw out the meaning of the sacred texts, no less diligent attention must be devoted to the content and unity of the whole of Scripture, taking into account the living tradition of the entire Church and the analogy of faith.
>
> It pertains to exegetes to work according to these rules in order to understand and expound more profoundly the meaning of sacred Scripture so that the judgement of the Church might mature, as it were, by preparatory study. For all of what has been said about the way of interpreting Scripture is subject finally to the judgement of the Church, which carries out the divine commission and ministry of guarding and interpreting the word of God.

This text lists three procedures as part of reading and interpreting Holy Scripture 'in the same Spirit in which it was written', which are necessary 'in order rightly to draw out the meaning of the sacred texts'. There is, first, attention 'to the content and unity of the whole of Scripture' – what may be called 'canonical criticism'. There is, secondly, an account of 'the living tradition of the entire Church'. This must refer to the Fathers and liturgies of both East and West. And, finally, there is '*analogia fidei*', a traditional phrase which emphasizes the fact that not only is the Bible as a whole invested with a multifaceted but consistent message, but also each part of the sacred text must be understood as compatible with others, indeed as deriving from and contributing to an understanding of the whole.

The unity of Scripture

The first consequence of the fact that Scripture is written by the Holy Spirit and must be interpreted in the same Spirit is that 'no less diligent attention must be devoted to the content and unity of the whole of Scripture'. Such a manner of reading and interpreting has been instinctive for most of Christian history. It

---

[8] Today the word 'intention' applies more to the will, i.e., 'what the author wishes to say'. For the ancients the *intentio mentis* signified that reality that the person was 'intending', that is, regarding. Cf. the discussion of Husserl, below.

suffices to look at any patristic writing to perceive this: any part of Scripture may be invoked to shed light on another part. With the advent of historical study and increased attention to the author and the author's intention, the tendency has been to consider a book or part of a book as an isolated entity. Thus, we have the modern phenomenon of studies devoted to 'the theology of Jeremiah', or Mark, or Deutero-Isaiah, and so on. Other procedures that are not as useful – that are, in fact, wrong – attempt to determine a more primitive layer of composition, seeking to discern its theological direction and then attributing to the final redaction a different direction. The assumption of most of this work is that an 'orthodox' layer was superimposed upon a more primitive and inclusive view. The multiplicity of opinions resulting from this procedure is evidence enough of its shaky foundation, and it often betrays a theological bias on the part of the investigator.[9]

In reaction to this atomizing and pluralizing understanding of the Scriptures, recently there has been a return to the more instinctive manner of considering the totality of the text. This return seeks to retain what has been gained through attention to the individual authors and books, but to integrate it with 'the whole of Scripture'. I am, of course, speaking of the approach linked with the name of Brevard Childs, which concentrates in a reflective way on the whole canon as mediating the divine message by holding all its parts in an overarching unity in diversity.[10] Though the insight is extremely important, there remain weaknesses in Childs's approach. Some of these weaknesses result from an understandable lack of recourse to a magisterium; some from the sheer vastness of the historical information that has to be integrated; and some from a lack of philosophical insights, particularly the concept of analogy, which could help in portraying the transposition process by which the various components of the final text have been formed into a whole.[11] Bernard Lonergan gives a good description of this process in his reflection on the process of conversion. Lonergan uses the term 'sublation' where I prefer 'transposition' because of the distance it allows us from Hegel.

> What sublates goes beyond what is sublated, introduces something new and distinct, yet so far from interfering with the sublated or destroying it, on the contrary needs it, includes it, preserves all its proper features and properties, and carries them forward to a fuller realization within a richer context.[12]

---

[9] I have discussed this more at length in my review of *Christology, Controversy and Community*. For an example of this procedure that finds irreducible diversity in the New Testament see Osiek, 'Family'.

[10] See Childs, *Biblical Theology of the Old and New Testaments* and *The New Testament as Canon*. See also Théobald (ed.), *Le Canon des Écritures*.

[11] For a treatment of some of these problems see Noble, *Canonical Approach*.

[12] Lonergan, *Method in Theology*, 241.

The living tradition of the Church

The canon is both a work of tradition and its inspired expression. Surrounding the canon of Scripture and bearing it along is the whole life of the Church, and the exegete must place himself within this movement in order to take 'into account the living tradition of the entire Church'. Surprising as it may seem, there has been hardly any philosophical reflection on the nature of what we call tradition. A recent study by Jorge Gracia can serve as an effective beginning.[13] Gracia's main contention is that tradition is action that is voluntary, intentional, repeated by members of social groups and significant for their identity. To the observation that, at least in the Roman Catholic view, tradition should have verbal content, Gracia replies:

> Accordingly, when Roman Catholics talk about beliefs as constituting a tradition, for example, they can be taken to be referring to the very actions of believing rather than to certain doctrines or to their textual formulation ... what counts in religious faith is the very actions of believing in which people engage and, second, ontologically it is such actions that exist – doctrines exist only insofar as someone holds them.[14]

The advantage of this statement is that it places liturgy and the whole of Christian living at the very heart of tradition. It should be complemented by the nuanced work of Yves Congar, for instance, who takes a broader view of the process of transmission,[15] and I should point out that the very soul of tradition is to be found in the action of the Holy Spirit by which those divine realities 'handed on' (*tradere*) are rendered present, accessible and life-giving.[16] I cite Gracia here because his work serves to highlight exactly what can be lacking in modern historical study of the Scriptures, particularly when the action of the Holy Spirit in the past and in the present is methodologically excluded. Tradition may also simply be described as *sacra doctrina*, an expression that applies to many facets of that activity by which God manifests and communicates himself and a knowledge of his plan so that we can know why we were created and set our lives in that direction. It includes God's original activity of self-manifestation, which culminated in Jesus Christ who is the revelation of God and the source of that divine gracious activity by which we can attain the end to which God has freely called us. The effective subject of this teaching activity is

---

[13] Gracia, *Old Wine*. One should also consult McLean, *Hermeneutics*.
[14] Gracia, *Old Wine*, 94.
[15] Congar, *Tradition and Traditions*.
[16] *Dei Verbum*, §8; *Catechism of the Catholic Church*, par. 78.

the Church, whose prophetic function, exercised principally through the magisterium, consists in preserving the authenticity of what has been and is being 'handed on' by the Holy Spirit. By extension, the term *sacra doctrina* applies to all the derivative human acts, initiated and sustained by the Holy Spirit, by which this originating activity is perpetuated and made available, in many forms, to subsequent generations of God's people.[17]

The analogy of faith

The last 'rule' to be mentioned by the document is '*analogia fidei*'. The term is found in Romans 12:6 (*analogia tēs pisteōs*), preceded by *metron pisteōs* in Romans 12:3. Both expressions seem to refer to testing prophecy to determine its genuineness, and the 'faith' referred to is rather the faith of other prophets as the process is described in 1 Corinthians 14:29–33. However, since a norm was already involved even in this type of charismatic faith, it was not long before the term took on the overtones of 'corresponding to the overall teaching of the Church', specifically the creeds. Later still, the expression also referred to the analogical relation between what is known naturally and what is revealed.[18] The *Catechism of the Catholic Church*, commenting on this passage of *Dei Verbum*, defines the analogy of faith this way: 'By "analogy of faith" we mean the coherence of the truths of faith among themselves and within the whole plan of Revelation'.[19]

One of the most important expressions of this analogy of faith is found in the fact of the canon itself. Attention to this fact would have prevented the tendency in much historical critical investigation to understand the 'pluralism' of the New Testament to be a conglomeration of conflicting views that would entitle one to continue the centrifugal movement in several new directions.

The teaching office of the Church

The final two sentences of §12 speak of the relationship between exegetical work and the teaching office and function of the Church. The first sentence urges exegetes to work according to the 'rules' just elaborated so that the judgement of the Church 'might mature'. A good example of such collaboration can be seen in the way the documents of Vatican II are the fruit of the biblical, liturgical, patristic and theological work of the previous 150 years,

---

[17] For a fuller discussion of this see Martin, '*Sacra Doctrina*'.
[18] See Scheffczyk, 'Analogy of Faith'.
[19] *Catechism of the Catholic Church*, par. 114.

especially that of the *Ressourcement* movement and much solid work of Protestant exegetes. The final sentence enunciates the Catholic principle that the Church has the divine mandate and ministry of preserving and interpreting the Scriptures, and all other efforts are subject to the authority of the Church's judgement. This principle is well expressed by Thomas Aquinas: 'Faith adheres to all the articles of faith because of one reason (*medium*), namely because of the First Truth proposed to us in the Scriptures understood rightly according to the teaching of the Church (*secundum doctrinam Ecclesiae*)'.[20]

Reading the Scripture in the Spirit in which it was written means first acknowledging that 'no prophecy of scripture is a matter of one's own interpretation, because no prophecy ever came by the impulse of man, but men moved by the Holy Spirit spoke from God' (2 Pet. 1:20–21). Aquinas sums up the process within God's people that leads from original revelation to interpretation. The fact that the transmission and reception process is much more complex than the ancients thought does not detract from the solidity of his understanding:

> After the level of those who receive revelation directly from God, another level of grace is necessary. Because men receive revelation from God not only for their own time but also for the instruction of all who come after them, it was necessary that the things revealed to them be passed on not only in speech to their contemporaries but also as written down for the instruction of those to come after them. And thus it was also necessary that there be those who could interpret what was written down. This also must be done by divine grace. And so we read in Genesis 40:8, 'Does not interpretation come from God?'[21]

Aquinas also considers that all of the authors of the New Testament were prophetically endowed because they could correctly interpret the Old Testament: 'They are also called prophets in the New Testament who expound the prophetic sayings because Sacred Scripture is interpreted in the same Spirit in which it is composed.'[22]

---

[20] *Summa Theologiae* II–II, 5, ad 2. For a judicious account of how the Church asserts the meaning of a biblical text see Gilbert, 'Textes Bibliques'.

[21] *Summa Contra Gentiles* 3, 154.

[22] *Ad Romanos* (on Rom. 12:8), Marietti ed. §978. For the background of this principle see de la Potterie, 'Interpretation of Holy Scripture'. We find in that study this text from Origen describing the responsibility of a bishop or priest: 'To learn of God by reading the divine Scriptures and by meditating on them with great frequency, or teach the people. But he must teach what he has learned of God, not from his own heart or any human sense, but what the Spirit teaches' (*In Lev. Hom.* 6,6 [*Sources Chrétiennes* 286, 297]; text is on p. 225 of de la Potterie's study).

The Challenge of Catholic Biblical Theology since *Dei Verbum*

A rethinking of history

Perhaps the best way to sum up the shortcomings of the historical-critical methods is to cite this passage from Brian Daley, who is pointing to the need for a retrieval of the patristic approach as an important corrective:

> '[H]istorical reality' – like physical reality – is assumed to be in itself something objective, at least in the sense that it consists in events independent of the interests and preoccupations of the scholar or narrator, something accessible through the disciplined, methodologically rigorous analysis of present evidence such as texts, artifacts and human remains ... As a result, modern historical criticism – including the criticism of Biblical texts – is *methodologically* atheistic, even if what it studies is some form or facet of religious belief, and even if it is practiced by believers. Only 'natural', inner-worldly explanations of why or how things happen, explanations that could be acceptable to believers and unbelievers alike, are taken as historically admissible ... So God is not normally considered to count as an actor on the stage of history. God's providence in history, the divine inspiration of Scriptural authors and texts, even the miracles narrated in the Bible are assumed to be private human interpretations of events, interior and non-demonstrable, rather than events or historical forces in themselves.[23]

To my knowledge, there is no other Catholic biblical theologian who is engaged at this moment in the effort to relocate the relatively new discipline of history, possessed of a legitimate autonomy within its own realm, within the larger framework of a Christian philosophy of time. Rather, the hegemony of modern historical study has reduced reflections on time to its own non-transcendent, 'atheistic' (to use Daley's term) dimensions. I would like to offer here a few reflections on how we must proceed in order to retrieve the ancient, largely Augustinian, understanding of time and bring it to bear on the modern science of history.[24]

It is interesting to observe that Thomas Aquinas, when considering the vice of 'curiosity', deals with the pursuit of knowledge that does not ultimately lead to the knowledge of the highest truth:

---

[23] Daley, 'Patristic Exegesis', 191. See also Plantinga, 'Two (or More) Kinds of Scripture Scholarship'.

[24] In what follows I am indebted to a study by Lamb, 'Temporality and History: Reflections from St. Augustine and Bernard Lonergan', to be published as part of the proceedings of a symposium held at the Intercultural Forum of the John Paul II Cultural Center. I thank Fr. Lamb for his permission to draw on this study. Also helpful in this regard is von Balthasar, *Theology of History*.

> While the good of man consists in the knowledge of what is true, the highest good of man does not consist in the knowledge of any truth but in the perfect knowledge of the highest truth, as the Philosopher says in Book 10 of the Ethics. And thus there can be a vice in the knowledge of some truths, insofar as such a desire is not ordered in a suitable manner to the knowledge of the highest truth in which consists the greatest happiness.[25]

While not wishing to call secular historians 'vicious', I do think it is important to recognize that Christians have a solemn obligation not to rest with 'facts', but to relate our modern knowledge of history to the first cause of all history. This is especially incumbent upon us since, in the incarnation, the Word has come among us and is in fact not only he through whom all things have 'been made' (Jn. 1:3), but also the One 'sustaining all things by his powerful word' (Heb. 1:3). This means that there is an interior and vertical dimension to events: they are brought about by agents who are *subjects*, that is persons with a spiritual capacity to know and will and to effect change. Because persons have an interiority, history has an interiority – a vertical dimension which relates it to the reality of the Word incarnate in history. This is what the Christian tradition referred to as 'Mystery'.

> A time without mystery, even if one could conceive of such a thing, would be a time that is empty, strictly linear. Mystery is what opens up temporality and gives it its depth; it is what introduces a vertical dimension: it makes of time the time of revelation and unveiling. Thus time acquires meaning.[26]

This is also what Henri de Lubac is referring to when he speaks of the 'S/spiritual dimension of history':

> God acts *within* history, God reveals himself *within* history. Even more, God inserts himself *within* history, thus granting it a 'religious consecration' which forces us to take it seriously. *Historical* realities have a *depth*; they are to be understood *spiritually*: *historika pneumatikôs* ... and on the other hand, *spiritual* realities appear in the movement of becoming, they are to be understood *historically*: *pneumatika historikôs* ... The Bible, which contains revelation, thus also contains, in a certain way, the *history* of the world.[27]

For modern history, time is succession – a dubious and uneven march toward an indeterminate future. The study of history, now capable of genuine reconstruction and insight, records this march. As we have seen, it resolutely eschews

---

[25] *Summa Theologiae* II–II, 167, 1, ad 1. The translation is my own.

[26] Lacroix, *Histoire et Mystère*, 7.

[27] De Lubac, *Catholicisme*, 119. Translation is from de la Potterie, 'Spiritual Sense' (emphasis original).

any consideration of transcendence, any search for a causality that exceeds the forces and resources of what is fundamentally a closed system.[28] I would propose, in contrast to this, that we use the term 'temporality' to describe the nature of human existence: temporality includes succession in a vision of presence. I derive this understanding from St Augustine. God, the Creator, who is eternity, is necessarily present in the action of sustaining all that is.

Temporality, the proper mode of creation's existence, is not just succession; it is succession with the dimension of presence. In this sense time is intrinsic to creation: 'God, in whose eternity there is no change whatsoever, is the creator and director of time ... the world was not created *in* time but *with time*'.[29] Therefore to understand time as intrinsic to creaturely existence,[30] and not an exterior and neutral 'container' for the changes of the past and future, is to advance toward an understanding of history that includes its 'mystery'. Augustine and many others have pointed to this dimension of the events narrated in the Bible. The 'mystery' is the eternally present christological dimension of the events of salvation history as this history moves through the succession of 'before and after'.

Practitioners of the historical-critical method sometimes point to the advantage we have in being able to establish a 'parallel' account of an event recorded in Scripture. This can sometimes be very helpful in entering more deeply into the event as mediated by the sacred text.[31] However, most of the time the result of historical study is then assumed to be the norm against which the biblical text is judged (the historical-*critical* method). This approach establishes a 'parallel' understanding of what the text 'means', but it gives us no idea of what and how the *text itself* is mediating. This is an apt time to recall the expression of *Dei Verbum* that 'the economy of salvation' takes place by 'events and words that are intrinsically bound to each other' so that 'the works accomplished by God in the history of salvation, manifest and confirm the teaching and the realities signified by the words, while the words proclaim the works and bring to light the mystery contained in them'. This means, in effect, that the historical method has not so much failed as that it has not really been tried. As K. Lawson Younger, Jr expresses it:

---

[28] The relation between this view and the pre-Christian pagan view of reality can be seen in the study by Sokolowski, *The God of Faith and Reason*.

[29] *De Civitate Dei* 11, 6; translation is that of M. Lamb. '*Cum igitur Deus, in cuius aeternitate nulla est omnino mutatio, creator sit temporum et ordinator ... procul dubio non est mundus factus in tempore sed cum tempore.*'

[30] While succession, an aspect of time, is clearly present in material creation, created spirits also have succession in that they go from potency to act.

[31] I am thinking, for example, of studies such as de la Potterie, 'Multiplication of the Loaves'; Latourelle, *Miracles of Jesus*.

While it is perfectly valid (and important) to ask questions concerning which events were narrated, it is equally valid and important to ask questions concerning the *way in which events were narrated*. In fact it is the latter questions which reveal the texts' ultimate purpose.[32]

This, I would suggest, is the task yet to be undertaken, especially in regard to biblical narrative. It will require greater literary sensitivity and demand greater faith sympathy with the realities mediated, precisely as mediated in the sacred text. It means, to cite *Dei Verbum* once again, that the interpreter must investigate what realities the sacred author is talking about (not just what he is 'saying'), and how he wants them understood as he used 'contemporary literary forms in accordance with the situation of his own time and culture'.

An Ancient Understanding of History as Christocentric

I wish to move now to a consideration of the ways in which historical investigation can in the future contribute to an understanding of both how the ancients themselves understood the transcendent dimension of the events in Israel's history and the literary mode in which they expressed this. I acknowledge that little more has been done to date than point to the deficiency and Eurocentrism of our methods, yet this calling of our attention is important and can, I think, profit from a deeper appreciation of the particular understanding of history that goes by the name 'spiritual sense'. It is there that Catholic biblical theology has begun to make a significant contribution.

I will present briefly the current state of the question, leaving to a longer study a more complete treatment of this extremely important dimension of biblical theology – one that is based on an understanding of the relation between the Testaments. The term 'spiritual sense', or 'spiritual understanding', refers to a Spirit-conferred experience of the realities mediated by the sacred text. It is most often used of such an understanding of the realities mediated in the Old Testament, now recognized as an anticipated and ontological participation in Christ.

Undoubtedly the author most responsible for helping twentieth-century theology become aware again of what was for the ancients an absolutely foundational understanding of revelation was Henri de Lubac.[33] Beginning with his study on Origen,[34] de Lubac showed that what was present amid the occasional exuberances of Origen was a profound understanding of the relation between

---

[32] Younger, *Ancient Conquest Accounts,* 63. Cited in Brettler, *Creation of History,* 1 (italics added).

[33] See de Lubac, *Medieval Exegesis* and *Sources of Revelation*.

[34] De Lubac, *Histoire et Esprit*.

the events narrated in the Old Testament and the mystery of Christ related in the New Testament. We are dealing not primarily with a theory of text, but with a theology of history. Using the traditional term 'allegory' from Galatians 4:24, which in ancient times nearly always alluded to this specifically theological procedure, de Lubac asserts:

> Let us immediately, however, clarify that to discover this allegory, one will not find it properly speaking in the text, but in the realities of which the text speaks; not in history as recitation, but in history as event.[35]

The meaning of the Old Testament text is to be found, therefore, not in the exterior comparison of texts, but in the interior recognition of economic participation. Let two texts suffice, out of a countless number that could be adduced. 'Holy Scripture, in its way of speaking, transcends all other sciences because in one and the same statement, while it narrates an event, it sets forth the mystery.'[36] The two words 'event' and 'mystery' refer in turn to the literal sense, the event, and then the same event as it is now seen to have been a participated anticipation of the mystery of Christ. Augustine has much the same to say: 'We must seek the mystery [the plan of God revealed in Christ] in the event itself, not only in the text [of the OT].'[37]

This spiritual sense of the Old Testament is basically a christological sense, as we have seen. However, the New Testament authors did not think that our present existence totally fulfilled the Old Testament. Often they based themselves on the threefold division implied in Hebrews 10:1: 'For the law has only a shadow (*skian*) of the good things to come and not the true form (*autēn tēn eikona*) of these realities ...' The law only possessed a shadow or sketch; we possess the realities, but 'in icon'. That is, we possess them not according to their proper mode of existence, but rather in signs and symbols, until we are with Christ in heaven; it is still true of the 'good things' that they are yet 'to come' in their fullness. Ambrose, who spoke of 'shadow', 'image' and 'truth', already expressed this understanding of the Hebrews text.[38] Such a view of history is the common denominator between sacred text and sacrament, particularly the Eucharist. The sacraments fulfil the events of the Old Testament in the act by which Christ makes himself present 'in icon', even as he anticipates the fullness of his presence 'in truth'.

---

[35] *Medieval Exegesis*, II, 86.

[36] Gregory the Great, *Moralia* 20, 1 (PL 76.135): '*Sacra Scriptura omnes scientias ipso locutionis suae more transcendit, quia uno eodemque sermone dum narrat gestum, prodit mysterium.*'

[37] '*In ipso facto, non solum in dicto, mysterium requirere debemus.*' On Psalm 68 (PL 36.858).

[38] '*Primum igitur umbra praecessit, secuta est imago, erit veritas. Umbra in lege, imago vero in evangelio, veritas in caelestibus.*' On Psalm 43 (CSEL 64.204).

Thomas Aquinas echoes this common threefold understanding of God's plan when discussing the threefold states of interior worship to which exterior worship must correspond:

> One state was in respect of faith and hope, both in the heavenly goods, and in the means of obtaining them … Such was the state of faith and hope in the Old Law. Another state of the interior worship is that in which we have faith and hope in heavenly goods as something future; but in regard to those means by which we are brought into the heavenly goods [we have faith and hope] as in things which are either present or past. And this is the state of the New Law. The third state is that in which both are possessed as present; wherein nothing is believed in as lacking, nothing hoped for as being yet to come. Such is the state of the Blessed.[39]

If we combine this notion of the threefold state with the understanding of Christ as fulfilling and sublating the realities mediated in the Old Testament we have the famous 'jingle' coined by the Danish Dominican Augustine, himself a disciple of Aquinas:

> *Littera gesta docet, quid credas allegoria,*
> *Moralis quid agas, quo tendas anagogia.*

> The letter teaches the events, allegory [teaches] what you should believe,
> The moral [teaches] what you should do, anagogy [teaches] where you should be going.[40]

The key to understanding this summary of the tradition is to know that '*allegoria*' refers to the christological understanding and that '*gesta*' refers to the events and persons of the Old Testament mediated principally through *narrative*. Thus there are fundamentally two senses: 'literal' and 'allegorical/spiritual/figurative/christological'. The 'moral' and 'anagogical' senses can be included under the christological sense in that they refer to the conduct and future of the whole Christ still living through time, in the age of 'icon' or 'image'. This is true of both Old and New Testament texts. It is important to note that for Aquinas these four 'senses' are not four meanings of a *text* but four dimensions of an *event*, which belong to Scripture by its nature ('*de necessitate Scripturae*').[41] In addition, Aquinas maintains that only Scripture can have this

---

[39] *Summa Theologiae* I–II, 103, 3; see also 106, 4 ad 1.

[40] De Lubac, 'Sur un Vieux Distique'. English translation in de Lubac, *Theological Fragments*. A more extended treatment is to be found in de Lubac, *Medieval Exegesis*. For a complete study of the distich, including variants and a critique of Augustine's vocabulary see Chatillon, 'Vocabulaire et Prosodie'. Chatillon also gives a variant found in Nicholas of Lyra: *quid speres anagogia*.

[41] *Quodlibetum* 7, art. 15, videtur 5. Cited by Michaud, 'Des Quatre Sens', 183.

spiritual sense. In the same *Quodlibetum* he asks the question 'Whether these same significations (the four senses) can be found in other writings?' He responds:

> Things are so ordered in their working out that from them a signification can be derived which is from him only who governs all things by his providence, and this is God alone ... Therefore in no branch of knowledge forged by human effort can there be found, properly speaking, anything but the literal signification, except only in this Scripture whose author is the Holy Spirit and for which human beings are instruments, as it is written: 'My tongue is the pen of a swiftly writing scribe'.[42]

With this mention of the Holy Spirit, we are led into the specificity of the sacred Scriptures and thus into the theology of inspiration. However, this cannot be treated separately from questions of language and history. I said above that the historical methods must be used to understand what the sacred authors are saying as they mediate the realities according to their own interpretation and in their own cultural and theological modes of expression. We must understand as well that the challenge posed by the dogmatic fact of scriptural inspiration obliges us to a profound philosophical and theological retrieval of the ancient understanding of inspiration and literature, using all that the philosophy of language and history has to offer. It is here that some creative work is being done in Catholic biblical theology, much of it, as we will see, centring on the traditional notion of 'inspiration'.

Some modern steps at recovery

The first step in such work is to bracket all the other ways, legitimate and exaggerated, in which the expression 'spiritual sense/understanding' was used in antiquity, except that which was defined above as 'a Spirit-conferred experience in faith of the realities mediated by the sacred text'. The second step is a careful analysis of each book of the New Testament in order to determine exactly how, in each case, the author actually reads the Old Testament as narrating events that find their full significance in the event of Christ and his church: this is the spiritual sense in its technical meaning. The third step is the development of a descriptive taxonomy of the ways in which the realities

---

[42] *Quodlibetum* 7, art. 16 (my translation). In the same vein, but this time from the side of the events themselves, we also read: 'The Jewish people were chosen by God that Christ might be born of them. Consequently the entire state of that people had to be prophetic and figurative ... Thus too, the wars and deeds of this people are expounded in the mystical sense [spiritual sense] but not the wars and deeds of the Assyrians or Romans, although the latter are more famous in the eyes of men' (*Summa Theologiae* I–II, 104, 2, ad 2). Translation from Levering, *Christ's Fulfillment*, 27.

mediated by the Old Testament text are actually viewed in the New Testament.[43]

Intimately connected to this three-step effort is a more philosophical and linguistic reflection on the nature of language and of text. This latter work, as it develops, will have a significant influence on issues in biblical theology, most notably in regard to inspiration and the relation between the Testaments. The discipline of semiotics associated with the names of Greimas, Pierce and Saussure has been applied to Scripture extensively in France. A leading figure in this work of studying the manner in which words and texts signify has been Jean Delorme.[44] A very ambitious attempt to approach Scripture with the results of semiotic study is that of François Martin, who has drawn attention to the work of over a century, particularly in France.[45] The same orientation, now in an extended context of literary mediation, is to be found in the studies of Oliver-Thomas Venard.[46] All of this research has taken the undoubted advance in the understanding of language and literature and applied it with fruit to biblical studies.

Notable among the insights of this line of thought would be the understanding of a text as an instance of communication. Authors compose texts in order to communicate something: a text is an instance of intersubjective communication. As Werner Jeanrond expresses it:

> Text composition and text reception stand to each other in a correlative relationship of communication. Text composition is the procedure which forms a text as a semantic potential, and reading is the procedure which realizes a written text as a form of sense. Text composition and reading – in other words, text production and text reception – are both guided by communicative intentions, in other words by that which the text has to say.[47]

A text may be defined as an act of communication consisting of a complex and interlocking linguistic sign organized according to the rules of a linguistic system. It is a multilevel reality that sublates more fundamental levels of literary components into a formal dynamic unity.[48] It is important here to note that the

---

[43] The first two steps are actually being implemented in a task force held annually as part of the meeting of the Catholic Biblical Association; the third must await the completion of the first two.

[44] For an overview of the work of semiotics and the Bible see Delorme, 'Sémiotique'.

[45] François Martin, *Pour une Théologie de la Lettre*. See also the assessment by Nodet, 'De l'Inspiration de l'Écriture'.

[46] See Venard, 'Esquisse d'une Critique des "Méthodes Littéraires"' and *Littérature et Théologie*.

[47] Jeanrond, *Text and Interpretation*, 83.

[48] I recall here the definition of sublation by Lonergan given above.

text 'needs, includes, and preserves' all the lower levels of linguistic utterance while it 'carries them forward to a fuller realization within a richer context'. An atomistic reading of the biblical text concentrates on the propositional dimension of the text and does not reach an understanding of the sense of the text as an integrated act of communication. Conversely, those who concentrate exclusively on the overall text ignore the fact that the propositional dimension, the various creedal formulae for instance, still operates on its own level of existence and must be respected as such even while its function in the overall structure is identified. This is once again the challenge of appreciating philosophically the process of 'transposition/sublation' referred to previously.[49]

Another contribution is the distinction between what is immanent in and what is manifested in and through a text. François Martin exploits this distinction in his own treatment of the spiritual sense, as defined above, of the Old Testament. All of this work needs to be deepened and rendered more precise. In addition, I think it needs the complementary work of Husserlian semiotics in order to more thoroughly eschew the danger of a certain Kantianism which can result in a kind of 'textism' that does not attain to the realities mediated by the text. In this connection I see the work of Robert Sokolowski as contributing that complementarity in what he calls a 'theology of disclosure'. Because the work of Husserl, especially as interpreted by Sokolowski, has not yet been applied to biblical studies, I would like to offer a few lines to indicate the contribution that I envisage.[50]

The primary contribution of the theology of disclosure, particularly as it is relevant to a retrieval of the Catholic reading of Scripture, is that it manages to bypass the 'egocentric predicament' created by the successive developments of a hermeneutics of suspicion. In Sokolowski's words:

> [According to modernity] ideas exist in the self-enclosed mind and they are immediately present to it. Ideas come between us and things. We have to get around them and outwit them if we are to reach the things themselves. To do so, we form hypotheses and build models in our minds, and we try to determine, by experiment, which of these hypotheses and models are false and which can be at least provisionally confirmed. In this way we hope to get beyond appearances to the things themselves, to the things that always remain absent and hidden from us.
>
> The suspicion of appearance in modernity has made manifestation the central issue in the philosophy of the last five centuries. Appearances are the metaphysical problem of modernity.
>
> The literary and philosophical movements called structuralism and deconstructionism claim that words and images refer only to other words and

---

[49] For a more extended discussion of this point see Martin, *Feminist Question*.

[50] The lines which follow are taken partially from Martin, 'Reading Scripture', 164–65.

images: there are only texts that refer to other texts, codes that become reinterpreted into other codes; there is no center, nothing beyond the merely apparent to which our words, images, and consciousness can be related.[51]

An appreciation of what is meant by 'intentionality' in the phenomenological view can enable us to account for the faith experience of Christians when they approach the sacred text in faith and come into contact with God and the divine realities of salvation. Again, the thinking of Husserl can help us. After distinguishing between indications and expressions (*Anzeigen* and *Ausdrücke*), Husserl goes on to discuss the reality of 'sign': 'something that is a material entity but is also saturated with the presence of thinking'.[52] In the matter of linguistic signs – that is, words – Husserl distinguishes between an empty intention and fulfilment. If while standing at the window I say to you, 'your uncle is coming to the house', you, who are not at the window, can possess the meaning even though as yet you do not perceive the referent. If, however, you come to the window, your intention of this fact moves from being empty to being filled. The reality contained in my words now becomes for you an intuitively fulfilled intention. Obviously, this example of sense perception applies to all other levels as well. 'According to Husserl, what the expression expresses *is the content of this intuitional act*. The expression does not express its own meaning; rather it expresses the content of the act that fulfills the signitive act that constitutes the expression'.[53]

Thus words are not empty 'signifiers', nor simply actualizations of a linguistic potential; rather, because of the presence to the speaker/writer of the *reality* expressed by the words, the words themselves become saturated by the thing itself. Who has not had the experience of listening to someone speak and experiencing within oneself the fact that this person '*knows* what they are talking about'? This happens because the reality intended by the speaker is present in his words and we experience that fact as the words reach us. Though much more must be said in order to gain a satisfactory understanding of the mystery of understanding and mediating in and through language, I have wished here only to point to this direction of epistemological thinking that has begun to make its mark on Catholic theology and is about to do the same in Catholic biblical study. While there could be discussion of variations on the historical critical method, approaches such as rhetorical criticism, social criticism, reader response criticism, and the like, I am convinced that they all suffer from the same incapacity to accord to reality its transcendent dimension and to accord

---

[51] Sokolowski, *Eucharistic Presence*, 183–86.

[52] Sokolowski, 'Semiotics', 171.

[53] Sokolowski, 'Semiotics', 174 (emphasis original).

to mind the transcendent source of its own light and capacity for language.[54] Allow me to conclude with a significant paragraph in Sokolowski's study that, as I see it, indicates clearly the way out of the anti-transcendent straitjacket that has bound so much of Catholic and other biblical study.

> These descriptions of Husserl bring out the special mode of being of words. They show that words are transparent, that when we hear someone speak or when we read a text or even when we see someone using sign language, we go right through the words to the things being signified and expressed by them. The word, as Husserl says, 'is one with' the thing it names, it fits that thing, it belongs with it in a special kind of belonging that is not like any other relationship.[55]

The semiotics of Husserl allow us to contextualize the advances made in the understanding of word and text and to step out of the Kantian dilemma that puts them at risk. However, in order to arrive at a genuinely transcendent epistemology, this achievement of Husserl must be integrated with what in the Catholic tradition is considered classical metaphysics. By that I mean the understanding that the light of the mind is itself 'a certain participation in divine light'; it is, in fact, 'nothing else but the imprint of the divine light in us'.[56] Knowing is therefore an actualization of our reality as the image of God.

> God's image in humankind can be considered in three ways. The first way is humankind's natural aptitude for knowing and loving God, an aptitude that consists in the very nature of the mind that is common to all humankind. Another way is where humankind is actually or habitually knowing and loving God, but still imperfectly; and this is through the conformation of grace. The third way is where humankind is actually knowing and loving God perfectly; and this is the image according to the likeness of glory.[57]

---

[54] Consider for instance this remark of Aquinas: 'Though there be many participated truths, there is but one absolute Truth which by its own essence is Truth, namely the Divine Being itself, by which Truth all words are words. In the same way there is one absolute Wisdom, raised above all, namely the Divine Wisdom by participation in whom all wise men are wise. And in the same way (there is) the absolute Word by participation in whom all who have a word are said to be speaking. This is the Divine Word, which in Himself is the Word raised above all.' Thomas Aquinas, *Super Evangelium S. Joannis Lectura*, ch. 1, Lectio 1, 33.

[55] Sokolowski, 'Semiotics', 176.

[56] Aquinas, *Summa Theologiae* I, 12, 11 ad 3; I–II, 91, 2.

[57] *Summa Theologiae* I, 93, 4. For an excellent study of this theme see Merriell, *Image of the Trinity*.

Concluding Reflections

Catholic biblical theology is in approximately the same situation as Protestant biblical theology, but the resources to which it has recourse are different. Striving as it does for integration, Catholic thought must elaborate a thorough philosophical understanding of the act of knowledge, the spiritual depths of language and the nature of temporality. This philosophical effort is animated and directed by faith. As the encyclical *Fides et Ratio* expresses it: 'reason is stirred to explore paths which of itself it would not even have suspected it could take'.[58]

Once having freed modern thought from its anti-transcendent bias, Catholic thought will be able to retrieve what is authentic in the previous centuries and integrate what is sound in modern achievements in order to construct a solid theological system. We must remember, however, that such a system is not the ultimate goal of the theological effort. All theological reflection must ultimately bring the believer and the community into transforming union with the word of God. Allow me to conclude with these words of Henri de Lubac, one of the most important figures in our Christian effort to serve the Church:

> [S]ince Christian mysticism develops through the action of the mystery received in faith, and the mystery is the Incarnation of the Word of God revealed in Scripture, Christian mysticism is essentially an understanding of the holy Books. The mystery is their meaning; mysticism is getting to know that meaning. Thus, one understands the profound and original identity of the two meanings of the word *mystique* that, in current French usage, seem so different because we have to separate so much in order to analyze them: the mystical or spiritual understanding of Scripture and the mystical or spiritual life are, in the end, one and the same.[59]

---

[58] Pope John Paul II, *Fides et Ratio*, §73.
[59] De Lubac, 'Mysticism and Mystery', in *Theological Fragments*, 35–70, at 58.

Bibliography

Abbott, W.M. (ed.), *The Documents of Vatican II* (Piscataway, NJ: New Century Publishers, 1966)

Balthasar, H.U. von, 'Il Senso Spirituale della Scrittura', *Ricerche Teologiche 5* (1994), 5–9

—, *A Theology of History* (Communio Books; San Francisco: Ignatius, 1963; reprint, 1994)

Brettler, M.Z., *The Creation of History in Ancient Israel* (London and New York: Routledge, 1995)

Brown, R.E., J.A. Fitzmyer and R.E. Murphy (eds.), *The Jerome Biblical Commentary* (Englewood Cliffs, NJ: Prentice Hall, 1988)

Chatillon, F., 'Vocabulaire et Prosodie du Distique Attribué a Augustin de Dacie sur les Quatre Sens de l'Écriture', in *L'Homme Devant Dieu: Mélanges offerts au Père de Lubac*, II: *Du Moyen Age au Siècle des Lumières*, (Paris: Aubier, 1964), 17–28

Childs, B.S., *Biblical Theology of the Old and New Testaments: Theological Reflection on the Christian Bible* (London: SCM Press; Minneapolis: Fortress Press, 1992)

—, *The New Testament as Canon: An Introduction* (Philadelphia: Fortress Press, 1984)

Congar, Y., *Tradition and Traditions: An Historical Essay and a Theological Essay* (trans. M. Naseby and T. Rainborough; New York: Macmillan, 1967)

Daley, B., 'Is Patristic Exegesis Still Usable?' *Comm* 29 (2002), 185–216

Delorme, J., 'Sémiotique', in *Dictionnaire de la Bible Supplément* (ed. É. Cothenet and J. Briend; Paris: Letouzey et Ané, 1996), 281–333

Farmer, W.R. (ed.), *The International Bible Commentary: A Catholic Ecumenical Commentary for the Twenty-first Century* (Collegeville, MN: Liturgical Press, 1998)

Fitzmyer, J.A., 'The Interpretation of the Bible in the Church Today', *ITQ* 62 (1997), 84–100

Gilbert, M., 'Textes Bibliques dont l'Église a Défini le Sens', in *L'Autorité de l'Écriture* (ed. J.-M. Poffet; Paris: Cerf, 2002), 71–94

Gracia, J.J.E., *Old Wine in New Skins: The Role of Tradition in Communication, Knowledge and Group Identity* (The Aquinas Lecture 2003; Milwaukee: Marquette University Press, 2003)

Harrington, D.J. (ed.), *Sacra Pagina* (Collegeville, MN: Liturgical Press, 1991–)

Hays, R., 'Response to Robert Wilken, "In Dominico Eloquio"', *Comm* 25 (1998), 520–28

Jeanrond, W., *Text and Interpretation as Categories of Theological Thinking* (trans. T. Wilson; New York: Crossroad, 1988)

La Potterie, I. de, 'The Multiplication of the Loaves in the Life of Jesus', *Comm* 16 (1989), 499–516

—, 'The Spiritual Sense of Scripture', *Comm* 23 (1996), 738–56

—, 'Interpretation of Holy Scripture in the Spirit in Which It Was Written', in *Vatican II: Assessment and Perspectives*: I (ed. R. Latourelle; New York: Paulist Press, 1988), 220–66

Lacroix, J., *Histoire et Mystère* (Tournai: Castermann, 1962)

Latourelle, R., *The Miracles of Jesus and the Theology of Miracles* (trans. M.J. O'Connell; New York: Paulist Press, 1988)

Levering, M., *Christ's Fulfillment of Torah and Temple* (Notre Dame, IN: University of Notre Dame, 2002)

Lonergan, B., *Method in Theology* (New York: Herder & Herder, 1972)

Lubac, H. de, *Catholicism: Christ and the Common Destiny of Man* (trans. L.C. Sheppard and E. Englund; San Francisco: Ignatius, 1988)

—, *Histoire et Esprit: L'Intelligence de l'Écriture d'après Origène* (Théologie 16; Paris: Aubier, 1950)

—, *Medieval Exegesis: The Four Senses of Scripture*, I–II (trans. M. Sebanc and E.M. Macierowski; Ressourcement; Grand Rapids: Eerdmans, 1998–2000)

—, *Sources of Revelation* (trans. L. O'Neil; New York: Herder & Herder, 1968)

—, 'Sur un Vieux Distique: La Doctrine du Quadruple Sens', in *Mélanges Offerts au R.P. Fernand Cavallera* (Toulouse: L'Institut Catholique, 1948), 347–66

—, *Theological Fragments* (trans. R.H. Balinski; San Francisco: Ignatius, 1989)

Martin, Francis, *The Feminist Question: Feminist Theology in the Light of Christian Tradition* (Grand Rapids: Eerdmans, 1994)

—, 'Reading Scripture in the Catholic Tradition', in *Your Word is Truth: A Project of Evangelicals and Catholics Together* (ed. C. Colson and R.J. Neuhaus; Grand Rapids: Eerdmans, 2002), 147–68

—, Review of D. Horrell and C.M. Tuckett (eds.), *Christology, Controversy and Community: New Testament Essays in Honor of David R. Catchpole* (NovTSup XCIX; Leiden: Brill, 2000), *CBQ* 64 (2002), 608–10

—, '*Sacra Doctrina* and the Authority of its *Sacra Scriptura* in St. Thomas Aquinas', *ProEcl* 10 (2001), 63–75

Martin, François, *Pour une Théologie de la Lettre: L'Inspiration des Écritures* (Cogitatio Fidei 193; Paris: Cerf, 1996)

McLean, G.F. (ed.), *Hermeneutics, Tradition and Contemporary Change* (Cultural Heritage and Contemporary Change; Series I: Culture and Values 30; Washington, DC: The Council for Research in Values and Philosophy, 2003)

Merriell, D.J., *To the Image of the Trinity: A Study in the Development of Aquinas' Teaching* (Studies and Texts 96; Toronto: Pontifical Institute of Medieval Studies, 1990)

Michaud, J.-P., 'Des Quatre Sens de l'Écriture: Histoire, Théorie, Théologie, Herméneutique', *EgT* 30 (1999), 165–97

Navarre University Theology Faculty (ed.), *The Navarre Bible (in the RSV and New Vulgate with a Commentary by the Faculty of Theology, University of Navarre)* (Dublin: Four Courts Press, 1988–)

Noble, P.R., *The Canonical Approach: A Critical Reconstruction of the Hermeneutics of Brevard S. Childs* (Leiden: Brill, 1995)

Nodet, E., 'De l'Inspiration de l'Écriture', *RB* 104 (1997), 237–74

Osiek, C., 'The Family in Early Christianity: "Family Values" Revisited', *CBQ* 58 (1996), 1–24

Plantinga, A., 'Two (or More) Kinds of Scripture Scholarship', *Modern Theology* 14 (1998), 243–77

Pope John Paul II, *Fides et Ratio* (Washington, DC: United States Catholic Conference, 1998)

Pope Pius XII, *Divino Afflante Spiritu* (Washington, DC: National Catholic Welfare Conference, 1943)

Scheffczyk, L., 'Analogy of Faith', in *Sacramentum Mundi: An Encyclopedia of Theology* (ed. K. Rahner, et al.; New York: Herder & Herder, 1968), 25–27

Sokolowski, R., *Eucharistic Presence: A Study in the Theology of Disclosure* (Washington, DC: Catholic University of America Press, 1993)

—, *The God of Faith and Reason: Foundations of Christian Theology* (Notre Dame, IN: University of Notre Dame Press, 1982)

—, 'Semiotics in Husserl's *Logical Investigations*', in *One Hundred Years of Phenomenology* (ed. D. Zahavi and F. Stjernfelt; Boston: Kluwer Academic Publishers, 2002), 171–83

Théobald, C. (ed.), *Le Canon des Écritures: Études Historiques, Exégétiques et Systématiques* (Lectio Divina 140; Paris: Cerf, 1990)

Thomas Aquinas, *Summa Contra Gentiles* (Rome: Marietti, 1893)

—, *Summa Theologiae* (Ottawa: Commissio Piana, 1953)

—, *Super Epistulas S. Pauli Lectura* (Rome: Marietti, 1953)

—, *Super Evangelium S. Joannis Lectura* (Rome: Marietti, 1952)

Venard, O.-T., 'Esquisse d'une Critique des "Méthodes Littéraires"', in *L'Autorité de l'Écriture* (ed. J.-M. Poffet; Paris: Cerf, 2002), 259–98

—, *Littérature et Théologie: Une Saison en Enfer, I: Thomas d'Aquin Poète Théologien* (Geneva: Solem, 2000)

Williamson, P., 'The Place of History in Catholic Exegesis: An Examination of the Pontifical Biblical Commission's *The Interpretation of the Bible in the Church*', in *'Behind' the Text: History and Biblical Interpretation* (ed. C. Bartholomew, et al; SHS 4; Carlisle: Paternoster; Grand Rapids: Zondervan, 2003), 196–226

Younger, K.L., Jr, *Ancient Conquest Accounts: A Study in Ancient Near Eastern and Biblical History Writing* (JSOTSup 98; Sheffield: Sheffield Academic Press, 1990)

4

The Theology of the Old Testament by Marco Nobile

A Contribution to Jewish-Christian Relations

Nuria Calduch-Benages

The purpose of this chapter is to present the work of Marco Nobile, the second Italian to publish a theology of the Old Testament,[1] and to situate his theology in the wider context of current developments in Catholic biblical theology, specifically the theology of the Old Testament, in Europe and the Americas. In doing so, I shall pay special attention to its hermeneutical perspective and its specific contribution to the current debate concerning the discipline of biblical theology.

Nobile is a Franciscan friar from Veneto, a biblical scholar who at present serves as rector of the Pontificio Ateneo Antonianum in Rome. His *Theology of the Old Testament* is published as part of a collection of biblical studies that has set an editorial limit on the length of the work, resulting in its being extremely succinct (about 240 pages of text).[2] Another study dedicated to the theology of the New Testament, which has been entrusted to Giuseppe Segalla, will complement Nobile's volume. In lively and pedagogical language, Nobile guides his readers through Old Testament texts to arrive at a lucid theological synthesis. His study is intended not solely for scholars and students of theology, but also for the general reader who wishes to understand the First Testament in an organic and profound way.

---

[1] The first is another Franciscan, A. Mattioli, author of *Dio e l'uomo*.

[2] Nobile, *Teologia*.

The Current Situation of Biblical Theology

After the crisis of the so-called 'biblical theology movement' in the 1960s and 1970s, interest in biblical theology has revived notably in the last 15 years, as the increasing number of publications demonstrates.[3] In fact, in this short period of time no less than five major theologies of the Old Testament have appeared (Horst Dietrich Preuss, Josef Schreiner, Walter Brueggemann, Otto Kaiser, and Rolf Rendtorff),[4] as well as two important though polemical attempts to present a pan-biblical theology – that is, a biblical theology of the entire Bible, Old and New Testaments (Brevard S. Childs, Charles H.H. Scobie).[5] Apart from these massive studies, numerous other contributions have appeared (monographs, articles, volumes of collected essays and congress volumes) which are concerned with other sectors of biblical science. Furthermore, two periodicals dedicated to the field have appeared: *Horizons in Biblical Theology* (Pittsburgh, since 1979) and *Jahrbuch für biblische Theologie* (Neukirchen, since 1986).[6]

Even though 'biblical theology today is a vibrant, living organism of interest to both the academy and the church',[7] we should not ignore the fact that biblical theology is – to use Barr's expression – a 'contrastive notion'. That is, it is a notion that cannot stand on its own but needs to be contrasted with other concepts (operations or modes of argument) in order to ensure its validity and to define its own identity.[8] Indeed, scholars have generally applied biblical theology only in contrast with other possible approaches to the Bible. And it is precisely this contrastive nature which has constituted the main characteristic of the discipline since its birth – hence its fluctuating and certainly ambiguous nature. Appreciated by some and discarded by others, biblical theology remains a discipline that is hard to define, a discipline that has always manoeuvred between biblical exegesis and dogmatic theology (cf. the famous discourse by

---

[3] Hasel: 'There is today unprecedented interest in biblical theology' ('Nature', 203); Barr: 'In fact scholarly activity in the area of biblical theology, or what appears to be close to it, continues to flourish' (*Concept*, 1).

[4] Preuss, *Theologie*, I–II; Schreiner, *Theologie*; Brueggemann, *Theology*; Kaiser, *Der Gott des Alten Testaments*, I–III; Rendtorff, *Theologie*, I–II.

[5] Childs, *Biblical Theology*; Scobie, *Ways*.

[6] See Reventlow, 'Theologie', and Barr, *Concept*, 1–2.

[7] Perdue, *Collapse*, 7.

[8] Cf. Barr, *Concept*, 5–17. For Barr, biblical theology shows a different face depending on which of the following it is contrasted with: 1) doctrinal (systematic, dogmatic or constructive) theology; 2) non-theological study of the Bible; 3) history of religion and corresponding approaches; 4) philosophical theology and natural theology; 5) the interpretation of *part* of the Bible as distinct from the larger complexes taken as *wholes* (p. 5).

Johann Philipp Gabler in 1787).[9] It is a discipline that touches upon the history of religion, philosophical and natural theology. It can encompass the entire Bible or limit itself to one Testament. What, then, is biblical theology? From among the many definitions, I favour Andrew T. Lincoln's definition, though he himself describes it as minimalist, according to which biblical theology 'is theology developed on the basis of the unity of the Bible and its two Testaments. It is biblical because it takes into account the whole Bible and it is theological because it engages in interpretation and reflection on the subject matter of the Bible'.[10]

Not only the definition, but also the methodology, structure and contents of biblical theology remain a matter of debate among scholars to this day. In his introduction to the recent volume of contributions to the ninth Wheaton Theology Conference, Scott J. Hafemann points out three major challenges that biblical theology will have to confront in the near future: biblical theology and the question of diversity (mapping out the content of the biblical witness); biblical theology and the question of the canon (working on the development of this content throughout the biblical canon); biblical theology and the question of conflict (striving to describe a pan-biblical theology that incorporates the Old and the New Testaments into an integrated whole).[11] Only ten years earlier, in his analysis of the current state of biblical theology, Pokorny considered the three major problems of the discipline to be: revelation and history (the problem of criteria); revelation and theology (the problem of hermeneutics); and revelation and the Bible (the problem of the Old and New Testaments).[12] Although they use different terminology, both authors coincide in essential points of a debate that remains open to new contributions. In this line Nobile presents a biblical theology of the Old Testament, one of the few originating from southern Europe, which seeks to answer the questions mentioned above from an essentially interreligious perspective.

The Theology of the Old Testament by Marco Nobile

In his introduction, Nobile raises the 'problem' of a theology of the Old Testament (Can there be a theology of the Old Testament today?) by giving a historical overview of the discipline. But first he gives his own definition of Old Testament theology: 'the systematic study of the belief of ancient Israel'. According to Nobile, the belief of Israel is the subject matter of investigation,

---

[9] See Sandys-Wunsch and Eldredge, 'J.P. Gabler's …' (for the English version).

[10] See Lincoln, Ch. 12, 'Hebrews and Biblical Theology'.

[11] Hafemann, *Biblical Theology*, 16–20.

[12] Pokorny, 'Problem'.

and the notion 'systematic' defines that which makes the investigation a theological one. That is, it is not a mere accumulation of historical and conceptual data, but rather a treatise that organizes the data into a harmonious report that speculatively transcends the data.[13] His historical panorama of biblical theology (Johann Philipp Gabler, Hermann Gunkel, Karl Barth, Walter Eichrodt, Gerhard von Rad, Wolfhart Pannenberg, Rolf Rendtorff, Karl Rahner, Oscar Cullmann, James Barr) concludes with the mention of two relatively recent projects, one of which has given rise to enormous polemic. These are *Old Testament Theology in a Canonical Context* (1985) by Brevard S. Childs and another work, less known perhaps because published only in French, *Le Dieu de la Promesse et le Dieu de l'Alliance* (1986) by Jacques Vermeylen. These books are methodologically quite different – in certain aspects they even oppose each other – but Nobile prefers to consider them as complementary. While the latter follows a diachronic route of the evolution of Israelite belief and presents itself as a new and up-to-date history of the religion of Israel, the former is methodologically situated at the opposite pole. According to Childs, the scholar who wants to design a biblical theology has to accept, first, the body of texts as a given fact, and second, the essentially Christian nature of the theology of the Old Testament.[14] In a certain way Childs and Vermeylen represent the two extremes in one of the more hotly debated issues regarding the theology of the Old Testament: should it be conceived as a history of the Israelite religion or as a systematic theology?

For Nobile, the historical perspective is very closely connected with the hermeneutical question – that is, with the interpretative operation that the scholar or believer applies to the Old Testament (or to the Bible in general) in order to understand it thoroughly. For this reason he presents a brief history of biblical hermeneutics, focusing especially on the modern era, beginning with Friedrich Schleiermacher and continuing with Wilhelm Dilthey, Martin Heidegger, Hans Georg Gadamer and Paul Ricœur. A theme emerges in the last section of the introduction, and again towards the end of the book, that can be considered a peculiar characteristic of Nobile's work: the Hebrew question.[15] Christians share the Old Testament with the Jews, and yet the problem of a theology of the Old Testament is a Christian problem. This point raises an endless number of questions. How do we reconcile the legitimacy of a Hebrew approach to the Scriptures with the necessity of submitting them to a Christian hermeneutic? How do we avoid the false alternatives of an acceptance of the Hebrew reading of the sacred text – leaving Christ in the margin – or a Christian manipulation of the Old Testament? Nobile expounds his position,

---

[13] Nobile, *Teologia*, 20.
[14] Childs, *Old Testament Theology*, 17–18.
[15] Nobile, *Teologia*, 245–56.

illustrating it with three significant quotations. The first is from the theologian
Dietrich Bonhoeffer, taken from a sermon given in a Nazi prison during
Advent, 1943: 'Time and again I discover how I think and feel in an Old Testa-
ment way; in the past I have read more the Old Testament than the New ...
Whoever wants to be and to feel too soon and too directly in a New Testament
way, for me is not a Christian.'[16] The second is from the biblical scholar Franz
Mussner: 'Without the construction (*Aufbau*) of "a theology after Auschwitz,"
there can not be an authentic demolition (*Abbau*) of Christian anti-Judaism.'
Finally, Nobile quotes Pope John Paul II, speaking 20 years after the promulgation of *Nostra Aetate*, the declaration on the relationship of the Church with
non-Christian religions:

> Jews and Christians must get to know each other better. Not just superficially as
> people of different religions, merely coexisting in the same place, but as members of
> such religions which are so closely linked to one another (cf. *Nostra Aetate*, 4) ... For
> Christians these relations [with Jews] have special theological and moral dimensions
> because of the Church's conviction, expressed in the document we are commemo-
> rating, that 'she received the revelation of the Old Testament through the people
> with whom God in his inexpressible mercy designed to establish the ancient Cove-
> nant, and draws sustenance from the root of that good olive tree into which have
> been grafted the wild olive branches of the Gentiles' (*Nostra Aetate*, 4).[17]

After carefully analysing the three quotations Nobile reaches a conclusion or,
better, expresses his deep desire: 'May our theology be a book that Christians
feel as their own and that Jews understand as something not strange.'[18]

In the first part of his book Nobile analyses the theological themes of the
Old Testament according to its classical division: Torah (connected with the
Deuteronomistic work), Prophets and Writings. He insists on the unity of the
text and favours reading it in its final form. For example, in the section Genesis
– 2 Kings he studies the themes of election and rebellion, divine faithfulness
and human weakness. The chapter on prophetic literature is Nobile's specific
field of expertise. His doctoral dissertation on Ezekiel at the Pontifical Biblical
Institute of Rome,[19] in which he illustrates the novelty of his exegetical position, made a notable impact among scholars. In his dissertation he proposes and
defends what he calls '*uno schema cultuale di fondazione*'. This is an expression
Nobile coined and can perhaps be translated as 'a foundational cultic scheme'.
It is one of Nobile's key ideas and undergirds especially his presentation of the

---

[16] All of these quotations can be found in Zenger, 'Versuch', 275–76.

[17] Here I quote the original English text in *Insegnamenti di Giovanni Paolo II*, 1078,
1080.

[18] Nobile, *Teologia*, 45.

[19] Nobile, *Una lettura*.

historic and prophetic literature. The expression is not to be understood in the sense of the 'ritual pattern' theory created by the Scandinavian and Anglo-American schools. According to them, the ritual pattern is a model originating from Mesopotamia or from Egypt, and from this place it expanded progressively. The 'cultic scheme' proposed by Nobile, on the other hand, is characterized by two methodological aspects. First, the word 'scheme' is chosen because some texts from Ezekiel seem to follow a structure oriented to the instauration of cult and the foundation of the temple. Second, the presence of this cultic scheme in the book of Ezekiel does not necessarily imply that it corresponds to a historically celebrated ritual. Nobile does not even raise the question of this last possibility. His only claim is to have discovered a literary scheme that gives unity to the whole book.

What we are dealing with here, in general terms, is a ritual scheme that articulates in a tripartite structure the foundational elements of many religions, including the Hebrew religion. In fact, it corresponds to an anthropological pattern that occurs both on the level of the individual and of the community. According to this pattern, a human being or a human society, in order to establish itself, projects itself outward and makes its foundational elements ritually visible in a series of institutions. This ritual accomplishment is found especially in archaic or premodern cultures, in which the distinction between what is civil and what is religious does not yet exist. Concretely speaking, this means that every form of social organization (the city), every official institution (the law), or every religious institution (the temple) needs to be legitimized by the divinity. This foundational scheme consists of three moments: first, a theophany or some legitimate apparition of the divinity; second, a conflict, frequently symbolized by a struggle between the godhead and his adversaries, ending with the elimination of the adversaries (a foreign nation, impurity, injustice – in short, the forces of evil); and third, the founding of the sanctuary (temple) or of a sacred institution (the law). The founding of the temple – seen as an '*axis mundi*' that establishes the borders of the three main cosmic zones (heaven, earth and hell) and at the same time favours a mutual relation among all of them – means that the forces of evil are subjugated and controlled in the underground 'abyss'. In other words, the destruction of the temple, in the event that it happens, will not be a local disgrace but a real catastrophe of cosmic range.

According to Nobile, this anthropological scheme of a cultic nature is found in Genesis 12:6–7, where the foundation of the sanctuary of Shechem is preceded by a theophany (cf. also 33:18ff., where the theophany is lacking). The same scheme appears in 26:23–25 for the sanctuary of Beer-Sheba and in 28:10–22 (cf. also 35:1) for that of Bethel. In these three episodes the fight against the enemies is lacking. This element, however, is present in Judges 6:11–32 at the foundation of the sanctuary of Ophrah by Gideon, who has

previously experienced a theophany (6:11–24). This passage recalls the fight of
Elijah against the prophets of Baal (1 Kgs. 18:20–24).[20] Again the same scheme
is found in Exodus 3 – 15[21] and also in various prophetic books: Isaiah, Jeremiah, Ezekiel, Zephaniah and Amos. This does not mean, as has already been
said, that such texts reflect a historical ritual or a ritual that was actually performed. It is, rather, a universal anthropological formula that can be found in
human societies. In Ezekiel, these three steps of the scheme can be distinguished more clearly than in the other prophetic books. First, the theophany
and the prophetic calling constitute the opening of the book (Ezek. 1 – 3).[22]
Second, the conflict, or '*pars destruens*', appears as a fight of God against the sin
of Israel (Ezek. 4 – 24) and against the foreign nations ('*ammīm rabbīm*) and cha-
otic waters (*mayim rabbīm*; Ezek. 25 – 32; 38 – 39). Third, the '*pars construens*'
culminates in the founding of the sanctuary and the promulgation of the laws
for the people (Ezek. 40 – 48).[23] In Hosea, Micah, Joel, Zechariah and Jonah,
Nobile discovers another pattern of internal structures.[24]

In the second part of his book, Nobile offers a systematic synthesis of a more
existential nature as the fruit of his analysis of Old Testament texts, always
respecting the autonomy and internal reference of the Hebrew Scriptures
before relating them to the New Testament (in the line of Gerhard von Rad
and Rolf P. Knierim).[25] This synthesis is articulated on the basis of the main
themes which, according to Nobile, characterize the dialogue between God
and his people – the latter being understood as historical reality (Israel) and as
anthropological reality (humankind). This dialogue is conceived as a revelatory
process. God reveals the conditions of the relationship (covenant). Such conditions are not atemporal but are situated in an ongoing history that is made up of
the following elements: a) an origin (creation) which establishes the beginning
of the universe and of humankind; b) a complex development involving devia-
tions, ruptures and returns, which is illuminated by a prophetic reading of history; c) a goal which is slowly depicted by a series of elements that are manifest
in the structure of reality and in the life of certain institutions (monarchy,
temple, law, the social organization of Israel). It is a frame of reference that
gradually emerges from an attentive reading of nature and of history (a
sapiential attitude). Nobile studies the following themes: revelation, God and

---

[20] See also the tradition of the ark in 1 Sam. 4 – 6 and 2 Sam. 6.

[21] Nobile, *Teologia*, 81–83, referring to the Exodus epic: 1) theophany of Moses (Ex. 3
     – 4); 2) fight between God and the Pharaoh (Ex. 5 – 11); 3) victory over the enemy
     (Ex. 12 – 14), and poetic commentary with liturgical connotations (Ex. 15).

[22] Nobile, 'Ez 37,1–14'.

[23] Cf. Nobile, 'Ez 38–39 ed Ez 40–48'.

[24] Cf. Nobile, 'Il valore strutturante'.

[25] Von Rad, *Old Testament Theology*, II, 385–404; Knierim, *Task*, esp. 1–20.

the human being, the world of the Old Testament, the problem of evil, life and death, time, and the spirituality of the Old Testament (the practice of faith), in which he speaks briefly of the Psalms. A weakness of Nobile's work in this second part, which is perhaps due to the enormous effort of synthesizing so much material, should be pointed out: it is not clear by what criterion he made his selection, since he nowhere gives a convincing justification of it.[26]

In the epilogue of his *Teologia*, 'Old and New Testament: Points of Theological Contact', Nobile aims to reap the fruit of his investigations and to define precisely the position of his Old Testament theology, thus preparing the transition to New Testament theology. I would like to draw attention to five relevant points that Nobile makes here: 1) A theology of the Old Testament is intimately connected with the state of contemporary exegetical investigations; it can not be an abstract theological discourse separated from the contingency of the scientific investigation. This does not mean that the theological discourse is precarious by nature, but rather that it has to be dynamic and always progressing and deepening in the knowledge of the word of God. 2) Precisely because it is a theological discipline, a theology of the Old Testament presupposes a system of conceptual co-ordinates that derive from one's faith; in other words, the theology of the Old Testament as such can only be undertaken by a Christian (in line with Brevard S. Childs).[27] The hermeneutic approach to the Mikra by Jews will obviously be different. No theology of the Old Testament should renounce its own confessional or ideological perspective, because this perspective contributes to the pluralism of theological research. 3) A theology of the Old Testament has to take into account the aforementioned dilemma concerning the nature of the discipline: Old Testament theology as a history of the Hebrew religion (thus Georg Fohrer or Antonius H.J. Gunneweg),[28] versus Old Testament theology as a systematizing of the biblical data according to a pre-existent dogmatic scheme (with notable divergences this position is adopted by Brevard S. Childs, for whom both Testaments, each in its own way, would give testimony to Jesus Christ).[29] 4) In an Old Testament theology one has to accept the 'participating distance' between the 'thing' transmitted by the word of God and the 'I' of the reader. This is necessary in order to avoid the trap of subjectivism, on the one hand, which imposes on the text ideological or personal prejudices and, on the other hand, the danger of positivistic objectivism which pretends to arrive at the intention of the historical author by

---

[26] Cf. Nobile, *Teologia*, 176.

[27] Cf. by contrast Dunn, Ch. 7, 'The Problem of Biblical Theology': 'Is a Jewish theological interpretation of their own Scriptures not equally "biblical theology"?' Cf. Levenson's study on why Jews are not interested in biblical theology in *Hebrew Bible*, 33–61.

[28] Fohrer, *Geschichte*; Gunneweg, *Biblische Theologie*.

[29] Childs, *Biblical Theology*. Cf. the criticism of Reventlow in 'Theologie', 65–66.

means of technical disciplines (philology, archaeology and others) while rejecting the insights of hermeneutics. 5) Finally, in order to engage in an Old Testament theology one has to appreciate the Hebraistic nature of the Old
Testament – for this is an indispensable condition for reaching a solution to the
'Hebrew question', either at a historical level or at a theological level. Nobile
affirms that this is not a matter of an emotional predisposition, but of a
hermeneutical attitude that is more respectful of the reality of the text and its
history, compared to what has gone on before generally, and that seeks to penetrate deeper into the Christian truth. In order to arrive at this goal, then, one
has to wear the 'Hebrew vest', just as did those who transmitted to us the faith
in Christ, the apostles.[30]

The Contribution of Nobile's Work to Jewish-Christian Relations

Without neglecting fundamental issues such as the search for a central or unifying principle, the canon of the Scriptures or the diachronic reading of the texts,
the main problem of biblical theology is, according to James D.G. Dunn, the
question of the two Testaments. The dynamic of biblical theology is determined and defined 'by texts which are Israel's Scripture (the Torah or Tanak as
a whole) and not *merely* the "*Old* Testament", but which are also Christian
Scripture ("the Scriptures" for the New Testament writers) and which therefore have some sort of defining role for the texts which were to become the
"*New* Testament"'.[31] Although he has a different approach, Nobile can be situated in the same line of thought.

Nobile raises three questions in his epilogue: Are there two revelations, or is
there just one revelation? Is the Old Testament Hebrew or Christian? What is
the hermeneutical approach of the New Testament to the Old Testament?
These issues reflect his preoccupation with the hermeneutical question and
with the so-called Hebrew question, without in any way wanting to impose a
Christianization of the Old Testament.

With regard to the first question, Nobile holds that the Old and New Testaments constitute a single process of revelation, especially seen from the point of
view of 'the history of salvation'. At the origin of both Testaments there is the
one God who initiated the revelatory process, which finds its fulfilment only in
the New Testament.[32] Although this way of understanding the unity of the

---

[30] Cf. Nobile, *Teologia*, 248–49.

[31] Dunn, Ch. 7, 'The Problem of "Biblical Theology"'.

[32] Cf. Pontifical Biblical Commission, *Jewish People*, n. 85: 'In both Testaments, it is the
same God who enters into relationship with human beings and invites them to live in
communion with him; the one God is the source of unity.' Cf. also n. 64.

biblical revelation may present some difficulties, it is part and parcel of the Christian belief and its tradition. In other words, the historical dimension of the revelatory process, which unites the two Testaments, remains a firm point in the debate.[33] Let me, however, indicate three main difficulties. First, the New Testament concept of history should be understood in the light of the eschatological, or apocalyptic, Hebrew expectations and not in an anachronistic way – that is, according to our modern conception of historical evolution or of history '*tout court*'. Second, the relation between the Old and the New Testament revelation is usually defined by the categories of 'promise' (for the Old Testament) and 'fulfilment' (for the New Testament). It is evident that the application of these categories, the former directed to the future and the latter rooted in the present, may on certain occasions be very reductive. Third, and this is according to Nobile the most serious difficulty to overcome, one has to take into account that the exclusive use of the category of salvation history introduces a double criterion into the process of revelation, splitting it along two lines: the revelation of the ephemeral and the revelation of the absolute. In this case, the Old Testament would be read as something that happened in the past (without consequences for the present), while the New Testament would enjoy the privilege of being what in reality is valid today and always. The one Bible, then, would offer two types of revelation – one better than the other for being more complete and perfect. The Scriptures understood as Old Testament do not simply speak of the past. They speak, rather, of a mystery that certainly is bound up with history – but that only today in Christ can reveal itself fully. From the point of view of truth, the past has the value of a perennial present.

With regard to the second question (Is the Old Testament Jewish or Christian?), Nobile answers that the Christian hermeneutical criterion differs from the Jewish criterion. In the case of the Hebrew Scriptures or Old Testament, the criterion with which Jews and Christians read the text is meta-textual. That is, it is a criterion that is not found materially in the text. From the historical-cultural point of view, the Christian reading of the text is influenced by its faith tradition, whereas the Jewish reading is guided by its oral tradition – made up of the rabbinic traditions, Midrashim, Mishna and the Babylonian and Palestinian Talmudim. Consequently the theological interpretation of the Scriptures by Christians on the one hand, and by Jews on the other, cannot but be different.[34] This does not imply, however, that there cannot be a positive relationship between the two hermeneutics.

Though far from denying the difficulty of such an enterprise, Nobile maintains that it is possible to establish a dialogue on the level of faith between

---

[33] Cf. Pontifical Biblical Commission, *Jewish People*, n. 85: 'Since it is a project for inter-personal relationships, God's plan is realized in history.'

[34] Cf. Pontifical Biblical Commission, *Jewish People*, n. 11.

Christian and Jewish hermeneutics of the Scriptures, if in their theological interpretation of the Old Testament Christians do not limit themselves to the category of 'salvation history' but also make use of the category 'Logos of God'. Precisely in the use of this latter hermeneutical category, post-biblical Hebrew thought could be a very effective instrument for us. Nobile affirms that the universal truth of Christ contained within the Old Testament is not only expressed in the vertical dimension of history, culminating in Jesus of Nazareth, but also in the horizontal dimension of the contemporaneity or eternity of the Logos. If we consider the Old Testament not solely as a writing that has collected 'prophecies' concerning Jesus of Nazareth, but also as a development of the revelation of the perennial Logos, who is Christ, then the Old Testament will always have something new to say to us, for it speaks of an eternal truth that is outside of time.[35] Therefore, the omnipresence of the Logos, present in the Old Testament in multiple and various forms, is, according to Nobile, the factor that legitimizes the two readings of the Scriptures – the Jewish and the Christian. Nobile maintains, at least as a working hypothesis, that in the Scriptures 'beyond a Christian Old Testament and a Hebrew Mikra, which theologically are irreducible to one another, a theological channel of communication can exist, which – without diminishing the Christian or Jewish peculiarity – leads to a reciprocal attention to the respective reception of revelation'.[36]

Nobile also addresses the issue of the hermeneutical approach of the New Testament to the Old Testament, taking into consideration the relation between the two Testaments from the point of view of an Old Testament scholar. The New Testament is a Christian reading of the Old Testament. In other words, the New Testament writings use the Old Testament for both understanding and giving authority to the 'Christian event'. The New Testament is full of explicit and implicit references to the Old Testament to such an extent that, globally speaking, one could say that in the New Testament the totality of the Old Testament is represented. It is evident that the relationship between the two Testaments cannot be determined by the quantity of cited texts alone. That would be a positivistic and restrictive criterion. The 'hermeneutical route' which Nobile proposes does not entail moving away from the Old to the New Testament and staying there for ever. Rather, the approach consists in passing continuously from the New to the Old Testament in order to understand the depth not only of what God has said, but also of what God is saying, which in some broad measure is already contained in the Old Testament. To sum it up: 'only if we manage to deepen our knowledge of the treasures of the eternal discourse of the God of the Old Testament, we shall be able to understand in an adequate way the mystery which is revealed in the

---

[35] Cf. Nobile, *Teologia*, 253.
[36] Nobile, *Teologia*, 254.

New Testament. Or the other way around: only when we thus trace the roots of the New Testament will it be possible to appreciate fully the timeless meaning of the Old Word.'[37]

Conclusion

In the first pages of his *Concept of Biblical Theology*, James Barr notes three aspects which, in his opinion, could help to clarify the present state of biblical theology: 1) the fact that biblical theology is practised by biblical scholars, whether of the Old or New Testament; 2) the innovative character of biblical theology, inasmuch as it is searching for something which as yet remains unknown; and 3) the ecumenical[38] potential of biblical theology. I would like to underline especially the last aspect, since the ecumenical dimension is the most remarkable feature of the work of Marco Nobile.

The Bible is the basis of two religions, Judaism and Christianity, and the biblical texts are at the basis of biblical theology (both Jewish and Christian). Therefore all attempts to make progress in the field of biblical theology have to be situated in the heart of the Jewish-Christian dialogue. Instead of accentuating the differences between the distinct theological traditions, biblical theology would have to be capable of finding common ground and creating room for exchange. 'Dialogue is possible, since Jews and Christians share a rich common patrimony that unites them. It is greatly to be desired that prejudice and misunderstanding be gradually eliminated on both sides, in favour of a better understanding of the patrimony they share and to strengthen the links that bind them.'[39]

More than twenty years ago Samuel Terrien affirmed: 'The time is ripe for an ecumenical theology of the Bible. In Holy Scripture is found the only ground common to all the families of Christendom for the stimulus and control of theological thinking.'[40] In this quote Terrien uses 'ecumenical' in its more narrow sense, relating to the unity of Christians. The theology of Nobile, however, goes far beyond that. Its 'ecumenical potential' is not used towards intra-Christian unity but to reinforce and deepen Jewish-Christian relations. This is, in my opinion, the most valuable contribution of Nobile's work to studies on biblical theology.

---

[37] Cf. Nobile, *Teologia*, 255–56.

[38] Here the adjective is used in its broader sense, including relations between Christianity and Judaism.

[39] Pontifical Biblical Commission, *Jewish People*, n. 87.

[40] Terrien, 'Play of Wisdom', 125.

100 Nuria Calduch-Benages

Bibliography

Barr, J., *The Concept of Biblical Theology: An Old Testament Perspective* (Minneapolis: Fortress Press; London: SCM Press, 1999)

Brueggemann, W., *Theology of the Old Testament: Testimony, Dispute, Advocacy* (Minneapolis: Fortress Press, 1997)

Childs, B.S., *Old Testament Theology in a Canonical Context* (London: SCM Press, 1985; Philadelphia: Fortress Press, 1986)

—, *Biblical Theology of the Old and New Testaments: Theological Reflection on the Christian Bible* (London: SCM Press; Minneapolis: Fortress Press, 1992)

Fohrer, G., *Geschichte der israelitischen Religion* (Berlin: de Gruyter, 1969)

Gunneweg, A.H.J., *Biblische Theologie des Alten Testaments: Eine Religionsgeschichte Israels in biblisch-theologischer Sicht* (Stuttgart: Kohlhammer, 1993)

Hafemann, S.J. (ed.), *Biblical Theology: Retrospect and Prospect* (Leicester: Apollos; Downers Grove, IL: InterVarsity Press, 2002)

Hasel, G.F., 'The Nature of Biblical Theology: Recent Trends and Issues', *AUSS* 32 (1994), 203–15

Insegnamenti di Giovanni Paolo II, vol. 8.1 (Vatican City: Libreria Editrice Vaticana, 1985)

Kaiser, O., *Der Gott des Alten Testaments: Theologie des Alten Testaments*, I: *Grundlegung* (UTB 1747; Göttingen: Vandenhoeck & Ruprecht, 1993)

—, *Der Gott des Alten Testaments: Wesen und Wirken. Theologie des Alten Testaments*, II: *Jahwe, der Gott Israels, Schöpfer der Welt und des Menschen* (UTB 2024; Göttingen: Vandenhoeck & Ruprecht, 1998)

—, *Der Gott des Alten Testaments. Theologie des Alten Testaments*, III: *Jahwes Gerechtigkeit* (UTB 2392; Göttingen: Vandenhoeck & Ruprecht, 2003)

Knierim, R.P., *The Task of Old Testament Theology: Substance, Method and Cases* (Grand Rapids: Eerdmans, 1995)

Levenson, J.D., *The Hebrew Bible, the Old Testament, and Historical Criticism: Jews and Christians in Biblical Studies* (Louisville, KY: Westminster John Knox Press, 1993)

Mattioli, A., *Dio e l'uomo nella Bibbia d'Israele: Teologia dell'Antico Testamento* (Casale Monferrato: Marietti, 1981)

Nobile, M., *Una lettura simbolico-strutturalista di Ezechiele* (Doctoral dissertation, PIB, Rome, 1982; only an abstract has been published: 'Estratto della dissertazione di laurea per il conseguimento del dottorato al Pontificio Istituto Biblico di Roma', Roma 1982)

—, 'Ez 37,1–14 come costitutivo di uno schema cultuale', *Bib* 65 (1984), 476–89

—, 'Ez 38–39 ed Ez 40–48: I due aspetti complementari del culmine di uno schema cultuale di fondazione', *Anton* 62 (1987), 141–71

—, 'Il valore strutturante e teologico di "shûb" e "yashab" nel libro di Osea', *Anton* 67 (1992), 472–89

—, *Teologia dell'Antico Testamento* (LOGOS; Corso di studi biblici 8.1; Leumann, Torino: Elledici, 1998)

Perdue, L.G., *The Collapse of History: Reconstructing Old Testament Theology* (Minneapolis: Fortress Press, 1994)

Pokorny, P., 'The Problem of Biblical Theology', *HBT* 15 (1993), 83–94

Pontifical Biblical Commission, *The Jewish People and their Sacred Scriptures in the Christian Bible* (Vatican City: Libreria Editrice Vaticana, 2002)

Preuss, H.D., *Theologie des Alten Testaments*, I–II (Stuttgart: Kohlhammer, 1991–92)

Rad, G. von, *Old Testament Theology*, I–II (New York: Harper & Row, 1965, 1968; London: SCM Press, 1975)

Rendtorff, R., *Theologie des Alten Testaments: Ein kanonischer Entwurf*, Band 1: *Kanonische Grundlegung*; Band 2: *Thematische Entfaltung* (Neukirchen-Vluyn: Neukirchener, 1999, 2001)

Reventlow, H. Graf, 'Theologie und Hermeneutik des Alten Testaments', *TRu* 61.1–2 (1996), 48–102; 123–76

Sandys-Wunsch, J., and L. Eldredge, 'J.P. Gabler and the Distinction between Biblical and Dogmatic Theology', *SJT* 33 (1980), 133–58

Schreiner, J., *Theologie des Alten Testaments* (NEchtB, Ergänzungsband zum Alten Testament, I; Würzburg: Echter, 1995)

Scobie, C.H.H., *The Ways of Our God: An Approach to Biblical Theology* (Grand Rapids: Eerdmans, 2003)

Terrien, S., 'The Play of Wisdom: Turning Point in Biblical Theology', *HBT* 3 (1981), 125–53

Vermeylen, J., *Le Dieu de la Promesse et le Dieu de l'Alliance* (LD 126; Paris: Cerf, 1986)

Zenger, E., 'Zum Versuch einer neuen jüdisch-christlichen Bibelhermeneutik. Kleine Antwort auf H. Seebass', *TRev* 90 (1994), 274–78

5

Mission as a Matrix for Hermeneutics and Biblical Theology[1]

Christopher J.H. Wright

Introduction: Bible and Mission

A personal pilgrimage

I remember them so vividly from my childhood – the great banner texts around the walls of the missionary conventions in Northern Ireland where I would help my father at the stall of the Unevangelized Fields Mission, of which he was Irish Secretary after twenty years in Brazil. 'Go ye into all the world and preach the Gospel to every creature', they urged me, along with other similar imperatives in glowing gothic calligraphy. By the age of twelve, I could have quoted you all the key ones – 'Go ye therefore and make disciples ...' 'How shall they hear ...?' 'You shall be my witnesses ... to the ends of the earth'. 'Whom shall we send? ... Here am I, send me'. I knew my missionary Bible verses. I had responded to many a rousing sermon on most of them.

By the age of twenty-one I had a degree in theology from Cambridge, where the same texts had been curiously lacking. At least, it is curious to me now. At the time there seemed to be little connection at all between theology and mission in the minds of the lecturers, or in my own mind, or, for all I knew, in the mind of God either. 'Theology' was all about God – what God was like, what God had said and what God had done and what mostly dead people had speculated on all three. 'Mission' was about us, the living, and what we've been doing since Carey (who of course was the first missionary, we so erroneously thought).[2]

---

[1] With this paper, the Scripture and Hermeneutics Seminar revisits an important dimension of scriptural hermeneutics that was opened up in the first volume in the series by H.D. Beeby, 'Missional Approach'

[2] It was this experience as a theological student that I was reflecting on in one of my editorials for *Themelios*, an international journal for students of theology and

'Mission is what we do.' That was the assumption, supported of course by clear biblical commands. 'Jesus sends me, this I know, for the Bible tells me so.' Many years later, including years when I was teaching theology myself as a missionary in India (another curious thought: I could have done precisely the same job in a college in England, but that would not have been considered 'mission'), I found myself teaching a module called 'The Biblical Basis of Mission' at All Nations Christian College – an international mission training institution in south-east England. The module title itself embodies the same assumption. Mission is the noun, the given reality. It is something we do and we basically know what it is; biblical is the adjective, which we want to use to explain what we already know we should be doing. The reason why we know we should be doing it – the basis, foundation or grounds on which we justify it – must be found in the Bible. As Christians, we need a biblical basis for everything we do. What, then, is 'the biblical basis for mission'? Roll out the texts. Add some that nobody else has thought of. Do some joined-up theology. Add some motivational fervour. And the class is heart-warmingly appreciative. Now they have even more biblical support for what they already believed anyway, for these are All Nations students after all. They only came because they are committed to doing mission.

This mild caricature is not in the least derogatory in intent. I believe passionately that mission is what we should be doing, and I believe the Bible endorses and mandates it. However, the more I taught that course, the more I used to introduce it by telling the students that I would like to rename it: from 'The Biblical Basis of Mission', to 'The Missional Basis of the Bible'. I wanted them to see not just that the Bible contains a number of texts that happen to provide a rationale for missionary endeavour, but that *the whole Bible is itself a 'missional' phenomenon*. The writings that now comprise our Bible are themselves the product of, and witness to, the ultimate mission of God. The Bible renders to us the story of God's mission through God's people in their engagement with God's world for the sake of the whole of God's creation. The Bible is the drama of this God of purpose engaged in the mission of achieving that

---

religious studies, in which I began:

> Think of a doctrine. Double it with variant interpretations. Divide by denominational distinctives. Add some technical jargon. Subtract any practical relevance. Finally take away the doctrine you first thought of, and what are you left with? Probably the sum of the average theological student's awareness of the relation between his theological study and the mission of the church. He is hardly to be blamed for this, since Western theology at least has been carried on for centuries with little or no direct relation to it. (*Themelios* 15.2 [1990], 39)

Dan Beeby agrees, commenting, 'Notoriously, biblical studies, on the whole, proceed comfortably without even a nodding acquaintance with mission or missiology', Beeby, 'Missional Approach', 278.

purpose universally, embracing past, present and future, Israel and the nations, 'life, the universe and everything'. Mission is not just one of a list of things that the Bible happens to talk about, only a bit more urgently than some. Mission is, in that much-abused phrase, 'what it's all about'. For that reason, mission could provide a framework both for our hermeneutical approach to reading the Bible and for organizing our account of biblical theology.

Some definitions

At this point it would be as well to offer some definition of the way I am planning to use the term 'mission', and the related words: missionary, missional and missiological.

Mission: It will be immediately clear from my reminiscences above that I am dissatisfied with popular use of the word mission (or more commonly in the USA, 'missions') solely in relation to human endeavours of various kinds. I do not at all question the validity of Christian engagement in mission, but I do want to argue for the theological priority of *God's* mission. Fundamentally, our mission (if it is biblically informed and validated) is our committed participation, at God's invitation and command, in God's own mission in the world through history.

Furthermore, I am dissatisfied with accounts of mission which stress only the 'roots' of the word in the Latin verb *mitto*, 'to send', and which then see its primary significance in the dynamic of sending or being sent. Again, this is not because I doubt the importance of this theme within the Bible, but because it seems to me that if we define mission only in 'sending' terms we necessarily exclude from our inventory of relevant resources many other aspects of biblical teaching which directly or indirectly affect our understanding of God's mission and the practice of our own. Generally speaking, I will use the term mission in its more general sense of a long-term purpose or goal that is to be achieved through proximate objectives and planned actions. Within such a broad mission (as applied to any group or enterprise), there is room for subordinate missions, in the sense of specific tasks assigned to a person or group which they are to accomplish as steps toward the wider mission. In the secular world, 'mission statements' seem to be much in vogue. Even restaurants (whose purpose in life one would have thought rather obvious) sometimes display them on their front windows, in an effort to link the task of feeding customers to some wider sense of 'mission'. Companies, schools, charities – even some churches (whose purpose in life ought to be more obvious than it is, even to their own members) – feel it helps them to have a 'mission statement', which summarizes the purpose for which they exist and what they hope to accomplish. The Bible presents to us a portrait of God that is unquestionably purposeful. The God who walks the paths of history through the pages of the Bible pins a mission statement to every signpost on the way. A missional hermeneutic of the Bible sets out to explore that divine mission and all that lies behind it and flows from it in relation to God himself, God's people and God's world.

Missionary: The word is usually a noun, referring to people who engage in mission, usually in a culture other than their own. It has even more of a flavour of 'being sent' than the word mission itself. Thus missionaries are typically those who are sent by churches or agencies to work in 'mission', or 'on missions'. The word is also used as an adjective, as in 'the missionary mandate', or 'a person of missionary zeal'. Unfortunately, the word has also generated something of a caricature, the missionary stereotype, as a regrettable side effect of the great nineteenth- and twentieth-century mission effort of the Western churches. The term 'missionary' still evokes images of white, Western expatriates among 'natives' in far-off countries. And it still evokes this image – all the more regrettably in churches which ought to know better, and certainly ought to know that already the majority of those engaged in cross-cultural mission are not Western at all, but from the growing indigenous churches of the majority world. As a result, many mission agencies which now build networks and partnerships with majority world churches and agencies prefer to avoid the term 'missionary' because of these unreconstructed mental images and describe their personnel as 'mission partners' instead.

Because of the predominant association of the word missionary with the activity of sending and with cross-cultural communication of the gospel – that is, with a broadly centrifugal dynamic of mission – I prefer not to use the term in connection with the Old Testament. In my view (which is not agreed by all), the people of Israel were not expected by God to 'send missionaries' to the nations.[3] So I would not, for example, choose to speak of 'the missionary message of the Old Testament' (the title of an early and excellent book by H.H. Rowley in 1944).[4] There are many biblical resources that profoundly enrich our understanding of mission in its broadest sense (and especially the mission of God) that are not about 'sending missionaries'. It is probably inappropriate, therefore, to refer to those texts and themes as 'missionary'.[5]

---

[3] Walter C. Kaiser, Jr, *Mission in the Old Testament*, takes the view that it was God's intention that Israel from the beginning should have engaged in some form of 'sending and going' mission to the nations. I do not find convincing biblical support for this.

[4] Rowley, *Missionary Message of the Old Testament*.

[5] Interestingly, though, the term *missio Dei* (mission of God) in its earliest use referred to the inner sending of God – that is, the Father sending the Son into the world, and the sending of the Holy Spirit by the Father and the Son. It is in this sense (among others) that John Stott can speak of our 'missionary God' ('Our God Is a Missionary God', ch. 19 in Stott, *Contemporary Christian*, 321–36).

Unfortunately, until recently, 'missionary' was the only English adjective formed from 'mission'. Another adjective, however, is being rightly welcomed into wider use.

Missional: This adjective denotes something that is related to or characterized by mission, or has the qualities, attributes or dynamics of mission (in the sense defined above). Missional is to the word mission what covenantal is to covenant, or fictional to fiction. Thus, we might speak of a missional reading of the exodus, meaning a reading that explores its dynàmic significance in God's mission for Israel and the world and its relevance to Christian mission today. Or we might say that Israel had a missional role in the midst of the nations – implying that they had an identity and role connected to God's ultimate intention of blessing the nations – which is not to say that Israel had a missionary mandate to go to the nations (whereas we could certainly speak of the missionary role of the church among the nations).

Missiology and missiological: Missiology is the study of mission. It includes biblical, theological, historical, contemporary and practical reflection and research. Accordingly, I will normally use 'missiological' when that theological or reflective aspect is intended. From the example above, one might equally speak of a missiological reading of exodus – but it would be less appropriate to speak of Israel having a missiological role in the midst of the nations. It is, in fact, because neither 'missionary role' nor 'missiological role' seems quite right in the latter case, that the word 'missional' is increasingly helpful.[6]

'This is what is written'

Mission, I suggested above, is what the Bible is all about in the sense that we could as meaningfully talk of the missional basis of the Bible as of the biblical basis of mission. Now this is a bold claim. One would not expect to be able to turn any phrase that began 'The biblical basis of ...' around the other way. There is, for example, a biblical basis for marriage, but there is not, obviously, 'a marital basis for the Bible'. There is a biblical basis for work, but work is not 'what the Bible is all about'. So is this not a rather exaggerated, even conceited, assertion? Indeed, in view of the enormous variety of the contents of the Bible, and the huge scholarly literature devoted to exploring every highway and

---

[6] Beeby also uses these words distinctively. He refers to 'a vocabulary of "mission", "missional", and "missiological". These all belong together – the praxis, the adjectival, the science' ('A Missional Approach', 278). He does not explicitly define the difference between 'missionary' and 'missional', but where he uses 'missionary' it has an active sense which sometimes includes its strong element of 'sending'.

byway of genre, authorship, context, ideology, date, editing and history of all these documents, does it make sense to speak of the Bible being 'all about' anything?

I take some encouragement in persisting with the claim from the words of the risen Jesus as recorded in Luke 24.[7] First to the two on the road to Emmaus, and then later to the rest of the disciples, Jesus made himself as Messiah the focus of the whole canon of the Hebrew Scriptures that we now call the Old Testament (vv. 27 and 44). So we are accustomed to speaking of the christological focus, or centre, of the Bible. For Christians, the whole Bible revolves around the person of Christ. Jesus went on, however, beyond his messianic centring of the Old Testament Scriptures to their missional[8] thrust as well.

> Then he opened their minds so they could understand the Scriptures. He told them, 'This is what is written: The Christ will suffer and rise from the dead on the third day, and repentance and forgiveness of sins will be preached in his name to all nations, beginning at Jerusalem.' (Lk. 24:45–47)

The whole sentence comes under the rubric 'this is what is written'. Luke does not present Jesus as quoting any specific verse from the Old Testament, but he claims that the mission of preaching repentance and forgiveness to the nations in his name is 'what is written'. He seems to be saying that the whole of the Scriptures (which we now know as the Old Testament), finds its focus *and* fulfilment *both* in the life and death and resurrection of Israel's Messiah and in the mission to all nations, which flows out from that event. Luke tells us that with these words Jesus 'opened their minds so they could understand the Scriptures', or, as we might put it, he was setting their hermeneutical orientation and agenda. The proper way for disciples of the crucified and risen Jesus to read their Scriptures is from a perspective that is both *messianic* and *missional*.

Paul, though he was not present for the Old Testament hermeneutics lecture on the day of resurrection, clearly found that his encounter with the risen Jesus and his recognition of Jesus as Messiah and Lord radically transformed his own way of reading the Scriptures. His hermeneutic now had the same double focus. Testifying before Festus he declares,

---

[7] In 1971 Henry C. Goerner, in *Thus It Is Written*, also took this text as a starting point for a biblical theology of mission.

[8] The use of 'missional' rather than 'missiological' here seems appropriate in light of the definitions above, since Jesus was not only offering a fresh theological reflection on the Scriptures, but also committing his disciples to the mission such reflection must now mandate: '… must be preached'; 'You are witnesses …'.

'I am saying nothing beyond what the prophets and Moses said would happen – that the Christ [Messiah] would suffer and, as the first to rise from the dead, would proclaim light *to his own people and to the Gentiles [nations].*' (Acts 26:22–23)

It was this dual understanding of the Scriptures which had shaped Paul's CV as the apostle of the Messiah Jesus to the Gentiles.

Down through the centuries, it would probably be fair to say, Christians have been good at their messianic reading of the Old Testament, but inadequate (and sometimes utterly blind) in their missional reading of it. We read the Old Testament messianically, or christologically, in the light of Jesus – in the sense of finding in it a whole messianic theology and eschatology which we see as fulfilled in Jesus of Nazareth. In doing so we follow his own example, of course, and that of his first followers and the authors of the Gospels. But what we have so often failed to do is to go beyond the mere satisfaction of ticking off so-called messianic predictions that have 'been fulfilled'. And we have failed to go further because we have not grasped the missional significance of the Messiah.

The Messiah was the promised one who would embody in his own person the identity and mission of Israel, as their representative, king, leader and saviour. Through the Messiah as his anointed agent, YHWH the God of Israel would bring about all that he intended for Israel. But what was that mission of Israel? It was nothing less than to be 'a light to the nations', the means of bringing the redemptive blessing of God to all the nations of the world, as originally promised in the title deeds of the covenant with Abraham. For the God of Israel is also the creator God of the entire world. Through the Messiah, therefore, the God of Israel would also bring about all that he intended for the nations. The eschatological redemption and restoration of Israel would issue in the ingathering of the nations. To fully recognize Jesus as Messiah, then, we also need to recognize his role in relation to the mission of Israel for the sake of the nations. Hence, a messianic reading of the Old Testament has to flow on to a missional reading – which is precisely the connection that Jesus makes in Luke 24.

Now, we recognize that the christological focus of the Bible operates in many different ways – some direct and others much more indirect. To speak of the Bible being 'all about' Christ does not (or should not) mean that we try to find Jesus of Nazareth in every verse by some feat of imagination. It means that the person and work of Jesus become the central hermeneutical key by which we, as Christians, articulate the overall significance of these texts in both Testaments. The same is true of the missiological focus. To say that the Bible is 'all about mission' is not about trying to find something relevant to evangelism in every verse. We are referring to something deeper and wider in relation to the Bible as a whole. We are thinking of the purpose for which the Bible exists, the God the Bible renders to us, the people whose identity and mission the Bible invites us to share, and the story the Bible tells about this God and this people and indeed about the whole world and its future. This is a story that encompasses past, present and future, life, the universe and everything. There is the closest connection between the biblical grand-narrative and what is meant here by biblical mission. To attempt a missional hermeneutic, then, is to ask: Is it possible, is it valid, is it profitable, for Christians to read the Bible as a whole from a missional perspective, and what happens when they do?

Before outlining some contours of an approach that would answer those questions, we shall look first at several ways in which the Bible is related to mission in contemporary writing on the matter. While these ways have their own validity and significant contributions to make, they do not seem quite adequate to what I have in mind as a comprehensively missional approach to biblical hermeneutics.

Steps Toward a Missional Hermeneutic

Beyond 'biblical foundations for mission'

There are more than enough books offering biblical foundations for Christian mission.[9] Some are tracts to the already converted, providing justification for the task to which writer and readers are already committed. Some pay no attention to critical scholarship; others, perhaps, too much.[10] Too many, more culpably, pay scant attention to the bulk of the Bible itself – the Old Testament. What all of these texts seek to do, however, is clear: to find appropriate biblical justification and authority for the mission of the Christian church to the nations. This may be in order to encourage those already engaged in such mission with the assurance that what they do is biblically grounded, or to motivate those who are not yet engaged in it with the warning that they are living in disobedience to biblical imperatives.

Such work, which might be called, 'biblical apologetic for mission', is of great importance. It would, after all, be a shattering thing if the church were suddenly seized by the conviction that all the missionary effort of two thousand

---

[9] Some of the more helpful texts on the subject include: Blauw, *Missionary Nature of the Church*; Burnett, *God's Mission*; Hedlund, *Mission of the Church*; Koestenberger and O'Brien, *Ends of the Earth*; de Ridder, *Discipling the Nations*; Senior and Stuhlmueller, *Biblical Foundations for Mission*.

[10] There is, of course, a proper place for the critical disciplines in our ground-laying work for biblical theology, but we also need to go beyond those foundations to the Bible's missiological thrust. Cf. Bosch, 'Hermeneutical Principles', and Van Engen, 'Relation of Bible and Mission', 34.

years was grounded in no clear warrant of Scripture. From time to time, of course, there have been voices that argued exactly thus. Indeed, it was in response to such voices, that argued theologically and biblically (as they thought) that mission to the nations was not required of good Christian citizens, that William Carey developed his biblical case for 'the conversion of the heathens' and became one of the first in the modern period to do so.[11]

The illustrious example of Carey, however, points to a shortcoming inherent in many 'biblical foundations for mission' projects. Carey built the whole of the biblical section of his case upon a single text, the so-called Great Commission of Matthew 28:18–20, arguing that it was as valid in his own day as in the days of the apostles, and that its imperative claim on the disciples of Christ had not lapsed with the first generation (as the opponents of foreign mission argued). While we would probably agree with his hermeneutical argument, and grant that his choice of text was admirable, it leaves the biblical case vulnerably thin. We might defend Carey with the consideration that it was an achievement in his context to make a biblical case for mission at all, albeit from a single text. Less defensible has been the continuing practice in many missionary circles to go on and on building the massive edifice of Christian missionary agency on this one text, with varying degrees of exegetical ingenuity. If you put all your apologetic eggs in one textual basket, what happens if the handle breaks?

What happens, for example, if all the hyperbole built on the word 'Go' is dissolved by the recognition that it is not an imperative at all in the text, but a participle, an assumption – something taken for granted. Jesus did not command his disciples to go; he assumed they would go, and he commanded them to make disciples. A better translation would be, 'As you go, therefore, disciple all the nations ...'

What happens if one questions the common assumption that this text gives some kind of timetable for the return of Christ: he will come back just as soon as we have all the nations 'discipled'? And is discipling a task that can ever be said to be completed (noting in passing that the text does say 'disciple', not

---

[11] There were, of course (contrary to popular mythology), Protestant missionaries long before William Carey. However, Carey was among the first to include a clearly argued biblical case for establishing a missionary society – in his use of Mt. 28:18–20 as his key text in his justly famous *An Enquiry into the Obligations of Christians, to Use Means for the Conversion of the Heathens* (1792). David Bosch comments:

> Protestants ... have always prided themselves on the fact that they do what they do on the basis of what Scripture teaches. Still, in the case of the earliest Protestant missionaries, the Pietists and the Moravians, very little of a real biblical foundation for their missionary enterprises was in evidence. Wm. Carey was, in fact, one of the very first to have attempted to spell out such a foundation for the Church's missionary mandate ('Hermeneutical Principles', 438).

'evangelize')? Does not every fresh generation of long-evangelized nations need fresh discipling? The Great Commission is an expanding and self-replicating task, not a ticking clock for the 'end-times'.

What happens, if, even more controversially, one heeds the voices of critical scholars who question whether the Great Commission, in these precise words in Matthew's Gospel, was ever actually spoken by Jesus?[12] In response to such a claim one might make several moves. One could seek to defend the authenticity of Matthew's text against the sceptics. One could argue that, even if this text is not a transcripted recording of words from the mouth of Jesus, it does authentically express the inevitable implication of his identity and achievement as understood by the post-resurrection church engaged in mission. Or one could search for more texts to back up this one.

The last option is the commonest. Most books offering a biblical basis of mission see their task as assembling as many texts as possible, texts which can be said to mandate, or in more indirect ways support, the missionary enterprise. Now this is also important as far as it goes. Such biblical inducement to mission engagement is needed in churches that seem rather selective in their reading of the Bible. There are many ordinary and worthy Christians who, in their personal piety, relish those Scriptures that speak to them of their own salvation and security, Scriptures that encourage them in times of distress, Scriptures that guide them in their efforts to walk before the Lord in ways that please him. But they may be surprised when they are confronted with such an array of texts that challenge them in relation to God's universal purpose for the world and the nations, the multicultural essence of the gospel and the missional essence of the church. Equally, there are many theological scholars and students whose understanding of theology is bounded by the horizon of the classical shape of the curriculum, in which mission in any form (biblical, historical, theological, practical) seems remarkably absent. If it can be shown (as I believe it certainly can) that there is a substantial number of texts and themes in the Bible that relate to Christian mission, then missiology may regain respectability in the academy (of which there are encouraging signs already).

However, whether we are able to present one text or many as a biblical basis of mission, the same danger that attends all prooftexting is still present. We have already decided what we want to prove (that our missionary practice is biblical), and our collection of texts simply ratifies our preconception. We thereby use the Bible as a mine from which we extract our gems – 'missionary texts'. These texts may sparkle, but simply laying out the gems on a string is not yet what one could call a missiological hermeneutic of the whole Bible itself. Such a collection of texts does not even provide an adequate whole-Bible

---

[12] This is the position argued by Alan Le Grys, *Origins*. Cf. James LaGrand, *Earliest Christian Mission*.

grounding for mission. Commenting on this text-assembly approach, David Bosch observes,

> I am not saying that these procedures are illegitimate. They undoubtedly have their value. But their contribution towards establishing the validity of the missionary mandate is minimal. This validity should not be deduced from isolated texts and detached incidents but only from the thrust of the central message of both Old and New Testaments. What is decisive for the Church today is not the formal agreement between what she is doing and what some isolated biblical texts seem to be saying but rather her relationship with the essence of the message of Scripture.[13]

What that 'central message ... the essence of the message of Scripture' might be, is of course precisely the issue we are wrestling with in these pages. To be able to say that it is 'mission' requires a lot more than just a list of benevolent texts. It also requires some careful definitions – but that lies ahead.

A final limitation of this 'list of texts' approach is that it has a suspicion of circularity. The danger is, as we have said, that one comes to the Bible with a massive commitment to the task of mission already in place, with a heritage of hallowed history, with methods and models in the present, and with strategies and goals for the future. All of this we have assumed to be biblically warranted. So in searching the Scriptures for a biblical foundation for mission, we are likely to find what we brought with us – our own conception of mission, now comfortingly festooned with biblical luggage tags. To establish a biblical grounding for *mission per se* is legitimate and essential. To claim to find biblical grounding for *all our missionary practice* is much more questionable. Some would say it is impossible – even dangerous. Rather than trying to find biblical legitimation for our activities, we should be submitting all of our missionary strategy, plans and operations to biblical critique and evaluation. Marc Spindler articulates this point well:

> If 'mission' is understood as the sum total of all actual missionary activities in the modern period or as everything undertaken under the banner of 'missions,' then an honest biblical scholar can only conclude that such a concept of mission does not occur in the Bible ... It is therefore anachronistic and hence meaningless to attempt to base all modern 'missionary' activities on the Bible, that is, to seek biblical precedents or literal biblical mandates for all modern missionary activities. Mission today must, rather, be seen as arising from something fundamental, from the basic movement of God's people toward the world [sc. with the good news of salvation through Jesus Christ] ... The genuineness of our biblical grounding of mission stands or falls with the orientation of modern missions to this central thought. All 'missionary' activities that have grown up in history must be reassessed from this perspective. Once again, a biblical grounding of mission by no means seeks to legitimate

---

[13] Bosch, 'Hermeneutical Principles', 439–40.

missionary activities that are actually being carried out. Its goal is, rather, evaluation of those activities in the light of the Bible.[14]

But in order to do that evaluative task, we have to have a clearer understanding of that 'something fundamental' – mission in its biblical sense, or, more precisely, a missiological framework of biblical theology.

Beyond multicultural hermeneutical perspectives

Slowly and somewhat reluctantly, the world of Western academic theology is becoming aware of the rest of the world. The impact of missiology has brought to the attention of the theological community in the West the wealth of theological and hermeneutical perspectives that are, in some cases at least, the product of the success of mission over the past centuries. Mission has transformed the map of global Christianity. From a situation at the beginning of the twentieth century when approximately 90 per cent of all the world's Christians lived in the West or North (i.e., predominantly in Europe and North America), the beginning of the twenty-first century finds at least 75 per cent of the world's Christians in the continents of the South and East – Latin America, Africa and parts of Asia and the Pacific. The whole centre of gravity of world Christianity has moved south – a phenomenon described, not entirely felicitously, as 'the next Christendom'.[15] We live in an age of a multinational church, and multidirectional mission. And, appropriately, we now live with multicultural hermeneutics. People will insist on reading the Bible for themselves. There is a great irony that the Western Protestant theological academy, which has its roots in precisely a hermeneutical revolution (the Reformation) that claimed the right to read Scripture independently from the prevailing hegemony of mediaeval Catholic Scholasticism, has proved so impervious to those of other cultures who choose to read the Scriptures through their own eyes.[16]

   This is a phenomenon that goes right back to the Bible itself, of course. The New Testament was born out of a hermeneutical revolution in reading those Scriptures we now call the Old Testament. And within the early church itself

---

[14] Spindler, 'Biblical Grounding', 124–25.

[15] Jenkins, *Next Christendom*. Cf. C.J.H. Wright, 'Future Trends in Mission', and bibliography there cited.

[16] Ignorance (whether innocent or wilful) of major issues in non-Western Christianity that non-Western theology must grapple with, was illustrated for me at a combined faculty meeting of several London theological colleges. A Ghanaian lecturer at All Nations said that in his pastoral work in Ghana he spent at least 50% of his time helping believers, pastorally and theologically, in the area of dreams and visions and the spiritual world. A British lecturer at another college commented with ill-concealed disdain to me over lunch, 'I rather thought we'd grown out of that kind of thing.'

there were different ways of handling those same Scriptures, depending on the context and need being addressed. Both Jewish and Greek Christians, who had come to faith in Jesus through the church's mission, felt that the Scriptures addressed and made claim upon them in different ways, such that Paul, in Romans 14 – 15 for example, had to insist that they accept one another even in the face of such radical differences of interpretation.

So a missional hermeneutic must include or at least recognize the multiplicity of perspectives and contexts from which, and within which, people read the biblical texts. Reflecting on such plurality, James Brownson argues that it is a *positive* thing with biblical roots.

> I call the model I am developing a *missional* hermeneutic because it springs from a basic observation about the New Testament: namely, the early Christian movement that produced and canonized the New Testament was a movement with specifically *missionary* character. One of the most obvious phenomena of early Christianity is the way in which the movement crossed cultural boundaries and planted itself in new places. More than half of the New Testament was in fact written by people engaged in and celebrating this sort of missionary enterprise in the early church. This tendency of early Christianity to cross cultural boundaries is a fertile starting point for developing a model of biblical interpretation. It is fertile, especially for our purposes, because it places the question of the relationship between Christianity and diverse cultures at the very top of the interpretative agenda. This focus may be of great help to us in grappling with plurality in interpretation today. … The missional hermeneutic I am advocating begins by affirming the reality and inevitability of plurality in interpretation.[17]

However, it would be inadequate to think that a missional hermeneutic of the Bible amounted only to aggregating all the possible ways of reading its texts, from all the multicoloured church and mission contexts around the globe. That is, of course, a fascinating and enriching thing to do. It is the common witness of those, including myself, who have lived and worked in cultures other than their own, that reading and studying the Bible through the eyes of others is a challenging, mind-blowing and immensely instructive privilege. But are we left only with plurality? And if so, are we consigned to a relativism that declines any evaluation? Are there any boundaries as to readings of biblical texts that are 'right' or 'wrong' – or even just 'better' or 'worse'? And how are those boundaries or criteria to be defined?

Brownson goes on from his discussion of a missional hermeneutic of diversity to argue for 'a hermeneutic of coherence'. The plurality of interpretative stances requires that we speak and listen to one another with respect and love,

---

[17] Brownson, 'Missional Hermeneutic', 232–33. See also Wright, 'Mosaic of Pluralisms'.

affirming our common humanity and our common commitment to the same biblical texts. 'Once we have affirmed plurality, however, we need also to grapple with how the Bible may provide a center, an orienting point in the midst of such diversity. What does it mean to speak *the truth* in love?'[18] The answer Brownson offers is the shape, the content and the claim of the biblical gospel itself. He agrees with scholars who have found a core of non-negotiable affirmations in the varied New Testament presentations of the gospel, and he insists that this must provide the hermeneutical framework or matrix for assessing the claims to validity that different readings of the text make.

> An understanding of the hermeneutical function of the gospel is critical to a healthy approach to plurality and coherence in biblical interpretation. Interpretation will always emerge out of different contexts. There will always be different traditions brought to bear by various interpreters ... In the midst of all this diversity, however, the gospel functions as a framework that lends a sense of coherence and commonality.[19]

While agreeing wholeheartedly with this, I would go further and point out that the gospel (which Brownson discusses in exclusively New Testament terms) begins in Genesis (according to Paul in Galatians 3:8). I would thus want to bring a whole-Bible perspective to the question of what Brownson calls 'a hermeneutic of coherence'. This surely is also implied in Luke's messianic and missional hermeneutic of the Hebrew canon in Luke 24, as mentioned above. Luke, who had lived and worked with Paul and who wrote the turbulent story of the earliest theological controversies in the church in Acts, knew perfectly well the diversity of interpretation of Old Testament texts even within the first generation of those who followed the Way of Jesus. Nevertheless, the words of Jesus 'opened their minds so they could understand the Scriptures'. In other words, Jesus provided the hermeneutical coherence within which all disciples must read these texts. That is, we must read in the light of the story that leads up *to* Christ (messianic reading), as well as the story that leads *on from* Christ (missional reading). Together, these form the story that flows from the mind and purpose of God in all the Scriptures for all the nations. That is a missional hermeneutic of the whole Bible.

Beyond advocacy readings and postmodern hermeneutics

The diversity of contextual approaches to reading the biblical texts includes those that are explicit in their advocacy stance – that is, readings done in the midst of, and on behalf of, or in the interests of, particular groups of people. As

---

[18] 'Missional Hermeneutic', 239 (his italics).
[19] Brownson, 'Missional Hermeneutic', 257–58.

against the rather blinkered view of theology that developed in the West since the Enlightenment, which likes to claim that it is scientific, objective, rational and free from either confessional presuppositions or ideological interests, theologies have emerged that declare such disinterested objectivity to be a myth – and a dangerous one, in that it conceals hegemonic claims. These theologies argue that contexts do matter. They argue that, in the act of reading and interpreting the Bible, the questions of who you are, where you are and whom you live among as a reader, all make a difference. The Bible is to be read precisely in and for the context in which its message must be heard and appropriated. So these approaches to the Bible and theology came to be called 'contextual theologies' within the Western academy. This term in itself betrayed the arrogant ethnocentricity of the West, for the assumption was this: other places are 'contexts' and do their theology for those contexts, while we, of course, have the real thing – the objective, 'contextless' theology. This assumption is being rightly challenged, and the West is seen for what it is – a particular context of human culture, not necessarily any better or any worse than any other context for reading the Bible and doing theology. But it is the context within which a certain mode of being Christian emerged and sustained itself for centuries and then came to have a dominant position in the world, largely through missionary activity and the churches and theologies that have resulted from such mission. It is the cultural context that culminated in the great tower of Babel that we call Enlightenment modernity, which is now in the process of fragmenting, like its Genesis prototype, into the scattered diversity of postmodernity.

What many of these newer theologies have in common is their advocacy stance. That is, they arise from the conviction that it is fundamental to biblical faith to take a stand alongside the victims of injustice in any form. Thus, the Bible is to be read with a liberationist hermeneutic – that is, with a concern to liberate people from oppression and exploitation. The earliest to make its impact on theological thinking in the West in the twentieth century[20] was Liberation Theology from Latin America. Theology was not to be done in the study and then applied in the world. Rather, action for and on behalf of the poor and oppressed was to be undertaken as a first priority and then, out of that commitment and praxis, theological reflection would follow. This presented a radical paradigm challenge to the standard Western way of 'doing theology'. Other examples include Dalit Theology from India, Min Jung Theology in

---

[20] The contemporary time frame is deliberate, since earlier centuries have seen their own theological developments with liberationist orientation. The Anabaptist movements of the radical Reformation, for example, developed a range of hermeneutical strategies in their struggle against the intense persecution they encountered from both Roman Catholic and mainline Protestant churches and states.

Korea and Black Theology in Africa and among African Americans. Feminist movements have also generated a broad and influential hermeneutic and theology, which have probably been more influential in the West than any of the others. All of these approaches to the text offer a hermeneutic which is intentionally 'interested'. That is, they read 'in the interests' of those they speak on behalf of – the poor, the outcasts, Blacks, women and so on.

So could a missional hermeneutic be presented as a liberation theology for missionaries? Or missiologists? The idea is mooted only half in jest. Given that 'missionaries' in popular mythology are seen as the compromised adjuncts of colonialism and almost synonymous with Western arrogance and cultural totalitarianism, it might be more natural to propose a liberation theology *from* missionaries (which is what some radical forms of non-Western theology have in fact advocated). However, the multinational nature of the global church has generated a new reality that is hardly yet acknowledged in the churches of the West, let alone in the popular culture and media there. And that reality is that more than half of all the Christian missionaries serving in the world today are not white and Western. It is the churches of the majority world that are now sending the majority of people into all kinds of cross-cultural mission work. So one is as likely to meet an African missionary in Britain as a British one in Africa. One encounters Brazilians in North Africa, Nigerians in parts of West Africa where few white people now venture, and Koreans almost anywhere in the world. While it remains true that the United States still sends the greatest number of missionaries to other parts of the world, the country that has the *second* highest number of cross-cultural missionaries (missionaries serving cross-culturally in their own country) is India.[21] There are at least thirty times more Indian nationality missionaries than there are Westerners serving as missionaries within India.

What simply cannot be said of this new phenomenon of world mission is that all of these Christian missionaries are agents of oppressive colonial powers, or that they operate as a religious veneer to political or economic imperialism. On the contrary, for the most part, Christian mission as carried out by the churches of the majority world operates out of powerlessness and relative poverty, and often in situations of considerable opposition and persecution. Such missionaries may not qualify as an oppressed class on the scale of, say, the poor in Latin America, or the Dalits in India (though many Indian missionaries are also Dalits). But they could do with some liberation from the oppressive stereotypes and unjust caricatures that still surround their calling, as well as from the marginalization that mission experiences in many churches and that missiology

---

[21] And there are recent estimates that suggest that the number of Protestant cross-cultural missionaries within India may already have surpassed the total number sent around the world from the United States.

still battles with in the strongholds of theological academia. So, yes, a missional hermeneutic is 'interested'. It reads the Bible and develops a biblical hermeneutic 'in the interests' of those who have committed their own personal life story into the biblical story of God's purpose for the nations. But this hermeneutic does so with the even stronger conviction that such commitment should be the normal stance for the whole church. For, on this reading of Scripture, a church that is governed by the Bible cannot evade the missional thrust of the God and the gospel revealed there.

However, a missional hermeneutic goes further. It is not content to take its place as just one of several liberationist, advocacy or 'interested' theologies on offer – though even as such, I contend, it has a right to exist, a right to advance and defend its own validity.[22] Rather, a broadly missional reading of the whole Bible actually subsumes liberationist readings into itself. Where else does the passion for justice and liberation that breathes in these various theologies come from, if not from the biblical revelation of the God who battles with injustice, oppression and bondage throughout history right to the eschaton? If not from the God who triumphed climactically over all such wickedness and evil – human, historical and cosmic – in the cross and the resurrection of his Son, Jesus Christ? Biblically, all true liberation, all truly human best interests, flow from God – not just any god, but the God revealed as YHWH in the Old Testament and incarnate in Jesus of Nazareth. So, inasmuch as the Bible narrates the passion and action (the mission) of this God for the liberation not only of humanity but also of the whole creation, a missional hermeneutic of Scripture must have a liberationist dimension.

The rise of 'contextual theologies', and then the recognition that all theology is in fact contextual, including the Western 'standard' variety, have coincided with the arrival of postmodernism and its massive impact on hermeneutics (as on all academic disciplines). Whereas the Western theological academy (built as it largely was on an Enlightenment modernity worldview, which privileged objectivity and sought a singular all-embracing theological construct) had difficulty with theologies which seemed so situated in local and historical contexts, the postmodern shift welcomes and elevates precisely such plurality. Postmodernism, however, not only celebrates the local, the contextual, the particular – it goes on to affirm that this is all we've got. There is no

---

[22] For a penetrating reflection on the plurality of readings of the biblical texts in the postmodern academy, and the impact that this has had on the traditional hegemony of Western theology, particularly in the field of Old Testament studies, see Walter Brueggemann, *Theology of the Old Testament*, 61–114. It seems to me that a missiological reading has as much right to set out its stall in the marketplace of contemporary hermeneutics as any other. Cf. also my own comments in 'Mosaic of Pluralisms'.

grand narrative (or metanarrative) that explains everything, and any claims that there is some truth-for-all that embraces the totality of life and meaning are rejected as oppressive power plays. Thus radically postmodern hermeneutics delights in a multiplicity of readings and perspectives but rejects the possibility of a single truth or unitive coherence.

Christian mission ever since the New Testament church, on the other hand, has wrestled for two thousand years with the problems of multiple cultural contexts yet sought to sustain the conviction that there is an objective truth-for-all in the gospel that addresses and claims people in any context. I would go further and argue that Israel in the Old Testament wrestled with a similar dynamic, namely the need to relate the faith of YHWH to changing cultural and religious contexts through the millennium and more of Israel's history. Cultural plurality is nothing new for Christian mission. It is, rather, the very stuff of missional engagement and missiological reflection.[23]

In an interesting and complex article, Martha Franks explores the way Christian theology of mission within the span of the twentieth century has moved from a fairly 'flat' presentation of a single biblical message, through a more historically nuanced understanding (as in the theology of Gerhard von Rad), to a recognition of the plurality within the Bible and within the contexts of mission (as in Donald Senior and Carroll Stuhlmueller). She observes how Lesslie Newbigin, for example, sensitively balances the particularity of election with the plurality of the Bible's vision for all nations and cultures and sees the fullness of the gospel brought into ever more visible glory through the two-way task of cross-cultural mission. She then goes on to link this to the concerns of postmodernism and claims that Christian mission has long preceded postmodernism in recognizing the validity of multiple contexts as 'home' for the gospel. Mission has never been merely a matter of transferring an object from one subject to another. Rather, the living dynamic of the gospel has been such that, while it has an unchanging core because of its historical rootedness in the Christ-event, it has been received, understood, articulated and lived out in myriad ways, both vertically through history and horizontally in all of the cultures in which Christian faith has taken root.

> Newbigin ...argues that mission work in the world's plurality is 'two-way.' Hearing the new understandings of the gospel that arise when the message of Christ is brought to new contexts is an important part of understanding the whole meaning of the Lordship of Jesus. This insight from mission work is sympathetic to the similar suggestion of postmodernism with regard to the meaning of texts – that communi-

---

[23] Andrew Walls provides richly stimulating surveys of the way the Christian church throughout history has developed ever-growing pluriformity though taking root in culture after culture, while preserving the essential non-negotiable and trans-cultural objective core of the gospel. See Walls, *Missionary Movement*.

cation between people, even when it is by book, is always 'two-way.' ... Moreover, Newbigin's understanding of mission points to the fact that Christian missiology has long preceded the postmodern world in recognizing the possible problem of the fact that transplanting language and concepts from one context to another leads to wholly new ways of understanding them. Having centuries of experience with the very problem on which the postmoderns have tumbled, it is appropriate to respond to the challenge of postmodernism not with revulsion, but with counsel. We know about these questions. We have something to offer.[24]

What we have to offer, I contend, is a missional hermeneutic of the Bible – the Bible which glories in diversity and celebrates human cultures, which builds its most elevated theological claims on utterly particular and sometimes very local events, which sees everything in relational, not abstract, terms, and which does the bulk of its work through the medium of stories. All of these features of the Bible – cultural, local, relational, narrative – are welcome to the postmodern mind. Where the missional hermeneutic will part company with the radical postmodern is in its insistence that through all of this variety, locality, particularity and diversity, the Bible is nevertheless actually *the* story. This is the way it is. And within *this* story, as narrated or anticipated by the Bible, there is at work the God whose mission is evident from creation to new creation. This is the story of God's mission. It is a coherent story with a universal claim. But it is also a story that affirms humanity in all of its cultural variety. This is the story that gives a place in the sun to all the little stories.[25]

Contours of a Missional Hermeneutic

The Bible as the product of God's mission

A missional hermeneutic of the Bible begins with the Bible's very existence. For those who affirm some relationship (however articulated) between these texts and the self-revelation of our creator God, the whole canon of Scripture is a missional phenomenon in the sense that it witnesses to the self-giving movement of this God towards his creation and towards us, human beings in God's own image, but wayward and wanton. The writings that eventually came to comprise the collected canon now called 'the Bible' are themselves the product of, and witness to, the ultimate mission of God.[26]

---

[24] Franks, 'Missiology of Scripture', 342.
[25] Richard Bauckham explores the constant biblical oscillation between the particular and the universal, and its implications for a missiological hermeneutic, with special attention to its relevance to postmodernity, in *Bible and Mission*.
[26] H.D. Beeby, in *Canon and Mission*, makes this point very strongly.

The very existence of the Bible is incontrovertible evidence of the God who refused to forsake his rebellious creation, who refused to give up, who was and is determined to redeem and restore fallen creation to his original design for it. ... The very existence of such a collection of writings testifies to a God who breaks through to human beings, who disclosed himself to them, who will not leave them unilluminated in their darkness ... who takes the initiative in re-establishing broken relationships with us.[27]

Furthermore, the processes by which these texts came to be written were often profoundly missional in nature. Many of them emerged out of events, or struggles, or crises, or conflicts, in which the people of God engaged with the constantly changing and challenging task of articulating and living out their understanding of God's revelation and redemptive action in the world. Sometimes these were struggles internal to the people of God themselves; sometimes they were highly polemical struggles with competing religious claims and worldviews that surrounded them. So a missional reading of such texts is very definitely not a matter of *first*, finding the 'real' meaning by objective exegesis, and only then, *secondly*, cranking up some 'missiological implications' as a homiletic supplement to the 'text itself'. Rather, the task of a missional reading is to see how a text often has its origin in some issue, need, controversy or threat, which the people of God needed to address in the context of their mission. The text in itself is a product of mission in action.

This is easily demonstrated in the case of the New Testament.[28] Most of Paul's letters were written in the heat of his missionary efforts: wrestling with the theological basis of the inclusion of the Gentiles; affirming the need for Jew and Gentile to accept one another in Christ and in the church; tackling the baffling range of new problems that assailed young churches as the gospel took root in the world of Greek polytheism; confronting incipient heresies with clear affirmations of the supremacy and sufficiency of Jesus Christ, and so on. And why were the Gospels so called? Because they were written to explain the significance of the *evangel* – the good news about Jesus of Nazareth, especially

---

[27] Taber, 'Missiology and the Bible', 232.

[28] Marion Soards surveys four current issues in New Testament studies (first-century Judaism, the life of Jesus, Pauline theology and the character of the early church) and shows how they are relevant to mission studies also. But he concludes with a converse comment in line with the point being made here: 'Mission studies should remind biblical scholars that many of the writings that we study (often in painstaking and even painful detail) came to be because of the reality of mission. An awareness of, and a concern with, the key issues of mission studies may well help biblical studies find foci that will bring deeper appreciation of the meaning of the Bible' (Soards, 'Key Issues', 107). With this I fully agree. Cf. also Koestenberger, 'Place of Mission', and the works referred to there.

his death and resurrection. Confidence in these things was essential to the missionary task of the expanding church. And the person who wrote the largest portion of the New Testament, Luke, shapes his two-volume work in such a way that the missionary mandate to the disciples to be Christ's witnesses to the nations comes as the climax to volume one and the introduction to volume two.

But we can also see how many of the texts of the Old Testament emerged out of Israel's engagement with the surrounding world in the light of the God they knew in their history and in covenantal relationship. People produced texts in relation to what they believed God had done, was doing, or would do, in their world. The Torah records the exodus as an act of YHWH that comprehensively confronted and defeated the power of Pharaoh and all his rival claims to deity and allegiance. It presents a theology of creation that stands in sharp contrast to the polytheistic creation myths of Mesopotamia. The historical narratives portray the long and sorry story of Israel's struggle with the culture and religion of Canaan, a struggle reflected also in the preexilic prophets. Exilic and postexilic texts emerge out of the task that the small remnant community of Israel faced to define their continuing identity as a community of faith in successive empires of varying hostility or tolerance. Wisdom texts interact with international wisdom traditions in the surrounding cultures, but they do so with staunch monotheistic disinfectant. And in worship and prophecy, Israelites reflect on the relationship between their God, YHWH, and the rest of the nations – sometimes negatively, sometimes positively – and on the nature of their own role as YHWH's elect priesthood in their midst.

All of the items referred to in the last paragraph deserve chapters of their own (and I hope to do justice to them eventually in a forthcoming book in this field). The point here is simply that the Bible is, in so many ways, a missional phenomenon in itself. The individual texts within the Bible often reflect the struggles of being a people with a mission in a world of competing cultural and religious claims. And the canon eventually consolidates the recognition that it is through these texts that the people whom God has called to be his own (in both Testaments) has been shaped as a community of memory and hope, a community of mission, failure and striving.

In short, a missional hermeneutic proceeds from the assumption that the whole Bible renders to us the story of God's mission through God's people in their engagement with God's world for the sake of the whole of God's creation.

Biblical authority and mission

'*The Great Commission*': the phrase itself implies an imperative, a mandate. So it also presupposes an authority behind that imperative. We find this, and other similar missionary imperatives, in the Bible. So our involvement in mission is, at one level, a matter of obedience to the authority of Scripture, regarded as the word of God. A 'biblical basis of mission', therefore, seeks out those biblical texts that express or describe the missionary imperative, on the assumption that the Bible is authoritative. A 'missional hermeneutic of the Bible', however, explores the nature of biblical authority itself in relation to mission. Does a missional approach to the Bible help us in articulating what we mean by biblical authority?

This is not the place for a full account of the Christian doctrine of the authority of the Bible. One aspect, however, is important for our purpose here. Many people subconsciously bring a military concept of authority to their understanding of the authority of the Bible. Authority is what gives the officer the right to issue commands. Commands are to be obeyed. The Bible is our authority. It issues the commands and tells us what to do, or what not to do. Authority, then, is simply a matter of orders on the one hand and obedience on the other. In missionary circles, military metaphors of this sort frequently surround the Great Commission. This text is said to provide the church's 'marching orders', for example – as well as the whole range of other military metaphors that follow – warfare, mobilization, recruits, strategies, targets, campaigns, crusades, front line, strongholds, the missionary 'force' (i.e., personnel) and so on. The language of authority seems easily converted into the language of mission, with the military metaphor functioning as the dynamic connector.

However, even if we strongly affirm our acceptance of biblical authority, the association of authority primarily with military-style command does not sit comfortably with much of the actual material in the Bible. There are, of course, many commands in the Bible, and indeed the psalmists celebrate these commands as a mark of God's goodness and grace (in, for example, Psalms 19 and 119). Those commands that we do have from God are to be cherished for the light, guidance, security, joy and freedom that they bring (to mention a few of the benefits praised by the psalmists). But the bulk of the Bible is not command – either in the sense of issuing commands to its first readers or to future generations thereof. Much more of the Bible is narrative, poetry, prophecy, song, lament, visions, letters and so on. What is the authority latent in those forms of utterance? How does a poem or a story, or somebody's letter to somebody else, tell *me* what *I* must do or not do? Is that even what it was intended to do? And more importantly in relation to our task here, how do such non-imperative sections of the Bible connect to mission, if mission is seen primarily as obedience to a command? I would suggest that it is partly because we have so tightly bound our understanding of mission to a single (although undeniably crucial) imperative of Jesus that we have difficulty making connections between mission and the rest of the Scriptures, where those other Scriptures are not obviously or grammatically imperative. We do not perceive any missional authority in such texts because we conceive authority only in terms of commands.

We need to widen our understanding of the word 'authority' considerably. In his majestic apologia for evangelical biblical ethics, *Resurrection and Moral Order*, Oliver O'Donovan argues that authority is a dimension of reality, which constitutes sufficient and meaningful grounds for action. The created order itself, by its objective reality, provides an authority structure within which we have freedom to act (both in the sense of permission to act and a wide range of options).[29] Authority is not just a list of positive commands; authority includes legitimating permission. Authority authorizes; it grants freedom to act within boundaries. Thus, the authority of my driving license (or my bishop's license) is not to order me every day where I must drive or what sacred service I must render. Rather, they authorize *me* to make those choices – giving me freedom and authority to drive where I wish, or to take services, preach, baptize and so on. In those contexts I am an *authorized* person, liberated by, while still subject to, the authority of the realities that stand behind those documents (the laws of the land and the road; the canons of the church).

Authority, then, is the predicate of reality, the source and boundary of freedom. Now, as O'Donovan argues, the created order itself as the fundamental reality structure of our existence is also a structure of authority. A physical brick wall, for example, by its simple real existence constitutes an authority. You have freedom on this side of it, or on that side of it. But your freedom ends when you attempt to run through it at high speed. It exerts its authority rather abruptly. Gravity as a force in the physical universe is an authority built into the way the universe exists. For us humans, gravity authorizes an immense freedom of action on and above the surface of the planet, provided that we 'work with it'. But it also sets limits to that freedom. You may freely choose to step off a cliff, but the authority of gravity will decree it to be the last free choice you make. Reality kicks in.

Now, how do these considerations help us to understand the authority of the Bible? If authority is the predicate of reality, then the authority of the canon of Scripture is that it brings us into contact with reality – or rather several connected realities, each of which has its own intrinsic, predicated authority. Reading and knowing the Scriptures cause us to engage with reality. That knowledge in turn functions to authorize, and to set boundaries around, our freedom to act in the world. And, more specifically for our purpose here, these

---

[29] I have discussed this insight of O'Donovan's further in relation to the authority of Scripture in an age of historical and cultural relativism in C.J.H. Wright, *Walking*, ch. 2. I also develop further the discussion that follows above in relation to Old Testament ethics in *Old Testament Ethics*.

realities (the realities of the biblical God, story, and people – as outlined below) authorize our action in mission. They make our mission appropriate, legitimate, and indeed necessary and inevitable. The authority for our mission flows from the Bible because the Bible reveals the reality on which our mission is based. I have three realities in mind, which are rendered to us first by the Old Testament Scriptures and then confirmed in the New. In these biblical texts we encounter the reality of *this God*, the reality of *this story*, and the reality of *this people*.

The reality of this God. It is becoming increasingly important in any talk of 'God' to be clear whom we are talking about. 'God' is merely an Anglo-Saxon monosyllable that in its origins would more commonly have been plural, 'the gods' – the generic term for the deities of the early tribes and settlers of northern Europe. The Bible introduces us to the very specific, named and biographied God known as YHWH, the Holy One of Israel (and other titles). This is the God whom Jesus called Abba, the one worshipped as LORD by Israelites, and as Father, Son and Holy Spirit by Christians. This is not a generic 'god' at all. While the Bible does insist that there is much that has been disclosed about this God through the natural world around us (which is in fact this God's creation), it is fundamentally the texts of the canon of Scripture in both Testaments that bring us knowledge of this God. Not only is YHWH the God 'enthroned upon the praises of Israel' (Ps. 22:3), he is the God rendered to us by the lips and pens of Israel.[30] YHWH is the reality to which the Old Testament Scriptures testify. His, therefore, is the authority that they mediate, because we have no other access to YHWH's reality than through these Scriptures. This 'rendering of God' in the Old Testament includes both God's identity and God's character. The point here is simply this: if the God YHWH who is rendered to us in these texts is really God, then that reality authorizes a range of responses as appropriate, legitimate and indeed imperative. These include not only the response of worship, but also of ethical living in accordance with this God's own character and will, and a missional orientation that commits my own life story into the grand story of God's purpose for the nations and for creation. Mission flows from the reality of this God – the biblical God. Or to put it another way: mission is authorized by the reality of this God.

The reality of this story. That the Old Testament tells a story needs no defence. The point is much greater, however. The Old Testament tells its story as *the* story, or rather, as a part of that ultimate and universal story that will embrace the whole of creation, time and humanity within its scope. In other words, in

---

[30] It will be evident that I am indebted here to the fascinating study of Dale Patrick, *The Rendering of God*.

reading these texts we are invited to embrace a metanarrative, a worldview which, like all worldviews and metanarratives, claims to explain the way things are, how they have come to be so, and what they ultimately will be.

The story that engages us in the Old Testament answers the four fundamental worldview questions which all religions and philosophies answer in one way or another:[31]

- '*Where are we?*' (What is the nature of the world around us?) Answer: We inhabit the earth, which is part of the good creation of the one living, personal God, YHWH.
- '*Who are we?*' (What is the essential nature of humanity?) Answer: Each one of us is a human person made by this God in God's own image, one of God's creatures but unique among them in spiritual and moral relationships and responsibility.
- '*What's gone wrong?*' (Why is the world in such a mess?) Answer: Through rebellion and disobedience against our creator God, we have generated the mess that we now see around us at every level of our lives, relationships and environment.
- '*What is the solution?*' (What can we do about it?) Answer: Nothing in and of ourselves, but the solution has been initiated by God through the choice and creation of a people, Israel, through whom God intends eventually to bring blessing to all nations of the earth, and ultimately to renew the whole creation.

Now the reality of this story is such that it includes us in its scope, for it points to a universal future that embraces all the nations. It is the story that is taken up without question (though not without surprise) in the New Testament. It is the story that stretches from Genesis to Revelation – not merely as a good yarn, or even as a classic of epic literature, but fundamentally as a rendering of reality – an account of the universe we inhabit and of the new creation we are destined for. We live in a storied universe. And once again, such a rendering of reality carries its intrinsic authority. For if this is truly the way things are, how they have become so and where they are going, then there are all kinds of implications for how we ought to respond personally and collectively. Again, worship, ethics and mission all spring to mind. These responses, including mission, are authorized by the reality of this story.

The reality of this people. The third reality that the Old Testament Scriptures render to us is that of the people of Israel. Ancient Israel, with their distinctive view of their own election, history and relationship to their God, YHWH, is a

---

[31] It will likewise be evident here that I am indebted to the analysis of J. Richard Middleton and Brian J. Walsh, *Truth Is Stranger than It Used to Be.*

historical reality of enormous significance to the history of the rest of humanity.[32] Christian mission to the nations is deeply rooted in the calling of this
people, and in the way they saw themselves and their story. In Old Testament
terms, the story had a past and a future, and both are important in shaping ethical and missional response – for, like Israel, the church is also a community of
memory and hope.

Israel's *celebration of its past* is legendary. It was the very stuff of their existence, for it rendered to them not only their own identity and mission, but also
that of YHWH, their God.

> Sing to the LORD, praise his *name*; proclaim his *salvation* day after day.
> Declare his glory among the nations, his *marvellous deeds* among all peoples.
> (Ps. 96:2–3, my italics)

The name, salvation and glory of YHWH were all bound up with 'his marvellous deeds'. YHWH was known through what he had done, and Israel knew
that to preserve YHWH's identity they must tell this story – whether to themselves or (in some way that remained a mystery in Old Testament times) to the
nations. For in the telling of the story stood the rendering of the God who was
its prime character. So Israel told the story as a bulwark against idolatry (Deut.
4:9ff.). They told the story as an explanation and motivation for the law (Deut.
6:20–25). They told the story as a rebuke to themselves (Amos 2:9–11; Mic.
6:1–8; Pss. 105–106), or to YHWH himself (Pss. 44, 89). They told the story as a
comfort and anchor for hope (Jer. 32:17–25). Israel's whole theology
depended on its memory, and Israel's memory was constitutive of their
peoplehood. The same identity as the people of God with this storied memory
constitutes also for us the authority for our mission.

But the story Israel told also had an *anticipated future* right at its beginning.
They were a people with a future in the purposes of God. The call of Abraham
included the promise that through his descendants God intended to bring
blessing to all the nations of the earth. That vision shone with greatly varying
degrees of clarity or obscurity in different eras of Israel's life, but there is in
many places an awareness of the nations as spectators both of what God did in
and for Israel, and of how Israel responded positively or negatively (Deut. 4:5–
8; 29:22–28; Ezek. 36:16–23). Ultimately, Israel existed *for the sake of* the
nations. So there is a teleological thrust to Israel's existence as a people and the

---

[32] Among Old Testament scholars there is, of course, considerable debate over their
historical reconstruction of the events by which Israel emerged in the land of Canaan
and into the annals of history. But that historical debate need not concern us here
since, by whatever process, Israel certainly did emerge and produce a society and a
body of traditions and texts which have had an unquestionably profound impact on
subsequent human history.

story they narrated and projected. Here is a God with a mission and a people with a mission, to be a light to the nations so that ultimately 'all flesh will see the glory of the LORD'. Such a vision undoubtedly generated a range of responses within Israel itself. For if this is the future guaranteed by the faithfulness of God, how should this affect the way Israel should live now? The question remains authoritative for us, too. For we share the same vision of the future, a future which to the eyes of faith is a reality, 'the substance of things hoped for', and thereby an ethic-generating and mission-mandating authority for those who live in its light.

So the reality of this people, rendered to us through the texts of the Old Testament, carries authority for an ethic of gratitude in view of God's actions for Israel in the past and carries authority also for our missional intentionality in view of God's purposes for humanity in the future.

These three features of the Old Testament – God, story and people – are affirmed as realities also for Christian believers in the New Testament. They are all, in fact, focused on Jesus in such a way that their authority and missional relevance is not only sustained but enhanced and transformed for those who are 'in Christ'. At this point we are approaching the missiological significance of a truly *biblical* (i.e., cross-testamental) theology.

For in Jesus we meet *this God*. The New Testament typically addresses the issue of 'Jesus and God' not so much in the categories of ontology, but of identity and character. Jesus is the one who explicitly shares the identity and character of YHWH and who ultimately accomplishes what only YHWH could.[33] So to know Jesus as saviour and Lord is to know reality, the way, the truth and the life, the word, the creator, sustainer and heir of the universe. And as for Israel, so for us, such reality carries its own authority for how we are to live and act in God's world.

And in Jesus we have the climax of *this story*, and the guarantee of its final ending. This story is also our story, for if we are in Christ then, according to Paul, we are also in Abraham and heirs according to the promise. Our future is the future promised by God to Abraham, achieved by Jesus and to be enjoyed by the whole of redeemed humanity from every nation, tribe, people and language (Rev. 7:9–10). Our lives also, then, are to be shaped by the gratitude that looks back to what God has promised and by the mission that looks forward to what he will accomplish.

And in Jesus we have become part of *this people*, sharing the comprehensive range of identity and responsibility that was theirs. For through the cross and the gospel of the Messiah Jesus, we have become citizens of God's people,

---

[33] See especially N.T. Wright, *Jesus and the Victory of God*, and Richard Bauckham, *God Crucified*.

members of God's household, the place of God's dwelling (Eph. 2:11 – 3:13).
Such an identity and belonging generate an ethical and a missional responsibility in the church and the world, which the New Testament spells out in some
detail.

So then, our mission certainly flows from the authority of the Bible. But
that is far richer and deeper than simply obeying a biblical command. Rather,
obedience to the Great Commission, and even the Great Commission itself,
are set within the context of these realities. The Great Commission is not
something extra or exotic. Rather, the authority of the Great Commission is
embedded in the reality of the *God* whose universal authority Jesus has been
given, in the reality of the *story* it presupposes and envisages, and in the reality of
the *people* who are now to become a self-replicating community of disciples
among all nations. This is the God we worship, this is the story we are part of,
this is the people to whom we belong. How should we then live? What then is
our mission?

Biblical indicatives and imperatives in mission

Another way of looking at this issue is to focus on the point often observed in
biblical theology, namely that biblical *imperatives* are characteristically founded
on biblical *indicatives*. An indicative is simply a statement of reality (or claims to
be). It is an affirmation or declaration or proposition: this is so; this is how
things are. By situating its imperatives in these indicative contexts, the Bible
effectively grounds their authority in that reality.

A familiar example of this is the way the Old Testament law is set within a
narrative context. The narrative expresses the indicative: this is what has happened in your history, and these are the things that YHWH your God has done.
Then the law expresses the responsive imperative: now then, this is how you
are to behave in the light of such facts. Exodus 19:3–6 classically articulates this
order:

> You have seen what I have done ... (the indicative),
> Now then, if you will obey me fully and keep my covenant, then ... (the imperative).

The Decalogue notably begins not with the first imperative commandment,
but with the indicative statement of God's identity and Israel's story (so far): 'I
am the LORD your God, who brought you up out of Egypt, out of the house of
bondage' (Ex. 20:2). In other words, the indicative of God's grace comes
before, and is the foundation and authority for, the imperative of the law and
responsive obedience. This fundamental priority of grace over law is even
more explicit in the answer the father is instructed to give his son when he asks
(as countless Christians have done ever since, and might have saved themselves

much theological blood, sweat and ink by attending to the father's answer), 'What is the meaning of all this law?' The father responds not simply with a reinforced imperative ('Just do it'), but with a story – the exodus story, the old, old story of YHWH and his love – the indicative of redemption. The very meaning of the law is grounded in the gospel of God's saving grace in history (Deut. 6:20–25).

Now when we think of the Great Commission, it is sometimes pointed out that, whereas the text is never actually given that title in the Gospels themselves, Jesus did emphatically endorse the Great *Commandment*, in so many words. Asked about the greatest commandment in the law (a familiar debating point in his day), he pointed to the magnificent Shema of Deuteronomy 6:4–5 about loving God with all our heart and soul and strength, complementing it with Leviticus 19:18, the command to love our neighbours as ourselves. But what we must not miss is that both of these commandments are founded on indicatives about the identity, uniqueness, singularity and holiness of YHWH as God. 'Hear, O Israel: The LORD our God is one LORD'; 'You shall be holy, for I the LORD your God am holy'. It is *the reality of YHWH* that constitutes the authority for these greatest commandments, on which, Jesus declared, hang all the rest of the law and the prophets.

Now here, then, we have a very clear imperative – to love God with the totality of our being and to love our neighbour as ourselves. This could easily be described, with even more textual justification, as 'the great commission', for it governs the whole of life regardless of our specific calling. This fundamental twin commandment certainly precedes, underlies and governs the so-called Great Commission itself, for we cannot make disciples of the nations without love for God and love for them.

And so it is no surprise, therefore, to find that, when we come to the Great Commission, it too follows the same formula: indicative followed by imperative. Jesus begins with the monumental cosmic claim, words that echo the affirmation of Moses about YHWH himself (Deut. 4:35, 39), that 'all authority in heaven and on earth has been given to me'. This is the reality behind the command. The identity and the authority of Jesus of Nazareth, crucified and risen, is the cosmic indicative on which mission stands authorized. But in order to understand all that such a claim for Jesus implies and includes, we need the whole of the Scriptures – as he himself affirmed when, in Luke's version, he drew both the significance of his own messianic identity and the anticipation of the church's missional future from the bold indicative, 'this is what is written'. We need, in other words, a missional hermeneutic of the *whole* Bible and its great indicatives – not just a narrow obedience to a single imperative text.

A missional hermeneutic, then, is not content simply to call for obedience to the Great Commission (though it will assuredly include that as a matter of non-negotiable importance), nor even to reflect on the missional implications of the Great Commandment. For behind both it will find the *Great Communication* – the revelation of the identity of God, of God's action in the world and of God's saving purpose for all creation. And for the fullness of this communication we need the whole Bible in all its parts and genres, for God has given us no less. A missional hermeneutic takes the indicative and the imperative of the biblical revelation with equal seriousness and interprets each in the light of the other.

That is to say, like biblical and systematic theology, biblical missiology revels in exploring the great affirmative themes and traditions of the biblical faith in all their complexity, profundity and remarkable coherence. But biblical missiology recognizes that if all this indicative theology is indicative of *reality*, then that carries a massive missional implication for those who claim this worldview as their own. If this is how it really is with God, humanity and the world, then what claim does that make upon the life of the church and individual believers? But, on the other hand, a missional hermeneutic of the whole Bible will not become obsessed with only the great mission imperatives, such as the Great Commission, or be tempted to impose upon them one assumed priority or another (e.g., of evangelism as the only 'real' mission, or social justice, or liberation, or ecclesiastical order). Rather, we will set those great imperatives within the context of their foundational indicatives, namely, all that the Bible affirms about God, about creation, about human life in its paradox of dignity and depravity, about redemption in all its comprehensive glory, and about the new creation in which God will dwell with his people. A missional hermeneutic, then, cannot read biblical indicatives without their implied imperatives. Nor can it isolate biblical imperatives from the totality of the biblical indicative. It seeks a holistic understanding of mission from a holistic reading of the biblical texts.

The biblical, theocentric worldview and the mission of God

However, even if we accept, returning to the introduction, that Jesus offers us a messiah-focused and mission-generating hermeneutic of the Scriptures, we may still query the claim that somehow there is a missional hermeneutic of the whole Bible such that 'mission is what it's all about'. This uneasiness stems from the persistent, almost subconscious, paradigm that mission is fundamentally and primarily 'something we do'. This is especially so if we fall into the reductionist habit of using the word 'mission' or 'missions' as more or less synonymous with evangelism. Quite clearly the whole Bible is not just 'about evangelism', and I am certainly not trying to claim that it is – even though evangelism is certainly a fundamental part of biblical mission as entrusted to us. To be sure, evangelism *is* something we do and it *is* validated by clear biblical imperatives. But it will not bear the weight of the case for saying that the whole Bible can be hermeneutically approached from a missional perspective.[34]

The appropriateness of speaking of 'a missional basis of the Bible' becomes apparent only when we shift our paradigm of mission from our human agency to the ultimate purposes of God himself; from mission as 'missions' that we undertake, to mission as what God has been purposing and accomplishing from eternity to eternity; from an anthropocentric conception to a radically theocentric worldview.

In shifting our perspective in this way and trying to come to a biblical definition of what we mean by mission, we are in effect asking the question, *Whose mission is it anyway?* The answer, it seems to me, could be expressed as a paraphrase of the song of the redeemed in the new creation. 'Salvation belongs to our God who sits on the throne, and to the Lamb' (Rev. 7:10). Since the whole Bible is the story of how this God, 'our God', has brought about his salvation

---

[34] At this point, therefore, I am in disagreement with David Filbeck, *God of the Gentiles*. Filbeck also wants to see the whole Bible as relevant to mission – including especially the Old Testament, but he defines mission wholly in terms of evangelism.

> When we speak of missions in this book we are referring only to crossing boundaries of language and custom into cultures other than our own with the express purpose and goal of winning the lost to belief in Jesus Christ as Lord and Savior and establishing God's Kingdom, Christ's Church, to be a light or witness for God in those cultures.

> Any other work that a missionary might do to advance this cause; such as building a hospital, teaching grade school, experimenting with planting a new variety of rice or vegetable, etc., while beneficial, is not included. These good works come and go according to the needs of time and place, and because of their very nature do not need biblical justification in an age of humanism. (p. 11)

I agree with Filbeck when he argues, as I do above, that mission provides theological coherence to the Bible, including the relationship of the Testaments.

> Indeed, it is this missionary dimension, so often neglected in modern theological interpretation, that unifies both Old and New Testaments and coordinates their various themes into a single motif. It is the logical connection between the Testaments that many modern theologians unfortunately seem to despair of ever finding ... In short, the dimension of missions in the interpretation of the Scriptures gives structure to the whole Bible. Any theological study of the Scriptures, therefore, must be formulated with the view of maintaining this structure. The missionary dimension to the interpretation of the Old Testament as displayed in the New Testament, I believe, accomplishes this in a way that no other theological theme can hope to match. (p. 10)

But I would not wish to confine my understanding of the missional significance of the Old Testament, as Filbeck does, to what it has to contribute to our theology of *evangelism* only:

> This hermeneutic, in addition to stating that the overall intent and meaning of the Old Testament is missionary in nature, also maps out how every aspect of the Old Testament should be analyzed to show how it relates and, more crucially, contributes to the task of evangelizing non-Christian populations in the world today. (p. 19)

for the whole cosmos (represented in concentric circles around God's throne in the magnificent neck-craning vision of Revelation 4 – 7), we can affirm with equal validity, 'Mission belongs to our God'. Mission is not ours; mission is God's. Certainly, the mission of God is the prior reality out of which flows any mission in which we ourselves get involved. Or, as it has been nicely put, it is not so much the case that God has a mission for his church in the world, as that God has a church for his mission in the world. Mission was not made for the church; the church was made for mission – God's mission.[35] A missional hermeneutic of the Bible, then, begins there – with the mission of God, and traces the flow of all other dimensions of mission as they affect human history from that centre and starting point.

The phrase *missio Dei*, 'the mission of God', has a long history. It seems to go back to a German missiologist, Karl Hartenstein. He coined it as a way of summarizing the teaching of Karl Barth 'who, in a lecture on mission in 1928 had connected mission with the doctrine of the trinity. Barth and Hartenstein want to make clear that mission is grounded in an intratrinitarian movement of God himself and that it expresses the power of God over history, to which the only appropriate response is obedience.'[36] So the phrase originally meant 'the sending of God' – in the sense of the Father's sending of the Son and their sending of the Holy Spirit. All human mission, in this perspective, is seen as a participation in, an extension of, this divine sending.

The phrase became popular in ecumenical circles after the Willingen world mission conference of 1952, through the work of Georg Vicedom.[37] It had the strength of connecting mission to the theology of the Trinity – an important theological gain. Mission flows from the inner dynamic movement of God in personal relationship. But in some circles the concept of *missio Dei* then became seriously weakened by the idea that it referred simply to God's involvement with the whole historical process – and not to any specific work of the church. The affirmation that mission was God's came to mean that it was not ours! Such distorted theology virtually excluded evangelism.

In spite of such misuse, however, the expression can be retained as expressing a major and vital biblical truth. The God revealed in the Scriptures is personal, purposeful and goal orientated. The opening account of creation portrays God working towards a goal, completing it with satisfaction and resting, content with the result. And from the great promise of God to Abraham in Genesis 12:1–3 we know this God to be totally, covenantally and eternally

---

[35] See Kirk, *What Is Mission?*, ch. 2, 'God's Mission and the Church's Response', 23–37.

[36] Hoedemaker, 'People of God', 163. Hoedemaker provides an interesting, and critical, survey of the history of the phrase *missio Dei*, and its weaknesses.

[37] Vicedom, *Mission of God*.

committed to the mission of blessing the nations through the agency of the people of Abraham. In the wake of Genesis 3 – 11 this is good news indeed for humanity – such that Paul can describe this text as 'the gospel in advance' (Gal. 3:6–8). From that point on, the mission of God could be summed up in the words of the hymn, 'God is working his purpose out as year succeeds to year', and as generations come and go.[38]

As we have already argued, the Bible presents itself to us fundamentally as a narrative – a historical narrative at one level, but a grand or metanarrative at another.[39] The narrative begins with the God of purpose in creation. It moves on to the conflict and problem generated by human rebellion against that purpose. Most of its narrative journey is spent in the story of God's redemptive purposes being worked out on the stage of human history. And it finishes beyond the horizon of its own history with the eschatological hope of a new creation. This has often been presented as a four-point narrative: creation, fall, redemption and future hope. This whole worldview is predicated on teleological monotheism: that is, the affirmation that there is one God at work in the universe and in human history, and that this God has a goal, a purpose, a mission which will ultimately be accomplished by the power of God's word and for the glory of God's name. This is the mission of the biblical God.

To read the whole Bible in the light of this great overarching perspective of the mission of God, then, is to read 'with the grain' of this whole collection of texts that constitute our canon of Scripture. In my view this is the key

---

[38] Beeby argues this fundamental orientation in approaching the Bible:

> The thesis [of his paper] is that the Bible read as scripture centres on the *missio Dei*. It is the record of the word and works of the loving, revealing God who created in love and redeems in love. It is a universal history brought about by the *dabar* of the Triune God. ('Missional approach', 272)

[39] It is of course not just a single narrative, like a river with only one channel. It is, rather, a complex mixture of all kinds of smaller narratives, many of them rather self-contained, with all kinds of other material embedded within them – more like a great delta. But there is clearly a direction, a flow, that can be described in the terms used above. Richard Bauckham sees the importance of the fact that 'the Bible does not have a carefully plotted single story-line, like, for example, a conventional novel. It is a sprawling collection of narratives …'. It is not an aggressively totalizing story that suppresses all others (the accusation that postmodernism makes against all metanarratives). Rather,

> these inescapable features of the actual narrative form of Scripture surely have a message in themselves: that the particular has its own integrity that should not be suppressed for the sake of a too readily comprehensible universal. The Bible does, in some sense, tell an overall story that encompasses all its other contents, but this story is not a sort of straitjacket that reduces all else to a narrowly defined uniformity. It is a story that is hospitable to considerable diversity and to tensions, challenges and even seeming contradictions of its own claims. (*Bible and Mission*, 92–94)

assumption of a missional hermeneutic of the Bible. It is nothing more than to accept that the biblical worldview locates us in the midst of a narrative of the universe behind which stands the mission of the living God.

Glory be to the Father and to the Son and to the Holy Spirit,
as it was in the beginning, is now, and ever shall be, world without end, Amen.

This is not just a liturgically conventional way to end prayers and canticles. It is a missional perspective on history past, present and future, and one day it will be the song of the whole creation.

From this theocentric starting point, *God with a mission*, we can in summary see the other major dimensions of mission flowing through the Bible. In its opening chapters we meet *humanity with a mission* on the planet that had been so purposefully prepared for their arrival – the mandate to fill the earth and subdue it and to rule over the rest of creation (Gen. 1:28). This delegated authority within the created order is moderated by the parallel commands in the complementary account, 'to serve and to keep'[40] the garden (Gen. 2:15). The care and keeping of creation is our human mission. The human race exists on the planet with a purpose that flows from the creative purpose of God himself. Out of this understanding of our humanity (which is also teleological, like our doctrine of God) flows our ecological responsibility, our economic activity involving work, productivity, exchange and trade, and the whole cultural mandate. To be human is to have a purposeful role in God's creation.

Then, against the background of human sin and rebellion in Genesis 3 – 11, we encounter *Israel with a mission*, beginning with the call of Abraham in Genesis 12. Israel came into existence as a people with a mission entrusted to them from God for the sake of God's wider purpose of blessing the nations. Israel's election was not a rejection of other nations but was explicitly for the sake of all nations. This universality of God's purpose, that nevertheless embraces the particularity of God's chosen means, is a recurrent theme and a constant theological challenge (to Israel as much as to contemporary theologians). With Israel, of course, we embark upon the longest part of the biblical journey, and the great themes of election, redemption, covenant, land-gift, worship, ethics and eschatology all await our missiological reflection.

Into the midst of this people – saturated with Scriptures, sustained by memory and hope, waiting for God – steps *Jesus with a mission*. Jesus did not just arrive. He had a very clear conviction that he was sent. The voice of his Father at his baptism combined the identity of the Servant figure in Isaiah (echoing the phraseology of Is. 42:1) and that of the Davidic messianic king (echoing the

---

[40] My own translation of the two Hebrew words, preserving the usual meaning of the simple verbs.

affirmation of Ps. 2:7). Both of these dimensions of his identity and role were energized with a sense of mission. The mission of the Servant was both to restore Israel to YHWH and also to be the agent of God's salvation reaching to the ends of the earth (Is. 49:6). The mission of the Davidic messianic king was both to rule over a redeemed Israel according to the agenda of many prophetic texts, and also to receive the nations and the ends of the earth as his heritage (Ps. 2:8). Jesus' sense of mission – the aims, motivation and self-understanding behind his recorded words and actions – has been a matter of intense scholarly discussion. What seems very clear is that Jesus built his own agenda on what he perceived to be the agenda of his Father. Jesus' will was to do his Father's will, so he said. God's mission determined his mission. In Jesus, the radically theocentric nature of biblical mission is most clearly focused and modelled. In the obedience of Jesus, even to death, the mission of God reached its climax. For 'God was in Christ reconciling the world to himself ' (2 Cor. 5:19).

Finally, the biblical narrative introduces us to ourselves as *the church with a mission*. As the quotation from Luke 24 in the introduction above indicates, Jesus entrusted to the church a mission that is directly rooted in his own identity, passion and victory as the crucified and risen Messiah. Jesus immediately followed the text quoted with the words, 'You are witnesses' – a mandate repeated in Acts 1:8, 'you will be my witnesses'. It is almost certain that Luke intends us to hear in this an echo of the same words spoken by YHWH to Israel in Isaiah 43:10–12.

> 'You are my witnesses,' declares the LORD, 'and my servant whom I have chosen, so that you may know and believe me and understand that I am he.
> Before me no god was formed, nor will there be one after me.
> I, even I, am the LORD, and apart from me there is no saviour.
> I have revealed and saved and proclaimed – I, and not some foreign god among you.
> You are my witnesses,' declares the LORD, 'that I am God.'

Israel knew the identity of the true and living God, YHWH; therefore they were entrusted with bearing witness to that in a world of nations and their gods. The disciples now know the true identity of the crucified and risen Jesus; therefore they are entrusted with bearing witness to that to the ends of the earth.[41] The church's mission flows from the identity of God and his Christ. When you know who God is, when you know who Jesus is, witnessing mission is the unavoidable outcome.

---

[41] It is probable that, in its immediate context (Luke 24 and Acts 1), the language of 'witness' refers primarily to the role of the apostles as direct eyewitnesses of the Lord Jesus Christ, and especially of his resurrection. However, since that specific and unique apostolic witness forms the basis of the continuing witness by all believers to the gospel of Christ, it is not inappropriate to discern the wider and long-term missional implications of the term here.

Paul goes further and identifies his own mission with the international mission of the Servant of the LORD. Quoting Isaiah 49:6 in Acts 13:47 he declares quite bluntly, 'this is what the Lord has commanded *us*: "I have made you a light for the nations, that you may bring salvation to the ends of the earth."' This is a missiological hermeneutic of the Old Testament if ever there was one. As the NIV footnote shows, Paul has no problem applying the singular 'you' (which was spoken to the Servant), to the plural 'us' (himself and his small band of church planters). So again, the mission of the church flows from the mission of God and the fulfilment of God's mandate.

Mission is not just something we do (though it certainly includes that). Fundamentally, mission is not even something we initiate. Mission, from the point of view of our human endeavour, means the committed *participation* of God's people in the purposes of God for the redemption of the whole creation. The mission is God's. The marvel is that God invites us to join in.

Mission arises from the heart of God himself, and is communicated from his heart to ours. Mission is the global outreach of the global people of a global God.[42]

Conclusion: Framework or Map?

Putting these perspectives together, then, a missional hermeneutic means that we seek to read any part of the Bible within a framework provided by the mission of God and all its ramifications in the biblical revelation. This means reading texts:

- in the light of God's purpose for his whole creation, including the redemption of humanity and the creation of the new heavens and new earth;
- in the light of God's purpose for human life in general on the planet, and of all the Bible teaches about human culture, relationships, ethics and behaviour;
- in the light of God's historical election of Israel, their identity and role in relation to the nations, and the demands he made on their worship, social ethics and total value system;
- in the light of the centrality of Jesus of Nazareth, his messianic identity and mission in relation to Israel and the nations, his cross and resurrection;
- in the light of God's calling of the church, the community of believing Jews and Gentiles who constitute the extended people of the Abrahamic covenant, to be the agent of God's blessing to the nations in the name of, and for the glory of, the Lord Jesus Christ.

---

[42] Stott, *Contemporary Christian*, 335.

Now the validity of any framework for hermeneutics or for biblical theology must always be open to critique, and the one who offers it must be humble enough to recognize that ultimately it is the text that must govern the framework, and not the other way round. Since I began with some personal reminiscence, perhaps I will be allowed to end with another. In 1998 I was invited to give the Laing Lecture at London Bible College (now the London School of Theology) with the title, '"Then they will know that I am the Lord": Missiological Reflections on the Ministry and Message of Ezekiel'. At the time I was working on my exposition of Ezekiel in the Bible Speaks Today series, and this was a useful opportunity to expose these reflections to friendly criticism. And that is what they got. In his response, Anthony Billington, lecturer in hermeneutics at London Bible College, while warmly appreciating the lecture's content, raised questions over the validity of using missiology as a framework for interpreting Ezekiel (or any other biblical text). There are, of course, many frameworks within which people read the text (feminist, psychological, dispensational, etc.). This is not intrinsically wrong, said Billington, since we all start somewhere with some framework of assumptions. But, he went on, the question is:

> Does this or that particular framework *do justice* to the thrust of the text in its biblical-theological context? Or does it *distort* the text? In other words, it's not that the bringing of a framework to a text is necessarily wrong in and of itself, nor even that the text may not be illuminated in significant ways when we do – for it frequently is. The question is more what sort of *control* the framework exercises over the text, and whether the text is ever allowed to *critique* the framework at any point.[43]

I agree entirely with Billington's concern. All I would ask is that the missional framework I propose be evaluated for its heuristic fruitfulness. Does it in fact 'do justice' to the overall thrust of the biblical canon? Does it illuminate and clarify? Does it offer a way of articulating the coherence of the Bible's overarching message?

There is, however, a sense in which *any* framework necessarily 'distorts' the text to some degree. The only way not to distort the biblical text is simply to reproduce it as it is. Any attempt to summarize it, or provide some system or pattern for grasping it or some structure to organize its content, cannot but distort the givenness of the original reality – the text itself. In this respect, a hermeneutical framework for reading the Bible (like any scheme of biblical theology) functions rather like a map. As cartographers will agree, every existing map and any possible map is a distortion to some degree of the reality it portrays. Maps of the world are the clearest examples of this. There is simply no way of producing on a two-dimensional plane the reality of the three-

---

[43] From Anthony Billington's unpublished written response to my lecture.

dimensional globe without distortion. So all world maps ('projections') compromise on where the unavoidable distortion occurs – the shape of the continents, or their relative area, or the lines of latitude and longitude, or distortion at the poles, or compass orientation and so on. The choice will depend on who the map is for and what it is intended primarily to show.

With larger-scale maps of smaller areas (e.g., for walking in the countryside or finding one's way in a city), the question becomes one of what to include or exclude from the symbolic representation that all maps are. Not every feature of the real landscape can be on a map, so the question again is, what purpose is the map intended to serve? What are the most significant features that the person using this map will need to see clearly? What can then be omitted – not because they don't exist in the geographical reality, but because they are not of primary relevance to this particular way of viewing that reality? Somewhere there must be maps of the sewers of London. They are doubtless of crucial importance to local authority engineers, but they are of limited value to a tourist. The map of the London Underground is a classic and brilliant representation of that system – invaluable to the tourist underground, but of very limited value on the streets above. It distorts and omits in order to simplify and clarify, and indeed it provides a much more comprehensible framework for understanding London by tube than any map would do that showed all the Underground lines in their actual twists and turns, distances and directions. Furthermore, we all know that the Underground map is a distortion of reality for the purpose for which it was designed – to enable us to navigate the actual reality of the trains simply and safely. The degree of distortion is justified and accepted for what it is, and we do not accuse it of falsehood, or of misleading the public. Distortion, in this context, is not at all the same thing as inaccuracy. In its own terms, the London Underground map is a comprehensively accurate document.

I think there is some value in this analogy – that is, of comparing hermeneutical frameworks to maps. The given reality is the whole text of the Bible itself. No framework can give account of every detail, just as no map can represent every tiny feature of a landscape. But, like a map, a hermeneutical framework can provide a way of 'seeing' the whole terrain, a way of navigating one's way through it, a way of observing what is most significant, a way of approaching the task of actually encountering the reality itself (just as a map tells you what to expect when you are actually 'in' the terrain it portrays). A missional hermeneutic such as I have sketched above seems to me to fulfil some of these 'mapping' requirements. It does not claim to explain every feature of the vast terrain of the Bible, nor to foreclose in advance the exegesis of any specific text. But when you encounter on your hike some feature of the landscape that is not marked on your map, you do not deny its existence because it has no place on your map. Nor do you necessarily blame the map for choosing not to

include it. Rather, the map enables you to set that feature in its proper geographical location and relationship with the other features around you. The
more I have attempted to use (or stimulate others to use) a missional 'map' of
the Bible, orientated fundamentally to the mission of God as argued above, the
more it seems that not only do the major features of the landscape stand out
clearly, but also other less well-trodden paths and less scenic scholarly tourist
attractions turn out to have surprising and fruitful connections with the main
panorama.

Bibliography

Ådna, J., and H. Kvalbein (eds.), *The Mission of the Early Church to Jews and Gentiles* (Tübingen: Mohr Siebeck, 2000)

Bauckham, R., *God Crucified* (Carlisle: Paternoster; Grand Rapids: Eerdmans, 1999)

—, *Bible and Mission: Christian Witness in a Postmodern World* (Carlisle: Paternoster; Grand Rapids: Baker Academic, 2003)

Beeby, H.D., 'A Missional Approach to Renewed Interpretation', in *Renewing Biblical Interpretation* (ed. C.G. Bartholomew, C. Greene and K. Möller; SHS 1; Carlisle: Paternoster; Grand Rapids: Zondervan, 2000), 268–83

—, *Canon and Mission* (Harrisburg, PA: Trinity Press International, 1999)

Billington, A., T. Lane and M. Turner (eds.), *Mission and Meaning: Essays Presented to Peter Cotterell* (Carlisle: Paternoster, 1995)

Blauw, J., *The Missionary Nature of the Church* (New York: McGraw Hill, 1962)

Bosch, D.J., 'Hermeneutical Principles in the Biblical Foundation for Mission', *ERT* 17 (1993), 437–51

Briggs, R.S., 'The Uses of Speech-Act Theory in Biblical Interpretation', *CurTM* 9 (2001), 229–76

Brownson, J.V., 'Speaking the Truth in Love: Elements of a Missional Hermeneutic', in *The Church between Gospel and Culture* (ed. G.R. Hunsberger and C. Van Gelder; Grand Rapids: Eerdmans, 1996), 228–59

—, *Speaking the Truth in Love: New Testament Resources for a Missional Hermeneutic* (Harrisburg, PA: Trinity Press International, 1998)

Brueggemann, W., *Theology of the Old Testament: Testimony, Dispute, Advocacy* (Minneapolis: Fortress Press, 1997)

Burnett, D., *God's Mission, Healing the Nations* (Carlisle: Paternoster, rev. edn., 1996)

Filbeck, D., *Yes, God of the Gentiles Too: The Missionary Message of the Old Testament* (Wheaton, IL: Billy Graham Center, Wheaton College, 1994)

Franks, M., 'Election, Pluralism, and the Missiology of Scripture in a Postmodern Age', *Missiology* 26 (1998), 329–43

Goerner, H.C., *Thus It Is Written* (Nashville, TN: Broadman Press, 1971)

Groot, A. de, 'One Bible and Many Interpretive Contexts: Hermeneutics in Missiology', in *Missiology: An Ecumenical Introduction* (ed. A. Camps, L.A. Hoedemaker and M.R. Spindler; Grand Rapids: Eerdmans, 1995)

Hedlund, R., *The Mission of the Church in the World* (Grand Rapids: Baker, 1991)

Hesselgrave, D.J., 'A Missionary Hermeneutic: Understanding Scripture in the Light of World Mission', *IJFM* 10 (1993), 17–20

Hoedemaker, L.A., 'The People of God and the Ends of the Earth', in *Missiology: An Ecumenical Introduction* (ed. A. Camps, L.A. Hoedemaker and M.R. Spindler; Grand Rapids: Eerdmans, 1995)

Jenkins, P., *The Next Christendom: The Coming of Global Christianity* (Oxford: Oxford University Press, 2002)

Kaiser, W.C., Jr, *Mission in the Old Testament: Israel as a Light to the Nations* (Grand Rapids: Baker, 2000)

Kirk, J.A., *What Is Mission? Theological Explorations* (London: Darton, Longman and Todd; Minneapolis: Fortress Press, 1999)

Koestenberger, A.J., 'The Place of Mission in New Testament Theology: An Attempt to Determine the Significance of Mission within the Scope of the New Testament's Message as a Whole', *Missiology* 27 (1999), 347–62

Koestenberger, A.J., and P.T. O'Brien, *Salvation to the Ends of the Earth: A Biblical Theology of Mission* (Leicester: Apollos, 2001)

LaGrand, J., *The Earliest Christian Mission to 'All Nations' in the Light of Matthew's Gospel* (Grand Rapids: Eerdmans, 1995)

Le Grys, A., *Origins of the Mission of the Early Church* (London: SPCK and Triangle, 1999)

Martin-Achard, R., *A Light to the Nations: A Study of the Old Testament Conception of Israel's Mission to the World* (trans. J.P. Smith; Edinburgh and London: Oliver and Boyd, 1962)

Middleton, J.R., and B.J. Walsh, *Truth Is Stranger than It Used to Be: Biblical Faith in a Postmodern Age* (London: SPCK; Downers Grove, IL: InterVarsity Press, 1995)

Patrick, D., *The Rendering of God in the Old Testament* (OBT; Philadelphia: Fortress Press, 1981)

Ridder, R.R. de, *Discipling the Nations* (Grand Rapids: Baker, 1975)

Rowley, H.H., *The Missionary Message of the Old Testament* (London: Carey Press, 1944)

Scobie, C.H.H., 'Israel and the Nations: An Essay in Biblical Theology', *TynBul* 43.2 (1992), 283–305

Senior, D., and C. Stuhlmueller, *The Biblical Foundations for Mission* (London: SCM Press, 1983)

Soards, M.L., 'Key Issues in Biblical Studies and Their Bearing on Mission Studies', *Missiology* 24 (1996), 93–109

Spindler, M.R., 'The Biblical Grounding and Orientation of Mission', in *Missiology: An Ecumenical Introduction* (ed. A. Camps, L.A. Hoedemaker and M.R. Spindler; Grand Rapids: Eerdmans, 1995), 123–43

Stott, J., *The Contemporary Christian: An Urgent Plea for Double Listening* (Leicester: Inter-Varsity Press, 1992)

Taber, C.R., 'Missiology and the Bible', *Missiology* 11 (1983), 229–45

Van Engen, C., 'The Relation of Bible and Mission in Mission Theology', in *The Good News of the Kingdom* (ed. C. Van Engen, D.S. Gilliland and P. Pierson; Maryknoll, NY: Orbis Books, 1993), 27–36

Vicedom, G.F., *The Mission of God: An Introduction to a Theology of Mission* (Saint Louis: Concordia, 1965)

Walls, A.F., *The Missionary Movement in Christian History: Studies in the Transmission of Faith* (Maryknoll, NY: Orbis Books; Edinburgh: T. & T. Clark, 1996)

Wright, C.J.H., 'Future Trends in Mission', in *The Futures of Evangelicalism: Issues and Prospects* (ed. C. Bartholomew, R. Parry and A. West; Leicester: Inter-Varsity Press, 2003), 149–63

—, 'Christ and the Mosaic of Pluralisms: Challenges to Evangelical Missiology in the 21st Century', in *Global Missiology for the 21st Century: The Iguassu Dialogue* (ed. W.D. Taylor; Grand Rapids: Baker, 2000), 71–99

—, *Old Testament Ethics for the People of God* (Leicester: Inter-Varsity Press; Downers Grove, IL: InterVarsity Press, 2004)

—, *Walking in the Ways of the Lord: The Ethical Authority of the Old Testament* (Leicester: Inter-Varsity Press; Downers Grove, IL: InterVarsity Press, 1995)

Wright, N.T., *Jesus and the Victory of God* (London: SPCK, 1996)

6

Story and Biblical Theology

Craig G. Bartholomew and Michael W. Goheen

Introduction

Grand or *meta*-narrative is an unlikely item on an agenda for biblical studies today. In our 'postmodern' era we have learned to adopt an attitude of 'incredulity towards metanarratives',[1] and within academic biblical studies we have been trained to emphasize diversity and to be suspicious of attempts to read the Bible as a (unified) whole. Despite these hostile forces, our contention in this chapter is that there is much to be gained from the recovery of reading the Bible as a grand narrative. Not only do we think this possible – and thus wish to commend it as a major way of doing biblical theology – but we also think it important if Scripture is to function as God's word in the life of his people.

At our St Andrews consultation on biblical theology and biblical interpretation we participated in a lively evening discussion about biblical theology and teaching the Bible. The starting point for discussion was an early draft of our *The Drama of Scripture*, a telling of the biblical story for first-year undergraduate students.[2] We contend that if we really want to recover the authority of Scripture in our lives, then we urgently need to recover the Bible as a grand story that tells us of God's ways with the world from creation to re-creation, from the garden of Eden to the new Jerusalem. Only thus will we see our way clear to indwell God's story and relate it to all of life today. Consequently our book attempts to tell the story in some two hundred pages, from Genesis to Revelation.

Needless to say, this approach to biblical theology did not go uncontested at the consultation. Debate was vigorous. We therefore welcome the opportunity presented by this volume to explore in more detail our proposal and its critique. Our case proceeds as follows: First we take note of the burgeoning interest in narrative in philosophy and theology. Flowing from this is a concern

---

[1] Lyotard, *Postmodern Condition*, xxiv.
[2] Bartholomew and Goheen, *Drama*.

with reading the Bible as an overarching story coming from various branches of theology – systematic, practical, ethics and missiology – but sadly not from within biblical studies. In the context of the literary turn within biblical studies from the 1970s onwards, a considerable amount of fertile work has been done on the Bible and its stories.[3] With few exceptions, however, this has not been extended to the Bible as a whole. The impetus in that direction has generally come from outside of biblical studies. This is not to say that the category of 'story' has been completely neglected by biblical theology. Thus we explore James Barr's recent comments in this respect and take note of earlier emphases on story in the history of biblical theology. From this we move on to N.T. Wright's work as the rare example of a major biblical scholar in whose work story, in the grand sense, is central. We conclude by trying to answer some of the major objections to our approach.

The Impetus Toward Narrative from Philosophy and Theology

Recent decades have seen a veritable explosion of interest in narrative, and this across a variety of disciplines. In philosophy Paul Ricœur, Alasdair MacIntyre, Charles Taylor and others have taken up the theme of narrative with vigour. Ricœur explores the way in which narrative is foundational to the world and how humans live in it. There is, according to Ricœur, an 'incipient "configuring" or "emplotting" process that is the experiential foundation of the human capacity to write literature and history'.[4] MacIntyre attends to the way in which all human life and thought is traditioned, and he is well known for his advocacy of the Aristotelian tradition for contemporary ethics. MacIntyre believes that our life decisions are shaped and ordered by our sense of how they fit within a larger story or tradition[5] and insists that, 'I can only answer the question, "What am I to do?" if I can answer the prior question, "Of what story do I find myself a part?"'[6]

In theology, narrative has been appropriated in a variety of ways. One can distinguish between the following emphases in this respect:

- An emphasis on Scripture as *the* story.
- An understanding of the importance of *our* communal *story* for theology. All our lives are storied by virtue of the cultural contexts in which we live, and theology needs to take this cultural, communal context seriously.

---

[3] One of the best examples is Sternberg, *Poetics*.
[4] Stiver, *Philosophy*, 137.
[5] See MacIntyre, *After Virtue*, ch. 15.
[6] MacIntyre, *After Virtue*, 216.

- Each of our lives is individually a story, and thus *personal narrative* has theological implications.

Stiver discerns three major theological schools that have developed, each of which majors on one of the above three aspects.[7] The Yale school (1), associated with Hans Frei and George Lindbeck, emphasizes the narrative shape of Christianity as a particular religion and asserts that Christians should appropriate this narrative and its language and allow it to 'absorb the world'.[8] Stanley Hauerwas has stressed in comparable ways the importance of narrative for theological ethics.[9] The Chicago school (2), associated with Ricœur and David Tracy, is less interested in the particularity of the Christian narrative than in the philosophical and cultural relevance of narrative. This moves in the direction of general hermeneutics and ways of correlating theology with contemporary culture. The California school (3), associated with James McClendon, attends to the relationship between theology and personal narrative and thus develops the importance of biography and autobiography for theology today.

All three of these approaches have implications for narrative approaches to biblical theology. For our purposes the Yale school is of particular interest, with its concern with the overarching Christian narrative. An example of work in this tradition is that of George Stroup, *The Promise of Narrative Theology*. Stroup is excited about the possibility that narrative holds for a recovery of the gospel in the church. In the process of exploring the possibilities of a narrative theology he pays considerable attention to narrative and the Bible. He recognizes the diversity of the Bible; much of it cannot be described as narrative.[10] Even those parts of the Bible that fit the genre of narrative differ in form, structure and function.[11] Nevertheless, Stroup says,

> At the center of Scripture is a set of narratives and these narratives are the frame around which the whole of Scripture is constructed. Apart from these narratives the Prophets would not be intelligible and without the frame of the Gospel narratives it would be difficult to understand the full meaning of the parables, epistles, creeds, and hymns of the New Testament.[12]

---

[7] Stiver, *Philosophy*, ch. 7.

[8] Frei quotes Auerbach's striking contrast between Homer's *Odyssey* and the Old Testament story: 'Far from seeking, like Homer, merely to make us forget our own reality for a few hours, it seeks to overcome our reality: we are to fit our own life into its world, feel ourselves to be elements in its structure of universal history ... Everything else that happens in the world can only be conceived as an element in this sequence; into it everything that is known about the world ... must be fitted as an ingredient of the divine plan' (Frei, *Eclipse*, 3).

[9] See Hauerwas, *Peaceable Kingdom*, and Hauerwas and Jones (eds.), *Why Narrative?*

[10] Stroup, *Promise*, 80 and 136ff.

[11] Stroup, *Promise*, 137.

[12] Stroup, *Promise*, 145.

According to Stroup there are good reasons why narrative is such a primary genre in the Bible. At a philosophical and sociological level, the identity of a community or person requires the interpretation of historical experience, and narrative is the best genre for this. And, since God's action is central to Christian faith, it is not surprising that much of the Bible takes the form of narrative. Stroup explores Deuteronomy and Mark in this respect. He notes that,

> The Christian community gives expression to its identity by means of a narrative that begins, 'A wandering Aramean was my father' ... culminates in the confession 'that Christ died for our sins in accordance with the scriptures' ... and continues in the narrative history of the church through the ages as it witnesses to the coming kingdom of God.[13]

Stroup makes an admirable attempt to take the Bible seriously in his narrative theology. His work thereby foregrounds the fecundity, as well as the complexity, of narrative for theological interpretation of the Bible. Narrative figures prominently in the Bible but, from Stroup's perspective, there is considerable diversity among biblical narratives, and there is much material that is not narrative. Indeed there seems to be something of a tension in this respect in Stroup's work – on the one hand Scripture seems to range from the wandering Aramean to the Christ and thus to have something of an overall narrative shape, while on the other hand Stroup confines himself to individual narratives. Stroup's work is thereby an impetus for closer examination of the Bible and narrative as a whole.

The Impetus Toward Narrative from Practical Theology and Theological Ethics

This impulse toward narrative comes not only from theology and philosophy, but also from various branches of practical theology – specifically pastoral theology, ethics, homiletics and missiology. All of these disciplines are in one way or another concerned to bring the Bible to bear on the concrete life of the Christian community. The significance of understanding the Bible as one unfolding story emerges, it would appear, when the focus is on how the Bible shapes our lives.

Central to this interest in narrative among practical theologians is the recognition that human beings interpret and make sense of their world through a story. That is to speak of story, not in literary categories, but as the essential shape of a worldview. As pastoral theologian Charles Gerkin says: 'All things human are in some way rooted in, or find their deepest structural framework

---

[13] Stroup, *Promise*, 146.

in, a narrative or story of some kind.'[14] Hence Gerkin wants to establish the practice of pastoral care on the solid foundation of a unified biblical narrative.

> This sense in which practical theological thinking is grounded in narrative is, of course, rooted in the faith that *the Bible provides us with an overarching narrative in which all other narratives of the world are nested.* The Bible is the story of God. The story of the world is first and foremost the story of God's activity in creating, sustaining and redeeming the world to fulfil God's purposes for it. The story of the world is the story of God's promises for the world. It is also the story of the vicissitudes of God's gracious effort to fulfil those promises.[15]

Gerkin qualifies the statement above in terms of the plurality of the stories of God's activity in the Bible that leads to tension between biblical themes. Nevertheless, he insists that 'the stories of the Bible taken together disclose a way of seeing the world and human life in the world as always held within the "plot" of God's intentional purposes and direction. Life in the world is life nested within that overarching narrative.'[16] It is this narrative context in which pastoral theology must take place.

Similarly, Stanley Hauerwas wants to situate ethics in the context of the biblical story. The first task of ethics is not to articulate ethical standards but to 'rightly envision the world' so that our life as a Christian community is consistent with the world as it exists.[17] To rightly understand the world we must attend to the biblical story. For Hauerwas, too, story is fundamentally a worldview category.

> My contention is that the narrative character of Christian convictions is neither incidental nor accidental to Christian belief. There is no more fundamental way to talk of God than in a story. The fact that we come to know God through the recounting of the story of Israel and the life of Jesus is decisive for our truthful understanding of the kind of God we worship as well as the world in which we exist.[18]

Like Gerkin, Hauerwas recognizes that this story is a complex story with many different subplots and digressions. Nonetheless, it provides an overarching narrative that enables the Christian church to understand its ethical calling.

In homiletics, Sidney Greidanus, Edmund Clowney and Graeme Goldsworthy underscore the importance of the biblical story for preaching:

> ... biblical theology involves the quest for the big picture, or the overview of biblical revelation ... If we allow the Bible to tell its own story, we find a coherent and mean-

---

[14] Gerkin, *Widening the Horizons*, 26.
[15] Gerkin, *Widening the Horizons*, 48.
[16] Gerkin, *Widening the Horizons*, 49.
[17] Hauerwas, *Peaceable Kingdom*, 29.
[18] Hauerwas, *Peaceable Kingdom*, 25.

ingful whole ... If God has given us a single picture of reality, albeit full of texture and variety, a picture spanning the ages, then our preaching must reflect the reality that is thus presented.[19]

The quest for the big picture is important for two reasons. The first is *hermeneutical*: one cannot properly interpret the text to be preached apart from the context of the biblical story. Clowney highlights two aspects of biblical theology – progression and continuity. This leads to two dimensions of biblical interpretation. Since the Bible is *progressive* revelation it has an epochal structure. One must interpret the biblical text in light of the particular epoch, the 'immediate theological horizon' or 'total setting of the revelation of that period'.[20] Of course the total setting is not only theological but also historical, cultural, literary, linguistic and so on. Since the Bible is a progressive *unity*, a second dimension is required: the preacher must interpret the text in light of the whole biblical story.[21] Likewise, Greidanus believes that the interpreter must see the message of the text not only in its immediate historical-cultural context but 'also in its broadest possible context, that is, Scripture's teaching regarding history as a whole'. That is because

> Scripture teaches one universal kingdom history that encompasses all of created reality: past, present, and future ... its vision of history extends backward all the way to the beginning of time and forward all the way to the last day ... the biblical vision of history spans time from the first creation to the new creation, encompassing all of created reality.[22]

The second reason for stressing the whole story is *homiletical*: the preacher's task is to call God's people to live in the biblical story. Lesslie Newbigin suggests that preaching must 'challenge' the cultural story with the biblical story.[23] Preaching calls God's people to indwell the biblical story: 'Preaching is the announcing of news, the telling of a narrative. In a society that has a different story to tell about itself, preaching has to be firmly and unapologetically rooted in the real story.'[24] Preaching in this way 'can only

---

[19] Goldsworthy, *Preaching*, 22.

[20] Clowney, *Preaching*, 88.

[21] Clowney, *Preaching*, 98.

[22] Greidanus, *The Modern Preacher*, 95.

[23] Newbigin borrows the term 'challenging relevance' from Alfred Hogg. Preaching must be made relevant to the hearers by entering into their cultural story and discourse. But it must also challenge that story ('Missions', 335–36).

[24] In another place Newbigin, *Word*, 204–205, speaks of his personal Bible reading, but his words could as easily be applied to his understanding of preaching:

> I more and more find the precious part of each day to be the thirty or forty minutes I spend each morning before breakfast with the Bible. All the rest of the day I am bombarded with the stories that the world is telling about itself. I am more and more skeptical about these

happen when the Bible in its canonical wholeness recovers its place as scripture'.[25]

The Impetus Toward Narrative from Missiology: Missionary Encounter Between Two Stories

Within missiology, Newbigin is known for emphasizing the foundational importance of understanding the Bible as one story[26] for mission and missions.[27] His notion of a missionary encounter illustrates how much is at stake in this respect. For Newbigin, a missionary encounter is the normal posture of every church in its culture when it is faithful to the gospel.

All of human life is shaped by some story: 'The way we understand human life depends on what conception we have of the human story. What is the real story of which my life story is a part?'[28] The only question is which one? In contemporary Western culture there are 'two quite different stories' on offer as the 'real story' of the world – the humanist story that flows from the classical philosophy of Greece and Rome, and the story that is told in the Bible.[29] These stories offer two 'incompatible' ways of viewing the world. The primary difference between them is the location of reliable truth. The biblical story locates truth in the story of God's deeds and words in history, centred in Jesus Christ, while the classical humanist story finds truth in timeless ideas that can be accessed by human thought. In the West, that missionary encounter takes place between the story of the Bible as it is embodied in the church and the cultural story of the West.

For Newbigin, both the biblical and the rationalist-humanist story have to do with *history*, an interpretation of what really happened. One story begins in our evolutionary past and sees history in terms of the progressive development of human mastery over nature by science and technology that leads to a world of freedom and material prosperity. The other story begins with the creation of

---

stories. As I take time to immerse myself in the story that the Bible tells, my vision is cleared and I see things in another way. I see the day that lies ahead in its place in God's story.

[25] Newbigin, 'Missions', 336.

[26] For a comparable emphasis see Walker, *Telling the Story*.

[27] For Newbigin, 'mission' is the sending of the whole church into the world to bear witness to the gospel in life, word and deed. In other words, all of life is mission! 'Missions' is part of that mission, specifically to take the good news to places where it has not yet been heard.

[28] Newbigin, *Gospel*, 15.

[29] Newbigin, *Proper Confidence,* 2; *Gospel*, 15.

the world and ends with its renewal, and leads through a narrow road marked by Israel, Jesus and the church. God's work in Israel and in the church, and especially in Jesus, offers a clue to the meaning of history. The Bible tells the story of the coming of God's rule over the whole creation. These stories are not mere literature or linguistically constructed discourses. They interpret past history and look to the goal of history. Consequently, these stories make claims to be *universal* history.[30] They offer answers to the origin and destiny of the whole world and also offer a clue to the meaning of world history and human life within it. The Bible is universal history: it sets forth a story of the whole world from its beginning to its end. It is the true story of the world, and all other stories are at best partial narratives, which must be understood within the context of the biblical story. Newbigin was challenged to see the Bible as universal history by Chaturvedi Badrinath, a Hindu scholar of world religions, who once said to him:

> I can't understand why you missionaries present the Bible to us in India as a book of religion. It is not a book of religion – and anyway we have plenty of books of religion in India. We don't need any more! I find in your Bible a unique interpretation of universal history, the history of the whole of creation and the history of the human race. And therefore a unique interpretation of the human person as a responsible actor in history. That is unique. There is nothing else in the whole religious literature of the world to put alongside it.[31]

As universal history, these stories make absolute and totalitarian claims on our lives.[32] They claim to understand the world as it really is and interpret the true meaning of history. Thus the way we understand all of human life depends on what we believe to be the true story of the world. While the origin and authority of the humanist story is encapsulated in the phrase 'I discovered', the biblical story finds its origin and authority in 'God has spoken'.[33]

A missionary encounter occurs when the church believes the Bible to be the true story of the world and embodies, or 'indwells',[34] the comprehensive claims of that story as a counter-cultural community over against the dominant cultural story. Since both stories make comprehensive and absolute claims,

---

[30] 'Universal history' is the term Newbigin most often uses to point to the comprehensive scope of the biblical story. For disadvantages in the use of the term 'universal history' see Buss, 'Meaning of History'.

[31] Newbigin, *Walk*, 4. See also Newbigin, *Gospel*, 89.

[32] In the words of Loughlin, *Telling*, 37, the biblical story is 'omnivorous': it seeks to overcome our reality.

[33] Newbigin, *Gospel*, 60.

[34] Employing Michael Polanyi's terminology, Newbigin speaks of 'indwelling' the biblical story. For more see *Gospel*, 33–38.

only one story can be *the* basic and foundational story for life. Newbigin charges that the Western church is 'an advanced case of syncretism' because it has allowed the biblical story to be accommodated into the more comprehensive Enlightenment story.[35]

If the church is to be faithful to its missionary calling, it must recover the Bible as one true story: 'I do not believe that we can speak effectively of the Gospel as a word addressed to our culture unless we recover a sense of the Scriptures as a canonical whole, as the story which provides the true context for our understanding of the meaning of our lives – both personal and public.'[36] If the story of the Bible is fragmented into bits (historical-critical, devotional, systematic-theological, moral), it can easily be absorbed into the reigning story of culture. Newbigin's recognition of this, and thus his passion for the importance of seeing the Bible as one story, comes from his missionary experience. In India he saw how easy it was for the Bible to be absorbed into a more comprehensive and alien worldview. The Bible as one comprehensive story in contrast to the comprehensive worldview of Hinduism was a matter of life and death.

Part of Newbigin's call for a missionary encounter in the West was to challenge biblical scholars to equip the church by helping to recover the Bible as one story.[37] He believed that, while historical-critical scholarship had brought much insight into Scripture, it also had capitulated to the Enlightenment story as the controlling story. While it claimed to be objective and neutral, in fact much biblical scholarship was 'a move from one confessional stance to another, a move from one creed to another'.[38] Or, as he put it elsewhere: 'The Enlightenment did not (as it is sometimes supposed) simply free the scholar from the influence of "dogma"; it replaced one dogma by another.' The power of the Enlightenment story is such that it is difficult to convince modern biblical scholars 'to recognize the creedal character of their approach'.[39]

It is apparent from the above that the impetus toward the recovery of the Bible as one story has been polyphonic – voices in philosophy, theology, ethics and practical theology push us in this direction. Where is biblical studies in all of this?

---

[35] Newbigin, *Other Side*, 23.

[36] Newbigin, 'Response'.

[37] Newbigin's response was twofold. 1) He sought to stir up discussion among biblical scholars. He approached George Caird, professor of the interpretation of holy Scripture at Oxford. Caird told him: 'You are asking for a total revolution in the way biblical scholars see their job.' Nevertheless, this initiative led to a group of younger biblical scholars beginning to discuss these issues. See Newbigin, *Unfinished Agenda*, 249. 2) He wrote a number of papers himself, challenging the unrecognized faith assumptions that shaped critical biblical scholarship.

[38] Newbigin, *Proper Confidence*, 80

[39] Newbigin, 'Role of the Bible', 1.

Story and Biblical Theology

Story has a long history in biblical theology, and we cannot review it in detail here. In Craig Bartholomew's introduction, he notes that Irenaeus worked with a narrative understanding of the Bible as a whole.[40] The redemptive-historical approach to the Bible, stemming from Calvin and exemplified in Geerhardus Vos and Herman Ridderbos,[41] also works with an understanding of the Bible as one unfolding story, although it precedes the contemporary stress on literature and narrative.[42]

In his *The Concept of Biblical Theology*, Barr devotes a chapter to 'story' in which he notes that, from the 1960s onwards, he and others stressed the importance of story as a category in Old Testament studies. Story in this context is deliberately set against *history*, partly as a reaction to the emphasis on the acts of God in the biblical theology movement (BTM). Story embraces material that is historical as well as that which includes myth and legend, and above all divine speech. Story focuses attention on the beginning, the progression and the culmination as being more important than the historical realities behind the text. Barr notes that G. Ernest Wright and others in the BTM had already indicated the importance of story in biblical theology, but he asserts that they made little of the actual story character of the Bible so that story functioned in their works more as an idea.[43]

---

[40] Loughlin, *Telling*, xii, mentions Augustine, Aquinas and Hamann as important figures in this narrative tradition.

[41] There is a 'redemptive-historical' school that developed in the Netherlands from the late nineteenth century and reached its zenith in the twentieth century between the world wars. This tradition is not broadly known but is rich in resources for biblical theology. It is a tradition that has had a formative influence on the authors of this article. We mention here only one more recent representative of this school, Herman Ridderbos. For a discussion of this redemptive-historical school in its historical development and its outworking in homiletics, see Greidanus, *Sola Scriptura*. A leader in this movement, B. Holwerda, summarized this redemptive-historical approach in 1940 as follows:

> The Bible does not contain many histories but one history – the one history of God's constantly advancing revelation, the one history of God's ever progressing redemptive work. And the various persons named in the Bible have all received their own peculiar place in this one history and have their peculiar meaning for this history. We must, therefore, try to understand all the accounts in their relation with each other, in their coherence with the centre of redemptive history, Jesus Christ. (Holwerda, *Begonnen*, 80, trans. and quoted by Greidanus, *Sola Scriptura*, 41)

[42] See, e.g., Ridderbos, *When the Time Had Fully Come*; *Redemptive History and the New Testament Scriptures*; *The Coming of the Kingdom*; *Paul: An Outline of His Theology*.

[43] It remains a relevant question as to the extent to which we can draw on the BTM in this respect today. See Bartholomew, 'Introduction', in this volume. For a relevant

Barr continues to see great value in approaching the Bible as story, as long as we don't set this against historical criticism. 'That the story is a totality and to be read as such would seem to agree with the "holistic" emphasis of many literary and canonical tendencies of today. But the fact that it is a totality does not mean that it has to be swallowed whole, uncritically.'[44] Barr, as we will see below, defends taking the whole of the Bible as story. Making Genesis the starting point enables us to avoid past mistakes, such as isolating the exodus from its broader narrative context. A story approach also connects with current understandings of communal and personal identity.

Brevard Childs is less positive towards story and biblical theology than Barr. He discusses narrative under literary approaches to biblical theology. His major concern with narrative is that, 'The threat lies in divorcing the Bible when seen as literature from its theological reality to which scripture bears witness.'[45] Barr, by comparison, finds a story approach to the Bible helpful theologically in that it alerts us to the Bible as the raw data of theological reflection. We will explore Childs's objection below. We find Barr's positive approach to story and biblical theology helpful, even if we disagree with him on the relation of the story to history. We agree with Barr that story is one way of doing biblical theology, and, like him, while we have no desire to rule out other approaches we think that this approach holds real potential for biblical theology. In our view there is room for a whole smorgasbord of ways of doing biblical theology, although we suspect that the narrative shape of Scripture is fundamental and will need to be taken into account by all readings, even if it is not their central concern.

The fact remains, however, that there is little sign of this sort of biblical theology being written. For all of the insights of older story approaches to biblical theology, things have moved on since then, and there would appear to be considerable scope for new work in this area if, as Barr asserts, story has a lot to offer biblical theology – not least in approaching the Bible as a whole. What would such an approach look like today?

N.T. Wright and the Recovery of Story in Biblical Studies

N.T. Wright is a biblical scholar who believes there is much at stake in recognizing the Bible as one story. In fact, the theological authority of the biblical story is tied up with its overarching narrative form. He offers a rich metaphor to explicate this authority.[46] Imagine that a Shakespearean play is discovered, but

---

source of the BTM on story and biblical theology see Rhodes, *Mighty Acts.*
[44] Barr, *Concept*, 352.
[45] Childs, *Biblical Theology*, 723.
[46] Wright, 'Bible', and *New Testament*, 139–43.

most of the fifth act is missing. The decision to stage the play is made. The first four acts and the remnant of the fifth act are given to well-trained and experienced Shakespearean actors who immerse themselves both in the first part of the play and in the culture and time of Shakespeare. They are told to work out the concluding fifth act for themselves.

This conclusion must be both consistent and innovative. It must be consistent with the first part of the play. The actors must immerse themselves in full sympathy in the unfinished drama. The first four acts would contain their own cumulative forward movement that would demand that the play be concluded in a way consistent and fitting with that impetus. Yet an appropriate conclusion would not mean a simple repetition or imitation of the earlier acts. The actors would carry forward the logic of the play in a creative improvisation. Such an improvisation would be an authentic conclusion if it were coherent with the earlier acts.

This metaphor provides a specific analogy for how the biblical story might function authoritatively to shape the life of the believing community. Wright sees the biblical story as consisting of four acts – creation, fall, Israel, Jesus – plus the first scene of the fifth act that narrates the beginning of the church's mission. Furthermore, this fifth act offers hints at how the play is to end. Thus the church's life is lived out consistently with the forward impetus of the first acts and moving toward and anticipating the intended conclusion. The first scene of act five, the church's story, begins to draw out and implement the significance of the first four acts, especially act four. The church continues today to do the same in fresh and creative ways in new cultural situations. This requires a patient examination of, and thorough immersion in, what act four is all about, how act four is to be understood in light of acts one through three, and how the first scene of act five faithfully carries forward act four.

This divine drama, told in Scripture, 'offers a story which is the story of the whole world. It is public truth.'[47] Thus it is to be normative: it is to function as the controlling story[48] for the whole life of the Christian community. The biblical narrative is an authoritative worldview. A worldview expresses the deepest and most basic (yet often unconscious) beliefs through which human beings perceive reality. Worldviews operate at a presuppositional and precognitive level and have to do with the ultimate concerns that grip people's lives. Worldviews function as a lens through which the whole world is seen, as a

---

[47] Wright, *New Testament*, 41–42.

[48] Wright speaks of the biblical narrative as a 'controlling story' (*New Testament*, 42). His use is similar to Wolterstorff's notion of 'control beliefs' (*Reason*, ch. 1). Wolterstorff speaks in the context of scholarship. Control beliefs are those fundamental beliefs that function foundationally to guide our theoretical work. For Wright, a 'controlling story' is that foundational story that gives shape and meaning to our lives.

blueprint that gives direction for life, as a grid according to which a people organize reality, and as a foundation which, though invisible, is vital in giving stability and structure to human life. The biblical and Western worldviews come in the shape of a grand story, a 'worldview-story'.[49] A community's life will always be shaped by a worldview-story. A culture is a community whose praxis and life is shaped by a controlling story. In the West, the Enlightenment and now its postmodern counterpart offer a public and comprehensive story that shapes Western culture.[50]

Both the biblical and the Western worldview-stories claim to be public truth. The Christian community – including biblical scholarship – is faced with a clash of stories: since both are comprehensive and claim the whole of one's life, loyalty can be given to only one grand story. Wright is concerned that biblical scholarship often does not carry out its work under the authority of the controlling story of Scripture. Rather, the Enlightenment, modernist, Western worldview-story is the lens through which many scholars view the Bible.

When this happens, biblical scholarship becomes reductionistic: Scripture is reduced to only a literary or historical phenomenon. One passes beyond these reductionist readings of Scripture, Wright believes, by taking into account the worldview-story of both the original writers and readers of the New Testament, as well as the worldview-story of contemporary readers and interpreters. It is the worldview of the original writers that gives meaning to the events they narrate. Historical study is always a matter of event and interpretation, the outside-happenedness and inside-meaning of an event. The earliest writers of the New Testament believed they were narrating actual events that possessed ultimate significance because God was acting in a climactic way in history. But the biblical authors and readers are not the only ones with a worldview: when the modern reader comes to the Bible, he or she does not come as a neutral and objective observer but also with a particular worldview lens.

---

[49] Wright's term, *New Testament*, 135. He uses this term to set off story as a comprehensive worldview from the various stories that express that worldview. The communal nature and narrative structure are important for Wright's understanding of worldview. This can be seen in what he does with Walsh and Middleton's four worldview questions. According to Walsh and Middleton, all worldviews provide answers to four foundational questions: Who am I?, Where am I?, What is wrong?, and What is the solution? (*Transforming Vision*, 35). Wright turns these questions into the plural to indicate the communal nature of our worldviews. In *Jesus* he highlights the importance of story when he suggests a fifth question: 'What time is it?' He explains: 'Since writing *The New Testament and the People of God* I have realized that "what time is it?" needs adding to the four questions I started with … Without it, the structure collapses into timelessness which characterizes some non-Judaeo-Christian worldviews' (*Jesus*, 443).

[50] Wright, *New Testament*, 139.

A worldview-story is public and comprehensive: it offers a lens through which to view everything else, including what adherents of other worldviews are 'really' up to. Biblical scholars, who may be unaware of their Western worldview lens,[51] or who have consciously embraced the Enlightenment vision as normative, look at the biblical texts and offer an account of what the biblical authors were 'really' up to. The biblical authors believed that God was acting in the historical events they proclaimed. One must either believe those claims or reject them on the basis of other beliefs embodied in another story. If that story is the Enlightenment story, theological claims do not stand up well, and so they are dismissed. But to accept the authority of the Western story and dismiss the theological claims of the original writers would be to abandon the comprehensive and public claim of the biblical story. Enlightenment modernism then subsumes Christianity within it and makes the biblical story one more private religious option.[52]

It is possible, though, to work the other way round: to embrace the biblical story as the true and comprehensive story, and to understand Enlightenment modernism and its postmodern reaction from within it. Then the biblical story becomes the controlling story for biblical scholarship. This is how Wright wants to proceed. The task of biblical interpretation, then, will not be a matter of 'purely literary' or 'purely historical' study, divorced from worldview and theology. Rather, it will be 'possible to join together the three enterprises of literary, historical and theological study of the New Testament and to do so in particular by the use of the category of "story"'.[53]

Theological interpretation will be as important as literary or historical. Theology is concerned with claims about God embodied in a worldview – whether there is a God, his relation to the world, and whether or not he is acting to set the world right.[54] The theological beliefs of the biblical authors and the Bible's modern interpreters will be essential to biblical scholarship: '"theology" highlights what we might call the god-dimension of a worldview

---

[51] A Chinese proverb highlights the difficulty in seeing one's own cultural story and assumptions: 'If you want to know about water don't ask a fish.' Newbigin speaks of his experience prior to India, before the 'immense power and rationality of the Vedantin's vision of reality' enabled him to understand the formative power of Western culture on him: 'My confession of Jesus as Lord is conditioned by the culture of which I am a part. It is expressed in the language of the myth within which I live. Initially I am not aware of this as a myth. As long as I retain the innocence of a thoroughly western man, unshaken by serious involvement in another culture, I am not aware of this myth. It is simply "how things are" ... No myth is seen as a myth by those who inhabit it: it is simply the way things are' (Newbigin, 'Christ and Cultures', 3).

[52] Wright, *New Testament*, 137.

[53] Wright, *New Testament*, 139.

[54] Wright, *New Testament*, 127.

... As such it is a non-negotiable part of the study of literature and history, and hence of New Testament studies.'[55]

. The recovery of the Bible as one controlling story is important for Wright because that story provides the true worldview context for biblical scholarship, allowing all dimensions of the biblical text – theological, literary and historical – to find full expression.

An important part of the recovery of the Bible as one story will be the work of Christian theology. For Wright, Christian theology is not the abstract arrangement of timeless truths or propositions in some overarching system. Rather, it is occupied with articulating the biblical story. Christian theology claims to be telling the true story about the Creator and his world; it tells us what God is doing in history to restore his creation.[56] So Wright is interested in 'working in line with some recent studies in narrative theology'.[57] Narrative theology, or telling the story, will be a necessary part of the church's task as they live in 'act five' of the biblical story: 'the retelling of the story of the previous acts, as part of the required improvisation, is a necessary part of the task all through'.[58] Israel retold the story of creation and sin. Jesus retold the story of Israel in his parables. The gospel writers retold the story of Jesus. 'This may suggest, from a new angle, that the task of history, including historical theology and theological history, is itself mandated upon the followers of Jesus from within the biblical story itself.'[59]

A narrative biblical theology can play a role in making the church – including biblical scholars – aware of the grand story that ought to be shaping their whole lives. However, this approach is not popular among biblical scholars because of a number of criticisms that have been levelled against it.

Arguments Against Reading the Bible as a Grand Story

It will be obvious from the above that we believe there are compelling reasons for a narrative biblical theology. However, we are well aware that few biblical scholars agree or work in this way. In this final section we attempt to answer some of the major objections to our approach.

---

[55] Wright, *New Testament*, 130–31.

[56] For Wright's summary of the biblical story see *New Testament*, 132.

[57] Wright also wants to distance himself from a narrative theological approach that doesn't take history seriously. He says: 'Unlike most "narrative theology", however, I shall attempt to integrate this approach with a historical focus. And this combined approach grows out of the analysis offered above of worldviews and how they work' (*New Testament*, 132).

[58] Wright, *New Testament*, 142.

[59] Wright, *New Testament*, 142.

There is a variety of genres and theologies in Scripture and they simply cannot be contained within the single genre 'story'.

While biblical scholars nowadays recognize the value of a narrative approach to the many stories in the Bible, most are still opposed to treating the whole Bible as a large story. After all, they say, Scripture contains a variety of genres such as wisdom, law and prophecy, which simply are not narrative, and a variety of theologies. Furthermore, even the narratives in Scripture exhibit diversity – there are stories like Jonah and fourfold repetitions of the Jesus story like the Gospels. How can all of these possibly form a single unfolding story?

This is an important argument because it is vital that any viable biblical theology do justice to the diversity of material in Scripture, both in terms of genre and theological interests, and not force a false uniformity upon the Bible. However, we do not think that a narrative reading of the Bible imposes a false unity on the Bible, provided one has an appropriate understanding of narrative and provided one takes note of the narrative contexts of non-narrative biblical writings.

We like Peterson's description of the Bible as 'a sprawling capacious narrative',[60] because it resists a simplistic understanding of the Bible as a story. Clearly the Bible is not a single-volume, closely-knit story. It consists of 66 books, each with its own history. Nevertheless, an understanding of narrative like that of Peterson leaves ample room for reading this collection of books as a single story from creation to re-creation. Thus Gerard Loughlin, for example, draws on the 'narrative mechanics' of Gérard Genette to explain how the four Gospels can fit within a narrative approach to the Bible. Central to Genette's approach is a distinction between the narrative account and the story of what actually transpired.[61] The difference between the order in which events occur in the story compared with the narrative Genette calls *anachrony*, and he proposes a trajectory of anachrony from full agreement between story and narrative to radical discordance. Genette calls the tendency for narrative to go back in time *analepsis* and suggests that the fourfold repetition of the Gospels can be understood as an example of repeating analepsis.[62] According to Loughlin:

---

[60] 'Living into God's Story'. This article originally appeared on the website 'The Ooze: Conversation for a Journey' (www.theooze.com). It can be accessed at http://www.churchcrossing.com/articles.cfm?fuseaction=articledetail&id=122

[61] See the distinction between history and history writing in Greidanus, *Modern Preacher*, 82–94.

[62] Repetition is, of course, a great characteristic of literature. See Sternberg, *Poetics*. It should also be noted that literature slows down at key points in the plot. In the biblical story there can hardly be a more important point than the Christ event – this is another way of accounting for the fourfold Gospel.

The story is not given apart from its telling in narrative, but the narrative is not the same as the story. The order of the narrative can be different from that of the story; the narrative's duration is nearly always different from the story's duration; the narrative can tell many times what happened only once, and tell once what happened many times; and the distance between narrative and story can differ greatly, as also the instant of telling. Given these differences between story and narrative, we can see how the Bible can tell one story in various different ways. It does not narrate every part of the story – there are ellipses, as well as pauses; while other parts are told repeatedly, and from different instants of narration.[63]

Loughlin's account demonstrates well how contemporary theories of narrative provide adequate room for reading the Bible as a single story. But what of the variety of genres in the Bible such as law, prophecy and wisdom? It is quite correct that these are different genres to that of narrative, but in our opinion these writings in the Bible cannot be understood apart from the underlying narrative context.[64] All biblical law is embedded in a narrative context, as the Ten Commandments clearly demonstrate. They must be read in the context of 'I am the LORD your God who brought you out of Egypt …'. Of course, biblical law has a long history and reached the form in which we have it after considerable development, but nevertheless in its canonical form it is positioned in relation to the law given by Moses at Sinai – this is its narrative context in Scripture. Similarly with the prophets – the prophetic books are invariably linked into the story of Israel, indeed they cannot be understood apart from such links, whatever we make of the development underlying the final form as we have it. The Old Testament wisdom books are also linked closely into Israel's story, most particularly through association with Solomon and the God of Israel, who is the creator God. The book of Psalms undoubtedly grew into its present form over a long period of time. Nevertheless, in its final form it is associated especially with David and serves as a carefully edited volume to teach God's people how to respond to him through all the challenges of life.

We do not for a moment deny the value of a healthy historical criticism in reading the Bible.[65] However, we do wish to privilege the final form of Scripture as we have it, and we maintain that in this final form all the books, in one way or another, are closely connected to God's unfolding story. As Newbigin says, 'the Bible is essentially narrative in form … It contains, indeed, much else:

---

[63] Loughlin, *Telling*, 62.

[64] Loughlin, *Telling*, 62, suggests that we think of law, proverbs, psalms and songs as narrative 'pauses'.

[65] See the relevant essays in Bartholomew, et al. (eds.), *'Behind' the Text*. As Greidanus, *Modern Preacher*, 29, says, 'The critical question here is, "What kind of historical-critical method is applied to the Bible?"'

prayer, poetry, legislation, ethical teaching, and so on. But essentially it is a story.[66] In this respect we find James Barr's comments very helpful:

> But in my conception all of the Bible counts as 'story.' A people's story is not necessarily purely narrative: materials of many kinds may be slotted into a narrative structure, and this is done in the Hebrew Bible. Thus legal materials are inserted and appear, almost entirely, as part of the Moses story. In this case they are incorporated into the narrative. Others are more loosely attached: songs and hymns of the temple and of individuals, mostly collected in the Book of Psalms but some slotted into the narratives as in Samuel, Kings and Chronicles. It does not matter much what weight we place on the 'Solomonic' authorship of Wisdom books: whether because they came from Solomon, or because they were general lore of Israel, they are part of the story also.
>
> In the New Testament, the letters of great leaders and an apocalyptic book like Revelation form part of the story, along with the more strictly narrative writings. Thus in general, although not all parts of the Bible are narrative, the narrative character of the story elements provides a better framework into which the non-narrative parts may be fitted than any framework based on the non-narrative parts into which the story elements could be fitted.[67]

For these reasons, then, we do not think that the variety of genres in the Bible militates against reading it as a grand story. Just as in Job the polyphonic voices contribute to the whole, so the diverse genres contribute to the unfolding of this sprawling and capacious story of God's dealing with the world and his people, culminating in the new heavens and earth.

The issue of conflicting theologies in the Bible is a harder issue to deal with, and we can only make some initial comments here. For many biblical scholars it is perfectly obvious that the Bible is full of diverse and conflicting theologies and worldviews, often even within a single book,[68] whereas for most believers the Bible as a whole represents a unified perspective on reality.[69] Reading the Bible as a sprawling, capacious story helps us to an extent with this because it alerts us to the subtle unity of the whole and allows for considerable diversity among the sub-plots of the plot. Different parts of the story come from and relate to different times and address different audiences and contexts. There is development in the story, and so climax and dénouement occur at certain points which illuminate what comes before and cast it in a new light, and so on and so forth. Thus, for example, the fact that Old Testament wisdom literature

---

[66] Newbigin, *Open Secret*, 81.

[67] Barr, *Concept*, 356.

[68] Davies, 'Ethics', is a good example.

[69] Levenson, *The Hebrew Bible*, and Goldingay, *Theological Diversity*, are helpful sources in beginning to tackle this issue.

does not articulate a strong eschatology does not, in our opinion, mean that it expresses a theology in contradiction to the historical books and Paul's Epistles. Rather, with its limited focus on the order in creation and theodicy it contributes to the overarching story and biblical theology. In many ways the proof of the pudding is in the eating, and we suggest that a story approach to the Bible may yield a surprising sense of the coherence within which there is considerable movement and diversity.

Reading the Bible as a story undermines its reference to God and what he has done in and through Jesus Christ.

Brevard Childs levels this criticism against narrative approaches to biblical theology. In his *Biblical Theology* Childs includes narrative theology under 'Literary Approaches to Biblical Theology'.[70] Referring to Barr and Frei, he says that 'initially the appeal to the subject matter of the Bible as "story" served to shift the focus away from the perplexing problems of historical referentiality'.[71] Later he criticizes this narrative approach because it also sidesteps theological issues: 'many modern "narrative theologies" seek to avoid all dogmatic issues in the study of the Bible and seek "to render reality" only by means of retelling the story'.[72] The problem can be seen, notes Childs, by the fact that liberals and conservatives agree on the centrality of narrative but disagree on the nature of the biblical story. Again he notes that 'it has become increasingly evident that narrative theology, as often practised can also propagate a fully secular, nontheological reading of the Bible. The threat lies in divorcing the Bible when seen as literature from its theological reality to which scripture bears witness.'[73]

We share Childs' concern with this sort of literary approach to the Bible.[74] Today the tendency is indeed to understand story and narrative in primarily literary terms. James Barr notes a shift in the paradigm of biblical theology that moves from 'revelation in history' as the primary category to a 'literary mode of reading'.[75] Story is then qualified in a literary way: narrative is a literary structure that creates a symbolic world. Or, to put it another way, story is qualified in a linguistic way: the Bible offers a merely linguistically constructed narrative world. In this paradigm, the historical and theological dimensions of the biblical story are muted at best.

---

[70] Childs, *Biblical Theology*, 18–21.

[71] Childs, *Biblical Theology*, 18.

[72] Childs, *Biblical Theology*, 81.

[73] Childs, *Biblical Theology*, 723.

[74] See in this respect George Steiner's devastating review of Alter and Kermode's *Literary Guide to the Bible*.

[75] Barr, *Concept*, 351.

However, we do not think that attending to the narrative, literary dimension of the Bible of necessity takes one in this direction. The Bible *is* literature, but it is also history and theology, and a vital element in any literary approach to the Bible is how one relates the literary aspect to these other two, as N.T. Wright, Sternberg and Thiselton indicate.[76] In our opinion, a healthy story approach to the Bible opens up its theological witness to God in a powerful way because it does justice to the books in which God has revealed himself to us.[77] Through God's story, the true nature of the world and its creator and redeemer are shown to us, and we are invited to participate in that story. In other words, we wish to assert a narrative realism in terms of the relationship between *this* story and our world and its creator.

The underlying issue here, we suspect, is the relationship between the biblical story and our view of the world. In this respect it should be noted that we position ourselves somewhere between the Yale school and the Chicago school. We endorse the Yale school's emphasis on the particularity of the Christian story and on our need to indwell that story and allow it to absorb the world rather than vice versa. However, we share with the Chicago school an interest in the relationship between the Christian story and the nature of the world and its ontology. Indeed, we think that we know from Scripture *and* experience that the world and human life have a narrative shape that fits with the biblical story. Thus the shape of the Bible as story is perfectly designed to get us in touch with the true nature of reality.

It may also be important to note that it is unhelpful to think of 'story' as merely a *literary* category. Narrative is fundamental to history writing and, we suggest, to doctrine and theology. From our perspective, story provides a way of approaching the Bible that facilitates an integration of all three of these aspects of the Bible.[78]

In terms of the Bible as a grand story and theology, we should also draw attention to some of the insights that developed in our earlier dialogue with Oliver O'Donovan in *A Royal Priesthood*. A narrative, biblical theological type of reading of the Bible is fundamental to O'Donovan's highly creative political theology in his *The Desire of the Nations*.[79] However, O'Donovan rightly points out that *sola narratione* is insufficient for theological analysis. We need to develop theological concepts normed by Scripture in order to do theological

---

[76] Wright, *New Testament*, Sternberg, *Poetics*, and Thiselton, 'Models'.

[77] Seeing the Bible as story challenges the reductionism that takes place so that 'When the Epic of God is "pinned down and classified like a butterfly in a collector's case" (J.B. Metz), the narrative quality of faith is dissolved into propositionalism.' Fackre, 'Narrative', 199.

[78] See our discussion of Wright, above.

[79] See Bartholomew, 'Introduction' (2002).

analysis. O'Donovan's work is an excellent example of how reading the Bible in relation to its narrative shape may lead one to the theological realities it deals with rather than away from them.

Reading the Bible as a story undermines the critical question of historical reference.

For Barr, the attraction of 'story' is that it sidesteps the issue of historical reference and enables us to proceed with an approach to the Bible as a whole.[80] Many scholars have similarly found a literary approach to the Bible refreshing in that it enables one to get on with creative readings of the Bible without always getting bogged down in speculative analyses of that which lies behind the Bible.[81] For others, this very sidestepping is what is so disconcerting since there is much at stake theologically in God having acted *in history*. The issue of the Bible and historical reference is exceedingly complex at points, and we cannot deal with it adequately here.[82] Some proponents of a narrative approach to the Bible are content to leave the issue of historical reference to one side. While we welcome their work on the Bible as a story, we ourselves think that the issue of historical reference remains important.

Newbigin argues strongly for the importance of historical reference: 'the whole of Christian teaching would fall to the ground if it were the case that the life, death and resurrection of Jesus were not events in real history', and 'it is of the very essence of the matter that the events and places which you read in your Bible are part of the real world and the real history – the same world in which you live.'[83] What is at stake, Newbigin asks, in defending the events of the biblical story as things that really happened in history? His answer offers a highly nuanced discussion that cannot be reproduced here,[84] but at the heart of his argument is the contention that we can only understand our own lives as they are interwoven into the larger story of humankind. This story forms one single fabric of interconnected events. Is there meaning in that story? The Bible's answer is that the meaning of history as a whole is given in certain events, which are also an inextricable part of that history.[85] Those events form a

---

[80] Sidestep, but not ignore! For Barr, historical questions remain crucial.

[81] E.g., Ellingsen, *Integrity of Biblical Narrative*, who asserts that we should get on with preaching the biblical stories with the same flair and imagination with which they were written without insisting that they must have happened.

[82] Readers should consult Volume 4 of the Scripture and Hermeneutics Series, *'Behind' the Text*, in this respect.

[83] Newbigin, *Gospel*, 66, 68.

[84] Newbigin, *Gospel*, 66–79; *Open Secret*, 81–90.

[85] 'Within the Christian tradition the Bible is received as the testimony to those events in which God has disclosed ("revealed") the shape of the story as a whole, because in

narrative continuity beginning in Israel and running through Jesus and the church. In those particular events in Israel and the church, but especially in Jesus – in that historical story – God reveals the meaning and purpose of the human story as a whole. It is essential that those events, which give meaning to the whole, form a part of the history and world in which we live.[86] Our story is part of a story being enacted by God's providential control and redemptive action in history. These events do not illustrate the truth about the world; rather, in these events we find the truth about the world:

> The Bible does not tell stories that illustrate something true apart from the story. The Bible tells a story that is the story, the story of which our human life is a part. It is not that stories are part of human life, but that human life is part of a story.[87]

We agree with Gabriel Fackre, Avery Dulles and many others who insist that, if the biblical story is true, then it requires 'a reality that corresponds to it'.[88] This inclines us towards a maximalist understanding of the historicity of the Bible but it does *not* close down for us the thorny issues of *how* the Bible reached its present form in relation to the events that underlie the biblical text.[89] Old Testament legal texts, to take one example, evidence a complex history, and any approach to the Bible as a true story must take full account of this textual history.

Whichever view one takes in relation to the biblical story and history, it is important to note that reflection on the historicity of the biblical story needs to *first* wrestle seriously with the shape of that story. This is precisely what has *not* been done in biblical studies. Biblical scholars have too often leapt to diachronic analysis or questions of historicity without first attending closely to the shape of the texts in front of them. As the literary turn has pushed us to attend to the shape of the biblical texts in their final form we find inevitably that the historical questions look quite different in the light of synchronic analysis of the texts. Similarly, we suggest that detailed attention to the Bible as a grand story should *precede* attention to the question of historical reference.[90]

Jesus the beginning and the end of the story, the alpha and omega, are revealed, made known, disclosed' (Newbigin, *Open Secret*, 85).

[86] 'The biblical story is not a separate story: it is part of the unbroken fabric of world history. The Christian faith is that this is the place in the whole fabric where its pattern has been disclosed, even though the weaving is not yet finished' (Newbigin, *Open Secret*, 88).

[87] Newbigin, *Open Secret*, 82.

[88] Fackre, 'Narrative', 197.

[89] On the maximalist-minimalist distinction see Bartholomew, 'Introduction' (2003), 5, 6. For an example of a believing approach to these historical questions in relation to the Ten Commandments see Bartholomew, '*Warranted*', 75, 76.

[90] This is what makes Sternberg's comments about the historicity of the Hebrew Bible so interesting. See Sternberg, *Poetics*, 32–35. The typical strategy of biblical scholars

The Bible may well be able to be read as a grand narrative, but it shares in this respect in the oppressive character basic to all metanarratives.

'Under' historical criticism, believing scholars had to struggle for some sense of the unity of Scripture.[91] Nowadays the battle has far more to do with ideology; even – perhaps especially – if the unity of the Bible as a story can be defended, the argument is that precisely as such a grand story it is deeply oppressive, as are all metanarratives. This critique of metanarratives, associated in particular with Jean-François Lyotard and Michel Foucault, has arisen as modernity began to unravel with the environmental crisis and the wars and holocaust in a century supposed to epitomize 'progress'. In the process, the grand narratives of science and progress have come in for scathing critique. In the process, the pendulum has swung right across so that all grand stories tend to be regarded with acute suspicion; all we can tolerate are small, local stories.

Apart from the fact that the biblical story is a non-modern metanarrative, it remains questionable whether grand narratives can in fact be avoided. In our opinion, 'the postmodern' suspicion of grand narrative – indeed its general neglect of narrative altogether – does not mean that it avoids taking a (grand) position on reality. It is possible that its rejection of grand story may conceal its own, coercive commitments. In our opinion, grand narratives or worldviews[92] cannot be avoided – part of being human means indwelling and living out some such basic narrative, albeit unconsciously.[93] Unavoidably, these narratives compete with each other and claim to tell the truth about the world in which we live, and undoubtedly some are much healthier than others. Thus, it is not a question of whether we indwell a grand narrative, but rather of which

---

in this respect is redolent of Lash's point ('When?', 143) that 'In the self assured world of modernity, people seek to make sense of the Scriptures, instead of hoping, with the aid of the Scriptures, to make some sense of themselves.' However, as Lash, 'Performing', 42, says, 'The performance of the New Testament enacts the conviction that these texts are most appropriately read as the story of Jesus, the story of everyone else, and the story of God.'

[91] See Levenson, *Hebrew Bible*, for a sense of just how fragmenting historical criticism can be.

[92] Perhaps the category of 'worldview' can help to express the foundational significance of the biblical story. A worldview is the articulation of the most basic beliefs you have about the world, and through which you view everything else. Wolters (*Creation Regained*, 2) offers the following definition of a worldview: 'the comprehensive framework of one's basic beliefs about things'. The Scripture offers a 'narrative framework' that offers a lens for understanding and a map for guiding us in the world. Story is foundationally a worldview category.

[93] In this respect see Wolters, *Creation Regained*.

one we indwell. Our contention is that the norm for the Christian story is the Bible, which itself has the shape of a grand story. Christians should therefore make every effort to allow their metanarratives to be normed by Scripture.[94]

Is the biblical story oppressive? This is a debate now developing in biblical studies, funded by the appropriation of post-colonial discourse, liberation theology, feminism, queer reading and so on. As Richard Bauckham rightly notes in his chapter in this volume on monotheism, once one has argued that monotheism is central to the whole Bible, one still has to attend to the ideological critique clamouring for attention. In our view it is vital to *first* attend to the shape of the biblical story as a whole before engaging in ideological critique. Scripture is authoritative in its totality, and questions of ideology must be seen in the context of Scripture as a whole.

It is important to note that in the history of the church the biblical story has been used as an oppressive metanarrative. This has happened when the Bible was linked with coercive political and military power. This, however, in our opinion, is to betray the biblical story. The cross stands at the centre of the story and is the hermeneutical clue for the entire story. When one sees the cross as the central clue, the Bible can again be seen as the liberating story we believe it to be. Newbigin argues that what makes any metanarrative inherently oppressive is that it looks to an intrahistorical triumph for its cause.[95] The biblical story is unique at just this point; it looks to an event, which points us to God's triumph beyond history. The cross points to the unique way in which the victory of God has been gained – through suffering and weakness and waiting for the final vindication of God at the end of history. Living in the biblical story means following the same path, protecting a freedom that will allow a response to the gospel that is uncoerced.

Conclusion

Andrew Walker challenges us to face the fact that,

> We are on the way to postmodernity, and already we are caught in an electronic field of blinding imagery and synthesized sounds. Where are our candles, smells and elec-

---

[94] We recognize that in practice Christians will tell the biblical story in different ways. And we believe that all tellings of the biblical story are contextual. For example, Kings tells the story differently during the exile than Chronicles after the exile. Their contexts determined their selection, arrangement and interpretation. In this way different tellings can be mutually enriching. Our concern at this stage is to encourage Christians to get on with telling the story so that these differences can emerge and then enrichment and/or real debates can begin.

[95] Newbigin, *Word*, 204.

tric bells? Where are our images of light and shade, our music of splendour, our divine dramas, the sacred dance? We have a story but no one can see it. We tell the story, but no one can hear it.[96]

Our contention, however, is that in biblical theology we do not tell the story! There is, in our view, far too little energy directed towards telling the biblical story as a grand narrative. In practical theology, missiology and ethics there is a growing chorus of voices calling for such a reading of the Bible, and we think that an answer to that call is long overdue in biblical theology. In our opinion, the objections to a narrative biblical theology do not stand up to critical scrutiny, and while we do not argue that this is the only way to do biblical theology, we think that it is an important approach. Some of the recent, creative trends in biblical interpretation such as literary and rhetorical methods position biblical scholars well to attend to the biblical story with creative nuance and detail – we long for scholars to move in this direction, and we agree with Newbigin and Wright that there is much at stake in this respect.

In our own *The Drama of Scripture* we have made an attempt to tell the story of the Bible. Doubtless our attempt is deeply influenced by our own theological traditions and inadequate in all sorts of ways. We acknowledge this openly, but we would much prefer a response of multiple, better attempts to tell the story than a rehash of the arguments against such an approach. As Walker says,

> in the act of telling the story, modern theologians cannot make people believe it. What they can do, however, is to stand up for the story, and learn again to tell it in the way it was meant to be told. ... It is the Church's grand narrative, which is essential not only for its own identity but for the salvation of the world.[97]

---

[96] Walker, *Telling the Story*, 197.
[97] Walker, *Telling the Story*, 53.

Bibliography

Barr, J., *The Concept of Biblical Theology: An Old Testament Perspective* (Minneapolis: Fortress Press, 1999)

Bartholomew, C.G., 'Introduction', in *A Royal Priesthood? The Use of the Bible Ethically and Politically* (ed. C.G. Bartholomew, J. Chaplin, R. Song and A. Wolters; SHS 3; Carlisle: Paternoster; Grand Rapids: Zondervan, 2002), 1–45

—, 'Introduction', in *'Behind' the Text: History and Biblical Interpretation* (ed. C.G. Bartholomew, C.S. Evans, M. Healy and M. Rae; SHS 4; Carlisle: Paternoster; Grand Rapids: Zondervan, 2003), 1–16

—, '*Warranted* Biblical Interpretation: Alvin Plantinga's "Two (or More) Kinds of Scripture Scholarship"', in *'Behind' the Text: History and Biblical Interpretation* (ed. C.G. Bartholomew, C.S. Evans, M. Healy and M. Rae; SHS 4; Carlisle: Paternoster; Grand Rapids: Zondervan, 2003), 58–78

Bartholomew, C.G., C.S. Evans, M. Healy and M. Rae (eds.), *'Behind' the Text: History and Biblical Interpretation* (SHS 4; Carlisle: Paternoster; Grand Rapids: Zondervan, 2003)

Bartholomew, C.G., and M.W. Goheen, *The Drama of Scripture: Finding Our Place in the Biblical Story* (Grand Rapids: Baker Academic, 2004)

Buss, M.J., 'The Meaning of History', in *Theology as History* (ed. J.M. Robinson and J.B. Cobb; New York: Harper Books, 1967), 135–54

Childs, B.S., *Biblical Theology of the Old and New Testaments: Theological Reflection on the Christian Bible* (Minneapolis: Fortress Press, 1992)

Clowney, E.P., *Preaching and Biblical Theology* (Phillipsburg, NJ: Presbyterian and Reformed Publishing, 1979)

Davies, P.R., 'Ethics and the Old Testament', in *The Bible in Ethics: The Second Sheffield Colloquium* (ed. J.W. Rogerson, et al.; JSOTSup 207; Sheffield: Sheffield Academic Press, 1995), 164–73

Ellingsen, M., *The Integrity of Biblical Narrative* (Minneapolis: Fortress Press, 1990)

Fackre, G., 'Narrative Theology from an Evangelical Perspective', in *Faith and Narrative* (ed. K.E. Yandell; Oxford and New York: Oxford University Press, 2001), 188–201

Fee, G., and D. Stuart, *How to Read the Bible for All Its Worth: A Guide to Understanding the Bible* (Grand Rapids: Zondervan, 1982)

Frei, H., *The Eclipse of Biblical Narrative* (New Haven: Yale University Press, 1974)

Gerkin, C.V., *Widening the Horizons: Pastoral Responses to a Fragmented Society* (Philadelphia: Westminster Press, 1986)

Goldingay, J., *Theological Diversity and the Authority of the Old Testament* (Grand Rapids: Eerdmans, 1987)

Goldsworthy, G.L., *Preaching the Whole Bible as Christian Scripture* (Downers Grove, IL: InterVarsity Press, 2000)

Greidanus, S., *Sola Scriptura: Problems and Principles in Preaching Historical Texts* (Toronto: Wedge, 1970)

—, *The Modern Preacher and the Ancient Text* (Grand Rapids: Eerdmans, 1988)

Hafemann, S. (ed.), *Biblical Theology: Retrospect and Prospect* (Downers Grove, IL: InterVarsity Press, 2002)

Hasel, G., *Old Testament Theology: Basic Issues in the Current Debate* (Grand Rapids: Eerdmans, 4th edn, 1991)

Hauerwas, S., *The Peaceable Kingdom: A Primer in Christian Ethics* (Notre Dame: University of Notre Dame Press, 1983)

Hauerwas, S., and L.G. Jones (eds.), *Why Narrative? Readings in Narrative Theology* (Grand Rapids: Eerdmans, 1989)

Holwerda, B., 'De Heilshistorie in de Prediking' in *Begonnen Hebbende van Mozes* (Terneuzen: Littoij, 1953), 79–118

Lash, N., 'Performing the Scriptures', in *Theology on the Way to Emmaus* (London: SCM Press, 1986), 37–46

—, 'When Did Theologians Lose Interest in Theology?', in *Theology and Dialogue: Essays in Conversation with George Lindbeck* (ed. B.D. Marshall; Notre Dame: University of Notre Dame Press, 1990), 131–47

Levenson, J.D., *The Hebrew Bible, The Old Testament and Historical Criticism: Jews and Christians in Biblical Studies* (Louisville, KY: Westminster Press, 1993)

Loughlin, G., *Telling God's Story: Bible, Church, and Narrative Theology* (Cambridge: Cambridge University Press, 1996)

Lyotard, J-F., *The Postmodern Condition: A Report on Knowledge* (trans. G. Bennington and B. Massumi; Minneapolis: University of Minnesota Press, 1984)

MacIntyre, A., *After Virtue* (Notre Dame: University of Notre Dame Press, 2nd edn, 1984)

Newbigin, L., 'Christ and Cultures', *SJT* 31 (1978), 1–22

—, *The Other Side of 1984: Questions for the Churches* (Geneva: World Council of Churches, 1983)

—, 'The Role of the Bible in Our Church' (unpublished remarks given at a meeting of the United Reformed Forward Policy Group, 17–18 April 1985)

—, *The Gospel in a Pluralist Society* (Grand Rapids: Eerdmans, 1989)

—, 'Response to "Word of God?" by John Coventry SJ', *The Gospel and our Culture Newsletter* 8 (1991), 2

—, *Unfinished Agenda: An Autobiography* (Edinburgh: St Andrews Press, exp. and rev. edn, 1993)

—, *A Word in Season: Perspectives on Christian World Missions* (Grand Rapids: Eerdmans, 1994)

—, *The Open Secret: An Introduction to the Theology of Mission* (Grand Rapids: Eerdmans, rev. edn, 1995)

—, *Proper Confidence: Faith, Doubt, and Certainty in Christian Discipleship* (Grand Rapids: Eerdmans, 1995)

—, 'Missions', in *Concise Encyclopedia of Preaching* (ed. W.H. Willimon and R. Lischer; Louisville, KY: Westminster John Knox Press, 1995), 335–36

—, *A Walk through the Bible* (Louisville, KY: Westminster John Knox Press, 1999)

Pannenberg, W., 'Response to Discussion', in *Theology as History* (ed. J.M Robinson and J.B. Cobb Jr; trans. W.A. Beardslee, et al., New York: Harper & Row, 1967), 221–76

Rhodes, A., *The Mighty Acts of God* (Richmond, VA: CLC Press, 1964)

Ridderbos, H.N., *When the Time Had Fully Come: Studies in New Testament Theology* (Grand Rapids: Eerdmans, 1957)

—, *Redemptive History and the New Testament Scriptures* (trans. H. De Jongst; rev. R. Gaffin; Phillipsburg: Presbyterian and Reformed Publishing, 2nd rev. edn, 1988)

—, *The Coming of the Kingdom* (trans. H. De Jongst; Phillipsburg: Presbyterian and Reformed Publishing, 1962)

—, *Paul: An Outline of His Theology* (trans. R. DeWitt; Grand Rapids: Eerdmans, 1975)

Steiner, G., 'Review of R. Alter and F. Kermode: *The Literary Guide to the Bible*', *The New Yorker* (11 Jan. 1988), 94–98

Sternberg, M., *The Poetics of Biblical Narrative* (Bloomington: Indiana University Press, 1987)

Stiver, D., *The Philosophy of Religious Language: Sign, Symbol and Story* (Oxford: Basil Blackwell, 1996)

Stroup, G.W., *The Promise of Narrative Theology: Recovering the Gospel in the Church* (Atlanta: John Knox Press, 1981)

Thiselton, A.C., 'On Models and Methods: A Conversation with Robert Morgan', in *The Bible in Three Dimensions* (ed. D.J.A. Clines, et al.; JSOTSup 87; Sheffield: JSOT Press, 1990), 337–56

Walker, A., *Telling the Story: Gospel, Mission and Culture* (London: SPCK, 1996)

Walsh, B.J., and J.R. Middleton, *The Transforming Vision: Shaping a Christian Worldview* (Downers Grove, IL: InterVarsity Press, 1984)

Wolters, A., *Creation Regained: Biblical Basics for a Reformational Worldview* (Grand Rapids: Eerdmans, 1985)

Wolterstorff, N., *Reason within the Bounds of Religion* (Grand Rapids: Eerdmans, 2nd edn, 1984)

Wright, N.T., 'How Can the Bible Be Authoritative?', *VE* 21 (1991), 7–32

—, *The New Testament and the People of God* (London: SPCK, 1992)

—, *Jesus and the Victory of God* (London: SPCK, 1996)

7

The Problem of 'Biblical Theology'
James D. G. Dunn

Introduction

Nine years ago I wrote a piece for a German symposium on biblical theology, edited by C. Dohmen and T. Söding and published in 1995. It attempted to pose what I saw as the key problem of biblical theology – that the very concept is contested and inextricably caught in the tension between the claims of two distinct religions, Judaism and Christianity, regarding the same texts, the same Bible. The concern of the paper was to indicate the character of the problem, to clarify its complexity and to outline its chief subject matter. I did not attempt to resolve the problem, since I regard it as irresolvable so long as Judaism and Christianity remain distinct. And even to begin a discussion of the aspects of the problem indicated would have required at least a small book. But to be clear on the fact and nature of the problem, to pose the problem itself as sharply as possible so that it cannot be easily dismissed or marginalized seemed to me to be still an important and valuable challenge. And though the recent course of my life and my current research interests have left me insufficient time to maintain reading in this area, it still seemed to me a contribution of potential value to pose the same problem afresh in the current symposium, using the unpublished English version of the 1995 article. The point is that the problem is the same – it will not go away – so that a formulation which reflects more of the 1990s than of the first decade of the twenty-first century can pose it just as sharply. If anything, the ongoing dialogue between Jews and Christians and the growing respect for the convictions of each by the other make it increasingly important to recognize and to face up to the problem. As in ecumenical dialogue within Christianity, once the initial enthusiasm over how much is agreed has passed, the dialogue can only progress if the central problems (here of a contested understanding of 'Bible') are taken on board.

Posing the Problem

The problem I wish to focus on is posed by the titles of three major studies on the theme of biblical theology from the early 1990s – *Biblische Theologie des Neuen Testaments*, the title chosen both by Hans Hübner and by Peter Stuhlmacher, and *Biblical Theology of the Old and New Testaments*, by Brevard Childs. The problem is that 'biblical' is being used in these titles in different ways. 1) The titles assume a Christian perspective, in which there is already an entity called 'the New Testament', and, explicitly or implicitly, another entity called 'the Old Testament'. In this perspective the 'Bible' is the Christian Bible made up of these two Testaments. 2) At the same time, a 'biblical theology of the New Testament' is inevitably an attempt to expound the New Testament writings from within (albeit within the canon), where a major explanatory key is the New Testament writers' use of the Old Testament.[1] But since for the New Testament writers there was as yet no New Testament as such, 'Bible' here denotes only the (Jewish) Scriptures.

Thus the very titles used in the enterprise of 'biblical theology' immediately press upon us the recognition that these writings are described as 'Bible/Scripture' because they function as Bible/Scripture for two different religious communities – the Jewish and the Christian. The point would have been difficult to avoid anyway, since the interdependence of a text, particularly a religious text, with its interpretative community, the community for which it is Scripture, is more or less self-evident ('Scripture' for whom?) and has rightly been an emphasis in recent broader hermeneutical discussion. It is this, however, which causes tension between the two usages of 'biblical theology'. For, on the one hand, Christianity is unique among world religions in the fact that it has absorbed the Scriptures of what is universally understood to be a quite separate religion and has claimed them as its own. But is the Old Testament only 'Bible' as Old Testament, that is, as interpreted by and in the light of the New Testament? If on the other hand, the Jewish Scriptures are 'Bible' independently of the Christian writings, should they not be allowed(!) to have their own voice independently of the New Testament?[2] Is a Jewish theological interpretation of their own Scriptures not equally 'biblical theology'? Childs sees the issue and poses it a number of times,[3] but he clearly understands 'biblical theology' as a Christian enterprise through and through.[4] My point, however, is that biblical theology, whether as a merely

---

[1] So particularly Hübner, *Biblische Theologie*, 1:28.

[2] Cf. Rendtorff, *Canon and Theology*.

[3] Childs, *Biblical Theology*, e.g., 77–78, 91, 444–45.

[4] Childs, *Biblical Theology*, 85–88.

descriptive exercise[5] or as also a prescriptive exercise (feeding faith and praxis), cannot be carried forward without close regard for the fundamental issues of self-identity and mutual recognition at the heart of Jewish/Christian dialogue.

This problem cannot be ignored. It is, in fact, constitutive of 'biblical theology' properly so called. Of course Christians could ignore the fact that their Old Testament is also the Jewish Bible and affirm that their 'biblical theology' is concerned only with their Bible. But that would immediately run counter to central concerns of the New Testament writers themselves, for whom the Jewish Scriptures were the only Bible. It was crucial to earliest Christian self-understanding and to New Testament apologetic generally that the gospel they were proclaiming was in direct continuity with those writings which were already recognized as Scripture by Jews as a whole and not just by Christians. And Jews, insofar as they might be interested in a subject called 'biblical theology',[6] could even more readily ignore those writings added to their Scriptures by the Christians and confine their interests to their Bible alone. But that would too easily sideline the question whether Jesus ought to be counted as one of their own prophets (or rabbis, or messiah?); and once Jesus the prophet from Nazareth is brought into play, dialogue with Christians becomes inescapable and cannot easily be excluded from the proper concerns of a Jewish biblical theology. Here the issues of continuity/discontinuity are at the heart of biblical theology.

In other words, the dynamic of biblical theology is that its subject matter is determined and defined by texts which are Israel's Scripture (the Torah or Tanak as a whole) and not *merely* the '*Old* Testament', but which are also Christian Scripture ('the Scriptures' for the New Testament writers) and which therefore have some sort of defining role for the texts which were to become the '*New* Testament'. Does 'New' indicate movement onto a different plane of revelation, with 'Old' subordinated to a merely background role? Or is 'New' a new form of the 'Old', with each vital to a proper reception and understanding of the other?

The Fundamental Nature of the Problem

Recognition of these dimensions of the problem helps to focus on this as the fundamental problem of biblical theology. Other questions, however important in themselves, simply serve to feed into this central problem.

---

[5] Cf. Räisänen, *Beyond New Testament Theology*.
[6] But see Levenson, 'Why Jews Are Not Interested'.

The search for a centre

One of these has been *the question of, or search for, a centre or unifying principle*. It is certainly possible to assert one such for the New Testament – Jesus himself, or faith in Jesus as Christ and Lord, or some such formulation. But the quest for such a single formulation in regard to the Jewish Scriptures has never been satisfactorily resolved.[7] And when Christian New Testament is added to Jewish Tanak, the objective becomes even more elusive; to assert that Jesus is the unifying centre of the Christian Bible simply re-poses the fundamental problem afresh. The issue, however, can be reformulated in the light of our initial reflections, for the interrelation of Scripture and religious community reminds us that unifying principles are likely to be several and not single. *Diversity* is also constitutive of both these religious groups and their Scriptures.[8]

The issue for biblical theology at this point, then, is whether, given the diversity within the Jewish Scriptures, the further diversity of the New Testament is simply an extension of the same diversity? If we can talk now of 'Judaisms' in late Second Temple Judaism, and of 'Christianities' already within first-century Christianity, what is the overlap between these Judaisms and Christianities? Is the self-understanding embodied in the New Testament documents still part of the spectrum of a diverse Jewish self-understanding expressed in or based upon their (Jewish) Scriptures? The fundamental question of biblical theology is whether the diversity *between* the Testaments involves a discontinuity that decisively undermines claims to continuity.

The question of canon

The counterpart to the question of unity and diversity is that of *canon*, which writers on biblical theology inevitably find unavoidable, since canon defines the content and scope of the 'Bible'. The difficulty in this case is that for the crucial period when the New Testament was being written, but was not yet 'the New Testament', the boundaries of the canon were fuzzy (the scope of the Writings, Hebrew or Greek, and the status of ben Sira, etc., not to mention the subsequent issues of the status of the *gilyonim* and the *sifrei minim*, and on the Christian side, of Hebrews, Revelation, etc.). This degree of indeterminateness at just the stage where 'biblical' is already ambiguous would seem to call in question the very viability of the enterprise – if we do not know clearly what is 'in the Bible' how can we speak with clarity of a 'biblical theology'? – especially as the fundamental problem is whether any of the traditions and writings now in the New Testament belong wholly within the fuzzy area round the Hebrew/Greek canon of the Jewish Bible.

---

[7] Cf., e.g., Reventlow, *Hauptproblem*, ch. 4.
[8] See, e.g., Goldingay, *Theological Diversity*, and Dunn, *Unity*.

Canon, however, is in effect coterminous with community[9] – an observation which prompts a line of reflection complementary to the last. For the fact is that there was a similar fuzziness round the community known as 'Israel' (what happened to the ten tribes, the status of proselytes, alien residents, Jewish 'sinners', etc.?); and yet there was a sufficiently identifiable entity called 'Israel', and subsequently 'Jew' and 'Judaism'. Just so there was an identifiable entity called 'Scripture' (singular). In both cases identity can be recognized and sufficiently defined, even when the boundaries remain blurred. If, then, the question of canon and its limits remains obscure, the problem can and must focus more on the central features round which community cohered and which identified the community as that community which acknowledged that Scripture. And the fundamental problem of biblical theology can thus be redefined as the question of how the New Testament writers (and the Christianity they were beginning to define) handle the identity markers that gave, and still give, the Jewish Scriptures (and community) their coherence.

Synchronic versus diachronic readings

To cite but one other issue: if 'Bible' is only to be defined as such from the time that both canons were regarded as closed, then the temptation is to read the biblical documents synchronically, with the character and content of the resultant biblical theology determined by the concerns of the community of the period chosen, so that we have to speak properly of a patristic biblical theology, or a reformation biblical theology, or a social-scientific biblical theology, or whatever. But the fundamental problem of biblical theology as defined above, as defined indeed (I would claim) by its own subject matter, makes a diachronic reading of the biblical texts unavoidable. For the texts in question functioned as 'Bible' for communities whose self-perception was changing and developing, and the symbiotic relation between Scripture and community means that the 'biblical theology' they were enacting changed and developed too. The religion of Israel (still less the religion of the patriarchs) embodied within the Jewish Scriptures is not synonymous with the Judaism which recognized these Scriptures as canonical, no more than the ministry and proclamation of Jesus or even the theology of Paul is identical with the Christianity which agreed the New Testament canon. A biblical theology conceived exclusively or even primarily in synchronic terms cannot hope to cope fully with the diverse and changing emphases of the biblical texts whose scriptural force was always context-related to one degree or other. Worse still, it cannot cope with the fundamental problem of whether the changed and changing emphases of the New Testament writers fall within the scope of a

---

[9] Sanders, *Canon*, xv.

dynamic biblical theology which can be recognized as such by Jew as well as Christian.

The fundamental problem of biblical theology, therefore, must focus on that vital period of overlap, when there was still a possibility that some or all of the New Testament writings might be included within the diversity and still-developing corpus of the only Scripture then recognized by Jews and first Christians, when Second Temple Judaism was not yet rabbinic Judaism, when the faith and worship of Paul and the other *Christianoi* was not yet 'Christianity'. Beyond that period the term 'biblical' loses the flexibility which allows it to be used in a way which both recognizes the Jewish Scriptures as 'Bible' in their own right and takes seriously the character of the New Testament writings as Scripture in the making. Beyond that period the term 'biblical' becomes fixed and confessional, a question-begging provocation to Jews whose Scriptures comprise the bulk of the Christian Bible, and the term is unable even to express fully the mindset and theology of Jesus and the New Testament writers themselves.

The problem, of course, is not limited to the strictly biblical material. Wherever there is claim to an ongoing revelation (we believe in the Holy Spirit), that claim will stand in tension with the authority of canonical texts. To say 'Scripture *and* tradition' is fine, until it becomes an issue of Scripture versus tradition. If the resolution in such a case lies along the lines of a concept of Scripture as 'living tradition', as I believe, then that simply reinforces the importance of according particular weight to the living dynamic of biblical theology which comes to expression in the very writing of the New Testament documents themselves.

The Central Subject Matter of Biblical Theology

The most obvious test of the viability of biblical theology thus defined, therefore, is provided by the central defining features embodied within their Scriptures by which each community recognized itself over a period as a recognizable religion. These features are, on one hand, the enduring identity markers of monotheism, Israel and Torah,[10] and on the other hand of Jesus, cross and resurrection.[11] The fundamental issue for biblical theology is how these relate to each other – whether the message of Jesus or the gospel about Jesus introduced a radical disjuncture with the central features of what we may fairly call Israel's biblical theology.

---

[10] Dunn, *Partings*.
[11] Dunn, *Unity*.

The unity of God

There is no doubt that *the unity of God* is a fundamental defining characteristic of Jewish faith. Whatever its prehistory, by the time we can speak of a Jewish Bible the issue is clear-cut, as expressed classically in the Shema, Second Isaiah, ben Sira and the resistance of the Maccabees to Hellenistic syncretism. It is true that attempts have recently been made to argue that Israelite religion made room for a second god, 'the great angel'.[12] But the attempts founder precisely on good biblical theology reasoning. Whereas some passages read atomistically may seem to give scope to such an argument, the same passages read biblically – that is, as part of or consonant with the Scriptures of the religion which confessed the Shema – have to be understood as themselves an expression of that same monotheism.

What is often forgotten is that God so understood is one of the equally fundamental presuppositions of New Testament theology. The point is often missed, simply because explicit Christian claims regarding God appear so rarely. A doctrine of God built only from the New Testament would have to work with allusion and inference more than with explicit exposition. Consequently, a New Testament theology which dealt only with items of faith which were clearly documented and expounded in the New Testament might well omit a section on God – taking it for granted, as the New Testament writers seem to, or subordinating it under Christology, as in effect many New Testament theologies do. *Theo*logy in the narrow sense is what Nils Dahl has called 'the neglected factor in New Testament theology'. Here again it is, in effect, biblical theology that saves us from a reading of New Testament theology that is too dependent on the merely explicit. For, of course, the reason why the theme is so neglected is because for the New Testament writers it was axiomatic; the point of significance for biblical theology is precisely that these writers felt no need to reformulate the doctrine of God.[13] It is only a biblical theology reading of the text, then (constantly aware of the biblical theology out of which the New Testament writers themselves were writing), which prevents a serious mistake being made here. The point emerges not from a reading of the New Testament as part of the Christian Bible, but from a reading of the New Testament itself which respects the theological perspectives, taken-for-granteds and allusions of a faith which was biblically shaped and informed through and through.

The key issue, of course, is whether Christian faith in Jesus as expressed within the New Testament breaches that monotheism. It is a key issue for biblical theology, for if the conclusion is affirmative, then it actually becomes

---

[12] See Barker, *Great Angel*.
[13] Childs, *Biblical Theology*, 367.

questionable whether New Testament Christology can be counted part of biblical theology. It could only be so in terms of a Christian faith that rode roughshod over one of the fundamental Jewish axioms; it could only be a biblical theology in which Jewish Scripture was no more than *Old* Testament, wholly subservient to New. It is a key issue, in other words, because it helps define what biblical theology is.

In fact it can be strongly argued that New Testament Christology stays within the bounds of the monotheism expressed in the Jewish Scriptures, that the high wisdom Christology of Paul or John or the angel Christology of Revelation simply extended the vigour of the wisdom reflection and the powerful impact of apocalyptic visions already present in the Jewish Scriptures, and extended beyond them in alternative patterns by other Jewish writers of the Second Temple period (Jewish apocalypses, Philo, etc.).[14] It is true that many assume that early Christianity did breach Jewish monotheism, and indeed the rabbis were soon to take it for granted that the Christian *minim* had abandoned the creedal belief in the unity of God. But here again biblical theology, properly so called, can provide a crucial check. For biblical theology at this point cannot simply be content with a description of New Testament Christology as going beyond Jewish monotheism (though that could arguably be a task and conclusion to which *New Testament* theology came). The *biblical* theology question is rather whether the monotheism of the Jewish Scriptures continues to be a controlling element in New Testament Christology – that is, not simply in helping exegetes to fill out the axiomatic character of the earliest Christian monotheistic presupposition, but also as a continuing controlling element which, properly respected, should prevent subsequent Christian interpretation of New Testament Christology from ignoring its monotheistic framework. It is the proper biblical theology respect for the emphasis of the Jewish Scriptures in their own right that prevents Christianity from lapsing into a bitheism or tritheism.

Israel

A second defining theme of biblical theology has to be *Israel*. For Israel is constitutive of the Jewish Scriptures. Not only is the theme of God's choice of and expectation for the people of Israel an integrating motif running through the bulk of these Scriptures, but, of course, they are primarily Israel's Scriptures. It is only as Israel's Scriptures and because they were acknowledged by Israel that they are Scriptures in the first place. Christians did not attempt to decide their canonical status (even as Old Testament) independently of the de facto prior decision of Israel on the subject. The fact that the Christian canon of the Old Testament coincides so completely with that of the Hebrew Bible simply

---

[14] Dunn, *Partings*, chs. 9 – 11.

documents the point. The fuzziness of the Christian canon(s) of the Bible – the status of the Old Testament apocrypha or of writings like 1 Enoch (in the canon of the Ethiopian church) – simply reflects the degree of fuzziness which pertained in late Second Temple Judaism itself.

Of course the horizon of the Jewish Scriptures stretches beyond Israel herself – a crucial factor in biblical theology. Of major importance within the Jewish Bible is the recognition of the one God as creator, as God of all creation and all peoples; and its soteriology extends to new creation and includes thought of Israel herself as a light to the nations. Nevertheless, the election of Israel, and the understanding of God as the God of Israel, is so fundamental within Jewish self-understanding, so axiomatic for Jewish biblical theology, that the issue of continuity between Jewish and Christian self-understanding on this point is inescapable as a fundamental question of biblical theology.[15]

In blunt terms the issue is whether Christianity can somehow claim to be part of Israel, incorporated within (eschatological) Israel. It comes to focus in such specific questions as whether Jesus' hope was (simply) for the restoration of Israel; to what extent Paul's argument in Romans 9 – 11 is an affirmation (or denial?) of Israel's election; and how to evaluate the assumption of the opening verses of James and 1 Peter that the letters were addressed to (the twelve tribes[!] in) the Diaspora. Of course it would be possible to develop the old covenant/new covenant antithesis of Hebrews in particular, and to argue with the most emphatic voices of the second century (Barnabas, Justin, Melito) that the Christians have replaced the Jews as the real people of God. But that early line of Christian self-understanding opened up the whole fateful *adversus Judaeos* tradition with its evil outworking in Christian anti-Semitism, so that for other than biblical theology reasons it must be resisted.

In fact, however, biblical theology considerations are sufficient to refute such a line of interpretation. For the attempts of the first Christians to define themselves were wholly within the parameters provided by the Jewish Scriptures; the very attempt was itself an exercise of biblical theology. To be more specific, the question whether Paul's argument in Galatians 3 and Romans 4, that the gospel fulfils the third strand of the promise to Abraham (the blessing for the nations), is viable and persuasive is first and foremost a question for biblical theology. That is, it is a question to be answered primarily in terms of the biblical theology of the Jewish Scriptures (not just with reference to Genesis. 12:3, etc., as Christian Old Testament). If it were simply a matter of *Christian* exegesis of the patriarchal promises, the nerve of Paul's own theological concern at this point would be cut (he wanted the argument to be persuasive as an exegesis of his own people's Scriptures) – which is to say, the nerve of biblical theology at this crucial point would be cut.

---

[15] Cf. Stuhlmacher, *Biblische Theologie*, 38.

A major consideration here may well be the fact that the most confrontational terms ('Judaism' and 'Christianity') are themselves so marginal to the biblical texts. 'Judaism' appears in literature first in 2 Maccabees (2:21; 8:1; 14:38), as designating a nationally conscious religion rebelling against hellenizing attempts to obliterate its distinctive identity. And in the New Testament it features only in Galatians 1:13–14, where again it expresses a polemically self-assertive religious identity. Not dissimilar is the emergence of the name 'Christianity'. For although the designation 'Christian' is already attested in Acts 11:26, the term 'Christianity' itself first appears only in Ignatius (*Magn.* 10:3; *Philad.* 6:1) – again, significantly, in polemical antithesis, this time with 'Judaism'. In other words, had these terms, 'Judaism' and 'Christianity', featured more prominently in the biblical texts, biblical theology would almost inevitably have found itself pushed in the same confrontational direction. But with 'Israel' as the primary self-identifying term both in the Jewish Scriptures and in the New Testament, it becomes a fundamental and defining concern of biblical theology to clarify what it is that constitutes Israel as Israel.

'Who is Israel?' is therefore a question integrally bound up with the question, 'What is biblical theology?' The fact that it is still a vital question for Israel today (Is 'Israel' a geographical/national or a religious entity? Do non-religious Jews belong to it, or proselytes to liberal Judaism?), as well as retaining foundational significance for Christianity (Where do Christians come in the Jew/Gentile dichotomy?), also means that biblical theology cannot be content to serve a merely antiquarian, descriptive function in the modern world.

The law

A third fundamental issue for biblical theology has to be *the law*. The issue is not to be short-circuited by observing that the Hebrew 'Torah' is not an exact synonym with the Greek 'law', as several have pointed out. The observation simply indicates that the issue is more complex. In fact Deuteronomy itself provides a bridge between the two uses, for in it *torah* denotes the collection of commandments which spell out Israel's covenant obligations ('all this law' – 4:8), and the equation Torah = Pentateuch is already implicit in 30:10 ('this book of the law'). But the issue is not to be either sidelined or resolved into semantics or questions of translation. For the fact is and remains indisputable that the Torah, 'the book of law', is central to both the Jewish Scriptures and to Jewish self-understanding. The Torah is the heart of the Jewish Scriptures, the canon within the canon of the Jewish Bible. 'To speak of canon is first to speak of Torah'[16] – the Prophets and Writings are simply the first and second commentaries on it. The Torah/law stands at the centre of the covenant with Israel and of Jewish life, at least from early Second Temple Judaism onwards.

---

[16] Sanders, *Torah*, x.

Consequently, a Christianity that disowns the law/Torah disowns a fundamental part of its own defining heritage. This was not seen clearly enough in a Christianity which defined itself too straightforwardly as gospel versus law, and which tended to heap on the religion of law (= Judaism) the antipathy and moral outrage which the justified/righteous reserve for the self-made/godless. Consequently, here too Christianity gave scope and comfort to anti-Semitic forces within the church, and here again the nerve of biblical theology was cut.

The *Tendenz* was unfortunate, to say the least, since closer attention to some broad themes in the New Testament should have prevented it – particularly the recognition of the concern in Matthew and Acts to demonstrate that Jesus and Paul are not to be dismissed as hostile to the law (e.g., Mt. 5:17–20; Acts 21:23–26), and Paul's own concern to argue that faith sustains the law and love fulfils the law (as in Rom. 3:31 and 13:8–10). It is fundamental to a correct exegesis of these texts to recognize that they were not written as 'Christian' texts already self-consciously distant from 'Jewish' concerns. Rather, they saw themselves as engaged in what we can properly call an intra-Israel debate about the meaning and application of the Torah – a debate shared with, and to some extent overlapping with, other intra-Israel debates of the time, as between Sadducee and Pharisee and Essene, or between apocalyptist and wisdom writer and rabbi. In other words, it was a debate about biblical theology. As such it was taking place within the New Testament writings and is to a greater or lesser degree constitutive of the gospel they sought to proclaim and the theology they expressed. This wrestling with its own subject matter and the interrelationship of its parts is integral to and definitive for biblical theology.

It is crucial that, in a period marked by renewed interest in biblical theology, this point be recognized. Otherwise exegesis and interpretation become drawn inexorably into categories determined primarily by later debates (such as those which characterized the Reformation). Otherwise the tendency to order the material under superimposed paradigms (promise and fulfilment, typology, salvation-history)[17] becomes a too easy and attractive solution. Otherwise we heal too lightly (by appeal to messianic torah or Zion torah)[18] the hurt and pain of the Christian Jew caught in the tensions between the revelation of the past and the revelation newly given, wrestling with the puzzle of how the people of the law could fail to recognize in the Spirit of Christ the hope of the law written in the heart. Otherwise we become caught up in a biblical theology of a barren kind, dominated by static categories and by a false dialectic between the Testaments (understood as 'Old' and 'New'). Only when we realize that the issue of the law, including the law and the promise, including the gospel and the law, was an issue of existential anguish and self-identity, was itself a biblical theology

---

[17] See, e.g., Barker, *Great Angel*, chs. 6 – 8.
[18] Cf. Gese, *Zur biblischen Theologie*, ch. 3.

debate in progress at the time, into which the New Testament (as well as other Second Temple Jewish) writers entered and to which they were making their contribution – only so can we hope to retain the dynamic character of the biblical theology of the Bible (Jewish and Christian) itself.

Conclusion

Biblical theology does not comprise the whole task of theology. Nor does it break down simply into Jewish biblical theology (of different kinds and periods) and Christian biblical theology (of different kinds and periods). The beginning of biblical theology is the recognition that the texts in focus are the Bible of two world religions. At the heart of biblical theology is the interface between a Jewish biblical theology and a Christian biblical theology – the interface that is the New Testament itself. The fundamental issue in biblical theology is whether the New Testament belongs to both – to both Bibles, to both biblical theologies. Is the New Testament, properly speaking, part of the revelation given by the one God of Israel to his people Israel, part of Israel's reflection on and response to that revelation? Inescapable in biblical theology is the ambiguity of self-understanding: does Jesus mark the continuity, even climax, of Israel's prophetic tradition, or its completion and rounding off? Is Paul the Jew become Christian apostle an apostate or the one who in the event fulfils most fully Israel's vocation to be a light to the Gentiles? Is Christianity an/the eschatological renewal of Israel or the abrogation of Judaism? It is the mark of biblical theology that such crucial questions can never be completely resolved, will never be resolved until the coming (parousia) of the Messiah, and that such ambivalence infuses and influences all other issues within biblical theology. But it is also that deep and deeply felt concern to be true to sacred tradition while being open to new insights, solutions and even revelation that makes biblical theology so invigorating and challenging – for today as it was in the biblical period itself.

Bibliography

Baker, D.L., *Two Testaments, One Bible* (Leicester: Inter-Varsity Press, 2nd edn, 1991)

Barker, M., *The Great Angel: A Study of Israel's Second God* (London: SPCK, 1992)

Childs, B.S., *Biblical Theology of the Old and New Testaments: Theological Reflection on the Christian Bible* (London: SCM Press; Minneapolis: Fortress Press, 1992)

Dahl, N.A., *Jesus the Christ: The Historical Origins of Christological Doctrine* (Minneapolis: Fortress Press, 1991)

Dunn, J.D.G., *Unity and Diversity in the New Testament* (London: SCM Press, 2nd edn, 1990)

—, *The Partings of the Ways between Christianity and Judaism* (London: SCM Press, 1991)

—, 'Das Problem "Biblische Theologie"', in *Eine Bibel – zwei Testamente: Positionen Biblischer Theologie* (ed. C. Dohmen and T. Söding; Paderborn: Schöningh, 1995), 179–93

Gese, H., *Zur biblischen Theologie: Alttestamentliche Vorträge* (München: Chr. Kaiser, 1977); ET *Essays on Biblical Theology* (Minneapolis: Augsburg, 1981)

Goldingay, J., *Theological Diversity and the Authority of the Old Testament* (Grand Rapids: Eerdmans, 1987)

Hübner, H., *Biblische Theologie des Neuen Testaments* (3 vols; Göttingen: Vandenhoeck & Ruprecht, 1990–95)

Levenson, J.D., 'Why Jews Are Not Interested in Biblical Theology', in *The Hebrew Bible, the Old Testament, and Historical Criticism: Jews and Christians in Biblical Studies* (Louisville, KY: Westminster John Knox Press, 1993), 33–61

Räisänen, H., *Beyond New Testament Theology* (London: SCM Press, 1990)

Rendtorff, R., *Canon and Theology* (Minneapolis: Fortress Press, 1993)

Reventlow, H. Graf, *Hauptprobleme der alttestamentlichen Theologie im 20. Jahrhundert* (Darmstadt: Wissenschaftliche Buchgesellschaft, 1982); ET *Problems of Old Testament Theology in the Twentieth Century* (London: SCM Press, 1985)

Sanders, J.A., *Torah and Canon* (Philadelphia: Fortress Press, 1972)

—, *Canon and Community: A Guide to Canonical Criticism* (Philadelphia: Fortress Press, 1984)

Stuhlmacher, P., *Biblische Theologie des Neuen Testaments* (Göttingen: Vandenhoeck & Ruprecht, 1992)

Great Themes of the Bible

8

Biblical Theology and the Problems of Monotheism
Richard Bauckham

Introduction

That the issue of 'monotheism' is a central issue for biblical theology hardly needs arguing. But there are a number of specific ways in which 'monotheism' has been problematized in recent biblical studies (hence the plural 'Problems of Monotheism' in my title). Major studies of the historical origins and development of 'monotheism' in ancient Israel, contextualized in the ancient Near Eastern context, have repeatedly challenged any traditional reading of the Old Testament's own telling of Israel's story. How far ancient Israel was 'monotheistic' at all before the latest strata of the Old Testament literature is very debatable, as is also therefore the extent to which Old Testament texts should be read in a 'monotheistic' way. For biblical theology, the methodological question of the role that a reconstructed history of ancient Israel should play in a biblical theology becomes unavoidable if these historical debates are taken seriously by biblical theologians.

However, the problems of 'monotheism' are not confined to the Old Testament. Some recent studies have questioned how far it is really correct to describe early Judaism (in the period up to and including the period in which the New Testament was written) as 'monotheistic', and this question about early Jewish 'monotheism' is closely related to much recent debate about the origins and character of early Christology. Do the New Testament writers presuppose 'monotheism' as the Old Testament and Jewish form of religious faith, not repudiating it but somehow incorporating their innovatory understanding of Jesus into it? Or does their high Christology arise from Jewish traditions that were not 'monotheistic'? The old question of how heirs of Jewish monotheism could have come to include Jesus in the deity of the one God has been posed and answered in a variety of fresh ways in the light of debates about 'monotheism' in the Old Testament and early Judaism. We have a fresh opportunity for considering 'monotheism' as a truly pan-biblical issue, not one confined to the specialisms of either Testament.

I have put 'monotheism' and 'monotheistic' in inverted commas through-out the previous paragraphs in order to alert us at once to the fact that the term 'monotheism' itself can become problematic and potentially misleading if we do not take the trouble to be clear precisely how we are using it. An important recent contribution to this whole area of debate has argued forcefully that not only is the term a peculiarly modern one, but that the set of ideas it evokes are characteristically Enlightenment ones, seducing us into reading the biblical writings in terms of a view of religion that belongs to the Enlightenment and is inappropriate to the texts. This claim provides a fruitful point of entry for us into the complex of 'problems of monotheism' with which we shall be con-cerned in this chapter.

There is one large and important area of discussion in which it is unfortu-nately not possible to engage within the scope of this chapter. This can be broadly characterized by the question: 'Is monotheism bad for people?' Critiques of monotheism as leading to absolute monarchical forms of govern-ment (in church as well as state), hierarchical structures in society, a dualistic exaltation of the male over the female, exclusion of the other and violence against the other, have been multiplying in recent years.[1] Such critiques pose searching questions for biblical theology, and they are not unrelated to the rather narrower historical and exegetical issues with which this chapter is con-cerned. But they also require serious engagement with the post-biblical history of ideas. The fact that they cannot be addressed in the present context should not be mistaken for failure to appreciate their importance.

Monotheism as a Misleading Category

A major contribution to our topic has been made by Nathan MacDonald in his recently published book, *Deuteronomy and the Meaning of 'Monotheism'*, a revised version of his Durham doctoral thesis, *One God or One Lord? Deuteron-omy and the Meaning of 'Monotheism'* (2001). MacDonald argues that the idea of 'monotheism' (like 'polytheism') is an invention of the Enlightenment that is inappropriate for understanding the Old Testament and that the use of this cat-egory has seriously distorted Old Testament scholarship's account of Israel's faith in YHWH. Tracing the invention of the word 'monotheism' and its early use by the seventeenth-century Cambridge Platonists, he associates it with the

---

[1] E.g., Ciholas, 'Monothéisme et violence'; Ochshorn, *Female Experience*; Ruggieri, 'God and Power'; Duquoc, 'Monotheism and Unitary Ideology'; Moltmann, *Trinity*; Hampson, 'Monotheism'; Schwartz, *Curse of Cain*.

intellectualization of religion in seventeenth-century English thought, which tended to identify religion with a body of theoretical knowledge and to judge the truth or falsity of a religion by the truth or falsity, rationally assessed, of the propositions that constituted it. 'Monotheism' was an organizing principle in the categorization of religions according to their intellectual claims, and, as such a principle, made the question of the number of gods a priority in the classification and evaluation of religions. The term 'monotheism', especially as subsequently taken over by the Deists, became associated with the Enlightenment's philosophical construction of a rational, ethical and universally evident religion. The identification of emergent 'monotheism' in ancient Israel was thus in danger of being a mere projection of Enlightenment beliefs and values and of being understood within a developmental understanding of the necessary progress of humanity through various stages towards ethical monotheism, which, being rationally compelling, is bound to prevail everywhere.

MacDonald shows how this Enlightenment idea of monotheism has influenced major accounts of Israelite religion from Wellhausen onwards. He acknowledges that von Rad is an exception in that he deliberately distinguished Israelite 'monotheism' from the modern conception that, he observes, derives from the Enlightenment. In my view, Yehezkel Kaufmann is also more of an exception than MacDonald allows. Whatever other criticisms may be made of Kaufmann's claim that the 'basic idea of Israelite religion is that God is supreme over all',[2] there is nothing peculiarly modern about it (whereas Enlightenment Deism was by no means happy with an *actively* sovereign God like Kaufmann's YHWH): it is the teaching of traditional Judaism, Christianity and Islam.[3] Allowing that Kaufmann's understanding of universalism is not the Enlightenment concept,[4] MacDonald nevertheless takes the fact that Kaufmann understands Israelite monotheism as in *any* sense universalistic to align him with the Enlightenment notion. The same seems to be true of transcendence.[5] MacDonald's discussion of Kaufmann shows that he needs the specifically Enlightenment idea of monotheism to do more work than it can. From his perspective he evidently needs to critique not only the influence of Enlightenment monotheism on Old Testament scholarship, but also the influence of the entirely traditional, pre-modern belief of the 'monotheistic' religions (Judaism, Christianity and Islam) in the transcendence, unrivalled sovereignty and universal deity of the one God. However, he is on firmer

---

[2] Quoted by MacDonald, *Deuteronomy*, 36, 37. MacDonald refers to the criticism of Kaufmann's claim by J. D. Levenson, *Creation*.

[3] MacDonald himself writes that 'YHWH's universal control provides the background of election' (*Deuteronomy*, 167).

[4] MacDonald, *Deuteronomy*, 39.

[5] MacDonald, *Deuteronomy*, 40.

ground, in my view, in seeing the persistence of the influence of the Enlightenment concept in the developmental models applied to Israelite religion, in light
of the impact of the new archaeological evidence for Israelite polytheism, by
two representatives of recent scholarship, Robert Gnuse and Walter Dietrich.

These matters are preliminary to MacDonald's study of Deuteronomy,
which argues that 'Deuteronomy does not, at any point, present a doctrine of
God that may be described as "monotheism"', while 'the description of Deuteronomy's message as "monotheistic" obfuscates at least as much as it enlightens'.[6] The following seem to me the most important ways in which he
distinguishes Deuteronomy's 'doctrine of God' from Enlightenment
monotheism:

1) Deuteronomy does not deny the existence of other gods. MacDonald
observes, with many others, that the Shema and the first commandment of the
Decalogue require monolatry, the exclusive devotion of Israel to YHWH, but
do not deny the existence of other gods. They may even be said to presuppose
their existence in treating them as real competitors for Israel's devotion.[7] Less
usual, though not unprecedented,[8] is MacDonald's denial that Deuteronomy
itself teaches that YHWH is the only god. (MacDonald, in line with his thesis,
translates אלהים as 'god', except on the few occasions when it has the article,
for which he uses 'God'.) The two key statements in chapter 4 – 'so that you
would acknowledge that YHWH is God (האלהים); there is no other besides
him' (4:35) and 'acknowledge … that YHWH is God (האלהים) in heaven above
and on the earth beneath; there is no other' (4:39) – he takes to mean that
YHWH is unique (the only god who is God) and is the only god *for Israel*.[9]

2) The 'intellectualization' of religion implicit in 'monotheism' is lacking in
Deuteronomy. 'Monotheism' 'represents a call to recognize the objective state
of metaphysical affairs'. That there is only one God is presented as 'a fact that
one must assimilate', part of a body of objective knowledge about the world
that is rationally accessible. 'In Deuteronomy, however, the recognition of
YHWH's oneness is a call to love YHWH, a love expressed in obedience and
worship'.[10] This does not mean that MacDonald denies that Deuteronomy
makes cognitive truth-claims about YHWH, but that he sees these as inseparable from the relational requirement of devotion to YHWH.

3) By contrast with the facile intellectual recognition of monotheism as a
fact, Deuteronomy – here exemplified in the Shema – requires of Israel (not
others) a love of or devotion to YHWH that is 'all consuming and incomparably

---

[6] MacDonald, *Deuteronomy*, 209–10.

[7] MacDonald, *Deuteronomy*, 77, 210.

[8] Cf. Gnuse, *No Other Gods*, 206, with references to other scholars in n. 47.

[9] MacDonald, *Deuteronomy*, 79–85.

[10] MacDonald, *Deuteronomy*, 210.

demanding'.[11] The emphasis is on a demand that is supremely difficult to fulfil. Moreover, it is not self-evident, as it is for the 'ethical monotheism' of the Enlightenment, what the obligation entails, since it is not a matter of general ethical values but of specific concrete acts of obedience laid down by YHWH for his own people Israel.

4) Deuteronomy presumes that, devotion to YHWH being as difficult and demanding as it teaches, Israel will easily forget YHWH and needs careful disciplines of remembrance. This distinguishes it from the Enlightenment view of monotheism as an intellectual step in human history that, once made, could not conceivably be reversed, so obvious is its intellectual superiority to polytheism. MacDonald quotes Schleiermacher: 'as soon as piety has anywhere developed to the point of belief in one God over all, it may be predicted that man will not in any region of the earth remain stationary on one of the lower planes. ... There is nowhere any trace, so far as history reaches, of a relapse from Monotheism, in the strict sense'.[12] The modern conception of a historical progress in which monotheism is a necessary stage has strongly influenced Old Testament scholars' ideas about a monotheistic development or monotheistic breakthrough in Israel.

5) Finally, there is a strong contrast between the universalism of Enlightenment monotheism (the meaning of which is especially clear when it is seen as the opposite pole from particularism) and the centrality of Israel's election in Deuteronomy. For the Enlightenment approach, true monotheism required the one God to be freed from any special attachment to Israel (this approach has strongly influenced New Testament as well as Old Testament scholarship). By contrast, for Deuteronomy, YHWH's 'uniqueness cannot be recognized apart from his election of Israel. For Deuteronomy there is no access to YHWH apart from this relationship ... This is true not only for Israel, but also for the nations ... How the nations respond to Israel determines their response to YHWH'.[13]

These arguments are very important and, in my view, largely convincing. My serious reservations concern the first point and will be explained below. Of course, MacDonald's study is confined to Deuteronomy. But points 2) – 5) seem to me to be broadly valid for much of the Old Testament (though some different things might also need to be said about the wisdom literature and about Genesis), and certainly they expose very sharply and usefully the ways that Enlightenment ideas of monotheism have distorted study of the Old Testament.

What I find disappointing in MacDonald's work is his failure to deal systematically with the issue of YHWH's uniqueness vis-à-vis the other gods. Given

---

[11] MacDonald, *Deuteronomy*, 210.

[12] MacDonald, *Deuteronomy*, 124.

[13] MacDonald, *Deuteronomy*, 180.

that Deuteronomy affirms the uniqueness of YHWH (as alone God [4:35, 39; 7:9] and as alone 'god of gods' [10:17]) without denying the existence of other gods, in what does that uniqueness consist? In his conclusion he writes that 'monotheism'

> does not capture what it means in Deuteronomy to say that 'YHWH is God' (הָאֱלֹהִים). 'Monotheism' has been generally understood, with exceptions such as Albright, as the denial of the existence of other gods, but one. In Deuteronomy the existence of other gods is not denied. Nevertheless it is still claimed that 'YHWH is God', or 'god of gods'. This claim to be a unique divinity is based not on creation, or YHWH's role in parcelling out the nations to other gods, but on YHWH's faithfulness, mercy and jealousy demonstrated by his election of Israel. In his particular actions for his people, YHWH shows that he is God. We might say, to use the language of theological discourse, that YHWH's claim to be God is not primarily an ontological claim, but more a soteriological one (though such a claim carries with it ontological implications).[14]

There are several questions to ask about this passage: a) What is the sense of 'primarily' in the last sentence?[15] One could say that the claim is *primarily* soteriological *in the order of knowledge,* but not in the order of being. In other words, YHWH is unique (even apart from his election of Israel), but Israel recognizes this uniqueness only through what he does for Israel. This would be parallel to the 'Nicene' argument in the Trinitarian debates of the fourth century, which proposed (against Arius) that Christ could only save, in the sense claimed by Christian soteriology, if he were fully divine. On the other hand, MacDonald's statement could mean that YHWH's claim to be God is *primarily* a soteriological one *in the order of being.* In other words, he is unique as a result of what he has done for Israel. In this case, his election of Israel constitutes his uniqueness. The penultimate sentence of the passage ('In his particular actions for his people, YHWH shows that he is God')[16] seems to me to make best sense if MacDonald intends the first of these two possible senses of 'primarily', but the

---

[14] MacDonald, *Deuteronomy*, 215.

[15] Lang, *Monotheism*, 55, makes a superficially similar point in relation to his view that monotheism was a response to the political circumstances of exile: 'There is a dimension of doctrine in monotheistic thought, it is true; but, unlike later scholastic speculation, Yahweh-aloneists and Jewish monotheists are not primarily concerned with dogma and doctrine. Theirs is a theology of hope ... In theological jargon one could say that soteriological monotheism is older than monotheistic dogma, or that hope precedes belief.' Lang seems to make two points: one about the main concern of Jewish monotheists ('not primarily concerned with dogma'), the second a chronological one ('soteriological monotheism is older than monotheistic dogma').

[16] Cf. also, e.g., MacDonald, *Deuteronomy*, 195: 'YHWH's uniqueness was *revealed* in his electing actions on Israel's behalf ' (my italics).

unclarity is disturbing if one is looking to his work for an answer to the question how Deuteronomy understands the uniqueness of YHWH.

b) How does what is said here about YHWH's unique claim to be God differ from the claim that he is the national god of Israel (and Israel should worship him exclusively because he has so extravagantly committed himself to Israel as his people), whereas other gods are similarly the national gods of their peoples (even though they cannot claim to have benefited their peoples in the outstanding way that YHWH has benefited Israel)? Is YHWH unique only in, so to speak, taking his commitment to his people more seriously than other national gods do and therefore requiring more exclusive allegiance than other national gods do?[17] I do not think MacDonald intends to say this (and I am sure Deuteronomy does not), but he says nothing else in his conclusion that enables us to give more content than this to the assertion of YHWH's uniqueness.

c) An understanding of YHWH's uniqueness vis-à-vis the other gods also requires that we know more about the other gods than simply that Deuteronomy does not deny their existence. If all that matters is that Israel is not to worship them, we seem to be back with the idea that YHWH's uniqueness really is nothing more than his election of Israel. His difference from other gods would be only that he is more committed to his people than they are. MacDonald is well aware that Deuteronomy has more than this to say about the contrast between YHWH and other gods,[18] but he does not draw these insights into a systematic presentation of the nature of YHWH's uniqueness.

MacDonald's failure to conclude more about YHWH's uniqueness than he does in the passage quoted above from his conclusion probably results from his concern to distinguish Deuteronomy from Enlightenment monotheism's assumption that the uniqueness of the one and only God is simply a fact to be recognized. He wants to stress that YHWH's uniqueness is knowable to Israel (and to anyone else) only in the context of Israel's relationship with YHWH. The problem is that this concern seems to lead him to reduce YHWH's uniqueness to that relationship. But this is not necessary. Given that Israel can *recognize* YHWH's uniqueness only from what YHWH does for Israel, it does not follow that this uniqueness cannot include what YHWH objectively is, even independently of Israel.

Deuteronomy seems to me to require an account of YHWH's uniqueness that takes full account of such passages as these: 'YHWH is God (הָאֱלֹהִים) in heaven above and on the earth below' (4:39); 'heaven and the heaven of heavens belong to YHWH your god, the earth with all that is in it' (10:14); 'YHWH

---

[17] Cf. Morton Smith's opinion that, while the theology of the Old Testament is in general 'the common theology of the ancient near East', what does require explanation is 'Yahweh's abnormal jealousy' ('Common Theology', 26).

[18] MacDonald, *Deuteronomy*, 92, 195–97.

your god is god of gods and lord of lords, the great god' (10:17); and the divine self-declaration of 32:39 in relation to what is said about the gods in the Song of Moses. But in order to establish my point I want particularly to engage with MacDonald's exegesis of the crucially important passage Deuteronomy 4:32–40.

The two key statements of YHWH's uniqueness (vv. 35, 39) come as the climaxes to the two sections verses 32–35 and verses 36–39:

> For ask now about former ages, long before your own, ever since the day that god created human beings on the earth; ask from one end of heaven to the other: has anything so great as this ever happened or has its like ever been heard of? [33]Has any people ever heard the voice of a god speaking out of a fire, as you have heard, and lived? [34]Or has any god ever attempted to go and take a nation for himself from the midst of another nation, by trials, by signs and wonders, by war, by a mighty hand and an outstretched arm, and by terrifying displays of power, as YHWH your god did for you in Egypt before your very eyes? [35]To you it was shown so that you would acknowledge that YHWH is God (האלהים); there is no other besides him (אין עוד מלבדו).

> [36]From heaven he made you hear his voice to discipline you. On earth he showed you his great fire, while you heard his words coming out of the fire. [37]And because he loved your ancestors, he chose their descendants after them. He brought you out of Egypt with his own presence, by his great power, [38]driving out before you nations greater and mightier than yourselves, to bring you in, giving you their land for a possession, as it is still today. [39]So acknowledge today and take to heart that YHWH is God (האלהים) in heaven above and on the earth beneath; there is no other (אין עוד).

> [40]Keep his statutes and his commandments, which I am commanding you today for your own well-being and that of your descendants after you, so that you may long remain in the land that YHWH your God is giving you for all time. (NRSV, altered)

MacDonald takes Israel's recognition of YHWH as האלהים in verse 35 to be the consequence of his election of Israel, while in verse 39 it is the consequence of his revelation at Horeb.[19] I do not think this is adequate. The passages seem to me to stress in both cases YHWH's supreme power, and it is because of YHWH's exercise of power on their behalf that Israel is to recognize him as האלהים. In the second case (while MacDonald must be right to see a connection between heaven and earth in v. 36 and heaven and earth in v. 39), the recognition that YHWH is 'God in heaven above and on the earth beneath' implies not just his presence in heaven and earth (as MacDonald argues), but also his power throughout heaven and earth. The parallel in Joshua 2:11 surely strongly

---

[19] MacDonald, *Deuteronomy*, 191–96.

supports this interpretation.[20] What makes YHWH, by comparison with the gods of the nations, 'the God' (or 'god of gods and lord of lords, the great god' as 10:17 puts it) is his unrivalled power. Thus, although it is only in what he does for Israel that Israel recognizes YHWH to be 'the God', this status is not only what he is in relation to Israel, but also what he is in any case and particularly in relation to the other gods. Of course, it is essential to Israel's relationship with YHWH that he exercises his power in love for Israel, in electing and favouring Israel, but he would not be 'the God' were he not powerful enough to make his election and favour effective in ways that are beyond the power of other gods.

The phrase with which verses 35 and 39 conclude – אֵין עוֹד (מִלְּבַדּוֹ) – is found, in this and other forms, quite frequently elsewhere and is generally considered a 'monotheistic formula'. MacDonald argues that here the meaning is that YHWH is the only god for Israel – not absolutely. I find his linguistic argument about the use of אֵין אוֹד[21] unconvincing, since it cannot apply in several other instances of this formula where YHWH is the subject (1 Kgs. 8:60; Isa. 45:5, 6, 14, 18, 22). He has shown only that when אֵין אוֹד is used there can be a limitation supplied by the context, but not that the phrase itself entails a limitation. 1 Kings 8:60 is the closest parallel[22] to Deuteronomy 4:35, 39. Solomon (at the dedication of the temple) prays that YHWH will 'maintain the cause of his servant and the cause of his people Israel' (v. 59)

so that all the peoples of the earth may know that YHWH is God (הָאֱלֹהִים); there is no other (אֵין אוֹד) (1 Kgs. 8:60).[23]

This is presumably a direct echo of Deuteronomy 4, and it is worth noting that at the outset of his dedication prayer Solomon says that 'there is no God like you in heaven above or on earth beneath' (8:23). The conclusion of verse 60 can surely not mean that all the peoples of the earth will know that YHWH is the only god *for Israel*. What they will recognize is that YHWH alone is 'the God'. They need not deny that there are other *gods,* but they will recognize the uniqueness of YHWH as the only one who can be called '*the God*'. It is in this category that 'there is no other'. This seems to me a good meaning also in Deuteronomy 4:35, 39. This interpretation agrees with MacDonald that the claim that 'YHWH is God (הָאֱלֹהִים)' is a claim for uniqueness that does not deny the

---

[20] Eccl. 5:1 (English 5:2), to which MacDonald especially appeals, is a considerably more remote parallel. (He gives the reference [*Deuteronomy,* 195] wrongly as Eccl. 5:6.)

[21] MacDonald, *Deuteronomy,* 81–84.

[22] Note also 2 Sam. 7:22, 28.

[23] Other instances of the formula 'YHWH is God (הָאֱלֹהִים)' or 'you are God (הָאֱלֹהִים)' are found in Josh. 22:34; 2 Sam. 7:28; 1 Kgs. 18:21, 37, 39 (*bis*); 2 Kgs. 19:15 = Isa. 37:16; 2 Chr. 33:13; Isa. 45:18.

existence of other gods, but allows (מלבדו) אין עוד to reinforce this uniqueness as such rather than reducing it again to its significance only for Israel.

What Israel is able to recognize about YHWH, from his acts for Israel, that distinguishes YHWH from the gods of the nations is that he is 'the God' or 'the god of gods'. This means primarily that he has unrivalled power throughout the cosmos. The earth, the heavens and the heaven of heavens belong to him (10:14). By contrast, the gods of the nations are impotent nonentities, who cannot protect and deliver even their own peoples. This is the message of the Song of Moses (see especially 32:37–39). The need to distinguish among 'the gods' between the one who is supreme (YHWH) and the others who are not just subordinate but powerless, creates, on the one hand, the usages 'the God' and 'the god of gods', and, on the other hand, the contemptuous terms 'non-god' (32:17: לא אלה; 32:21: לא אל) and 'their mere puffs of air' (32:21: הבליהם). Though called gods, the other gods do not really deserve the term, because they are not *effective* divinities, acting with power in the world.[24] YHWH alone is the God with supreme power:

> See now that I, even I, am he;
> there is no god besides (or 'with') me.
> I kill and I make alive;
> I wound and I heal;
> and no one can deliver from my hand. (32:39)

This is not Enlightenment monotheism, and nothing of what MacDonald writes about the existential and relational import of YHWH's uniqueness should be surrendered. But we do seem here to be at least approaching the 'monotheism' of the 'Abrahamic' religions in their traditional forms, as well as 'monotheism' as Kaufmann understood it. It is not enough to observe that Deuteronomy does not deny the *existence* of other gods. We should also recognize that, once we do attend to the ontological implications that MacDonald admits Deuteronomy's 'doctrine of God' must have, this theology is driving an ontological division through the midst of the old category 'gods' such that YHWH appears in a class of his own.

The Quest of the Historical Monotheism

MacDonald's work, apart from his introductory survey of scholarship, is, of course, limited to Deuteronomy and to the final form of the text. He attempts

---

[24] Cf. Schmidt, *Faith*, 279: The Old Testament 'regarded the gods not as nothing, but as good for nothing; it does not deny their existence but their power and effectiveness'.

neither to place this in a historical context in relation to the historical place of other Old Testament texts, nor to place it in a canonical context of the rest of the texts read synchronically. The larger task of biblical theology clearly requires that one attempt at least one of these tasks, but whether the first is necessary or desirable for biblical theology immediately raises questions about the method and nature of biblical theology. In some ways, the issue of monotheism is similar, in Old Testament theology, to the issue of the historical Jesus in the New. Has New Testament theology any need to take an interest in the historical reconstruction of Jesus attempted in the quest of the historical Jesus, or are the canonical renderings of Jesus in the four Gospels the only proper and sufficient concern of New Testament theology? Similarly, is a history-of-religions account of the origins and development of ancient Israel's exclusive Yahwism relevant to the understanding of faith in YHWH that must be central to an Old Testament theology, not to mention a pan-biblical theology? James Barr, for one, thinks that this is one of the key areas in which an absolute demarcation between the history of religion and biblical theology should not be maintained and where the results of history-of-religions scholarship are important for biblical theology.[25] Some of those who have contributed recently to the study of the origins and development of exclusive Yahwism in Israel are also convinced of the relevance of their results to biblical theology.[26]

The question arises particularly acutely because, as MacDonald points out, 'from its conception "monotheism" has been tied to questions of origin',[27] and this is also true of the discussion of monotheism in Israel and the Old Testament. To put a blunt question: Did YHWH reveal his exclusive deity to Israel at the time of the origins of the nation before the settlement in the land, as Deuteronomy claims, making this claim the basis for Israel's exclusive devotion to YHWH? Of course, historical study could never answer the theological question about the action of YHWH as such, and even a scholar like Robert Gnuse, who is deeply concerned with the theological implications of the historical work in this field, does not ask this theological question as such. But he would have to answer it negatively, because, like many recent scholars,[28] he thinks that Israelite religion was originally indistinguishable from Canaanite religion and that exclusive Yahwism was a late development of the monarchical period. (Others would not date it earlier than the exile.) Can we affirm the theological

---

[25] Barr, *Biblical Theology*, 137–38. The other two of the three examples he gives are in fact closely connected with the issue of monotheism: the 'convergence' of deities (YHWH and El), and 'sexuality in the deity' (including the evidence for a female consort of YHWH).

[26] E.g., Dietrich, 'Werden und Wesen'; Gnuse, *No Other Gods*; Becking, 'Only One God'.

[27] MacDonald, *Deuteronomy*, 53.

[28] E.g., Niehr, 'Rise of YHWH'.

teaching of the Old Testament while allowing that the historical 'facts' could have been as different from the Old Testament's own narrative as this? Could YHWH really be as the Old Testament portrays him if, historically, even the claim of exclusive Yahwism has merely been projected back through fictionalized history from the exile all the way to Moses? The status of 'history' in Old Testament theology is, of course, a familiar issue,[29] but this instance of it seems to me to pose the problem most acutely.

As in the case of the historical Jesus, I would be reluctant simply to let history and theology go their separate ways, and so, though I can speak only as a novice in the field, it may be worth observing that I seriously doubt that the emerging consensus that Israelite religion was in origin simply Canaanite religion really has a historically persuasive basis in the evidence. Archaeology has indeed shown that the worship of gods besides YHWH, especially the goddess Asherah, was widespread in Israel and Judah in the monarchical period.[30] This is hardly inconsistent with the biblical narratives, which require only the supposition that, in addition to widespread polytheistic practice, there was a tradition of exclusive Yahwism – the tradition from which the biblical writings derive – which, whatever its varying degrees of influence and strength over centuries, went back to a much earlier period. It is important not to confuse such a tradition, which can be regarded as normative only as a theological judgement or in historical retrospect from its achievement of normative status in practice in the post-exilic period, with the religion of Israel in the pre-exilic period, understood as the practice of most Israelites and evidenced by the archaeology as well as the texts, insofar as they can be considered reliable evidence for the practices they criticize. While archaeology provides no evidence of the existence of exclusive Yahwism before the end of the monarchical period (for which period the amulets from Ketef Hinnom and the tomb graffiti from Khirbet beit Lei are plausibly evidence of such),[31] the evidence it offers for the nature of Israelite religion is in total very small and can hardly be said to make it even probable that exclusive Yahwism did not exist.

The conclusion that exclusive Yahwism did not exist until the late monarchical period results mainly from treating the biblical texts not just with historical scepticism but with historical scepticism based on very considerable ideological suspicion of the texts, along with the use of religio-historical models for interpreting the non-biblical evidence and making a plausible story out of it. Such models are inescapable in any history of religions and the smaller

---

[29] Cf., e.g., Barr, *Biblical Theology*, ch. 21.

[30] The evidence is especially well presented and discussed in the essays in Becking et al. (eds.), *Only One God*.

[31] Vriezen, 'Archaeological Traces'; and Hess, 'Yahweh and his Asherah', offer balanced and sensible assessments of what the archaeological evidence shows.

the amount of evidence and the more ambiguous it is the more it is the models that control the conclusions drawn from the evidence. Once the biblical texts have been discounted as reliable evidence, not only because of very late datings given them but also because they are so ideologically shaped, the remaining evidence is, it must surely be admitted, rather easily malleable according to the models and analogies employed. While the historical reconstruction may indeed fully respect the integrity of this evidence, it is not so easy to tell whether an alternative historical reconstruction might not do so just as well. Ironically, there is a clear danger of historiography that is no less ideologically shaped than it considers that of the Deuteronomists to have been. In particular, most such reconstructions seem controlled by a developmental model, however nuanced, that envisages a series of steps that advance by stages towards full monotheism and cannot reckon with serious departure from monotheism once this has been attained.

I find two instances of the way Robert Gnuse deals with proposals that are not in line with the emerging consensus rather revealing. One of the valuable aspects of his book is the careful presentation of the work of most recent scholars in this field and the development of his own critical synthesis out of his assessment of these. The major recent study that is probably most out of line with what Gnuse identifies as the mainstream within which he situates himself is *The Rise of Yahwism* (first edition, 1990) by Johannes C. de Moor.[32] This very learned work, which handles a wide range of ancient Near Eastern sources with expertise, proposes 'a new paradigm for the early history of Yahwism'.[33] As far as origins go, de Moor proposes that exclusive worship of El in the form of YHWH-El originated, in the context of a wider tendency to put one god above others, among 'proto-Israelites' in late thirteenth-century Canaan, and that a form of this cult that can be more precisely identified as exclusive Yahwism originated with Moses (whom de Moor argues in detail to have been the Egyptian chancellor Beya of Egyptian texts) at the end of the twelfth century.[34]

This is how Gnuse evaluates de Moor's work:

> It is brilliantly argued, but it is incredibly hypothetical. He has reconstructed detailed history on the basis of apparently archaic sounding poetry in the Bible, a dangerously subjective procedure. His theory is possible, but not probable. Such a theory is difficult to refute, but also impossible to prove. Any hypothesis which increasingly turns literary allusions into specific historical reconstructions becomes less likely to have been the true historical scenario. De Moor's theory runs counter to the direction in

---

[32] Writing in 1997, Gnuse refers to the 1990 edition. I have used the revised and enlarged 1997 edition.

[33] De Moor, *Rise of Yahwism*, 9.

[34] The dating of Beya at 'the end of the 13th century' in de Moor's concluding summary (*Rise of Yahwism*, 372) seems to be a mistake.

which scholars are moving in their understanding of monotheistic evolution, so he will convert few readers to his hypothesis.[35]

The judgement that de Moor's work is very speculative is fair, but I wonder whether it is really *more* 'hypothetical' or its use of evidence *more* 'subjective' than the reconstructions Gnuse favours. The really decisive point against de Moor seems to be Gnuse's final sentence, which puts remarkable faith in a scholarly trend just because it is a scholarly trend, even given that Gnuse identifies this trend as 'a paradigm shift'.[36] (Gnuse himself is aware that many factors – not just the evidence – go into the making of scholarly trends.) What I find valuable is Gnuse's admission that de Moor's theory is 'possible'. He does not claim that there is evidence against it, only that the evidence for it is weak. This is a revealing indication of the status of all historical claims in this area. I have adduced this example not because I wish to defend de Moor's theory (I lack the competence to assess it in detail), but because Gnuse's treatment of it seems to me to illustrate how far a controlling model can be the decisive factor in both making and judging historical reconstructions in this area.

My second instance of Gnuse's evaluation is not of a particular reconstruction but of a proposed model for interpreting the evidence. This is from Werner Schmidt's fine work, *The Faith of the Old Testament* (first published in 1968), which Schmidt himself characterized as standing midway between a history of Israelite religion and a theology of the Old Testament,[37] not in principle unlike the way Gnuse seems to position his own work. To characterize the way in which exclusive Yahwism related to other cults, Schmidt spoke of a 'double process of recognition and rejection'.[38] YHWH took over some characteristics of other gods, while being sharply distinguished from other characteristics of the other gods. This was a process of recognizing what was compatible and rejecting what was incompatible with Israel's core faith in YHWH. But such a process presupposes some criterion for such distinctions. Schmidt writes:

> It remains unsatisfactory however simply to state this polarity of contact and rejection. After the religio-historical comparison has been made, the question (for which there is historical justification too) is bound to arise: what made possible for Israel this history in which it deprived Yahweh's opponents of their power? What was the criterion which allowed rejection on the one hand, borrowing and change on the other? This is a difficult problem, and one to which the same answer cannot be given

---

[35] Gnuse, *No Other Gods*, 109.

[36] Gnuse, *No Other Gods*, 12.

[37] Schmidt, *The Faith*, ix (J.R. Porter's foreword to the English edition).

[38] Schmidt, *The Faith*, 180.

in every case. But Yahweh's demand for exclusivity and the prohibition of images are bound to be cited as the decisive criterion.[39]

Gnuse, who praises these categories of 'recognition', 'rejection' and 'core' (i.e., the criteria that guided the double process of recognition and rejection), correctly notices that the first two come close to the two categories which Mark Smith, in his much more recent major work, identifies as 'convergence' and 'differentiation' of deities.[40] What he does not note is the way that Schmidt's model supplies a clear deficiency in Smith's, in that the latter lacks an equivalent to Schmidt's category of 'core'. Smith's model provides an enlightening *description* of the relationship between YHWH and the other gods, but it lacks any clear explanation of the process.[41] But this advantage in Schmidt's model is lost in Gnuse's evaluation:

> Schmidt's categories are excellent for future discussion, except for his propensity to date the process too early [Schmidt considers the 'core' of Yahwism, as he identifies it, to date from the pre-settlement period] and to articulate the 'core' too concretely. The exclusivity of Yahweh and the aniconic portrayal were probably not important factors in the pre-exilic religion of Israel, as archaeology and the newer critical understanding of the biblical texts indicate ... The so-called 'core' of Yahwistic faith was probably more nebulous and would be difficult to define.[42]

But the historically explanatory value of the 'core' is entirely lost when thus reduced to the nebulous and indefinable! It seems to me that Schmidt quite correctly saw that it is a necessary *historical* question (as well as one important for Old Testament theology) to ask about the criteria that guided the double process of recognition and rejection or the already early core of faith in YHWH that accounts for its distinctive later development. His answer is, of course, as a historical explanation a hypothesis, but has a lot of plausibility to it.[43] Gnuse rejects it, not really on grounds of hard evidence (the archaeology actually favours the early origin of Yahwistic aniconism rather than disproving it[44]) but because he

---

[39] Schmidt, *Faith*, 180.

[40] Smith, *Early History*.

[41] This is explicit: Smith, *Early History*, 155–56, shows, from one point of view, laudable historical caution.

[42] Gnuse, *No Other Gods*, 239.

[43] For a similar historical argument, see Albertz, *History of Israelite Religion*, 61–62: 'there must have been a potential for difference within Yahweh religion which distinguished it from the usual polytheistic religions, a potential to which opposition groups which saw the exclusive worship of Yahweh as the only possibility of overcoming crises could appeal'.

[44] See esp. Mettinger, *No Graven Image*. He distinguishes *de facto* aniconism, which is as old as Israel itself (194), from 'the programmatic prohibition of images of the deity',

is committed to a different model – so much so that, in my judgement, he has failed to recognize the superiority of Schmidt's model in accounting for the evidence.

These two examples of Gnuse's reasons for rejecting alternatives to the emerging consensus suggest that one should not have too much confidence in the historical basis for this consensus (i.e., for the view that Israelite religion was originally indistinguishable from Canaanite religion and that exclusive Yahwism was a late development). But Gnuse's work must retain our attention for the next stage of our argument also, because Gnuse is not only an enthusiastic champion of the emerging consensus. He is also its theologian, convinced that it has important implications for biblical theology.

The thread that runs through the whole of Gnuse's book is his evolutionary understanding of the emergence of monotheism from Israelite religion. This is for him not only a heuristic model for historical understanding of what happened but also a crucially important theological category. He draws from much of the recent scholarship the impression that monotheism did not develop simply in a gradual process over a long period, as the evolutionary model has in the past tended to suggest, but through a combination of evolution and revolution – that is, 'an evolutionary process which occurs in revolutionary fashion'. He envisages 'a series of intellectual revolutions over a period of years which culminated in the exile', when 'true' monotheism emerged out of the politico-religious crisis of the period.[45] (Gnuse uses a variety of terms to describe the culmination of the development, Deutero-Isaiah's monotheism, with its denial of the existence of other gods: true monotheism, absolute monotheism, theoretical monotheism, pure monotheism, radical monotheism.)

The development through intellectual 'leaps' precipitated by specific circumstances has been a fairly common picture, while Mark Smith already spoke of a combination of evolution and revolution.[46] Gnuse's contribution is to show that this combination need not involve abandoning a biological model of evolution, since contemporary understanding of the latter itself incorporates the idea of periodic 'leaps' forward, rather than a purely gradual process. He calls this model 'Punctuated Equlibria'. It is quite unclear to me how this

---

which he attributes probably to the influence of Deuteronomistic theology (135, but cf. 196 for a possibly earlier date). Considering Israelite aniconism as such a form of a more general phenomenon of West Semitic aniconism, he does not see it as one of Israel's *differentia specifica*, though it may well be that 'the express veto on images' is (195–96). He perhaps does not allow sufficiently for the way that, in a given historical context, Yahwistic aniconism could be seen as distinctive and differentiating.

[45] Gnuse, *No Other Gods*, 69.

[46] Gnuse, *No Other Gods*, 102.

explicitly biological model is supposed to function. Is it no more than an illustration (with 'pedagogic' usefulness, as Gnuse sometimes says), or is it supposed to have some explanatory value? Does the fact that the historical developments can be plotted in a way that resembles biological evolution somehow make that way of plotting them more convincing? Even for someone who believes as strongly as Gnuse does in the overall progressive nature of human intellectual and religious history, as well as in biological evolution, I cannot see any reason at all why the former should be supposed to advance in the same way as the latter.[47]

Old Testament scholars have often attached to their accounts of the development of monotheism in ancient Israel remarks to the effect that monotheism was the great Jewish contribution to the world or that what happened in Israel laid the foundations for the modern world.[48] But Gnuse claims for the emergence of Israelite monotheism its status as 'a great evolutionary advance for humanity'[49] by placing it within a world-historical scheme of evolutionary intellectual advance. Along with comparable intellectual breakthroughs in the 'Axial Age' in Greece, Persia, India and China, it belongs to the third great stage of intellectual evolution, succeeded either at the Renaissance or the Enlightenment by the modern intellectual world to which we belong.[50] Of course, this is a prime instance of the influence of the Enlightenment model such as Nathan MacDonald claims, but Gnuse not only envisages monotheism in highly intellectualizing terms (he often speaks of the Israelite intelligentsia achieving intellectual breakthroughs, and he more often speaks of intellectual history than of intellectual and religious history, as though the intellectual were the important aspect). He also sees the whole value of the developments he describes as consisting in the way they lead humanity on from one stage of intellectual development to the next, with the modern age as the culmination of the process. Thus, however much or little Enlightenment ideas of monotheism have influenced his understanding of the content of Israelite faith in

---

[47] Even James Barr's moderate defence of evolutionary models of Israelite religion (*Biblical Theology*, ch. 7), while in my judgement associating the ideas of biological evolution and historical development too closely, does not seem to think there can be a useful comparison between the *ways* in which the two processes operate.

[48] Halpern, 'Brisker Pipes', 107, ends his quite sober interpretation of the historical development in this extraordinary way: 'The resultant communal religion remains at the heart of Western culture; the successful socialization of the radical monotheistic insight illustrates the interaction between the theory and the reality. In that sense, synthetic monotheism, as it may be called, was a movement towards theoretical empiricism, toward the "scientific method." It is in that sense that it has contributed most to the progress and progressiveness of Western thought.'

[49] Gnuse, *No Other Gods*, 125.

[50] Gnuse, *No Other Gods*, 233–36.

YHWH, it is especially important to notice that the significance he sees in the development of this faith is quite different from the way any Old Testament writer could conceivably have seen it.

Gnuse has accomplished something theologically interesting. In effect, he has adopted a reconstruction of the historical evolution of monotheism in Israel which replaces the biblical narrative of Israel's history with YHWH, and at the same time he has supplied a new theological understanding – a modernist salvation history – that corresponds to the new historical reconstruction, replacing the Old Testament's own theological account of Israel's history with YHWH. The procedure is parallel to that of radical reconstructions of the historical Jesus, which, since nineteenth-century liberalism, have frequently been inextricably linked with theologies alternative to those of the Gospels. It is merely rather surprising that Gnuse sees his work, in its theological aspect, as biblical theology.

Although Gnuse accords the emergence of monotheism in Israel world-historical significance, precisely this evaluation distances us modern people from it: 'We may be built upon biblical thought, but we have moved beyond it, too.'[51] The revolutionary breakthrough achieved by Israel's monotheistic intellectuals in the exile is, like all such evolutionary breakthroughs, but the beginning of a further process of evolution – 'the Judaeo-Christian tradition' – in which 'the implications of radical monotheism are [still] being worked out in terms of their social and religious imperatives'.[52] (One wonders why the Muslim world is not also part of the evolutionary process deriving from Israelite monotheism.) In other words, 'the implications of monotheistic religion are unfolding still in our own age. Perhaps, this is *the cardinal conclusion* to be drawn from contemporary critical studies *for the theological task before us*'.[53] Gnuse is oblivious to such obvious questions as: If Western intellectual development is the leading edge of human evolution, does it not look rather as if a new evolutionary breakthrough to some kind of postmodern atheism is already in process?

Gnuse's more detailed thoughts on the implications for biblical theology revolve around the difference between the old biblical theology's penchant for a contrastive picture of Israel's distinctiveness vis-à-vis her Canaanite environment and his evolutionary picture of difference emerging from major continuity. About this difference he makes two interesting points. One is that, whereas the old biblical theology fostered a dialectical model of the church's opposition to the world, with a corresponding attitude to social and political change, the new understanding will stress continuity and look for gradual processes of

---

[51] Gnuse, *No Other Gods*, 235.

[52] Gnuse, *No Other Gods*, 273.

[53] Gnuse, *No Other Gods*, 275 (my italics).

greater justice and equality, sensing the presence and activity of God in the human cultural processes of the whole contemporary world.[54] To this one might respond that drawing any such conclusions from biblical theology to the actual possibilities for change in specific social and political situations is hardly the way to do applied theology.

The second implication of his evolutionary picture is that we should abandon the 'quest to find something unique in biblical thought, that was so much in fashion ... We should not search for the unique, but rather for how old ideas were transformed'.[55] This seems to me a more insightful comment. It is surely true that the old fashion in Old Testament theology for outlining the Old Testament's theological ideas as in contrast at every point to the Near Eastern context 'produced forced generalizations'.[56] It would be refreshing to look for the Old Testament's own critiques of its religious environment rather than at historically reconstructed contrasting worldviews. We might discover that, in the last resort, it is not so much an issue of unique ideas as of YHWH's own uniqueness. As Peter Machinist shows, while Old Testament scholars find it increasingly difficult to locate anything truly unique in Israel's religion, a strong sense of the uniqueness of YHWH and of Israel (and the two as closely connected) pervades the writings of the Hebrew canon.[57] Gnuse reduces this to Israel's position as a kind of evolutionary bridgehead to the intellectual future of humanity, Machinist himself to Israel's sociological need for a 'counter-identity' in the face of the older and dominant cultures of Egypt and Mesopotamia.

In a quest for the unique identity of YHWH in Old Testament theology, we should surely be looking not only to the 'monotheistic' claims, which may or may not have convincing parallels in other ancient cultures, but to the fact that these claims (that YHWH is the unique creator and sovereign lord of all reality) are made with no diminution of the particularity of YHWH the God of Israel. Particularity of this kind *cannot* be reduced to a general religious idea and so absorbed either into the general religious climate of the ancient world or into an ongoing process of intellectual evolution. What gets lost in the massive intellectualization of the subject by Gnuse is not simply the sense that Israelite religion was more than a set of ideas about reality, but also the particularity of YHWH. Gnuse's God does not, of course, really do any of the particular things the Old Testament's YHWH does, while his election of Israel becomes Israel's remarkable intellectual achievement as a signal contribution to the intellectual evolution of humanity. The most important warning that arises from consideration of Gnuse's work is that biblical 'monotheism', whether or not we choose

---

[54] Gnuse, *No Other Gods*, 277–78.
[55] Gnuse, *No Other Gods*, 271.
[56] Gnuse, *No Other Gods*, 271.
[57] Machinist, 'Question', 420–42.

to use the word and however we find it necessary to define it, is a claim about the God who defines himself by his covenant with Israel and the particular name YHWH that cannot be abstracted from his particular identity in his history with Israel.

Gnuse's is not the only attempt to draw theological conclusions from the emerging consensus about the origins of monotheism in Israel. There are also those for whom the triumph of monotheism in the postexilic period was not at all a good thing, but a victory for oppressive patriarchal religion over the generous diversity of preexilic polytheism, in which YHWH had a consort and female spirituality found expression both in the household religion evidenced by the commonly found figurines of Asherah and also in cult centres not reserved for the exclusive worship of a single male god. Again, in its happy recovery of what it was really like from behind the ideological suppression and distortions of the canonical accounts, this resembles nothing so much as some forms of the quest of the historical Jesus, in which the real Jesus is rescued from the dogmatic Christology imposed on him by the Gospels. Of course, there is no real future for Old Testament theology, even of a suspicious and reconstructive kind, in this direction. If the attractive religious paradigm is that of Israel when Israelite religion was very much like most other ancient Near Eastern religious cultures, then there can be no good reason for continuing to be religiously interested in Israel in particular. Ancient polytheistic religion is, after all, much better documented outside Israel, and has left much more impressive religious literature elsewhere than the few polytheistic fragments that might be recoverable from the monotheistic censuring to which Israel's religion was subject in the literature that survives in the Old Testament.

The Old Testament: A Monotheistic Book?

Nathan MacDonald's book makes an indispensable contribution in demonstrating the inappropriateness of the categories of Enlightenment monotheism for understanding Old Testament faith in YHWH. However, not everyone who speaks of 'monotheism' has the Enlightenment model mainly in view. There are those whose thinking is much more influenced by the ways in which the Jewish and Christian traditions have read the Bible and understood the uniqueness of the God of Israel and the Christian God. There are also those who, as MacDonald recognizes in the case of von Rad, are well aware of at least some of the differences between Old Testament and modern 'monotheism' but continue to find it appropriate to speak of 'monotheism' in the former case, while seeking to avoid misunderstanding. My sense is that those New Testament scholars and scholars of early Judaism who speak of 'Jewish monotheism' in the Hellenistic and Roman periods are less influenced by the Enlightenment model than Old Testament scholarship has been. What term other than 'Jewish monotheism' could one use to characterize the very strong awareness that Jews of the post-biblical periods certainly had of the uniqueness of their God by contrast with the many and various gods worshipped by all other people they knew? (Perhaps one might propose 'mono-Yahwism', were that not reminiscent of the 'YHWH-alone' movement of the late monarchical period hypothesized by Morton Smith and Bernhard Lang. I use 'exclusive Yahwism' as a general term to cover what may be no more than monolatry as well as what I call 'Jewish monotheism'.) I shall continue to speak of 'late Second Temple period Jewish monotheism' ('Jewish monotheism' for convenience) for the kind of religion that I find in the Jewish literature of that period and that seems to me presupposed by the New Testament. The most important task is not that of finding a fully satisfactory label, but that of characterizing accurately just how the uniqueness of YHWH was understood.

This is itself a controversial subject, on which I am writing at length elsewhere.[58] But it seems to me relevant to our understanding of the Old Testament, as biblical theologians, in the sense that what I am calling 'Jewish monotheism' is what Jews in the period of the formation of the Hebrew canon found in these Jewish Scriptures. This category is not alien to the texts in the way that Enlightenment monotheism is. Arguably what I call 'Jewish monotheism' is the theology of the canon in the sense that it was the theological context for the formation and editing of the canonical collection and the way in which this collection was intended to be read by those who made it the Scriptures of that very scriptural religion, early Judaism. It would seem quite appropriate at least to consider whether it can be read in that way without violence to a historically informed understanding of the texts. I am not suggesting that all the ways in which early post-biblical Judaism read the biblical texts are valid for us. I am only wondering whether and how the basic understanding of the uniqueness of YHWH that the Hebrew canon's first readers found in it can also be found in it by us. If I am correct that this is also the understanding of the God of the Old Testament that is presupposed by the New Testament in the course of its also very innovatory christological reading of the Old, then the issue is also vital for the task of 'pan-biblical' theology.

For Jewish monotheism, the one God has a unique name, YHWH, and a unique relationship with his chosen people Israel, to whom he has revealed not only the supreme power he exercises in mighty acts of salvation and judgement in relation to Israel, but also the moral dispositions (in the classic characterization of Ex. 34:6–7) that characterize his dealings with Israel. All these elements of YHWH's particular identity as the God of Israel are essential to Jewish monotheism, as are the requirements on Israel summed up in the first commandment

---

[58] For the time being, see my short account in *God Crucified*, ch. 1.

of the Decalogue and in the Shema, which make Israel's monotheism no mere matter of intellectual belief but a matter of distinctive cultic practice and loving obedience that encompasses the whole of life.[59] (This is inadequately called monolatry, but it is true that Jews of the late Second Temple period were peculiarly conscious of the obligation to worship only YHWH and that this, with its negative corollary of non-participation in anything implicated in the cult of other gods, marked out Jewish monotheism most obviously in religious practice.)

This God of Israel is the one and only Creator of all things and sovereign Lord over all things. Among the many other things that late Second Temple period Jews said about the uniqueness of their God, these two aspects of his unique relationship to all other reality were the most commonly cited, repeatedly used to put YHWH in an absolutely unique category. Most Jewish writers had no hesitation in making clear that, in this sense, YHWH is the only true God there is and ought to be acknowledged as such by all people. All pagan worship of other gods was giving to others what only the one Creator and Lord of all things ought to receive. Much Jewish literature of the period can be said to hold to an eschatological monotheism that expected that, since YHWH is the one and only Lord of all reality, he must come to be acknowledged as such universally in the end. But this universalism was not in tension with the particularity of YHWH's election of Israel, for other nations would come to recognize precisely YHWH, the God of Israel, as the only true God. It would be his salvific acts on Israel's behalf that would create this universal recognition and recognition of the one God, Creator and Lord of all, would be inseparable from recognition of his special relationship to his covenant people. While in the diverse literature of early Judaism there are certainly more universalistic perspectives and more particularistic perspectives, often related to specific contextual factors such as diaspora Jewish apologetic or Palestinian Jewish resistance to Roman rule, on the whole it is fair to say that universalism and particularism are not contradictory aspects. Jewish monotheism is characterized by its way of relating YHWH's particularity as Israel's God with his universality as Creator and sovereign Lord of all.

This is the kind of Jewish reading of the Jewish Scriptures that the New Testament seems everywhere to presuppose. Most would allow that parts of these Scriptures give strong support to this kind of 'monotheism', but is it a plausible or valid canonical reading of the whole? Several writers have proposed that the Hebrew canon as a whole can be described as 'monotheizing', if not 'monotheistic', literature. This distinction is made by James Sanders, in a

---

[59] Barclay, *Jews*, 429, is right to find the term 'monotheism' inadequate if it is taken to place 'the emphasis on a concept – the belief that there is one, and only one, being rightly called "God" – and obscures the significance of *cultic practice* in defining acceptable or unacceptable religion'.

brief treatment that claims that 'every bit of [the Bible] monotheizes – more or less well'. He explains that each era from which biblical writings come 'left a residue of idioms derived from the polytheisms of its culture, precisely because of the struggle to monotheize'. [60] After a few examples, he concludes:

> The Bible is a monotheizing literature displaying the struggles of generations over some fifteen to eighteen centuries to pursue the Integrity of Reality. In this sense the Bible is a paradigm; it conjugates the nouns and verbs of the divine integrity in a plethora of different kinds of situations and conditions. To monotheize, in this sense, is not to progress or evolve toward monotheism, but rather to struggle within and against polytheistic contexts to affirm God's oneness, both in antiquity and today. [61]

These are very suggestive remarks, especially noteworthy for the way in which they allow polytheistic materials to be seen as subject to a monotheizing dynamic without proposing a developmental or evolutionary model. Unfortunately, Sanders has not pursued his suggestions any more fully, and nor, so far as I am aware, has anyone else. Sanders appears to be speaking about the individual biblical writings rather than about a 'monotheizing' editing of them to form the canon, but his model seems at least to require a process of 'monotheizing' selection of material as part of the process of canon formation. Similarly, any plausible proposal that the process of canonization was in part a 'monotheizing' process cannot attribute the 'monotheizing' purely to canonical editors, but must presuppose the prior existence of some 'monotheizing' literature. It could, however, also be open to the presence in the canon of material that is not itself obviously 'monotheizing' at all but that 'monotheizing' editors did not consider resistant to a 'monotheizing' reading encouraged by other parts of the canon.

Bernhard Lang, who, unlike Sanders, appears unsympathetic to the canonical suppression of polytheistic aspects of Israelite religion, emphasizes the role of the editors of the canon, who were 'committed monotheists', [62] and explains that the exclusion of unequivocal polytheism from the canon results not only from the exclusion of explicitly polytheistic writings but also from the more subtle methods of 'assimilating, adopting and re-interpreting traditions which may conserve polytheistic elements within a monotheistic context'. [63] One of his examples is the Israelite goddess Wisdom in Proverbs 1 – 9, where the polytheistic material has survived only because it could be read monotheistically, in a way that reduced Wisdom to 'a mere figure of poetic speech'. [64] Again, this

---

[60] Sanders, *Canon*, 51.

[61] Sanders, *Canon*, 52.

[62] Lang, *Monotheism*, 53.

[63] Lang, *Monotheism*, 50.

[64] Lang, *Monotheism*, 53; see further Lang, *Wisdom*.

promising proposal has not been followed up by further argument that 'polytheistic' texts in the Old Testament are limited to ones that could be read in a monotheistic way, consistent with the explicit monotheism of other parts of the canon.

John Sawyer's article, 'Biblical Alternatives to Monotheism', implicitly counters Lang's argument by arguing that there are three categories of text in the Old Testament. There is 1) a small group of 'texts in which monotheism is explicit: that is to say, statements in which the existence of other gods apart from Israel's God, Yahweh, is denied';[65] and 2) 'a second group of texts which, although not originally monotheistic, have under the influence of the [monotheistic] Deuteronomic texts, been so interpreted'.[66] But there is also 3), a third category of texts 'which are explicitly and embarrassingly polytheistic texts'.[67] With reference to the second category, he asks: 'Can a few explicitly monotheistic passages be used to change the meaning of other texts whose meaning is less explicit?'[68] After discussing the third category, he claims to 'have demonstrated that the plain meaning of the biblical text as a whole is far from monotheistic'.[69] In a response, Ronald Clements argued that

> Read diachronically, in the light of a critical awareness of the varying stages through which the Israelite religious tradition passed, monotheism does not seem to have been all that prominent a feature … Nevertheless when read synchronically, as a connected body of religious texts which are believed to offer a coherent and unified revelation, the idea of monotheism would appear to be very important.[70]

The disagreement between Sawyer and Clements seems to be over two points: whether it is proper to read some texts in conformity with others in the canon if this means 'changing' their original meaning; and whether there are texts that cannot even be plausibly subjected to such a reading.

I shall return to these issues after making a further, crucially important point about Jewish monotheism. The essential element in what I have called Jewish monotheism, the element that makes it a kind of monotheism, is not the denial of the existence of other 'gods', but an understanding of the uniqueness of YHWH that puts him in a class of his own, a wholly different class from any other heavenly or supernatural beings, even if these are called 'gods'. I call this YHWH's transcendent uniqueness. (Mere 'uniqueness' can be what distinguishes one member of a class from other members of it. By 'transcendent

---

[65] Sawyer, 'Biblical Alternatives', 173.
[66] Sawyer, 'Biblical Alternatives', 174.
[67] Sawyer, 'Biblical Alternatives', 176.
[68] Sawyer, 'Biblical Alternatives', 175.
[69] Sawyer, 'Biblical Alternatives', 179.
[70] Clements, 'Monotheism', 338.

uniqueness' I mean a form of uniqueness that puts YHWH in a class of his own.) Especially important for identifying this transcendent uniqueness are statements that distinguish YHWH by means of a unique relationship to the whole of reality: YHWH alone is Creator of all things, whereas all other things are created by him; and YHWH alone is the sovereign Lord of all things, whereas all other things serve or are subject to his universal lordship. I think that a dynamic of distinguishing YHWH's uniqueness as in this sense transcendent is how the 'monotheizing' that Sanders rightly identifies throughout the biblical texts largely occurs (though I would not insist that there are not individual texts and perhaps whole biblical books where this dynamic cannot be identified). It is in this manner that the biblical texts, in Sawyer's words, 'struggle within and against polytheistic contexts to affirm God's oneness'.

From this perspective it is clear that explicitly monotheistic texts are far from confined to those in Sawyer's first category, which he defines as 'statements in which the existence of other gods apart from Israel's God, Yahweh, is denied'.[71] For example, a text like Nehemiah 9:6, which Sawyer does not count as monotheistic, can now be seen to be a very strong expression of the monotheistic dynamic:

> You are YHWH, you alone; you have made heaven, the heaven of heavens, with all their host, the earth and all that is on it, the seas and all that is in them. To all of them you give life, and the host of heaven worships you. (NRSV, altered)

By attributing to YHWH the creation of all other reality, by emphasizing that all other creatures without exception have been created by YHWH, this text is making an absolute distinction between the unique identity of YHWH and all other reality. The fact that other heavenly beings, YHWH's retinue, 'the host of heaven', are included does not qualify the uniqueness of YHWH but, on the contrary, serves to underline YHWH's uniqueness by making it unequivocally clear that YHWH does not belong to a class of heavenly beings that includes him along with the host of heaven, but is absolutely distinguished from the host of heaven in that he created them. This text makes the transcendent uniqueness of YHWH as clear as could be.

This example illustrates how it is not the existence of heavenly beings besides YHWH that is at stake in the 'monotheizing' dynamic of the texts and the canon, but the nature and status of such beings. Within the Hebrew canon, most 'gods' besides YHWH fall into one of two categories. They are either members of YHWH's retinue, serving his rule, or they are impotent nonentities. In the former case, they are called by a variety of terms (gods, sons of gods, sons of the Most High, holy ones, watchers, the host of YHWH, the host of heaven). They

---

[71] Sawyer, 'Biblical Alternatives', 173. He reckons with only twenty-five such texts, mostly in the Deuteronomic writings and Deutero-Isaiah.

accompany YHWH as warriors or attendants, and they assemble in YHWH's presence in heaven. We should avoid the 'etymological fallacy' of determining the significance of this heavenly retinue of YHWH by reference to its origins in a properly polytheistic context rather than its functions in the biblical text. Despite the rather misleading sense suggested by the commonly used English term 'divine council', the assembly around YHWH are not counsellors. He does not consult them in an open decision-making process in which they contribute advice on which he acts. Unless we count Satan's unsolicited suggestions, which YHWH allows him to implement, in Job 1:9–12; 2:4–7, the only instance of advice given by one of the assembly to YHWH is in 1 Kings 22:19–22, where YHWH asks for a volunteer to lead Ahab to his death and, when 'a spirit' offers to do it, asks him 'how?' and approves of his suggestion. Not even this degree of participation in planning or decision-making occurs anywhere else. In Isaiah 6, there is only YHWH's request for a volunteer (6:8). When Jeremiah speaks of prophets standing in 'YHWH's council' (סוֹד, a word which implies intimacy, a circle which is privy to YHWH's plans, but not necessarily for debate or advice), he expects them to hear YHWH's decrees announced in the assembly, not to be involved in or present at some kind of discussion (Jer. 23:18, 22). The general point is that these 'gods' are not independent powers but servants of YHWH who no more qualify his unique status than do human beings who worship and obey YHWH. YHWH's retinue are the attendants of an absolute monarch, whose sheer numbers evidence his greatness and whose constant praises serve precisely to define and to proclaim his transcendent uniqueness.

The other category of 'gods' consists of the gods of the nations, reduced to the status of powerless nonentities by the biblical texts' insistence on YHWH's uniquely supreme power, and ridiculed as 'non-gods' and 'nothings', as we observed in the first section above in the case of Deuteronomy 32. Again, the monotheizing dynamic is apparent not in absolutely denying their existence, but in denying them a status that could conceivably detract from YHWH's transcendent uniqueness.

The mere use of אלהים or other terms for divine beings is not decisive for Jewish monotheism; everything depends on how such beings are defined in relation to YHWH. However, it is interesting – and deserves much more attention than it has received – to observe some steps toward linguistic distinctions, such as the use of אלהים with the article in some cases to distinguish 'God' from 'the gods' (see above on Deuteronomy's usage), the use of אלהים with a meaning something like 'the deity' (e.g., in Gen. 1), and the contemptuous descriptions of the foreign gods or idols by such terms as 'non-gods' (לֹא אֵל) or אלילים, a deliberate malformation of אלהים (as in Ps. 96:5: 'For all the gods [אלהי] of the peoples are אלילים, but YHWH made the heavens').[72] In the

---

[72] See H.D. Preuss in *TDOT* 1.285–87.

literature of later Second Temple Judaism the words for 'god' (in Hebrew, Aramaic and Greek) almost entirely cease to be used for the heavenly beings who serve YHWH, except in the Qumran community's own compositions and in the special case of Philo (whose use of θεός is strongly affected by Hellenistic use), and even the use of 'holy ones' strongly declines.[73] There is clearly a concern to reduce the use of terms that could designate both YHWH and other heavenly beings. The Qumran community continued to use almost all the biblical terms for heavenly beings to describe the angels (as they were now most often called), perhaps as a deliberate continuation of scriptural usage, but it would be a mistake to think the community less monotheistic than other Jews of the period. Terminology was affected by monotheizing, but not always decisively.

Sawyer distinguished a group of explicitly monotheistic texts (which I have argued should be much larger than he allows) from a category of texts which were not originally monotheistic but have been interpreted as such under the influence of the explicitly monotheistic texts. He doubts that such interpretation – 'changing' the original meaning of texts – is legitimate. I think this is too stark a contrast and propose that my concept of a monotheizing dynamic can help us identify more continuity between these two types of text. Let us take Sawyer's examples: in the first category he focuses on the texts that use the formula 'and there is no other [besides YHWH]', while in the second category he focuses on the passages which emphasize the incomparability of YHWH. Not all of the texts in the former category say exactly that there is no other *'god,'* besides YHWH, as 2 Samuel 7:22 and Isaiah 45:5, 14, 21 do. More typically, they put YHWH in a class of his own, for example:

'YHWH is the God (האלהים); there is no other besides him.' (Deut. 4:35)

'There is no Holy One like YHWH, no one besides you.' (1 Sam. 2:2)

'That all the people of the earth may know that YHWH is the God (האלהים); there is no other.' (1 Kgs. 8:60)

'I am YHWH, and there is no other.' (Isa. 45:5, 6, 18)

'I, YHWH, am your God, and there is no other.' (Joel 2:27)

Compare some of the 'incomparability' texts:

'Who is like you, YHWH, among the gods?' (Ex. 15:11)

---

[73] Similarly, statements of YHWH's incomparability, common in the Old Testament, are in the post-biblical literature almost entirely confined to the Qumran community's writings. This is doubtless because they state YHWH's incomparability *among the gods.*

'For who is like me? Who can summon me? Who is the shepherd who can stand before me?' (Jer. 49:19; 50:44)

'For who in the skies can be compared to YHWH?
Who among the sons of gods is like YHWH? …
YHWH God of hosts, who is as mighty as you, YHWH?' (Ps. 89:6, 8)

The 'incomparability' texts usually say that YHWH is incomparable among 'the gods' (though sometimes the comparison is more generally with any creature at all) and so seem superficially polytheistic, in the sense of admitting the existence of other heavenly beings. In fact, however, they are expressions of the 'monotheizing' dynamic that is constantly driving a line of absolute distinction between YHWH and other 'gods'. The effect of 'there is none like YHWH' is precisely to put YHWH in a class of his own, exactly as the first category of texts do in denying that there is any 'other' besides YHWH. Whether the existence of other gods is denied or whether YHWH is simply said to be in a class of his own by comparison with them is of small importance to the general sense of all these texts. This is confirmed by the fact that examples of the two kinds of text sometimes occur in close association with each other, for example:

'There is no one like you, and there is no god besides you.' (2 Sam. 7:22)

'I am God, and there is no other; I am God, and there is no one like me.' (Isa. 46:9).

There remains Sawyer's third category of texts, the 'explicitly and embarrassingly polytheistic' ones. The most important texts here are those which depict the battle between YHWH and the chaos monsters (Rahab, Leviathan, the Sea), whether these represent the forces over which YHWH triumphed when he created the world (Ps. 74:13–14) or the persistent threat of chaos or evil that threatens creation and will require a further victory of YHWH in the future (Isa. 27:1). This topic deserves a full discussion for which this is not the place. But the idea that there are powers opposed to God which God must defeat is part and parcel of the traditional monotheistic religions, along with, of course, the conviction that God is unquestionably able to defeat such powers of evil and can be expected to do so in the end. Jon Levenson is right to argue that there is real theological loss when this theme in the Hebrew Bible is dismissed in favour of an impression of YHWH's power as serene supremacy that is never challenged.[74] But the recognition of YHWH as the sole Creator of all things and the sole sovereign Lord of all things need not require that. What matters is that, as Herbert Niehr puts it,

---

[74] Levenson, *Creation*.

> No other divinity is the subject of the processes of creation or the taming of chaos in the [Hebrew Bible]. YHWH alone is the creator and he alone fights chaos. The [Hebrew Bible] texts show that he is a universal god having power over everything in heaven and earth and that he is the supreme god fulfilling deeds other gods cannot fulfil.[75]

In other words, YHWH's defeat, restraint or taming of chaos (in a variety of texts) does not, in the perspective of Jewish monotheism, put his sole deity in doubt but precisely demonstrates his sole deity.

Recognition of the 'monotheizing' dynamic in the form I have proposed does not prevent us recognizing in the Hebrew Bible material that in a wide variety of ways resembles the language and myths of Canaanite and other Near Eastern religions. Rather, it shows us the way such material is constantly being re-functioned to serve the purpose of asserting and characterizing the transcendent uniqueness of YHWH. The texts were composed in cultures in which polytheism was always near to hand and had to be engaged. As Sanders put it, there is in the texts a 'struggle within and against polytheistic contexts to affirm God's oneness'.[76] They are texts in which (with some possible exceptions, such as Ecclesiastes[77]) we do not see monotheism securely achieved and taken for granted, but rather the many creative ways in which it is constantly being recovered and rethought. Moreover, as Nathan MacDonald's work makes very clear, in distinguishing Deuteronomy from Enlightenment monotheism, exclusive Yahwism in the biblical tradition is not an easily made intellectual proposition but a demand for radical and complete devotion to YHWH. So the 'monotheizing' dynamic always works in favour of a recognition of YHWH's transcendent uniqueness that is inseparable from his uniquely demanding requirement of loyalty and devotion from his covenant people.

So my proposal does not suppress the diversity of the texts, but it does show how the whole of the Hebrew Bible can be read in accordance with early Jewish monotheism. It rejects a developmental reading of the texts. Not only is

---

[75] Niehr, 'Rise of YHWH', 67.

[76] Sanders, *Canon*, 52.

[77] Cf. Frydrych, *Living*, 107–108: 'Qoheleth's perspective is thoroughly monotheistic, in the most rigid sense of that word. There is not a single hint in the book that Qoheleth is prepared to consider more than one deity, or a force of any kind, in operation alongside God, nor is there any apologetic against polytheistic views. This latter fact is of some interest, for Hellenistic influence on the society of Qoheleth's day was significant, and the documented tension between traditional Judaism and the penetrating Hellenism would have been impossible to escape. Yet, this tension is not at all reflected in the book. We have to conclude from this that Qoheleth has in mind an audience that needs no convincing with respect to the monotheistic perspective he puts before them.'

an evolutionary account of the emergence and development of monotheism simply not the story the canonical narratives of Israel tell. Recent scholarship also seems to me to have made the idea that we can stratify all the texts chronologically (with minute dissection of the texts into earlier and later layers and interpolations) and thereby construct a developmental reconfiguration of the biblical material hugely problematic. All attempts to do this are hopelessly speculative because the texts have not been preserved in such a way as to make it possible. Undoubtedly the texts emerge out of a complex history, but they do not contain sufficient or sufficiently clear traces of their own pre-history to make tradition history a viable vehicle for biblical theology.[78] What they do contain is a dialectic of 'convergence' and 'differentiation' (Mark Smith's terms) or 'recognition' and 'rejection' (Werner Schmidt), driven by the core apprehension of YHWH's uniqueness. I use these terms not to describe a developmental history, as Smith and Schmidt do to some extent, but to characterize what is happening throughout the texts in many different ways. There is no evolution visible in the texts, but there is a dynamic.

Finally in this section, I must comment on the significance of the parallels in ancient Near Eastern religious texts to much of the kind of language I have identified as 'monotheizing' or monotheistic in the Old Testament. Here, for example, is part of a Sumerian prayer to the moon god Nanna-Suen (Sin):

> O lord, who decides destinies in heaven and on earth, whose saying no one can alter, who holds water and fire in his hands, who guides living creatures – who among the gods is as you are?
> Who is exalted in heaven? You alone are exalted!
> When you have spoken your word in heaven, the Igigi [gods of heaven] pray to you, when you have spoken your word on earth, the Anunnaki [gods of the earth or underworld] kiss the ground. ...
> O lord, your rule has no counterpart in heaven nor your heroic power among your divine brothers on earth,
> mighty one, exalted king, whose 'divine powers' no one dares to wrest from you, none of the gods can be compared with your deity.[79]

Such prayers, addressed to many different gods, are not uncommon in the religious literature of Mesopotamia. There seem to be various explanations, which Gnuse reports thus:

---

[78] Therefore I disagree with Barr, *Biblical Theology*, 61, when he suggests that 'the idea of monotheism' is one of those topics in biblical theology for which 'a historical framework with dating of different sources would very likely prove necessary'.

[79] Beyerlin (ed.), *Near Eastern Religious Texts*, 105–6. This text is no later than the seventeenth century BC.

Mesopotamia produced several deities who received apparently exclusive veneration, most notably Marduk and Sin in Babylon and Ninurta and Ashur in Assyria.
However ... the existence of other gods is not denied, thus suggesting that each
deity, when worshipped exclusively, merely absorbed the other gods temporarily
and with respect for their continued existence. In some texts the elevation of one
god was connected to the rhetoric of imperial aspiration of a conquering empire, in
others the deity was symbolically representative of all the gods, and in prayers and
laments the petitioner addressed the deity with exaggerated language of exclusivity
in order to motivate the god to act.[80]

Quite similar material appears also in Egypt (quite apart from the atypical episode of Akhnaton's cult of Aton), where, for example, it was possible to praise
Amon-Re as the sole creator of all things, including even the gods.[81] But different gods were variously praised as creator of the world, on different occasions
or by different worshippers each praising their own personally favoured god.
There was also an Egyptian tendency to merge deities.[82]

   It is quite true that many such statements are, considered in themselves,
semantically indistinguishable from similar ones about YHWH in the Old Testament.[83] The tendency to exalt one god to a *sui generis* position as compared
with the others really is a 'monotheizing' move, whatever the reasons for it, as
is the tendency to absorb features of various gods into one. However, these
tendencies never, apparently, relate consistently and permanently to only one
god. It seems not to have been thought inconsistent for the same kinds of language to be applied to more than one god on different occasions or by different
individuals. Perhaps this also happened in preexilic Israel. But what characterizes the Old Testament as a canonical collection of literature is that this kind of
language is invariably reserved for YHWH with whom all other gods are consistently contrasted. There is nothing occasional or optional about its application
to YHWH. Thus the Old Testament language that can be paralleled elsewhere
nevertheless needs, within the Old Testament, to be understood in its context
as part of the Old Testament's overall delineation of the unique identity of
YHWH.

---

[80] Gnuse, *No Other Gods*, 268; cf. his fuller survey on pp. 154–61. Cf. Lohfink, 'Polytheistic', 142: 'Theoretical polytheism among Israel's neighbours, in practice, always
   left open the possibility of monolatry – the tendency, indeed, toward monolatry.
   Divine figures could split themselves up, then join together again. New gods could
   step in ... But it always happened that the man who worshipped one of these gods
   more or less consciously summed up in that divinity all that godhead meant to him.'
[81] See the hymn in Beyerlin (ed.), *Near Eastern Religious Texts*, 13–16.
[82] Gnuse, *No Other Gods*, 161–74.
[83] Machinist, 'Question', 423.

The Shema in the New Testament

Some scholars have proposed connections between non-monotheistic material in the Old Testament and Christology in the New Testament. John Sawyer, for example, thinks his view that the Old Testament is not predominately monotheistic helps to explain how belief in the divinity of Christ and the doctrine of the Trinity developed.[84] Bernhard Lang argues that an old tradition of two gods in Israel persisted in early Judaism and fed into New Testament Christology,[85] while Margaret Barker has pursued this approach in much more detail, arguing that in the older Israelite tradition that survived alongside monotheism El and YHWH were distinct gods, father and son, and that the early Christians identified Jesus with YHWH.[86] In my view there is no good evidence for the idea that non-monotheistic forms of Israelite religion survived through the Second Temple period to be available to the early Christians. The literature of early Judaism is uniformly monotheistic. But there is in any case another reason not to make this kind of connection between non-monotheistic Israelite religion and the New Testament: it is clear that the New Testament writers presuppose the kind of Jewish monotheism that I have described in the last section and that is found throughout early Jewish literature. Their christological innovations proceed on the basis of this presupposed monotheism and they do not intend to depart from it.

In the present chapter we shall confine ourselves to three important instances of the New Testament's appropriation of the Shema,[87] which, as a considerable amount of evidence shows, was central to the Jewish faith of the period, recited twice daily by observant Jews and echoed frequently in the literature. The first example does not involve Christology, the second and third do.

Romans 3:28–30

> For we hold that a person is justified by faith apart from works prescribed by the law. Or is God the God of Jews only? Is he not the God of Gentiles also? Yes, of Gentiles also, since God is one; and he will justify the circumcised on the ground of faith and the uncircumcised through that same faith. (NRSV)

---

[84] Sawyer, 'Biblical Alternatives', 179.

[85] Lang, 'Monotheismus'; and *Hebrew God*, 197.

[86] Barker, *Great Angel*.

[87] Other allusions to the Shema are Mt. 22:37; Mk. 12:29–30, 32; Lk. 10:27; Gal. 3:20; 1 Tim. 2:5; Jas. 2:19.

In this passage, with its obvious allusion to the Shema ('God is one'), Paul draws a relatively novel[88] conclusion from the understanding of the Shema that was normal in the late Second Temple period. Indeed, the form of the allusion itself (εἷς ὁ θεός) is itself more or less standard. The usual form is εἷς θεός (ἐστι) (*Sib. Or.* 3:11; *Sib. Or.* frag. 1:7, 32; Josephus, *Ant.* 4.201; Ps-Sophocles; Philo, *Opif.* 171; *Spec.* 1.30), though James 2:19 has εἷς ἐστιν ὁ θεός. It follows from reading the Shema as 'YHWH our God, YHWH is one',[89] which is probably also how the Septuagint (κύριος ὁ θεὸς ἡμῶν κύριος εἷς ἐστιν) should be understood. The words were understood to mean that YHWH, the God of Israel ('our God') is the one and only God of all reality, the one Creator and Lord of all. In this way the words express exactly that combination of particularity and universalism that is characteristic of early Jewish monotheism.

Paul takes up precisely that combination. He does not deny that God is, in a distinctive sense, the God of his people Israel, but he insists that, since he is the one and only God there is, he must also be the God of Gentiles. In itself even this might not be controversial. But he interprets it to mean that Gentiles do not have to become Jews in order to be 'justified'. Mark Nanos puts it well:

> Gentiles are forbidden to become Jews ... because to do so would be to deny the universalistic oneness of God (he is the One God of all the nations), which would implicitly deny his election of Israel and the privilege of Torah, because if he is not the One God of all outside Israel who believe in him then he is not the One God of Israel; he is not the One God at all. His oneness has been compromised if he is *only* the God of Israel, *only* the God of the circumcised, *only* the God of Torah, and not *also* the God of the nations, not *also* the God of the uncircumcised, and not *also* the God of those outside the Torah.[90]

Although there is no indication that Paul had it in mind, there is a kind of Old Testament precedent for insisting that YHWH is not the one God unless he is the God of the nations as well as the God of Israel. In the only echo of this part of the Shema within the Hebrew Bible, Zechariah 14:9 predicts that 'YHWH will become king over all the earth; on that day YHWH will be one and his name one.' The thought is evidently that YHWH cannot be truly one until he is in fact universally acknowledged as the one true God. The passage goes on to envisage an annual pilgrimage of the nations to worship YHWH by celebrating the Feast of Tabernacles in Jerusalem. The festival was associated with God's gift of the rains, and so it is appropriate that the punishment of any nation that

---

[88] Probably Philo comes closest in what he says about proselytes in *Spec.* 1.52.

[89] For convincing arguments that this is also the meaning within Deuteronomy, see Moberly, 'YHWH is One'; MacDonald, *Deuteronomy*, 62–70.

[90] Nanos, *Mystery*, 184.

does not make this pilgrimage to Jerusalem will be drought (Zech. 14:16–19). But the gift of the rains was also associated with the Shema (Deut. 10:13–14 – this passage was probably part of the twice-daily recitation of the Shema), and so it seems that Zechariah 14 envisages a universalizing of the Shema. All peoples will be YHWH's peoples, all will love YHWH as the Shema requires, all will therefore worship him at the Feast of Tabernacles, and all will receive the paradigmatic divine blessing on those who love him. Thus Paul's characteristically radical conclusion from the Shema is in line with the way the Shema was understood even within the Old Testament. Israel's election, as God's people, becomes paradigmatic (and so never simply dissolved in an undifferentiated universalism) rather than exclusive.

1 Corinthians 8:1–6

Now concerning food sacrificed to idols: we know that 'all of us possess knowledge.' Knowledge puffs up, but love builds up. Anyone who claims to know something does not yet have the necessary knowledge; but anyone who loves God is known by him.

Hence, as to the eating of food offered to idols, we know that 'no idol has real existence in the world,' and that 'there is no God but one.' Indeed, even though there may be so-called gods in heaven or on earth – as in fact there are many gods and many lords – yet

for us there is one God, the Father,
from whom are all things and for whom we exist,
and one Lord, Jesus Christ,
through whom are all things and through whom we exist. (NRSV, altered)

It is widely recognized that in verse 6 Paul offers a Christian formulation of the Shema. But we should first notice how throughout his discussion of the issue of food offered to idols Paul draws on the tradition of Jewish monotheistic rhetoric and especially on Deuteronomy. The issue, of course, is a very traditional issue of Jewish monolatry in a pagan religious context. Thus the two statements that Paul takes up in verse 4, in order to explain them in the following verses, are typically Jewish monotheistic formulae: 'we know that "no idol has real existence in the world," and that "there is no God but one"' (οἴδαμεν ὅτι οὐδὲν εἴδωλον ἐν κόσμῳ καὶ ὅτι οὐδεὶς θεὸς εἰ μὴ εἷς). No doubt, these statements come from the Corinthians' letter, but the Corinthians may have been citing back to Paul what he himself had taught them, and in any case the assertions are typically Jewish monotheistic ones. The designation of other gods as 'idols' can, of course, only be Jewish. The two statements together are reminiscent of the common Jewish monotheistic formula which claims that there is no other God besides YHWH, especially those versions of this formula which give it an explicitly cosmic context, like the ἐν κόσμῳ ('in the world')[91] of 1 Corinthians 8:4, which Paul echoes in the εἴτε ἐν οὐρανῷ εἴτε ἐπὶ γῆς ('in heaven or on earth') of the following verse, and especially also those versions of the formula which link it with an allusion to the Shema's assertion of the uniqueness of God. For example:

> YHWH is God; there is no other besides him.... YHWH is God in heaven above and on the earth beneath; there is no other. (Deut. 4:35, 39)

> For there is no other besides the Lord, neither in heaven, nor on the earth, nor in the deepest places, nor in the one foundation. (*2 Enoch* 47:3J)

> He is one, and besides him there is no other. (Mk. 12:32)

The first of the two statements is probably best translated: 'no idol has real existence in the world'. The alternative translation, 'an idol is a nothing in the world', is tempting, because it could echo the biblical use of הבל (' a vapour, a mere puff of air', i.e., nothing of any consequence) for the pagan gods, as in Deuteronomy 32:21 and elsewhere.[92] But the linguistic parallel between the two statements favours the former translation, which also makes better sense of 'in the world'. This last phrase also makes it obvious that 'idol' here does not mean the physical object as such (which, of course, undeniably exists) but the pagan god supposedly pictured by it, which in Jewish usage could also be called εἴδωλον. When Paul returns to the topic in chapter 10, now in order to urge the Corinthians to 'flee from the worship of idols' (10:14), he is aware that his argument might seem to contradict his agreement with the Corinthians that 'no idol has real existence in the world':

> What do I imply then? That food sacrificed to idols is anything, or that an idol is anything (εἴδωλόν τί ἐστιν)? No, I imply that what pagans sacrifice, they sacrifice to demons and not to a god. I do not want you to be partners with demons. (10:19–20, NRSV, altered)

Paul's point may be that what the idol-worshippers think the idol represents – a god – does not exist, but, as Jewish tradition believed on the basis of Deuteronomy 32:21 and Psalm 106:37, evil spirits exploit their fantasy, so that, though they do not know it, they are actually worshipping 'demons'.[93] (The alternative view is that both in 8:4 and 10:19 Paul means that pagan gods do not exist *as*

---

[91] The biblical prohibition of idolatry is associated with specific rejection of the worship of anything in the cosmos: Deut. 4:15–19; 5:8.

[92] Cf. also *Jub.* 20:8 ('all those who trust in them trust in nothing'); *2 Bar.* 41:2; *2 En.* 34:1. LXX translates הבל as οὐδὲν on one occasion, in Isa. 49:4, though the reference there is not to gods or idols.

[93] *1 Bar.* 4:7; *Jub.* 11:4–5, 17; *1 En.* 19:1; 99:7; *Sib. Or.* frag. 1:22; 8:47, 386, 394.

gods, that is, there is nothing godlike about them, but they do exist as minor supernatural forces – δαιμόνια.)

In any case, what matters most here is Paul's resort to the Song of Moses, a classic resource for the Jewish insistence on the exclusive worship of YHWH. He cites Deuteronomy 32:17: 'They sacrificed to demons and not to a god' (LXX: δαιμονίοις καὶ οὐ θεῷ). The Hebrew of this verse probably means 'to demons, to what is not divine (לא אלה)'.[94] As a translation of this, the Septuagint Greek should mean 'to demons and not to a god', or 'to demons, that is no-god', though a reader who did not know the Hebrew *Vorlage* could read it as 'to demons and not to God'. This meaning is possible in Paul's use of the allusion, but 'to demons and not to a god' is more appropriate to the Pauline context.[95] The same words Paul cites from Deuteronomy 32:17 are also echoed in *1 Baruch* 4:7 (δαιμονίοις καὶ οὐ θεῷ); *Jubilees* 11:17; *1 Enoch* 19:1; and *Sibylline Oracles* fragment 1:22.[96] They are a Jewish monotheistic commonplace. But Paul is well aware of their context in the Song of Moses, understood as recounting the history of Israel's idolatrous behaviour to which Paul had appealed in the earlier part of chapter 10.

He goes on to allude to the same passage of the Song of Moses again in 10:22: 'Or are we provoking the Lord to jealousy? Are we stronger than he?'. The first question alludes to Deuteronomy 32:21: 'They have provoked me to jealousy with what is not a god' (LXX: ἐπ' οὐ θεῷ).[97] This is the only occasion on which Paul speaks of the divine jealousy (unless 2 Cor. 11:2 counts). His choice of the allusion shows that he takes very seriously the Jewish understanding of monolatry as required by God's jealous desire for the sole devotion of his covenant people (Ex. 20:5; Deut. 4:23–34; 5:9; 6:15; 32:16, 19, 21). In this sense God's jealousy is closely connected with the Shema. This makes it all the more noteworthy that Paul here attributes the divine jealousy of Deuteronomy to Jesus Christ. In Deuteronomy 32:21 YHWH speaks in the first person, but in turning the passage into a third-person statement Paul could supply κύριος from verse 19. But since 'the cup of the Lord' and 'the table of the Lord' in the preceding verse must refer to Christ, this must be one of those quite frequent occasions on which Paul interprets the κύριος of an Old Testament YHWH

---

[94] *1 En.* 19:1 paraphrases this as 'sacrifice to demons as to gods'; cf., similarly, *Sib. Or.* 8:394: 'dead demons, as if they were heavenly beings'.

[95] Fee, *First Epistle to the Corinthians*, 472; Bell, *Provoked*, 253–54.

[96] Note also Pseudo-Philo, *L.A.B.* 25:9 ('the demons of the idols'). Several of these passages understand the demons to be spirits of the dead (connecting Deut. 32:17 and Ps. 106:37 with Ps. 106:28; Deut. 26:14): *Jub.* 11:27; *Sib. Or.* frag. 1:22 ('sacrifices to the demons in Hades').

[97] The second question is probably an ironic reference to 'the strong' in the Corinthian church, but it may also allude to Deut. 32:39, which declares YHWH's unrivalled and unchallengeable power.

text as Jesus.[98] The implication for Jewish monotheism and Christology is remarkable: the exclusive devotion that YHWH jealously requires of his people is required of Christians by Jesus Christ. Effectively Jesus assumes the unique identity of YHWH.

This is coherent with the suggestion that Paul already has the Song of Moses in mind in 10:4 ('the rock was Christ'), alluding to the description of YHWH as Israel's Rock that is characteristic of the Song (Deut. 32:4, 15, 18, 31; note the close association with the theme of Israel's idolatry in verse 18).[99] But more certainly and more importantly, Paul has already prepared for his christological appropriation of the themes of monolatry and jealousy by means of his reformulation of the Shema in 8:6.

Paul has the Shema in mind from the beginning of chapter 8, for 'loves God' in verse 3 is already an allusion to it.[100] He is well aware that the faith of the Shema is not just a matter of objective knowledge that God is unique, but of wholehearted devotion to the one God. Thus in verse 5 he is already shifting the emphasis from the mere existence or otherwise of gods (which v. 4 stressed) to the question of allegiance, devotion and worship. The sense in which there are 'many gods and many lords' (v. 5) is that pagans give allegiance and worship to them, whereas 'for us' (v. 6) there is one God and one Lord. While the phrase 'many gods and many lords' is accurate – the term κύριος was used in many Greek cults – it also makes a neat contrast with the one God and one Lord of Paul's remarkable rewriting of the Shema. The carefully structured formulation reads:

ἀλλ' ἡμῖν εἷς θεὸς ὁ πατὴρ
    ἐξ οὗ τὰ πάντα καὶ ἡμεῖς εἰς αὐτόν,
καὶ εἷς κύριος Ἰησοῦς Χριστὸς
    δι' οὗ τὰ πάντα καὶ ἡμεῖς δι' αὐτοῦ.

but for us [there is] one God, the Father,
    from whom [are] all things and we for him,
and one Lord, Jesus Christ,
    through whom [are] all things and we through him.

In stating that there is one God and one Lord, Paul is unmistakably echoing the monotheistic statement of the Shema ('YHWH our God, YHWH, is one'),

---

[98] Thiselton, *First Epistle to the Corinthians*, 778.

[99] Fee, *First Epistle to the Corinthians*, 449; Bell, *Provoked*, 254.

[100] If 'being known' by God (8:3) should be understood in terms of divine election (cf. Amos 3:2), then the association in that verse between loving God and being known by God could be further explored as a Deuteronomic theme related to the Shema (cf. Deut. 7:7–9) which Paul also reflects in Rom. 8:28–29.

whose Greek version in the Septuagint reads: 'The Lord our God, the Lord, is one' (κύριος ὁ θεὸς ἡμῶν κύριος εἷς ἐστιν). Paul has taken over all of the words of the Septuagint version of the Shema: 'The Lord our God, the Lord, is one' (κύριος ὁ θεὸς ἡμῶν κύριος εἷς ἐστιν),[101] but rearranged them in such a way as to produce an affirmation of both one God, the Father, and one Lord, Jesus Christ.

If Paul were understood as *adding* the one Lord to the one God of whom the Shema speaks, then, from the perspective of Jewish monotheism, he would certainly be producing, not christological monotheism, but outright ditheism. Over against the many gods and many lords (v. 5) whom pagans worshipped, the Shema demands exclusive allegiance to the unique God alone. Even if 'Lord' in verse 6 means no more than 'lords' in verse 5 – and it must certainly mean at least this – there can be no doubt that the *addition* of a unique Lord to the unique God of the Shema would flatly *contradict* the uniqueness of the latter. Paul would not be reasserting Jewish monotheism in a Christian way, nor modifying or expanding the Shema, but repudiating Judaism and radically subverting the Shema. The only possible way to understand Paul as maintaining monotheism is to understand him to be including Jesus in the unique identity of the one God affirmed in the Shema. But this is in any case clear from the fact that the term 'Lord', applied here to Jesus as the 'one Lord', is taken from the Shema itself. Paul is not adding to the one God of the Shema a 'Lord' the Shema does not mention. He is identifying Jesus as the 'Lord' whom the Shema affirms to be one. In this unprecedented reformulation of the Shema, the unique identity of the one God *consists of* the one God, the Father, *and* the one Lord, his Messiah (who is implicitly regarded as the Son of the Father).

Paul rewrites the Shema to include both God and Jesus in the unique divine identity. But the point might not have been sufficiently clear had he not combined with the Shema itself another way of characterizing the unique identity of YHWH. Of the Jewish ways of characterizing the divine uniqueness, the most unequivocal was by reference to creation. In the uniquely divine role of creating all things it was for Jewish monotheism unthinkable that any being other than God could even assist God (Isa. 44:24; *4 Ezra* 3:4; Josephus, *C. Ap.* 2.192). But to Paul's unparalleled inclusion of Jesus in the Shema he adds the equally unparalleled inclusion of Jesus in the creative activity of God. No more unequivocal way of including Jesus in the unique divine identity is conceivable, within the framework of Second Temple Jewish monotheism.

As well as dividing the wording of the Shema between God and Jesus, Paul also divides a description of God as the Creator of all things between God and Jesus. The description in its undivided, unmodified form is used elsewhere by Paul – in Romans 11:36a: 'from him and through him and to him [are] all

---

[101] The ἡμῶν appears as the ἡμῖν and repeated ἡμεῖς of Paul's formulation.

things' (ἐξ αὐτοῦ καὶ δι᾽αὐτοῦ καὶ εἰς αὐτὸν τὰ πάντα), where the context is one of Jewish monotheistic praise of the uniqueness of God.

It is true that there are some non-Jewish Hellenistic parallels to the formulation which relates 'all things' (τὰ πάντα) to God by a variety of prepositions. The best examples are in Pseudo-Aristotle, *De Mundo* 6 (ἐκ θεοῦ πάντα καὶ διὰ θεοῦ συνέστηκε); Marcus Aurelius, *Medit.* 4.3 (ἐκ σοῦ πάντα, ἐν σοὶ πάντα, εἰς σὲ πάντα); and *Asclepius* 34 (*omnia enim ab eo et in ipso et per ipsum*). The point of such formulae is that they describe God as the cause of all things, indicating the various types of causation (as standardly recognized in ancient philosophy) that are appropriate to God's relation to the world by means of the various prepositions: that is, efficient causation (ἐκ), instrumental causation (διὰ; or ἐν), and final causation (εἰς).[102] But such formulae would clearly be very congenial to Jewish usage, since Jews were in any case much in the habit of describing God as the Creator of 'all things' (e.g., Isa. 44:24; Jer. 10:16; 51:19; Sir. 43:33; Wis. 9:6; 2 Macc. 1:24; 3 Macc. 2:3; *1 En.* 9:5; 84:3; *2 En.* 66:4; *Jub.* 12:19; *Apoc. Ab.* 7:10; *Jos. Asen.* 12:1; *Sib. Or.* 3:20). Josephus (*B.J.* 5.218), without the use of the prepositions, says much the same as the non-Jewish Hellenistic formulations: 'all things are from God and for God' (τοῦ θεοῦ πάντα καὶ τῷ θεῷ). Philo explicitly takes up the standard philosophical set of types of causation and applies to God's relation to the world the three which can be so applied: God himself is the efficient cause ('by whom [ὑφ᾽ οὗ] it was made'), his Word is the instrumental cause ('by means of which [δι᾽ οὗ] it was made'), and the final cause ('on account of which [δι᾽ ὅ]') is 'the display of the goodness of the Creator' (*Cher.* 127). In Hebrews 2:10, God is the final and instrumental cause of his creation: the one 'on account of whom (δι᾽ ὅν) are all things and through whom (δι᾽ οὗ) are all things'.

We can therefore be confident that Paul's formulation – 'from him and through him and to him [are] all things' (Rom. 11:36) – is neither original to Paul nor borrowed directly from non-Jewish sources, but was known to him as a Jewish description precisely of God's unique relationship to all other reality. When he uses it in Romans 11:36 there is no christological reference, but when he incorporates it into his christianized version of the Shema in 1 Corinthians 8:6, he divides it between God and Christ, just as he divides the wording of the Shema between God and Christ. The relationship to God expressed by the first and the last of the three prepositions (ἐκ and εἰς) is attributed to the one God, the Father ('from whom [are] all things and we for him'), while the

---

[102] Material and formal causation could not appropriately describe the relationship between God and the universe. Ephesians 4:6 uses a different kind of formula, which also relates God to all things by means of three different prepositions, but has the prepositions governing πάντα: 'one God and Father of all, who is above (ἐπὶ) all and through (διὰ) all and in (ἐν) all.'

relationship expressed by the second of the three prepositions (διά) is attributed to the one Lord, Jesus Christ ('through whom [are] all things and we through him'). The fact that in Romans 11:36 all three prepositions apply to God, whereas in 1 Corinthians 8:6 one of them applies to Christ, does not mean that they no longer all describe the Creator's relationship to the whole of creation. On the contrary, it means precisely that Christ is included in this relationship as the instrumental cause of creation.

The variation between 'all things' and 'we' in 1 Corinthians 8:6 results from Paul's desire to situate himself and his readers within the 'all things' who are thus related to their Creator. In this way Paul is continuing the emphasis of the ἡμῖν ('for us') with which he began his adaptation of the Shema, and reflecting the Shema's own reference to 'the Lord *our* God'. He wishes it to be clear that the God whose unique identity is characterized by being the Creator of all things has that identity not only for all things in general, but specifically *for us*, who therefore owe exclusive allegiance to this God. The fact that Paul associates 'all things' with one preposition ('from whom all things'), 'we' with another ('we for him'), and both 'all things' and 'we' with the last preposition ('through whom all things and we through him'), is a rhetorical variation adapted to the needs of verbal symmetry. Paul does not mean that 'we' are not also 'from God' or that 'all things' are not also 'for God'. The whole is a condensed form of what would otherwise have been the more cumbersome and less symmetrical formulation:

> one God, the Father,
> from whom [are] all things and we from him,
> for whom [are] all things and we for him,
> and one Lord, Jesus Christ,
> through whom [are] all things and we through him.

By formulating his version of the Shema in terms both of God's relationship to 'all things' and of his relationship to 'us', Paul reflects the two aspects of the divine identity according to the Shema as Jews of this period understood it: the one God is both the God of his covenant people and the universal God.

In conclusion, therefore, we can say that Paul is carefully and profoundly faithful to Jewish monotheism's understanding of the Shema in both its affirmation that YHWH, the God of Israel, is the one and only God and in its requirement that this one God's people be exclusively devoted to him. The only (!) novel element in Paul's reformulation is the inclusion of Jesus Christ within the unique divine identity so understood.

John 10:30

I and the Father are one.

It is surprising that this does not seem to have been previously recognized as an allusion to the Shema, but we have already noticed (in the discussion of Rom. 3:28–30) that the formula 'God is one' was a common abbreviation of the Shema. It is true that in all Greek echoes of the Shema the word for one is masculine (εἷς), as we should expect, whereas in John 10:30 it is neuter (ἕν). But this is a necessary adaptation of language. Jesus is not saying that he and the Father are a single person, but that together they are one God. The statement should perhaps be understood as Jesus' understanding of the Shema, corresponding to the allusion to the Shema by 'the Jews' in John 8:41: 'we have one Father, God' (cf. Mal. 2:10).

Jesus' assertion of oneness with the Father occurs twice more in John's Gospel, both in the prayer of chapter 17, where Jesus prays that his disciples 'may be one, as we are one' (17:11: ὦσιν ἓν καθὼς ἡμεῖς; 17:22: ὦσιν ἓν καθὼς ἡμεῖς ἕν). This analogy between the oneness of Jesus and his Father, on the one hand, and the oneness of the disciples, on the other, has been used to argue that the former indicates no more than closeness of association or concurrence of will. But again the background in Jewish monotheistic reflection will clarify the issue considerably. Jewish writers sometimes say that to the one God there corresponds 'one' of something else in what belongs especially to him in the world: one holy city, one temple, one altar, one law, and especially one chosen people (*2 Bar.* 48:23–24; Josephus, *Ant.* 4.201; 5.111; *C. Ap.* 2.193; Philo, *Spec.* 1.52, 67; cf. also *2 Bar.* 85:14). Such formulations presumably lie behind the creedal list of seven 'ones' (also related to the Shema) in Ephesians 4:4–5: 'one body and one Spirit ... one hope of your calling, one Lord, one faith, one baptism, one God and Father of all' (cf. 1 Cor. 12:13).

For the particular case of one people corresponding to the one God, there may be an Old Testament source. In the Old Testament this correspondence is found only in 2 Samuel 7:22–23,[103] but the context in David's prayer makes this an important passage, which would have been well known, and could easily have been connected with Ezekiel 37:15–28, where the repeated use of 'one' does not apply to God but does to Israel, who are to be 'one nation' under 'one king' (37:22) or 'one shepherd' (37:24). In Ezekiel 34:23 the 'one shepherd' is

---

[103] Only the people are explicitly called 'one', but the parallel between v. 22 (about YHWH) and v. 23 (about Israel) is so clear that it is natural to think that a correspondence between the 'one' people and the 'one' God is implicit. Against correcting 'one' (אֶחָד) to 'another' (אַחֵר) in v. 23, in accordance with the LXX, see N. Lohfink and J. Bergman in *TDOT* 1.200.

'my servant David'. This last passage evidently influenced John 10:16 ('one flock, one shepherd'), showing that John's interest in oneness language has Old Testament roots.

The Jewish topos that correlates one God with one people, of course, in no way implies that God is a unity in the same sense as his people are. Josephus and Philo understand the correspondence in the sense that service and worship of the one God unites the people of God into one (Josephus, *Ant.* 5.111; Philo, *Spec.* 1.52; 4.159; *Virt.* 7.35). The divine singularity draws the singular people of God together into a relational unity. It is this kind of unity that the Johannine Jesus desires for his people. He prays that his disciples be a single community corresponding to the uniqueness of the one God in which he and his Father are united (17:11, 22).

The Johannine Jesus' claim to oneness with the Father amounts to including himself with his Father in the unique identity of the one God as understood in Jewish monotheism. Within this divine identity there is the uniquely intimate relationship of the Father and the Son. The oneness statements are clearly related to the statements of reciprocity: 'I am in the Father and the Father is in me' (10:38; 14:10, 11; cf. also 14:20; 17:21, 23). The first of these, in 10:38, is the climax of Jesus' defence of his earlier claim that 'I and the Father are one' (10:30). Both are taken to be blasphemous and clearly they are in some sense equivalent claims. Evidently, this reciprocal indwelling – the closest conceivable intimacy of relationship – is the inner reality of the oneness of Father and Son. Their unity does not erase their difference, but differentiates them in an inseparable relationship.[104] We should also notice that the terms 'Father' and 'Son' entail each other. The Father is called Father only because Jesus is his Son, and Jesus is called Son only because he is the Son of his divine Father. Each is essential to the identity of the other. So to say that Jesus and the Father are one is to say that the unique divine identity comprises the relationship in which the Father is who he is only in relation to the Son, and *vice versa*. It is in the portrayal of this intra-divine relationship that John's Christology steps outside the categories of Jewish monotheistic definition of the unique identity of the one God. It does not at all deny or contradict any of these (especially since the Shema asserts the uniqueness of God, not his lack of internal self-differentiation), but from Jesus' relationship of sonship to God it redefines the divine identity as one in which Father and Son are inseparably united in differentiation from each other.

There is much else in New Testament Christology to show that early Christians presupposed the Jewish monotheism of the late Second Temple period and its monotheistic reading of the Hebrew Bible. But these three case studies of New Testament interpretation of the Shema are examples that make

---

[104] Appold, *Oneness Motif,* 281–82.

the point with reference to early Judaism's central affirmation of the uniqueness of YHWH. The christological innovations – remarkable as they are – cannot be properly understood unless they are seen to work with – not at all to abandon – precisely the contours of early Jewish monotheism. With the inclusion of Jesus in the unique identity of YHWH the faith of the Shema is affirmed and maintained, but everything the Shema requires of God's people is now focused on Jesus. Exclusive devotion is now given to Jesus, but Jesus does not thereby replace or compete with God the Father, since he himself belongs to the unique divine identity. Devotion to him is also devotion to his Father.

Bibliography

Albertz, R., *A History of Israelite Religion in the Old Testament Period*, I (trans. J. Bowden; London: SCM Press, 1994)

Appold, M.L., *The Oneness Motif in the Fourth Gospel* (WUNT 2/1; Tübingen: Mohr [Siebeck], 1976)

Barclay, J.M.G., *Jews in the Mediterranean Diaspora from Alexander to Trajan (323 BCE – 117 CE)* (Edinburgh: T. & T. Clark, 1996)

Barker, M., *The Great Angel: A Study of Israel's Second God* (London: SPCK, 1992)

Barr, J., *The Concept of Biblical Theology: An Old Testament Perspective* (London: SCM Press, 1999)

Bauckham, R., *God Crucified: Monotheism and Christology in the New Testament* (Carlisle: Paternoster; Grand Rapids: Eerdmans, 1998)

Becking, B., 'Only One God: On Possible Implications for Biblical Theology', in *Only One God? Monotheism in Ancient Israel and the Veneration of the Goddess Asherah* (ed. B. Becking, M. Dijkstra, N.C.A. Korpel and K.J.H. Vriezen, London: Sheffield Academic Press, 2001), 189–201

Bell, R.H., *Provoked to Jealousy: The Origin and Purpose of the Jealousy Motif in Romans 9–11* (WUNT 2/63; Tübingen: Mohr [Siebeck], 1994)

Beyerlin, W. (ed.), *Near Eastern Religious Texts Relating to the Old Testament* (trans. J. Bowden; London: SCM Press, 1978)

Ciholas, P., 'Monothéisme et violence', *RSR* 69 (1981), 325–54

Clements, R.E., 'Monotheism and the Canonical Process', *Theol* 87 (1984), 336–44

Dietrich, W., 'Über Werden und Wesen des biblischen Monotheismus: Religionsgeschichtliche und theologische Perspektiven', in *Ein Gott allein? JHWH-Verehrung und biblischer Monotheismus im Kontext der israelitischen und altorientalischen Religionsgeschichte* (ed. W. Dietrich and M.A. Klopferstein; Freiburg, Switzerland: Universitätsverlag, 1994), 13–30

Duquoc, C., 'Monotheism and Unitary Ideology', in *Monotheism* (ed. C. Geffré and J.-P. Jossua; *Concilium* 177 [1/1985]; Edinburgh: T. & T. Clark, 1985), 59–66

Fee, G.D., *The First Epistle to the Corinthians* (NICNT; Grand Rapids: Eerdmans, 1987)

Frydrych, T., *Living under the Sun* (VTSup 90; Leiden: Brill, 2002)

Gnuse, R.K., *No Other Gods: Emergent Monotheism in Israel* (JSOTSup 241; Sheffield: Sheffield Academic Press, 1997)

Halpern, B., '"Brisker Pipes than Poetry": The Development of Israelite Monotheism', in *Judaic Perspectives on Ancient Israel* (ed. J. Neusner, B. Halpern and E.S. Frerichs; Philadelphia: Fortress Press, 1987)

Hampson, D., 'Monotheism', in *Dictionary of Ethics, Theology and Society* (ed. P.B. Clarke and A. Linzey; London and New York: Routledge, 1996), 582–85

Hess, R.S., 'Yahweh and his Asherah? Epigraphic Evidence for Religious Pluralism in Old Testament Times', in *One God, One Lord in a World of Religious Pluralism* (ed. A.D. Clarke and B.W. Winter; Cambridge: Tyndale House, 1991), 5–33

Lang, B., *Monotheism and the Prophetic Minority* (Sheffield: Almond Press, 1983)

—, *Wisdom and the Book of Proverbs: A Hebrew Goddess Redefined* (New York: Pilgrim Press, 1986)

—, 'Der monarchische Monotheismus und die Konstellation zweier Götter im Frühjudentum: Ein neuer Versuch über Menschensohn, Sophia und Christologie', in *Ein Gott allein? JHWH–Verehrung und biblischer Monotheismus im Kontext der israelitischen und altorientalischen Religionsgeschichte* (ed. W. Dietrich and M.A. Klopfenstein; Freiburg, Switzerland: Universitätsverlag, 1994), 559–64

—, *The Hebrew God* (New Haven and London: Yale University Press, 2002)

Levenson, J.D., *Creation and the Persistence of Evil: The Jewish Drama of Divine Omnipotence* (Princeton: Princeton University Press, 2nd edn, 1994)

Lohfink, N., 'The Polytheistic and the Monotheistic Way of Speaking about God in the Old Testament', in *Great Themes from the Old Testament* (trans. R. Walls; Edinburgh; T. & T. Clark, 1982)

MacDonald, N., *Deuteronomy and the Meaning of 'Monotheism'* (FAT 2/1; Tübingen: Mohr Siebeck, 2003) [a revised version of his Durham doctoral thesis, *One God or One Lord? Deuteronomy and the Meaning of 'Monotheism'* (2001)]

Machinist, P., 'The Question of Distinctiveness in Ancient Israel', in *Essential Papers on Israel and the Ancient Near East* (ed. F.E. Greenspan; New York: New York University Press, 1991), 420–42

Mettinger, T.N.D., *No Graven Image? Israelite Aniconism in Its Ancient Near Eastern Context* (CN[OT] 42; Stockholm: Almqvist & Wiksell, 1995)

Moberly, R.W.L., '"YHWH is One": The Translation of the Shema', in *From Eden to Golgotha: Studies in Biblical Theology* (South Florida Studies in the History of Judaism 52; Atlanta: Scholars Press, 1992), 75–81

Moltmann, J., *The Trinity and the Kingdom of God* (trans. M. Kohl; London: SCM Press, 1981)

Moor, J.C. de, *The Rise of Yahwism: The Roots of Israelite Monotheism* (BETL 91; Leuven: Leuven University Press/Peeters, 1997)

Nanos, M.D., *The Mystery of Romans* (Minneapolis: Fortress Press, 1996)

Niehr, H., 'The Rise of YHWH in Judahite and Israelite Religion: Methodological and Historical Aspects', in *The Triumph of Elohim: From Yahwisms to Judaisms* (ed. D.V. Edelman; Contributions to Biblical Exegesis and Theology 13; Kampen: Kok Pharos, 1995), 48–50

Ochshorn, J., *The Female Experience and the Nature of the Divine* (Bloomington: Indiana University Press, 1981)

Ruggieri, G., 'God and Power: A Political Function of Monotheism?', in *Monotheism* (ed. C. Geffré and J.-P. Jossua; *Concilium* 177 [1/1985]; Edinburgh: T. & T. Clark, 1985), 16–27

Sanders, J.A., *Canon and Community: A Guide to Canonical Criticism* (Philadelphia: Fortress Press, 1984)

Sawyer, J.F.A., 'Biblical Alternatives to Monotheism', *Theol* 87 (1984), 172–80

Schmidt, W.H., *The Faith of the Old Testament* (trans. J. Sturdy; Oxford: Basil Blackwell, 1983)

Schwartz, R.M., *The Curse of Cain: The Violent Legacy of Monotheism* (Chicago: University of Chicago Press, 1997)

Smith, M.S., *The Early History of God: Yahweh and the Other Deities in Ancient Israel* (San Francisco: Harper & Row, 1990)

Smith, M., 'The Common Theology of the Ancient Near East', in *Studies in the Cult of Yahweh,* I (ed. S.J.D. Cohen; Religions in the Graeco–Roman World 130/1; Leiden: Brill, 1996), 15–27

Thiselton, A.C., *The First Epistle to the Corinthians* (NIGTC; Carlisle: Paternoster; Grand Rapids: Eerdmans, 2000)

Vriezen, K.J.H., 'Archaeological Traces of Cult in Ancient Israel', in *Only One God? Monotheism in Ancient Israel and the Veneration of the Goddess Asherah* (ed. B. Becking, M. Dijkstra, N.C.A. Korpel and K.J.H. Vriezen, London: Sheffield Academic Press, 2001), 45–80

9

The Unity of Humankind as a Theme in Biblical Theology

Stephen C. Barton

Introduction: Humankind at Risk

In his recent book *The Dignity of Difference: How to Avoid the Clash of Civilizations*, Chief Rabbi Jonathan Sacks draws to our attention serious threats to the future of humankind arising especially out of the process of globalization. According to Sacks, if tribalism of various kinds is a threat to peaceful human coexistence, so also is universalism – of which globalization is the most powerful current manifestation. In place of both tribalism and universalism, Sacks calls for a practice of acceptance of the other, the stranger, based on a full recognition of 'the dignity of difference':

> Today we are inclined to see resurgent tribalisms as the great danger of our fragmenting world. It is, but it is not the only danger. The paradox is that the very thing we take to be the antithesis of tribalism – universalism – can also be deeply threatening, and may be equally inadequate as an account of the human situation. A global culture is a universal culture, and universal cultures, though they have brought about great good, have also done immense harm. They see as the basis of our humanity the fact that we are all ultimately the same. We are vulnerable. We are embodied creatures. We feel hunger, thirst, fear, pain. We reason, hope, dream, aspire. These things are all true and important. But we are also different. Each landscape, language, culture and community is unique. Our very dignity as persons is rooted in the fact that none of us – not even genetically identical twins – is exactly like any other. Therefore none of us is replaceable, substitutable, a mere instance of a type. That is what makes us persons, not merely organisms or machines. If our commonalities are all that ultimately matter, then our differences are distractions to be overcome. This view, I will argue, is profoundly mistaken. It is a mistake that has been made several times in the history of the West, and we are in the process of making it again in the form of globalization.[1]

---

[1] Sacks, *Dignity*, 47–48.

However we might wish to nuance this particular articulation of the way the world is, religious and social commentators like Sacks have made an important contribution in pressing with urgency and insight the case for a recognition of current threats to humanity and in suggesting how we might respond appropriately. What needs to be acknowledged, furthermore, is that this is the context in which we do our biblical theology today.

This chapter, therefore, is an attempt to explore one theme of critical generic relevance to current tensions and crises. It is the theme of *the unity of humankind* as this is portrayed in the classical and biblical traditions, and especially in the texts of the New Testament. I explore this theme in the twofold conviction that the biblical tradition offers profound reflection of ongoing relevance to the quest for human unity and that this resource merits careful attention and ongoing appropriation.[2]

Why Unity? Unity of What Kind?

Before we proceed to texts and traditions, attention to the context(s) in which the discourse of unity or 'oneness' arises is crucial if we are to understand the semantic and rhetorical weight the discourse is intended to carry and the interests it is meant to serve.

Let me give an example or two to illustrate what I mean. In the modern ecumenical movement, the appeal of and for the unity of the churches plays a central role. The legitimating slogan is taken from John 17:21: 'that they may all be one'. Underpinning this is the creedal and theological tradition of the church as 'one, holy, catholic and apostolic'.[3] What is interesting in such an appeal is how the discourse of unity – including the prayer of Jesus cited as a powerful dominical warrant – is made to underpin the politics of ecumenism. This is no bad thing: evaluation would require further discussion. My point here is that we can better understand the meaning(s) and force of 'unity' in ecumenical discourse if we understand its *political and ideological setting*.[4] Furthermore, in the specific context of ecumenical politics, it may be the very ambiguity or polysemic character of 'unity' language that gives it its appeal: different constituencies can use the same kind of discourse in ways which both convey (the appearance of) unity – thereby giving ecumenical institutions and processes their *raison d'être* and influence – while preserving (the reality of) diversity and even discord.

---

[2] For studies of particular relevance in the area of New Testament studies, see Borgen, 'Jesus Christ'; Dahl, 'Christ', 'One God' and 'Gentiles'; Meeks, 'Body'; and Schlier, 'Unity'.

[3] See on this Dulles, *Catholicity*.

[4] For an early account along these lines, see Wilson, *Religion*, 151–205.

A second example comes from even closer to home, perhaps: the attempt to establish (or impugn) the unity of Scripture in the face of its apparent diversity.[5] Once again, what is interesting is not so much whether such attempts meet with success but why they are undertaken in the first place. Nor is it difficult to see that at least one of the reasons has to do with the question of *authority*. The authority of Scripture is said to rest on its unity, on the basis that, at some fundamental level at least, it 'speaks' with one voice. Therefore it can be trusted to reveal what is true and people can (be told to) live their lives in accordance with its teaching. Interesting also is the way in which this kind of argument (for the unity of Scripture) is more important – or important *in different ways* – for some groups or churches than for others: typically, for Protestants more than for Catholics and Orthodox, and, within Protestantism, for evangelicals more than for liberals, and so on.

A significant irony emerges out of such examples. The irony is that the discourse of unity – precisely because it is always embedded in particular cultures and sub-cultures and is always the expression of particular interests – is at one and the same time a means of articulating *difference*. As a way of saying 'yes' to one way of seeing the world, it is necessarily also a way of saying 'no' to other ways. As a way of affirming who 'we' are and to whom 'we' belong in unity, it is also a way of saying who 'they' are and from whom we are (in unity!) separating.

An important corollary of this claim – that unity is invariably unity *up to a point* and that claims about unity are a way of establishing *boundaries* – is that the discourse of unity is an *ordering* discourse: it helps to define not only those outsiders with whom we are not 'one', but also what it means to be a member of those who claim to be united together as 'one'. Thus, members of a particular solidarity may be expected (and expect each other) to be certain kinds of people, behave in certain kinds of ways, believe certain things, and so on. The totalitarian possibilities of this kind of ordering of society go back to antiquity: Plato's *Republic* (cf. especially Book IV) is a case in point.[6] Obviously, totalitarianism is not the only possibility, but the example shows that the discourse of 'unity' and 'oneness' is bound up inextricably with the ordering of society and the exercise of power.

To put it another way, these observations bring home the fact that the discourse of 'unity' and 'oneness' is ideological – in the sense that it is an expression of identity, power and interests in particular social and cultural settings. Unless we take this point seriously, acknowledge it openly and find ways of evaluating it appropriately (i.e., in relation to the truth about the oneness of God and the sovereignty of God over all things), anything we say about 'unity'

---

[5] For two distinguished attempts, see: Dunn, *Unity*; and Reumann, *Variety*.

[6] See on this Schofield, 'Approaching', 190–232, esp. 217–24.

will be either hopelessly bland ('mere rhetoric') and therefore virtually mean-
ingless, or it will be a potential cloak for (intended or unintended) power plays
of one kind or another.

The Unity of Humankind in the Greco-Roman Tradition

The moral and theological reflection that comes to us in the New Testament is
likely to have been influenced not only by the traditions of Israel and early
Judaism, but also by the philosophical and political traditions and practices of
the Greco-Roman world. Within these traditions – and perhaps especially in
the utopian traditions – considerable attention was given, over time, to the
theme of the unity of humankind.[7] Here, I can only summarize briefly some of
the ideas that form part of the backdrop to early Christian belief and practice in
this area.[8] It is interesting, in the context of Greco-Roman thought, to ask
whether or not early Christian ideas of unity appear surprisingly parochial and
particularist, or whether it is more a case of Christian ideas (like those of Judaism) representing a particularism *of a different kind*.

   Striking, first of all, in the ancient Greek tradition, is the fact that, whereas in
Homer there is a general sense of humanity as *anthrōpos* (humankind) transcending differences of language and culture, the rise of the Greek city-states
brought in addition a strong awareness of human diversity, and, from the time
of the Persian Wars, the sense of a fundamental division between Hellene and
'barbarian'. At the same time, from the fifth century on, the concept developed
of humankind as a specific type of being marked off both from the gods and
from animals. Humankind is both united and distinguished by certain physical
characteristics, by the gift of *logos* (speech and, hence, reason), by the possession
of the *technai* (the crafts which make material civilization possible), and by the
acceptance of a common standard – summed up in the term *dikē* (justice) – able
to serve as a moral basis for distinguishing civilized from uncivilized.

   In the fourth and third centuries, the concept of humankind was dominated
by two strains of thought. One was *pan-Hellenism*, of which Isocrates was a
prominent spokesman and advocate. H.C. Baldry's comment is significant:

> In a sense this was a tendency towards a wider unity, but it also deepened the dividing
> line between Greek and 'barbarian'; and the shift of view which now saw the antith-
> esis as one between cultures rather than between races, bringing some foreigners by
> birth on to the Greek side of the fence, did little as yet to weaken the division itself ...

---

[7] Of general relevance is Ferguson, *Utopias*.

[8] I am drawing on Baldry, *Unity*. My thanks to Professor Christopher Rowe of
Durham for drawing this work to my attention.

> The unity of the Hellenistic world was to a large extent a projection of the unity of Greece, not a unification of mankind.[9]

In other words, unity in its Hellenistic conception was unity up to a point, unity of a certain (culturally hegemonic) kind, unity that ordered the world in a particular way and that itself created distinctions.

The second influential strain of thought in the Greek view of the unity of humankind from this period was *the distinction between wisdom and folly*, a conception of an 'aristocracy of the wise' common in the Socratic tradition, Cynicism, Epicureanism and in Zeno and early Stoicism. Once again, Baldry makes a comment directly pertinent to our concerns:

> To all this [distinction between wisdom and folly] there was a corollary: not unity of all men, but unity of the wise; the conception of an aristocracy of the possessors of wisdom which transcends the normal barriers between human beings, bringing within the same circle rich and poor, man and woman, Greek and foreigner, perhaps even free man and slave.[10]

How intelligible, in this light, and at a later period, is the behaviour of 'the wise' whom Paul confronts in the house churches in Corinth; how strange and provocative the 'foolishness' of his response (cf. especially 1 Cor. 1 – 4)! Baldry's comment helps us to see that part of what is at issue in Corinth is not anything as straightforward as Corinthian social stratification set over against the Pauline doctrine of unity in 'the body of Christ', but a much more complex dialectic *between different models of unity*, each predicated on different understandings of what it means to be human.

A broader idea of the unity of humankind develops from the beginning of the third century on, and the impact of Rome appears to have been decisive.[11] Here, the idea is based not so much on philosophical concepts of cosmic unity (as in the Stoicism of one of Zeno's successors, Chrysippus), nor on developing ideas (in medical texts, for example) about humankind as a species, but on a greater awareness of human geography, of the geographical unity of the world as an aggregate of peoples, along with a sense – evident in the *Universal History* of Polybius – of the unity of human history.

Influential also in the second century and subsequently are certain philosophical developments. In the writings of Posidonius there is a continued interest in the 'human geography' dimension, the idea of a whole human race made up of many diverse parts. In Panaetius, there is a stress on the unity of humankind in its common possession of reason. In Antiochus, there is a

---

[9] Baldry, *Unity*, 177.

[10] Baldry, *Unity*, 178.

[11] See further, Baldry, *Unity*, 190ff.

combination of Stoic and Peripatetic views, such that the Peripatetic doctrine of universal human kinship (*oikeiotēs*) is linked with the Stoic theory of 'aware-ness of what is akin to oneself' (*oikeiōsis*), 'and so the notion of human unity, implicit in early Stoicism, could be made explicit and given definite form by a pattern of kinship extending from self-love to a bond connecting the entire human race'.[12] Finally, these developments reach a point of philosophical and conceptual maturity in the works of the Roman aristocrat Cicero, according to whom all humankind (the *genus humanum*) shares in *ratio* and *humanitas* and has the potential for *sapientia*.

This centuries-long tradition of Greco-Roman thought is an important backdrop to early Christian ideas about the unity of humankind. To tease out points of analogy and dis-analogy, of continuity and discontinuity, is a task to be taken further. Here, however, we may observe just a few points. First, it is clear that early Christian ideas about the unity of humankind did not develop in a vacuum. They will have resonated in all kinds of ways with the world around them.[13] In their own way, they may even have exerted a certain appeal to those whose anthropological horizons were broad enough to take in questions about the identity and fate of humankind as a whole. Second, it is clear also that long-ings for and aspirations towards the unity of humankind such as there may have been in antique society will have found in early Christianity an unusual and provocative conception and practice, with unity a matter not of the possession of reason, but of the gift of faith, and where *sophia* or *sapientia* come not from Epicurus's garden but from the garden of Eden and the garden of Gethsemane.

The Unity of Humankind in the Bible and Early Judaism

That unity or 'oneness' is a pervasive motif in biblical thought is impossible to deny. Without doubt, its foundation in belief and cult is monotheism, the one-ness of God, as given classic expression in the Shema: 'Hear, O Israel: The Lord our God is one Lord; and you shall love the Lord your God with all your heart, and with all your soul, and with all your might' (Deut. 6:4–5 RSV).[14] The body of the people of God is to be one people in love of God because the God they worship is one. As such, the people's oneness is testimony to the oneness of God.

---

[12] Baldry, *Unity*, 194–95.

[13] See further, Appold, *Oneness*, 163–93, for a useful excursus entitled, 'Religious-his-torical Profile of the Oneness Motif'.

[14] On the questions of translation posed by the ambiguity of the Hebrew, and for a convincing solution, see Moberly, 'Yahweh', 209–15. On the meaning and signifi-cance of the Shema, see Moberly, 'Interpretation'.

But that is to begin, theologically speaking, with election, with the unity of Israel as 'a kingdom of priests and a holy nation' (Ex. 19:5–6), a unity which subsequently becomes a model and metaphor for the church (cf. 1 Pet. 2:9; Rev. 1:6; 5:10). For our theme of the unity of *humankind*, we need to go back a step, to go (as it were) from Exodus back to Genesis, from election back to creation, from Moses (and before him, Abraham) back to Adam.[15]

In brief, Genesis 1 – 11 offers a profound reflection on the human condition, on what all humankind has in common. Humankind is a unity because, in its representative figure Adam ('earthling' or 'earth creature'), it is created by God in the image of God (Gen. 1:26–27; 5:1–2). Thus, the genealogies (e.g., Gen. 5) show that the whole human race is descended from a single progenitor: it is a single family descended from a single father – as such, all its members are children (or sons) of Adam (cf. Ps. 115:16). Conversely, it is worth noting, with Jon Levenson, that 'it is humanity in general and not any people in particular that is created. Israel is not primordial. It emerges in history, twenty generations after the creation of the human species in the image of God (or the gods, 1:26–27) ... It is neither descended from the gods nor divine itself. All people are created equally in the divine image.'[16]

The high valuation of humankind as all alike created in the divine image is the reason why homicide is a capital offence (Gen. 9:6). It also finds expression in the wonder of the psalmist at God's favour toward humankind (Ps. 8:4–6):

> What is man, that thou art mindful of him,
> And the son of man that thou dost care for him?
> Yet thou hast made him little less than God,
> And dost crown him with glory and honour.
> Thou hast given him dominion over the works of thy hands;
> Thou hast put all things under his feet ...[17]

Other parts of the biblical tradition also express the unity of humankind in the sense that God's providence is directed towards all that he has made. Thus, the psalmist speaks of how 'The Lord is good to all, And his compassion is over all that he has made ... Thou openest thy hand, thou satisfiest the desire of every living thing' (Ps. 145:9, 16). And from the prophetic literature comes the book of Jonah, one of the main points of which is its ironic and subversive display of God's concern for the well-being of all his creatures, even the pagan Ninevites: 'And should not I pity Nineveh, that great city, in which there are more than a

---

[15] See further, Greenberg, 'Mankind', 369–93.

[16] Levenson, 'Horizon', 147.

[17] As Greenberg, 'Mankind', 371, says of these words: 'God-like attributes attach to all human beings; they are not a specifically Israelite property.'

hundred and twenty thousand persons who do not know their right hand from their left, and also much cattle?' (Jon. 4:11).[18]

But if humankind is united through its connection in creation with Adam, it is united also through its connection with Noah. For after the universal destruction in the flood, God makes a covenant with humankind – and not only with humankind, but with the whole created order (cf. Gen. 9:8–17). This covenant brings with it a demand for moral responsibility, the focus of which is the preservation of what the flood, in response to human depravity, had endangered – namely life, human life in particular (Gen. 9:4–6). And this becomes the basis in Second Temple and Rabbinic Judaism for the tradition of the 'Noachide commandments'. These commandments are understood as a kind of natural law or constitution of universal application. Thus, for example, the Book of Jubilees (7:20–39) has Noah teaching his sons 'the ordinances and commandments and all the judgments that he knew':

> And he exhorted his sons to observe righteousness,
> And to cover the shame of their flesh,
> And to bless their Creator,
> And to honour father and mother,
> And love their neighbour,
> And guard their souls from fornication and uncleanness and all iniquity ...
> Whoso sheddeth man's blood, and whoso eateth the blood of any flesh,
> Shall be destroyed from the earth ...[19]

By virtue of its association with the primeval period – that is, the period before the covenants with Abraham and Moses – this code came in Judaism to represent a kind of public ethics, an area of common moral ground making possible day-to-day relations between Jews and Gentiles. Markus Bockmuehl has argued, furthermore, that this tradition was influential in the formation of early Christian ethics – of rules governing and making possible a common life shared by both Jewish converts and Gentile converts.[20] Be that as it may, we have in the covenant with Noah, as in the creation of Adam, a strong biblical presupposition of the unity of humankind created and sustained by the one true God.

What, then, of Israel? Do not the covenants with Abraham and Moses represent the triumph of particularity, the coming into being of one kind of unity ('a peculiar people') that undermines the unity of humankind as a whole? Theologically speaking, what is the relation between creation and election, between Israel and 'the nations'? Understandably, this is a question that has

---

[18] See Greenberg, 'Mankind', 371–72.

[19] Cited in Greenberg, 'Mankind', 374.

[20] Bockmuehl, 'Commandments', 72–101.

attracted significant attention in recent scholarship[21] and cannot be pursued in detail here. It must suffice to make a few summary observations.

First, it is important not to over-emphasize the distinction between the creation of humankind and the election of Israel, between (as it were) Genesis and Exodus or (more precisely) between Genesis 1 – 11 and Genesis 12ff. The story of creation is the prelude to and an integral part of the story of election: the themes of the Pentateuch are introduced from Genesis on.[22] On the theological side, it is the one God who acts throughout in freedom and sovereignty. To give but one example: the God who creates the world by separating one part of creation from another (e.g., light from darkness) is the same God who orders the life of the nations by separating one nation from the rest to be a 'light' to all. On the anthropological side, the story of Adam epitomizes the story of Israel and the story of Israel is a development of and response to the story of Adam, Noah and the Tower of Babel.

Second, Israel's role as 'a kingdom of priests and a holy nation' (Ex. 19:6) is a particular role and a privileged role, certainly: but it is also a *representative* role set against a universal horizon. The primary aspect of this role is that of *witness to the oneness of God*:

> You are my witnesses, says the Lord,
> And my servant whom I have chosen,
> That you may know and believe me
> And understand that I am He.
> Before me no god was formed,
> Nor shall there be any after me. (Isa. 43:10)

Thus, Israel's identity and self-understanding is always being negotiated in the context both of its relationship with God and also of its relations with 'the nations'. As John Barclay puts it: 'Much Jewish theology thrived precisely in the tensions inherent in being God's people in God's wider world.'[23]

One manifestation of this is Israel's respect for the non-Israelite. Hence, the insistence on care for the 'stranger' or 'resident alien' (cf. Ex. 23:9; Lev. 19:33–34; Deut. 23:7–8). Hence also the acceptance of proselytes, a practice demonstrating that Gentiles were not excluded from membership of God's chosen people. Another manifestation is Israel's high regard for 'righteous Gentiles' – Gentiles who revered God or who played a significant and positive part in God's designs and/or whose behaviour accorded in fundamental ways with

---

[21] Especially noteworthy are a number of Jewish scholarly contributions, including: Lafer, 'Universalism', 177–211; Segal, 'Universalism', 1–29; and Levenson, 'Horizon', 143–69. For a recent Christian contribution, see Bauckham, *Bible*.

[22] See Clines, *Pentateuch*.

[23] Barclay, 'Universalism', 211.

God's will, such as Jethro (Ex. 18), Rahab (Josh. 2), Naaman (2 Kgs. 5), Job and Cyrus (Isa. 44:24 – 45:10). Yet another is found in Israel's worship, not least in the period of the Second Temple, in the understanding that the temple was the 'navel' of the world – the place where Gentiles could come and stand before God (in the Court of the Gentiles), and the place to which all the nations would come for salvation in the eschatological future.[24] Thoroughly expressive of this view of Israel's representative, priestly role and responsibility is Jesus' temple protest culminating in the saying: 'Is it not written, "My house shall be called a house of prayer *for all the nations*?" But you have made it a den of robbers' (Mk. 11:17 and par.).

We may conclude, therefore, that the particular oneness of Israel is not a contradiction of the oneness of humankind. Here, Levenson's comment is salutary. Speaking of the biblical distinction between Israel and the nations, he says: '[This] distinction does not coincide with the distinction between good and bad … The difference between the chosen and the unchosen is not … the difference between the saved and the damned.'[25] Rather, it appears to be the case that these two 'unities' coexist side by side and help to define each other. *That* they stand side by side is certainly interesting: but *how* they stand side by side is much more interesting. Theologically, the relation is understood fundamentally in terms of *revelation and blessing*: God makes himself known for salvation and judgement, blessing and cursing, in creation and in election, both among the nations as a whole and in Israel in particular. Historically and sociologically, the relation takes a whole variety of forms and expressions which are a matter of ongoing vigilance and constant negotiation, from the relative cosmopolitanism of Philo and Josephus, along with those who stand in the broad streams of the wisdom tradition, to the sectarianism of the Qumran Covenanters and those who stand in the narrower, more world-confronting, streams of apocalypticism.

The Unity of Humankind in the New Testament

Against this wide background of the classical and biblical traditions, in both of which the theme of the unity of humankind is well developed and that in a variety of ways (only some of which I have been able to touch upon), I turn now to consider in a little greater depth three New Testament texts – Galatians, Ephesians and the Gospel of John – where the motif of unity is prominent. My aim in so doing is to better understand the meaning(s) of unity in its originating

---

[24] On the significance of the temple, see especially Hayward, *Temple*, esp. 1–17. An important testimony to the acceptance of Gentile participation in temple worship in Jerusalem is Isa. 56:6–8, on which see Levenson, 'Temple', 291–93.

[25] Levenson, 'Horizon', 158–59.

contexts in the New Testament and early Christianity, with a view to its appropriation in a biblical theology relevant for today.[26]

'All one in Christ Jesus': Eschatological unity in Paul

In Galatians 3:26–28, Paul cites what Wayne Meeks calls an early 'baptismal reunification formula'[27] to sum up the astonishing, world-shattering consequences of the coming of Christ and, with Christ, the gift of divine sonship for Gentiles as well as Jews on the basis of their justification by faith:

> For *you are all sons of God* through faith in Christ Jesus [*Pantes gar huioi theou este dia tēs pisteōs en Christō Iēsou*]. For as many of you as were baptized into Christ have put on Christ. There is neither Jew nor Greek, there is neither slave nor free, there is no male and female; for *you are all one* in Christ Jesus [*pantes gar humeis heis este en Christō Iēsou*].

Two points are of particular interest for present purposes. The first springs from the literary observation of the way in which the statement is organized carefully to form an *inclusio*, such that 'you [Gentiles and Jews] are all sons of God ... in Christ Jesus' stands in parallel with 'you [Gentiles and Jews] are all one in Christ Jesus'. Here we have one answer to our question, what kind of unity? In addressing Gentile Christians tempted by 'Judaizers' to doubt their status as full members of God's new creation, the unity of which Paul is speaking is *a unity of identity and status as eschatological 'sons of God'* by virtue of their belonging by faith to the Son of God (cf. Gal. 4:4–5). Paul wants his Gentile converts to be convinced that they are not 'second-class citizens' in the kingdom of God. On the contrary, on the basis of the assent of faith (*dia tēs pisteōs*) and the rite of baptism which together bring them into relationship with Christ (*en Christō Iēsou*), Gentiles and Jews alike are 'all one' as God's 'sons'. Their unity of identity and status, in other words, is eschatological and christological.[28]

The second point is the way in which categories rooted in creation and salvation history are reinterpreted – even transcended – something made even more emphatic by the inclusion of two categories which, strictly speaking, are redundant to the rhetorical context.[29] On the one hand, the term 'sons of God',

---

[26] My treatment of the New Testament is not exhaustive, by any means. Other texts relevant to our theme include: Acts, *passim*; Rom. 3:29–30; 5:12ff.; 1 Cor. 8:4–6; 12; Rev. 5:9–10.; 7:9 and *passim*. For an analysis of 1 Corinthians as a call to unity, see Barton, '1 Corinthians', an analysis indebted to Mitchell, *Paul*.

[27] See Meeks, 'Image', 165–208.

[28] So, too, most recently, Campbell, 'Reconciliation', 39–65.

[29] That is to say, given that, in context, Paul is addressing relations between (Christian) Jews and (Christian) Gentiles, the categories slave/free and male/female are, at least at a surface level, unnecessary. So, too, Betz, *Galatians*, 182.

normally reserved for Jews (cf. Rom. 9:4), is applied equally to Gentiles. On the other, the binary oppositions of Jew/Greek, slave/free, male/female – conventional in Jewish and Hellenistic texts as ways of characterizing natural differences both in human society and in the ordering of the cosmos – are negated in a quite radical way.[30] It is as if creation and human society are declared dismantled, unmade. In their place there is a '*new creation*' – and Paul uses the very expression *kainē ktisis* in the climactic statement of Galatians 6:15 (cf. also 2 Cor. 5:17) – in which those previously identified in terms of their ethnicity (Jew/Greek), class (slave/free), or gender (male/female) are now identified differently, as all alike 'sons of God'.

Paul's doctrine of anthropological unity in Christ is rhetorically powerful. But it is not put forward in a vacuum. The situation is one of genuine crisis, as the anathemas Paul invokes on his opponents in the letter's opening show (Gal. 1:8, 9). Thus, he speaks of unity for a particular reason, and the unity of which he speaks is unity of a particular kind. He speaks of unity because the teaching and practice of the 'Judaizers' threaten, first, the unity within the churches themselves (Gal. 5:9); second, the unity of the churches with Paul their apostle (Gal. 4:11–20); and third, the unity that the believers have with God on the basis of their knowing and being known by him (Gal. 4:8–9).

But why does he speak of *this kind* of unity – unity that transcends the anthropological distinctions and oppositions accepted almost universally in antiquity as fundamental to the right ordering of society and cosmos? The answer must be that the teaching and practice of the 'Judaizers' open the way for a reassertion of those very same distinctions and oppositions: and this, in Paul's view, represents a betrayal of the gospel of new creation, a return to the 'slavery' of the old dispensation, a separation from Christ, a denial of the life of the Spirit, and a fall from grace (Gal. 5:1–6).

Thus, Paul's doctrine of unity, as expressed in Galatians, is quite context-specific and content-specific. The specific context is the crisis in Jew-Gentile relations in the Galatian churches. The specific content is the negation and transcendence of cosmic oppositions in the death of Christ: an eschatological transformation of reality, the corollary of which is a 'no' to the Judaizers' attempts effectively to reduce Christian unity to ethnic uniformity, and a 'yes' to Christian unity as Spirit-inspired love and mutual burden-bearing after the pattern of Christ irrespective of differences of ethnicity, class and gender.

Clearly, the locus of this eschatological and christological unity is the community of the church, understood as 'the Israel of God' (Gal. 6:16). The unity, in other words, has a particularity about it – a particular centre of gravity, a particular social location and form – and that is how it is able to manifest the particular revelation of the grace of God in the gospel of Christ. Ironically, however,

---

[30] Excellent on this is Martyn, 'Antinomies', 410–24.

it is also why the disputes and schisms to which Paul refers in Galatians are all ecclesial: to do with relations between the apostles in their respective missions, between the Jerusalem church and the churches of the Diaspora, between Jewish converts and Gentile converts within local (house) churches in Galatia, and so on.

We may say, then, that if the unity of the new creation in Christ is a gift, it is also a challenge. If it is a source of almost unprecedented potential social amity, it is also a source of anxiety and controversy. If it makes possible a realization of the 'freedom' (*eleutheria*) so highly prized in biblical tradition and in the social philosophy of antiquity, it is also a limit and constraint. Without these elements of challenge, controversy and constraint, without the sense of unity 'up to a point', unity itself would be undermined and the world-transforming power of the gospel would be impugned.

But can we speak of a conception in Galatians of the unity of *humankind*, or is what Paul says about unity limited only to Christian believers? Is Paul's vision of oneness in Christ a universal vision, or is it a vision only for the church? Here we touch again on the large question of what Levenson aptly calls 'the universal horizon of biblical particularism'.[31] With respect to Paul in Galatians, what we may fairly say is that Paul does clearly work with a theological anthropology of universal scope: the death of Christ is, after all, the unmaking and remaking of the creation, the negation and transcending of the oppositions basic to that order of things which 'in Christ' pertain no longer. However, as we have seen, that universal vision is profoundly particularist. It is *biblical*, in the sense that it represents a transformation and reinterpretation of the biblical narrative of creation and election, of Adam and Abraham and Moses. It is *christological*, both in that the turning point of the narrative is the death and resurrection of Christ and in that 'the gospel of Christ' is, for Paul, the non-negotiable foundation for everything else. It is *eschatological*, in that the new life it offers to all is life according to the direction of the Spirit. And, although its social manifestation and practical outworkings have wide ramifications, its centre of gravity is *ecclesial*: 'So, then, as we have opportunity, let us do good to all [*pros pantas*], but especially to those who are of the household of faith [*tous oikeious tēs pisteōs*]' (Gal. 6:10).

So it is not the case that the Judaism Paul is leaving behind is 'particularist' and the gospel of Christ 'universalist'.[32] Rather, as biblical faith and the religion of Judaism are *universalist in a particularist way*, so also is the gospel Paul preached and practised. The difference is not between universalism and particularism, but between one kind of particularism and another. It is impossible to understand Paul's deep anxiety over the influence of 'Judaizers' in Galatia and

---

[31] Levenson, 'Horizon'.
[32] So also Barclay, 'Multiculturalism', 197–214.

elsewhere without an appreciation that what are at issue are questions much more to do with *divergences over the particularities of Christian faith* than with its universal horizon. That helps to explain why the emphasis in relation to unity is first and foremost on the unity of the church. It also explains why Paul is willing to put unity *at risk*, even and especially in an ecclesial context. In the end, Paul's ultimate concern is not with unity for its own sake, whether ecclesial unity or the unity of humankind, but with unity as an expression of the truth of the gospel of new creation in Christ. True unity is the kind of unity that is grounded upon, and bears witness to, the world-negating and world-transforming truth of the gospel. It is unity received as gift and grace (Gal. 6:18).

'[T]o bring all things back into unity in Christ': Cosmic reunification in Ephesians

In its dramatic elucidation of the meaning, effect and challenge of the gospel of Christ for humankind, the Letter to the Ephesians is astonishing among the texts of the New Testament for the preponderance of the language of *reconciliation expressed as reunification*.[33] This gains its intelligibility in part against a background in ancient philosophy, from the pre-Socratics on, according to which the visible plurality and diversity of substances and beings are declensions from an original unity, a unity towards which all things will ultimately return. It also gains intelligibility from the biblical narrative of creation, election and redemption – in particular, creation as the manifestation of the God who is One, as nevertheless alienated from the true source of its life in God, and as called (above all, in representative form, in the people of Israel) back into oneness with God through obedience to one law and true worship in one temple.

For the author of Ephesians, these streams of understanding about the origins and goal of the cosmos – and correspondingly about what it means to be human – have taken now a decisive, new direction, which he identifies at the climax of his opening paean of praise to God:

> For he [God] has made known to us in all wisdom and insight the mystery of his will, according to his purpose which he set forth in Christ as a plan for the fullness of time, *that all things might be brought back into unity in Christ [anakephalaiōsasthai ta panta en tō Christō]*, things in heaven and things on earth. (Eph. 1:9–10)

Following the strong precedent of the christological monotheism of the earlier Pauline tradition (cf. 1 Cor. 8:6; 15:28), according to which cosmic reunification in God is both guaranteed through the reconciling death and resurrection

---

[33] I am indebted especially in this section to the profound essay by Max Turner, 'Mission and Meaning in Terms of "Unity" in Ephesians', and I am grateful to him for sharing it with me. See also Turner, 'Ephesians', 1222–44.

of Christ (cf. Rom. 5:9–11; 2 Cor. 5:17–21) and inaugurated in the church as the eschatological oneness of the body of Christ (cf. Gal. 3:28; 1 Cor. 12:13; Col. 3:11), Ephesians develops a vision of the reunification of humankind 'in Christ' of almost unique intensity. Two texts are particularly important. The first is Ephesians 2:11–18:

> Therefore remember that at one time you Gentiles in the flesh, called the uncircumcision by what is called the circumcision, which is made in the flesh by hands – remember that you were at that time separated from Christ, alienated from the commonwealth of Israel, and strangers to the covenants of promise, having no hope and without God in the world. But now in Christ Jesus you who once were far off have been brought near in the blood of Christ. For he is our peace, who has made us *both one* [*ta amphotera hen*], and has broken down the dividing wall of hostility, by abolishing in his flesh the law of commandments and ordinances, that he might create in himself *one new humanity* [*eis hena kainon anthrōpon*] in place of the two, so making peace, and might reconcile us both to God *in one body* [*en heni sōmati*] through the cross, thereby bringing the hostility to an end. And he came and preached peace to you who were far off and peace to those who were near; for through him we both have access *in one Spirit* [*en heni pneumati*] to the Father. So then you are no longer strangers and sojourners, but you are fellow citizens with the saints and members of the household of God, built upon the foundation of the apostles and prophets, Christ Jesus himself being the cornerstone, in whom the whole structure is joined together and grows into a holy temple in the Lord; in whom you also are built into it for a dwelling place of God in the Spirit.

If the gospel 'mystery' concerns the revelation of the reunification of the cosmos in Christ (Eph. 1:9–10), what comes to the fore in this latter text is the claim that the beginning of this cosmic reunification is taking place *in the church*. How so? Not just in the more traditional (Jewish and Judaizing) idea of the 'coming near' of the Gentiles to join Israel and share Israel's covenantal benefits (cf. Isa. 57:19), but there is something more radical: the unification of *both Gentiles and Jews* in a quite new solidarity described variously as 'one new humanity', 'one body', 'the household of God' and 'a holy temple in the Lord'.[34]

This new solidarity enjoys a oneness of relationship both 'vertical' ('access in one Spirit to the Father') and 'horizontal' ('he is our peace, who has made us both one'). Throughout the passage, the language of alienation, separation, distance and hostility is set in contrast with the language of reconciliation, unification, proximity and peace. To put it another way, as if to emphasize the extent of the transformation already taking place, the author elaborates his vision in terms of powerful multidimensional and overlapping images of identity and incorporation to do with space ('far off' vs. 'brought near'), place

---

[34] So also Lincoln, *Ephesians*, 163.

('dividing wall' vs. 'holy temple'), time ('at one time' vs. 'but now') and per-sons-in-relationship ('hostility' vs. 'peace'; 'strangers' vs. 'fellow-citizens'; 'commonwealth of Israel' vs. 'household of God'). The temple imagery at the climactic end of the passage is especially significant. Not only does it express the unity into which the church as the new humanity is growing but, as the place/people where God dwells, it expresses also the meeting – the *uniting* – both of heaven and earth and of the future in the present.

It cannot be doubted that this represents an exalted vision of the church and its calling: to be the place and the people whose supernatural, eschatological unity embodies and displays in the present the unification of the whole cosmos in Christ which is yet to come (cf. also Eph. 3:6, 8–10). What this vision means for *how church members are to live* is elaborated in the second half of the letter (chs. 4 – 6). Once again, the motif of unity and what makes for unity predominates:

> I, therefore, a prisoner of the Lord, beg you to lead a life worthy of the calling to which you have been called, with all lowliness and meekness, with patience, forbear-ing one another in love, eager to maintain *the unity of the Spirit* [*tēn henotēta tou pneumatos*] in the bond of peace. There is *one body and one Spirit* [*hen sōma kai hen pneuma*], just as you were called to the *one hope* [*en mia elpidi*] that belongs to your call, *one Lord* [*heis kurios*], *one faith* [*mia pistis*], *one baptism* [*hen baptisma*], *one God and Father of us all* [*heis theos kai patēr pantōn*], who is above all and through all and in all. (Eph. 4:1–6)

Pivoting on the 'therefore' in Ephesians 4:1, this passage constitutes an opening exhortation to corporate performance in everyday sociality of that cosmic rec-onciliation and reunification inaugurated in Christ that has been the focus of Ephesians 1 – 3. First, the virtues and practices that sustain a Spirit-inspired common life (e.g., humility and patience) are set out (Eph. 4:1–3). These uni-fying virtues and practices are then reinforced by a statement of the church's unifying creedal confession, where the emphasis on unity is conveyed in the powerful rhetorical crescendo of the sevenfold repetition of the word 'one' (Eph. 4:4–6). In this confession, there is a reminder of major reunification themes from the first half of the letter (cf. Eph. 2:14–17 [one body]; 2:18–22 [one Spirit], 1:12, 18 [one hope]) and a recapitulation of (what was probably) the believers' traditional baptismal affirmation, itself indebted to biblical monotheism as summed up in the Shema (cf. 'one Lord', v. 5). So practices of unity and the confession of the oneness of God go hand in hand and are mutu-ally reinforcing. This is strengthened even further by the reminder that the unity into which the church is called to grow is *given already* in Christ – the One who liberates and 'fills' the cosmos, and who is able therefore to give to his people the gifts of leadership and nurture that will enable them to grow as one body into union with himself as 'the head' (Eph. 4:7–16).

In Ephesians 4:17 – 6:9, the author proceeds to elaborate on the virtues and practices needed to sustain the church's identity and mission as the reconciled, unified new creation. Prominent here is paraenesis in (broadly speaking) two crucial areas of social ethics: the ethics of communication (or speech ethics) and the ethics of marriage and the household. In respect of the former, and on the grounds that 'we are members one of another' (Eph. 4:25), believers are to eschew alienating and hostile forms of speech such as lying, slander and anger, and are to practise instead acts of communication which edify, bestow grace, forgiveness and harmony, and culminate in doxology (cf. Eph. 4:25 – 5:20). In respect of marriage and the household – and within a 'Christianized' patriarchal order of things which is taken for granted – believers are to live their common life in ways that express the profound unity-in-love of Christ and the church (Eph. 5:21 – 6:9). Worth noting here, and not sufficiently acknowledged, is that one of the reasons so much space is given to household relations is that, perhaps better than any other set of social relations, they – especially *nuptial* relations – are able to represent and embody the new creation unity of Christ and 'his body', the church.[35] Significant in this respect is the appeal to Genesis 2:24 ('… and the two shall become *one flesh [sarka mian]*'), interpreted typologically by the author as referring to the 'great mystery' of Christ and the church (Eph. 5:31–32). The primal unity of the man and the woman in the garden of Eden prior to the alienation of the fall is the supreme type for the eschatological unity of Christ and the church in the 'now' of the new creation, and this eschatological unity is, in turn, to find expression not only in the nuptial and household relations of believers, but also in the life of the church as a whole.

There can be no doubt, therefore, that in Ephesians the motif of unity or oneness is all pervasive and the theme of reconciliation as reunification predominates. If we ask 'why unity?' and 'unity of what kind?', we come to recognize again that the usage is situated and context-specific: it has an 'edge'. There is an *intra-mural* dimension to this. In speaking of the reunification of the cosmos in Christ and its realization in the church, the author is seeking to inculcate a truly radical self-understanding of the church as a new solidarity, God's new household-temple. What was true formerly of Israel is true now of the church. The boundaries of the oneness of the people who belong to the one Lord and one God have been redrawn: to embrace Gentiles as well as Jews. Because of Christ, the space/place, time and people where God dwells and with whom he is one have been and are being transformed. But there is an *extra-mural* dimension also. As the place/people where the apocalyptic 'mystery' of cosmic reconciliation in Christ is being revealed, the church is a light in the darkness of an alienated world (cf. Eph. 4:17–23; 5:7–20). In its very

---

[35] A point well made by Lincoln, *Ephesians*, 364–65; cf. also his *Theology*, 123.

particularity, it is a witness to the possibility of a new humanity characterized by reconciliation – with God and with neighbour.

'I and the Father are one': Oneness in the Gospel of John

The Gospel of John is quite distinctive among the gospels in its emphasis on the 'oneness' of the Father and the Son and the 'oneness' of believers both with the Son and with one another.[36] Taken as a whole, and from the prologue on, the Gospel represents a claim that the one true God has made his presence, name and glory uniquely known in the person of the Son with whom he is one, believing and abiding in whom makes possible entry into 'life' and brings a new oneness into being, an eschatological unity of people drawn from every nation. In short, oneness is a principal vehicle and theological shorthand for John's Christology, soteriology and ecclesiology.

If we ask why the motif of oneness (and its corollaries in a wide range of reciprocity statements) is so pervasive in John, we are led to suggest – partly on the basis of the profound and mutual hostility that marks so many of the encounters between Jesus and his interlocutors – that oneness in John has both a defensive, apologetic character and a constitutive, identity-defining character. At the heart of the *apologetic* aspect is the issue of monotheism – one God and God as one.[37] Here, the fundamental claim that the Son is 'one' with the Father is a defence against the accusation that believing/abiding in Jesus as the Son 'from the Father' is a blasphemous departure from faith in the one true God (e.g., Jn. 10:31–39). In relation to *identity-formation*, the oneness theme represents what is fundamental for the evangelist in Christology, soteriology and ecclesiology. It represents the claim that, as the Son from the Father, the Word of God incarnate, Jesus is the Messiah, the one who uniquely and truly reveals God and the way to God and who is able therefore to bring into being a single, united people gifted with 'eternal life', sharing in the glory of God and able to worship God 'in Spirit and truth'.

We may take two of the most important texts as exemplary.[38] In John 10, Jesus reveals himself as 'the good shepherd' who knows his sheep by name and

---

[36] Fundamental in the scholarly literature is Appold, *Oneness*, and, most recently, Hayward, 'Unity'.

[37] The recognition that 'monotheism' (and related issues) was a key point of controversy in the development of Christology is a growth point in current New Testament studies. See, for example, Hurtado, *One God*; Bauckham, *God Crucified*; and Stuckenbruck and North (eds.), *Monotheism*. Curiously, Appold misses this point: 'the evangelist shows no interest in using the oneness term to express the monotheistic aspect of faith' (*Oneness*, 13 n. 1).

[38] The Johannine texts where 'one [*heis*]' has theological significance are at 10:16, 30; 11:52; 17:11, 21–23. In addition to these 'oneness' texts, however, there is a very

whose death on their behalf will bring into '*one* flock [*mia poimnē*]' under '*one* shepherd [*heis poimēn*]' sheep from different folds (10:11, 14–16). Furthermore, in so laying down his life in conformity with the Father's will, Jesus the Good Shepherd can affirm at the end of the discourse, 'I and the Father are *one* [*hen*]' (Jn. 10:30).

A number of observations are pertinent for our present purposes. First, taking account of the immediately preceding episode of the healing of the blind man and the controversy with the Pharisees in John 9, the context is highly polemical. It is one of charge and countercharge on matters christological, and of excommunication and alternative adherence on matters of belonging. So Jesus' claim to be 'the *good* shepherd' who acts in union with the Father and who creates by his sacrifice 'one flock' out of many has as its corollary an exceptionally powerful and pointed challenge.[39] The leadership he offers and the new solidarity he creates represent a stark alternative to Pharisaic leadership and the solidarity of the synagogue. The repeated references to the 'division [*schisma*]' Jesus generates are not coincidental (cf. Jn. 9:16; 10:19). The oneness Jesus makes possible represents both salvation and judgement, both the drawing of new lines in space, time and human society and also the drawing of boundaries marking out real points of difference.

A second observation concerns the role of *sacrifice* both 'vertically' in expressing the oneness of the Son with the Father – the Son as embodying the sanctifying presence of the Father (Jn. 10.36) – and 'horizontally' in bringing the new oneness of sheep into being. Although it is not made explicit, it is as if, as the one who 'lays down his life for the sheep' (Jn. 10:11, 15, 17, 18 [*bis*]), Jesus inaugurates a fundamental *shift* in the order of reality and in the ordering of human community. By his death, Jesus the Messiah gives life. The point is made repeatedly elsewhere (e.g., Jn. 1:29; 2:17–22; 3:14–16; 6:52–58, etc.). In the immediate context, it is reinforced dramatically in the succeeding episode where the raising to life of Lazarus precipitates the plot to destroy Jesus. Significantly, in that episode, the 'good shepherd' motif recurs with the calling of Lazarus from the tomb by name (Jn. 11:43; cf. 10:3–4, 27; also 5:22–29). Also significant is the fact that the motif of oneness recurs, specifically in relation to the sacrificial death of Jesus: 'He [Caiaphas] did not say this of his own accord, but being high priest that year he prophesied that Jesus should die for the nation, and not for the nation only, but to gather *into one* [*eis hen*] the children of God who are scattered abroad' (Jn. 11:51–52).

---

wide range of texts which express the fundamental *unity* and mutual reciprocity of Father and Son, as well as the unity of Father, Son and believers, and of believers with one another.

[39] The force of the challenge is reinforced, of course, by the scriptural resonance of the shepherd/sheep metaphor used by Jesus with the condemnation of the leaders of Israel in Ezekiel 34. Note especially the reminiscence of Ezek. 34:23 and 37:24 in the 'one shepherd, one flock' motif of Jn. 10:16.

There is an undoubted interest in unity of a provocatively inclusive kind here. The references to 'other sheep that are not of this fold' in 10:16 and to 'children of God scattered abroad' in 11:52 – along with such episodes as the extended encounter with the Samaritans (Jn. 4) and the coming of the Greeks to see Jesus (Jn. 12:20–26) – imply an inclusive solidarity where the boundaries of the people of God are able to be redrawn because of Jesus' sacrifice in death.[40] But boundaries remain: they are redrawn but not discarded. To put it another way, because the centre – understood now in terms of the death of the Good Shepherd – has shifted, the periphery has shifted (but not dissolved) also, allowing the inclusion of some previously excluded and the union of some previously separated.

The other text of major import in relation to oneness in John is the prayer of Jesus prior to his ascent to the Father via the cross, in chapter 17. Particularly relevant is the following:

> Holy Father, keep them in thy name, which thou hast given me, *that they may be one, even as we are* [hina ōsin hen kathōs hēmeis]. . . . I do not pray for these only, but also for those who believe in me through their word, *that they may all be one* [hina pantes hen ōsin]; even as thou, Father, art in me, and I in thee, that they also may be in us, so that the world may believe that thou hast sent me. The glory which thou hast given me I have given to them, *that they may be one even as we are one* [hina ōsin hen kathōs hēmeis hen], I in them and thou in me, *that they may become perfectly one* [hina ōsin teteleiōmenoi eis hen], so that the world may know that thou has sent me and hast loved them even as thou hast loved me. (17:11b, 20–23)

Although the passage invites extended literary analysis, I can offer here only the following observations.[41] First, the words are part of Jesus' prayer of departure that constitutes the climax of his ministry to the disciples in the upper room. In its form as a prayer – by far the most extended prayer in the Gospel (cf. 12:27–28) – and as something of a 'last will and testament',[42] it carries enormous rhetorical and theological weight. Second, the structure of the petitions for unity in verses 20–21 and 22–23 is remarkable for its repetitive *parallelismus membrorum*, the effect of which is to highlight the central themes of (as we shall see) oneness and witness. Third, and directly relevant to the theme of oneness, the purpose construction, 'that they may be one [hina ōsin hen]', occurs no less than four times in the prayer (17:11, 21, 22, 23) and nowhere else in John. So its presence in the prayer is significant and emphatic. Fourth, this prayer of Jesus is not for the world but for the disciples. This is implicit in the wider context of

---

[40] Significant in this connection also is the titulus placed by Pilate on Jesus' cross and written in Hebrew, Latin and Greek (Jn. 19:20).

[41] See further, Appold, *Oneness*, ch. VII.

[42] The allusion is to Käsemann's famous study, *Testament*.

the prayer in the upper room ministry of Jesus to the disciples alone (in Jn. 13 – 17); it becomes explicit in the words of Jesus himself, 'I am praying for them; I am not praying for the world but for those whom thou hast given me...' (17:9).

These observations at the literary level open the way for certain comments and suggestions at the thematic level. It is clear, for example, that the petitions for unity are petitions on behalf of the disciples: so their thrust is primarily ecclesial. Like Paul and Ephesians, it would appear, the evangelist's focal interest is not the unity of humankind in general but the unity of disciples of Jesus in particular. Why so? The principal reason is theological and evangelical. As Appold has rightly pointed out,[43] *the oneness of which the Gospel of John speaks is revelational*. It is a oneness that expresses the truth of revelation especially in relation to Christology, soteriology and ecclesiology. Thus, and at the risk of oversimplification, the oneness of disciples with each other (the moral/ ecclesiological aspect) is revelatory of and grounded in the oneness of individual disciples with the Son (the soteriological aspect), and this in turn is revelatory of and grounded in the oneness of the Son with the Father (the christological aspect).

Where does this leave humankind in general? Given the strong polarities and dualities that are so characteristic of John's worldview,[44] it comes as no surprise that humankind does indeed have a unity, a unity also defined in relation to revelation, but where the relation to revelation is primarily negative. This solidarity in opposition to revelation is represented variously: 'the darkness' that has not overcome the light (1:5); 'his own' who did not receive him or believe in him (1:11); 'the world', that body of humanity that loves darkness rather than light because of its moral turpitude (3:19); 'the Jews' or 'the Pharisees', catch-all terms for those who reject Jesus' claim to equality with God and seek to kill him (5:18; cf. 7:1; 8:59); children of the devil, the one 'who was a murderer from the beginning, and has nothing to do with the truth' (8:44), and so on.

On the basis of the foregoing, it is possible to interpret John as the proponent of a rather sombre duality of *opposed unities* – a worldview that is the product, perhaps, of a minority group under pressure and provocation (cf. 16:1–4) forced to adopt a sectarian stance of exclusivism and withdrawal. On this view, the heavy emphasis in Jesus' prayer of departure on the oneness of disciples both present and future can be understood as directed at the establishment and maintenance of group identity and solidarity in a context of social hostility. Here, 'oneness' is a shorthand for boundary marking in space, time and society which defines the self – as one who belongs in what Raymond Brown called 'the community of the beloved disciple' – and the other.[45] Some

---

[43] Appold, *Oneness*, 47.

[44] On the question of 'dualism' in John, see further Charlesworth, 'Comparison'.

[45] Brown, *Community*.

such sociological explanation has become a virtual consensus in recent Johannine scholarship.[46] While certainly debatable on aspects of method and content, this kind of explanation helps to contextualize the language of oneness and unity in John and to remind us that – as in Paul – such language is ideological, ordered to the marking of the differences of belief and practice that both unite and separate.

But the duality of opposed unities is *not static*. Jesus' prayer for the oneness of the disciples – as a manifestation of the oneness he shares with the Father – places the disciples in a dynamic relation with the world, a relation of *witness*. That is the force of the repeated and parallel *hina*-clauses in verses 21 and 23: 'that they may all be one ... *so that the world may believe* that thou hast sent me ... that they may become perfectly one *so that the world may know* that thou hast sent me and hast loved them even as thou hast loved me.'

Thus, if Johannine oneness is revelatory, a manifestation of the truth about Christ, salvation and the church, its purpose is *missiological*. Just as the oneness of Father and Son manifests itself in the sending of the Son, out of love, into the world, so the oneness of the Son and those who believe in him manifests itself in love for one another and in mission to the world.

Conclusion

The traditions and texts that I have begun to explore in this chapter have the potential to continue to speak. The biblical texts in particular express in a most profound way a universal vision of the unity of humankind as the revelation of the oneness of God in creation. They show also how that universal vision is *sustained, complicated and enriched* within the boundaries of a particular unity, the people of God, whose oneness displays the oneness of God in salvation and reconciliation.

In terms of our present situation, the material I have explored provokes the following reflections by way of the beginnings of a process of appropriation. First, at its most profound, the vision of the unity of humankind is *grounded in the vision of the oneness of God*. It is essential, therefore, that our understanding of what it means to be human, both as individuals and corporately, flows from our faith in the sovereignty of God in creation and the love of God in redemption. To put it another way, the unity of humankind is, theologically speaking, a matter of revelation: it comes to us as gift. It is an invitation to share in the life of the God who is One.

---

[46] See, for example, Meeks, 'Sectarianism'; Martyn, *Theology*; and Ashton, *Understanding*.

Second, in so far as Christ is the one in whom God's wisdom is made known and in whom creation finds its meaning and goal, it follows that *true human unity consists in growing into Christ*, acknowledging the lordship of Christ, practising the imitation of Christ, learning in our personal and political relations to die and rise with Christ. This does not come naturally. It involves patterns of identity-transforming common life that are eschatological, a sharing already – however partially – in the life of heaven. The power for this comes from *the eschatological Spirit*, whose heavenly gifts make life in union with one another and with God possible.

Third, this conception of the unity of humankind implies *an ecclesiology*: it finds its most potent expressions and interpretations in particular faith communities able over time to sustain cultures and practices that are truly catholic – that is, where unity is achieved, not at the cost of difference, but as its more complex and profound manifestation. Of critical importance in fostering and deepening such catholicity are symbolic forms of communication that both situate the particular in a universal context (and ultimately in God) and allow the universal to be 'earthed' materially and politically in the particular. The *sacraments* of baptism and Eucharist are just such symbolic forms. The sacraments mediate communication of the deepest, most transforming, most unifying kind – communication as communion.

Finally, this conception of human unity implies also *a missiology and a way of life*. Paul's mission is one of reconciliation, of offering himself up in the service of his heavenly Lord in order to make the new creation unity of Jews and Gentiles a reality. The challenge of Ephesians is to allow the reconciling fullness of Christ that believers share by grace to manifest itself in a sanctified common life, constituting thereby a light in the world's darkness. In the Gospel of John, the unity in love of Jesus' disciples arises out of the mission of the Son as the One sent by the Father with whom he is one, and leads in turn to the sending of the disciples into the world to witness to the truth. In each case, the way of life consonant with mission is the way of love, reconciliation and what makes for peace.

Trinity, church, mission and the sanctified life: these are fundamental elements of a biblical theology of the unity of humankind. It is here (or hereabouts) that Christians will want to begin as they seek to respond to current threats to humankind, including the challenges of tribalism and globalization that Jonathan Sacks so eloquently describes.[47]

---

[47]   For help in improving this essay, I am grateful to John Barclay, Markus Bockmuehl, Walter Moberly, Robin Parry and Bernd Wannenwetsch, and to the members of the New Testament Research Seminar in the Department of Theology, University of Durham.

Bibliography

Appold, M.L., *The Oneness Motif in the Fourth Gospel* (Tübingen: Mohr/Siebeck, 1976)

Ashton, J., *Understanding the Fourth Gospel* (Oxford: Clarendon Press, 1991)

Baldry, H.C., *The Idea of the Unity of Mankind* (= *Grecs Et Barbares,* Entretiens Tome VIII; Geneva: Vandœuvres, 1962)

Barclay, J.M.G., '"Neither Jew Nor Greek": Multiculturalism and the New Perspective on Paul', in *Ethnicity and the Bible* (ed. M.G. Brett; Leiden: Brill, 1996), 197–214

—, 'Universalism and Particularism: Twin Components of Both Judaism and Early Christianity', in *A Vision for the Church: Studies in Early Christian Ecclesiology* (ed. M. Bockmuehl and M.G. Thompson; Edinburgh: T. & T. Clark, 1997), 207–24

Barton, S.C., '1 Corinthians', in *Eerdmans Commentary on the Bible* (ed. J.D.G. Dunn and J.W. Rogerson; Grand Rapids: Eerdmans, 2003), 1314–52

Bauckham, R., *God Crucified: Monotheism and Christology in the New Testament* (Carlisle: Paternoster Press, 1998)

—, *The Bible and Mission: Christian Witness in a Postmodern World* (Carlisle: Paternoster, 2003)

Bauckham, R. (ed.), *The Gospels for All Christians* (Grand Rapids: Eerdmans, 1998)

Betz, H.D., *Galatians* (Philadelphia: Fortress Press, 1979)

Bockmuehl, M., 'The Noachide Commandments and New Testament Ethics', *RB* 102 (1995), 72–101

Borgen, P., 'Jesus Christ, the Reception of the Spirit, and a Cross-National Community', in *Jesus of Nazareth: Lord and Christ* (ed. J.B. Green and M. Turner; Grand Rapids: Eerdmans, 1994), 220–35

Brown, R.E., *The Community of the Beloved Disciple* (New York: Paulist Press, 1979)

Campbell, D.A., 'Reconciliation in Paul: The Gospel of Negation and Transcendence in Galatians 3.28', in *The Theology of Reconciliation* (ed. C.E. Gunton; London and New York: T. & T. Clark, 2003), 39–65

Charlesworth, J.H., 'A Critical Comparison of the Dualism in 1QS 3:13 – 4:26 and the "Dualism" Contained in the Gospel of John', in *John and the Dead Sea Scrolls* (ed. J.H. Charlesworth; New York: Crossroad, 1972), 76–106

Clines, D.J.A., *The Theme of the Pentateuch* (Sheffield: JSOT Press, 1978)

Dahl, N.A., 'Christ, Creation and the Church', in *The Background of the New Testament and Its Eschatology* (ed. W.D. Davies and D. Daube; Cambridge: Cambridge University Press, 1956), 422–43

—, 'Nations in the New Testament', in *New Testament Christianity for Africa and the World* (ed. M.E. Glasswell and E.W. Fasholé-Luke; London: SPCK, 1974), 54–68

—, 'The One God of Jews and Gentiles (Romans 3:29–30)', in *Studies in Paul* (Minneapolis: Augsburg, 1977), 178–91

—, 'Gentiles, Christians, and Israelites in the Epistle to the Ephesians', in *Christians Among Jews and Gentiles* (ed. G.W. Nickelsburg and G. MacRae; Philadelphia: Fortress Press, 1986), 31–39

Dulles, A., *The Catholicity of the Church* (Oxford: Clarendon Press, 1987)

Dunn, J.D.G., *Unity and Diversity in the New Testament* (London: SCM Press, 1977)

Ferguson, J., *Utopias of the Classical World* (London: Thames & Hudson, 1975)

Greenberg, M., 'Mankind, Israel, and the Nations in the Hebraic Heritage', in *Studies in the Bible and Jewish Thought* (Philadelphia: Jewish Publication Society, 1995), 369–93

Hayward, C.T.R., *The Jewish Temple: A Non-biblical Sourcebook* (London: Routledge, 1996)

—, 'The Lord is One: Reflections on the Theme of Unity in St. John's Gospel from a Jewish Perspective', in *Exploring Early Jewish and Christian Monotheism* (ed. L.T. Stuckenbruck and W.E.S. North; London: T. & T. Clark International, 2004), 138–54

Hurtado, L.W., *One God One Lord* (Philadelphia: Fortress Press, 1988)

Käsemann, E., *The Testament of Jesus: A Study of the Gospel of John in the Light of Chapter 17* (London: SCM Press, 1968)

Lafer, G., 'Universalism and Particularism in Jewish Law: Making Sense of Political Loyalties', in *Jewish Identity* (ed. D.T. Goldberg and M. Krausz; Philadelphia: Temple University Press, 1993), 177–211

Levenson, J.D., 'The Temple and the World', *JR* 64 (1984), 275–98

—, 'The Universal Horizon of Biblical Particularism', in *Ethnicity and the Bible* (ed. M.G. Brett; Leiden: Brill, 1996), 143–69

Lincoln, A., *Ephesians* (Dallas: Word Books, 1990)

Lincoln, A., and A.J.M. Wedderburn, *The Theology of the Later Pauline Letters* (Cambridge: Cambridge University Press, 1993)

Martyn, J.L., *Theology and History in the Fourth Gospel* (Nashville: Abingdon Press, 2nd edn, 1979)

—, 'Apocalyptic Antinomies in Paul's Letter to the Galatians', *NTS* 31 (1985), 410–24

Meeks, W.A., 'The Man from Heaven in Johannine Sectarianism', *JBL* 91 (1972), 44–72

—, 'The Image of the Androgyne: Some Uses of a Symbol in Earliest Christianity', *HR* 13 (1974), 165–208

—, 'In One Body: The Unity of Humankind in Colossians and Ephesians', in *God's Christ and His People* (ed. J. Jervell and W.A. Meeks; Oslo: Universitetsforlaget, 1977), 209–21

Mitchell, M.M., *Paul and the Rhetoric of Reconciliation* (Louisville, KY: Westminster John Knox, 1992)

Moberly, R.W.L., '"Yahweh Is One": The Translation of the Shema', in *Studies in the Pentateuch* (ed. J.A. Emerton; VTSup 41, Leiden: Brill, 1990), 209–15

—, 'Toward an Interpretation of the Shema', in *Theological Exegesis: Essays in Honor of Brevard S. Childs* (ed. C. Seitz and K. Greene-McCreight; Grand Rapids: Eerdmans, 1999), 124–44

Reumann, J., *Variety and Unity in New Testament Thought* (Oxford: Oxford University Press, 1991)

Sacks, J., *The Dignity of Difference: How to Avoid the Clash of Civilizations* (London and New York: Continuum, 2002)

Schlier, H., 'The Unity of the Church in the New Testament', in *The Relevance of the New Testament* (London: Burns & Oates, 1968), 193–214

Schofield, M., 'Approaching the *Republic*', in *The Cambridge History of Greek and Roman Political Thought* (ed. C.J. Rowe and M. Schofield; Cambridge: Cambridge University Press, 2000), 190–232

Segal, A.F., 'Universalism in Judaism and Christianity', in *Paul in His Hellenistic Context* (ed. T. Engberg-Pedersen; Edinburgh: T. & T. Clark, 1994), 1–29

Stuckenbruck, L.T., and W. North (eds.), *Exploring Early Jewish and Christian Monotheism* (London: T. & T. Clark International, 2004)

Turner, M., 'Ephesians', in *New Bible Commentary* (ed. D.A. Carson et al.; Leicester: IVP, 1994), 1222–44

—, 'Mission and Meaning in Terms of "Unity" in Ephesians', in *Mission and Meaning: Essays Presented to Peter Cotterell* (ed. A Billington, T. Lane and M. Turner; Carlisle: Paternoster, 1995), 138–66

Wilson, B., *Religion in Secular Society* (London: Penguin, 1969)

Parts of the Bible and Biblical Theology

10

Zechariah 14 and Biblical Theology

Patristic and Contemporary Case Studies

Al Wolters

In this chapter I propose to bring together the themes of biblical theology and biblical interpretation by bringing them both to bear on a single chapter – Zechariah 14. I will do this by surveying three patristic and three contemporary commentaries that self-consciously seek to situate this chapter within the grand narrative of the Christian canon. Finally, in the light of this survey, I will venture a number of comments of my own as to how Zechariah 14 should be read in the context of the overall biblical story.

Introduction

By way of introduction, let me first say a few words about the term 'biblical theology', about the value of consulting the history of interpretation and about the difficulty of Zechariah 14.

For my purposes, I am going to define 'biblical theology' as the scholarly enterprise which seeks, on the basis of a belief in the unity of the Christian canon, to draw out the connections between any given part of the Scriptures and the overall biblical story, notably including references to the historical future – whether messianic, eschatological or world-historical in a more general sense. By the overall biblical story (or metanarrative) I understand the broad outline of the ecumenical Christian confession regarding creation, the fall of humankind into sin and the remedy for that fall in the history of Israel and the coming of Jesus of Nazareth as the Messiah, by whose death and resurrection a worldwide and multi-ethnic church was created – a church which sees itself as part of the story and looks forward to its consummation in Christ's second coming and the restoration of all things in him. This grand narrative includes the history that was actually experienced by the various writers of the Bible over the many centuries of its composition and formation, but it encompasses much more, since the biblical story reaches back to the creation of the world and stretches forward to the eschatological renewal of the world. As I use the term, therefore, 'biblical theology' looks at Scripture as both embodying and projecting an all-encompassing narrative 'world' and seeks to relate all of its variegated and seemingly contradictory parts to this one overarching *Geschichte*, which is both story and history.

I take it that the task of doing biblical theology is a perennial one, and that each successive generation of Christian biblical interpreters must meet this challenge afresh. There is no era of biblical interpretation which has been excluded from this task, or which has failed to contribute to it. Nevertheless, the rise of classical historical criticism, a characteristic product of the European Enlightenment, has in many ways subverted the project of doing biblical theology, since it deliberately set out to remove from academic biblical scholarship some of the fundamental assumptions governing that project, notably the inspiration and unity of the Christian canon, and the historical referentiality of much of its discourse, especially discourse about the future. As a result, most of the history of biblical interpretation was dismissed as 'pre-critical' and declared largely irrelevant to the academic study of Scripture. It is only recently, with the rise of postmodernism, that the modernist bias of this attitude has been more generally admitted in the academy, and that a greater interest has emerged in the history of biblical interpretation. Nevertheless, it is still true that most biblical scholars are woefully ignorant of anything in their discipline written more than a generation ago, and that even those who do have some appreciation for the history of interpretation have little interest in mining that history for the task of doing biblical theology. The time is ripe for the recovery within biblical studies of what Anthony Thiselton calls the 'post-history' of the biblical texts,[1] and to glean from that post-history some of the forgotten insights which it contains into the interconnectedness of the biblical documents and the metanarrative which they tell.

To emphasize the value of knowing the history of interpretation is of course not to be uncritical of it, either with respect to detailed questions of exegesis or with respect to the broader issues of biblical theology. It is undoubtedly true that much of patristic, medieval and early modern biblical interpretation contains material which needs to be discarded in the light of modern advances in archaeology, philology and literary criticism, or which deserves to be dismissed as arbitrary and fanciful because it is based on a doctrine of spiritual senses

---

[1] Thiselton, *1 Corinthians*, xvii, 196.

which had few methodological controls. Nevertheless, for the task of doing biblical theology these earlier eras of biblical interpretation continue to be valuable, if for no other reason than that they at least raised the question of how a given pericope resonates in the echo chamber of the Christian Bible as a whole. As we shall see, the patristic interpretation of Zechariah 14 provides ample evidence of this tantalizing mixture of the discardable and the valuable.

I have chosen Zechariah 14 to illustrate these points, in part because it is notoriously obscure. Jerome famously designated the book of Zechariah as a whole as an *obscurissimus liber*[2] and its final chapter is even more challenging than most of the others. As confirmation of this point we may refer to Luther's two commentaries on the book of Zechariah. The first one, published in Latin in 1526, breaks off at the end of chapter 13 and simply leaves chapter 14 without commentary.[3] The second one, published in German in the following year, does have a brief commentary on the fourteenth chapter, but this begins with the words, 'Here, in this chapter, I give up. For I am not sure what the prophet is talking about.'[4] Many other commentators have also testified to the difficulty of interpreting this chapter, and it is this very obscurity which makes Zechariah 14 an interesting test case for comparing patristic and contemporary approaches to doing biblical theology. Precisely because the meaning of the text seems to be so indeterminate, it gives unusual scope for different ways of understanding its relationship to the grand narrative of Scripture as a whole, and thus provides an apt occasion for the display of hermeneutical presuppositions.

The content of Zechariah 14, which could be entitled 'Jerusalem and the nations on the Day of the Lord', can be summarized in the following seven statements:

The Lord will first gather the nations in order to visit the horrors of war on Jerusalem, and then turn around and fight these nations (vv. 1–3).

Right through the Mount of Olives, where his feet will stand, the Lord will create a valley of escape from Jerusalem, and then arrive with his army (vv. 4–5).

There will be continuous daylight, continuous streams will flow eastwards and westwards from Jerusalem, and the Lord will be king of the whole earth (vv. 6–9).

Jerusalem will be lifted high in safety, and the surrounding countryside will be depressed and flattened (vv. 10–11).

---

[2] Jerome, *Commentarii*, 747.
[3] Luther, *Zechariah*, 152.
[4] Luther, *Zechariah*, 337.

The nations that fought against Jerusalem will be decimated by plague, panic and the attack of Judah, and their wealth taken (vv. 12–15).

The survivors of the nations will make an annual pilgrimage to worship the Lord in Jerusalem, and those who don't will be punished (vv. 16–19).

The commonest things in Jerusalem and Judah will be holy, and the ungodly will be absent (vv. 20–21).

In what follows we will discuss three representative patristic commentaries on this chapter, and three representative twentieth-century commentaries that can still be said to be engaged in the project of biblical theology. To restrict the scope of our discussion even further, and to allow a more detailed comparison of the six selected commentators, we will focus our attention especially on three features of the chapter: the initial assault of the nations on Jerusalem, the splitting of the Mount of Olives and the holiness of the horses' trappings.

Patristic Commentaries

The earliest patristic commentaries on Zechariah that we know of are those by Origen and Hippolytus (third century AD), but both of these are lost.[5] However, there are six patristic commentaries from the fourth and fifth centuries which are still extant: four in Greek (Didymus the Blind, Theodore of Mopsuestia, Cyril of Alexandria and Theodoret of Cyrrhus),[6] one in Syriac (attributed to Ephraem Syrus)[7] and one in Latin (Jerome).[8] For our purposes, we will select Theodore of Mopsuestia as a representative of the so-called 'Antiochene' school of interpretation, Didymus the Blind as a representative of the rival 'Alexandrian' school and Jerome as an especially influential exegete who belongs in a class by himself.

Theodore of Mopsuestia

Theodore of Mopsuestia is perhaps the foremost representative of the exegetical school associated with Antioch in Syria. Although he was later anathematized by various church councils in the West, he was held in high honour as an exegete in the Syriac churches, where he became known as

---

[5] See Doutreleau, 'Introduction', 30–33.

[6] On Didymus, Theodore, Cyril and Theodoret, see Doutreleau, 'Introduction', 34–41.

[7] On Ephraem Syrus, see Doutreleau, 'Introduction', 33–34.

[8] Jerome, *Commentarii*.

simply 'the Interpreter'. His hermeneutics is characterized by a strong rejection of allegory and a great reluctance to see Old Testament texts as referring to NT realities. In fact, the history to which the Hebrew Bible refers is in his view almost entirely restricted to the period ending with the Maccabean revolt in 168–165 BC. According to H.N. Sprenger, the most recent editor of Theodore's commentary on the Minor Prophets, his exegesis was characterized by two procedures: a historical-grammatical explanation of the lexical meaning of the text, and a typological interpretation of OT texts.[9] For the former he used the full arsenal of rhetorical categories which he had learned in his studies under the pagan rhetor Libanius and the Christian exegete Diodorus of Tarsus. With respect to the latter he was extraordinarily reticent, seeing typological references to the NT only on the basis of a prior meaning which makes sense on its own terms within the OT historical context. Although he is sometimes depicted as a forerunner of modern historical criticism,[10] his acceptance of typology, however restricted in actual practice, shows that this judgement needs to be significantly qualified.

Theodore's commentary on the Minor Prophets is one of his earliest exegetical works, written around 380.[11] His exegesis of Zechariah 14 needs to be seen in the context of his overall interpretation of Zechariah 9 – 14. Although he did not detach these chapters from the preceding eight, as modern critical scholarship has done, he does treat them together as predictions of the history of Israel in the OT era. Remarkably, however, he sees these predictions as referring first (in Zech. 9:1 – 11:3) to events happening in the lifetime of Zechariah's contemporary Zerubbabel in the sixth century BC, then (in Zech. 11:4 – 14:11) to the events surrounding the Maccabean revolt in the second century BC, and finally, in the middle of chapter 14, back to the sixth century again. This means that he interprets the famous passage in Zechariah 9:9 ('Behold, your king comes unto you'), which the NT applies to Christ, as referring properly to Zerubbabel.[12] Furthermore, he takes the verses that follow in chapter 9 to refer to Zerubbabel's victory over the forces of the house of Gog, Scythian invaders who were to threaten Jerusalem and be defeated by Zerubbabel. It is not until Zechariah 11 and the famous shepherd allegory that the scene suddenly changes to the Maccabean era. According to Theodore the subsequent chapters in Zechariah, including the first eleven verses of chapter 14, all contain predictions of the events of that pivotal era in Jewish history. Thus the description of the assault of the nations on Jerusalem in verse 1 has reference to the attack of the armies of Antiochus IV Epiphanes, and the Lord's

---

[9] Sprenger, 'Einleitung', 85.

[10] See for example Zaharopoulos, *Theodore of Mopsuestia*, 6–7, 176–85.

[11] Doutreleau, 'Introduction', 35; cf. Sprenger, 'Einleitung', 96.

[12] Theodore of Mopsuestia, *Commentarius*, 367.

intervention on behalf of the Jews in verse 3 refers to the divine aid which was given to the Maccabees.

Similarly, he interprets the dramatic description of the splitting of the Mount of Olives as a highly imaginative figure of speech. Theodore puts it this way: '[Zechariah] says all these things by way of hyperbole (ὑπερβολικῶς), as is his custom, and because by the greatness of the help which he supplies to his own people, and by his wrath against the enemy, he will appear, as it were, to shake all things.'[13] In other words, God's help and anger at the time of the Maccabean struggle were 'earth-shattering', as it were, but only in a metaphorical sense. Similarly, when the Septuagint text says in verse 6 that 'it will happen on that day that there will not be light', Theodore explains this as follows:

> [Zechariah] does not really mean 'light' … but just as it is customary to say 'the sun will be obscured', and 'the sun will go down on them' and all such expressions, meaning that those who are in distress have no sensation of light, but seem at the time to be, as it were, in a kind of darkness, so he speaks here as well. But because of the greatness of the events, he says, men will imagine they do not even see light.[14]

Again, the absence of light is for Theodore simply a figurative way of describing the great distress experienced by the oppressed Jews at the time of the Maccabees.

However, at the end of verse 11 Theodore discerns a transition in the text. He writes as follows:

> Now in these [foregoing] verses [Zechariah] has concluded the prophecy concerning the Maccabean events: the things which were to happen during that time, the sins which would be committed by them, the things that were to befall them at the hands of their enemies, as well as the great care concerning them which God would show by lending his decisive influence to the leaders of the good cause. But from this point on he takes up again what he had said before the foretelling of the Maccabean events, when in speaking of the blessings which would come to the nation through Zerubbabel he added the destruction of those connected with Gog. Here too he takes up again the foretelling of these blessings, because they were about to happen in the near future. He did this so that the fresh events surrounding Gog might be a guarantee of the events which were going to happen after a very long time (I mean the Maccabean ones), and so that the prophet would be able to conclude his prophecy with a view to a foretelling that would be of greater benefit.[15]

---

[13] Theodore of Mopsuestia, *Commentarius*, 394. All quotations from Theodore are my translations of the Greek.

[14] Theodore of Mopsuestia, *Commentarius*, 395.

[15] Theodore of Mopsuestia, *Commentarius*, 396–97.

In other words, Theodore sees the prophet reverting to the subject of his earlier predictions in Zechariah 9 and 10, where he had foretold how Zerubbabel was to defeat the forces of Gog. For the initial readers of Zechariah's prophecy this would be a foretelling 'of greater benefit' than the one about the Maccabees, because it would be fulfilled in those readers' lifetimes. Moreover, this fulfilled prophecy would function as a guarantee (πίστις) of the fulfilment of the one about the Maccabees, some four hundred years later.

Since the last half of chapter 14 now deals with a prophecy concerning Zerubbabel's battle with the armies of Gog, we understand how Theodore relates verse 20, which in the Septuagint speaks of a horse's 'bit' or 'bridle' (Greek χαλινός), to that military engagement. There was a widespread exegetical tradition in antiquity that, after the defeat of Gog's forces by Zerubbabel, the weapons of the former were dedicated to God.[16] Theodore understands the 'bridle' of our passage to stand by a kind of synecdoche (he uses the technical rhetorical term ἀπὸ μέρους) for those weapons, and writes as follows:

> [Zechariah] means to say that many things – too many to count – will also be dedicated to God by the Israelites from the spoils which they will take from the enemy. The blessed David did something similar after slaying Goliath, when he dedicated the sword to the Lord. The same thing is meant here too, that at that time they will offer to God even the bridles of the horses, which they have taken from the fallen. For by the bridle, as by a part (ὡς ἀπὸ μέρους), he meant to refer to the other military equipment and spoils which they were going to dedicate, each one bringing forward from the spoils what he thought best, according to his own purpose ... He meant by the bridle to refer to the dedicated items from the military equipment ... in accordance with the custom of divine Scripture to indicate many by a part (ἀπὸ μέρους), whenever it considers detailed precision superfluous, since here too it was superfluous to enumerate spears and swords and breastplates.[17]

In short, Theodore interprets Zechariah 14 as referring to two eras of Israel's history which were still future in the prophet's own day: first the distant Maccabean future, and then the immediate future when Zerubbabel was to defeat the Scythian forces under Gog. In this he follows his regular practice of understanding the Old Testament within its own historical horizon, without reference to the New Testament era. Furthermore, by bringing to bear such rhetorical categories as hyperbole and synecdoche he maintains the historical reference of this prophecy without resorting to a wooden literalism. The passage is interpreted within the context of the historical narrative of Scripture, including those parts which were yet future, but with a deliberate restriction to the Old Testament period.

---

[16] See the note by Ceslas van den Eynde in Ishodad of Merv, *Commentaire*, 7 n. 5.

[17] Theodore of Mopsuestia, *Commentarius*, 398–99.

We see from this example of Theodore's interpretation that it is a mistake to characterize the Antiochene school of patristic exegesis, of which he is the most prominent representative, as being concerned above all with the *literal* meaning of Scripture. Instead, it is more accurate to speak of its emphasis on the *historical* sense, which may be conveyed in highly figurative ways. In this the Antiochene school stood in opposition to the Alexandrian school, with its extensive use of allegory.

Didymus the Blind

We now turn to a representative of this second exegetical tradition, Didymus the Blind, who was an older contemporary of Theodore. He probably wrote his commentary on Zechariah in 387, less than a decade after Theodore's work on the Minor Prophets, but there is no indication that he was acquainted with the latter. His commentary on Zechariah 14 is quite extensive, running to some 55 pages in Doutreleau's edition. He wrote it at the request of Jerome, who was a great admirer of his and had visited him in Alexandria in 386.[18]

Although it had long been known that Didymus had written a commentary on Zechariah, it was presumed lost until 1941, when a large cache of Didymus' exegetical writings were discovered in a cave in Toura, just south of Cairo.[19] Among these was the largely intact commentary on Zechariah, consisting of a single codex of 414 sheets of papyrus. It was published, with an extensive introduction, notes and a French translation, by Louis Doutreleau in 1962. One of the surprises which emerged from the publication of this long-lost work was the degree to which Jerome, at whose urging it had originally been written, had relied on it in writing his own commentary. It became evident that the latter in many parts consisted of little more than a Latin translation of Didymus' Greek.[20]

In general, it can be said that Didymus, unlike Theodore, has very little interest in the historical sense of the text. Nevertheless, his treatment of the assault of the nations on Jerusalem in Zechariah 14:1–2 is an exception to this. He points out that spoils are often divided outside of a conquered city, rather than within it, and that it is especially painful when plundering and rape take place before the very eyes of the conquered citizenry. He then goes on to say: 'Such things, with all their inhumanity, happened to the inhabitants of Jerusalem and Judah when the people of Judea were captured by the nations on account of the guilt which they took upon themselves by killing the Lord.'[21] He clearly has in mind the destruction of Jerusalem in AD 70, and this is

---

[18] Doutreleau, 'Introduction', 23.

[19] Doutreleau, 'Introduction', 21.

[20] Doutreleau, 'Introduction', 130–35.

[21] Didymus the Blind, *Sur Zacharie*, 980–82 (V,28). All quotations from Didymus are my translations from the Greek.

confirmed by his subsequent reference to the Jewish historian Josephus and the calamities suffered by his people, which he describes. However, from this point on, history virtually disappears from Didymus' purview.

We see this illustrated in his exposition of the immediately following verses, which speak of the Lord going out to do battle, of his feet standing on the Mount of Olives and of the splitting of that mountain. He begins by making the philosophical point that God transcends corporeality and is therefore invisible. Such a view has hermeneutical consequences. Didymus writes, 'Since therefore this is the correct way of speaking and thinking about God, one must take the ways in which he is deliberately described in the divine Scriptures in rather corporeal terms in an intelligible sense appropriate to God (νοητῶς καὶ θεοπρεπῶς).'[22] Consequently, God does not really 'go out'.

> Just as we understand and comprehend the passages about his repentance and anger and similar emotions, in the same way, since he is incorporeal, we understand statements about his ascending and descending, and going out and coming in, in a way consonant with our intelligible conception (νόησις) of him. Therefore, [when we read] in the prophecy before us the expression 'The Lord will go out', we do not imagine a movement from place to place, for such movements are characteristic of bodies.[23]

Oddly enough, Didymus pays no attention in his commentary to the idea of the Lord doing battle on behalf of his people.

When the Septuagint text says in verse 4 that 'his feet will stand (στήσονται) on the Mount of Olives', Didymus understands the verb in its ingressive meaning, 'come to a standstill, halt', and interprets it in a spiritual sense. Other passages of Scripture speak of the Lord walking away from his people in anger, but here his feet are said to halt.[24] And they halt on the Mount of *Olives*, which suggests to Didymus a whole series of scriptural associations having to do with the olive. For example, the olive is said to be – no doubt because of the use of olive oil as a lighting fuel and a medicinal ointment –'a fruit which maintains and preserves the divine light and puts an end to sicknesses and troubles'.[25] The reference to olives is in turn related to the splitting of the Mount of Olives. This means that the olive groves on this mountain are divided into two kinds of spiritual olive trees – good ones facing east, and bad ones facing west.[26] Didymus then cites a series of biblical passages that illustrate both kinds of olive tree. In this way everything is spiritualized. Nothing that he writes has reference to the

---

[22] Didymus the Blind, *Sur Zacharie*, 984 (V,34).

[23] Didymus the Blind, *Sur Zacharie*, 986 (V,35).

[24] Didymus the Blind, *Sur Zacharie*, 988 (V,39).

[25] Didymus the Blind, *Sur Zacharie*, 988 (V,40).

[26] Didymus the Blind, *Sur Zacharie*, 990 (V,41).

actual mountain east of Jerusalem or its future history; everything has become a symbol of spiritual truth. It is also telling that he makes no comment about the connection – or lack of connection – between verses 1–2 (which he does interpret historically) and verses 2–4 (which he gives a quite different kind of interpretation).

The rest of Didymus' commentary on Zechariah 14 continues this non-literal and non-historical kind of exegesis. His usual procedure is to let a given word or phrase suggest one or more other places in Scripture where those same expressions occur, and to associate them with some point of orthodox theology or spirituality. There is almost no attempt to see coherence or connection, either logical or narrative, in the progression of the text. Individual texts, or individual words, are like pegs upon which Didymus hangs an unrelated series of points of doctrine. Old and New Testament texts are cited helter-skelter alongside each other, with little or no regard to their literary context or their place within the canon as a whole. Didymus' exegesis is not arbitrary, because it never strays from dogmatic orthodoxy, but it seems to be related to the text mainly through a process of imaginative association.

There is one further exception to his overall disregard for any future historical referent to the prophecy of Zechariah 14. This occurs in his commentary on verses 5b–6: 'And the Lord my God will come and all his holy ones with him. In that day there will be no light and there will be cold and frost for one day.' Of this Didymus writes: 'The text before us can (δύναται) refer to the second and glorious coming of the Saviour',[27] and he proceeds to back up this interpretation by various other Scripture references. What is striking about his statement here is its tentativeness; the text *can* be explained in this way, but it need not be. This tentativeness stands in stark contrast to Didymus' usual mode of confident assertion. He seems hesitant to commit himself to even this historical fulfilment in the eschaton.

As a final illustration of his overall spiritualizing approach we turn to his treatment of verse 20, on the holiness of the horse's bridle. He writes as follows:

> On the day, just explained, of the Feast of Tabernacles, to which one should go up and celebrate to worship the King, the Lord Almighty, 'that which is on the horse's bridle' will be called 'holy to the Lord Almighty.' And what is this but the one who restrains [...] the unbridled souls which lack understanding and other virtue. The sage forbids their frenzy and their unbridledness, and commands such frenzy-driven men: 'Do not be like a horse or a mule without understanding; with bridle and muzzle you shall squeeze their jaws when they do not come near to you.' [Ps. 31 (32):9] For how can the 'lustful horse who neighs after the wife of his neighbour' [Jer. 5:8], frenzy-driven by his shameful passions, not be restrained by his spiritual

---

[27] Didymus the Blind, *Sur Zacharie*, 1006 (V,69).

bridle?[28] So when his undisciplined impulse has been restrained by the horsebreaker, he will become tame, so that he will prove useful for battle, as is said about him in Proverbs: 'The horse is made ready for the day of battle, but help is from the Lord' [Prov. 21:31].[29]

Apparently basing himself on the general idea of the horse's bridle as something that restrains, Didymus explains the bridle of this passage as the word that restrains unbridled souls. By a process of association he then connects this thought with a number of different biblical texts: Psalm 31:9, by way of the word 'bridle' and the theme of animal restraint; Jeremiah 5:8, by way of the theme of horses with passions needing restraint; and Proverbs 21:31, by way of the theme of horsebreaking. Clearly, his discussion circles around the general idea of controlling the passions, but it has no reference to actual horses or to a historical future.

Jerome

Our third patristic commentator is Jerome. As we have mentioned, he was the one who had asked Didymus to write the commentary on Zechariah, and he himself drew heavily on the latter when he set about writing his own commentary almost 20 years later (in 406). His is the first commentary on Zechariah to be written in Latin, and it was to prove enormously influential in the Latin West until early modern times. Apart from the language in which it was written, what distinguishes Jerome's commentary is the fact that he works from the Hebrew text as well as from the Septuagint. In fact, he prefaces each section of the commentary with two Latin translations of the passage to be discussed: first Jerome's own translation of the Hebrew text, which with minor variations is the same as his recently completed Vulgate version, and second his translation of the Greek text of the Septuagint. It is striking that Jerome sometimes bases his commentary on the latter as well as the former. We need to bear in mind, of course, that the Septuagint had been the Old Testament of the Christian church for centuries, and many considered it to be inspired. Following this double translation, the general pattern (there are a few exceptions) is that Jerome first gives a literal or historical commentary on the text, in which he frequently refers to Jewish exegesis and the meaning of individual Hebrew words (often citing other ancient versions), and then moves on to a 'spiritual' interpretation, in which he is generally heavily dependent on Didymus. In fact, he relies so much on Didymus that he not infrequently repeats the latter's slips of

---

[28] I read the damaged text here as ἐπ[έχεται] τῷ πνευματ[ικῷ χαλινῷ] rather than Doutreleau's reconstruction ἐπ[άγεται] τῷ πνευματ[ικῷ ἐπιβάτῃ].

[29] Didymus the Blind, *Sur Zacharie*, 1076 (V,190).

the pen or textual mistakes.[30] However, he appears also to have had before him the commentaries by Origen and Hippolytus, which are now lost.[31] Because of his double emphasis on historical and spiritual interpretation, Jerome in some sense straddles the Alexandrian and Antiochene schools, although the latter would probably have disowned him for his ready acceptance of allegory. On the other hand, Jerome says of the Alexandrian interpreters Origen, Hippolytus and Didymus that 'their ἐξήγησις [exegesis] was entirely allegorical, and they hardly touched on even a few matters pertaining to history'.[32] Accordingly, he describes his own project as follows: 'I mixed the spiritual interpretation of our own exegetes (*tropologiam nostrorum*) with the historical interpretation (*historia*) of the Jews.'[33]

In many ways Jerome stands head and shoulders above his predecessors, certainly when it comes to philological erudition and scholarly humility. For one thing, he is acutely aware of the difficulty of his task. In a famous passage at the beginning of the second part of his commentary on Zechariah he writes:

> We pass from the obscure to the more obscure, and with Moses enter cloud and darkness. Deep calls to deep in the voice of the floods of God, and the Spirit goes curling round in coils, and turns back on its own paths; we endure labyrinthine wanderings, and we direct our blind footsteps by the thread of Christ.[34]

In his discussion of the assault of the nations on Jerusalem, Jerome closely follows Didymus' discussion, including the reference to Josephus. In punishment for the killing of Christ, God destroyed Jerusalem by the Romans. However, he also includes a reference to the Roman historian Tacitus and his (now lost) account of the destruction of Jerusalem in AD 70.[35] At the conclusion of his commentary on the initial two verses Jerome adds this telling comment:

> The Jews say that these things are to be fulfilled under Gog, and others that they were partly accomplished in the times of the Macedonians and Egyptians and various other peoples. As for us, leaving the variation in chronology (*temporis varietatem*) to the judgement of the Lord, let us explain what is written.[36]

This remark is significant because it informs us that Jerome was aware of a number of other views, both Jewish and Christian, with respect to the

---

[30] Doutreleau, 'Introduction', 130–31.

[31] Doutreleau, 'Introduction', 129.

[32] Jerome, *Commentarii*, 748. All quotations from Jerome are my translations from the Latin.

[33] Jerome, *Commentarii*, 748.

[34] Jerome, *Commentarii*, 795. I read *obscuriora* rather than *obscura* in line 118 (see the textual apparatus *ad locum*).

[35] Jerome, *Commentarii*, 878.

[36] Jerome, *Commentarii*, 878.

historical fulfilment of this prophecy, but that he himself was going to refrain from trying to identify the various historical referents of the predictions that follow, and to restrict his remarks to the textual level. It is significant that he does not deny that the chapter contains predictions that will find their fulfilment in history, but simply leaves that issue to the judgement of God. We also note in passing that the interpretation of 'the Jews' to which he alludes was apparently an eschatological one, and that the interpretation of 'others', presumably Christians, allowed for the *partial* fulfilment of the prophecy in a number of different historical epochs. Unfortunately, we do not know who these Christian interpreters were.

True to his declared intent, Jerome does not try to identify a historical fulfilment of the next few verses, which speak of the feet of the Lord standing on the Mount of Olives and its subsequent splitting. With some modifications he follows the allegorical interpretation of Didymus, including the latter's sentiments about anthropomorphic language.

> That God 'goes out' and 'fights' against the nations, and that his feet stand upon the Mount of Olives, and the other things contained in the sacred Scriptures which are expressed in an anthropomorphic and carnal way (ἀνθρωποπάθως *dicta et carnaliter*), we must understand in a manner worthy of God.[37]

But he concludes this section with another reference to the difficulty of the task, and to the literal eschatological interpretation of the Jews:

> As in other very difficult and obscure passages, we have said the foregoing to the best of our limited ability. The Jews, however, following the letter that kills, try to show that while God is standing upon the Mount of Olives the mountain itself is divided into two parts, so that the rift of the one part has its beginning facing the east and the other part extends its end to the west. In the very steep middle, one part is divided to the north and the other to the south.[38]

Apparently the standard Jewish interpretation of Zechariah 14 in Jerome's day understood it to have a literal historical fulfilment in the end times.

Jerome does make the occasional exception to his declared intent not to identify a future fulfilment after verses 1–2. One is found in his comments on verses 6–7, with their reference to the absence of light and the presence of cold and frost on the day of the Lord. Unlike Didymus, however, Jerome does not express himself tentatively. He writes, 'Clearly (*manifeste*) the second coming of the Saviour is being proclaimed'. He then expands on this as follows: 'When the day of his coming happens, there will be no light, but cold and frost, since

---

[37] Jerome, *Commentarii*, 878.
[38] Jerome, *Commentarii*, 880.

the love of all will have cooled, all will grow cold because of the many disasters which will befall them, and will lose the ardour of their former faith.'[39] Although he still understands the language in a figurative way, the reference is nevertheless to the historical future of Christ's return.

A second exception is of special interest. In commenting on verse 12, which graphically depicts the horrible physical disintegration of the nations who will wage war against Jerusalem, Jerome says that this obviously does not apply to the Romans who destroyed Jerusalem, as some have claimed. He then continues:

> We, however, will say that all the persecutors who have afflicted the church of the Lord have even in the present age – to say nothing of their future torments – received back the things they did to others. Let us read in the ecclesiastical histories what Valerian, Decius, Diocletian, Maximian, Maximin (the cruellest of them all), and recently Julian, have suffered, and then we will demonstrate by the facts that the truth of the prophecy has been fulfilled, even in a literal sense, because their flesh rotted and their eyes wasted away and their tongue was dissolved into a putrid and bloody mass.[40]

In other words, although Jerome understands Jerusalem here to refer to the church rather than the physical city, he nevertheless sees the prophecy as having been literally and historically fulfilled in the sufferings of the church's persecutors. Furthermore, this fulfilment takes place not only in the future pangs of hell, but in the historical reality of the present church age – and within that age on a number of different occasions spread over several centuries. This noteworthy comment – which expands on a passing remark in Didymus – stands in striking contrast to the general tenor of Jerome's allegorical understanding of this chapter.

We turn now to Jerome's treatment of the holiness of the horse's bridle in verse 20. In an introductory philological comment he writes,

> The Hebrew word *mesuloth* is translated by Aquila and Theodotion as βυθός, that is 'depth', and by Symmachus with περίπατος σύσκιος, that is, 'a shady walkway'. Only the Septuagint translated it as χαλινός, that is, 'bridle', which we also have followed in this passage, lest we seem to be introducing something new in a much-publicized question.[41]

Jerome does not immediately clarify what the 'much-publicized question' (*quaestio uulgata*) is which caused him to retain the translation 'bridle' in the

---

[39] Jerome, *Commentarii*, 882.

[40] Jerome, *Commentarii*, 889.

[41] Jerome, *Commentarii*, 897.

Vulgate, but he does indicate that he himself would have favoured the translation 'depth' or 'shady walkway', and would explain this as referring to the mystical knowledge of the depths of God. However, if the rendering 'bridle' is chosen he prefers the interpretation given by Didymus, that it represents the word of God, which restrains the passionate. In either case, a 'spiritual' interpretation is given which has nothing to do with real horses and their trappings.

As an aside, it is of interest to note that Jerome also makes a brief comment that may explain the mysterious *quaestio uulgata* that had inclined him to retain 'bridle' in the text against his better judgement. He writes:

> I heard a story from someone, told with pious intent, but ridiculous, that the nails of the Lord's cross, out of which Constantine Augustus made bits for the bridle of his horse, are here called 'holy to the Lord.'[42] I leave it up to the discretion of the reader whether this explanation should be accepted.[43]

This legend about the nails of the crucifixion being used for the bit of Constantine's horse was widespread in Jerome's day and is reported by other patristic writers, such as Eusebius and Theodoret. Jerome obviously did not believe the legend, but he was disinclined to upset those who did believe it by changing the Septuagint understanding of this verse. In any case, it is clear that those who did accept the legend saw in it a concrete historical fulfilment of Zechariah's prophecy.

Before leaving Jerome we should also say a bit more about the non-allegorical interpretation which he repeatedly opposes. In his comments on the restoration of Jerusalem in verse 10–11 he makes another reference to the literal eschatological interpretation which he attributes to the Jews of his day.

> The Jews and Judaizing Christians promise themselves in the last days a rebuilding of Jerusalem, with waters going out from its midst, which flow down to both seas, a time when circumcision is to be practiced again, and sacrifices are to be offered, and all the precepts of the law are to be observed, so that the Jews do not become Christians, but Christians become Jews. On that day, they say, when Christ will be seated to reign in a Jerusalem made of gold and jewels, there will be neither idols nor diverse worship of the deity, but the Lord will be one, and the whole earth will revert back to the desert, that is, to its ancient state.[44]

A little later he adds,

> Such are the literalistic pipe-dreams of the Jews, and of the chiliasts among us [*Haec Iudaei iuxta litteram somniant, et nostri chiliastai*] … who promise themselves, in return

---

[42] Instead of the *sanctum Domini* of the editions, I read *sanctum Domino* (as in the biblical text being expounded).

[43] Jerome, *Commentarii*, 898.

[44] Jerome, *Commentarii*, 885.

for self-control and brief fasting in this life, such exotic delicacies as onions, metrices, pheasants, and the Jewish rather than Ionian partridge ... And let them not set the Revelation of John against us, which must itself be explained spiritually.[45]

It is clear that Jerome is here polemicizing, not so much against the Jews, but against a group of Christians (witness their appeal to the book of Revelation) who had been influenced by Jewish hermeneutics and eschatology. They understand the new Jerusalem of the eschatological future as an actual city. Against them Jerome states baldly: 'But we for our part interpret the heavenly Jerusalem as the church.'[46] Finally, he writes on verse 16, about the surviving nations who will celebrate the Feast of Tabernacles: 'These things too the Jews, in a vain hope, predict will come to pass in the reign of a thousand years, of which this feast is a prelude.'[47] It would seem that the 'Jews' of which Jerome here speaks are Christian Jews whom he earlier called 'chiliasts', because of their interpretation of the millennium in Revelation 20.

Looking back over the three patristic writers whom we have discussed, we notice three salient points with reference to the project of biblical theology as we have defined it. The first is that all three church fathers, whatever differences they may have among themselves, nevertheless agree that this chapter should be understood as *Scripture*, and that as such it conveys to the church universal something about biblical teaching as a whole. The second is that, although all three implicitly assume that Zechariah 14 is part of the metanarrative of Scripture, and have no objection in principle to seeing this part of Scripture refer forward (either through predictive prophecy or typology) to later phases of that metanarrative in history, they in practice are remarkably reticent in availing themselves of this hermeneutical possibility. Theodore restricts himself to the historical horizon of the Old Testament, and both Didymus and Jerome, with only incidental exceptions, take refuge in an allegorical understanding which has very little to do with intra-story connections along the track of concrete fulfilment in space and time. The third point is that all three seem to espouse a doctrine of exegetical determinacy, that is, the view that a biblical text has a single reference to extra-textual reality that the exegete can identify. When the reference is to the historical future, this doctrine means that a prediction has only one identifiable fulfilment. The main exception to this is the place where Jerome (who in general is the most intellectually humble of the three) allows for multiple future fulfilment of the prediction that the church's persecutors will suffer bodily punishment.

---

[45] Jerome, *Commentarii*, 886.
[46] Jerome, *Commentarii*, 886.
[47] Jerome, *Commentarii*, 893.

Twentieth-century Commentaries

We now put on our seven leagues' boots and take a giant step from the late fourth and early fifth century of the Christian era to the late twentieth century. Before turning our attention to three representatives of the contemporary exegetical scene, it is necessary to make two general comments about the intervening millennium and a half. The first is that Christian exegetes since the patristic era, unlike Didymus and Jerome, have not been reticent in relating Zechariah 14 to later phases in the grand narrative of Scripture. In fact they have been quite open to doing so. The difficulty is that they have disagreed on how it should be done. Roughly speaking I believe it is possible to identify five different ways in which interpreters have made the connection between Zechariah 14 and the rest of the biblical story. I will simply list them here, but I refer the interested reader to a recent essay of mine for a fuller account.[48] The first view is similar to that of Theodore of Mopsuestia and sees all of Zechariah 14 as referring to the Maccabean Revolt in the early second century BC. Among those holding this view was Hugo Grotius in the seventeenth century.[49] A second position is that which takes the chapter to refer to the church age, that is, the period from the ascension to the second coming of Christ. A representative of this position, which has been very widely held, was Martin Luther.[50] The third interpretation is that of John Calvin, who understood our chapter to refer in the first instance to the time period between the Babylonian exile and the New Testament, and indirectly, by analogy, to the church age as well.[51] Calvin seems to have been unique in taking this approach. Fourthly we have the common view that Zechariah 14 has reference to the end times associated with the second coming. This appears to have been the prevailing view in the Middle Ages, but it was also adopted by many modern expositors, for example C.F. Keil in the nineteenth century.[52] All of these views assume that the language of our chapter must be understood figuratively, depicting in graphic imagery historical realities which might in fact be quite different. The fifth position, which is that of the dispensationalist movement which arose in the nineteenth century, breaks with this tradition. Like the fourth position it takes the historical referent of the chapter to be the time of Christ's return, but it insists that the fulfilment will be literal. A prominent representative of this tradition is Charles L. Feinberg.[53] Apart from the connection between this last view and dispensationalism, a remarkable feature of this variety of

---

[48] Wolters, 'Zechariah 14.

[49] Grotius, *Opera Omnia Theologica*, 1.563–65.

[50] Luther, *Zechariah*, 336–47.

[51] Calvin, *Zechariah and Malachi*, 405–55.

[52] Keil, *Minor Prophets*, 400–21.

[53] Feinberg, *God Remembers*, 192–205.

interpretations is that there is very little correlation between one's confessional or ecclesiastical affiliation and one's view of the fulfilment of Zechariah 14.

A second observation about the time period between the patristic and contemporary eras is that the rise of historical criticism in the late eighteenth century has had the effect of undercutting all efforts to understand a part of the Old Testament as having reference to later phases of the biblical story, or indeed to any future reality. As a matter of principle, the commitment to the inspiration of Scripture, to the unity of the Christian canon and to the reality of predictive prophecy was ruled out of court as a dogmatic prejudice which has no place in critical biblical studies. Consequently, critical commentaries on Zechariah 14 began to have quite a different focus. A small number of interpreters in the nineteenth century, for example, assuming (as was then the fashion) that Zechariah 9 – 14 was preexilic, understood Zechariah 14 as the work of a prophet who had foreseen the fall of Jerusalem to Nebuchadnezzar in 586 BC and had mistakenly predicted that God would intervene on Israel's behalf after an initial defeat. This was the view of Ferdinand Hitzig and others.[54] More recently, commentators in the tradition of classical historical criticism, for example Paul D. Hanson,[55] have sought to deduce from the text of Zechariah 14 the date and ideological commitment of the anonymous author, and in this way to situate him within the contending ideological parties of postexilic Israel. Within this tradition of scholarship there is no room for asking the question how this chapter fits into the project of doing biblical theology. Zechariah 14 is deliberately viewed in abstraction from the biblical story as a whole.

Nevertheless, despite the enormous prestige of mainline historical criticism, that project has not died, and there continue to be published commentaries which seek to contribute to it in some measure. As three examples of such commentaries I have chosen those by Merrill Unger (1963), A.S. van der Woude (1984) and Elizabeth Achtemeier (1986). It would have been easy to choose other examples, but these three in my opinion represent a fair cross-section of contemporary scholarly commentaries that have not succumbed to the critical elimination of biblical theology.

Merrill Unger

Unger's commentary is a classic example of dispensationalist exegesis, in which chapters 9 – 11 of Zechariah are taken to refer to the events leading up to and surrounding the first coming of Christ, and chapters 12 – 14 to the events surrounding his second coming. In this context chapter 14, to which Unger devotes by far the longest section of his commentary, represents the 'grand finale

---

[54] Hitzig, *Kleine Propheten*, 384–91.

[55] Hanson, *Dawn of Apocalyptic*, 369–401.

of Israel's hope for the future'.[56] He begins his discussion with a hermeneutical preface, in which he states unequivocally: 'Chapter 14 is *wholly prophetic* from the standpoint of the present age, and the only method of interpretation that will unlock its meaning is the *literal*.'[57] Somewhat confusingly, however, he then also speaks of the necessity of 'dealing discriminatingly with figurative language as a graphic vehicle for presenting such literal truth'.[58] Accordingly, he interprets the siege and fall of Jerusalem in verses 1–2 as referring to the literal battle of Armageddon as described in Revelation 16.[59] Similarly, he explains the account of the Lord's feet standing on the Mount of Olives as follows:

> How can the Lord's (Jehovah's) feet stand on the Mount of Olives? Because they are the feet of his resurrected humanity, which ascended to heaven from the same locality, and because '*this same Jesus* who was taken up ... into heaven shall *so* come *in like manner*' as the disciples witnessed Him 'go into heaven' (Acts 1:11).[60]

In other words, Yahweh will appear in the person of Jesus at his second coming, and his feet will stand on the same place from which Jesus ascended to heaven.

It is consistent with this overall approach that Unger assumes a future geological upheaval in the area around Jerusalem, so that the Mount of Olives will actually split in two, and the Judean hill country (with the exception of Jerusalem) will drop several hundred feet in elevation, leaving the capital perched atop a promontory. From that elevated position two literal streams will flow – one to the Dead Sea, and one to the Mediterranean. This will be during the time of the millennium, a literal thousand-year period of peace and prosperity. In commenting on these verses, Unger constantly polemicizes against the traditional Christian exegesis which understands the language here as figurative. On the two streams emanating from the future Jerusalem (v. 8) he writes:

> These waters will be *literal* waters although they reflect and imply spiritual blessings. To phantomize or mysticalize them is just as arbitrary and destructive of the real meaning of the passage as to phantomize or mysticalize the capture and deliverance of Jerusalem (vss. 1–3), or the second advent of Messiah, or the earthquake and the topographical changes accompanying it (vss. 4–7).[61]

In many ways Unger's view seems to be similar to that of the Christian *chiliastai* opposed by Jerome.

---

[56] Unger, *Zechariah*, 254 (pp. 254–71 deal with ch. 14).
[57] Unger, *Zechariah*, 239 (Unger's italics).
[58] Unger, *Zechariah*, 239.
[59] Unger, *Zechariah*, 242.
[60] Unger, *Zechariah*, 245 (Unger's italics).
[61] Unger, *Zechariah*, 255 (Unger's italics).

The mention of the millennium also alerts us to the fact that Unger is working with a fairly precise chronology of prophetic eschatology. He writes that the 'day of the Lord' of which Zechariah speaks in this chapter can be defined as follows:

> [It] is that prophetic period embracing the final phase of Israel's chastisement and trouble, followed by her salvation and deliverance at the second advent of Messiah (the quintessential phase) and extending throughout the subsequent period of kingdom peace and prosperity, commonly called the millennium.[62]

This is, of course, the well-known eschatological sequence of premillennial dispensationalism.

Unger's comments on the last two verses of the chapter are also worth noting. He states that the reason why the horses' 'bells' (the now-standard rendering of the Hebrew *měṣillôt*) and the temple pots will be considered holy, is 'to emphasize the fact that *every* phase of life in the kingdom will be sanctified and holy and nothing would any longer be considered secular'.[63] Finally, it is striking, in the light of Unger's insistence on the literal sense, to see how he explains the very last words of the chapter, which state that 'there will be no more a Canaanite in the house of the Lord of hosts'. He writes: 'The term *Canaanite* is best taken as a morally and spiritually unclean person'.[64] It seems that the term 'Canaanite' is not, after all, to be taken literally.

A.S. van der Woude

One of the finest commentaries on Zechariah to appear in recent decades is the relevant volume by A.S. van der Woude in the Dutch series 'De Prediking van het Oude Testament'.[65] Although much closer to the mainstream of critical scholarship than Unger, van der Woude nevertheless takes seriously the canonical status of the prophetic book as an integral part of the overall biblical story. This comes out clearly in the final section of his commentary, which is entitled 'The proclamation of Zechariah 14'.[66] Like Unger, van der Woude interprets the chapter as referring to the end times, but unlike him does not take the language to be literal, or to be more specific than speaking of 'the eschaton' in general terms.

It is worth quoting his reflections at greater length:

---

[62] Unger, *Zechariah*, 255 (Unger's italics).

[63] Unger, *Zechariah*, 270

[64] Unger, *Zechariah*, 270.

[65] Van der Woude, *Zacharia* (pp. 251–70 on ch. 14).

[66] Van der Woude, *Zacharia*, 269.

The riddle of our chapter therefore requires a serious reflection on the reality which is here depicted as the ultimately decisive one, and which therefore makes a claim to give guidance in the here and now. The aspect that is most easily grasped is the intensity and horror of the destruction and obliteration which will characterize the end time according to vv. 1–2 and vv. 12–15. They are an extrapolation of our dread of a universal catastrophe which will consume everything and everyone. The eschaton is preceded by a concentration of suffering and misery which the church has not previously experienced. Judgement begins with the household of God. The King of the whole earth has a controversy, not only with a world that has broken faith with Him, and grants him no room in earthly affairs, but also (and in the first place) with his church. Therefore salvation comes about via the nadir of judgement. God's kingdom is born in hellish pain. This is a frightening prospect for people of faith who believe they possess religious guarantees, as well as for a humanity which imagines it can achieve its salvation in and through an evolutionary process. But our author does not lead us to a radical pessimism: God does not permanently abandon his church and his world because of their sin and guilt, but he preserves a remnant for the new earth. But eschatology does not only involve human beings, let alone human souls, but it is cosmic in scope. All of reality is included in God's saving action. This is true not just in a manner of speaking, but empirically. The earth too will be renewed. In all of this the central truth is that the God of Israel will become what he already is: the King of the whole earth, and that he will also be obeyed and worshipped as such. At that time the dark sides of our guilt-ridden existence will fall away: the night and the uncomfortable cold will make way for the eternal day, the desert for the fertile earth, the obstructing mountains for the broad plain, impiety for worship, the profane for the holy. Reality remains earthly, but it is transformed into light, out of light and darkness. Out of this profound conviction that God will one day establish his kingdom and achieve his purpose with the world, the author of Zechariah 14 dares to translate the language of faith into realistic terms, and by means of his faith-inspired metaphors to penetrate to the concrete, visible and tangible world.[67]

Elizabeth Achtemeier

Finally, we turn to the brief commentary on Zechariah by the late Elizabeth Achtemeier.[68] She begins her exposition as follows:

Zechariah 14 is essentially an explication of 13:9 [the immediately preceding verse which depicts how the remnant is purified by fire] with its covenant formula. The fourteenth chapter explains how that renewed relationship between God and his people will come about, what the nature of the covenant relationship will be, and what consequences it will have for all the nations of the earth.[69]

---

[67] Van der Woude, *Zacharia*, 269–70 (my translation from the Dutch).
[68] Achtemeier, *Nahum–Malachi*, 107–69 (165–69 on ch.14).
[69] Achtemeier, *Nahum–Malachi*, 165.

It is clear that she is here equating Jerusalem, in the tradition of classical biblical theology, not just with the city in Judea, or with the Old Testament covenant people, but with God's people in a broad salvation-historical sense. The assault of the nations on Jerusalem shows that '[t]he Kingdom comes only after God's conquest of evil and only after his thorough-going purgation of his people's sin'. The splitting of the Mount of Olives shows that God is 'Lord over his creation'.[70] Verses 6–8 depict the presence of God 'in traditional terms that picture a veritable new creation: The polarities of the original creation (day and night, cold and heat, summer and winter) are done away.' She goes on to say: 'Then in the act that forms the goal of all human history God will take his throne as king over all the earth (v. 9).'[71] The description of Zechariah 14 is clearly taken as a depiction of the eschaton as understood in the biblical metanarrative, but without the specifics supplied by various New Testament eschatological texts.

Achtemeier concludes her discussion of the chapter as follows:

> Despite the gruesomeness of some of the details that the prophet presents to us in this chapter, it nevertheless portrays for us a magnificent vision – of the whole earth cleansed and made faithful and obedient to God; of every people included in the covenant relationship with the Lord; of all nations worshipping at his throne, proclaiming him sole King over their lives for all time. In short, we are presented in this chapter with the picture of the Kingdom of God come on earth.[72]

In a concluding paragraph she relates this to the New Testament: 'The future Kingdom of God is no longer only prophetic hope. Now it is guaranteed by the resurrection of Jesus Christ – his victory over human evil and death.'[73]

The three contemporary commentators whom we have discussed all agree in taking Zechariah 14 to refer to the eschaton. This reflects the fact that the earlier views that related this chapter to pre-eschatological periods of history have fallen into disfavour. However, there is a marked difference between Unger and the other two in the way in which they understand the connection between the textual description and its referent. Unger emphasizes the literal nature of the description and relates it to the events surrounding the second coming of Christ as foretold in the New Testament and understood in premillennial dispensationalism. Van der Woude and Achtemeier, on the other hand, do not assume a literal mode of representation and speak of the eschaton in much more general terms. However, although the latter two agree in their general hermeneutical approach, they also differ among themselves

---

[70] Achtemeier, *Nahum–Malachi*, 165.

[71] Achtemeier, *Nahum–Achtemeier*, 166.

[72] Achtemeier, *Nahum–Malachi*, 168.

[73] Achtemeier, *Nahum–Malachi*, 169.

theologically. Van der Woude, influenced by Dutch neo-Calvinism, stresses that the end times will bring a recreation, a cosmic renewal of concrete earthly reality, while Achtemeier, under the influence of the Barthian tradition, emphasizes that the eschatological future will bring about 'a veritable new creation', in which the natural polarities of the old creation are eliminated. The one sees a restoration of the original created order, the other its abandonment and replacement.

With this we complete our brief consideration of three patristic and three contemporary commentators on Zechariah 14 who have engaged in some sense in the project of biblical theology. Our survey has of necessity been exceedingly sketchy and selective. We turn now to a series of six concluding theses, or reflections, which are prompted by our overview.

Conclusions

An important lesson to learn from our survey is that of exegetical and hermeneutical humility. No one can afford to be dogmatic about the interpretation of Zechariah 14. When such giants of the Christian exegetical tradition as Theodore, Jerome, Luther and Calvin come to such radically different readings of this chapter, it behoves us to be modest in our claims. Here we can learn from Jerome, who recognized the extraordinary difficulty of this text and acknowledged the limits of his own interpretative abilities. There is a certain wisdom in his resolve to explain only what is written, and to leave the question of historical fulfilment to the judgement of God.

At the same time, the difficulty of the enterprise should not deter Christian interpreters from seeking to correlate what Zechariah prophesies about the future day of the Lord with what the entire canon teaches about the overall story of God's dealings with humanity and the cosmos from creation to eschaton, and with the concrete historical events that go into that story. To take flight into a-historical allegory, after the manner (with some exceptions) of Didymus and Jerome, or to deny the unity of the canon and thus of the biblical metanarrative, after the manner of mainline historical criticism, is to eliminate a perspective which the Scriptures themselves everywhere presuppose, and which has been at the core of historic Christian orthodoxy for two millennia.

It is illegitimate, and indeed a doomed attempt, to insist on the exclusive propriety of a 'literal' reading of this or any other chapter of Scripture. Apart from the fact that all language may be said to be metaphorical,[74] it is impossible to read more than a few sentences in ordinary prose without having to

---

[74] See, e.g., Hesse, 'Cognitive Claims', 40.

recognize imagery of various kinds. Here Theodore, with his appreciation for how rhetorical figures of speech make language idiomatic and oblique, is wiser than Unger. It is crucial to recognize, as Theodore did, that the use of figurative language does not somehow compromise the ability to tell the truth about historical states of affairs.

The task of doing biblical theology of necessity involves broader theological commitments that may not be of a hermeneutical sort. The different interpretations of our chapter given by van der Woude and Achtemeier are instructive in this regard. Though they agree that it refers in non-literal terms to the climax of the biblical story, their own fundamental understanding of the relation between creation and redemption decisively affects what they take the text to be saying about the last things.

The diverse interpretations which leading Christian interpreters have given of Zechariah 14 should alert us to the possibility that it allows multiple historical fulfilments. Here Jerome's comments about verse 12 are particularly illuminating. That verse speaks of the horrible physical sufferings which will be experienced by the enemies of Jerusalem (which Jerome understands to mean the enemies of the church). But he goes on to say that this prediction can be said to have come literally true in the lives of a number of prominent Roman persecutors of the Christian church – not only in the afterlife, but also during their lifetime on earth. In other words, the truth of this prophecy was borne out in a number of different events in that part of the grand narrative of Scripture that is church history.

I would submit that we can generalize this example to apply to the chapter as a whole. Everything in Zechariah 14 has had, and will have, multiple historical fulfilments, perhaps coming to a climax at the consummation of the biblical story. In fact this is true in general of the 'day of the Lord', of which this pericope is a description. The mistake that interpreters have made is to correlate these predictions too exclusively with a narrowly defined set of events in history. The prophecy of Zechariah 14 is fulfilled in subsequent history, but not only in certain limited phases or events of subsequent history. It is fulfilled in every phase of the history of Jerusalem – both in the history of Jerusalem as the geographical capital of the Old Testament nation of Israel, and in the antitypical prolongation of that holy city in the New Testament church of God in every phase of its history from Pentecost to the eschaton. It finds its fulfilment in the Maccabean struggle in the second century BC, and in the persecution and deliverance of Christians in the Sudan today, and in the time of the antichrist and Christ's return. In a sense, all of the proposed historical interpretations are right, but they are also all wrong to the extent that they deny the validity of the others.

Bibliography

Achtemeier, E., *Nahum–Malachi* (IBC; Atlanta: John Knox Press, 1986)

Calvin, J., *A Commentary on the Twelve Minor Prophets*, V: *Zechariah and Malachi* (trans. J. Owen; Edinburgh: Calvin Translation Society, 1849; repr. Edinburgh: Banner of Truth Trust, 1986)

Didymus the Blind, *Didyme l'Aveugle: Sur Zacharie* (trans. L. Doutreleau; SC 83–85; Paris: Éditions du Cerf, 1962)

Doutreleau, L., 'Introduction', in Didymus the Blind, *Sur Zacharie*, *Didyme l'Aveugle: Sur Zacharie* (trans. L. Doutreleau; SC 83–85; Paris: Éditions du Cerf, 1962), I.13–188

Feinberg, C.L., *God Remembers: A Study of Zechariah* (Portland, OR: Multnomah Press, 4th edn, 1979)

Grotius, H., *Opera Omnia Theologica* (3 vols.; London: Moses Pitt, 1679)

Hanson, P.D., *The Dawn of Apocalyptic: The Historical and Sociological Roots of Jewish Apocalyptic Eschatology* (Philadelphia: Fortress Press, rev. edn, 1979)

Hesse, M.B., 'The Cognitive Claims of Metaphor', in *Metaphor and Religion* (Theolinguistics 2; ed. J.P. van Noppen; Brussels: Vrije Universiteit Brussel, 1983), 27–46

Hitzig, F., *Die zwölf kleinen Propheten* (Leipzig: Hirzel, 3rd edn, 1863)

Ishodad of Merv, *Commentaire d'Išo 'dad de Merv sur l'Ancien Testament*, IV: *Isaïe et les Douze* (trans. C. van den Eynde; CSCO 304; Scriptores Syri 129; Louvain: Secrétariat du CSCO, 1969)

Jerome, *S. Hieronymi Presbyterii Opera*, I: *Opera Exegetica 6, Commentarii in Prophetas Minores* (ed. M. Adriaen; Turnholti: Brepols, 1970)

Keil, C.F., *Minor Prophets* (K&D 10.2; Grand Rapids: Eerdmans, 1989)

Luther, M., *Luther's Works: Minor Prophets III. Zechariah* (ed. H.C. Oswald; Saint Louis: Concordia Publishing House, 1973)

Sprenger, H.N., 'Einleitung', in *Theodori Mopsuesteni Commentarius in XII Prophetas: Einleitung und Ausgabe* (ed. H.N. Sprenger; GO V.1; Wiesbaden: Harrassowitz, 1977), 1–151

Theodore of Mopsuestia, *Theodori Mopsuesteni Commentarius in XII Prophetas: Einleitung und Ausgabe* (ed. H.N. Sprenger; GO V.1; Wiesbaden: Harrassowitz, 1977)

Thiselton, A., *The First Epistle to the Corinthians* (NIGTC; Grand Rapids: Eerdmans; Carlisle: Paternoster Press, 2000)

Unger, M., *Zechariah: Prophet of Messiah's Glory* (Grand Rapids: Zondervan, 1963)

Wolters, A., 'Zechariah 14: A Dialogue with the History of Interpretation', *Mid-America Journal of Theology* 13 (2002), 39–56

Woude, A.S. van der, *Zacharia* (POut; Nijkerk: Callenbach, 1984)

Zaharopoulos, D.Z., *Theodore of Mopsuestia on the Bible: A Study of His Old Testament Exegesis* (New York: Paulist Press, 1989)

11

Paul and Salvation History in
Romans 9:30 – 10:4

William J. Dumbrell

Introduction

Purpose

The thesis of this chapter is that a salvation-history approach to biblical theology provides an understanding of what was at stake in Paul's continuing clash with Jewish Christianity, echoes of which continue to be seen in letters such as Ephesians and the Pastoral Epistles.

The passage chosen to illustrate the general questions that this chapter takes up is Romans 9:30 – 10:4. Romans 10:4 particularly has given rise to many exegetical studies, but interaction with these studies is not the present consideration. While this chapter will result in a different reading of this passage, this is not the result of a different exegesis based on the same presuppositional stance. The difference in meaning is reached by applying a different presuppositional grid – namely, that Paul is speaking not about Israel historically (the traditional view) but about post-cross Israel still offering obedience to the Jewish law under a Mosaic covenant whose validity and institutions ceased with the death of Christ. Not a great deal of attention, therefore, needs to be drawn to different exegetical results, and so this will not be done.

This section of Paul is chosen because, in a relatively small context, major questions of Pauline approach to Israel, law and covenant are present. In short, this chapter is concerned with the macrodynamics of Pauline theology. These are traceable, I believe, from the manner in which Paul deals with the problem under discussion in Romans 9 – 11, which is the future of national Israel. Several other Pauline contexts from Romans, Galatians or Corinthians could also have served to achieve the same result, since the question being raised is that of fundamental Pauline presuppositions in the matter of his approach to post-cross Israel.

The issues to be raised in this chapter – the operation of the new covenant instituted by Jesus, the distinction between national and believing Israel, the Pauline attitude to the Mosaic law – are all products of the often overlooked post-cross focus of Paul in his theology and ministry. They are not presented here as novel. It is suggested, however, that when collaboratively related, as they often are in key Pauline contexts such as Romans 9:30 – 10:4, they provide a very different hermeneutical stance, since they reflect Paul's understanding of basic changes in national Israel's relationship to God which were brought about by the cross. Occasionally such changes are referred to, but in my experience they are rarely exploited.[1]

This brings me to the nub of the question for this chapter: that of Paul's attitude to non-Christian Israel in his day. Were they, for him, still the people of God? This issue is taken up in some detail in the body of this chapter. It is a complex issue on which there will always be different evaluations of whether ethnic Israel continues in an election relationship to God. My short answer, to stem from this chapter, is no.

Method

Biblical interpretation, I argue, is dependent upon one's understanding of the movement of the whole Bible in its various stages or on what documents this movement and assesses it, namely a biblical theology. Biblical theology, as I see it, is the progressive, descriptive, unfolding of the stages whereby the whole of the canonical 'story' develops from the basic deposit of Genesis 1 – 3 until the full purpose of God is reached in the descent of the new creation in Revelation 21 – 22.

An approach to biblical theology rests for me on the five following points. First, biblical theology provides the macro view of revelation in history. Secondly, on my view we cannot construct an Old Testament theology or a New Testament theology but only a biblical theology, since we are concerned to track the course of revelation within an interdependent canon. Thirdly, there cannot be a centre around which this theology is organized since biblical theology is concerned to trace a divine movement whose intention on my view is discernible in Genesis 1 – 3 and completed in Revelation 21 – 22. Fourthly, my belief in a unitary thread of purpose connecting the whole Bible, which the

---

[1] Two recent writers who have recognized a difference brought into being by the cross, yet without fully capitalizing upon it, are R.H. Bell and T.R. Schreiner. Bell, *No One Seeks*, 248, notes that in Rom. 1:18 – 3:20 Paul does not reckon with sacrifice as means of atonement, since with the sacrifice of Christ all cultic atoning practice was considered invalid. Schreiner, *Law*, 3, 62–3, also refers incidentally to the absence of atonement for Judaism following the death of Christ.

biblical narratives themselves reveal, means that there cannot be within the one canon competing or differing theologies though there may be different emphases within a unitary theology. Fifthly, while the manner in which the final form of the text came into being, or the question of the communities which may have been formative in the production of the text, are matters of historical interest and indeed historical concern, and while attention must always be directed to ongoing work in this area, the task of biblical theology, generally speaking, is to commence with the formed and accepted canonical text.[2]

Approach

In all of this I am saying that particular exegesis is part of a connected whole, and that in the final analysis exegesis must take into account the full content of the canon. So this chapter will ask: where in the development of the Bible's unfolding purpose does Paul stand, and to what biblical developments does he look back for guidance on the issues of ministry that he faces?

Salvation History and Covenant

Paul's initial question in 9:30 looks back to 9:24–29 and advances reasons for how the situation described in those verses has come about. In this verse Paul is not talking about Gentiles in general, but saved Gentiles, whose place in the divine economy he had discussed in 9:24–29.[3] God always had in mind their incorporation into Israel, while, by the same purpose, Israel would be constituted by a believing remnant comprised of Jews and Gentiles, since salvation was always by grace and never by race – a point that Paul made clear in Romans 9:6–13. The fulfilment of divine purposes, which the death of Christ achieved, brought several new facts into this beginning of the kingdom of Christ.

First, there was the fact that the death of Jesus had introduced Jeremiah's renewed covenant with Israel (cf. Lk. 22:20). Paul's statement in 9:30 then signifies that some Gentiles, who had not pursued righteousness (i.e., a right standing with God), were now in a right relationship with God through faith, as members of the new covenant. All of this reflects the primary thrust of the New Testament, that the death of Christ introduced a totally new factor into the history of Israel and of the world. With the rending of the veil of the temple immediately consequent upon the death of Jesus (Mk. 15:38), Israel and her institutions had been dismissed, and access to God was now available

---

[2] My publications illustrate my approach; cf. *The End of the Beginning*.
[3] Correctly, the NRSV, against many versions.

independently of the temple. Israel's commission to be a light to the nations, the world's evangelist, was to be transferred to the new body to emerge at Pentecost, the church or the restored or remnant Israel. In theological terms, this great salvation-history change meant extensive present difficulties and an eventual rupture between Christianity and Judaism, built around the principal factors of the inauguration of the new covenant and the consequent free admission of the Gentiles into the new body without acceptance of the Mosaic law.

Second, it seems clear that most of the problems that beset the early Christian church, reflected in such letters as Romans, Corinthians and Galatians, and even in later letters such as Ephesians and the Pastoral Epistles, were occasioned by the continuance of now irrelevant Jewish institutions in Jerusalem until AD 70 and the influence that this exercised upon Jewish-Christian communities.

Third, most of the Pauline material deals with day-to-day missionary concerns related to contemporary issues. It may be an obvious point to make, but in many key passages, including Romans 9:30 – 10:4, Paul is talking about Israel in a *post-cross* situation, and thus about the change in Israel's national standing brought about by the death of Christ.

I argue that the divisions within Jewish and Gentile Christianity which are so obvious in Romans and Galatians are best explained by Jewish Christian insistence upon interpreting Jesus within the Mosaic covenant. Paul, on the other hand, sees the new covenant instituted by Jesus as liberating the new Pentecost community to pursue the wider aims of the Abrahamic covenant, and thus to present to the Gentiles (and Jews) a gospel of covenant admission by free grace. This new covenant relationship, possible from Pentecost onwards, was really exploited only by Paul in the early Christian period. In my judgement, these divisions were not resolved by the Christian church until the fall of the Jewish temple in AD 70 decisively moved the Jewish church out from under the shadow of Judaism. I will now examine what I regard as these fundamental changes in hermeneutical approach made necessary by the cross. Then I will apply them to a contested Pauline context, Romans 9:30 – 10:4.

The New Covenant in the New Testament

Jesus' institution

Covenant theology has not been given the high profile it deserves in the considerations of New Testament theology, bearing in mind the thoroughly Jewish character of the early church, for whom a covenant connection and perspective would have been axiomatic. Max Turner suggests that the importance of the covenant concept in the New Testament (and in the Old

Testament!) is not to be determined by the frequency of its mention.[4] The single mention in the Gospels, at Luke 22:20 and parallels, comes at a crucial point and offers a major interpretation of the passion narrative. The Pauline church used Luke's formula (cf. 1 Cor. 11:25; Lk. 22:20). Turner notes the use of covenant language in Luke 22:29, 'I appoint unto you a kingdom' (a point which is evidnt from the use of the verb *diatithemi*; cf. the cognate noun *diatheke*, Lk. 22:20), commenting that 'covenant' and 'kingdom' were well established and correlated biblical concepts. All of this means that God's in-breaking salvation provides the fulfilment of the Abrahamic covenant (Lk. 1:72–75), which was what the Sinai covenant was designed to effect, and would have effected, had Israel seen it as the way for God's people to live. W. Foerster notes that salvation, kingdom of God, messianic jubilee and new covenant are overlapping descriptions with only slightly different nuances.[5] That Jesus himself had instituted by his death the new covenant of Jeremiah 31:31–34, and identified the Lord's Supper as a continual memorial of that death, is sufficient in itself to expect that the new covenant would be a vital New Testament doctrine. The inauguration of the new covenant leading to the new creation becomes, indeed, the major blessing to stem from the death of Jesus.

That Jesus' foundation is 'new' is implied, if not stated, in Matthew and Mark. In Luke, Jesus' imagery of a new covenant in his blood recalls Exodus 24:8, where Moses sealed the Sinai covenant by blood, in what may have been an act of imprecation leading to the ratification of the Sinai covenant for Israel following the exodus. Covenant blood was understood in the Targums of Pseudo-Jonathan and Onkelos as atoning.[6] Similarly, Matthew's addition, 'for the forgiveness of sins' (26:28), makes explicit what is already implicit in the expression 'blood of the covenant'. By 'forgiveness of sins', Jesus alludes to Jeremiah 31:31–34 and points to the effect of his sacrifice. Since Jesus is presented as a servant figure,[7] his action at the supper recalls the sacrificial self-giving of the servant of Isaiah 53:12, who bore the sins of 'many' – that is, all (cf. Is. 53:12). We are also reminded of Isaiah 42:6; 49:6–8, where the servant was to be given for a covenant of the people (i.e., Israel) and from her covenant base to be a light to the Gentiles – that is, to bring God's salvation to the ends of the earth. Jesus thus understood his death as sacrificial and as a vicarious atonement (cf. Mk. 10:45; 1 Cor. 15:3; 2 Cor. 5:21), making possible the completion of Israel's mission in fulfilment of her covenant to be a light to the Gentiles.

---

[4] Turner, 'Sabbath'.

[5] Foerster, *TDNT* VII, 990–91 (cf. Gal. 4:24; Eph. 2:12; 1 Cor. 11:25; 2 Cor 3:6; and Heb. *passim*).

[6] Cf. Lane, *Hebrews*, 245.

[7] Cullmann, *Christology*, 65, 93; France, *Jesus*, 123.

'I will not drink … until the kingdom of God comes' (Lk. 22:18) indicates that just as the Passover looked forward to the day when Israel would share in the messianic banquet, so does the Lord's Supper. Indeed Paul and the Pauline churches interpreted the death of Jesus as a Christian Passover sacrifice (1 Cor. 5:7), and Luke's attention to the detail of the Last Supper is consistent with his heavy emphasis on the Isaian new exodus.[8] Jesus did not see his death as a tragedy or an error, but as the crowning act of his ministry in which he poured out his blood in a once and for all redemption and liberation.

What would have been Jesus' understanding of the dimensions of this new covenant? In alluding to Jeremiah 31:31–34 (Lk. 22:20), Jesus, according to Luke, would have been referring to the prophet's promise to an Israel on the point of exilic disintegration, of the renewal of the Sinai covenant beyond the impending judgement. It is clear that a renewal is in mind, not only from the semantic possibilities of Hebrew *hadash*, 'new', which the LXX by its *kaine diatheke* exploits, but also by the connection with the Sinai covenant to which Jeremiah 31:32 points. Thus Jesus' new covenant must be understood as the continuation of an arrangement with Israel, and not as a replacement for that arrangement. What 'Israel' is in view, the evidence of the four Gospels and early Acts makes clear. However, the purpose of the Sinai covenant, to enable the fulfilment of the Abrahamic covenant through Israel, could now be put into commission in the new Spirit-filled Israel of Pentecost.

So Paul, with his Abrahamic emphasis, never hints that God has abandoned his covenant with Israel. Paul makes it clear, however, that the bulk of Israel had rejected the risen Jesus as the Jewish Messiah, but that not all Israel are the continuing Israel (Rom. 11:1–10; 9:6; cf. Gal. 6:16). It is only thus the question of the identity of Israel that is a Pauline concern. How, then, will the 'new covenant' operate with national Israel rejected (cf. Mt. 21:43; Jn. 19:15)? Presumably it would permit the complete operation of the Sinai covenant in a way that was prevented by Israel's disobedience in the Old Testament. The new covenant will facilitate a restored, obedient Israel to fulfil the commission imposed by virtue of its election as the people of God (Ex. 19:5–6).[9] That commission was, for Israel, a charge to be a light to the world. What the implementation of the new covenant will mean for an obedient, restored Israel in the new, post-cross era is world mission. Mission will now take a different form. Israel will no longer be called upon to attract the nations to Jerusalem and her temple by her difference as a kingdom of God nation. The mission of restored Israel will now be in the wider world since, with the death of Jesus, the notion of a literal, this-world promised land had disappeared. In its place the world itself emerges as

---

[8] Strauss, *Davidic Messiah*, 297–305.
[9] For an exegesis of this passage see my *Covenant and Creation*, 84–89.

the new promised land, a type of the final antitype of the new creation.[10] Luke will take up that factor in the Acts of the Apostles.

Jesus had virtually confined his ministry to Israel, with only occasional contact with Gentiles. In various incidents, however, Jesus had understood that a subsequent ministry to the Gentiles would occur, occasioned by his death.[11] By instituting a new covenant, Jesus thought clearly in terms of a world role for his restored Israel. Jesus lived and died as a loyal Jew. The burden of his ministry was to and for Israel, but he came to see that his concept of renewal for Israel would be achieved not through his ministry to the nation, but by his death for Israel and his resurrection, which would bring in a new Israel to be in fact the New Testament church, which began on Jewish foundations.

Christ's sacrificial death as both victim and priest consummated the old order and inaugurated the new. In ratifying the Sinai covenant (Ex. 24:1–11), Israel had called down death upon itself for disobedience (Ex. 24:8–11). The cross was the summit of Israel's disobedience, but it also dealt with it. After the old covenant had been completed by such a sin offering as Jesus was,[12] a new covenant could now be introduced.

The new covenant was God's final arrangement with his people. The Last Supper was a Passover meal commemorating the release from bondage (cf. Ex. 12:2–27; 13:8–9), designed to introduce the new covenant and the rule of the kingdom of God. The Passover connotation of the Last Supper made such an introduction of the new covenant associated with a further exodus redemption particularly comprehensible. By its Passover analogies, the Last Supper signified a 'new exodus', to be followed by the establishment of a covenant. Likewise, Paul's understanding of Christ's death was cast in Passover terms in 1 Corinthians 5:7, to be followed by a new covenant inaugurated by it in 1 Corinthians 11:25. The eating of the Supper was not merely a commemorative act, but it was also an act of proclamation of Jesus' intentions and expectations (cf. 1 Cor. 11:26). In later Christian terms, to partake of the Supper was to signify commitment to the new covenant, celebrating deliverance from sin and entrance into the new covenant.

Thus, in the light of Jesus' major interpretation of his death as required to inaugurate the new covenant of Jeremiah 31, we need to be expectant of the post-cross effect of covenant change. It is difficult to overestimate the profundity of Paul's theology of covenant change in a post-cross Jewish environment, especially when Jewish institutions were still intact and given the fact that Jewish experience was always understood in covenant terms.

---

[10] As well as in rabbinic thinking, cf. Paul in Rom. 4:13 and the Epistle to the Hebrews generally.

[11] Specifically at Jn. 12:20–26.

[12] Rom. 8:3; 2 Cor. 5:21. Cf. Rom. 3:25 as a Day of Atonement allusion. Cf. Bailey, *Jesus*.

The new covenant in Paul

Paul was a Hebrew of the Hebrews, as to the Torah, a Pharisee, the son of a Pharisee, educated at the feet of Gamaliel in Jerusalem (Acts 22:3), a member of the royal tribe of Benjamin, circumcised as he should have been on the eighth day (Phil. 3:5). We may justly assume that for Paul as a Jew, God's covenant with Israel always remained an unquestioned assumption through which everything else was experienced. The keeping of the Torah, by this time itself a shorthand term for covenant, but also a word with broad implications in Judaism, subsuming both 'grace' and 'covenant', stood as the standard demanded from God's people. For Israel, the relationship to Torah was a fundamental expression of covenant status.[13] The community of the covenant embraced those who accepted the Torah and whom the Torah bound to God, for the Torah was the covenant 'identity marker' of Israel. Proper covenant response was zeal for the law.

E.P. Sanders maintains that in the Tannaitic period the basic Jewish theological concepts are assumed rather than stated.[14] What Paul generally presumed as basic to Israel's faith did not need to be stated, though in Christian terms there are eight occurrences of *diatheke* in the (undisputed) letters of Paul.[15] Galatians 4:24 mentions two covenants. The only occurrence of 'new covenant' in Paul, other than the traditional Lord's Supper reference at 1 Corinthians 11:25, is in 2 Corinthians 3:6.

2 Corinthians 3:1–6 may be taken as illustrative of Paul's new covenant thinking. The context suggests that a group of itinerant Jewish preachers coming to Corinth after Paul's initial ministry had challenged Paul's authority and had slighted his demeanour and delivery. Paul claims they are false apostles who disguise themselves as 'ministers of righteousness' (11:15), that is, as ministers concerned with expounding the necessity of being connected with the Mosaic covenant (cf. 3:1–11). The more narrow connection with the law and the Mosaic covenant that Paul assumes in 3:6 seems to make them Judaizers.[16] In developing the analogy with the ministry of Moses to Israel in Exodus 34, Paul sets himself forth as a minister of the new covenant of Jeremiah 31:31–34, involved in its delivery (2 Cor. 3:6). His opponents, in contradistinction, are presumably ministers of the old covenant. By doing so, he presents himself as in analogy with Moses, but he underlines the distinction between himself and Moses. The Sinai covenant and the obligations for Judaism stemming from it

---

[13] The Mekilta on Ex. 20:6 has 'By Covenant is meant nothing other than the Torah'. Cf. Dunn, *Partingsa*, 25, 98, 299 n. 1.

[14] Sanders, *Paul*, 420–21.

[15] Rom. 9:4; 11:2; 1 Cor. 11:25; 2 Cor. 3:6, 14; Gal 3:15, 17; 4:24; cf. Eph. 2:12.

[16] Barnett, *Second Corinthians*, 32–34, recognizes this.

seem to have been the content of the ministry of the Judaizing false apostles to Corinth, who probably saw the Christian era as a continuation but consummation of the Jewish era. For them, the Mosaic covenant was to be seen as the continuing covenant into which Jesus had been incorporated as its fulfilment. Paul describes the contrast between his work and the *current ministry* of the Judaizing false apostles[17] as a contrast between an external communication on stone tablets[18] without spiritual significance and the writing of the law upon the hearts of believers, which is a result of the operation of the new covenant[19] as evidence of a new, transforming covenant experience.[20] While the description of the Mosaic law as on 'tablets of stone' (v. 7) expressed national Israel's final Sinai position in the Old Testament,[21] in 3:3b Paul is pointing in these terms to an external ministry operating in Corinth with no spiritual results, since the Mosaic covenant was now defunct.

With Paul's 'not of the letter, but of the Spirit', the contrast is not between his ministry and that of Moses, but between his ministry and that of the false apostles.[22] The old covenant ministry to Israel had produced no significant national change. Now, in Paul's day, the Christian gospel was being supplemented by formalistic and legal demands requiring full obedience, perhaps to what was regarded as the continuing Mosaic structure undistinguished by any

---

[17] Contra S.J. Hafemann, *Paul*, 173, who regards the contrast as one between two ministries, Paul's and Moses'.

[18] Ex. 24:12; 31:18; 32:15; 34:1; Deut. 9:10. Paul's allusion in 3:3b seems to be to the current ministry of the false apostles.

[19] Hafemann, *Paul*, 171. In describing the Mosaic covenant as a ministry of death (v. 7), Paul may be referring to its present effects in the post-cross situation. Though the Sinai covenant proved to be so for national Israel and could always become simply this, this was not its intention, as is indicated by the frequent reference in the Old Testament to a remnant of believers, for whom the Sinai covenant was operating with blessing. The renewal of the Sinai covenant contemplated in Jer. 31:31–34 indicates that, as given by God to control Israel's ministry, it could achieve its purpose. Only unbelief would vitiate it, as proved to be the case. Its total fulfilment would thus demand a further divine intervention and initiative.

[20] The place of the law in valid Sinai covenant experience was in the heart. The newness of the new covenant does not result from this requirement, but rather from the expectations of the final resolution of the problem of sin by the transformation of believers at the Parousia. See my *Covenant and Creation*, 181–85.

[21] I refer to the further Sinai covenant resulting from Israel's golden calf disobedience, in which Moses, as Israel's covenant mediator from that episode on, receives a continuing spiritual experience (during the covenant acceptance or at Sinai?) denied to that of national Israel (Ex. 34:29–35). Thereafter, until the advent, national Israel continued to receive mediated revelation, never again to experience the openness to the divine presence which had been the case in Ex. 19. Cf. my *Faith of Israel*, 40–41.

[22] Contra Hafemann, *Suffering*, 214.

inner liberation. The nature of the contrast, as 2 Corinthians 3:6 makes very clear, is not between the Mosaic age and Paul's age, but between the Mosaic age continuing in the Christian age at Corinth and the new covenant ministry conducted by Paul.

It is beyond doubt that the Mosaic covenant, which Jesus and John the Baptist came to revive and to reapply to Israel, in the time of its operation was neither a ministry of death nor a ministry of condemnation. The Sinai covenant itself as divinely imposed was deficient only in the area of human obedience to it. It was intended to be, and was, an instrument of salvation and national blessing. Indeed, in both old and new covenants such a contrast in experience between letter and Spirit was possible and indeed actual. In the Old Testament there is abundant evidence from the Psalms and other personalized evidence that the Old Testament saints put the old covenant into valid operation. What Paul has said in verse 6 about the contrast between the Spirit and the letter, while it always applied throughout the currency of the Mosaic covenant, seems mainly to refer to the difference between two current bases for ministry operating in Corinth, as 3:1–3 and the present tense of verse 6 ('kills') imply. As opposed to the ministry of the 'false apostles', Paul's gospel, applied in regeneration through the Spirit, was producing changed lives.

Covenant in Hebrews

The Epistle to the Hebrews also attests the covenant dilemma that confronted Christian Jews until AD 70. The temple, with all of its institutional attractions – sacrifice, priesthood and worship structures – continued to function after the death of Christ. Hebrews counters its continuing attraction by pointing to the institutions of the new covenant age, which replicated but nevertheless replaced those of the old covenant (priesthood, sanctuary, Day of Atonement, sacrifice, altar). We remind ourselves that Christian doctrine did not evolve overnight, even given such remarkable encounters as Paul's on the Damascus Road. Hebrews, a pre-AD 70 composition in my judgement, written probably to a Diaspora house church, instances the pull that the continuation of the Jerusalem temple exercised on Jewish thinking. The problem that the audience of the Epistle to the Hebrews faced had to be resolved by recognizing and accepting the new covenant cultic equivalents mentioned above, indicating that the area from which the influence had come was again probably Jerusalem itself. In general terms, Acts and the Pauline Epistles appear to concur that many of the pre-AD 70 struggles resulted from the perseverance of Jewish institutionalism.

It seems clear, therefore, from such major works of the New Testament, that the understanding of the death of Christ in new covenant terms was not an incidental theological issue. The death of the Jewish Messiah, finally having come, shook Jewish foundations. The Christian claim that this Jesus was the

Messiah and the one who inaugurated a new covenant based upon a new exodus called for the repentance of national Israel, as indeed the early church in Acts preached. If Christian claims were true, then the new age had arrived! It was understandable that Jewish interests resisted this to the death, for the incoming of the Gentiles into the religious structure of Israel would mean the end of Israel's ethnic nationalism. The cross, not the fall of Jerusalem, was the end of the Jewish age, which lingered on as obsolescent (Heb. 8:13) until AD 70, when the inevitability of the parting of the ways between Jews and Christians was clear and Jewish Christians were then forced to come to terms with the logic of the events.[23]

National and Believing Israel

Any total contrast between letter and Spirit or indeed between law and Spirit applied to the two Testaments as an explanation of differences misconceives the unitary biblical view of salvation by grace and the presence of these opposites in New Testament experience. The problem for national Israel in the Old Testament was that national experience was always external, merely of the letter. By national Israel I understand the leadership of Israel, depicted in the Old Testament as disobedient to the Sinai covenant from the exodus onwards. But this national result does not tell the complete story of piety within Israel in the period. In the Old Testament the emphasis is almost exclusively upon nationalistic Israel as a failed entity, which never responded to its national commission to be a light to the nations (Ex. 19:5–6; Is. 49:6). But within Israel there was undoubtedly a core of faithful dedicated to obedience to the covenant. They are present only in the personalized writings of the Old Testament (Psalms and Proverbs principally) and in tales of pious individuals (Caleb, Ruth, Hannah, etc.). The term 'remnant', used by the prophets from Isaiah on (perhaps also in Amos), overlaps perhaps, but as a more political term. The prophetic ministry of Jesus, which initially with John the Baptist sought the reformation of the nation, quickly came to terms with the impossibility of this aim, fulfilling in this paradoxical way the will of God for his ministry (Mk. 3:31–35; Mt. 12:46–50; Lk. 8:19–21). Jesus, while still addressing the nation, makes the relationship to himself personal. It is probable that the key parable of the sower not only reflects the negative response of Israel to Jesus, but reflects also the response of national Israel, throughout its history, to the divine word. Jesus, in

---

[23] Bauckham, 'Parting', argues that the real divisions between Judaism and Christianity came mainly after AD 70, and he may well be correct. But we must not undervalue the cracks at the seams that appear within the New Testament itself. Nor must we confine the Pauline problems with Judaism to the early Pauline Epistles alone.

'prophetic-remnant' fashion, gathers around him an Israel within an Israel. The *ekklesia* that Jesus will build will in fact be this alternate profile of Israel. This is not the place, however, to enter into a full-scale discussion of the role of national Israel in the Gospels and beyond. The fact remains that the church begins on the day of Pentecost with a believing Israel called in response to national Israel's failure. In short, the new covenant with Israel never involved national Israel but was a reality only for the new or restored Israel. For restored Israel, the operation of the new covenant meant ministry to the world. In the early Christian period such an attitude was vigorously opposed by national Israel's representatives, for whom the initial Sinai and Mosaic covenant continued.

At the death of Jesus, the Jewish era had passed away and Jewish institutions had been divinely discarded. While Paul never makes this point a formal conclusion, it seems clear, particularly from Galatians, that this is the understanding that guided Paul's thought. The formal break between the covenant eras required a considerable lapse of time, and also an overlap, after the death of Christ, until the distinction between competing covenant communities became plain and required a choice. In short, it required the later destruction of the temple and the cessation of temple sacrifice, priesthood and so on, to set the emerging Christian structures on a course completely independent from Judaism, and to permit the respective communities to reflect on the differences which divided Judaism from Christianity.

Paul and Law in the Light of the Cross

Galatians 3:19–24

Romans 9:30 – 10:4 majors on different attitudes to the law and a brief review is now required of Paul's attitude to the Mosaic law. Such basic Pauline attitudes come in Galatians 3, and the supposed contradiction in Pauline thinking about the law, which appears superficially between Galatians 3 and Romans 7, may be elucidated and explained by what has been written above. The relationship of the Mosaic law to the present Christian position in Galatians 3:19–24 serves as the crux of Paul's argument in Galatians 3. Now, in verses 19–20, Paul expounds the purpose and function of the Mosaic law and its relationship to the Mosaic covenant. In verse 19 Paul asks, 'Why then the law?' raising the question of the law's purpose, taken up in verses 19–25. If the law cannot procure salvation (as he has argued), then what is its function? Paul initially tells us that the law was 'added' (by God, to the previous promise to Abraham). The word 'added' indicates the law's subsidiary place in God's purposes, but not necessarily its inferiority. Law was added 'for the sake of transgressions', where the Greek preposition could mean result or goal – that is, to produce transgressions or to identify transgressions. Reading it with Romans 7, especially verse 7, the argument here seems to indicate that the place of law in salvation history was not merely to identify transgressions, but to multiply transgressions; that is, to enable sin to be seen as a covenant breach and so, in a negative way, to remove every basis other than faith for participating in the promises. The Abrahamic promise was permanent, but the addition of law in the form of the Sinai covenant was temporary. As associated with the Mosaic covenant, the Mosaic law was temporary; but insofar as it voiced divine principles, the law, as Paul will later make clear, is 'holy, and just and good' (Rom. 7:12; i.e., as divine revelation and when put within its proper revelational context).

Paul refers to the giving of the law through Mosaic mediation (v. 19 seems not to refer to the initial covenant revelation of Ex. 20).[24] Probably Paul is thinking here of the effective covenant for Israel in the Old Testament, that based on the second conclusion of the covenant in Exodus 34:1–28. The divine appearances to Israel and its elders (Ex. 19:24) seemed so direct as to rule out the possibility of covenant mediation in chapters 19 – 20. The national sin of the golden calf resulted in Moses' breaking of the two covenant tablets (Ex. 32:19; cf. Akkadian *tuppam hepu* for contract breach), and thus the rescinding of the Exodus 20 – 24 covenant through the symbolism of the broken tablets.

Withdrawal of direct divine guidance to the promised land and the substitution of angelic leadership then occurred (Ex. 32:34). This could well have created the context for Paul to associate angels with the subsequent law giving in the second covenant of Exodus 34:1–28. Exodus 34:10, with *karat berit*, points to a new, not an affirmed or renewed, covenant.[25] The notion of angels as participants present at the giving of the law was popular in Paul's time (cf. Deut. 33:2 LXX; Josephus, *Ant.* 15.136; *Test. Dan.* 6; *Jub.* 1:29 – 2:1; Acts 7:38, 53; Heb. 2:2). Paul's view may draw some biblical support from Psalm 68:18 (MT 68:17) where angels are associated with the giving of the law, understanding the 'chariots' of God as angels accompanying him at Sinai. The subsequent

---

[24] The Decalogue, with its second singular address, was heard by all Israel (cf. the implications of Ex. 20 and certainly Deut. 4:10–12). The covenant code of Ex. 21 – 23 was given through Moses, but this speaks more for the derivative nature of the law than for the necessity of mediation.

[25] Dumbrell, *Covenant and Creation*, 16–26. This conclusion has been challenged by P.R. Williamson, *Abraham*, in continuity with T. Alexander, but a semantic analysis of the occurrence of *karat berit* sustains my contention that it alone is used as an initiation formula. Cf. my *Faith of Israel*, 29, 34–35, 63. The second giving of the Sinai covenant at 34:10 includes, of course, all the legal apparatus of the first. Its major purpose seems to have been to place constraints upon Israel as a judgement upon its blatant covenant disobedience of Ex. 32.

distinction between Moses and national Israel (Ex. 34:29–35) would clearly underline such an enclosure in sin for national Israel, as the subsequent verses in Galatians 3 attest.

The simplest and best interpretation offered for the difficult and very laconic Galatians 3:20 is that offered by Terence Callan, that the concept of a mediator suggests plurality, and thus any transaction in which the mediator is involved is inferior to one in which God acts directly.[26] On this view, the verse offers a further pejorative view of law as finally given in the Sinai covenant and as mediated through Moses. Such an activity of Moses (Ex. 34) occurred within the context of Israel's gross national disobedience of Exodus 32 – 34, when, after Moses' intercession, a further covenant was imposed, but this time not with Israel directly as in Exodus 20, but through Moses.[27] The result was that, when the covenant was finally imposed as conclusive, Yahweh's requirement of mediation served to stress the sin of Israel. After Sinai, Israel remained continuously under mediators until the advent of Christ.

Paul adds a further point in verses 21–22. Unlike promise, the law cannot impart life. Paul, who seems to have been conscious of the thought that might arise from what he had said, asks whether law and promise contradicted each other. Since God had given both, law must have been compatible with promise; but since the Messiah had not yet come, the law, though never contrary to promise, became for national Israel a kind of jailer (cf. vv. 23–25). For believing Israel as opposed to national Israel, however, in the Old Testament the law was written in the 'heart'[28] as presumably it was always meant to be,[29] and its fulfilment was always a delight. In regard to Paul's use of the Mosaic law, there is then a conflict between Romans 7 and Galatians 3 only if we lose sight of Paul's purpose in Galatians of addressing national disobedience to the Sinai covenant.[30] Righteousness, which indicates the believer's right status with God, never came through law but through promise, through incorporation into the

---

[26] Callan, 'Pauline Midrash'.

[27] It may seem that Mosaic mediation for Israel commenced earlier with the giving of the Covenant Code from Ex. 20:22ff. But Ex. 21:1 (cf. 'judgements') indicates that what follows in chapters 21 – 23 is derivative and not primary legislation, which can thus be secondarily 'given through Moses'.

[28] Dumbrell, *Covenant and Creation*, 178–81, referring to Pss. 37:31; 40:8 (MT v. 9; *me'eh*, 'inward parts'); Is. 51:7. Contrition in the Old Testament is an exercise of the heart: Pss. 51:10 (MT 12), 17 (MT 19); 73:1, 13; Prov. 22:1; Is. 57:15. A return to Yahweh is the result of a change of heart (Jer. 3:10), and for the nation to repent is to circumcise the heart (Jer. 4:4; cf. 9:25; Ezek. 44:7, 9).

[29] As was the intended case for the nation (cf. Deut. 10:16; 30:6).

[30] Israel's national disobedience to the Sinai covenant is implicit in Paul's remarks at Gal. 3:19, 21.

promise-structure, the covenant relationship, and thus in regard to the new covenant by incorporation into the person of the Promise-Keeper, Messiah Jesus. With a strong adversative at the beginning of verse 21, Paul indicates the real situation. So far from conveying life, law was used by Scripture (Paul seems to have the whole of the Old Testament in mind, for the argument of verse 22 seems to demand this) to confine the whole Jewish nation under sin.

Verses 23–24 point to the experience of national Israel provided with the Mosaic covenant. Before this faith (i.e., the faith referred to in v. 22, Christian faith)[31] came as a possibility, the Mosaic law operated as a power to confine 'us' (i.e., disobedient Israel generally).[32] Paul is pointing to the Old Testament effects of Israel's unbelief, which gave law a judgmental role against the nation. Though it is not stated here since it is not germane to his argument, Paul is aware of the distinction between national Israel and the believing remnant who, though suffering under disobedient leadership, because of their covenant standing would not have been so personally confined (cf. Rom. 9:6; cf. the punctuated comments throughout Ps. 119 'O how I love thy law', etc.; cf. vv. 24, 35, 47, 92, 97, 113, 127, 159, 163, 167). He is directing his arguments in this chapter (and in 4:1–7) against Jews who, at the time of writing, still placed their confidence in the Mosaic covenant. The Mosaic law's restrictive supervision was to continue until its era was over, that is, until salvation through faith in Christ and thus entrance to the new covenant was finally available. This meant that, with the death of Christ, the era of national Israel had finished. With the coming of *this* faith in Christ (cf. the Greek article in v. 23), the Mosaic law, with the demise of national Israel, had no further role to play in the era of the new covenant.

Verse 24 elaborates on verse 23 with the image of the *paidagogos*, the family slave/retainer. His role, which is ambivalently assessed in the literature of the period, seems to have been a negative one of restrictive, oppressive supervision.[33] In 'until Christ came', Paul is speaking chronologically of successive periods of salvation history, with the Christian period making it quite clear what was always the case, that justification was by faith. Paul's point is that the coming of Christ should have awakened national Israel to the role of the law. The Mosaic law's role in the history of salvation had ceased with Christ's death.

---

[31] The genitive *'Iesou Christou* in v. 22 is objective, not subjective. For a very trenchant criticism of the popular subjective interpretation of this sequence in this and other cases, see Seifrid, *Christ*, 139–46, who argues strongly and correctly for the genitive in the phrases as objective.

[32] Cf. Donaldson, 'Curse of the Law', 95–96, who argues that Paul's use of 'we' in Gal. 3 refers to Jews as opposed to Gentiles.

[33] Cf. Longenecker, *Galatians*, 148.

'Now that faith has come' – Law in Galatians 3:25–29

Now that this new covenant faith was available (v. 25), the Mosaic law had no further restrictive role to play. This, however, does not mean the end of divine law as the guiding motif for life within the new covenant. Paul's point has been that the covenant with Abraham was always primary, and that the Sinai covenant occupied a complementary role for national Israel within that of the covenant with Abraham. The Mosaic covenant was always temporary, transient and an anticipation of the fulfilment of the Abrahamic, except that it provided a reflection of what comprised godly conduct.

The result (v. 26) was that all the Galatian believers, from both Jewish and Gentile backgrounds, have been brought to a new experience as the true sons of God by their faith (or by this faith, i.e., not by ethnic connection). They have inherited adoption as sons, formerly Israel's position (Ex. 4:22–23; Deut. 14:1–2; Hos. 11:1), which is now for all in Christ Jesus.[34] Thus 'all one in Christ Jesus' (v. 28) means that for all who now belong to Christ Jesus, the normal differences implying relative worth or inequality deriving from birth – that is, ethnic (Jew or Greek), social and economic (slave or free) or gender (male and female), do not affect membership in the people of God by rebirth. Paul is not arguing that these differences have no place in our current society. The argument of the chapter is concluded in verse 29 with what is really its statement of purpose: that if the category of belonging to Christ applies, then distinctions vanish. As Abraham's seed, believers share in the promises to Abraham. Thus those in Christ are the true 'sons of Abraham', not Jews as such. The chapter thus concludes with the full identification of believers with the faith of Abraham, toward which the argument has been moving.

Under the Sinai covenant, works of the law did not win grace; at best they are simply the necessary evidence of a grace-impelled life. They could not be a condition of covenant entrance, which in the Old Testament (as in the New)

---

[34] 'In Christ' in 3:28 is the correlate of 'sons of God' in 3:26, and the correlate of baptism in 3:28 (cf. v. 29), where belonging to Christ means being Abraham's seed, heirs according to promise (v. 29). This strongly confirms that 'in Christ' meant, for Paul, membership in the historical though now eschatological people of God. This means that those baptized (i.e., in an affirmation of the faith, not mere baptism as such; cf. v. 26) with reference to Christ (and not Judaism) have identified themselves with Christ (v. 27). 'Christ Jesus' is the normal Pauline order for his 'in Christ' formula, which indicates a transfer of dominion and thus membership in the new people of God (as opposed to being 'in Adam') by incorporation into Israel's Messiah, Jesus of Nazareth, and thus sharing in the Abrahamic 'seed' promises. Paul's 'clothed themselves with Christ' conveys the sense of sharing Christ's nature as a result of being united to Christ and his sphere of dominion, so as to begin that transformation into his image through the ongoing work of the Spirit.

was by grace alone. In the New Testament the phrase 'works of the law', as noted above, is not a generalized term for self-effort. It has, describing post-cross conditions, a definite reference to a Sinai covenant connection and membership.[35] Paul does not feel any need in Galatians (or elsewhere)[36] to particularize '*nomos*', since for Paul there is only one law, the Mosaic law. When 'law' appears as an absolute term in Galatians (and indeed in Paul generally) the reference is to the Mosaic law. The Christian alternative is 'the law of Christ' (6:2). In the course of time, obvious markers of Jewishness such as food laws and circumcision and Sabbaths became the flag leaders for indications of law observance, but the Mosaic law had no claim on Christians in the New Testament.

Jewish law performance in the New Testament period, even the most misguided legalistic law performance – and certainly very much of Jewish Torah performance was legalistic – was the attempt to respond to grace by maintaining the covenant. What upholds justification, as well as initiating it, is faith. Admittedly, Christian faith will show itself in 'works' (not, however in 'works of the [Mosaic] law'), since under the new covenant as well as the old, what demonstrates faith is obedience to the will of God. In both old and new covenants, what facilitated obedience was the law in the heart of the believer, put there by the Holy Spirit in both Testaments.

Paul was keenly aware of the salvation-history changes that had swept into Judaism as a result of the cross. He understood that the death of Christ had now enabled Judaism to fulfil its biblical commission of being a servant race, facing the world as a true kingdom of God people. A significant minority of Jews in Jerusalem initially embraced this wonderful new opportunity for Judaism, and they laboured to keep the emerging new Jewish Christian movement within the boundaries of existing Jewish institutionalism as far as that could be done. Much of the political detail of this Jewish endeavour is to be seen in the Acts of the Apostles. More importantly, the results of this attempt to perpetuate the past within the contours of the new movement are to be found in the Pauline Epistles.

The curse of the law – Galatians 3:10

The salvation-history principle underlying Paul's logic, to be seen later in Romans 9:30–33, may be briefly illustrated by referring to the Galatians 3 context in which the Mosaic law and its claims are most fully discussed. Paul's reasoning in Galatians 3:10, where the issue may be seen at its clearest, may be understood in terms of the salvation-history change which underlay his

---

[35] Cf. Martin, *Christ*, 24–25, for discussion.

[36] Martin, *Christ*, 21–31, supplies a survey of views on Paul's use of *nomos*.

preaching.[37] The 'for' (Greek *gar*, v. 10) introduces a section (3:10–14) designed to explain by reference to Scripture (perhaps used by the opponents) the reason for the implied dichotomy in verses 6–9 between faith and Torah in regard to what constitutes sonship of Abraham. However, the logic of the two parts of verse 10 creates the problem, for it is against supposed law-keepers that Paul directs the curse of the law (3:10a), originally directed against covenant transgressors (Deut. 27:26). To solve the problem, traditionally an unstated minor premise has been thought to have been intended by Paul, namely, 'no one in fact has fulfilled the law', to be placed between the two halves of the verse to explain the progress of the argument. This then leads to the conclusion of the verse that the curse of the law falls on those who transgress the law, since the law cannot be kept in its entirety (Deut. 27:26). That Old Testament verse had called for law performance, the absence of which called down a curse. The implied premise does control the movement from verse 10a to 10b, but to the bare notation of covenant curses in Deuteronomy 27 must be added, of course, the contingency provided for national and personal atonement through the sacrificial system which negated the effect of the curse. Thus the bald statement of liability of Deuteronomy 27 was open, as is all Old Testament law, to mitigation by sacrifice acceptable to God.

In verse 10 Paul turns the normal approach to Deuteronomy 27 around, stating that all who rely on the works of the Mosaic law are under a curse. Added to this, he asserts in Galatians 3:21 that law keeping could never be the way of salvation, even if perfect obedience were possible. For salvation is based on promise; but law is a response to covenant obligation, not the precursor of covenant.

Paul's reference to 'as many as are of the works of the law' in 3:10a, however, has present Sinai covenant relationships in mind, and this is the point of the verse. Greek *ek* plus the genitive is used to denote a member of a certain class or party,[38] who are not here identified by their actions, but by their covenant orientation – that is, membership of the Sinai covenant. To be 'of the works of ' the Torah is not the same as fulfilling or doing the law, so that Deuteronomy 27:26, 'cursed is everyone who does not observe and obey all the things written in the book of the law', may add an expectation of conduct from those who falsely believe themselves to be covenant members. To be cursed (Old Testament, literally, 'to be devoted to destruction') is to be cut off from God, to be outside the covenant of grace. So Galatians 3:10 says that in the 'now' of the new covenant age, all the Jews who rely on obedience to the law in order to stay in the covenant are under the curse of the law, since the Mosaic covenant which offered atonement through sacrifice ceased with the cross.

---

[37] See my fuller treatment of this verse in 'Abraham and the Abrahamic Covenant'.

[38] Cf. Caneday, 'Redeemed'.

True, the Mosaic law cannot be kept perfectly, but this is not Paul's point. By Christ's unprecedented saving act, he established a new covenant and a new kind of forgiveness. By his ignoble death, Jesus appeared as one cut off from the Mosaic covenant, devoted to destruction. Yet in that death Christ perfectly fulfilled the law as the one true and unblemished sin offering and atoning sacrifice. But God had now vindicated the one who had been publicly pronounced accursed.

This meant that continuing post-cross members of the Sinai covenant would always find themselves under its curse for disobedience, because all had solemnly sworn they would do and obey all the words the Lord had said. Of course, biblically, salvation is never achieved by human effort, and Paul merely draws out the illogic of the Judaizing position. In their endeavours to impose Mosaic covenant law on the Galatians, the Judaizers were given impetus by conduct such as Peter's at Antioch. At the same time, apart from anything else, the Judaizers are shown by Paul in Galatians 3 to be in serious theological confusion. By their demand for the imposition of the Mosaic law on Christian converts, they were in fact making demand for Christian incorporation into the Mosaic and Sinaitic structure. In particular, by requiring the Galatians to submit to circumcision, food laws, Sabbath keeping and so on, they were not merely making demands for the acceptance of Mosaic law in terms of ethical principles. They were assuming the continuance of the Mosaic covenant and insisting upon its continued recognition. This was a serious category mistake, which presumed the continued existence of institutions of sacrificial atonement whose validity had been decisively ended by the cross. That is why the Abrahamic connection, and a requisite understanding of what Abrahamic sonship meant, were so critical to Paul's presentation in Galatians 3. In Galatians 3:10 (and in Gal. 2:14–21, etc.), Paul is making a salvation-history point. He is not reflecting on the history of Israel generally, but on the present constitution of Israel, on Jews who have refused to see the work of Jesus Messiah as terminating the Sinai covenant and determining a new covenant relationship ensuring Israel's continuing position. Indeed, they had probably endeavoured to fit Jesus into the Sinai compact, which they saw as continuing and ensuring national Israel's supremacy. It was true that the Sinai covenant had continued, but with a different Israel, who was now to implement the commission given to Israel to witness to the world of the new reality of Christ's kingship established by the ascension.

The curse of the law now, says Paul, will come on those who were of the 'works of the (Mosaic) law' – that is, upon all who were continuing post-cross members of the Sinai covenant, since all would fail to keep the law. By substituting 'book of the law' in Galatians 3:10 for 'this law' in both the MT and the LXX, Paul extends the application of Deuteronomy 27:26 to the whole of the Old Testament law. Under the normal operation of the old covenant, atonement through sacrifice after personal confession of sins committed deliberately would have been available, so that within the atonement system the curse did not operate. Paul's implied point, however, is that there is no forgiveness available for Mosaic covenant-keepers, since the curse is to be applied universally to adherents of the Sinai covenant, whether law-keepers or law-breakers, with no redress possible. This was because the sacrificial system for the removal of the curse of the law and for forgiveness of transgressions was no longer available.[39] In short, Paul is arguing, the day of the Sinai covenant is over, and those who continue to resort to it have now no means of institutional forgiveness available for their inevitable sinning.

In critical contexts such as Galatians 2:14–21 and 3:10–14, Paul is not reflecting on the history of Israel generally, but is making a salvation-history point in regard to the present constitution of Israel. This point is directed to Judaizers and Jews who have refused to see the work of Jesus Messiah as terminating the Sinai covenant and as determinative of a new covenant relationship. Still attempting to live under the Sinai arrangement, they were under the curse invoked in Deuteronomy 27:26 for non-fulfilment of covenant obligations, since the sacrificial system which they needed for imperfect obedience had been annulled. Under the operation of the new covenant, in force since the death of Christ, forgiveness is available through a different system of non-cultic atonement.[40] It must now come through acceptance that Jesus in his death provided a sufficient atonement for all sin – past, present and prospective. Christ's death as a sin offering was in itself the great inclusive Day of Atonement (Rom. 3:25). With the death of Christ, the temple in Jerusalem was itself profaned (Mk. 15:38). While the temple continued to function in Jerusalem until September AD 70 and was doubtless considered effective by Judaism at large, the reality of the matter was that the death of Christ brought Israel's institutional system to a conclusive end, never to be reactivated.

The post-cross situation, therefore, found national Israel endeavouring to keep a Mosaic law which no longer had Christian validity. But here again, if the position is not nuanced, contradiction seems to arise between Pauline

---

[39] As mentioned above, the customary approach to Gal. 3:10 is to insert a middle term such as 'no one can keep the law', as implied between 3:10a and 3:10b. The verse is then seen as Paul's approach to Christian Judaism, which is continuing Israel's legalistic approach to justification. One recent writer who has recognized the difference without fully capitalizing upon it is Bell, *No One Seeks*, 248, noting that Paul in Rom. 1:18 – 3:20 does not reckon with sacrifice as a means of atonement, since with the sacrifice of Christ all cultic atoning practice was considered invalid. As I have independently noted, when it is understood that Paul is writing from a post-cross situation in Gal. 3 and generally, many issues, including the interpretation of the vexed 3:10, fall into place.

[40] 1 Jn. 1:9; cf. 2:2.

pronouncements in Romans 7 and Galatians 3. With the death of Christ the Mosaic code had gone, but not the demand for Christians to produce the fruit of the Spirit (Gal. 5:22) or to fulfil the 'law of Christ' (Gal. 6:2).

Application to Romans 9:30 – 10:4

Translating these salvation-history perspectives into the exegesis of Romans 9:30 – 10:4, (some) Gentiles, not 'pursuing righteousness',[41] nevertheless had found it by faith (v. 30) through the preaching of Christ, as Israelite prophecy had foretold.[42] This is the inevitable conclusion, given Paul's argument in 9:6b–29. The survey Paul has made in chapter 9, clearly based upon his present missionary experience, is confirmed by the number of God's elect coming into the new covenant from the conversion of Gentiles.

At Romans 9:30, the righteousness that was in fact obtained is membership of the new covenant. In the Old Testament the denominative verb *SDQ* means 'to be righteous' (Qal), 'to declare righteous' (Hiphil) forensically or covenantally. It is widely agreed that righteousness – that is, right standing with God, or righteousness in covenant language, does not denote a property but actions taken which demonstrate the existence of a relationship. The word generally denotes conformity to a norm, and the norm to which conformity must be had in the Old Testament is the God-given covenant. We may take the relationship back to the God/creation relationship between humanity and a divine creation order.[43] The consistent obligation of humanity to return to such a relationship, however, falls within the salvation-history movement whereby Israel becomes Yahweh's evangelist to the world to bring about world renewal and the kingdom of God. To say that God is righteous means that with the conclusion of the biblical covenants through which God's

---

[41] This remark is an interesting aside by Paul. The phrase itself is not often taken up in discussion. The Gentiles concerned, as non-Jews, were not pursuing righteousness but were addressed by the gospel in which the righteousness of God was revealed. We are thus to understand the remark as a contrast with 9:31 and with the Jewish pursuit of righteousness, though the analogy is not complete since for the Gentiles the issue was initial acceptance with God, whereas for the Jews it was a continuation of an imagined acceptance on the post-cross basis of Mosaic law performance. Thus the point Paul seems to have in mind in 9:30 is the Gentile attainment of acceptance through Paul's law-free gospel.

[42] Paul's argument in Rom. 9 climaxes in the admission to the Gentiles in vv. 24–26, quoting Hos. 1:10 (directed in its context to Israel's future) on this point.

[43] As do Stuhlmacher, *Gerechtigkeit Gottes*, and more recently his pupil M.A. Seifrid in his *Christ, Our Righteousness*. There is no objection to this. The purpose of Old Testament covenants, however, is to put into action God's purposes, leading to the full implementation of the new creation, a point which Seifrid does not consider.

purposes for the world are to be enacted, he acts according to the tenor of his covenant undertakings. For me, such undertakings reach back to Genesis 1 – 2 as the basic biblical covenant.[44] So in the Old Testament God will intervene to bring about blessing or judgement based on covenant promises, according to circumstances. In the prime Old Testament example, Abraham's relationship was right (Gen. 15:6) when he trusted God's promises. He was thus justified (declared to be righteous), since his conduct was evidence of a continuing covenant relationship. Though the covenant was not formally and reassuringly affirmed until Genesis 15:18, its promise structure had begun with Abraham's call and commission in Genesis 12:1–3, and the place of biblical covenants was to affirm and give quasi-legal effect to relationships already established.[45]

In New Testament use the verb *dikaioō* ('treat as righteous') becomes descriptive of the change of status brought about by the action of the Holy Spirit in rebirth. To judge by the word's use, justification does not itself refer to the gift of rebirth, but simply to the change of status conferred by rebirth. To say that a believer is righteous in the Old Testament or New Testament is to say that the believer is acting, as prompted by God, in such a way as to initiate or maintain a relationship in the old or new covenants. Membership in the covenant on the basis of belief indicated by action is the understanding of both Testaments as to the meaning of 'righteousness' or 'to be righteous'. All of this means that the theological language drawn from the New Testament of 'justification by faith' refers to a status resulting from God's action in placing believers within the new covenant, by his forgiveness.

In his use of the past tenses in 9:30–33, Paul is reviewing a post-cross missionary situation, as the mention of Gentile conversions makes clear. Where has the cross left Israel and the Gentiles? Some Gentiles (there is no definite article in v. 30) are in, and much of Israel is out. The difference is the recognition or the non-recognition (in the case of Israel) of Christ as Jewish Messiah and divine Son of God. Paradoxically, explains Paul in Romans 9:31, Israel, following after a law that was designed to express covenant membership,[46] did not obtain membership in the new covenant. The problem Paul is raising at this point (v. 32) is *not* that of covenant membership and the righteousness it conferred *in the Old Testament era*. That arose in the Old Testament from a valid pursuit of Torah and was true of the pious and the remnant, though not true of the nation generally.

---

[44] See my *Covenant and Creation*, 11–46.

[45] See my *Covenant and Creation*, 21.

[46] Rom. 9:31 cannot be understood without the explanation that 9:32 supplies. It follows, from the reasons given in 9:33 for Israel's failure (her stumbling over Christ as the rock of offence), that the difficult phrase *nomon dikaiosunes*, 'law which aims at righteousness' in v. 31 has righteousness in view. Cf. Schreiner, *Romans*, 539, and the literature cited.

In verse 31 Paul is thinking of Israel's stance in regard to covenant relationships following the death of Christ. The 'but as' of verse 32 reflects Paul's judgement that Israel's action in the post-cross situation was generally illusory and self-defeating. From national Israel's post-cross point of view, Torah-keeping was a requirement for covenant standing, but for Paul such attempts were simply works based on Torah and of no Christian significance. The place of Torah as providing for the obedience of faith under the Sinai covenant was undoubted and unchallengeable, so long as the Sinai covenant was in force. But Paul is thinking of Israel's stance toward covenant relationships following the death of Christ. It follows from the reasons given in 9:33 for Israel's failure, her stumbling over Christ as the rock of offence (not the Torah),[47] that the difficult phrase *nomon dikaiosunes* in verse 31 must refer to Israel's *post-cross* continued pursuit of the Sinai covenant and her refusal to acknowledge the resurrected Jesus as Israel's Messiah.

The law of righteousness (v. 31) – that is, the law, which aimed at demonstrating the maintenance of the covenant,[48] was the legitimate goal that Israel, if rightly motivated,[49] ought to have pursued under the Mosaic covenant. But in the post-cross situation, which Paul is discussing in 9:30 – 10:4, Israel's rejection of Christ had created her spiritual stumbling, as the scriptural citations in verse 33 make abundantly clear. But Paul is indicating a double problem, which now confronted the nation. This is the national continuance of seeking to keep the Sinai covenant by law-based conduct not prompted by faith in Christ at a time when the Sinai covenant itself had been replaced by the new covenant inaugurated by the death of Christ. Wrongly motivated, the national Israel of Paul's day was endeavouring to perpetuate the wrong covenant. Their misguided attempt to bolster the Mosaic covenant would mean their divine

---

[47] Schreiner, *Romans*, 541, suggests that 'the idea that the stone here refers to the Torah can be confidently rejected' (with references cited).

[48] I.e., a law whose object was to maintain right standing (within the covenant). Martin, *Christ*, 137, correctly argues that since the Gentiles' pursuit was righteousness, it was righteousness for which the Jews were striving.

[49] As I have noted above, the requirement for obedience in the Old Testament was always to have the law in the heart. National Israel, even at Sinai, never met this requirement. We may adduce here the golden calf narrative, the second covenant made with Israel at Sinai (Ex. 34:10) and the distinction drawn in Ex. 34:29–34 between Moses and Israel. Never again in the OT was Israel directly addressed, but revelation was received through mediators, prophets, wise men, priests, etc., for Israel. John's Gospel notes this from another point of view, indicated by the incarnation (cf. Jn. 1:14). John's point of a new departure as a result of the incarnation attests the general New Testament approach to the new salvation-history movement in the New Testament, and is affirmed in a different sense by Paul in 2 Cor. 3:12–18.

rejection and the destruction of their religious symbols in AD 70. The new reality was that Jew and Gentile must enter the new covenant in the same way and stay in the covenant in the same way: by faith. The cross had revoked the national privilege for Israel of covenant entry by birth. In their final renunciation of Christ, the terrible 'We have no king but Caesar' (Jn. 19:15), by which they had jettisoned their national election at the cross, they had simply become part of their world ruled by political alliances, but with no standing as a nation within the kingdom of God.

Through my own study of Romans 9:30–33 I have concluded that N.T. Wright's exegesis of Romans 10:1–4 detailed below, reached by a slightly different route, is correct. In repeating his concern of Romans 9:1 at 10:1, Paul begins a new phase of the argument. Jews had zeal (10:2), but not according to knowledge which recognized the true state of the case; for they were, as Paul writes, ignorant of God's righteousness, his new covenant purposes. What is in view in verse 3 is not a righteousness that is imputed (cf. NRSV 10:3), but God's acquittal in demonstration of his dynamic fidelity to his covenant purposes. The Jews rejected God's message to the nation in Jesus, which was the fulfilment of God's Sinai covenant purpose. They did not understand the significance of the ministry of Jesus. Paul then goes on to support this conclusion in the familiar but greatly contested sentence in 10:4. Literally the verse runs, 'For the *telos* of the law Christ with a view to righteousness for every one who believes'. Apart from the interpretative difficulties of the sentence in its particulars, there are many difficulties in identifying the subject of the sentence, as well as the forms and the placements in the English syntax of the verb 'to be'.[50] Since, however, the context of the argument is Israel's rejection of Christ as the inaugurator of the new covenant, the sentence is best construed with N.T. Wright, 'Christ is the end of the law "with reference to righteousness" (i.e., covenant membership); it is (now) for all who believe'.[51] The first part of this sentence indicates the finality of the Jewish age. In submission to the Sinai covenant, Christ as a perfect sin offering ended the Mosaic law by fulfilling it (10:4), by demonstrating the complete covenant obedience that Moses had required of Israel, dying not only for Israel, but also for the world whose representative Israel was. That is to say, the time of the Sinai covenant came to an end with the death of Jesus, which ended the institutions of national Israel. Moreover, since the era of Jewish particularity had ended, the sacrifice of the cross, as the revelation of God's covenant righteousness, must be pleaded by all for forgiveness. Therefore the new covenant, which completed God's promise

---

[50] For a survey of interpretation of 10:4, see Schreiner, *Romans*, 544–48; Martin, *Christ*, 129.

[51] Wright, *Climax*, 242–45.

structure, is open to all on the basis of faith in Jesus, Saviour of the world, Israel's Messiah now enthroned as Lord of all.

Conclusion

In short, the thesis of this chapter is that the great movement in salvation history resulting from the death of Christ and the inauguration of the new covenant must regulate our approach to Pauline theology. Further, Paul is speaking in Romans 9:30 – 10:4 of a post-cross situation in which ethnic Israel stands rejected and has been replaced. These considerations of new covenant, new Israel, and law in Paul as a reference to Mosaic law no longer applicable to Christians, need to regulate our approach to the interpretation of Paul.

This chapter has suggested that biblical exegesis is dependent upon a canonical biblical theology. But this latter is itself an understanding of the progressive implementation of God's purposes through history. I have suggested that great salvation history changes proceeded, as we might necessarily expect, from the cross. God begins again with a new people of God. Old notions of election, covenant and law are dismissed or transformed by the keen and inspired mind of Paul. Several results accrue from this chapter. The questions of Paul's approach to Israel, to Jewish law and to the Jewish covenant all need to be further examined. It is my hope to be able to take all of these further.

Bibliography

Bailey, D.P., *Jesus as the Mercy Seat: The Semantics and the Theology of Paul's Use of Hilasterion in Romans 3:25* (Cambridge: Cambridge University Press, 1999)

Barnett, P.W., *The Second Epistle to the Corinthians* (NICNT; Grand Rapids: Eerdmans, 1997)

Bauckham, R., 'The Parting of the Ways: When, How and Why', *SJT* 35 (1993), 135–51

Bell, R.H., *No One Seeks for God* (WUNT 106; Tübingen: Mohr Siebeck, 1998)

Callan, T., 'Pauline Midrash: The Exegetical Background of Gal. 3:19b', *JBL* 99 (1980), 555–67

Caneday, A., 'Redeemed from the Curse of the Law: The Use of Deut. 21:22–23 in Gal. 3:13', *TJ* 10 (1989), 185–209

Cullmann, O., *Christology of the New Testament* (Philadelphia: Westminster Press, 1959)

Donaldson, T.L., '"The Curse of the Law" and the Inclusion of the Gentiles', *NTS* 32 (1986), 94–112

Dumbrell, W.J., 'Abraham and the Abrahamic Covenant in Galatians 3', in *The Gospel to the Nations: Perspectives on Paul's Mission* (ed. P. Bolt and M. Thompson; Leicester: Inter-Varsity Press, 2000), 19–31

—, *Covenant and Creation* (Exeter: Paternoster Press, 1984)

—, *The Faith of Israel: A Theological Survey of the Old Testament* (Grand Rapids: Baker, 2nd edn, 2002)

—, *The End of the Beginning: Revelation 21 – 22 and the Old Testament* (Eugene, OR: Wipf and Stock, 2001)

Dunn, J.D.G., *The Partings of the Ways: Between Christianity and Judaism and their Significance for the Character of Christianity* (London: SCM Press, 1991)

France, R.T., *Jesus and the Old Testament: His Application of Old Testament Passages to Himself and His Mission* (London: Tyndale Press, 1971)

Hafemann, S.J., *Paul, Moses and the History of Israel* (Tübingen: Mohr/Siebeck, 1995)

—, *Suffering and the Spirit* (WUNT 2/19; Tübingen: Mohr/Siebeck, 1986)

Lane, W.L., *Hebrews* (Waco, TX: Word Books, 1991)

Longenecker, R.N., *Galatians* (Waco, TX: Word Books, 1990)

Martin, B.L., *Christ and the Law in Paul* (Leiden: Brill, 1989)

Rae, M., 'Creation and Promise: Towards a Theory of History', in *'Behind' the Text: History and Biblical Interpretation* (ed. C. Bartholomew, C.S. Evans, M. Healy and M. Rae; SHS 4; Carlisle: Paternoster; Grand Rapids: Zondervan, 2003), 267–99

Sanders, E.P., *Paul and Palestinian Judaism* (Philadelphia: Fortress Press, 1977)

Schreiner, T.R., *Romans* (Grand Rapids: Baker, 1998)

—, *The Law and Its Fulfilment in Pauline Theology* (Grand Rapids: Baker, 1993)

Seifrid, M.A., *Christ, Our Righteousness* (Leicester: Apollos, 2000)

Strauss, M.L., *The Davidic Messiah in Luke-Acts: The Promise and Its Fulfilment in Lukan Christology* (JSNTSup 110; Sheffield: Academic Books, 1995)

Stuhlmacher, P., *Gerechtigkeit Gottes bei Paulus* (FRLANT; Göttingen: Vandenhoeck & Ruprecht, 2nd edn, 1966)

Turner, M., 'The Sabbath, Sunday and the Law in Luke-Acts', in *From Sabbath to the Lord's Day: A Biblical Historical and Theological Investigation* (ed. D.A. Carson; Grand Rapids: Zondervan, 1982), 99–157

Williamson, P.R., *Abraham, Israel and the Nations: The Patriarchal Promise and Its Covenantal Development in Genesis* (Sheffield: Sheffield Academic Press, 2000)

Wright, N.T., *The Climax of the Covenant* (Minneapolis: Fortress Press, 1992)

12

Hebrews and Biblical Theology
Andrew T. Lincoln

Biblical Theology and Hebrews

There is still no consensus about what is meant by the term 'biblical theology'.
If the proposal of this chapter is to make any sense, then some of its assumptions
about the context of the debate of which it is a part need to be spelled out at the
beginning. To do so will, however, inevitably incur the risk of revisiting briefly
what for some readers is well-trodden terrain. A minimalist definition of biblical theology might be that it is theology developed on the basis of the unity of
the Bible and its two Testaments. It is biblical because it takes into account the
whole Bible and it is theological because it engages in interpretation and reflection on the subject matter of the Bible.[1] But such a definition inevitably covers
up a host of issues. Some would claim that all theology worthy of the label
Christian theology is biblical theology, because it has to take account of the
Bible as, at very least, a major source of the Christian tradition, on which it
reflects in the light of contemporary concerns and modes of thought. Others,
however, would hold that biblical theology is simply that subdiscipline of theology that attempts to describe the theology contained in the Bible itself. Historically, of course, that is how biblical theology as a distinct discipline had its
origins, and it was seen as a way of breaking free from the shackles of dogmatic
theology. J.P. Gabler's famous lecture of 1787 was entitled 'On the proper distinction between biblical and dogmatic theology, and the specific objectives of
each'.[2] In it he insisted that the task of analysing the biblical data was a historical
task and to be sharply distinguished from the philosophical and dogmatic task
of articulating Christian belief in the present. His lecture is often seen as a

---

[1] Cf. also Watson, *Text and Truth*, 8: 'This expression [biblical theology] has been
applied in the recent past to an approach that emphasizes both the ultimate coherence of the two Testaments and the theological dimension of the interpretative
task.'

[2] For the English translation of the lecture, see Sandys-Wunsch and Eldredge, 'J.P.
Gabler's …', 133–58.

convenient marker of a divide from earlier thinking when scholastics, reformers and pietists could, for the most part, assume that their own theology was basically the same as the theology or theologies contained in the Bible. The inevitable result of Gabler's division of tasks was then a further division in which the historical task of describing the theology of the Old Testament was separated from that of describing the theology of the New Testament. The further consequences for academic biblical scholarship have been well documented and much discussed. Over the nineteenth and twentieth centuries, specialization and fragmentation within biblical studies turned the division of tasks in regard to the Old Testament and the New Testament into a major gulf between the practitioners. In the light of all the historical and critical distinctions that needed to be made and the increasing body of secondary literature to be accounted for, it became more and more difficult for individual scholars to be in control of the data in their own area and to find coherent ways of speaking about the unity and diversity of even one of the Testaments. So dealing adequately with the relation *between* the Testaments came to be thought of as beyond the capabilities of most scholars, and the further dogmatic task, which Gabler had always intended should be addressed, was almost completely lost sight of by biblical scholars.

On their side, most dogmatic theologians did not consider the Bible to contain real theology and regarded theology proper as having its main focus elsewhere. In the last century, probably von Rad in Old Testament studies and Bultmann in New Testament studies came closest to doing theology through their biblical analysis. From the theological side it was arguably Barth, though he would never have considered what he was doing as biblical theology, who provided the strongest example of how working with biblical texts can contribute to dogmatic theology. In the middle of the last century there was also the so-called 'biblical theology movement', whose main exponents were G.E. Wright on the Old Testament side and O. Cullmann on the New Testament side, with their emphases on the God who acts and on salvation history. Both Childs and Barr have charted the problems and perceived deficiencies of that approach.[3] Both of these scholars, in quite different ways, have also gone on to recognize that descriptive biblical theology is of limited use for the task of theology within the Christian church unless it is also qualified and directed by some overall theological construal.[4] Nevertheless, whether biblical theology can be done and how it is to be done have again become matters on the agenda of contemporary biblical studies and theology.[5] Not only biblical scholars such

---

[3] Cf. Childs, *Biblical Theology in Crisis*; Barr, *Old and New* and, on semantic problems in its practitioners' use of the Bible, *Semantics* and *Biblical Words*.

[4] Cf. Childs, *Biblical Theology of the Old and New Testaments*; Barr, *Concept*.

[5] For a recent collection of essays reflecting a variety of approaches, see Hafemann

as Childs and Barr, but also others such as Seitz, Watson and Moberly have made substantial contributions.[6] Further, there is an increasing tendency on the part of some contemporary theologians, such as Placher, Volf, Charry and Ford, to provide some close theological readings of biblical texts in their work.[7] A major reason for this revival of interest has been the loosening of the hold of the dominant modern paradigm that treated the Bible in a detached fashion as an ancient historical document and the accompanying recognition that the commitments of interpreters play a crucial role in interpretation. This has provided greater incentive for Christian scholars to bring to bear their convictions about the unity and significance of the Bible in their work. At the same time, of course, some aspects of the postmodern paradigm, which recognizes the interests of interpreters, challenge in their own way whether there is any viable unity in the Bible and whether theologies based on the Bible are beneficial rather than harmful in their effects.

Why, having given a very inadequate sketch of the context of the discussion about biblical theology, do we now turn to a discussion of one book in the New Testament? Of what relevance is an examination of the Epistle to the Hebrews to the more recent discussions of biblical theology? Is this simply another retreat to his own territory on the part of a New Testament specialist? One has to start somewhere and, if one's starting point is at the New Testament end of the canon, then of all the New Testament writings Hebrews provides us with the most focused and explicit treatment of the relationship between the new revelation in Christ and God's previous disclosure. One might want to argue that, in their different ways, Matthew, John, or Paul in Romans, come close – but they also treat a number of other major concerns. Hebrews, on the other hand, has as its almost all-encompassing concern issues of continuity and discontinuity between what was believed to have taken place in the life, death and resurrection of Jesus and God's inscripturated revelation. And, in pursuing this concern, Hebrews contains extended expositions of particular scriptural texts in a way that is matched by no other New Testament document.[8]

(ed.), *Biblical Theology*. Scobie's full-scale biblical theology, *Ways of our God*, designates its approach as 'intermediate biblical theology', standing between historical study of the Bible and use of the Bible as Scripture. Yet, apart from its selection of key themes, it remains primarily descriptive.

[6] Cf. Seitz, *Word Without End*; *Figured Out*; Watson, *Text and Truth*; Moberly, *From Eden to Golgotha*; *The Bible, Theology, and Faith*.

[7] Cf., e.g., Placher, *Narratives*; Volf, *Exclusion and Embrace*; Charry, *Renewing*; Ford, *Self and Salvation*.

[8] It is not surprising that Moody Smith, 'Use', 61, could write, 'Perhaps more than any other figure the unknown author of Hebrews deserves the title of the Old Testament theologian of the New'. Hofius, 'Biblische Theologie', has also seen the relevance of Hebrews for this topic.

It might be thought that there is one obvious objection that torpedoes my projected enterprise. If doing biblical theology in some way entails reflecting on the relationship between the two Testaments and hearing their distinctive witnesses together as Scripture, then in what sense can the writer to the Hebrews be said to be a biblical theologian? Obviously he did not have two written Testaments. Instead, his letter would one day become part of the varied witness of the second Testament. But before we decide that this chapter is taking us down a blind alley, it is worth recalling that the writer of Hebrews is by no means in a totally dissimilar situation to that of would-be biblical theologians. What he attempts to bring together, according to 1:1, 2, are God's speaking in the prophets and God's speaking in the Son. Whereas later Christians have these two stages of revelation analogously in the Old Testament and the New Testament, he had Jewish Scripture in its translated Greek form and early Christian traditions about Christ in the light of which he read Scripture and consciously reflected on the relation between the two.[9] Of course, those early Christian traditions were to be elaborated and applied in a variety of ways and genres until they reached the much fuller form in which we have them in our present canon, but they function as an equivalent in embryonic form of the later fuller collection. Might not, therefore, some of the same basic issues of continuity and discontinuity in relating old and new that are confronted in his thinking also be important for ours? In support of this stance it can be claimed that, in fact, one of the subdisciplines of biblical theology has always been the New Testament writers' use of the Old Testament. And the reason for this has been the conviction that, in thinking about the relation between the Testaments, the way the New Testament writers used their Scriptures has a significant part to play in coming to conclusions on the broader matter (though it is by no means the only consideration).[10] So, this chapter will first explore what is entailed in theological reading of Scripture within Hebrews itself, while keeping in view the broader concerns that have already been introduced. We will then take up the latter more explicitly by suggesting how Hebrews might connect with these concerns and will conclude by providing some pointers to a biblical theological approach to Scripture.

---

[9] Cf. also Hofius, 'Biblische Theologie', 108–109.

[10] It is interesting to observe that, although in one place in *Biblical Theology of the Old and New Testaments* Childs, arguably from an overemphasis on a so-called 'discrete witness' of the Old Testament, can backtrack on his earlier view that the New Testament use of the Old Testament is a central category for biblical theology and assert that 'there is no literary or theological warrant for assuming that the forces which shaped the New Testament can be simply extended to the level of Biblical Theology involving theological reflection on both testaments' (76), he can later state in an anachronistic formulation that 'the book of Hebrews represents an important theological attempt at resolving the relation between Old and New Testaments' (312).

Scripture and the Relationship between Old and New in the Rhetorical Structure of Hebrews

It is worth beginning by rehearsing briefly how far Scripture and the relation of old and new in revelation permeate the structure and rhetoric of Hebrews.

The use of Psalm 110:1, 4

As a word of exhortation (13:22), similar to a synagogue homily (cf. Acts 13:15), the pastoral sermon that constitutes the bulk of Hebrews makes extensive use of Scripture and so has prominent midrashic features in individual sections and in the whole composition. Its sermon can, in fact, be seen as an implicit midrash woven around Psalm 110:1, 4. These two verses contain the major theme of Hebrews – the exaltation of Christ at God's right hand (Ps. 110:1) and, more specifically, his exaltation as priest after the order of Melchizedek according to God's oath (Ps. 110:4). It is noticeable that a key verse, 8:1, puts its summary of the writer's message in terms of these two verses from the psalm – 'Now the point in what we are saying is this: we have such a high priest (i.e., not a Levitical one but one after the order of Melchizedek, who has just been discussed) [Ps. 110:4], one who is seated at the right hand of the throne of the Majesty in heaven [Ps. 110:1]'. Psalm 110:1 is there right at the beginning of the sermon; its wording is clearly alluded to in the prologue in 1:3, and then it is actually cited in 1:13. Psalm 110:4 is quoted for the first time in 5:6 and alluded to both in terms of the Melchizedek high priesthood and God's oath through chapters 5 – 7 (cf. 5:10; 6:17, 20; 7:3, 11, 15, 20, 24, 28) and is actually cited twice in this section in 7:17, 21. Then, as we have seen, the two psalm verses are combined in the wording of 8:1 about the main point of the argument. Psalm 110:1 is cited again twice in 10:12, 13 and picked up as a motif at the beginning of the final *paraenesis* or ethical exhortation section in 12:2.

Synkrisis

What has been traditionally talked of in terms of the superiority of Christ to older forms of revelation is seen in rhetorical terms as an example of *synkrisis* – a rhetorical form that compares representatives of a type in order to determine the superiority of one over another. *Synkrisis* functioned in Greco-Roman oratory as a means of praise or blame by comparison and made the comparison in terms of family, natural endowments, education, achievements and death. In Hebrews, various types of Christ or earlier figures are seen as lesser by comparison with him. Family relations (Christ as the divine Son), education (learning perfection through suffering) and death (his once-for-all sacrificial death) all feature in the comparison. This sort of argument structures the discourse because, as in an encomium (a discourse in praise of someone), the *synkrisis* is used for the purpose of moral exhortation. So the comparisons in Hebrews – of angels and the Son, of Moses and Christ, of Aaron and Christ, of the Levitical priesthood and Christ, of the old covenant and the new covenant – are in each case followed by *paraenesis*. Comparison also involves, of course, the argument that, if what God said and did then had such and such consequences, how much more/less is this the case now that God has spoken and acted in this final way in Christ. This overlaps with a Jewish *qal wahomer* type of exegesis, arguing from the lesser to the greater, and one prime example of this is in 9:13, 14: 'For if the blood of goats and bulls ... sanctifies those who have been defiled so that their flesh is purified, how much more will the blood of Christ ... purify our conscience ...' (cf. also 2:2, 3; 10:28, 29; 12:25, 26). This pastoral homily is, then, structured by the comparison and contrast between the two major stages and forms of God's speaking – in the earlier provisional and in the later final, in the old and in the new, in the law and the prophets and in the person of the Son.

Exordium

All of this strikes one immediately, of course, in the introduction, or exordium, of 1:1–4 about God's speaking in the Son. There is difference and discontinuity, because God's speaking in olden times is compared to God's speaking in these last days. The partial and piecemeal revelation through the prophets is compared to the focus of the final revelation in the Son. And there is immediately talk of superiority and inferiority in the comparison because this Son is much superior to the angels, whose mediatorship was considered to enhance the status of the revelation given in the law. Whereas the prophets mediated the divine word, the Son is the embodiment of that word and 'the exact imprint of God's very being' (1:2, 3). At the same time there is also, of course, continuity in the two stages, because in both it is God who has spoken (1:1, 2) and because what God said at the earlier stage can be shown to point to its fulfilment in the later – as the christological interpretation of scriptural texts in 1:5–14 immediately illustrates. This continuity/discontinuity dialectic is part of the comparison that structures the whole letter. The comparison of Christ with the angels, with Moses and with the priesthood in 1:5 – 10:39 is clearly one between the embodiment of the new revelation and the representatives of the old. But what the reader is confronted with from the beginning of this sermon is that what God has done in Christ is the decisive and determinative divine speech-act. According to Hebrews, this means – and this is the thrust of all that follows – that it should be impossible to drift back to an earlier stage of revelation or to hold a view of God's inspired oracles in

Scripture in which these simply sit alongside and are left undisturbed by the new word God has spoken in the Son.

Peroratio

Hebrews 12:18–29 contains all the main features one would expect of a peroratio, as it recapitulates the sermon's message, driving it home for the final time with heightened emotional appeal to the readers. It contains a last major *synkrisis* between the old and new, which paints a graphic picture designed to arouse both fear and gratitude, and is again followed by exhortation. Revelation and access to God for the Israelite covenant assembly at Sinai in Exodus 19 is compared with revelation and access to God for the new covenant assembly at Zion, and a contrast is made between the visible and tangible aspects of the old and the invisible and heavenly realities of the new. As in the comparison of the exordium, there is continuity in that God speaks on both occasions. But whereas the speaking at Sinai was so terrifying that it made the hearers beg not to be addressed further, the speaking from Zion is a gracious speaking through the sprinkled blood of Jesus, the mediator of the new covenant. Again the exhortation, with its 'how much less …' argument, exploits the interplay between the continuity and the discontinuity of the comparison as a vital element for the writer's urgent pastoral message. 'See that you do not refuse the one who is speaking; for if they did not escape when they refused the one who warned them on earth, how much less will we escape if we reject the one who warns from heaven!' (12:25).

Pastoral purpose

The exhortations accompanying the *synkrisis* prompt the question why the writer of Hebrews embarks on this large-scale enterprise of comparison between the new and the old. Of course, his sermon is not concerned with making comparison for its own sake. Rather, on what is arguably the most plausible construal of the letter's purpose, the various comparisons serve the writer's pastoral concern about Jewish Christians who were in danger of losing their hold on their confession about Jesus as the exalted Christ and who, under the pressures of marginalization and trials, were considering abandoning their distinctive christological beliefs in order to merge back into the security of their Jewish heritage. The writer reflects on and expounds his readers' relationship to God's earlier revelation in attempting to clarify for them their identity and its implications and in stressing what is entailed in their being Jewish *Christians*.

Some Features of Hebrews' Christological Reading of Scripture

Christology and confession

In Hebrews it is not just that the old is seen in the light of the new but, more specifically, that Scripture is read in the light of Christ and interpreted in such a way as to show the superiority and finality of what God has done in him. But what is meant by 'christological'? Where does the writer's view of Christ come from? It is not simply a cipher into which he can put any content he wishes. Rather, it is embedded in his early Christian tradition, which already contains interpretation of Jesus' earthly life, his death and exaltation, and his status as God's Son. So in 2:3, 4 he insists that the message of salvation is rooted in Jesus' own teaching and the apostolic message, 'confirmed to us by those who heard him'. And he sees this tradition maintained by the former leaders of the community to which he writes: 'Remember your leaders, those who spoke the word of God to you' (13:7). Most noticeably, he talks about 'the confession' (*homologia*) to indicate the source of the Christology he shares with his addressees. Hebrews 3:1 speaks of 'Jesus, the apostle and high priest of our confession'. Then 4:14, in speaking about Jesus, the Son of God, exhorts, 'Let us hold fast to our confession' and 10:23 repeats, 'Let us hold fast to the confession of our hope'. In line with this emphasis, as is commonly held, 1:2b, 3a right at the outset of the epistle take up the language of a confessional formulation. Yet it is also important to note that this christological confession was already related to and shaped by the Jewish Scriptures. In other words, interaction between the Jewish Scriptures and Christology does not take place for the first time when the writer brings his christological key to the reading of Scripture. Interaction has already been taking place in formulating the Christology that now provides the key. So there should be no room for thinking that a christological interpretation involves merely a one-way movement from the new to the old. In anticipation of this chapter's later reflections, this observation is already suggestive for thinking about biblical theology. For Christians, the reading of Scripture takes place within an ecclesiastical tradition with its confession about Christ. The christological convictions that provide the lenses through which Scripture is read come from a developing tradition. This, of course, immediately tells against the assumption, made by some proponents of biblical theology, that its task needs to be kept quite distinct from concerns of dogmatic theology. And, in line with this, even after some early Christian writings had themselves become part of a developing New Testament canon, the church recognized the need for a theological 'rule of faith' (Irenaeus) to manage the diversity of Scripture. At the same time, it is not as if the early Christian confession about Christ is fixed in its formulation, and it is particularly through bringing it into play with his reading of Scripture that the writer of Hebrews finds new ways of developing the tradition and of going beyond what in 6:1 he calls 'the basic teaching about Christ'. Indeed, Hebrews' central notion of Jesus as the great high priest is precisely an instance of this development. It is a piece of christological reflection and exploration that emerges from thinking about Jesus in relation to reading scriptural texts about priesthood and thereby enriches the theological tradition. As part of this process, the way in which Hebrews employs Melchizedek is particularly instructive. The writer is not content simply to employ Psalm 110:4 in proof-text fashion. He uses all of what the Jewish Scriptures say about this figure and does some creative biblical theology by reading Genesis 14 in the light of both Psalm 110:4 and his christological confession and, without obviously misreading the basic sense of the scriptural texts, he makes them cohere in an overall christological interpretation.

Clearly the Jewish Scriptures function in Hebrews as an authoritative and effective vehicle of communication for the writer's formulation of his word of exhortation. They provide the point of reference, the language and the symbols the writer and his readers have in common. Yet, for the writer, the more significant source of solidarity with his readers is, or should be, their common confession about Christ. Here, however, there is a difference between the strength of his adherence to the confession and the penetration of his insights into it and those of the readers. Nevertheless the Scriptures can be made to serve his attempt to bring the readers closer to his own level of understanding and assurance in regard to the christological confession.

The God who speaks in Scripture

The writer's exhortation underlines that the new message the readers have received about Christ stands in continuity with their heritage. It is the same God who speaks. So, for example, in 3:1–6 the structure of revelation is depicted as *one* house, with God as the builder, in which Moses as servant in the house testifies to the things that were to be spoken later about the one set over the house as Son. In this way God's speaking in the old order retains its validity. 'The message declared through angels was valid' (2:2) and even now can continue to be cited as the oracles of the living God. Yet this God of Scripture is now also characterized in terms of the divine actions in Christ and the Spirit. The first citations of Scripture in the sermon, in 1:5–13, are treated as the utterances of God. But then, in 3:7–11, Psalm 95 is quoted as the direct words of God's Spirit to the readers: 'Therefore, as the Holy Spirit says, "Today, if you hear his voice, do not harden your hearts as in the rebellion ..."' But Scripture can also be seen as the word of Christ, and one of the most striking illustrations of a christological functioning of Scripture is when its texts are in fact placed in the mouth of Christ – as occurs, for example, with Psalm 22:22 and Isaiah 8:17, 18 in Hebrews 2:12, 13 and with Psalm 40:6–8 in Hebrews 10:5–7. In the process, such texts can be slightly altered and updated in conformity to what the writer believes about Jesus so that their wording may be plausibly identified with his words. So here a christological reading functions as part of a conviction that the God of Israel is a triune God who speaks through Scripture. One can also say that in Hebrews' christological reading there remains a movement of thought from God to Christ alongside one from Christ to God.[11] The exordium reflects this. In 1:1, 2 it is the God who spoke to our ancestors through the prophets who in the last days has spoken in the Son. The speaking in the Son is decisive for the divine self-disclosure, so knowledge about Christ is essential to a true knowledge of God. Yet, at the same time, the prior speaking of the God of Israel through the prophets is the presupposition without which the final speaking in the Son would not properly make sense.

The messianic use of texts

Elsewhere, the Jewish Scriptures function christologically in a more traditional sense, with the old yielding its fullest meaning in the light of the new through the messianic use of texts. Some take up an already established messianic tradition of interpretation – for example, the use of Psalm 2:7 and 2 Samuel 7:14 in Hebrews 1:5 or the extensive use of Psalm 110:1. Others appear to innovate – for example, the use of Psalm 8:4–6 in Hebrews 2:6–9. With such messianic readings it is, of course, not a matter of proving various convictions about Christ's person or work from Scripture. These are already assumed as part of the Christian confession so that, when the Scripture is read with these convictions, certain of its features are found to lend themselves to this interpretation from the new perspective. At the same time, however, it has to be noted that, because of the writer's convictions about Christ as the pre-existent Son and as one with God, he now finds in such texts that which would never have been said of any human being, even of the Messiah.[12]

Typology

The typology of Hebrews has a christological and eschatological thrust, whereby Scripture is seen to provide foreshadowings, partial anticipations of

---

[11] It is strange that Barr, *Old and New*, 153–54, finds it necessary to set a Trinitarian reading of the Old Testament over against a christological one and to argue for a direction of thought from God to Christ and not from Christ to God. Theologically speaking, any proper christological approach will also be a Trinitarian one, and Father and Son will be mutually interpreting.

[12] Hofius, 'Biblische Theologie', 114–17, makes this point strongly.

the good things to come – the realities that have now become present in Christ. On the one hand, typology depends on some basic continuity, on correspondences between the various stages of the same God's working. And yet, on the other hand, discontinuity is introduced by the way the reality and finality of the antitype is shown to transcend, to be superior to its type. This can be seen, for example, in 3:7 – 4:13, where the resting place of the land becomes, through a link with God's Sabbath rest, a type of the rest of eschatological salvation inaugurated by Christ in God's new 'today' (cf. 3:13, 14). On the one hand, there is a discontinuity because believers are already entering the rest (4:3). But, on the other hand, since the consummation of the rest is still future, there is a continuity because they too need to be exhorted to make every effort to enter the rest, lest they fall through the same sort of disobedience that afflicted the wilderness generation (4:11). The interplay between continuity and discontinuity essential to typology is also what contributes to the effectiveness of the writer's *paraenesis*. The fulfilment in the antitype raises the stakes for Christian believers. As a result of God's oath, the wilderness generation fell by the sword (cf. Num. 14:43). But those the writer of Hebrews is addressing face something more fearful than any two-edged sword – the lethal weapon of God's word of judgement, which will expose the intentions of their hearts and render them defenceless before the consuming gaze of the one to whom account must be given (4:11–13).

Relativization of the old

The christological reading of Scripture in Hebrews entails some relativizing of the old revelation in the light of the new. This is seen in three main overlapping ways: 1) Scripture points beyond itself by indicating its own inadequacy. This then entails 2) a discontinuity between the old revelation and the new one in Christ, and 3) in the light of the latter the old can now be seen as having been ineffectual.

God's revelation in Scripture can be quoted to show its 'self-confessed inadequacy', as G.B. Caird phrased it.[13] Perhaps the clearest example of this phenomenon is in 8:8–13, where the words of Jeremiah 31 are employed to argue that its prophecy of a new covenant obviously entailed that the first one must be deficient in some way – otherwise there would have been no need for a new one. In 7:11 a similar point had been made in connection with Psalm 110:4. Why, the writer asks, does the psalmist speak here of a different priesthood after the order of Melchizedek, if the old Aaronic order was perfectly adequate? Understood in the full light of what God has now done in Christ, Scripture itself attests to the inadequacy of the earlier covenant and its priesthood.

---

[13] Caird, 'Exegetical Method', 47–49.

When the old revelation is seen particularly as inscripturated law covenant, the greatest stress on discontinuity emerges. This note is sounded in the theological argumentation that sets out Christ's superiority to the angels, to Moses and to the Aaronic priesthood – the representatives of the law. As 7:11–19 make clear, for Hebrews the law and the priesthood share the same transience. And, since there was clearly meant to be a change in the priesthood, the writer argues, of necessity there must also be a change in the validity and permanence of the law that established it (7:12). So the law, declared by angels (2:2), mediated by faithful Moses (3:2–5) and administered by the Levitical priesthood (7:5–28), is demonstrated to be not only preliminary but also imperfect, inferior to the new revelation in Christ. The strongest language is employed to express the discontinuity in the central theological section of the letter in 8:1 – 10:18. In 8:6–13, in the contrast between the first and second covenants, the former is said to be deficient and obsolete and ready to vanish away. And later in 10:8–10, again in terms of first and second and this time with special reference to sacrifices, the first – God's will as expressed in the law – is described as abolished in order to establish the second – God's will as embodied in Christ.

In context these texts clearly show that a christological reading of the Jewish Scriptures does not mean that the old simply leads into the new as a natural extension. In places, the new's fulfilment of the old is seen to entail not only that the old's institutions are no longer valid, but also that they never really worked properly at all. One of the reasons given in chapter 7 (cf. esp. vv. 18, 19) for the law's commandment about priesthood having been abrogated is that it was weak and ineffectual and the law was unable to make anything perfect – and perfection, or completion, is one of Hebrews' key notions for the eschatological salvation brought by Christ. This point is elaborated in 9:1 – 10:18. The first covenant's regulations for worship entailed two tents – a first or outer tent, into which the priests enter continually, and a second, inner tent, into which only the high priest goes, and then only once a year. Hebrews draws on the Jewish tradition that the divisions in the tabernacle or temple mirror the division between earth and heaven, the inaccessibility of the holy of holies representing the separateness from earth of God's holy presence in heaven. Yet instead of holding that the cosmic structuring reinforces the validity of these worship arrangements, Hebrews draws a different and radical conclusion about the ineffectiveness of all sacrifices performed in the earthly tents. 'By this the Holy Spirit indicates that the way into the sanctuary has not yet been disclosed as long as the first tent is still standing' (9:8). There was no genuine access to God in heaven while the old system was still operating. So what was going on with these sacrifices? Here Hebrews introduces another outer/inner distinction. The sacrifices and arrangements were temporary 'regulations for the body' (9:10) and purified the flesh (9:13), but they could not 'perfect the conscience of the worshiper' (9:9) or 'purify our conscience from dead works to worship the living God' (9:14). In contrast, Christ's once-for-all sacrifice brings him into the heavenly tent of God's presence (9:11, 12) and reaches the parts of humans other sacrifices cannot reach. A further aspect of this radical conclusion is spelled out in 10:1–4, where, in a formulation that appears to draw on both Jewish eschatological notions and middle Platonic terminology, the law is said to have 'only a shadow of the good things to come and not the true form of these realities' and so could have no power to deal with sin – 'it is impossible for the blood of bulls and goats to take away sins'. Finally, the innovative christological reading of Scripture in 10:5–11 makes the same point decisively. Christ is portrayed as quoting Psalm 40:6–8 on coming into the world: 'Sacrifices and offerings you have not desired ...'. Of course, this critique of sacrifices is not uncommon in the Jewish Scriptures themselves but is never absolute. Yet, with Christ's announcement of this critique and of his coming to do God's will, Hebrews draws a sharp contrast between the two. With the coming of Jesus it is not simply that God does not want sacrifices unless other acts of obedience accompany them or are made primary. Rather, God no longer wants those sorts of sacrifices at all (cf. 10:8, 9). Instead the offering of Christ's body is the once-for-all sacrifice for sins (10:10, 12, 14). It is not that sacrifices were never God's will but that, now that Jesus has come, sacrifices – and therefore, by implication, the functioning of the Jerusalem temple – are no longer God's will. Yet it is also not the case that the significance of blood sacrifices and priesthood can be left behind as obsolete, but that Christ is now for ever the perfect sacrifice and priest, providing immediate and full access to God's holiness.

Does Hebrews' Christological Reading Have a Coherent Hermeneutical Framework?

It has become clear, then, that in Hebrews the recognition of the Jewish Scriptures as the authoritative word of God is quite compatible not only with their serving as a vehicle for expressing the significance of Christ and the implications of the Christian gospel, but also, within this pastoral purpose, with parts of the earlier revelation of the Jewish Scriptures being seen as superseded by God's final word in Christ and as no longer functioning as regulative norms for the community's worship or ethics. For some interpreters, the task of biblical theology is to find the 'inner logic' that holds the Bible as a whole together. Is there a compelling hermeneutical logic to the christological approach to Scripture employed by Hebrews? A number of possible explanations might be offered.

Ceremonial/moral distinction

It is often thought that the difference Christ makes to the earlier stage of revelation can be summed up in terms of its ceremonial parts being done away with and its moral aspects remaining. In the post-apostolic church this distinction in dealing with the OT was most fully developed by Tertullian (cf. *De Pudicitia* 6:3–5), and on the surface it seems to be appropriate for Hebrews on the assumption that the obsolescence of the first covenant really refers to its ceremonial and cultic aspects, its priesthood and sacrificial system. It should be remembered, however, that this distinction deals only with the use of the law and not with other parts of Scripture, and even then it proves to be deficient as an explanation for Hebrews' treatment. It fails to do justice to the fact that for Hebrews, as we have seen, cultic and ceremonial aspects have become antiquated not simply in themselves but as part of a larger whole, the first covenant as such and its law. When Hebrews refers to the law, it is to the entire Sinaitic covenant, including its ethical commandments (9:19). What is said about priesthood cannot be separated neatly from ethical issues, because priests offered sacrifices for sins, including transgressions of moral laws. A change in the priesthood entails a change in the law as a whole (7:12); the two share the same transience. And because Jesus is the mediator of a better covenant, the first covenant as a whole is held to have become obsolete and about to disappear (8:6–13).

Promise/law perspective

Since, in addition to talking about the law having been changed, Hebrews also employs the language of promise, this raises the question whether Hebrews might contain a logic that compares with Paul's promise/law hermeneutic found in Galatians 3 and Romans 4. In fact, in 6:13 – 7:27 Hebrews does have its own intriguing version of this, in which promise is seen to be operative within Scripture both before and after law. As in Paul, the promise is linked with Abraham (6:13, 14; cf. also 11:8–19). But to the notion of promise, Hebrews adds that of God's oath from Genesis 22:16. The writer's interest in God's oath in Psalm 110:4 has already been noted, and this treatment of Abraham prepares for a return to that text. Hebrews 6:18 goes on to speak of two unchangeable realities, in which it is impossible that God should prove false – the divine promise and oath. Understanding Scripture in the light of what has happened in Christ, Hebrews can go on to say that Christian believers also have these realities. And 6:19, 20 make clear that the form in which they now have God's promise-oath is in the exaltation of Jesus on their behalf to heaven and his presence there as a high priest for ever after the order of Melchizedek. This is spelled out explicitly a little later in 7:20–22. In the better hope of the new covenant promise its high priest was addressed with an oath: 'The Lord has sworn and will not change his mind, "You are a priest for ever."' God has gone on oath and Jesus as high priest is the living embodiment of that oath, just as, as Son, he is God's final word (1:2). Now the law came later than the promise-oath to Abraham – at the time of the Levitical priesthood (7:11a), but the law does not supersede the promise-oath, because there would have been no need for a second promise-oath about a priest according to the order of Melchizedek if the law was meant to be permanent or if it was effectual (cf. 7:11b, 18). As 7:28 asserts, 'For the law appoints as high priests those who are subject to weakness, but the word of the oath, which came later than the law, appoints a Son who has been made perfect for ever'. But this creative christological reading has more to offer when the Genesis 14 account of Abraham and Melchizedek is brought into the picture. Now the law can already be seen to be relativized at the time of Abraham – before it was actually given. The argument is, briefly, as follows. The law gave the Levites the right to collect tithes from the rest of the people, who, like the Levites, are descended from Abraham (7:5). But this entire schema of law operative among Abraham's descendants is brought into question by the account of Abraham the patriarch – the father of them all – giving tithes to Melchizedek, who stood completely outside this system (7:4). In terms of the principle of solidarity, where the one represents the many, Abraham's action represents that of his descendants, including Levi, who can thereby be seen to be recognizing the superiority of the Melchizedek priesthood and the inferiority of the law, its priesthood and its tithing regulations (cf. 7:7–10). In the light of the one who now embodies the Melchizedek priesthood, by blessing Abraham who had received the promises, Melchizedek confirms the promise and at the same time, by collecting tithes from him, he relativizes the law as no longer valid (cf. 7:6).

This passage illustrates a promise/law hermeneutic operating more generally. Scripture witnesses to the one who fulfils God's promise-oath and, in the light of that fulfilment, Scripture can now also be seen to witness to the inadequacy and obsolescence of the law. This hermeneutic serves the theological point that the law is now to be seen as ineffectual in dealing with humanity's sin and that, with the certainty and immutability of the fulfilment of the promise-oath in Christ, God takes full and decisive responsibility for dealing with that sin once and for all.

Theological exposition/paraenesis

As a general rule, as G. Hughes in particular has pointed out,[14] there appears to be more of an emphasis on continuity in the sections of *paraenesis* and more of

---

[14] Cf. Hughes, *Hebrews and Hermeneutics*, 54–73.

an emphasis on discontinuity in the sections of theological exposition. Discontinuity is to the fore in the exposition of the comparison between God's word in Christ and the Mosaic law and covenant. But continuity is stronger in the exhortations. So the *paraenesis* of 3:7 – 4:13 is a midrashic application of Psalm 95 to the believers' lives. The exhortation to endurance and faithfulness in 10:36–39 makes direct use of the words of Habakkuk 2:3, 4. And throughout Hebrews 11 the faith of figures from the Jewish Scriptures is treated as a model for Christian believers. Then, in 12:5, 6, such believers can be addressed directly as sons or children by the exhortation of Proverbs 3:11, 12: 'My child, do not regard lightly the discipline of the Lord ...'. But in all such exhortation it is not as if the readers are simply thought of as in precisely the same situation as their earlier counterparts. Their new situation as believers in Christ is assumed, and it is the combination of the text with this situation that gives rise to a new form of the word of God that addresses them. This can be seen in the way the LXX wording of Psalm 8 can be exploited to fit the situation of Christian believers in 2:6–9; in the way the resting place of the land in 3:7 – 4:13 becomes the eschatological rest of salvation, into which believers already enter; or in the way it can be said of Moses in the creative anachronism[15] of 11:26 that 'he considered abuse suffered for the Christ to be greater wealth than the treasures of Egypt'.

The already/not yet of eschatology

The tension between the role of God's earlier revelation in some places continuing to provide God's word to the Christian community and yet in others being dismissed as obsolete can also be seen to reflect the writer's eschatology, as again G. Hughes in particular has persuasively shown.[16] In other words, one of the filters that determines for the writer how much continuity and how much discontinuity there will be as the Jewish Scriptures function for Christian believers is his experience of the end times, his belief about what has happened in the Son in these last days. In the theological sections, with their christological focus, the writer is stressing the 'already' of what God has done in Christ, the finality of its fulfilment of the old, its embodiment of permanent heavenly reality – and it is here that the earlier revelation is seen to be most relativized and outmoded by its own culmination. Yet the end has not fully

---

[15] Koester, *Hebrews*, 69, 72, 118, talks of the writer's creatively anachronistic depictions of both Abraham and Moses.

[16] Cf. Hughes, *Hebrews and Hermeneutics*, 66–73, 108–109, where he speaks of the Christian experience of the end as 'the hermeneutical "screen" which has been placed across the scriptures, allowing them to speak with immediacy or blocking them off as outdated'.

come, and believers have to press on to the ultimate eschatological goal, and it is here that the writer finds the closest continuity with the older revelation. Scriptural exhortations to faith, perseverance and endurance can still apply or be updated, as can their promises and threats of judgement, while believers' 'not yet' continues. So it is not only a relation between the present and the past that is operative in a christological reading of Scripture, but also a relationship between both of these and the future. The language of promise from Scripture comes into play again here (with the promise to Abraham, the promise of rest and a city to come, the promise of a new covenant), and with it the notion of promise and fulfilment. Indeed, the whole of Scripture can be seen as promise. The opening statement that in the past God spoke through the prophets is not to be interpreted narrowly. In fact, of the thirty-one actual scriptural citations in Hebrews, seven are from the Prophets, twelve from the Pentateuch, and twelve from the Writings (eleven from Psalms, and one from Proverbs). This suggests that, for Hebrews, all of Scripture is being viewed as prophetic. Scripture's promises witness to a future beyond its own boundaries, and that future itself then has two stages in the last days – present fulfilment and future consummation. Which of these two stages is in view determines the writer's choice and use of scriptural texts for his argument.

Quotation/retelling

But there is another pattern at work in regard to the christological interpretation of Scripture in which there appears to be a discrimination taking place between speech and narrative.[17] Strikingly, the actual quotations of Scripture all involve direct address and constitute an oracular authoritative word into the present. But scriptural narrative is never quoted. Instead, Hebrews deals with these parts of Scripture by retelling or paraphrasing them. This provides a more distancing effect than the direct address and allows the writer's Christian convictions to reshape the telling. In the retold narrative sections, the distinctive status of Israel's national institutions and past leaders is downplayed and scriptural narrative is reoriented to become the preparatory history of Christian believers in which its heroes (cf. the retelling in chapter 11) can be seen as pre-Christ Christian marginalized outsiders.

If finding one overall explanatory pattern is the aim in searching for a coherent hermeneutical framework for Hebrews' christological interpretation, then this has not proved to be possible. Instead, what appears to be the case is that the christological key produces a number of general patterns of coherence in the reading of Scripture. No one formulation of the logic, however, is able

---

[17] For an extended and persuasive account of this distinction, see Eisenbaum, *Jewish Heroes*, esp. 89–133.

adequately to capture the diversity of the moves between old and new generated by the writer's christological reading. Hebrews' approach to biblical theology is one which, at the same time as offering some guidelines, suggests that any search for one master method is likely to be a frustrating one. Rather, through its own intricate interweaving of the new and the old, it indicates that attempts to remain faithful to both in christological readings of Scripture can be open-ended, allowing for diverse and new approaches, for creativity, and for the emergence of further insights into the dialectic between the two stages of revelation.

Hebrews and Biblical Theology

At least one thing should be clear. The writer of Hebrews does his theology by reading Scripture. There is a sense in which it is not only the arguments and conclusions derived from such reading, but also the close readings themselves, done in the light of his christological convictions, that constitute his theology. In other words, a Christian reading of Scripture is both Hebrews' theological method and also, to a large extent, provides its theological content.

In this biblical theology a confident commitment to Christ and the Christian confession, shaped by ongoing tradition, is brought to the Jewish Scriptures in the conviction that they are God's word and that therefore both the earlier and the later form of that word need to be taken seriously. But such a description and our discussion of patterns of coherence are in danger of remaining much too abstract. They leave out two key elements – the writer who is doing the relating of the old and new and the audience (and its situation) for whom it is being done. This is not an argument for delving behind and outside the epistle for further information about the actual author and recipients, which would in any case be particularly problematic in the case of Hebrews. Rather, it is noting that justice needs to be done to what is clear from the letter's rhetoric and clues in its exhortation. Namely, its comparison of the old and the new is not some neutral objective attempt to come up with a comprehensively coherent way of relating the two groups of revelatory data. The comparison is made, as indicated briefly earlier, from a pastoral concern, arising from the pressing needs of a specific situation in the lives of a particular group of believers. The writer selects certain texts or passages of Scripture because they are perceived to be appropriate to his pastoral task, enabling him to work with the necessary theological questions and to provide a persuasive christological interpretation. If, as Jewish Christians, the addressees are to hold on to and grow in a distinctive Christian identity, they need to see *both* how their Christian confession is compatible with their Scriptures, fulfilling its symbols and promises, *and* how it is a final and determinative word from God, transforming their past and calling them to the continued faith in Christ and to the more strenuous appropriation of the worship and patterns of behaviour that this better form of God's word requires. So this is by no means a disinterested reading of Scripture. Yet at the same time its creative and agenda-driven readings for the most part, and to a remarkable extent, do not simply drown out any so-called 'discrete' witness of the texts. It is not as though the writer's christological convictions simply go hunting for scriptural prooftexts that will support them. The reading of the old in the light of the new is much more holistic than this. There is a dialectic at work in which reading Scripture can also shed further light for writer and readers on their new life in Christ. If the Jewish Scriptures are interpreted by what happened with Jesus, so also what happened with Jesus is interpreted by the Jewish Scriptures.

In the mix of ingredients for Hebrews' biblical theology, therefore, are pastoral concern and empathy leading to teaching and exhortation geared to a specific setting. And what makes this version of biblical theology effective is a further combination of qualities and characteristics that the writer brings to the task. Imagination and creativity are wedded to a mastery of contemporary exegetical and rhetorical skills and techniques in order to make his christological advocacy as persuasive as possible. At the same time, the writer's contemporary worldview shapes his understanding of what has happened in Christ and of its implications. That worldview is informed primarily by the Jewish eschatology found in apocalyptic writings, which saw history as divided into this age and the age to come and as being played out in the two halves of the cosmos – heaven and earth. But it appears that the writer is a Hellenistic Jew who has also been influenced by some of the thinking and formulations of the middle Platonism of his time.[18] So, for example, as we have observed, he contrasts earthly shadows with their true form in the heavenly invisible world (8:5; 10:1). He also contrasts the created and transient world of earth and heaven with a more permanent and stable realm and therefore associates believers with what will remain (12:26–29).

If Hebrews serves as a forerunner of biblical theology, then it is the type of biblical theology in which interpreters bring to their reading of the two Testaments as Scripture their Christian beliefs shaped by the theological tradition and by contemporary thought, the perceived needs and issues faced by the church in its life in the world, and a whole range of reading skills – all in order to discern how Scripture might speak afresh in this encounter and to provide as persuasive advocacy as possible for the message that emerges. And, for Hebrews, such a process can be attributed to the work of God's Spirit. The Spirit, who originally confirmed the Christian message to believers (2:3, 4), discloses the connection between Scripture and Christ (9:8) and enables God's scriptural word to speak

---

[18] For a good recent discussion of this aspect of the thought of Hebrews, see Schenck, 'Philo'.

again to the later situation of Christian believers (3:7; 10:15). This clearly runs counter to any notion of doing biblical theology purely as an academic enterprise in which the attempt is made to present a descriptive account of the relation between the Testaments or of a succession of its themes.

What appears to be going on instead in Hebrews is someone asking the following question: given the Jewish Scriptures and given what has happened in Christ, how do I now hear the word of God for this new setting in the life of God's people? It is not surprising, then, that the bulk of Hebrews takes the form of a sermon, or homily. It indicates that one of the primary settings for doing biblical theology in this sense is preaching.[19] In many churches preachers are presented with the opportunity for doing biblical theology every week when they look at the lectionary readings. How many, rather than picking one of the three readings (usually one from the New Testament), consider deliberately relating the Old Testament and the New Testament in an attempt to hear the word of God, given the diverse witness of both Testaments? Clearly this is not the only way God speaks to the church from Scripture. God speaks from individual passages and individual books, but our hearing and interpretation of these is consciously or unconsciously in some broader canonical and theological context. But Hebrews is also helpful here, because it relates God's word across the two great epochs and also listens to that word from particular scriptural passages interpreted within the larger patterns.[20]

But the same contextual issues entailed in biblical theology as preaching hold for more critical systematic reflection. That Hebrews itself has become part of the canon should not be thought to entail that the pastoral orientation of its message has been transcended and that one can now simply offer descriptions of the two Testaments taken together, shorn of Hebrews' elements of contingency, as the determinative word for any further theological reflection. The writer of Hebrews is clearly critical in his theological reflection, wrestling both with the issue of where the continuity between the two stages of revelation lies and where the discontinuity between them is such that parts of the former have to be critiqued and pronounced no longer directly applicable. Biblical theology which takes Hebrews as one possible model for its work will need to continue to be critical in the same way, not holding that questions of either continuity or discontinuity have been settled for all time. Instead, it will continue to work at fresh solutions in the light of central convictions about Christ and both the interpretative methods and the needs of its own time.[21]

---

[19] France, 'Writer', relates Hebrews to the tradition of modern expository preaching.

[20] France, 'Writer', 260–72, isolates and discusses seven such scriptural passages which the writer of Hebrews expounds.

[21] On biblical theology in the light of Hebrews as a critical discipline, see also Hofius, 'Biblische Theologie', 124–25.

Why do this sort of biblical theology? Scholars have enough to do keeping up with what have become the isolated disciplines of Old Testament or New Testament or theology. Unless we are to think of it as the scholarly domain of one or two geniuses who have the inclination to penetrate the worlds of these three disciplines, the mandate and motivation for the rest of us has to be similar to that of the preacher – the conviction that there are theological resources in Scripture taken as a whole that can speak to needs within the church and the world in our own time. This is, of course, to argue that biblical theology should be a consciously Christian theological and pastoral (in the broadest sense of the term) enterprise. It means that biblical theology is not a preliminary project, upon whose completion systematic or constructive theology depends, but that theological concerns are involved from the outset. It means, too, that biblical theology requires not only the reading skills traditionally thought to belong to biblical scholars. Biblical theology also requires the ability to participate in the present-day articulation of Christian faith traditionally thought to belong to Christian theologians and ethicists. This version of biblical theology also connects with the best insights of postmodernism in its critiques of a supposed objectivity that hides particular interests and of so-called totalizing projects.

There are two further and interrelated issues that Hebrews raises for biblical theology. If Hebrews can relativize and critique parts of its authoritative Scriptures in the light of what has happened in Christ (see above), should not any biblical theology that adopts its approach be prepared to critique and relativize parts of its Scriptures – including now, of course, the New Testament, in the light of its central confession about the gospel of the crucified and risen Jesus?[22] It is relatively easy, though by no means undisputed, to see what this might mean in areas where the New Testament writers applied the gospel to their own first-century context and issued exhortations also shaped by the patriarchy, the master-slave relationships and the views of sexuality of the time. In faithfulness to the same gospel, present-day Christians might well see it necessary to take up quite different ethical stances. Much more difficult, because the issue is so much more central to early Christian proclamation, is to see what it might mean for another area with which the New Testament, and particularly

---

[22] Hebrews, of course, carries out its critique because it views Christ as the definitive eschatological fulfilment of its Scriptures. This proposal does not imply that present-day interpreters have some further normative revelation that enables them to do something similar. It entails that the same norm, not an additional one, is applied to documents that are the human, and therefore culturally conditioned, witnesses to the eschatological fulfilment in Christ and are not simply to be identified with that fulfilment itself. It also entails recognizing that the fulfilment in Christ has both an already and a not yet aspect and that the specific implications of this for later settings remain to be worked out by responsible interpreters under the guidance of the Spirit.

Hebrews itself, confronts biblical theology – namely, what is commonly labelled as Christian supersessionism vis-à-vis Judaism. To discuss this issue at all adequately would require another chapter, but it should at least be briefly clarified.

What sort of attitude to Judaism would Hebrews have encouraged among its actual readers? Wilson rightly points out that this is a question to which not enough attention is paid.[23] His own answer is that 'the author would have encouraged his readers … to form a clear and unambiguous judgement: Judaism is defunct, because it has been surpassed'.[24] But if, as is most likely, author and readers were themselves Jews, this answer requires qualification. Indeed, the notion of this document's relation to Judaism could be held to be an anachronistic one, if it suggests that author and readers saw themselves as standing outside their religious heritage and having an attitude towards its basic set of convictions from which they had now distanced themselves by converting to the new religion of Christianity. Rather, from their own perspective, it was not so much that Judaism was defunct but more that their religion and its central symbols had now been decisively fulfilled in Christ. Because of this fulfilment, furthermore, new ways of expressing their worship of and obedience to Israel's God had become appropriate, and new ways of interpreting their Scriptures had become inevitable. Nevertheless, it is also the case that these Jewish Christians were a minority and that the conflict of their beliefs with those of the majority of Jews were already entailing decisions with social consequences about whether their primary allegiance lay with the majority or with their own small assemblies of Jewish Christians. Talking of Hebrews' attitude to Judaism is, in this qualified sense, not anachronistic, since it reminds us that what has come to be called 'the parting(s) of the ways' is already implicit in this epistle's exhortations.[25] Once the separation had clearly set in after 135 AD and Hebrews became a text whose later readers were primarily Gentile Christians who had little contact with the Judaism of their own time, then its denigration of the earlier stage of Judaism would easily have been thought to apply to Judaism as such.

For present-day Christian readers of Hebrews the issue may not be the document's supersessionism as such, but rather particular implications that have been drawn from this. After all, as Gordon suggests,[26] both Christianity and Judaism are supersessionist in regard to the religion of the Jewish Scriptures. Both abandoned the central form of worship that involved satisfying God by

---

[23] Wilson, *Related Strangers*, 110–11.

[24] Wilson, *Related Strangers*, 122–23.

[25] Dunn, *Partings*, 91, concludes, 'it is difficult to avoid talking of a parting of the ways in the case of Hebrews'.

[26] Gordon, *Hebrews*, 27–28.

means of animal sacrifices and developed new systems for dealing with the major concerns of holiness and sin. Both developed new sets of authoritative writings through which the Jewish Scriptures were to be interpreted. But these observations take us only so far. Judaism remains in strong continuity with its Scriptures in holding the study and practice of Torah to be its covenantal worship of the one true God. What Hebrews says about the passing of the old covenant, with its law, and the fulfilment of the promise of a new covenant in Christ stands in clear contradiction to this. So the issue, with which a fair amount of recent theology has been struggling[27] and with which biblical theology in particular must continue to wrestle, is whether, and if so how, it is possible to respect the continuing religious validity of the synagogue in its various forms while still holding to the claim at the heart of Hebrews and the New Testament witness as a whole – namely, that Jesus Christ is the decisive revelation of God for all human beings. This is a pressing issue because of the Shoah, but, once the matter has been brought to Christian attention and by whatever means, it becomes clear that the issue is also bound up with a significant difference between the position of present-day Christians and those of the New Testament period. The latter, including the writer of Hebrews, expected the theological tension between Christians and non-Christian Jews to be resolved within a generation by the Parousia of Christ at the end of the age. The biblical theology of Hebrews has as its primary concern to convince Jewish Christians of the distinctiveness and validity of their new confession and its implications in relation to their heritage. While not neglecting significant elements of continuity with the Jewish past, the emphasis in its rhetoric and theology is to stress the 'already' of God's decisive word in such a way as to draw strong negative deductions about central elements of that past in order to prevent its readers simply drifting back to their previous convictions. As with all powerful theological statements forged in particular and contingent settings, there are likely to be both gains and losses when these are appropriated by later generations who are removed from the original situations that produced them.[28] This is particularly so in the case of Hebrews. Over against the gains in insight into Christology, the atonement, the nature of Christian existence and the decisive newness of the covenant established in Christ have to be set the losses, once its later readers are primarily Gentile Christians, of any existential sense of continuity with a Jewish heritage and of their being encouraged to think of Judaism,

---

[27] See Soulen, *God of Israel*, for one recent attempt to deal with the continuing validity of Judaism from a Christian perspective.

[28] Cf. also Brown, *Churches*, 117, who contends with reference to the various New Testament theologies that 'for every theological insight one pays a price. The more brilliant the insight, the more likely that other aspects of truth will be put into the shade, often to be overlooked and forgotten.'

to take up Wilson's language, simply as 'defunct, because it has been surpassed'. When the 'not yet' of Hebrews has turned into over nineteen hundred years, in which both the Jewish synagogue has continued and Gentile Christian attitudes to Jews have often been lamentable and entailed tragic consequences, some different biblical theologizing from that of Hebrews, though no less faithful and creative, may well be required. With Hebrews, it will grapple with the consequences of an affirmation of God's once-for-all revelation in Christ, while attempting to do greater justice to the continuity as well as the discontinuity with Judaism, to God's continuing election of Israel and to the acknowledgement that 'God's history with Israel and the nations is the permanent and enduring medium of God's work as the Consummator of human creation and therefore ... also the permanent and enduring context of the gospel about Jesus'.[29]

The claim of this chapter as a whole has been that Hebrews is more than simply esoteric first-century exegesis of Scripture in the cause of promoting belief in Christ. Christians now find its interpretative project within their Scripture and its embryonic biblical theology compels them to ask how they construe the unity of the two Testaments in the light of their theological confession about Christ and their ecclesial and cultural setting. In their pursuit of and critical reflection on this task, Hebrews can remind them of the danger of thinking that there is one overall schema that will serve as a solution; of the interesting variety of factors, not simply Scripture texts themselves, to be taken up in enabling the combination of Old and New Testaments to speak afresh to new issues and new settings; and of the challenges to their traditional theological construals that may be entailed in the process.

---

[29] Soulen, *God of Israel*, 110.

Bibliography

Barr, J., *The Semantics of Biblical Language* (London: Oxford University Press, 1961)

—, *Biblical Words for Time* (London: SCM Press, 1962)

—, *Old and New in Interpretation* (London: SCM Press, 1966)

—, *The Concept of Biblical Theology: An Old Testament Perspective* (Minneapolis: Fortress Press; London: SCM Press, 1999)

Brown, R.E., *The Churches the Apostles Left Behind* (New York: Paulist Press, 1984)

Caird, G.B., 'The Exegetical Method of the Epistle to the Hebrews', *CJT* 5 (1959), 44–51

Charry, E., *By the Renewing of Your Minds* (Oxford: Oxford University Press, 1997)

Childs, B.S., *Biblical Theology in Crisis* (Philadelphia: Westminster Press, 1970)

—, *Biblical Theology of the Old and New Testaments: Theological Reflection on the Christian Bible* (London: SCM Press; Minneapolis: Fortress Press, 1992)

Dunn, J.D.G., *The Partings of the Ways between Christianity and Judaism* (London: SCM Press, 1991)

Eisenbaum, P.M., *The Jewish Heroes of Christian History: Hebrews 11 in Literary Context* (Atlanta: Scholars Press, 1997)

Ford, D.F., *Self and Salvation* (Cambridge: Cambridge University Press, 1999)

France, R.T., 'The Writer of Hebrews as a Biblical Expositor', *TynBul* 47 (1996), 245–76

Gordon, R.P., *Hebrews* (Sheffield: Sheffield Academic Press, 2000)

Hafemann, S.J. (ed.), *Biblical Theology: Retrospect and Prospect* (Leicester: Apollos; Downers Grove, IL: InterVarsity Press, 2002)

Hofius, O., 'Biblische Theologie im Lichte des Hebräerbriefes', in *New Directions in Biblical Theology* (ed. S. Pedersen; Leiden: Brill, 1994), 108–25

Hughes, G., *Hebrews and Hermeneutics* (Cambridge: Cambridge University Press, 1979)

Koester, C.R., *Hebrews* (AB 36; New York: Doubleday, 2001)

Lehne, S., *The New Covenant in Hebrews* (Sheffield: Sheffield Academic Press, 1990)

Moberly, R.W.L., *From Eden to Golgotha: Essays in Biblical Theology* (Atlanta: Scholars Press, 1992)

—, *The Bible, Theology, and Faith* (Cambridge: Cambridge University Press, 2000)

Placher, W.C., *Narratives of a Vulnerable God* (Louisville, KY: Westminster John Knox Press, 1994)

Sandys-Wunsch, J., and L. Eldredge, 'J.P. Gabler's "The Distinction between Biblical and Dogmatic Theology"', *SJT* 33 (1980), 133–58

Schenck, K.L., 'Philo and the Epistle to the Hebrews: Ronald Williamson's Study after Thirty Years', *Studia Philonica Annual* 14 (2002), 112–35

Scobie, C.H.H., *The Ways of our God: An Approach to Biblical Theology* (Grand Rapids: Eerdmans, 2003)

Seitz, C.R., *Word Without End: The Old Testament as Abiding Theological Witness* (Grand Rapids: Eerdmans, 1998)

—, *Figured Out: Typology and Providence in Christian Scripture* (Louisville, KY: Westminster John Knox Press, 2001)

Smith, D.M., 'The Use of the Old Testament in the New', in *The Use of the Old Testament in the New and Other Essays* (ed. J.M. Efird; Durham, NC: Duke University Press, 1972), 3–65

Soulen, R.K., *The God of Israel and Christian Theology* (Minneapolis: Fortress Press, 1996)

Volf, M., *Exclusion and Embrace* (Nashville: Abingdon Press, 1996)

Watson, F., *Text and Truth: Redefining Biblical Theology* (Edinburgh: T. & T. Clark, 1997)

Wilson, S.G., *Related Strangers: Jews and Christians 70–170 C.E.* (Minneapolis: Fortress Press, 1985)

Theological Interpretation and Biblical Theology

13

Systematic – In What Sense?

Trevor Hart

We systematic theologians stand among the biblical theologians in this volume as aliens in the land and I hope my essay will be received with the sort of generosity which the Old Testament urges upon its readers as appropriate for the treatment of such. The New Testament, of course, urges similar things with respect to enemies, but that seems to be stretching a point unnecessarily! But I find, in fact, that the direction which my reflections have taken goes some way toward undermining even alien status for a systematician among biblical theologians. So that has ruined my opening gambit.

For it is precisely the relationship between these two sorts or modes of theological work – systematic and biblical – that I want to say something about. What are the similarities between them (if any); where do the differences lie; and how might we think of them as related to one another? And I want to begin by asking a question about the nature and legitimacy of systematic theology as such. This may seem an odd thing for a systematic theologian to do, but there are different ways of understanding the adjective 'systematic', and not all are equally helpful. Some, indeed, have frequently aroused the suspicion of biblical theologians, and not always without cause.

System Addicts? Or, On the Need to Avoid both of Two Patron Saints

In preparing these observations I was driven back initially to some comments made by Jürgen Moltmann in the preface to *The Trinity and the Kingdom of God*. This volume is, Moltmann insists, the first in a series of 'systematic contributions to theology', rather than the opening instalment of a system of theology or a dogmatics. Systems, he warns, tend to be a hindrance rather than a help to serious theological reflection and judgement. In a system, in principle 'one has to be able to say everything, and not to leave any point unconsidered. All the statements must fit in with one another without contradiction, and the whole architecture must be harmonious, an integrated whole.'[1] Comprehensive theoretical systems, even theological ones are, we might say, mostly better suited to evoking a form of aesthetic appreciation than for opening up discussion and dispute, and lay tacit claim to a finality to which no product of human thought may legitimately aspire. Like certain sorts of imaginative literature, they may console us and gratify our deep-rooted human need for closure and completeness (a 'sense of an ending', and of some overall orderly pattern in terms of which to make sense of things), but the extent to which they do so is precisely the extent to which they part company with the texture of reality as we experience it, which is open-ended, complex and often elusive, resisting our efforts to pin it down. In their incessant bid to tidy up the inherently unsystematic phenomena which present themselves to us for consideration into a harmonious, overarching integrated whole, systems cannot easily accommodate that which does not seem to fit within their categories and are always tempted to exclude or distort it.

Furthermore, we might add, systems overlook the inherently contextual nature and shape (and therefore the provisionality) of all such intellectual engagements. The foundations and scaffolding around which they are constructed frequently result in an edifice that, viewed from any distance, looks unnervingly like what passes muster as serious philosophy in a particular time and place. Confident theological appeal to 'reason' has in practice often meant borrowing wholesale from both the insights and the errors of philosophers as divergent as Plato, Porphyry, Aristotle, Kant, Hegel, Marx, the Vienna Circle, Wittgenstein, Heidegger and Derrida. That theology should seek insights and tools from such sources for its own intellectual task is unsurprising, and in itself perfectly appropriate. When the borrowing is wholesale, though, and the result amounts to little more than the deployment of such biblical bricks, timber and other materials as may fit a systematic architecture constructed ultimately to the dictates of a philosophical blueprint, serious questions must be asked about the integrity of the project, and in particular about the fate of the surplus materials. Christian Scripture offers no neat system, and ambitious attempts to systematize it ought to attract suspicion rather than assent in the first instance from those whose concern is faithfulness to the text, and acknowledgement of its authority in the integrally related tasks of theological reflection and Christian discipleship. Procrustes is the obvious patron saint of systems of this sort, and if we would avoid the inadvertent offering of our theology at his shrine then our appeal to philosophy (and other intellectual engagements with reality) will be of a more eclectic and judicious sort.

---

[1] Moltman, *Trinity*.

It is possible that this emphasis, like so much else in Moltmann's work, arises from an appreciative but nonetheless critical reaction to the shape of the theology produced over several decades by his teacher Karl Barth. Barth's *Church Dogmatics* is certainly a bold and ambitious attempt to map the contours of Christian belief, and to do so in a systematic manner. It is wide-ranging even in its incompleteness (Barth intended further volumes and the project was interrupted by his death in 1968), and it is certainly structured around some clear theological principles. Yet, while it is certainly a dogmatics in this more traditional and proper sense, rather than a set of serial engagements or forays in the territory of Christian theology, Barth's writing is not guilty of systematizing in the more problematic sense we have identified. He has his philosophical and other influences and resources, to be sure; but there is no overarching intellectual authority to which the whole is subjected, and in terms of which it is organized, save what Barth takes to be the unitive pattern latent within the biblical text itself, and the unfolding of this within orthodox catholic dogma. Yet even here Barth is careful to leave the authority of the text as such in place, rather than effectively substituting the authority of dogma for it. Theology, he insists, is the product of human interpretative activity, and as such can only ever be partial and provisional in its claims. For any system, or even any formal doctrine, to claim the final word — even though that word be 'biblical' in every jot and tittle — would amount to a relativizing of the word rather than a submission to it as the primary source and norm for theology. For this reason, while we must seek the best interpretation available to us, and be prepared to take our stand upon it, we must also be willing to take it back time and again to its textual sources, and allow it to be measured and tested against the word which is not given all at once and once for all, but is 'new every morning'.

The practical faithfulness of Barth to this methodological commitment is perhaps most obviously seen in the shift that occurred in his understanding of the nature of the sacraments between the writing of the early volumes and his lengthy treatment of the theme in volume IV/4, the fragment on 'The Christian Life'.[2] As Barth himself acknowledges, the shift arose through the influence upon his thinking of his son Markus Barth's 1951 book *Die Taufe —ein Sakrament?* This exposition of the New Testament notion of sacrament and the logic of its understanding of baptism sent Barth himself back to his Bible to wrestle with the text again and provoked an unashamed if no doubt uncomfortable change of mind from his earlier published ideas. Not all would prefer the later Barth to the earlier on this subject, and one line of criticism which it is certainly possible to develop is that the later 'non-sacramental' version parted company at this particular juncture with some of the most basic emphases and principles of his own dogmatic vision, deliberately embracing

---

[2] *Church Dogmatics* IV/4.

views which fail to cohere with the wider whole developed over the best part of thirty years. The rights and wrongs of the particular theological move that Barth made need not concern us here. What matters for our purposes is the integrity with which he allowed the voice of the biblical text to continue speaking to him and to disrupt his thinking about a central doctrinal issue and, when it did so, his willingness to take a new direction, sacrificing if necessary the coherence of the pattern as he had earlier perceived it, and allowing it instead to evolve in accordance with what he now took to be a more adequate hearing of the word within the church.

If, then, one eschews systematizing of a strict sort in theology, may one nonetheless remain 'systematic' in a broader and more open-textured sense (as exemplified, I have suggested, in the *Church Dogmatics*)? Or is one, perhaps, compelled to choose instead a plastic figure of Heraclitus (patron saint of the contemporary fascination with particularity and flux) to hang from the rear-view mirror? It seems to me that the Christian theologian may and must remain systematic in this wider sense, and must do so for reasons having their basis in the substance of Christian doctrine itself (and therefore, ultimately, in the voice of Scripture). Faith in God as the sort of Creator to which Scripture testifies compels us, I think, to make the presumption that, finally, things hold together, that 'reality' is orderly and meaningful, a genuine universe rather than a 'pluriverse'; and this presumption places us under a moral obligation to approach it on these terms, seeking the unitive form or forms which hold it together, seeking links, connections, pattern. What Christian faith in God does not lead us to suppose, however (indeed, unless we arbitrarily limit the effects of human fallenness and sin to a zone located from the neck down, it suggests the very opposite) is that we are especially well-placed epistemically to know it. On the contrary, the eschatological shape of the story within which Scripture locates both God and his creatures (and the leitmotifs of fall and redemption shot through the story) places all our human bids to make sense of things under the sign of a divinely ordained provisionality ('for now we see in a mirror, dimly' and 'know only in part': 1 Cor. 13:12) and counsel humility rather than confidence about our epistemic capacities (as those who are, according to Paul, still *echthrois te dianoia*) to put reality in an intellectual stranglehold and force it to submit. Theology, it seems to me, should be practised consciously in this tension between an objectively rooted confidence that there is a wealth of divinely given meaning to be had, and an abiding appropriate realism about the inevitable shortfall and limits of our attempts to have it this side of the new creation. Recognition of this gap is vital, since it reminds us that reality (and in this context that reality known to us in and through Scripture) should be the measure and judge of our partial and provisional knowledge and statements about it, rather than vice versa.

Transformation and Convergence in the Frame of Knowing: The Distinctive Task of a Systematic Theology

We turn now, then, to the question of the relationship between 'systematic' theology in this sense and 'biblical' theology. Perhaps the first thing to say is that they share much in common. Indeed, one might be tempted to say that, in its concern to identify connections and to trace pattern at the level of *Scripture as a whole*, biblical theology is already involved in a 'systematic' enterprise, and is therefore a form of systematic theology. The presumption of presence in the text of Scripture as a whole, the conviction that the whole holds together and coheres, that some unitive form may and should be sought, is certainly one shared by systematic and biblical theology. Unity of form, of course, may be of different sorts, and seeking it certainly need not (though of course it may) mean the 'use of sweeping and wholesale' rather than 'careful and analytic' procedures with which James Barr charges the discipline.[3] Biblical theology, we might say, seeks (without overriding the particularity and diversity proper to the text) at least to identify and to unfold wider unifying patterns within the canon, thereby to offer some more organized interpretation of the faith which vibrates through what is intrinsically an 'unsystematic' body of literature, and so to offer an account of Scripture's own theological priorities and emphases. This latter point is important. One criticism which biblical scholars have sometimes levelled at systematicians is that, by beginning with questions arising within some particular intellectual or existential concern and *bringing these to* the text, systematic theology has often imposed artificial agendas upon its reading of the text, and 'hindered the Bible's own concerns and categories from emerging'.[4] Systematic theology, I shall suggest duly, cannot avoid some engagement of a fairly direct sort with the concerns and agendas of its day. Its engagement with these, though, should be informed and shaped by a logically prior sense of the internal coherence of that world of belief and practice reflected, directly and indirectly, within Scripture. Otherwise it is not clear in what sense Scripture may properly serve as a norm or authority for it. While there may be legitimate overlap between them, therefore, we might suggest that the distinctive contribution which biblical theology makes (and the key point of its value for systematic theology) is precisely this, that in its engagement with the text as a whole, its concern is to allow the text's own categories, concerns and emphases to speak. In terms of the ethics of interpretation, biblical theology is concerned chiefly to listen to the text, to hear what it has to say. Having listened to it, systematic theology may proceed to address questions to it which engage other concerns.

---

[3] Barr, *Scope and Authority*, 2.

[4] Goldingay, *Approaches*, 21.

With some such distinction as this in mind, Barth differentiates between the two tasks of laying bare 'what the apostles and prophets said' and that of determining 'what we must say on the basis of what the apostles and prophets said'.[5] It would be tempting to use this as a neat formula for differentiating biblical theology from systematic, understanding the one as an essentially descriptive task, and the other as a normative task with a more contemporary agenda. James Barr adopted just such a distinction in his inaugural lecture as Oriel Professor of the Interpretation of Holy Scripture in the University of Oxford.[6] But, tempting though such a clear-cut differentiation may be for a variety of reasons, it is misleading and finally unsustainable. There are a number of reasons for supposing so. First, although its primary concern is certainly with 'what the apostles and prophets said', we shouldn't overlook the fact that and the extent to which every exercise in biblical theology is itself a human activity rooted in and shaped by the interpreter's 'here and now'. Biblical theology cannot escape its place as a contemporary explication of the textual material it handles, and it can lay no claim to success in some supposedly dispassionate task of 'pure description'. It is always to some extent a work of theological construction as well as one of discovery. Its bids to recognize, clarify and explicate patterns in the text are highly skilled, and the results inevitably present for our consideration something other than the text itself as such presents. They are results for which particular interpreters must take responsibility, and they cannot be identified in any simple way with 'what the text says'. Of course it does not follow from this that all interpretations are equally faithful to the text, or equally valuable. If, though, we are to evaluate their relative worth then it will be by taking them back to the text and reading them alongside it, weighing their persuasive force as mediators illuminating its burden of meaning. To admit this is already to acknowledge that they are themselves 'other than' the text itself.

Second, given the nature, depth and complexity of the text in question, we should also reckon with the possibility that more than one such interpretation may be fruitful, granting us a more rounded sense of the text's key concerns. Perhaps some alternatives presented for our consideration will indeed prove to be incompatible and a choice between them compelled, but others may be complementary. There is no reason in principle to suppose that the text (or any individual part of it) is susceptible only of one interpretation, that there are not multiple patterns of meaningfulness fruitfully to be had from it, each offering its own irreplaceable insights. Thus Goldingay writes (about the Old Testament, but a similar point might be made about Scripture as a whole):

---

[5] Barth, *Church Dogmatics* Vol. 1/1, 16. See further, Vol. 1/2, 821.
[6] Barr, 'Does Biblical Study Still Belong to Theology?'.

If we have not yet discovered the single correct key to producing a satisfactory synthesis of OT faith, this suggests that there is no such key. Understanding the OT resembles understanding a battle or a person, or appreciating a landscape, rather than understanding the layout of an architect-planned new town. We can appreciate a landscape by starting from its roads, its contours or its water supplies, or by taking as its centre a hill, a church, an inn or a bus stop; each perspective will lead us to a different aspect of its understanding. Similarly, many starting points, structures and foci can illuminate the OT's landscape.[7]

Biblical theologies have variously been organized around concepts, symbols, narrative structure and key historical events or acts of God. The patterns traced in the text in each case are different, but each may serve to break its meaning open in significant ways. There are, no doubt, things to be said about the canon of Christian Scripture that need not be said about the Old Testament. There are patterns that seem to be analytic in its very identity as a Christian text as such. A biblical theology which did not, for example, at some stage identify the centre of theological gravity in the person of Christ, and read the Old Testament as the normative (albeit often presupposed rather than explicitly identified) context for making sense of the New Testament, would have to have its credentials as a 'Christian' theology called into question. But to insist upon this is not to deny the possibility of fruitful alternative, complementary approaches to this basic 'eschatological' reading.

Third, once we have acknowledged the contextual and creative particularity of the enterprise, we might suppose it important to consider other interpretations precisely in order to see whether their approach affords a view of aspects which our own has inadvertently overlooked. 'Indeed, in the history of Christian theology the openness of all knowledge and all explanations is actually constitutive; for it is their abiding openness that shows the power of their eschatological hope for the future'[8] or, we might say differently, their trust in the authority of God's word rather than their own adequacy as readings of it. Again, we are back with a tension between a legitimate bid for unity of form and recognition of the inherent vulnerability of every attempt to map it. Biblical theology is thoroughly rooted in the moment, and is doing much more than merely describing data.

A fourth reason why the distinction between a 'descriptive' biblical theology and a 'normative' systematics breaks down is summed up neatly by Brevard Childs: 'The enterprise of Biblical Theology is *theological* because by faith seeking understanding in relation to the divine reality, the divine imperatives are no longer moored in the past, but continue to confront the hearer in the present as

---

[7] Goldingay, *Approaches*, 28–29.

[8] Moltmann, *Trinity*, xiii–xiv.

truth.'[9] In other words, the *theological* enterprise as such is normative (anything less does not deserve the name theology), concerned with elucidating textual patterns with a prescriptive rather than a merely historical significance for the contemporary Christian reader, and whatever historical work it engages in is deliberately rather than merely accidentally engaged in with one foot firmly planted in the present context and its concerns. None of this means that the ethical attempt to let the text speak on its own terms and to listen to it as it does so is unworthy or futile. It does mean, though, that we should not pretend to do so in some disinterested manner, nor mistakenly suppose that we have attained 'sure conclusions' via some scholarly objectivity which excuses us from the ongoing task of subjecting our findings to the scrutiny of the text again and again and again.

Is there, then, further significant difference between the labours of biblical theology and those of the systematic theologian?

Perhaps the chief difference lies in the way in which systematic theology deliberately and extensively seeks to engage the distinctive priorities and emphases of Scripture (discerned at least in part through the work of biblical theologians) with those which confront it in wider intellectual concerns, the insights, claims and assumptions of other disciplines, and of the wider world. In this sense, by furnishing an orderly account of the former, and with its normative intent, biblical theology might be depicted as a stage on the way to a particular systematic engagement. But it does not aspire to this further explicit step. While, as we have seen, it cannot be done otherwise than with a foot firmly planted within the contemporary context, its concern is clearly not with this context as such, but with one which is other than it, and speaks to it an alien word. Biblical theology begins with the text and leads back to the text. This is its nature, even as a 'contemporary explication' of the text. The systematic theologian is also concerned with discerning, clarifying and extrapolating the unitive patterns of Scripture, and with their articulation in forms accessible (not necessarily amenable!) to the contemporary church. The work of discernment and clarification is closely related to that of the biblical theologian. That of extrapolation may take a further step, but will still be identifiably rooted in the concerns and emphases of Scripture itself. The fourth-century doctrine of the consubstantiality of Father and Son and the fifth-century doctrine of hypostatic union are both evidently several stages down the road of christological development from the language and conceptuality of Scripture. Yet, properly understood, each is securely rooted in the biblical testimony to Christ, and was offered to the church not as a philosophical complication of its faith, but precisely as a hermeneutical device to secure certain ways of reading key New Testament texts rather than other ways of doing so. No theological school was

---

[9] *Biblical Theology of the Old and New Testaments*, 86.

ever more willing to cite biblical prooftexts than the Arians. The question which had to be decided in AD 325 was not what the Bible said, but how what it said was to be made sense of; and the Nicene theologians and their successors insisted that the wider pattern or 'scope' of scriptural testimony concerning the 'Son' of God was secured by the doctrine of the *homoousion* rather than some of the available alternatives. The key term was certainly unbiblical in one sense (not to be found in any reliable concordance), but thoroughly biblical in the sense that mattered most.

Systematic theology, though, does not stop here. This work of discernment, clarification and extrapolation (all of which falls under the heading of 'interpretation' of the text) is its necessary starting point, but cannot be where it all stops. Unless the church is to remain isolated in an intellectual and cultural ghetto of its own making, and to deserve the label of irrelevance so often attached to it, it must engage critically and constructively with the wider understandings of the world which confront it. Of course, the matter is not even so simple as that. It is not as though Christians (and Christian theologians) were on one side of a notional line, and 'culture', or 'the world', on the other side. Very few of us will ever find ourselves in missionary circumstances of that sort. For us it is going to be more complicated, because we are products of and shaped by the very 'world' with which our theology must engage. The dialogue is one that must be carried on, as it were, within us as well as between us and others. But there will only be a dialogue at all if we are indeed Christians, and know ourselves in some clear sense to be 'in' the world but not finally 'of' it, at odds with it in the same moment that we discover the deep-rooted remnants of its abiding influence upon and within us. Drawing on the church's account (rendered in liturgy, ritual and praxis as well as in Scripture, preaching, doctrines and dogmas) of the 'internal coherence' of Christian faith and practice, systematic theology pursues this dialogue through a quest for a corresponding 'external coherence'; that is, a convergence of what it believes to be true on the basis of the gospel with other things which human learning at its best encourages us to believe about ourselves and the world in which we live.[10] Its mandate for this quest is no shallow pragmatism (and it fails in the task if, in the interest of a bloodless apologetics, it simply allows the *Wissenschaft* of its day to dictate to it what may count as warranted belief) but rather the biblical insistence that the God made known in Jesus Christ is no mere tribal deity, but Lord of heaven and earth. This being so, the theologian has every reason to anticipate the final unity of meaning and truth, even though it may not as yet be available for inspection. That which, as yet, we see through a glass darkly is nonetheless worth striving after in a process in which, to borrow from the title

---

[10] See further on this Hart, *Faith Thinking*, chs 8–11.

of one of T.F. Torrance's books, we may properly expect both *transformation* and *convergence* in the frame of our knowing as human beings.

As a systematic theologian, I tend to use biblical theology selectively and critically in my efforts to discern aspects of the internal coherence of Scripture. I use it precisely because it enables me to 'hit the ground running'. It does a huge amount of fruitful exegetical work for me which otherwise I would have neither time nor skill to do so well. But Brueggemann, Childs, Eichrodt, von Rad and many others sit alongside one another on my bookcase, and my habit is generally to consult more than one voice for reasons indicated above. Furthermore, I don't allow the voice of biblical theology to mediate my relationship with the text of Scripture entirely! I weigh the contributions of different offerings precisely by allowing each to drive me back to the text itself, comparing the persuasive force of each in the actual breach of reading. So, if – as I have suggested in this short chapter – all biblical theology is in some sense and to some extent properly 'systematic', so too systematic theology ought first and foremost to be biblical theology, listening to the authentic voice of the text and letting its priorities and concerns speak for themselves rather than imposing alien agendas upon it. To the extent that the work of biblical theologians facilitates this careful listening, and keeps systematics earthed in the world of the text, it provides a vital resource, while still leaving enough work to be done to keep the systematic theologian in a job. On both counts, this systematic theologian at least is very grateful!

Bibliography

Barr, J., *The Scope and Authority of the Bible* (London: SCM Press, 2002)

—, 'Does Biblical Study Still Belong to Theology?', in *The Scope and Authority of the Bible* (London: SCM Press, 1980), 18–29

Barth, K., *Church Dogmatics* (trans. G.T. Thomson; ed. G.W. Bromiley and T.F. Torrance; Edinburgh: T & T Clark, 1936–77)

Barth, M., *Die Taufe – ein Sakrament?* (Zollikon-Zurich: Evangelischer Verlag, 1951)

Childs, B., *Biblical Theology of the Old and New Testaments* (London: SCM Press, 1992)

Goldingay, J., *Approaches to Old Testament Interpretation* (Leicester: Apollos, 1990)

Hart, T.A., *Faith Thinking: The Dynamics of Christian Theology* (London: SPCK, 1995)

Moltmann, J., *The Trinity and the Kingdom of God* (London: SCM Press, 1981)

14

Biblical Theology and the Clarity of Scripture

John Webster

To put the matter in brief compass: normative (as opposed to historical or descriptive) biblical theology attempts to give a comprehensive account of the theological teaching of Scripture as a whole, and of the claims made by that teaching upon the mind and practice of the church of Jesus Christ. It undertakes this task on the basis of a conviction that, in the economy of God's revelatory and reconciling presence, such an account is both necessary and possible. It is necessary because the truthfulness and legitimacy of the church's thought and action rest upon its openness to divine instruction in its fullness and integrity: as such, biblical theology is a corollary of *tota scriptura*. It is possible, first, because in all of their variety the biblical writings together constitute a unified divine act of communication – a single, though a rich, complex and historically extended, divine word from which a coherent body of teaching can be drawn. From this perspective, biblical theology is a corollary of the unity of Scripture as the church's canon. And a comprehensive biblical theology is possible, second, because the coherent teaching that Scripture sets forth can be discerned by the Spirit-directed use of interpretative reason in the communion of saints. The possibility of biblical theology is, therefore, a corollary of the clarity of Scripture.

Affirming the viability of a comprehensive biblical theology is thus closely related to making judgements about the nature of Scripture. These include judgements about whether terms like 'Scripture' or 'canon' identify properties of the biblical texts in relation to God or simply indicate churchly use, or judgements about whether the distinction between the Old and New Testaments indicates episodes in the single drama of God's revelatory grace, or only a more or less awkward juxtaposition of two religious systems and their textual carriers. At least since Gabler, historians of biblical literature and religion have characteristically argued that canon, unity or clarity are dogmatic judgements, arbitrary impositions upon the biblical materials which cannot be warranted by historical description. These historians have, accordingly, been reluctant to develop a comprehensive biblical theology. From the vantage point of Christian dogmatics, overcoming such reluctance will require an account of the unity, canonicity and clarity of Scripture in relation to the economy of God's communicative grace and its reception in the church. What follows is a sketch of one part of the dogmatic background for a viable biblical theology, namely the importance of *claritas scripturae* for the tasks of interpretation.[1]

The Importance of *Claritas Scripturae*

Theological talk of the clarity of Holy Scripture is a corollary of the church's confession of the radiance of God in the gospel. The gospel attests that, in free majesty and love, the triune God establishes, maintains and completes fellowship with humankind, making himself present and so making himself known as maker, redeemer and giver of life. As the testimony of the prophets and apostles, Holy Scripture is inspired by God to serve his self-communicative presence. The clarity of Scripture is the work which God performs in and through this creaturely servant as, in the power of the Holy Spirit, the Word of God illumines the communion of saints and enables them to see, love and live out the gospel's truth. God lifts up the light of his countenance upon the saints through Holy Scripture, orders their interpretation of the biblical testimony and so builds them up in godliness.

Affirmations such as these are the common stock of classical Christian hermeneutics, though they are more usually familiar to us from sixteenth- and seventeenth-century Protestantism, in which they acquired greater dogmatic precision as well as a certain polemical prominence. They have, however, ceased to have much operative force either in the theology of Scripture or in the theory and practice of biblical hermeneutics and, if they remain present to us, it is most often in coarsened, rationalistic versions. Accounting for their decline would require a full account of the career of modern biblical hermeneutics and its neighbouring disciplines, which is well beyond the scope of these remarks. For the present purpose, it may suffice merely to identify an external factor (the changed relation to texts in some general hermeneutical theory) and an internal factor (dogmatic weaknesses in some late expressions of Protestant theology of Scripture) whose conjunction has done much to undermine theological confidence in the viability of this particular tract of Christian theological teaching.

First, decline of confidence in the hermeneutical viability of *claritas scripturae* is related to the prominence of that strand of hermeneutical theory which seeks

---

[1] I have attempted a parallel exercise in relation to canon in 'Dogmatic Location'.

to secularize and de-absolutize Scripture. In a very suggestive essay, Otto Marquard proposes that one of the commanding forces in the rise of literary hermeneutics and their application to the Bible was the experience of '*a hermeneutical war – a civil war over the absolute text*'.[2] Hermeneutics responds to bloody conflict over the interpretation of Scripture by 'inventing – thus turning itself into pluralizing, which is to say, literary, hermeneutics – the non-absolute text and the non-absolute reader'.[3] Hence '*literary hermeneutics* – by transforming the absolute text into the literary text and the absolute reader into the aesthetic reader – is *given precedence*, as a reply to the hermeneutic civil war over the absolute text'.[4] *Originalitas, non veritas, facit interpretationem*. The effect of this development on the notion of the clarity of Scripture is, of course, highly disruptive, for *claritas*, as conceived by the magisterial Reformers and their heirs, involves two affirmations: 1) that Scripture is indeed 'absolute', not in the sense that it is divine, but in the sense that it is the unsurpassable bearer to us of non-contingent divine revelation, and 2) that the interpretation of such a text cannot be *ad libitum* but must be according to the law which the text sets before us. The hermeneutical directive of the clarity of Scripture is thus an extension of the affirmation *sacra scriptura locuta, res decisa est*; whereas literary hermeneutics (of which hypermodern hermeneutical scepticism is only a late version) can be a near-infinite deferral of decision.

What of the second, internal factor? Post-Reformation theology of Scripture expounded *claritas* as part of a larger dogmatic ontology of the Bible. In doing so it offered an essential check against any strategies of secularizing Scripture, preventing clarity, along with efficacy, inspiration, authority or canonicity, from becoming simply attributes of the subjective *use* of Scripture, and insisting instead upon the objective (though not, of course, non-natural) character of Scripture as divine communication. The subsequent history of Protestant bibliology, however, demonstrated a certain limitation in those post-Reformation accounts, namely that, badly handled, the idiom of properties of Scripture could rather easily be separated out from talk of God's reconciling and revelatory activity in the church, and formalized or rendered abstract. If seventeenth-century dogmaticians were usually safeguarded from such formalization by, for example, linking *claritas* to efficacy, later accounts ran the risk of so talking of Scripture's clarity *in se* and *ante usum* that it became extracted from its proper dogmatic location and rendered as a natural property of the Bible qua text. This, in turn, made it possible to associate clarity with transparency of authorial intention or original meaning, in such a way that

---

[2] Marquard, 'Question', 20. Marquard's sketch might be filled out by J.S. Preus's study, *Spinoza and the Irrelevance of Biblical Authority*.

[3] Marquard, 'Question', 21–22.

[4] Marquard, 'Question', 24.

clarity was further distanced from its doctrinal setting and expounded in terms of rational accessibility. Clarity, in other words, becomes confused with historical evidentness; the context of clarity is not the self-communicative presence of God to the community of faith, but the transparency of a historical report to historical reason.

By way of contrast, what is attempted here is a dogmatic account of *claritas scripturae* that expounds the notion through a series of interconnected affirmations: about the self-communicative presence of God, about the ontology and properties of Scripture, about the church as the creature of the Word, and about sanctified interpreters and their acts. Amongst other things, it suggests that a well-rounded theological account of *claritas*, far from undermining the validity of hermeneutical work, recovers the proper vocation of hermeneutics, precisely by reinserting the activity of interpretation into the overall structure of God's communicative fellowship with humankind. And, moreover, the argument here is that attention to dogmatic factors is crucial in explaining the modern history of hermeneutics, and in articulating a Christian understanding of what it means to engage in the interpretation of Scripture. The history of modern theology has been deeply affected by general theory about texts, readers and reading communities and acts of interpretation, developed in relative isolation from theological considerations, and in such a way as to neutralize, absorb or even sometimes repudiate theological talk of the place of the biblical texts in the revelatory activity of God. In the matter of biblical interpretation, Christian theology has not always managed to keep hold of the rhythm of its own concerns, often looking to general theory to provide it with two things: 1) its *problematic* (that is, an account of the content and structure of hermeneutical reflection, of its primary questions, and of the ways in which they are to be approached), and 2) its *genealogy* (that is, a history of hermeneutics as a comprehensive science of interpretation, in terms of which specifically Christian traditions of biblical interpretation are to be understood). Once this problematic and its attendant genealogy acquire some authority in theology and demonstrate some success both in explaining how theological hermeneutics has come to be where it is and in recommending how it ought to be conducted, then almost inevitably theological factors tend to be compromised. They come to enjoy only a diminished status, or to be reconceived in the light of dominant hermeneutical conventions. Yet there is no necessity about such developments, and they could have been resisted by more thoughtful drawing upon the resources of Christian teaching about the nature of Holy Scripture, and by a measure of confidence that the church's dogmatic traditions can be of assistance to biblical hermeneutics as it pursues its vocation.

A dogmatic depiction of the topic is an attempt to give an orderly, reasoned portrayal of the church's confession. As a piece of dogmatics, it is, of course, wholly subordinate to the primary work of the church's theology, which is exegesis. Dogmatics, and in particular a theology of Scripture, cannot presume to anticipate or control exegetical work, to which it is an ancillary science. In the case of a doctrine of Scripture, the assistance dogmatics provides is as follows: it offers a description of the origin, nature and ends of Holy Scripture, and of its place in the divine economy. The scope of such an account stretches from consideration of the revelatory purpose and action of God, through an account of the inspiration, sanctification and canonization of the biblical texts to an account of the faithful reading-acts of Spirit-illumined readers in the fellowship of the saints. A doctrine of Scripture offers a theological ontology of Scripture and an ecclesiology and anthropology of its readers, in terms of which Christian exegetes can understand their place in the divine economy and so more fittingly perform the task to which they are appointed. That is, a doctrine of Scripture does not orient exegetical practice by determining particular results, but by portraying the field of exegetical activity, the divine and human agents in that field, the actions undertaken by these agents, and the ends which they serve. In this way it acts as an auxiliary to exegetical labour.

Until recently, there have been few modern precedents from which to take direction in discussing either the doctrine of Scripture in general or the particular issue of *claritas scripturae*. There are now signs that, having languished on the edges of theology for some time, bibliology is returning to theological debate. Among recent English-language works, notice should be taken of K. Vanhoozer, *First Theology* (esp. pp. 127–203); M. Horton, *Covenant and Eschatology* (pp. 121–276); and T. Ward, *Word and Supplement*. See also J. Webster, *Holy Scripture*. In German, there is an important study by A. Wenz, *Das Wort Gottes, Gericht und Rettung*. The question of *claritas scripturae* still awaits a thorough dogmatic exposition. The recent study of J. Callahan, *The Clarity of Scripture*, makes a beginning, but lacks doctrinal precision. There are treatments of the topic by U. Duchrow, 'Die Klarheit der Schrift und die Vernunft'; R. Muller, *Post-Reformation Reformed Dogmatics* II (pp. 340–57); A.C. Thiselton, *New Horizons in Hermeneutics* (pp. 179–203); K. Vanhoozer, *Is There a Meaning in this Text?* (pp. 314–17). The two-volume study by R. Rothen, *Die Klarheit der Schrift*, covers a good deal more than its title suggests and is best read as a critical account of the theology of Scripture in Luther and Barth. The best overall dogmatic treatment remains G.C. Berkouwer, *Holy Scripture* (pp. 267–98). Much of the specialist literature is devoted to interpretation of Luther's debate with Erasmus in *De servo arbitrio*. See in particular: F. Beisser, *Claritas Scripturae bei Martin Luther*; P. Hayden-Roy, 'Hermeneutica gloriae vs. hermeneutica crucis: Sebastian Franck and Martin Luther on the Clarity of Scripture'; R. Hermann, 'Von der Klarheit der Heiligen Schrift'; O. Kuss, 'Über die Klarheit der Schrift'; R. Mau, 'Klarheit der Schrift und Evangelium: Zum Ansatz des lutherschen Gedankens der claritas scripturae'; P. Neuner and F. Schröger, 'Luthers These von der Klarheit der Schrift'; H. Østergaard-Nielsen, *Scriptura Sacra et Viva Vox: Eine Lutherstudie*; S.D. Paulson, 'From Scripture to Dogmatics'; E. Wolf, 'Über "Klarheit der Heiligen Schrift" nach Luthers *De servo arbitrio*'.

By way of initial orientation, the following proposition may be offered: To confess the clarity of Holy Scripture is to acknowledge the radiant presence of God, who through Holy Scripture sheds abroad the light of the knowledge of his reconciling works and ways in the communion of the saints, assembled by the Word of God and illuminated by the Spirit to hear the gospel with repentance and faith.

Talk of the clarity of Holy Scripture is a *confession*. To confess is to articulate a truth which is given, presenting itself to the mind, will and affections in its irreducible spiritual character. To confess is also to commit oneself to act in accordance with and under the tutelage of that which is confessed. Confession is thus a recognition of, and a decision for, divine teaching. Consequently, confession does not take its rise in natural perception; its origins lie in the conversion of reason through divine instruction. Confession is the articulation of knowledge which comes to us in the course of the great work of reconciliation, which is purposed by God the Father, accomplished by God the Son, and brought to full effect by God the Holy Spirit. The clarity of Scripture is a matter for confession because it is not simply a linguistic or semantic property of the biblical text, perceptible *remoto Deo;* clarity is that which Scripture is by virtue of the presence and action of God, and that which is seen as it makes itself visible to faith. *Claritas scripturae* is 'a "confession" of faith that praise[s] the Word in its clarity'.[5]

Accordingly, in its character as confession, talk of the clarity of Scripture is also an *acknowledgement*. That is, such talk is not in any straightforward way a proposal on the part of the church or the individual reader; still less is it simply a statement of interpretative policy. It is grateful recognition and reception of that which Scripture antecedently is. As with the attributes of God, so here with the properties of Scripture: the logic of theological attribution is not ascription but acknowledgement. The properties of Scripture are not labels attached to Scripture, indicating our attitudes towards, interests in, or intended uses of the biblical text. To talk of *claritas scripturae* is to acknowledge that, by virtue of the action of God, Holy Scripture *is* clear.

But *claritas scripturae* is not a simple, but rather a complex, notion.[6] What it says about the nature and functioning of the biblical texts draws upon theological doctrine concerning the nature and purpose of God and God's relation to the world, concerning the church in relation to Word and Spirit, and concerning the nature of human interpreters and their acts in relation to Scripture. As

---

[5] Berkouwer, *Holy Scripture*, 273.

[6] My account of the complex character of the notion of *claritas scripturae* has some similarities to that offered by Callahan in *The Clarity of Scripture*, 11, who argues that 'the expression clarity of Scripture refers to how Christians account for the union of Scripture that is read, an appropriate reading of Scripture and Scripture's readers.

with all themes in bibliology, the domain of the clarity of Scripture is the *magnalia Dei*, the economy of God's reconciling and revelatory turn to the saints. Its explication therefore requires careful arrangement of materials drawn from across the dogmatic corpus: the doctrine of the Trinity, soteriology, ecclesiology and anthropology. This involves, in particular, reflection upon the fact that the triune God is himself light, and so radiantly present to his creatures, one who wills to be known and loved, and so one whose work of reconciling love can be described as calling his creatures out of darkness and into his marvellous light (1 Pet. 2:9). The clarity of Scripture is a refraction of the light which God is and which he sheds abroad. Similarly, talk of the clarity of Scripture involves an account of those who are illuminated by the divine presence, those for whom the Lord is light and salvation (Ps. 27:1). That company, which may be variously described as the fellowship of the saints, the community gathered around the word, or the *illuminati* of the Holy Spirit, is the setting in which the clarity of Scripture is made a matter of attention and confession, and in which Scripture's clarity guides the work of interpretation. To engage in the interpretation of the clear Word of God requires the Spirit's gifts of repentance and faith as those dispositions of human life in which the gospel may be heard.

All of this, then, constitutes the web of affirmations within which the theological logic of the notion of the clarity of Scripture is best displayed. We now turn to their fuller explication.

The Effective Illuminating Presence of God the Revealer

The setting of the clarity of Scripture is the effective illuminating presence of God the revealer who is in himself light and whose mighty work of reconciliation overthrows the darkness and ignorance of sin, restoring us to fellowship and establishing the knowledge of himself.

Holy Scripture is clear because God is light and therefore the one in whose light we see light. God is himself light. The splendour and inexhaustible self-sufficiency of God's triune being includes his limitless capacity to enlighten the world by manifesting himself as its true light. As light, God is the one who is glorious in himself and so one who is resplendent. The metaphor of light is particularly fitting to indicate the manner in which, in the depth of his being, God is one whose freedom and sovereignty include a turning to his creatures. For

---

Scripture, when read in a Christian manner, can be said to be clear in itself but not by itself (it has never been isolated from its readings or readers, historically or theologically)'. But though Callahan is keen to trace the connections between clarity and the activity of reading, he has little to say about revelation and runs the risk of detaching clarity as a hermeneutical practice from theology proper.

light is not light if it is self-enclosed: light shines, it suffuses or pervades. It does so by virtue of its own inherent potency, yet that potency is precisely the capacity to be self-diffusing, to shed itself abroad. God is light, omnipotent and therefore omnipresent light. The eminence which God is and in which he is the creator and Lord of all things includes the energy or impetus of his self-revelation. God is light, imparting and disclosing his glory, enlightening all things effectively and effortlessly, breaking forth by virtue of his own spontaneous and unfettered power. 'The true and living God is eloquent and radiant.'[7]

It scarcely needs to be said that this divine radiance by which all things are illuminated is no impersonal state of affairs. It is the presence of God the revealer. To speak of the light of God is to speak of a personal action and mode of relation, the free self-disposing of the Lord of all things existing towards and with his creatures. God's radiance is not a simple metaphysical formula but a matter of fellowship between himself and those whom he enlightens by manifesting himself, showing them the light of his presence. As the one who is in himself light, God faces his people, lifting up the light of his countenance and so illuminating them (Pss. 4:6; 44:3; 89:15). In sum: to say that God is light is to confess the effective, illuminating presence of God the revealer.

Yet more must be said. The confession that God is light has to be understood in terms of the divine resolve for fellowship. But this resolve does not run its course unhindered; it faces opposition from the very creature it seeks to enlighten and bless. Standing in God's light, illuminated by God, shown the light of God's countenance, the creature attempts to wrest itself free of fellowship with God and establish itself in independence from the creator as its own light and giver of life, its own source of light and truth. But to accomplish this act of rebellion the creature must resist, even deny, God's light. In defiance of the divine resolve, in an absurd and impotent yet, for all that, utterly destructive act of repudiation, the creature refuses to acknowledge the glory of God, his illuminating presence as creator. And so the creature falls into darkness and ignorance. This darkness and ignorance do not quench the light, for how could the creature extinguish the light of God's glory or rob the divine being of its splendour or place an insurmountable obstacle in the path of its radiance? Rather, the creature's act of defiance is a matter of wilful opposition to light, as a result of which the light becomes that which exposes the creature as sinner. The light whose purpose is to illuminate the creature continues to do so; but now what it discloses is the creature's wickedness, laying the creature open to judgement. 'And this is the judgement, that the light has come into the world, and men loved darkness rather than light, because their deeds were evil. For everyone who does evil hates the light, and does not come to the light, lest his deeds should be exposed' (Jn. 3:19–20). To 'hate' the light and to refuse to

---

[7] Barth, *Church Dogmatics* IV/3, 79.

'come to' the light are the elemental breaches of fellowship which form the essence of sin. From them flow ignorance and blindness, disordered and directionless existence. 'He who walks in the darkness does not know where he goes' (Jn. 12:35; cf. 1 Jn. 2:11; Prov. 4:19).

With this we reach the soteriological heart of what is to be said about God as light, expressed thus in our proposition: in his 'mighty work of reconciliation [God] overthrows the darkness and ignorance of sin, restoring us to fellowship and establishing the knowledge of himself'.

'In him was life, and the life was the light of men. The light shines in the darkness, and the darkness has not overcome it' (Jn. 1:4–5). God's Word is life and light. And this Word, in opposition to (and so in mercy upon) the defiant creature and its dark world, becomes flesh. In Jesus Christ the Word incarnate, the world is no longer permitted to hug itself in darkness or refuse to acknowledge that God is light. The sheer perversity of sin, its persistence in refusing the light, is simply overruled by virtue of one single reality: 'The light shines in the darkness, and the darkness has not overcome it'. The 'shining' is entirely undefeated by the darkness which it masters, overwhelms and scatters. And this is because it, or rather *he,* Jesus Christ, God's Word and light as human presence, is the glory of God. He is not simply a refraction of God's glory, still less a witness to the light (Jn. 1:8). He is the 'true light' (Jn. 1:9) in the world. To receive him is to behold God's self-manifestation, to see in him the glory of God, which is a 'glory as of the only Son of the Father' (Jn. 1:14). For he, Jesus Christ, is God of God and therefore light of light. In him there takes place the majestic and merciful disclosure of God. As the embodiment of God's glory, he is at one and the same time the accomplishment of reconciliation and the accomplishment of revelation. He is the definitive act in which fellowship with and the knowledge of God are restored. 'The Word became flesh and dwelt among us ... He has made him known' (Jn. 1:14, 18). He is the confirmation of the reality: 'God is light'; and he is the one in whom there occurs the fulfilment of the purpose of God, namely 'fellowship with him' (1 Jn. 1:6).

This fellowship, to which we are destined and appointed by God the Father and which is secured against human darkness by God the Son, the effulgence of the Father's glory (Heb. 1:3), is made continuously real by the illuminating ministry of the Holy Spirit. And so the apostle prays in Ephesians 'that the God of our Lord Jesus Christ, the Father of glory, may give you a spirit of wisdom and of revelation in the knowledge of him, having the eyes of your hearts enlightened' (Eph. 1:17–18). The God and Father of our Lord Jesus Christ is 'the Father of glory', the resplendent one who gives the Spirit in order to endow those whom the Son has reconciled with wisdom, revelation and knowledge. These benefits which flow from the Spirit's work are summed up as 'the enlightenment of the eyes of the heart'. Knowledge of the scope of God's luminous presence and activity (that is, of 'the riches of his glorious inheritance in the saints') originates not on the creaturely side of fellowship but on the side of the illuminating person of the Spirit. 'That you may know' is strictly subordinate to and dependent upon the giving of the Spirit and his enlightening of the eyes. Seeing God's glory is God's work.

This reconciling and revelatory presence of the triune God gives the frame for theological talk of the clarity of Holy Scripture. The economy of God's communication of himself by scattering the darkness of sin, reconciling lost creatures, overcoming ignorance and establishing the knowledge and love of himself, is the dogmatic location of the notion of *claritas scripturae*. Scripture is clear as the instrument of the reconciling clarity of God, whose light is radiantly present in Jesus Christ and the Holy Spirit. Establishing this dogmatic setting is a task of first rank in the doctrine of Scripture, and, once established, it must not simply be assumed or left to one side: it must be operative at every point, and rendered explicit. Unless this is done, and bibliology tied explicitly to reconciliation and revelation, disorder threatens. This disorder, which readily afflicts any theology of Scripture and its properties, results from the extraction of Holy Scripture from the divine economy. Once detached from operative language about the self-disclosure of God in the course of seeking and maintaining fellowship, the theology of Scripture becomes an isolated piece of teaching. It drifts away from a proper understanding of the origin and ends of Scripture (life with God who lifts up the light of his countenance); it runs the risk of attributing to the text perfections which are properly to be attributed to God alone; and it may thereby make the perception of Scripture's properties (including clarity) a matter of rational judgement rather than of faith in God's presence. The only effective safeguard is attentiveness to the architecture of the gospel, a sense of the scope and arrangement of Christian teaching, and a vigilance lest the pressures of confessional polemic or deference to non-theological literary and philosophical theory deform the theological structure and so prevent well-ordered exposition of *claritas* in relation to the being and work of God who is light.

We conclude this section with three instructive examples of the exposition of the doctrine of *claritas scripturae* in terms of its location in the economy of God as reconciler and revealer. First, *Luther*. The discussion of *claritas scripturae* in *De servo arbitrio*[8] is undergirded by a theological presupposition that Holy Scripture and its readers exist in a sphere which is illuminated by the presence of the risen Christ.

What still sublimer thing can remain hidden in the Scriptures, now that the seals have been broken, the stone rolled from the door of the sepulchre, and the supreme mystery brought to light, namely, that Christ the Son of God has been

---

[8] Luther, *Bondage*, 24–28, 89–99 (*WA* [*Weimarer Ausgabe*] 18, 606–609, 652–59).

made man, that God is three in one, that Christ has suffered for us and is to reign eternally?[9]

The clarity of Scripture, that is, is to be understood as a corollary of the fact that the 'supreme mystery' has indeed been 'brought to light'; Scripture is clear because the Bible and its readers stand after the resurrection in the realm of revelation, and because the *res* which Scripture signifies is itself utterly resplendent.

> The subject matter of the Scripture ... is all quite accessible, even though some texts are still obscure owing to our ignorance of their terms. Truly it is stupid and impious, when we know the subject matter of Scripture has all been placed in the clearest light, to call it obscure on account of a few obscure words.[10]

And so Luther continues in a celebrated passage:

> when the thing signified is in the light, it does not matter if this or that sign of it is in darkness, since many other signs of the same thing are meanwhile in this light. Who will say that a public fountain is not in the light because those who are in a narrow side street do not see it, whereas all who are in the marketplace do see it?[11]

What troubles Luther about Erasmus is, more than anything, his scepticism. What Erasmus takes as modesty before the hidden mysteries of God and as a refusal of speculation, Luther views as a perverse refusal to acknowledge that, in Christ's resurrection, what was once hidden has now become plain, and that the present time is no longer in half-light but is the domain of full revelation.

> Matters of the highest majesty and the profoundest mysteries are no longer hidden away, but have been brought to light and are openly displayed before the very doors. For Christ has opened our minds so that we may understand the Scriptures, and the gospel is preached to the whole earth.[12]

Accordingly, for Luther establishing clarity involves a great deal more than sorting out obscurities and identifying Scripture's plain (moral) teaching. It entails, rather, grasping the fact that the matter of Scripture is illumined and made plain by the light of the resurrection. What is so striking about Luther's account of *claritas* is his vigorous theological objectivity: Scripture *is* plain because it is illuminated by God's saving work. Failure to perceive this is not to be attributed to some defect in Scripture's clarity, for 'everything there is in the Scriptures has been brought out by the Word into the most definite light',[13] but to 'the blindness or indolence of those who will not take the trouble to look at the very clearest truth'.[14] In short: for Luther, *claritas scripturae* is a salvation-historical affirmation, a statement about the light of the

---

[9] *LW*, vol. 33, 25–26.

[10] *LW*, vol. 33, 26.

[11] *LW*, vol. 33, 26.

[12] *LW*, vol. 33, 26–27.

[13] *LW*, vol. 33, 28.

[14] *LW*, vol. 33, 27.

gospel in which Scripture stands and which must illumine the reader if Scripture's clarity is to be perceived.

Second, mention may be made of *Zwingli* in his 1522 account 'Of the Clarity and Certainty or Power of the Word of God'. Here much space is given over to the polemical assertion that to be *theodidacti* in interpretation of Scripture necessarily means the exclusion of human teachers: the affirmation 'taught of God' carries with it the negation 'not of men'.[15] Behind the polemic, however, is an attempt to set *claritas scripturae* in the wider context of God's fellowship with his creatures. It is for this reason that Zwingli begins his treatise apparently tangentially with discussion of the *imago dei*, expounding the image in terms of the relation between creator and creature: 'we are made in the image of God and ... that image is implanted within us in order that we may enjoy the closest possible relationship with its maker and creator'.[16] Hence the 'inward man ... delights in the law of God because it is created in the divine image in order to have fellowship with him'.[17] This furnishes Zwingli with the overarching context of the doctrine of the clarity of Scripture, which concerns the way in which the Word (God's communicative presence and action) illumines the 'inner man', so making Scripture clear: 'It is the Word of God, which is God himself, that lighteth every man' so that 'the comprehension and understanding of doctrine comes ... from above'.[18] There is, doubtless, the beginning of a problem here, particularly a competitive view of divine and human action: 'not *doctores,* not *patres,* not pope, not *cathedra,* not *concilia,* but the Father of Jesus Christ' teaches the church.[19] And this goes hand in hand with the interiorized, a-social anthropology that Zwingli presupposes. Nevertheless, the scope of Zwingli's treatise is such that he sets discussion of *claritas* in a larger frame of the saving relations of God and humankind and so resists an over-hasty concentration upon textual properties in and of themselves.

It is, however, to Zwingli's successor in Zurich, *Heinrich Bullinger,* specifically in the first three sermons of the first *Decade,* that we should turn for one of the most elegant and shrewd statements of the soteriological and revelatory setting of the theology of the clarity of Scripture.[20] The details of what Bullinger has to say in the third sermon about the relation of Scripture's clarity to the activity of exposition need not detain us at present. What is much more important is the way in which, in the first two sermons, Bullinger prepares for his account of the clarity of Scripture by setting out what is, in effect, a brief history of the revelatory acts of God, in which Bullinger traces 'the history of the proceeding of the Word of God, and by what means it shined ever and anon very clear and brightly in the world'.[21] For Bullinger, what is said of Scripture has its place in the fact that 'from the beginning ... of the world,

---

15 Zwingli, 'Clarity and Certainty', 89.
16 Zwingli, 'Clarity and Certainty', 65.
17 Zwingli, 'Clarity and Certainty', 67.
18 Zwingli, 'Clarity and Certainty', 79.
19 Zwingli, 'Clarity and Certainty', 79.
20 Bullinger, *Decades* I & II.
21 Bullinger, *Decades*, 48.

God by his Spirit and the ministry of angels, spake to the holy fathers', so providing that 'no age at any time should be without most excellent lights'.[22] Revelation is thus what Bullinger calls 'that lively tradition' of patriarchs and prophets, definitively summed up in the Son of God and then communicated in the ministry of the apostles. In sum, 'The Word of God is the speech of God, that is, the revealing of his good will towards mankind, which from the beginning, one while by his own mouth, and another while by the speech of angels, he did open to those first, ancient, and most holy fathers; who again by tradition did faithfully deliver it to their posterity.'[23] This theology of the Word is then related to the end of revelation and the manner of its reception. As regards its end, Bullinger's emphasis is soteriological: 'the Word of God is revealed, to the intent that it may fully instruct us in the ways of God and our salvation';[24] as regards its reception, what is required is a number of virtues which are themselves gifts of the Spirit – reverence, attentiveness, prayer, sobriety, faith.[25] What is most striking in Bullinger's presentation is his firm sense of the proper setting of doctrinal affirmations about the nature of Scripture, his sense, therefore, that talk about *claritas scripturae* ought only to be reached after full depiction of 'the history of the proceeding of the Word of God'. Moreover, Bullinger offers an especially fine example of the coordination of the doctrines of revelation and salvation with an untroubled and circumscribed hermeneutics that is surely the best index of good theological order in this matter.

Clarity as a Property of Holy Scripture as Text

The radiance of God's presence in the 'proceeding of the Word of God' avails itself of creaturely instruments. It presents itself in and through creaturely forms, electing and ordering the course of these creaturely realities, and acting through their service to accomplish its end, namely the publication of the *magnalia dei*. Of those forms, the chief is Holy Scripture, through which the clear Word of the gospel sounds forth. In propositional form: Holy Scripture is clear as the sanctified creaturely auxiliary of the communicative presence of God, through which the promise and instruction of the gospel are announced by the Holy Spirit.

Our next task, therefore, is to discuss the place of the biblical text in the divine economy, and, more specifically, to identify the senses in which clarity may be understood as a property of Holy Scripture as text. Discussion of this topic can easily drift into dualist assumptions that fail to give a properly integrated account of the relation between divine communicative activity and creaturely realities. One version of this dualism does not allow that a text, as a

---

[22] Bullinger, *Decades*, 39, 40.
[23] Bullinger, *Decades*, 56.
[24] Bullinger, *Decades*, 61.
[25] Bullinger, *Decades*, see p. 64.

verbum externum, can in and of itself play any role in the divine economy, for texts are mere natural products, obscure and indeterminate, and cannot be instrumental in God's self-clarification. The problem here is what Wenz identifies as a bifurcation of 'concrete and limited creaturely historical means' from 'God's saving action and work'.[26] And it usually results in one of two things: either a rejection of any sense that the text is itself clear, or (more often) a relocation of clarity in readers or reading communities, so that clarity is a property, not of the biblical text but of the processes of its reception. Another version of the dualism demonstrates the same disintegrated understanding of texts and divine communication, but this time by ascribing to the biblical texts properties or actions which are proper to God, in this way removing the text from the realm of natural, contingent history. On this model, Scripture is without qualification clear *in se*; its perspicuity is such that the divine self-clarification is identified with the text. These two forms of dualism, either naturalization or near-divinization of the text, are two faces of the same coin. Both lack a well-rounded theological treatment of the divine use of creaturely instruments that can coordinate the natural integrity of the text and the incommunicability of divine action. What is required, therefore, is a way of talking of the use of texts in the economy of God's revelatory grace that will compromise neither their naturalness nor their divine use. Such an account can then furnish the basis for a theological understanding of clarity as a textual property.

At the heart of such an account is, I suggest, a notion of Scripture as 'sanctified creaturely auxiliary of the communicative presence of God'. Scripture is, first, a sanctified text. By sanctification we refer to the work of the Holy Spirit in electing, shaping and preserving creaturely realities to undertake a role in the divine economy: creaturely realities are sanctified by divine use. This divine 'use', though it is gratuitous, is not simply occasional or punctilliar, arbitrarily employing the creaturely reality and then casting it aside. That is, sanctification has a properly horizontal dimension; it involves the election and overseeing of the entire historical course of the creaturely reality so that that reality becomes in itself a creature made suitable to serve the divine purpose. A sanctified creaturely reality is not extracted from its creatureliness, but ordered in such a way that it can fittingly assist in the work that is proper to God. Sanctified by the Spirit, the creaturely reality is given its own genuine substance as it is moulded to enter into the divine service.

This notion of sanctification can be applied to the nature of the biblical texts and their function in God's revelatory work. As the work of the Spirit, sanctification integrates communicative divine action and the creatureliness of those elements that are appointed to serve God's self-presentation. Thus, to speak of Scripture as *holy* is to articulate two convictions. First, because they

---

[26] Wenz, *Wort Gottes*, 295.

are sanctified, the texts are not to be defined and handled exclusively as 'natural' entities: they are fields of the Spirit's action in the publication of the knowledge of God. Second, sanctification does not diminish creatureliness; hence the texts' place in the revelatory economy of God does not withdraw them from human processes. It is *as*, not *despite*, what they are as creaturely that they serve God. The sanctified text is creaturely, not divine, and its place in the divine economy does not need to be secured by ascribing divine properties to the text.

From this, we may draw a fundamental principle for our understanding of the ontology of Scripture: Holy Scripture has its being in the formative economy of the Word and Spirit of God. It is what it is as a sanctified element in the proceeding of the divine Word; the movement of God's self-manifestation determines the text's substance and therefore its properties, including its clarity. At this point, three affirmations intersect. 1) It is proper to speak of the ontology of the text. However much the biblical texts are bound up with their reading and reception, they have a measure of durability and resistance and can be spoken of *in se*. They are more than a score for performance, much more than an empty space for readerly poetics. 2) The ontology of the biblical texts has to be explicated in theological terms. The confession that the Bible is Holy Scripture stands against the assumption that the being of this text is exhaustively defined by its occupation of a space in a natural field of communicative activity. This assumption is to be controverted because of its underlying claim that a 'natural' understanding of the text is more basic than an understanding of the text as Holy Scripture. The biblical text *is* Holy Scripture, its being defined not simply through membership of the class of texts, but by the fact that it is *this* text, sanctified, that is, Spirit-generated and preserved, in *this* field of action, the communicative movement of God. 3) Because the text of Holy Scripture has its being in this divine movement, talk of the properties of the text is a means of indicating that which Holy Scripture is as it fulfils its appointed task and serves God's glorious presence. What does this mean for theological portrayal of clarity as one of the properties of Holy Scripture?

As with the more general notion of sanctification, so here in the question of *claritas scripturae*: effective christological and pneumatological teaching are central to the success of the enterprise. Scripture's clarity is rooted in the fact that it is appointed to be the instrument of the Spirit's announcement of the gospel of Christ. In the power of the Spirit, Jesus Christ is the prophet of his own reality: he announces himself. Risen from the dead, he is the living Word who declares with divine authority and full effect the reality of, and the benefits which flow from, his reconciling achievement. Because Scripture is sanctified for the service of this Word, it 'enlightens', bringing the clear Word of God to bear upon the attentive listener. 'When the Word of God shines on the human

understanding,' writes Zwingli, 'it enlightens it in such a way that it understands and confesses the Word and knows the certainty of it.'[27] Drawing examples from the patriarchs' persuasion of the authenticity of divine commands,
Zwingli notes that 'God's Word brought with it its own clarity and enlightenment'.[28] Yet he is careful to add that this clarity is not a quality of the listener's
understanding, but the fruit of the Spirit's work in and through the text. Scripture is clear, that is, because of 'the light of the Spirit of God, illuminating and
inspiring the words in such a way that the light of the divine content is seen in
[God's] light'.[29]

Appeal to christological and pneumatological doctrine prevents the segre-
gation of the property of clarity from the revelatory work of God. In similar
fashion, careful delineation of the connection between the clarity of Scripture
and Scripture's efficacy (*efficacia scripturae*) prevents its isolation from its
dynamic presence in the communion of saints among whom the gospel is
announced by Scripture. Scripture is clear as it performs its task of serving the
illuminating presence of Jesus Christ in his church. Clarity is therefore what
might be called a historical property of Scripture, an attribute of the text which
has its being in the 'proceeding' of revelation. The idiom of the ontology and
properties of Scripture is dynamic.

This connection of clarity and efficacy is a routine aspect of most modern
dogmatic accounts of the topic and is often associated with Luther. To emphasize in this way that clarity is effectual helps block ideas that *claritas scripturae* is
something to hand, 'available' after the manner of a historical report.[30] Scripture
is clear as God is clear, namely in the event of his self-bestowal, as gift and not as
stored treasure. Moreover, this emphasis ensures that we keep in mind the relation between the clarity of Scripture and the end of Scripture, namely the publication of the promise and instruction of the gospel.

Nevertheless, there is a danger that clarity may be collapsed into or identified with
efficacia, with the result that clarity is scarcely a property of Scripture as text and much
more a property of the divine event of revelation to which Scripture is only somewhat loosely attached. One of the most influential accounts along these lines is
Beisser's influential study *Claritas Scripturae bei Martin Luther.*[31] Beisser proposes that,
for Luther, the clarity of Scripture is a function of Scripture's effectiveness as a 'living,

---

27 Zwingli, 'Clarity and Certainty', 75.
28 Zwingli, 'Clarity and Certainty', 77.
29 Zwingli, 'Clarity and Certainty', 78. On this theme in Luther, see R. Hermann,
   'Von der Klarheit', 10ff.; Mau, 'Klarheit der Schrift', 134ff.
30 See Mau, 'Klarheit der Schrift', 135; Wolf, 'Über "Klarheit der Heiligen Schrift"',
   726.
31 Beisser is followed, for example, by Duchrow, 'Klarheit der Schrift', and Thiselton,
   New Horizons.

spoken word',[32] so that the location of clarity is primarily in the event of proclamation.[33] Beisser is certainly correct to urge that *claritas* ought not to be viewed as a static *depositum* but as a living phenomenon, and therefore as one unavailable for disengaged inspection.[34] And he lays the right kind of emphasis on clarity as a function of the divine radiance: 'the clarity of Scripture is God's clarity'.[35] However, in protecting the notion of clarity from excessively formal or static conceptions, Beisser can hardly avoid an actualistic account of the matter: clarity, in effect, becomes oral clarification to which Scripture as *text* is not sufficiently related.[36] Beisser identifies a distortion that can be introduced into the theology of Scripture when clarity as textual property is discussed. But the safeguard is not to evacuate *claritas* into *viva vox evangelii*, on the grounds that to talk of Scripture as clear *in se* is objectifying. What is required is, rather, a dynamic (but not actualistic) ontology of Scripture that retains the idiom of properties and neither separates nor identifies clarity and efficacy.

Here we may look for instruction to what may at first blush appear to be an unpromising guide, namely Turretin. The received account of his theology of Scripture in the *Institutes of Elenctic Theology* is that it transforms a dynamic theology of Scripture into something static, and so reifies the clarity of Scripture as an objectified textual phenomenon. Callahan, for example, argues that Turretin represents a shift to 'the belief that clarity is a quality of Scripture itself, rather than something brought to the text by the reader (whether ecclesial official or Spirit-illumined believer)',[37]

---

[32] 'Dieses Wort ist klar, eindeutig und jedermann zugänglich. Sein Evidenz ist schlagend. Ein gesprochenes Wort wird gehört; das ist die Grundform dieser Evidenz. Dies darf aber nicht als ein mechanischer, automatisch ablaufender Vorgang verstanden werden. Denn evident ist das Wort eben nicht als festliegende Größe, sondern als gesprochenes Wort. Die Evidenz des Wortes hat nicht ein Depositum zur Basis, sondern sie entsteht, indem das Wort evident ergeht' (Beisser, *Claritas Scripturae*, 31).

[33] 'Das Wort ist äußerlich, aber obwohl es äußerlich ist, ist es eine geistliche Größe. Nimmt man hingegen den Buchstaben für sich allein, so erweist er sich als schwach, je ungeeignet. "Spiritus Sanctus lesset sich nicht, verbis bunden, sed rem profert." Es dürfte damit deutlich geworden sei, daß es bei Luther ein vorliegendes Depositum für das, was Gottes Wort ist, nicht gibt. Wirklich ist das Wort nicht, insoweit es im Buche steht, sondern weil es gepredigt wird, weil Gott selbst darin zu uns redet' (Beisser, *Claritas Scripturae*, 37). This is undergirded by Beisser's suggestion 'daß Luther die Bibel oder das Wort Gottes in erster Linie als mündliches, gepredigtes Wort ansieht' (141): 'wenn Luther von scriptura oder von verbum redet, so denkt er nicht primär an einen *Text*' (83).

[34] 'Unbeschadet der Öffentlichkeit dieses Wortes ist seine Klarheit nicht in erster Linie die der vernünftigen Allgemeingültigkeit, sondern sozusagen eine Klarheit aus der Hand Gottes. Das Wort ist klar, aber dies ist nicht allgemein, vernünftig feststellbar, sondern das Wort ist klar als *Gottes* Wort ... Insofern kann man sagen, daß das äußerliche Wort bei Luther ein geistliche Größe ist' (Beisser, *Claritas Scripturae*, 85).

[35] Beisser, *Claritas Scripturae*, 85.

[36] See Mau's critical comments on Beisser in 'Klarheit der Schrift', 130.

[37] Callahan, *Clarity of Scripture*, 144.

thereby sacrificing the confessional character of clarity. But this is to foreshorten Turretin's account. Clarity is not, for him, mere evidentness; it is rather concerned with the fact that in Scripture the mysteries of faith 'are so wonderfully accommodated by the Lord that the believers understand these mysteries sufficiently for salvation'.[38] Clarity as textual property is inseparable from both divine accommodation and from readerly activity, which together form the soteriological setting for a theology of Scripture's attributes. It is true that Turretin's account of clarity sometimes goes awry, notably at those points where Scripture itself is spoken of in a rather unqualified way as agent: the Scriptures, he writes, 'are luminous formally and effectively because like the sun they emit rays and impress themselves upon the eyes of the beholder'.[39] But this is a small slip, corrected almost immediately in Q. XVII.xi by talk of God as the efficient cause of Scripture. Only a slight adjustment to Turretin would be required to bring out more fully the dynamic element of what he has to say, and to relate it to the wider economy of salvation.

Clarity is therefore a property bestowed upon Holy Scripture by the work of the Spirit. Sanctified to do service to the glorious self-manifestation of God, appointed by Christ as a witness to himself, Scripture is clear because in and through its texts the Holy Spirit announces the gospel's promise and instruction. As the older theology put it, Scripture is clear concerning 'all things necessary for salvation'. Or in Calvin's phrase: the 'clearness' of Scripture is the way in which, by divine appointment, Scripture is 'a fit and proper guide to show us clearly the way'.[40] Clarity does not mean ease or immediacy of access or absolute semantic transparency. It means that this text is caught up in God's self-manifestation as the light of the world and becomes the means through which the Spirit makes plain the gospel. But *where* does the Spirit make the gospel plain, and *to whom*? These are the concerns of our final sections, on the church and the act of interpretation.

The Ecclesial Nature of Holy Scripture

The sphere of the clarity of Holy Scripture is the church, the creature of the Word of God; by the Word the church is generated and preserved, and by the Spirit the church sets forth the clear Word of God in traditions of holy attentiveness.

Holy Scripture is an ecclesial reality. This is not because Scripture is the church's invention, whether through production or authorization, and still less is it because the church is Scripture's patron, conferring some dignity on it by adopting it as its symbol system of choice. Rather, Scripture is an ecclesial

---

[38] Turretin, *Institutes of Elenctic Theology*, I, 143 (Q. XVII.iii).

[39] Turretin, *Institutes of Elenctic Theology*, I, 144f. (Q. XVII.viii).

[40] Calvin, *Hebrews*, 342.

reality because the place of Scripture is in the economy of salvation, and the economy of salvation concerns the divine work of restoring fellowship through the gathering of the *sanctorum communio*. A soteriology without an account of the church would be incomplete; and a bibliology uncoordinated to ecclesiology indicates a cramped grasp of the scope of the divine economy. By extension, because *claritas* has its sphere in soteriology, it has a necessary ecclesial component: the clear Word of God is the Word of God in, for and over the church. For clarity concerns the luminous character of the gospel of God of which Holy Scripture is the creaturely auxiliary. That luminosity, and the clarity of the text in and through which it bears testimony to itself, is not mere transparency available for inspection by standardly rational persons. It is spiritually perceived – perceived, that is, by those whom Christ and the Spirit gather into the faithful community who receive the Word with trust and fear of the Lord.

Failure to make sense of the ecclesial aspect of *claritas scripturae* is one of the chief weaknesses of Hodge's account of the matter. Although Hodge cautions that clarity does not spell the end of 'deference to the faith of the church',[41] his argument is driven by an antithesis between private judgement and church authority. 'What Protestants deny on this subject is that Christ has appointed any officer, or class of officers, in his Church to whose interpretation of the Scriptures the people are bound to submit as of final authority.'[42] That this is a degenerate version of what can be found in, for example, Zwingli and Turretin, can be seen in the next sentence: God 'has made it obligatory upon every man to search the Scriptures for himself, and to determine on his own discretion what they require him to believe and to do'.[43] Clarity is therefore a necessary condition for the 'right of private judgment' which is 'the great safeguard of civil and religious liberty'.[44] This is surely the wrong idiom for an account of the operations of Scripture. First, it assumes that office or tradition in the church are always instruments of suppression, and never act as guides. Second, it thinks of the fellowship of the saints by analogy from the civil realm (as an aggregate of individual bundles of rights and judgements). Third, 'judgement' is an odd description of the fear and trembling which the faithful have before the Word. And, most of all, the whole account is curiously deistic in its lack of language about the activity of God.

Similar problems surface in R.T. Sandin's attempt to depict clarity through the philosophy of Wittgenstein (with which he is not well acquainted), to whom Sandin attributes the view that 'all communication by means of language presupposes the self-identity and determinateness of what is spoken/heard (written/read)'.[45] By

---

[41] Hodge, *Systematic Theology*, I, 184.

[42] Hodge, *Systematic Theology*, I, 184.

[43] Hodge, *Systematic Theology*, I, 184.

[44] Hodge, *Systematic Theology*, I, 186.

[45] Sandin, 'Clarity of Scripture', 239.

extension, 'if there is a meaning in Scripture such meaning is clear', and the task of interpretation is simply a matter of removing obstacles in the recipient.[46] There are numerous problems here: the appeal to philosophy rather than theology; the assumption that there is no such thing as special hermeneutics; the absence of language about God; but, more than anything, a lack of any reference to the church as the sphere of meaning (all the more surprising in view of Wittgenstein's views on the social character of communication).

Scripture is clear in the gathering of the saints, which is the 'special sphere of influence' of Holy Scripture.[47] If this has, at least until recently, remained a somewhat muted theme in Protestant dogmatics, this is largely because in Reformation and post-Reformation polemic, *claritas* was a key weapon in protest against the authority of interpretative traditions and their agents. At its best, this polemic was not detached either from conviction of the ecclesial sphere in which Scripture functions or from the proper exercise of the office of interpretation. But the demands of polemic against the magisterium could lead to neglect of both. Zwingli's principle that 'enlightenment, instruction and assurance are by divine teaching without any intervention on the part of that which is human'[48] betrays an ecclesiological minimalism which already exposes the Protestant tradition to the threat of the hegemony of private judgement which has been noted in Hodge. Moreover, Zwingli may here (as, perhaps, in his sacramental theology) slip into a dualism in which God's work of illumination is immediate and contextless, making use of no auxiliaries and occurring in empty spaces which are simply the occasions of its imparticipable self-activation.

If we are not to be betrayed into some of these mistakes, what is required is judicious theological specification of both 'clarity' and 'church'. Clarity must be related to churchly acts of interpretation in a way that denies neither that Scripture is clear *in se* and *ante usum* nor that there is a legitimacy to ecclesial interpretation. The churchly component must be articulated in such a way that its role is not one of presiding over or supplementing and so 'clarifying' Scripture, but rather of receiving its inherent clarity in holy attentiveness. The clarity of Scripture, that is, constitutes a determination of the role of the church vis-à-vis Scripture, both in the sense of limiting the church's activity and in the sense of giving it a specific character and direction. The clarity of Scripture forms, checks and directs churchly interpretation.

This entails, first, that the church should not be considered to have any constitutive or co-constitutive role in the clarity of Holy Scripture. Scripture is not

---

[46] Sandin, 'Clarity of Scripture', 240.

[47] Barth, *Church Dogmatics* I/2, 685.

[48] Zwingli, 'Clarity and Certainty', 80.

an initial textual stage in divine revelation that is then completed by churchly activity. Nor is Scripture obscure raw material whose perspicuity derives from ongoing ecclesial clarification. The church does not illuminate Scripture but is illuminated by it and is wholly dependent upon Scripture to dispel its ignorance. For the church, too, Scripture is 'a lamp shining in a dark place' (2 Pet. 1:19), and its clarity is not generated but confessed and received in the church's traditions of reading.

Underlying this are two primary motifs in a theology of the clarity of Scripture. The first is that Scripture's clarity is closely attached to its sufficiency. Supplementation of Scripture is disallowed because, as the elected assistant to God's self-manifestation, Scripture is entirely adequate to the task to which it is appointed.

David Brown's recent account of 'tradition as revelation' in *Tradition and Imagination* falters at just this point. 'Revelation is ... a matter of God taking seriously our historical situatedness, our dependence on our own particular environment and setting, rather than attempting to override it. That being so, my contention is that the process of revelation had to continue beyond Scripture, since otherwise the tradition would have become stultified through being trapped within one particular epoch and its assumptions.'[49] Rejecting a 'deposit' view of revelation and contending that tradition is best understood as 'imaginative reappropriation of the past',[50] Brown presupposes that Scripture is 'part of a living tradition that is constantly subject to change'.[51] If such an account fails, it is partly because within its terms there can be no theologically significant distinction between Scripture and tradition (and therefore, of course, no operable versions of canon and dogma). But it is also because it mischaracterizes tradition itself, whose essential activity it conceives to be 'rewriting',[52] hardly a fitting term to describe the commentarial traditions which have had such importance in Christian reception of Scripture.[53] To say, on the other hand, that the church finds itself in the light of the clear Word of God, *having been* illuminated, is to suggest that Scripture is possessed of a measure of completeness, a hard edge which marks it off from those acts by which the church receives its radiance.

A second, related motif is that Scripture is the living Word of God, the *viva vox dei* which is not inert and obscure until activated by the church's acts, but *in se* the means of bestowing life and light. Clarity is not a property that Scripture acquires by virtue of the church's use; as a function of the light and life of the

---

[49] Brown, *Tradition and Imagination*, 8.

[50] Brown, *Tradition and Imagination*, 65.

[51] Brown, *Tradition and Imagination*, 107.

[52] Brown, *Tradition and Imagination*, 74.

[53] It is interesting that Brown's examples of tradition in this and the subsequent volume, *Discipleship and Imagination*, are largely drawn from imaginative literature, the plastic arts and popular piety.

gospel and the gospel's God, its clarity in an important sense precedes the church's reading.

> Here we may consider Rowan Williams's proposal that, over against 'closed' accounts of the interpretation of Scripture in which reading is merely a matter of passive reception of already constituted meaning, reading is properly 'dramatic' or 'diachronic'. 'The meanings in our reading,' he writes, 'are like the meanings in the rest of our experience, they are to be discovered, unfolded ... So long as our humanity remains unintelligible except as a life of material change, irreversible movement, it is unlikely, to say the least, that we could establish non-diachronic modes of reading as primary'.[54] Or again: 'Christian language takes it for granted ... that meanings are learned and produced, not given in iconic, ahistorical form. It grows out of a particular set of communal and individual histories, and its images and idioms are fundamentally shaped by this fact.'[55] And so Christian interpretation is unavoidably engaged in 'dramatic' modes of reading: 'we are invited to identify ourselves in the story being contemplated, to re-appropriate who we are now, and who we shall or can be, in terms of the story. *Its* movements, transactions, transformation, become *ours* ... [A] dramatic reading means that our appropriation of the story is not a static relation of confrontation with images of virtue or vice, finished pictures of a quality once and for all achieved and so no longer taking time, but an active working through of the story's movement in our own time.'[56] 'Dramatic' or 'diachronic' reading thus highlights both the *temporal* and the *active* character of our interpretation of texts; they are a matter of 'a complex of interwoven processes: a production of meaning in the only mode available for material and temporal creatures'.[57] The difficulty here is, once again, not the affirmation that there is an ecclesial component in the reception of Scripture, but that the ecclesial component is of such prominence that the text becomes an occasion for the church's activity of interpretation, work that is more poetic than receptive.

Clarity is not churchly clarification; the church's traditions of interpretation are authentic insofar as they are a receiving of the clear Word. The ecclesial basis for this is that the church is the creature of the Word. The church is that community which is brought into life and preserved in life by the communicative and reconciling action of the triune God, the one in whose presence and by whose gift the church has its life. That presence and gift are brought to bear upon the church by the action of the Spirit of the risen Christ in and through the prophetic and apostolic witnesses. Holy Scripture, therefore, is the instrument of Christ's rule in the church, and stands over against the church – not as a mere statutory norm, but as the sword of the Spirit. Scripture is not something

---

[54] Williams, 'Discipline', 49.
[55] Williams, 'Discipline', 49.
[56] Williams, 'Discipline', 50.
[57] Williams, 'Discipline', 55.

indefinite and opaque, but a divine action of illuminating force and clarity. The office of the church in the matter of interpretation is undertaken, therefore, with deference and submission, wholly subservient and posterior to the divine self-annunciation, whose lively and clear presence it indicates rather than completes or activates. What the church does is, in Bullinger's phrase, a matter of 'giving a setting out to the Word of God'.[58] The church interprets the Word by confessing and exhibiting its clarity. There is a parallel here to the churchly act of canonization: the church does not create the canon but confesses the canon and pledges itself to abide under the canon's rule and judgement. So in its acts of interpretation: the church does not create Scripture's clarity but confesses its antecedent character and so pledges itself to continue beneath its consolation and instruction, and thereby to test its interpretative acts against the clear Word, asking whether they are 'genuine audits corresponding to the Word of God or … no more than speculative constructs out of the Church's creative spirituality'.[59]

There are, doubtless, spiritualized versions of the sort of ecclesiology suggested here which all but eliminate the element of churchly reception and reduce the interpretation of Holy Scripture to something drastically internal and individualistic. But the issue is not whether the clarity of Scripture eradicates tradition: of course not. The church is visible; it is a historical form of common life and activity. The issue is, rather: what kind of tradition? My suggestion is that, in the light of the clarity of Scripture, the church's tradition is best understood as 'holy attentiveness'. Tradition is the church's movement of Spirit-generated and Spirit-governed hearing of the clear Word of the gospel that is borne to us by Holy Scripture. It is the *church's* movement, and therefore categorically different from the divine movement of self-manifestation and its creaturely auxiliary; it is not self-moved, and it can claim no perfection. It may, indeed, be corrupt; at certain points it may be a counter-movement to God's revelatory presence, especially when it seeks to preside over that presence as its guardian, or gives itself the task of bestowing on God's revelation a clarity which it lacks. But though it is frail, it stands under the hopeful sign of God's election, and as it is appointed by the Holy Spirit to serve the clear Word of God, so it is made a fitting instrument of hearing. To believe in the Holy Spirit is necessarily to believe in the holy catholic church, the communion of saints. And to believe in the church is to believe in the forgiveness of sins – to believe, that is, that the Spirit can purify a community of the Word of God and make it into a movement in which the Word gains a hearing for itself. Christian interpretation of Scripture exists in that movement, which is not a finished product but an inherited task. Finding ourselves in that movement and the human

---

[58] Bullinger, *Decades*, 72.
[59] Torrance, *Divine Meaning*, 6.

company which assembles around it, learning in its school, coming to envisage our own task through those who have also been appointed to attend to the Word, we are quickened to the task of responsible participation in the discernment of the clear Word. Our final task is to offer an initial sketch of that participation.

Responsible Participation in the Discernment of the Clear Word

Reconciled to God, drawn into the fellowship of the saints and illuminated by the Holy Spirit, the Christian interpreter of Holy Scripture is summoned and empowered humbly to venture interpretation of the clear Word of God as it is spoken in the words of Holy Scripture.

The clarity of Scripture does not eliminate readerly activity. It is certainly true that there is a correlation between the rise of some strands of general hermeneutical theory in theology and the decline of appeal to *claritas scripturae* in biblical hermeneutics, as attention shifts away from the biblical text as self-interpreting (that is, as the means of the Spirit's clarification of the gospel to the saints of God) towards the text as awaiting interpretative realization. But it would be improper to respond to this development by urging the claims of a naïve objectivism, in which Scripture's clarity is such that the interpreter is merely the wax on which the text leaves its clear impression. Clarity does not suspend interpretation; but what is of central importance is to offer a theological rationale for the necessity of interpretation, rather than remaining content with, say, the lightly theologized phenomenology of human subjectivity or reader-response theory which often do service at this juncture. In continuation of what has been said about the doctrine of the church, the necessity of interpretation must be grounded in a consideration of the ways and works of God among the saints.

Interpretation is necessary because Holy Scripture is an element in the economy of salvation, the economy whose theme is the renewal of fellowship between God and his human creatures. Interpretation is an aspect of the rebirth of our noetic fellowship with God. The history of reconciliation and revelation is not a unilateral divine history in which there is only a divine agent, with no creaturely coordinate. It is the history of God with us; because its *res* is fellowship, it has a genuine human coefficient. In it, the human creature is restored to *life*, from, with and for God, renewed to inalienable humanness, not to the spurious autonomy of the proud captains of the mind, but to the freedom to confess, to know as we are known. In this sphere of the knowledge of God, therefore, there can be no sense in which revelation is a declaration that achieves its end simply by being uttered. As creative and reconciling speech, revelation calls forth a hearer. It does so *ex nihilo*. The hearer does not precede the divine Word, and is not a creaturely *conditio sine qua non* for revelation's effectiveness. Revelation is effective *in se*, by virtue of its own self-moved and sovereign power. But that movement is a movement which calls into being a partner to this divine self-giving, one who participates, not only passively but as a real agent, in the movement of the knowledge of God. And as revelation presents itself through the textual form of Holy Scripture, the Word constitutes the creature as reader and interpreter, not just as observer but as one commissioned to act out the right use of Scripture. To say less would be to cut short the reach of the history of salvation.

Revelation is therefore summons and empowerment. It is grace, and therefore wholly creative; it is the self-presentation of the one who brings into being the things that are not. But he really does bring them into being, really does create them and appoint them to stand beneath his summons and to be empowered by him to live, and therefore to hear the clear Word of God and see the light of life.

This sketch of a theological grounding of the necessity of hermeneutics can be contrasted with two other recent Christian accounts of the same territory in which theological factors play a much less prominent role. The first is found in J.K.A. Smith's study *The Fall of Interpretation*. Smith's argument for the necessity of interpretation takes the form of a severe critique of what he claims is a long tradition in Western theology according to which interpretation is a result of the fall, a 'postlapsarian disease'[60] in which immediacy is replaced by hermeneutical mediation. Smith's counter-proposal 'understands interpretation and hermeneutical mediation as constitutive aspects of human being-in-the-world'.[61] Insofar as the proposal is doctrinally underwritten, it is by a theology of createdness, for which hermeneutics is 'an aspect of a good, peaceful creation'.[62] The result of this is 'an understanding of the *status* of interpretation as a "creational" task, a task that is constitutive of finitude and thus not a "labor" to be escaped or overcome'.[63] An immediate consequence is that Smith can make little positive sense of the notion of the clarity of Scripture, which he sees as expressive of a desire to 'return from mediation to immediacy, from distortion to "perfect clarity" and from interpretation to "pure reading"'.[64] Theological talk of clarity is therefore rejected as 'incipient Platonism (or gnosticism)',[65] resting 'on a dream of full presence',[66] infected with the 'myth of immediacy'.[67] This

---

[60] Smith, *Fall*, 18.
[61] Smith, *Fall*, 22.
[62] Smith, *Fall*, 22.
[63] Smith, *Fall*, 22–23.
[64] Smith, *Fall*, 38.
[65] Smith, *Fall*, 134.
[66] Smith, *Fall*, 135.
[67] Smith, *Fall*, 88.

account is unsatisfactory at a couple of levels. 1) It is historically underdetermined. There have been debased versions of the doctrine of the clarity of Scripture which confuse *claritas* with immediacy and which therefore think of interpretation as a curse from which we have to be redeemed. But neither the Reformers nor the Protestant dogmaticians construe clarity in that way, nor do they fail to emphasize that clarity does not disqualify the activities of interpretation. Smith offers few historical examples of how the immediacy excludes interpretation, and his account of the Western theological tradition is remarkably broad brush in its treatment. 2) In doctrinal terms, the most telling inadequacy of his account is Smith's extracting of the notion of *claritas* from its surrounding dogmatic structure. The classical Protestant construal of perspicuity is a complex arrangement of Christology, soteriology, pneumatology, ecclesiology and sanctification, all undergirded by a doctrine of the ways and works of God in revelation. Only when lifted out of that cluster of affirmations can clarity be reduced to a crude notion of transparency. Smith's inattentiveness to these dogmatic issues, which leads to a seriously stripped-down version of *claritas*, can be traced to the fact that, in the tradition of neo-Reformed philosophers like Dooyeweerd, but in distinction from more classical Reformed thinkers like Bavinck, Barth and Berkouwer, he considers philosophy foundational to the 'special science' of theology.[68] One of the corollaries of this is the development of a notion of creation that has little to do with the economy of reconciliation, but is in fact a metaphysics of human finitude with little real theological freight. In effect, Smith offers a philosophical rationale for the necessity of interpretation, and moreover one which bifurcates *claritas* and interpretation by deploying the wrong doctrinal materials.

Callahan, in *The Clarity of Scripture*, avoids some of these difficulties by providing more extensive theological foundations for his account of the necessity of interpretation. Yet here, too, interpretative acts on the part of readers are not adequately coordinated with divine activity, indeed, the doctrines of reconciliation and revelation, though they form the background of the account, rarely come forward to the front of the stage. In large part, this is because of Callahan's strong concern to ensure that 'the assertion of Scripture's clarity is immediately related to how readers read'.[69] In itself this is an uncontroversial, indeed a necessary, concern. But things go somewhat awry when the description of the reader is undertaken by talk of 'Christian interpretative frameworks',[70] of 'a pattern of Christian interpretative interests',[71] or of the reader's 'enactment or embodiment of the text's display of what was once offered',[72] all of which give the wrong sort of scope to the reader. Matters would be more securely stated by a more modest, soteriological idiom of 'faith', 'hearing', 'attention', and so forth, in order to avoid the impression that the relation of the reader to Holy Scripture is simply a particular instance of a general rule about texts and

---

[68] Cf. Smith, *Fall*, 187 n. 22.
[69] Callahan, *Clarity of Scripture*, 47–48.
[70] Callahan, *Clarity of Scripture*, 52.
[71] Callahan, *Clarity of Scripture*, 17.
[72] Callahan, *Clarity of Scripture*, 42.

their reception, an impression reinforced by Callahan's deployment of reader-reception hermeneutics in the latter part of his study.

The case for the necessity of interpretation is best made, not (as in Smith's work) through religious philosophy, or (as in Callahan's book) through a combination of theology and literary theory, but through a consideration of the movement of revelation. In this respect, T. Ward's account in *Word and Supplement* gives much greater space to theological factors. In distinguishing between sufficiency and self-sufficiency, and therefore highlighting the text's relations to its readers, he makes careful use of pneumatology, for it is the Spirit who 'brings the possibility of appropriate response to the text's illocutionary act'.[73] And Ward's account is mercifully free of the phenomenology of interpreting subjects that so clogs many discussions of reading. Yet even here theological arguments are set alongside philosophical and literary materials, especially speech-act theory, in a way which does not always leave space for a full deployment of the dogmatic materials, and which indicates that the book has a firm apologetic agenda.

In order to describe that to which the Christian is summoned and for which the Christian is empowered in the matter of the clear Word of God in its scriptural witness, we need to depict, first, the context or setting of interpretation, and then, second, the nature and activity of the interpreter.

The setting is best described by use of soteriological, ecclesiological and pneumatological teaching: the Christian interpreter is 'reconciled to God, drawn into the fellowship of the saints and illuminated by the Holy Spirit'. Of the soteriological and ecclesiological aspects, much has already been said: the Christian interpreter is one who has been extracted from the darkness of sin by the judgement and mercy of God, and set in the sphere of the church, the chosen race, the royal priesthood, the holy nation which is what it is by virtue of the divine call out of darkness into light. Christian interpretation of Holy Scripture is determined by this setting; the 'hermeneutical situation' (that is, the constitutive elements of the business of scriptural interpretation, God, text and readers, and the field of their interactions) is not an instance of something more basic but an episode in the history of salvation. At every point it is defined by the fact that it involves this God (the one who is light and who in Jesus Christ and the Holy Spirit is luminously present), this text (Holy Scripture as the assistant to that presence), and therefore this reader (the faithful hearer of this God in and through this text). Pneumatology has an especially important role in achieving the right kind of theological determinacy in an account of the anthropological, readerly element. As we have noted, theology readily succumbs to the temptation to depict the reader by deploying such bits of philosophical or literary phenomenology as appear companionable to its own interests. Pneumatology forestalls this, by demonstrating that the readerly

---

[73] Ward, *Word and Supplement*, 202.

element is ingredient within the compass of God's revelatory presence, and therefore that non-theological supplements are not only unnecessary but may, indeed, deform the content of a theological portrait of interpretation, most commonly by excessive belief in readerly competence. The Holy Spirit is the Lord and life-giver whose work in this sphere is to generate a genuine human correspondent to God's revealing work, that is, genuine acknowledgement and response to the divine summons, and a genuine capacity to hear and see. The 'circuit of the Spirit' thus embraces God's revelatory and inspiring acts and God's illuminating work, so that we do indeed have 'a world of revelation, where God and man are associated again in mutual understanding'.[74]

In this setting, what is to be said of readerly, interpretative activity? The act of interpretation repeats the basic motif of Christian existence, which is being drawn out of the darkness of sin and turned to the light of the gospel. Holy Scripture is clear; but because its matter is that to which we must be reconciled, readers can only discern its clarity if their darkness is illuminated. By what right do we pronounce Scripture to be obscure? Luther asks:

> With similar temerity a man might veil his own eyes or go out of the light into the darkness and hide himself, and then blame the sun and the day for being obscure. Let miserable men, therefore, stop imputing with blasphemous perversity the darkness and obscurity of their own hearts to the wholly clear Scriptures of God.[75]

Setting aside darkness and turning to the light are not within the competence of readers (theories of readerly virtue usually trip at this point). To discern the light of God is to discern that which itself gives the possibility of its own discernment. We see light in God's light. Interpretation of the clear Word of God is therefore not first of all an act of clarification but the event of being clarified. Reading, therefore, always includes a humbling of the reader, a breaking of the will in which there is acted out the struggle to detach our apprehension of the text from the idolatrous schemas that we inevitably take to it, and by which we seek to command or suppress it or render it convenient to us. 'Behold and see, if thou canst, O soul pressed down by the corruptible body, and weighed down by earthly thoughts, many and various; behold and see, if thou canst, God is truth.'[76] If that is a dynamic of reading, then reading Holy Scripture in its clarity involves subjection to the divine declaration.

> For it is not for us to sit in judgement on Scripture and divine truth, but to let God do his work in and through it ... Of course, we have to give an account of our understanding of Scripture, but not in such a way that it is forced or wrested according to our will, but rather so that we are taught by Scripture.[77]

---

[74] Senarclens, *Heirs*, 282.

[75] Luther, *Bondage*, 27.

[76] Augustine, *De Trinitate* VIII.iii.

[77] Zwingli, 'Clarity and Certainty', 92.

Reading the clear Word of God involves mortification; as Bullinger notes, true exposition of the clear Word must never be 'after our own fantasies'.[78]

Yet the matter cannot remain here. The reader is not simply mortified, stripped of deceit and interpretative hubris, but also vivified: exegetical reason is renewed, and interpretation made possible. Interpretation is not simply a passive letting-be of the text, but a venture of responsibility. The human coordinate to the clarity of Holy Scripture is thus not only negation but also what Barth calls 'freedom under the Word',[79] that is, responsibility for the interpretation of the Word which God has for the church. The church

> cannot allow the revelation attested by Scripture to flow over itself as a waterfall flows over a cliff. Rather, because God's revelation is attested by Scripture and because Scripture furnishes the documentary evidence of this movement of revelation and exists only within it, the church for its part must allow itself to be set in movement through Scripture.[80]

Because *claritas* is inseparable from *efficacia*, then 'the superiority of Scripture over against the church is not the idolatrous calm of icy mountain peaks towering motionlessly above a blossoming valley … Scripture is itself spirit and life'.[81] In terms of the relation of clarity to interpretation, this means that the churchly readers of Scripture are not simply 'spectators or even objects'[82] of the rule of Scripture in the church, but those responsible for its explanation.

> As the Word of God it requires no explanation … since as such it is clear in itself. The Holy Ghost knows very well what he has said to the prophets and apostles and what through them he wills also to say to us. This clarity which Scripture has in itself as God's Word, this objective *perspicuitas* which it possesses, is subject to no human responsibility or care.[83]

But this Word assumes the form of a human word, and so incurs the need of explanation. Yet the basic form of this explanation is 'the activity of subordination',[84] which Barth explains thus:

> When the Word of God meets us, we are laden with the images, ideas and certainties which we ourselves have formed about God, the world and ourselves. In the fog of

---

[78] Bullinger, *Decades*, 75.
[79] Barth, *Church Dogmatics* I/2, 695–740.
[80] Barth, *Church Dogmatics* I/2, 671–72.
[81] Barth, *Church Dogmatics* I/2, 673.
[82] Barth, *Church Dogmatics* I/2, 711.
[83] Barth, *Church Dogmatics* I/2, 712.
[84] Barth, *Church Dogmatics* I/2, 715.

this intellectual life of ours the Word of God, which is clear in itself, always becomes obscure. It can become clear to us only when this fog breaks and dissolves.[85]

Because of this, 'it is true that every interpretation of Scripture consists substantially in the interpretation which the Word gives of itself'.[86] Yet 'it is still the case that this self-illumination does not take place without us, and therefore terminates in that freedom to which as members of the church we are called, and therefore in a human activity in the service of the Word of God.'[87]

Revelation is a movement that moves. Impelled into hearing and responsibility by that movement, the Christian is also authorized and empowered for interpretation. Because they have their place in the formative economy of the clear Word of God, interpretative acts are neither constructive nor creative. But they are work, a straining of our powers to follow, an attempt to discern and articulate the clear Word which does not simply lie before us but which sets itself in relation to us as an address which we do not really hear until we are actively caught up in the movement of which both it and we are part.

Being caught up in this movement means *reading according to the law of the text*. Scripture's clarity has the character of law. The law of the text is its presentation to us of a definite order and a definite requirement. To read is to trace that order, following its lead, exploring, seeking to say again what it says to us, but all this as discovery of an inherent clarity, a repeating of what is there. We have been schooled by genealogists into acute suspicion of this law of the text, and to regard the associated hermeneutics as 'strict disciplinarian observance'.[88] But surely something more courageous is required of us than compliance with this convention of rebellion? Our almost obsessive scruple about the dangers of pathological versions of the text as law, our fretting at the question of whether texts will deceive, can often be a refusal to have a mature and responsible relation to a text without retreating into agonistics in which we have to master the text or it will surely master us. For the law of the text does not stultify any more than the moral law undermines ethical authenticity. As law the text quickens, summoning us and enabling us actively to discern the structure of its reality and the tasks which it sets before us.

Conclusion

The absence of the notion of *claritas scripturae* in the exegetical and hermeneutical practices of much mainstream Christianity is in part a function

---

[85] Barth, *Church Dogmatics* I/2, 716.
[86] Barth, *Church Dogmatics* I/2, 718.
[87] Barth, *Church Dogmatics* I/2, 718.
[88] Vattimo, *Beyond Interpretation*, 50.

of the fact that, for a variety of reasons, modern Christianity has come to share a widespread cultural assumption – namely that texts are not and cannot be a mode of *scientia*, and therefore that appeal to the biblical text will not get us very far. Theologians concerned to counter this assumption most often analyse the problem as one of authority: failure to appeal to the text is an exercise in disobedience. This is undoubtedly an aspect of the matter, from which modern Christianity has too readily disencumbered itself. But more is involved: an inability in a non-statutory culture to conceive of how appeal to a text could possibly be a mode of rational inquiry. For are not texts always and only instruments of power, occlusions of real (economic, political, gendered) relations? And cannot texts be resolved without residue into authors or contexts or readers, and so stripped of the determinateness necessary to exercise a statutory role?

A recovery of the role of texts requires at least three things. It involves a wider recovery of confidence in substantive rationality. It involves careful theological specification of the nature and properties of Holy Scripture, including clarity, in terms of its place in the wider tapestry of the self-manifesting presence of God among the saints. But it also involves coming to see that the very activity of interpretation is itself an episode in the struggle between faith and repudiation of God. We can cloak our own darkness by calling it the obscurity of the text; we can evade the judgement that Scripture announces by endless hermeneutical deferral; we can treat Scripture not as the clear Word of judgement and hope but as a further opportunity for the imagination to be puzzled, stimulated and set to work. 'Behold and see if thou canst ... But thou canst not: thou wilt slide back into those carnal and earthly things.' That is why the promise of *claritas scripturae* is inseparable from the prayer: 'Open my eyes, that I may behold wondrous things out of thy law' (Ps. 119:18). In the answer to that prayer is the recovery of the vocation of biblical theology and biblical interpretation.

Bibliography

Augustine, *De Trinitate libri XV* (CCSL 50; Turnholt: Brepols, 1968)

Barth, K., *Church Dogmatics* I/2 (Edinburgh: T. & T. Clark, 1956)

—, *Church Dogmatics* IV/3 (Edinburgh: T. & T. Clark, 1961)

Beisser, *Claritas Scripturae bei Martin Luther* (Göttingen: Vandenhoeck & Ruprecht, 1966)

Berkouwer, G.C., *Holy Scripture* (Grand Rapids: Eerdmans, 1975)

Brown, D., *Discipleship and Imagination: Christian Tradition and Truth* (Oxford: Oxford University Press, 2000)

—, *Tradition and Imagination: Revelation and Change* (Oxford: Oxford University Press, 1999)

Bullinger, H., *The Decades* I & II (Cambridge: Cambridge University Press, 1849)

Callahan, J.P., *The Clarity of Scripture: History, Theology and Contemporary Literary Studies* (Downers Grove, IL: InterVarsity Press, 2001)

Calvin, J., *The Epistle of St Paul to the Hebrews and the First and Second Letters of St Peter* (Edinburgh: Oliver and Boyd, 1963)

Duchrow, U., 'Die Klarheit der Schrift und die Vernunft', *KD* 15 (1969), 1–17

Hayden-Roy, P., 'Hermeneutica gloriae vs. hermeneutica crucis: Sebastian Franck and Martin Luther on the Clarity of Scripture', *ARG* 81 (1990), 50–68

Hermann, R., 'Von der Klarheit der Heiligen Schrift: Untersuchungen und Erörterungen über Luthers Lehre von der Schrift in *De servo arbitrio*', in *Studien zur Theologie Luthers und des Luthertums* (Göttingen: Vandenhoeck & Ruprecht, 1981), 170–255

Hodge, C., *Systematic Theology*, I (New York: Scribner, Armstrong, 1877)

Horton, M., *Covenant and Eschatology: The Divine Drama* (Louisville, KY: Westminster John Knox Press, 2002)

Kuss, O., 'Über die Klarheit der Schrift', in *Schriftauslegung: Beiträge zur Hermeneutik des Neuen Testamentes und im Neuen Testament* (ed. J. Ernst; Paderborn: Schöningh, 1972), 89–149

Luther, M. *The Bondage of the Will*, in *Luther's Works*, vol. 33 (Philadelphia: Fortress Press, 1972)

Marquard, O., 'The Question, To What is Hermeneutics the Answer?', *Contemporary German Philosophy* 4 (1981), 9–31

Mau, R., 'Klarheit der Schrift und Evangelium: Zum Ansatz des lutherschen Gedankens der claritas scripturae', *Theologische Versuche* 4 (1972), 129–43

Muller, R., *Post-Reformation Reformed Dogmatics* II: *Holy Scripture: The Cognitive Foundation of Theology* (Grand Rapids: Baker, 1993)

Neuner, P., and F. Schröger, 'Luthers These von der Klarheit der Schrift', *TGl* 74 (1984), 39–58

Østergaard-Nielsen, H., *Scriptura Sacra et Viva Vox: Eine Lutherstudie* (Munich: Kaiser, 1957)

Paulson, S.D., 'From Scripture to Dogmatics', *LQ* 7 (1993), 159–69

Preus, J.S., *Spinoza and the Irrelevance of Biblical Authority* (Cambridge: Cambridge University Press, 2001)

Rothen, R., *Die Klarheit der Schrift* (2 vols.; Göttingen: Vandenhoeck & Ruprecht, 1990)

Sandin, R.T., 'The Clarity of Scripture', in *The Living and Active Word of God* (ed. M. Inch and R. Youngblood; Winona Lake: Eisenbrauns, 1983), 237–53

Senarclens, J. de, *Heirs of the Reformation* (London: SCM Press, 1963)

Smith, J.K.A., *The Fall of Interpretation: Philosophical Foundations for a Creational Hermeneutic* (Downers Grove, IL: InterVarsity Press, 2000)

Thiselton, A.C., *New Horizons in Hermeneutics* (London: HarperCollins, 1992)

Torrance, T.F., *Divine Meaning: Studies in Patristic Hermeneutics* (Edinburgh: T. & T. Clark, 1995)

Turretin, F., *Institutes of Elenctic Theology* I: *First through Tenth Topics* (Phillipsburg: Presbyterian and Reformed Publishing, 1992)

Vanhoozer, K., *First Theology: God, Scripture and Hermeneutics* (Leicester: Apollos, 2002)

—, *Is There a Meaning in this Text? The Bible, the Reader and the Morality of Literary Knowledge* (Leicester: Apollos, 1998)

Vattimo, G., *Beyond Interpretation: The Meaning of Hermeneutics for Philosophy* (Cambridge: Polity, 1997)

Ward, T., *Word and Supplement: Speech Acts, Biblical Texts, and the Sufficiency of Scripture* (Oxford: Oxford University Press, 2002)

Webster, J., 'The Dogmatic Location of the Canon', in *Word and Church: Essays in Christian Dogmatics* (Edinburgh: T. & T. Clark, 2001), 9–46

—, *Holy Scripture* (Cambridge: Cambridge University Press, 2003)

Wenz, A., *Das Wort Gottes, Gericht und Rettung: Untersuchungen zur Autorität der Heiligen Schrift in Bekenntnis und Lehre der Kirche* (Göttingen: Vandenhoeck & Ruprecht, 1996)

Williams, R., 'The Discipline of Scripture', in *On Christian Theology* (Oxford: Basil Blackwell, 2000), 44–59

Wolf, E., 'Über "Klarheit der Heiligen Schrift" nach Luthers *De servo arbitrio*', *Theologische Literaturzeitung* 92 (1967), 721–30

Zwingli, H., 'Of the Clarity and Certainty or Power of the Word of God', in *Zwingli and Bullinger* (ed. G.W. Bromiley; London: SCM Press, 1953), 59–95

15

Biblical Theology and Theological Exegesis
R. R. Reno

Introduction

Stephen Fowl begins his recent book, *Engaging Scripture: A Model for Theological Interpretation*, with an observation germane to the topic of this volume. 'The discipline of biblical theology,' he writes, 'in its most common form, is systematically unable to generate serious theological interpretation of scripture.'[1] When I first read this sentence, I gave immediate assent. Influenced by Hans Frei's genealogy of modern biblical scholarship, *The Eclipse of Biblical Narrative*, I have long nurtured a critical suspicion of contemporary students of the Bible, even a suspicion of the work of scholars committed to serving the church with their learned expertise. More recently, reflection upon the spiritual logic of the modern critical tradition has deepened my conviction that the mental habits of contemporary intellectual life, habits often nurtured in the late eighteenth- and early nineteenth-century origins of historical-critical study of the Bible, have a moribund and sterile tendency.[2]

Unsystematic reading in the history of modern biblical interpretation has only reinforced my suspicions. The link between anti-dogmatic theological liberalism and the methodological programme outlined by Benjamin Jowett in his influential essay, 'On the Interpretation of Scripture' in *Essays and Reviews*, is patent.[3] His essay is a treasure trove of modernist truisms that continue to underwrite the methods of historical-critical biblical study.[4] One can be

---

[1] Fowl, *Engaging Scripture*, 1.
[2] See my two recent efforts to understand these contemporary mental habits, 'Postmodern Irony', and 'Fighting'.
[3] Jowett, *Essays and Reviews*, 330–433.
[4] Here are some gems. 1) 'If words have more than one meaning, they may have any meaning' (p. 37) – a classic case of the slippery slope fallacy. 2) 'A knowledge of the original language is a necessary qualification of the Interpreter of Scripture' (p. 390) – and yet, the Greek Fathers are miserable failures as exegetes. 3) 'The simple words

brought to despair by the ways in which modern historical critics of the Bible are so blissfully ignorant and uncritical of their own intellectual discipline.[5] This ignorance is compounded by the fact that, in the United States, biblical scholarship is overwhelmed with refugees from the most dominant form of American Christian modernism, fundamentalism. Thus, the shift from shrill biblicism to an equally shrill anti-biblicism is seamless, and the consensus is preserved. As Jowett proclaims, the dead hand of dogma corrupts the pure and original biblical faith. Exegesis disciplined by the doctrinal tradition of the church is to be opposed. Modern myths of pure access and foundational certainties triumph across the board.

Yet, the more I have thought about Fowl's assessment of our current situation, the less I have been satisfied with my own happy assent. For I worry that I have been judging the failures of biblical scholarship on the basis of my own half-baked ideas about theological exegesis, playing the superior critic of the critics with my own postmodern smugness. The more I have thought about the key comparative term in Fowl's assessment, the less confident I have become that I know just what might constitute the 'serious theological interpretation of scripture' that 'the discipline of biblical theology' fails to 'generate'. After all, one should hesitate to accuse a discipline of failing to deliver desired results if one cannot adequately characterize the *desideratum*. My goal, then, is to formulate an account of theological exegesis, to take a material stand by which to clarify what is lacking in contemporary biblical exegesis.

To achieve this goal, I will not attempt a theological definition of 'theological exegesis'. Instead, I wish to work inductively. I will begin with a modest survey of recent biblical commentaries, leavened with some backward glances to the patristic tradition of exegesis. My selection is ad hoc and limited, but I am increasingly convinced that one of the impediments to clear thinking about theological exegesis on the part of theologians is a drift toward abstraction. To exhort one and all to read the Bible 'theologically', or to read it 'for the church', offers little insight into what is necessary. Furthermore, digressions into Ricœurian, narrative and postmodern hermeneutical theory seem to produce more ideas than exegesis.[6] My hope is that attention to particular

---

of [Scripture the interpreter] tries to preserve absolutely pure from the refinements or distinctions of later times' (p. 338) – modernity is the great new beginning. 'The true use of interpretation is to get rid of interpretation, and leave us alone in company with the author' (p. 384) – Jowett has the same interpretive ideal as John Nelson Darby.

[5] For a richly compact and spiritually disciplined expression of this despair, see DiNoia's review of John P. Meier's *A Marginal Jew*.

[6] Recently, Rabbi Shalom Carmy told me that his teacher, Rabbi Joseph Soloveitchik, lamented that we live in an age of treatise, not commentary. One of my goals in this chapter is to offer remarks underdetermined by prevailing theories

exegetical performances will help bring the question of theological exegesis into focus, and do so at a level of textual specificity familiar to biblical scholars.

In what follows, I offer a commentary on some commentaries, moving from New Testament to Old Testament. This brief tour through instances of modern exegesis will allow me to formulate the problem – the problem of distance – that dominates most efforts to recover a theologically rich interpretation of Scripture. Insofar as I am able to give clear expression to this problem, I will be better able to suggest a way forward to a vigorous practice of theological exegesis.

New Testament

For focus, consider a relatively obscure verse from Paul's Epistle to the Romans – 8:26. The verse reads as follows: 'Likewise the Spirit helps us in our weakness; for we do not know how to pray as we ought, but the Spirit himself intercedes for us with sighs too deep for words' (RSV). This passage has a fruitful richness. It has philological puzzles: the rare word 'intercession'. The 'likewise' raises questions about the unit of text appropriate for fruitful exegesis. The parallel of the Spirit's intercession with the Son's intercession places the verse within a Trinitarian horizon. More importantly, for my purposes, the recent history of commentary is marked by telling failures and some useful successes.

Anders Nygren does not directly discuss Romans 8:26 in his *Commentary on Romans*. Instead, he offers comment on 8:18–30 as a whole unit, emphasizing the single theme of eschatological victory. For Nygren, these verses are best understood as Paul's expression of confidence in 'God's mighty acts'. The exegesis is interesting for two reasons: 1) it echoes Nygren's own theology of *Christus victor*, and 2) it reflects the a-Trinitarian pattern of so many New Testament commentaries. 'God' and 'Christ' are the only subjects of divine predicates in this exegesis. This is very striking, because I have the impression that this a-Trinitarian framework is not the result of historical-critical compunction. That is to say, Nygren is vigorously 'theological' in his reading of the text and spends little or no time discussing philological or historical questions.

Paul Achtemeier's commentary on Romans is more detailed than Nygren's, and he comments directly on 8:26, but like Nygren's, the exegesis is strikingly similar in theological consequence.[7] Furthermore, like Nygren, there is no operative Trinitarian language. So, when explaining the intercession of the Spirit, Achtemeier concludes, 'Without the Spirit, we are simply at a loss to know how to communicate with God.'[8] Achtemeier's exegetical

---

of interpretation, and in this way I hope to facilitate the writing of commentaries rather than contribute to the production of theory.

[7] Achtemeier, *Romans*.

[8] Achtemeier, *Romans*, 143.

approach does more than repeat Nygren's approach and theology. Achtemeier advances apologetic, doctrinal, intratextual and anagogical comments as well. For example, against those tempted to spiritualize pre-emptively, Achtemeier observes that the Pauline idea of creation's 'groaning' is not simply poetic. A polluted environment suffers. At the doctrinal level, Achtemeier treats all of Romans 8 as testimony that the doctrine of predestination produces confidence and not fear. 'We have confidence in our future with God only because that future is in God's hands.'[9] On this theme, he points to numerous OT passages that affirm that the future is in God's hands (e.g., Is. 44:6–8). And finally, Achtemeier offers an anagogical exegesis (though he may not see it as such) of 8:26–27. God will heed prayers 'characterized less by petitions for personal good than for the good of the community of God's people'.[10]

This anagogical approach to 8:26 is not unique to Achtemeier. Another commentator interprets the verse as reassuring us that even our feeble efforts in prayer will be appreciated by God.[11] Still another makes the anodyne comment on 8:26 that Paul is trying to remind us 'that we who are Christians are not the spiritual giants we would like to be'.[12] Compare these instances of spiritual interpretation with John Chrysostom. As a moralizing interpreter, Chrysostom often scans as a contemporary exegete. In his *Homilies on Romans*, his comment on this verse observes that 'we are ignorant of much that is profitable for us'.[13] Yet, the homiletical point is made in the context of a discussion of what might be called the pneumatic history of the church. Referring to 1 Corinthians 14, Chrysostom notes that 'God did in those days give all that were baptized certain excellent gifts'. This pneumatic plenitude stands in contrast to his own day. Exploiting the presence of the notion of intercession in Romans 8:26, Chrysostom observes that pneumatic potency has been concentrated in the ordained clergy who offer up prayers on behalf of the people. I do not want to commend Chrysostom's material analysis. The point is that the homiletical chestnut about our spiritual immaturity is placed within a briefly outlined scheme of pneumatological development. Chrysostom presumes that the history of the church provides an apt context for exegetical discernment, and the effect is to draw together his audience and the text.

In contrast, a Roman Catholic commentator, Hermann Schelkle, illustrates the abstractive move that is so characteristic of modern commentary.[14] For

---

[9] Achtemeier, *Romans*, 145.

[10] Achtemeier, *Romans*, 147.

[11] Black, *Romans*.

[12] Morris, *Epistle to the Romans*, 326.

[13] I draw all of the quotes in this paragraph from J.B. Morris's translation in the *Library of the Fathers*, Vol. 31, p. 251

[14] Schelkle, *Epistle to the Romans*.

Schelkle, theological abstractions such as 'redemption', 'sonship' and 'the new, transfigured corporeality' dominate. This approach is typical of much of what we think of when someone commends 'theological exegesis'. Modern theological interpretation relies on words and concepts ('redemption') that stand at least two removes from the text. That is to say, Schelkle is glossing the text with broad generalizations about 'the Christian view of salvation', a view that seems to float in an ether of ideas. There is little or no connective explication. It is as if an already highly ramified theological scheme were superimposed upon the text, and the exegesis moves from the particularity of the text to the generalities of the scheme.

I want to dwell on the difference between Chrysostom and this modern approach. I have little doubt that Chrysostom has some quite specific ideas about ministry, intercession and the economy of corporate prayer. Yet, notice how his exegesis does not discuss a 'theology of ministry', nor does he use the text to formulate a pneumatology. Chrysostom does not develop his comments at such a remove, either from the text or from what is going on in his church. Needless to say, we might judge Chrysostom's exegesis materially bad. The context of Romans 8 suggests that Paul might treat the silence (or inarticulateness) of the laity of Chrysostom's time as precisely the weakness that the Spirit brings before the Father, a reading well supported by the silent weakness of Jesus' intercession on the cross, which, in turn, has its own prophetic warrant in Isaiah 53. My purpose, however, is to highlight the formal success of Chrysostom's approach. He draws a detail of church practice into the text and, in so doing, he illuminates a Christian particularity (the practice of priestly prayer) with a textual particularity ('intercession' in the verse). Modern criticism, in contrast, titrates out theological propositions.

Just why modern exegesis moves away from particularity and toward abstraction is difficult to determine. For most scholars socialized into the historical-critical tradition, the biblical text is self-consciously isolated so that it is not 'contaminated' by anachronism. For this reason, the more ahistorical the theological concepts, the less threatening they are to the historical-critical method, and not surprisingly, we find that biblical scholars who offer theological comment tend to reach for the most abstractive and de-particularized formulations.[15] The effect is a superimposition of theological terminology. Notice how pre-critical exegesis does not tend to superimpose theological schemes on the NT as a form of commentary. Pre-critical exegesis may *presuppose* such

---

[15] For example, in his otherwise fine study of the intratextual logic of Paul's letters, Richard Hays explains Paul's exegetical ambitions as growing out of 'the hermeneutical priority of Spirit-experience' (*Echoes*, 108). It is precisely the lack of doctrinal, liturgical and historical specificity that commends a term such as 'spirit-experience'. It is a concept innocent of particular meaning, and therefore it cannot corrupt the exegesis.

schemes. One rightly notes, for example, that Chrysostom exploits the presence of 'intercession' in order to retail his view of pneumatic development that justifies a discrete clerical office with a special intercessory role. Nonetheless, to presuppose is not the same as to superimpose. For the church fathers, the actual practice of exegesis usually involves highly particular intratextual analysis in which the comment, as such, is closer to the literal sense – an interweaving of concerns rather than an isolation.

Origen's comment on Romans 8:26 illustrates. He parses the threefold use of 'groaning' in Romans 8 as a whole, connecting it to Paul's 'three appeals' to the Lord for relief from his torment (2 Cor. 12:8), which is, in turn, commended by a verse from the Psalms: 'My groaning is not hidden from you' (Ps. 38:9). And why are our groanings not hidden? Origen adverts to 1 John 2:1: 'We have an advocate with the Father, Jesus, the just.'[16] This allows Origen to turn to a reflection on the way in which the Spirit of God adopts a kenotic pedagogy, giving us words for our prayers that – now turning to 1 Corinthians 14:15 – turn out to be the singing of the Psalms and the recitation of the Lord's Prayer. Surely one can claim that Origen's comments presuppose something like a Trinitarian theology, as well as the liturgical practice of the church, but it would be absurd to say that his exegesis 'imposes' such things on the text. The skein of intratextual association *constitutes* the reading. Origen is not drawing out or proving theological propositions. His exegesis is densely allusive, and the 'theology' in the exegesis simply is the network of associations and allusions. It is not some further thought or inference made at a distance from the text. In short, Origen draws out no conclusions that might supersede or be superimposed upon the text.

One can speculate about the reasons why a modern commentator might not offer such a close reading. Romans 8 does not mention 'Father', and in general historical-critics feel it anachronistic to import a developed Trinitarian theology that would support exegetical comment on the interplay of Spirit, Son and Father in the dynamics of intercession. As a consequence, modern critics express the theological significance by recourse to concepts such as 'redemption', sterilized of the classical Trinitarian theology that defines these concepts in a rigorous fashion (e.g., 'redemption' in an Athanasian and not gnostic sense). In other words, instead of exegetically 'showing' the Christian vision of intercession – a 'showing' that the tradition has presumed requires a Trinitarian vocabulary – modern commentaries draw conclusions at a remove from the specificity of the text. The text provides *evidence* for a 'theology of x'. The text guides us toward the message; it is not the message itself.[17]

---

[16] See Origen's *Commentary on the Epistle to the Romans*, VII.6.

[17] In *The Eclipse of Biblical Narrative*, Hans Frei again and again shows how this move away from the text to its 'meaning' is the inevitable outcome of modern hermeneutical assumptions.

I find the appeal to theological abstractions and the drift away from textual particularity throughout the literature, and I want to be clear that I do not think historical-critical compunction is the sole explanation. Such a move is supported by the post-Trinitarian theologies of liberal Protestantism, as well as by the dangerously formal Trinitarianism of both Calvinist and Tridentine theologies in which the God-world-human person problems are expressed in such a rigidly metaphysical fashion that classical Nicene forms become conceptually subordinated.[18] Still further, much of the modern intellectual tradition privileges the 'drawing out' of truth.[19] Recall Bacon's image of torturing nature with experiment in order to gain her truths. Scientists have found general formulae and symbolic mathematical abstractions very useful, and this reinforces the sensibility of the modern intellectual in which inherited forms of life are reshaped into conceptual ramified formulations. Hegel was, of course, the master of this, and however much we might reject the grandiosity of his synthesis, our intellectual imaginations remain characteristically 'phenomenological' rather than 'literal' or 'material'.

This is not a treatise in the history of ideas, so I must leave speculation behind. What is crucial, for me, is the effect of modern intellectual sensibilities on biblical exegesis. 'Theology' is treated as something to be 'drawn out'. The upshot is a tendency to move away from the text as one moves toward its theological import. This move drains theological exegesis of its scriptural immediacy. Examples are legion. To read Luke Timothy Johnson is to read a theological exegesis in which scripturally saturated doctrinal vocabulary (e.g., Father) does not function in the exegesis. In his summation of the larger context for Romans 8:26, he writes, 'It is difficult to overstate the degree of intimacy between the divine and human freedom that Paul here presents.'[20] The abstract problem of divine and human freedom – itself a modern gloss on the particular arguments characteristic of the Pelagian controversy and then the Reformation – is warmed by the word 'intimacy', but the effect is negligible. To say that Romans 8:26 testifies to the false juxtaposition of divine and human agency in no way illuminates what makes the juxtaposition false, or how one might see the relationship accurately. The same holds for 'redemption' or 'realized eschatology' or other theological formulations used by modern commentators without a scripturally (or liturgically or ascetically) thicker connection to the text. The concepts are presented as giving meaning to the text rather than the text giving meaning to the concepts.

To my mind, the distance between the literal sense and theological abstractions is the single greatest failure of earnest and well-meaning attempts by

---

[18] For useful background analysis of this danger, see Placher, *Domestication*.

[19] Heidegger famously thought that this 'drawing out' characterizes Western philosophy since Plato.

[20] Johnson, *Reading Romans*, 131.

modern exegetes of the NT to produce theological exegesis. I have attempted
to illuminate this failure by recourse to some patristic exegetes. Now I wish to
attend to some successful instances of modern exegesis. They do not succeed
by being more synthetic and comprehensive. Nor do they manifest a uniform
approach. Instead, the success rests in the willingness of the commentators to
use scripturally saturated theological language, structured by Nicene assumptions and suggestive of intratextual links to other parts of Scripture. Rather than
'draw out' theological propositions, the movement is one of 'drawing
together' scriptural details.

The first example is minor, but telling. In his commentary, Roy Harrisville
observes that the weakness in which the Spirit helps us is 'our cruciform life'.[21]
Harrisville offers no further detail, but his exposition of weakness by recourse
to the crucifixion links Romans 8:26 to Jesus' passion, as well as to Paul's
appeals to the power of the cross in 1 Corinthians. To speak of 'our cruciform
life' instead of 'our spiritual life' stimulates intratextual reflection that pulls
other details of the biblical text closer to the reader, details that revolve around
the particularity of Jesus. Moreover, specific liturgical and ascetic practices are
present in 'cruciform', but not in a word such as 'redemption' or 'eschatological'. My point is that 'cruciform' is a scripturally saturated word. Jews have
eschatological beliefs. Muslims seek redemption. But 'cruciform life' is so close
to the claims and practices that make Christians Christian that Jews and Muslims would deny that theirs is a 'cruciform life'.

In his *Shorter Commentary on Romans*, Karl Barth offers a unified analysis of
the whole of Romans 8. Barth does not proceed verse by verse, but over the
course of his exposition he draws in textual detail. It is in the context of his
larger discussion of the middle section of Romans 8 that he offers his comment
on verse 26: 'In their joyless and powerless groaning God hears the voice of his
own Son …'.[22] Here Barth presumes that the help and intercession of the Spirit
is to draw us into Christ, the one who was crucified for our sakes. Thus, the
larger theme of 'groaning' (in the faithful, in creation, in the Spirit) is given a
paschal meaning. The 'intimacy' of divine and human – Luke Timothy Johnson's theme – is given content. The upshot is not simply a more scripturally
immediate exegesis. God is a person rather than principle (hearing the groans of
the Son), and we can see the connection between the Pauline teaching and the
larger narrative (not only of Jesus, but the Old Testament as well, echoing the
groaning and wailing of the Israelites in Egypt and Babylon). Here, we are
much closer to pre-critical tradition and a view of theology as a dense act of
exegetical 'showing' rather than exegesis that draws theological conclusions at
a remove from the text.

---

[21] Harrisville, *Romans*.

[22] Barth, *Shorter Commentary on Romans*, 102.

My final example parallels Barth's reading of 8:26. In her verse by verse reflections on Romans 8, Adrienne von Speyr gives an explicitly anagogical reading to verse 26.[23] She does not treat Paul's description of our weakness as a general reassurance that God will love us even in our failures. Nor does she speak of a generic intimacy between divine and human. Instead, she identifies a specific exchange. The verse teaches us that 'we may confide our insufficiency to the Son and the Spirit, that they may transform it into what is theirs, what can be heard and accepted by the Father'. Von Speyr does not identify any intratextual supports for her reading. One could imagine turning to Romans 5 and the way in which the Son takes on the greatest of our insufficiencies – death. Moreover, I am left wondering how and in what sense our insufficiency is transformed into something that might become a predicate of the Spirit and the Son. How, for example, can death become 'theirs', and what would a 'transformed death' be? Yet, I am convinced that the success of von Speyr's exegesis stems from the explicit and confident use of a Trinitarian horizon for interpretation. Indeed, I find myself thinking that Barth is disappointingly abstract when he makes 'God' the subject who hears the Son – though this is the way in which Paul speaks throughout Romans 8 and Barth is exhibiting an honourable Calvinist restraint by keeping as close as possible to the particularity of the text.

The lesson I draw from this brief survey of NT exegesis is simple. Drawing theological conclusions is not the same as offering theological exegesis. Luke Timothy Johnson is very free with his theological vocabulary, and he is often championed, along with Richard Hays and others, as a leader in the post-critical project. Yet, his approach is very different from the exegesis found in the church fathers and which is present in Barth and von Speyr. Exegesis that speaks of 'the divine-human relationship' or 'God's victory over death' functions differently from exegesis that speaks of the 'cruciform life' and 'the groans of the Son'. The former offers theological comment as a gloss or epitome at one or two removes from the text, while the latter organizes and expounds the text theologically. Both are theological, but only the latter intensifies and deepens the Nicene framework for Christian language and practice, a framework that is itself much closer to the text – not in the sense of relying on particular passages, but in the sense of being able to maximize affirmations of the plain sense. But I am jumping ahead of myself. We need to briefly survey some recent commentaries of the OT.

Old Testament

If modern NT commentators can speak of Jesus and God, but not the Father, Son and Holy Spirit in the NT, then the parallel problem in OT exegesis is that

---

[23] Speyr, *Victory*.

commentators can speak of God (and even then, the scholarly invention 'Yahweh' is likely to displace God), but they cannot speak of Jesus Christ. Here, the problem is not prophecy and fulfilment, narrowly understood. Rather, modern interpreters have rejected the larger figural assumptions of pre-critical OT exegesis. David is not a type of the King of kings. Moses is not a type of the one who fulfils the law. On a much larger scale, the history of Israel is not a prefiguration of the history of the church. For this reason, modern Christian commentators have an extremely difficult time seeing how the great bulk of the OT is, in fact, a text that teaches truths about Jesus Christ and the people who call him Lord rather than generic truths about God. As a consequence, Christian theological concerns must remain distant from the text.

The IBC commentary on 1 and 2 Kings illustrates this situation perfectly. Richard Nelson uses the canonical form of the text and places no emphasis on philological details. His stated purpose is to treat the text as a fully-fashioned whole and interpret it according to its own evident theological intent. As Nelson reports, the narrative 'offers us insight and perspective on the nature of God'.[24] Yet, this God has no clear relationship to the God who raises Jesus from the dead. At most, Nelson identifies exactly the abstractive theological features that make so much of New Testament commentary thin. For example, he observes that the tension in Kings is between the unconditional and conditional dimensions of God's promise (unconditional to David and his line; conditional to Solomon), and in this way, reports Nelson, 'the narrative offers one possible way of balancing [the] two opposing theological grammars' found in Augustine and Pelagius, Calvin and Arminius.[25]

This approach to theology is typical. The books of Kings are not concerned with Christ and the church. Rather, they are 'theological' only insofar as they address theological 'problems' such as 'grace and free will' or 'unconditional and conditional promises' that are shared with the New Testament and the subsequent Christian tradition. The logic of the analysis is a straightforward instance of 'normal science' at work. Christian theology has inherited problems x, y and z that transcend the particularity of the biblical texts. Attentive to the logical structure of such problems (e.g., the relation of transcendence and imminence, eternity and time, divine power and human freedom), the exegete shows how the structure of specific stories in the Old Testament addresses such problems. One offers a phenomenology (Hegel's notion of a conceptual account purified of particularity) of Israelite history, and this provides us with something relevant to an equally conceptual and de-particularized account of Christianity. 1 and 2 Kings may be about something entirely alien to Christianity – different time, different place – but they meet in the rarefied sphere of

---

[24] Nelson, *First and Second Kings*, 2.

[25] Nelson, *First and Second Kings*, 35.

'theology'. To be more provocative: they meet in a conceptual allegory of God, world and humanity.

Mark Throntreit's commentary on Ezra and Nehemiah in the IBC series offers further evidence of this presumption that theological exegesis involves jumping from the text to putatively 'theological questions'.[26] Consider Ezra 3:7 (the import of cedar from Lebanon for the reconstruction of the temple) as a test case. Throntreit offers nice intratextual clues, pointing out how the second temple recapitulates the first, and echoes Isaiah 60:13. Throntreit observes that foreigners participate in the rebuilding of the temple. However, there is no forward movement into the New Testament and Pauline teaching on the role of Gentiles. Later in the commentary, present Christian reality enters briefly. However, the theological interpretation that Throntreit gives to Ezra 10 and the expulsion of foreign wives is utterly vacant of any scriptural specificity: 'Of greater significance for contemporary readers is the message of these chapters regarding the need for continual reformation.'[27] A vague nostrum, 'continual Reformation', serves as the only link between past and present.

One intrepid commentator of a historical book, Gene Rice, does presume the classical link between Israel and the church, but just like so many New Testament commentators, the theological reflection is very, very distant from any scriptural (or historical) specificity.[28] Of 1 Kings 5:6 (Solomon's commandment to secure cedars from Lebanon for the construction of the temple), he writes, 'This passage is a reminder of the delicate relationship of Israel (and the church) to the world.' The most he can say about this 'delicate relationship' is that 'Israel's (and the church's) mission is not to condemn or to escape from the world but to transform it'.[29] Rice is important because he shows that one element of Christian exegesis of the Old Testament – a presumed relationship between Israel and the church – is insufficient. For Rice, the link is made, but he so consistently treats the history of Israel as an allegory for conceptual points (e.g., not to escape but to transform) that the theological pay-off leads away from, rather than into, scripturally saturated conclusions.

The same interpretive results obtain for all the contemporary efforts of Old Testament exegesis (except Peter Ochs's) in Stephen Fowl's collection, *The Theological Interpretation of Scripture: Classic and Contemporary Readings*. For example, Walter Brueggemann draws out nuggets such as the following. Moses' commission reveals a general truth about all Old Testament history: 'it is human agency in the service of Yahweh's solidarity with Israel'.[30]

---

[26] Throntreit, *Ezra–Nehemiah*.

[27] Throntreit, *Ezra–Nehemiah*, 57.

[28] Rice, *Nations*.

[29] Rice, *Nations*, 46.

[30] Fowl, *Theological Interpretation*, 161.

A contrast between contemporary and ancient exegesis is illuminating. Gregory of Nyssa's comment on the same passages (also included in the Fowl collection) defies epitome. Commenting on Exodus 4:3 where Moses' rod becomes a serpent, Gregory notes the link between 'serpent' and 'sin' in the larger canonical context. Then, turning to John 3:14 ('Just as Moses lifted up the serpent in the wilderness, so must the Son of Man be lifted up' – itself an echo of Num. 21:9), Gregory observes that while Jesus was not sin, he did assume our sin so as to destroy it. But, even here, there is no theological nugget. Instead, Gregory returns to the framework of Exodus, now pressing forward to Exodus 7:12, to make the point: 'But for our sake he became a serpent, in order to devour and consume the Egyptian serpents ...'.[31] The economy of atonement is expressed, but unlike the modern exegesis that moves toward conceptual allegory expressed as an abstract statement of the doctrine of atonement, Gregory treats theological exegesis as the discernment and expression of the logic of atonement within the immediacy of the textual idiom. *Theoria* – Gregory's term for spiritual or theological interpretation – is not resident in propositional truths (e.g., a correct conceptual account of atonement). *Theoria*, for Gregory, is the insight that allows one to arrange exposition of the text so that one sees its capacity to disclose the truth. The serpents can be brought into the service of expressing the victory over them. This is the 'conclusion' of the exegesis.

Moderns have objected that the literal ambience of Exodus does not control Gregory's exegesis, and they – we – worry about how one can reliably know what the text discloses and what arrangements of the text render more visible the truths of salvation. The 'arrangings', we worry, are whimsical deformations rather than wise illuminations. I do not want to gainsay these worries. I only wish to emphasize that, whether we think the specific allusions whimsical or wise, Gregory does not draw away from the semantic particularity of Exodus. On the contrary, he exploits that particularity (e.g., rods and serpents) in order to weave a larger account of Moses' role in the drama of redemption in Christ. For Gregory, to see the literal sense of Exodus as transparent to the figure of Christ is the culminating achievement of exegesis.[32]

No matter how we might judge the legitimacy of Gregory's exegesis, we must allow that his theological interpretation remains within the verbal atmosphere of the text – something one cannot say about conceptual allegories that dominate modern attempts to provide theological exegesis of the Old Testament. Gregory is not 'drawing out' a message in a moment of theological application. His reading involves 'drawing in' the text. In other words, Gregory reads the Scriptures in such a way that the very words of the text are the

---

[31] Fowl, *Theological Interpretation*, 111.

[32] *Life of Moses*, II.35.

privileged building blocks for theological insight. To turn the word 'serpent' into the idiom for expressing Christ's triumph over sin says more than any statement of doctrine.

The Problem Expounded

My survey of the commentaries is limited. Nonetheless, the modest effort has convinced me that announcing and urging theological seriousness in exegesis is insufficient. There are commentaries already available that *do* attempt to provide theological comment. In my judgement, however, the results are too often inadequate. The reason, it seems to me, is simple. For nearly all the commentators I read, theological exegesis means the theological inference one draws from the exegesis conducted by some other means. In other words, nearly all commentators treat 'theology' as a result of exegesis rather than a method of exegesis. They do not assume that the specific structure and content of classical Christian doctrine functions as an exegetical framework for organizing, focusing and developing textual analysis, and that the most basic form of theology simply is the web of textual allusion, typology and semantic interconnection – or perhaps more accurately, theology is the *habitus* that allows one to generate such an interpretive web. For most modern theological exegesis what counts as theological comment is eccentric. It arches out of the text and into a discussion of some *x*: the Pauline theology of grace, the Israelite theology of covenant, the priestly theology of sacrifice. Or it reaches even further into abstraction with discussions of 'grace and free will' or the 'covenant of grace' or 'a theology of redemptive divine excess'.

A brief focus on one of the most compelling spokesmen for the recovery of a theologically vigorous reading, Brevard Childs, illustrates the conceptual issues at stake in this problem. Childs argues that Christian exegesis should seek to discern the unity and cogency of the whole biblical text, hence his affirmation of canonical interpretation. However, I am struck by the way in which Childs assumes that this unity should be sought at a distance from the scriptural text. Here is how he states his approach in *Biblical Theology of the Old and New Testaments*: 'A major thesis of this book is that this basic problem [of the unity of the two Testaments] can only be resolved by theological reflection which moves from a description of the biblical witness to the object toward which these witnesses point, that is, to their subject matter, substance, or *res*.'[33]

I have no interest in quarrelling with the theory of language or interpretation entailed in the *signum/res* distinction. Indeed, that distinction may be a crucial exegetical premise for all Christian interpretation. However, Childs

---

[33] Childs, *Biblical Theology*, 80.

does not suggest the distinction as a premise. Instead, he is making a proposal about exegetical practice (hermeneutics in the old sense of the term). One should organize and frame reflection upon the biblical text with a sustained analysis of the text according to genre, within its historical context, attending to philological details, and so forth. On this basis, Childs wishes the interpreter to give space for the 'discrete voice' of the diverse parts of the canon (the Old Testament in particular). Only then can the classical questions of Christian theology be engaged, with the answers given by the exegete now properly disciplined by the biblical text in its 'literal historical' particularity.

This proposal captures the failure of so many well-intentioned and earnest modern attempts to provide theological exegesis, for it endorses the eccentric pattern that produces theological reflection at a distance from Scripture. Put simply, the operative assumption is that theology is something other than close textual analysis. To be sure, such reflection is disciplined by the text, but the key conceptual point is that the text is presumed to be at a remove from theology (whatever that might be), and the job of the Christian exegete is to bring the text to bear on this strangely non-scriptural form of reflection. To return to the *signum/res* distinction, Childs treats theological reflection as concerning the divine *res*, not the scriptural *signa*, and thus understood, the combination 'theological exegesis' is oxymoronic. One must discipline theological reflection with exegesis conducted by some other means.

I am all in favour of disciplining theological reflection with exegesis, but I do not think we should presume the separation implicit in Childs's approach. The patristic tradition has treated the scriptural *signa* and the puzzles they create as the proper concern of theology.[34] Theology is disciplined, not by an external science of exegesis, but by the task of making exegetical sense of the signs – not the least of which is the puzzle that the stated purpose of these *signa* is to bring us into fellowship with the divine res. For this reason, most of the pre-critical tradition has regarded theology as an exegetical project from start to finish.[35] It

---

[34] See Augustine's discussion of the temptation to seek the divine *res* without undergoing the pedagogy of the scriptural *signa* (*De doctrina christiana*, Preface). Certainly, in a broad sense, Childs agrees with Augustine. The difference rests in how to avoid the temptation. For Augustine, one must enter into the particularity of the way established by Jesus Christ. The divine *res* cannot be reflected upon. How could our finite minds take God as an object of inquiry? This is absurd, and we would be bereft were it not for the fact that 'the whole temporal dispensation was set up by divine providence for our salvation', and through the Scriptures we can discern and conform our minds to this dispensation, thus allowing the pedagogy of the finite to lift us toward that divine *res* which is beyond the argument and analysis that constitutes inquiry.

[35] Anselm is an interesting exception. See *Cur Deus homo*, I.4, where Anselm sets aside scriptural arguments in order to proceed *remoto Christo*. Even here, however, the background remains exegetical. For in the artful play on 'body' – of Christ, of truth,

treated theology as a discussion of questions that arise from the Scriptures (e.g., how can one say 'Jesus is Lord' and, at the same time, obey the first commandment?).[36]

What difference does this difference make? To my mind, it makes a great difference. Childs assumes that true theology must move from 'description' of what the text says to 'analysis' of its subject matter, and this subject matter is formulated with the abstracted and scripturally thin concepts that characterize so much unsuccessful theological exegesis. Notice how Childs's presumption that the subject matter of Scripture is God leads him to organize his material reflection around loci – for example, 'reconciliation with God' – that seem more perspicuous than the dispersed details of Scripture. Then, under such topics, he gives the impression that the real question is not 'how can Galatians be reconciled with Leviticus?' but rather 'what is the biblical view of justification?' So, he writes, 'Rather than seeing righteousness as an ethical quality or a virtue, the New Testament assumes the Old Testament's perspective of the righteousness of God as a relational term'.[37] The concept 'relational' does the work of linking the Old Testament to the New Testament. The concept is the *theoria* toward which the exegete works; it is a conceptual artefact resident in a domain of propositions independent of the specific literal world of Scripture. Nothing could be further from the *theoria* Gregory of Nyssa expounds in his *Life of Moses*.

Allow me to illustrate further this strategy of 'drawing out' theology from the text. To return to the commissioning of Moses in Exodus that occupied Gregory, consider Childs's theological reflections on the same passage in his Exodus commentary. Here is a sample of the level of abstraction. 'The being and activity of God are not played against each other, but included within the whole reality of the divine revelation.' 'History is the arena of God's self-revelation ...'. 'The divine reality of which this passage speaks encounters Moses as well as the writers of the New Testament in a particular situation and seeks to evoke a response of obedience within God's plan.'[38] 'History', 'divine reality', 'self-revelation', 'response of obedience': these are concepts that commend themselves because of their abstracted quality. The distance between

---

of scriptural words – Anselm suggests that his non-scriptural arguments allow 'the very body of truth to shine more brightly' (I.4). In this context and under the influence of a standard patristic equation of the carnal body of Christ with the carnal body of Scripture (see Origen, *C. Celsum*, VI.77), Anselm seems to be suggesting that his method of argument has an exegetical value. It allows the *corpus veritatis* – the body of the divine Word as depicted in Scripture – to shine more brightly.

[36] For a fully developed account of the way in which patristic doctrine emerges out of exegetical puzzles, see Behr, *Way*.

[37] Childs, *Biblical Theology*, 501.

[38] Childs, *Book of Exodus*, 88.

such high-level notions and the literal sense of the Old Testament is necessary in order to negotiate the diffuse particularity of Scripture. Theology must be done at arm's length, and the reified concepts of modern theology (self-revelation!) make this distance seem natural and normal.

Were the Christian intellectual tradition functional, we might allow that Childs's use of theological concepts presumed a scripturally saturated context for their meaning and use. The moment of abstraction can have a heuristic, orienting usefulness, and I have no interest in prohibiting it. However, I am convinced that in the late modern Western context, the Christian intellectual tradition is not functional, and Childs's theological comments reinforce rather than reduce the distance between what theologians say (or biblical scholars say in theological idioms) and Scripture. Concepts such as God, revelation, history, obedience, and so forth, are fixed mental objects rather than plastic concepts shaped to handle specific exegetical problems. For example, rather than treating 'God' as a highly ambiguous concept that exegetical pressure forced the church to specify at Nicea, Childs treats the concept as available for use in drawing out exegetical conclusions. He seems to think that exegesis terminates with the concept rather than using the concept as a magnet around which to draw scriptural particularity, or to change metaphors, as a screen on which to project the literal figures of the sort that Gregory provides. As a consequence, for modern exegetes, 'theology' seems to denote an abstracted, conceptual realm that expresses the results of interpretation. Theology is not an exegetical stance or method in itself. It is not a form of reading Scripture.

The irony is that by distancing theology from the immediate work of ordering and analysing scriptural signs, Childs cannot achieve his overarching goal of recovering a biblically disciplined theological practice. Theology is not disciplined by exegesis. It is so thoroughly deracinated that the literal sense can exert pressure only at a great distance, if at all. Or, to put the matter differently, once an eccentric trajectory is presupposed – exegesis concerns the scriptural *signa* and theology the divine *res* – the only hope is somehow to bring theological propositions into correspondence with scriptural propositions, with fundamentalists and non-fundamentalists differing only in what counts as correspondence. Thus, the basic forms of Christian modernism predominate. Something other than the texture and detail of the language and practice of the apostolic tradition is the 'essence of Christianity'. For a conservative or liberal rationalist, the former is important only as evidence to warrant the latter and, even when one drops implausible forms of rationalism, modern hermeneutics assumes that the linguistic particularity has meaning only insofar as it mediates something: consciousness, intention, Spirit, and so forth. As Stanley Fish might put the outcome, there is no text in biblical theology understood in this fashion.[39]

---

[39] Fish, *Is There a Text?*

Interpretation and the Divine Economy

I hope that my inductive approach has not been too tedious. I have circled back to the central problem a number of times: the abstractive nature of modern theological commentary; the project of 'drawing out' that leads away from the details of Scripture; the presumption that theology is a consequence rather than mode of exegesis. At this point, I wish to move out of the inductive and into the assertive by making some programmatic statements about the root problem facing contemporary exegesis and suggesting a way forward.

Modern theological readers drift toward abstraction, and their exegesis inscribes an eccentric trajectory away from the biblical text because they (we) cannot sustain a belief that human history, especially the history of the people of Israel and the Christian church (which includes the history of the composition, canonization and interpretation of the Scriptures) is so ordered that a deeper and more accurate understanding of that history will lead us toward a deeper knowledge and love of God. The issue is not the much confuted and confused question of the errancy or inerrancy of the scriptural text. This is a byway of modernism. Rather, the nub of the difficulty is that we simply find it difficult to suppose that the biblical text functions in manifold and complex ways as the privileged key to understand that natural-historical order that is shaped by God for his own purposes, purposes both revealed and brought to fruition in Jesus Christ. Or, to put the point in a different idiom, we cannot believe that the complex historical nexus of events, persons, oral traditions, compositions, editorial revisions, interpretive traditions and communally authoritative doctrine and discipline that constitute the many layers of the Scriptures (as well as the created order in which those events, persons, traditions, compositions and doctrines are anchored and from which they receive their being as concrete particulars) is the single witness of the Holy Spirit to the one redemption of all in Jesus Christ. As a consequence, we cannot see how organizing and connecting the myriad pieces of this natural-historical order in such a way that Jesus Christ is evident as the unifying hypothesis (Eph. 1:9–10) would constitute the most essential form of theology. For example, we cannot see how ordering what we make of the book of Judges (which may, in fact, be deeply informed by historical-critical methods) with what we make of the history of the early church (which, again, may involve a wealth of modern critical tools) is theology – the project of making the single witness more perspicuous and visible to the human mind. This blindness is the single greatest impediment to the recovery of an exegesis that is theological rather than an exegesis that draws out theological conclusions at a distance from the Scriptures.

Irenaeus calls the natural-historical order fulfilled in Jesus Christ the divine economy. His extended argument against gnostic exegesis, *Against Heresies*, is an attempt to show how presuming this divine economy clears the way for a maximally cogent interpretation of the Scriptures, where 'cogent' means not only the most plausible intratextual order but also an interpretation that presupposes a non-mythological ontology. What does this mean? Irenaeus' approach to exegesis presupposed that one finds truth by thinking through the way in which the great array of facts (e.g., God delivered Israel from Egypt, Gentiles are baptized into Christ, the world is not eternal, there are four different gospel stories, Joshua and Jesus have the same name – the list could go on and on) fits together into a single 'economy'. One looks for the truth in these facts and the myriad ways in which they interact, not in the concepts or abstractions one might legitimately use to facilitate the ordering of them. In this way, Irenaeus proceeds in much the same way as a modern scientist. The crux of the project of modern science is not the formula or theory (e.g., $E=mc^2$). Rather, what matters is the ability of the formula or theory to guide the scientist in ordering the world into a successful experiment.

The evident importance of structuring theory can easily create the impression that patristic theology is 'drawing out' conclusions from Scripture. Irenaeus offers epitomes of the divine economy such as the church's confession of faith in

> the one God, omnipotent, the maker of heaven and earth, the creator of man, who brought the deluge, and called Abraham, who led the people from the land of Egypt, spoke with Moses, set forth the law, sent the prophets, and who has prepared fire for the devils and his angels.[40]

I do not wish to criticize or commend Irenaeus' particular take on the structure of events from creation to consummation. It may be the case that any attempt to epitomize the divine economy, as any attempt to summarize a Shakespearean play, entails distortion.[41] Instead, my concern is formal. Epitome functions to guide Irenaeus' material judgements about how to structure the countless details of Scripture, and it is clear that arranging the details simply is theology for Irenaeus. Moreover, by so understanding theology, it follows methodologically, pedagogically and mystagogically that one given over to such a task will try to draw the diffuse elements of Scripture into ever closer and more intimate interconnections. In short, however flawed in particular exegetical judgements, Irenaeus will not seek a theology 'drawn out' or at a distance from the

---

[40] *Against Heresies*, III.3.3.

[41] See Kendall Soulen's analysis of the problems latent in Irenaeus' 'canonical narrative', *God of Israel*, 25–56. One of the perversions of modern reading of Irenaeus (and the Fathers in general) is the tendency to hunt for 'doctrine' amidst the unruly mass of exegetical performance. This magnifies the distortions by focusing our attention on the abstractions and epitomes that the Fathers rely upon for exegetical orientation.

Scripture. Theology is a practice of reading. It is not a conclusion drawn from reading.

Let me illustrate this point. Irenaeus' well-known description of Jesus Christ's saving work of recapitulation is no less exegetical than soteriological. Jesus Christ 'sums up' the economy of the Father, providing the decisive clue about just how to structure one's reading of the biblical text so as both to discern the reality of events described (which may well be spiritual rather than carnal) and to grasp the particular literal genius of the sacred text that both reveals and hides ('He made darkness his hiding place' [Ps. 18:11]) so that we are brought to see this reality as it is rather than as we imagine it to be. Thus, Adam does not 'fall' in an abstract sense. His disobedience comes from the fruit of the tree, and from the tree comes death. Jesus Christ recapitulates this scene, though now in the key of righteousness rather than sin. Christ's obedience triumphs over sin by his death on the tree of the cross, and the fruit of that tree is life. Or again, as sin comes from a woman (Eve), so righteousness comes from a woman (the Virgin Mary). Or again, just as the tree of transgression was the greatest victory of the devil, so the cross of Christ is his greatest defeat.[42] To my mind, the structured link of textual particularity is crucial. Irenaeus does not have a 'theology of original sin', nor does he have a 'theology of grace'. He has an integrated array of exegetical statements that bring the details of Scripture into certain patterns that make the divine economy visible. The presumption is that recapitulations of the patterns in the direct idiom of Scripture are more perspicuous than a conceptual statement of the patterns. To see Christ as the recapitulation of Old Testament detail is more powerful than a statement that he does so recapitulate – and very little is to be learned by an investigation of the concept of recapitulation. In this way, Irenaeus would seem to follow the first principle for the writing of modern realistic narrative: show it, don't say it.

For this reason, and not because of the advent of historical-critical methods, what Irenaeus is doing is very different from contemporary biblical theology, to say nothing of contemporary systematic theology. His description is better than any account I might give.

> One may bring out the meaning of those things which have been spoken in parables, and accommodate them to the general scheme of the faith; and explain the operation and dispensation of God connected with human salvation; and show that God manifested longsuffering in regard to the apostasy of the angels who transgressed, as also with respect to the disobedience of men; and set forth why it is that one and the same God has made some things temporal and some eternal, some heavenly and others earthly; and understand for what reason God, though invisible, manifested himself to the prophets, not under one form, but differently to different individuals;

---

[42] For Irenaeus' exposition of these recapitulations, see *Against Heresies*, V.19ff.

and show why it was that more covenants than one were given to mankind; and teach what was the special character of these covenants; and search out for what reason 'God hath concluded every man in unbelief that he may have mercy on all' (Rom. 11:32); and gratefully describe on what account the Word of God become flesh and suffered; and relate why the advent of the Son of God took place in these last times, that is, in the end, rather than in the beginning; and unfold what is contained in the Scriptures concerning the end, and things to come; and not to be silent as to how it is that God has made the Gentiles, whose salvation was despaired of, fellow-heirs, and of the same body, and partakers with the saints; and discourse on how it is that 'this mortal body shall put on immortality, and this corruptible shall put on incorruption' (1 Cor. 15:54) ...[43]

In short, for Irenaeus, theology defines the intellectual task of expounding 'the whole picture'. In that task, conceptual allegory will not do; one must depict the truth in and through the details, not in order to 'control' theology with exegesis, but because those details, the *signa*, are ordained by God to bring us into fellowship with his ineffable divine *res*. Thus, *expounding* the divine economy as a particularized sequence (and not reporting on a conceptual pattern in that economy, e.g., recapitulation) constitutes theology.

We need not think such an approach inaccessible in our age. As I attempted to show above, Karl Barth and Adrienne von Speyr do not turn from description of what the text says to formulate a theological conclusion. They offer a theologically ramified exposition of what the text says, and that *constitutes* their conclusion. A patristic interpreter such as Gregory of Nyssa is more difficult to characterize. However, one striking feature is clear. The intratextual project of intensifying the christological unity of the text is evident. For Gregory, what we would call 'theological propositions' (e.g., Jesus bore our sin though he was not a sinner) are expressed in terms of immediate scriptural idiom (e.g., 'For our sake he became a serpent, in order to devour and consume the Egyptian serpents'). In this way, what we think of as theology is not isolated and held at a distance from the text. The *theoria* that Gregory seeks to expound is found in his organization of the literality of the text so that its potency as a witness to Christ is perspicuous. Gregory shows the *theoria*, he does not say it.

Gregory's particular approach and exegetical techniques differ from Barth's, as do Barth's from von Speyr's, but the overall effect of their exegesis is similar. One feels as though the particular scriptural text under comment not only constitutes a part of a unified textual witness, but the particular text also enters into a mutually illuminating relationship with other particular forms of scriptural language and apostolic practice. This is theological exegesis – that is to say, exegesis that brings one to see, in some small way, how Scripture has an economy, a *theoria*, a 'divine genius'. To think with Scripture in this fashion is

---

[43] *Against Heresies*, I.10.3.

to begin to conform one's mind to that divine genius. This conformity, not the search for scripturally deduced doctrinal proposition, guides the mind toward that which the mind seeks but cannot comprehend: knowledge and love of God.

Postscript

A recent experience brought home to me that recovering theological exegesis of the sort I have commended will not be easy, even for those who champion it in theory. In May, I was in Vilnius, Lithuania, teaching a class on Christian hermeneutics. My mind was much preoccupied with the issues I have tried to clarify in this chapter, and I envisioned the lectures as a chance to work through some ideas about theological exegesis. One morning, I was preparing a class on Augustine's *De doctrina christiana*. In Book II, as Augustine discusses the proper use of scriptural signs, he introduces an example from the Song of Songs: 'Your teeth are like a flock of shorn ewes ascending from the pool, all of which give birth to twins, and there is not a sterile animal among them' (4:2). I immediately stopped and thought to invent an allegorical reading so that I might anticipate the great Augustine. I speculated, 'Indeed, like the shorn ewes, divine love is fertile and generative' – exactly the sort of 'theological' reading so prevalent in the contemporary literature. Then I read on. Augustine's reading of that passage, while allegorical, was like a blow to the head. He writes,

> It gives me pleasure to contemplate holy men, when I see them as the teeth of the church tearing men away from their errors and transferring them to its body, breaking down their rawness by biting and chewing. And it is with the greatest of pleasure that I visualize the shorn ewes, their worldly burdens set aside like fleeces, ascending from the pool (baptism) and all giving birth to twins (the two commandments of love), with none of them failing to produce this holy fruit.[44]

My improvised theological reading of this verse from the Song of Songs exemplifies the basic pattern of modern theological exegesis. My 'spiritual reading' moved from the particularized imagery of the Song of Songs to a vague spiritual nostrum about the nature of God and his grace. In contrast, classical exegesis provides a 'spiritual reading' that moves from particularized imagery to particularized teaching and practice. Whatever Augustine is doing in his exegetical comment, he is not leading his readers away from the specific practices of Christianity. He is not justifying or proving anything, and he certainly is not drawing a theological 'conclusion'. Instead, he is taking a complex image from a love poem (which I do not fully understand in that context – teeth

---

[44] *De doctrina christiana*, II.6.

giving birth?) and illuminating it by establishing an interpretive relationship to a (relatively) clear Christian practice (baptism) and teaching (love commandment). Here, as elsewhere in Augustine's vast body of writing, theology is not a separate moment of conclusion, standing at a distance from Christian particularity. It is an entry into the medium of the Scriptures, an entry made under the confidence that the Scriptures and the church to which they give life are *media divina*. It is this exercise in intimacy that we need to recover.

Bibliography

Achtemeier, P., *Romans* (IBC; Atlanta: John Knox Press, 1985)

Barth, K., *Shorter Commentary on Romans* (trans. D.H. van Daalen; London: SCM Press, 1959)

Behr, J., *The Way to Nicea: Formation of Christian Theology*, I (Crestwood: St. Vladimir's Seminary Press, 2001)

Black, M., *Romans* (NCB; London: Oliphants, 1973)

Childs, B.S., *The Book of Exodus: A Critical, Theological Commentary* (Philadelphia: Westminster Press, 1974)

——, *Biblical Theology of the Old and New Testaments: Theological Reflection on the Christian Bible* (London: SCM Press; Minneapolis: Fortress Press, 1992)

Chrysostom, *Homilies on Romans* (trans. J.B. Morris; *Library of the Fathers*, 31; Oxford: J.H. Parker, 1848)

DiNoia, J.A., review of *A Marginal Jew: Rethinking the Historical Jesus* by John P. Meier, *ProEccl* 2/1 (1991), 122–25

Fish, S., *Is There a Text in This Class? The Authority of Interpretive Communities* (Cambridge, MA: Harvard University Press, 1980)

Fowl, S., *Engaging Scripture: A Model for Theological Interpretation* (Oxford: Basil Blackwell, 1998)

—— (ed.), *The Theological Interpretation of Scripture: Classic and Contemporary Readings* (Oxford: Basil Blackwell, 1997)

Frei, H., *The Eclipse of Biblical Narrative* (New Haven: Yale University Press, 1975)

Harrisville, R., *Romans* (Minneapolis: Augsburg, 1980)

Hays, R., *Echoes of Scripture in the Letters of Paul* (New Haven: Yale University Press, 1989)

Johnson, L.T., *Reading Romans: A Literary and Theological Commentary* (New York: Crossroad, 1997)

Jowett, B., 'On the Interpretation of Scripture', in *Essays and Reviews* (London: John W. Parker and Son, 1860), 330–433

Morris, L., *The Epistle to the Romans* (Grand Rapids: Eerdmans, 1988)

Nelson, R., *First and Second Kings* (IBC; Atlanta: John Knox Press, 1987)

Nygren, A., *Commentary on Romans* (trans. C.C. Rasmussen; Philadelphia: Muhlenberg Press, 1949)

Origen, *Commentary on the Epistle to the Romans: Books 6–10* (trans. T.P. Scheck; Washington, DC: Catholic University Press, 2002)

Placher, W.C., *The Domestication of Transcendence: How Modern Thinking about God Went Wrong* (Louisville, KY: Westminster John Knox Press, 1996)

Reno, R.R., 'Postmodern Irony and Petronian Humanism', in *In the Ruins of the Church* (Grand Rapids: Brazos Press, 2002), 31–46

——, 'Fighting the Noonday Devil', *First Things* 135 (2003), 31–36

Rice, G., *Nations Under God: A Commentary on the Book of 1 Kings* (Grand Rapids: Eerdmans, 1990)

Schelkle, H., *The Epistle to the Romans: Theological Meditations* (trans. J.A. Kliest and J.I. Lilly; New York: Herder & Herder, 1964)

Soulen, K., *The God of Israel and Christian Theology* (Minneapolis: Fortress Press, 1996)

Speyr, A. von, *The Victory of Love: A Meditation on Romans 8* (trans. L. Wiedenhoerer; San Francisco: Ignatius, 1990)

Throntreit, M., *Ezra–Nehemiah* (IBC; Atlanta: John Knox Press, 1987)

16

Imaginative Readings of Scripture and Theological Interpretation

Stephen B. Chapman

In face of the biblical text we are not bound to imagine that the Word of God is present, we are not called upon to use any devices to make it present. But in face of the biblical text we are clamped or pincered by thankfulness and hope …

(K. Barth, *Church Dogmatics* I/2, 533)

… the human possibility of knowing is not exhausted by the ability to perceive and comprehend. Imagination, too, belongs no less legitimately in its way to the human possibility of knowing. A man without an imagination is more of an invalid than one who lacks a leg. But fortunately each of us is gifted somewhere and somehow with imagination, however starved this gift may be in some or misused by others.

(K. Barth, *Church Dogmatics* III/1, 91)

Critical Attentiveness

One response to the present sense of malaise concerning theological interpretation of the Bible has been a renewed appeal to the faculty of the imagination, both as an expression of what theological interpretation currently lacks and as a suggestive pointer toward a more promising hermeneutics. The intent of this chapter is to offer a number of particulars in evaluation of that appeal in order to identify where discernible pitfalls for theological interpretation are involved and where significant promise exists. Here at the outset, however, it will help to sharpen the provisional focus of this exploration by seeking a more precise understanding of what exactly is wrong with theological interpretation in its contemporary form.

James Barr, for example, questions the idea that a problem exists. He begins his recent massive book on biblical theology by carefully detailing a remarkable fluorescence of theological writing on the Bible throughout the 1990s.[1] The

---

[1] Barr, *Concept*, 1–2.

works he mentions include biblical theologies proper, *Festschriften*, other volumes of collected essays, methodological treatments and journals specifically devoted to the study of theology and the Bible. Barr estimates that in terms of sheer quantity, these works represent as high a degree of activity in this area as the field has ever seen, remarking dryly: 'If biblical theology is in decline, it seems not to be because of under-nourishment.'[2] Barr's rejection of what many would consider common wisdom[3] helpfully refocuses the question at hand. The problem, to take Barr's point seriously, is not that theological interpretation has been ignored but rather that the *right kind* of theological interpretation is not being done.[4] So why not?

Answers will immediately vary at this point, making it a challenge to gauge the reliability of further analysis. Because the diagnosis of a disease goes a long way toward suggesting its proper cure, Scripture scholars are sometimes prone to diagnose the particular theological illness for which they already like the medicine. However, in order to make a preliminary probe one might well begin with Stephen Fowl's identification of a crucial aspect to the problem in his criticism of Werner Jeanrond's 'overly formal' treatment of theological interpretation; Jeanrond proposes that theological interpretation is interpretation that attends to 'the question of God'.[5] Fowl elaborates:

> What sort of attention to these accounts really counts as theological interpretation? Does an interpretation that attends to the picture of God found in the Succession Narrative wholly in terms of the social and political forces that led to the production

---

[2] Barr, *Concept*, 2.

[3] See the description of the 'crisis in biblical interpretation' in Childs, 'Foreword', xv.

[4] Readers will note that while Barr's comments concern 'biblical theology', my own observations are framed in terms of 'theological interpretation'. By adopting this broader language, I mean to designate a larger class of activity. In other words, I consider all biblical theology to involve the kind of theological interpretation explored in this chapter, but I do not view all theological interpretation as taking the form of biblical theology. I understand biblical theology to entail a further degree of order or systemization, a feature that would raise additional methodological difficulties for the points under review here. Instead, this chapter can be thought of as exploring the hermeneutical *preconsiderations* for biblical theology and as responding to a more fundamental question: how is the biblical text to be read theologically? For a discussion of the *theological* danger specific to 'biblical theology' as an ordering or a system, see Barth, *Dogmatics* I/2, 483: 'Therefore a biblical theology can never consist in more than a series of attempted approximations, a collection of individual exegeses.' Whether Barth was right about this or not, his critique has set additional hurdles before the task of biblical theology.

[5] Fowl, *Scripture*, 29. For the work of Jeanrond to which Fowl primarily refers, see Jeanrond, 'Hermeneutics', esp. 88.

of that particular view of God count as theological? If so, then the vast majority of professional biblical scholarship has been theological for quite some time. Moreover, it is not clear that systematic theology has anything to contribute to that discussion.[6]

Fowl's isolation of the question regarding the *quality* of interpretive attention is exceptionally illuminating for diagnostic purposes. The problem, as he sees it, lies not so much with the object of theological interpretation ('God') but with the way in which that object is to be described and explained.

  Both of these tasks have emerged as pressing methodological difficulties: the way in which a 'particular view of God' can be identified within a text and *described*, and the way in which that 'particular view' is then to be *explained*.[7] Heightened awareness of such questions leads in turn to the realization that genuine theological interpretation involves a certain quality of attention throughout the entire process of wrestling with the biblical text – theological attention 'all the way down', as it were.[8] To be sure, descriptive work on a text is more open to the possibility of working neutrality and relative objectivity; it is in the explanatory mode that the need for explicitly theological reasons and formulations usually becomes more obvious. However, the idea that one can base theological 'explanation' directly on the foundation of neutral textual 'description' must be challenged, particularly since so much of what is now done in biblical studies involves the application of sociological categories, often generally dismissive of religion but masquerading as neutral description.[9] For example, when the Deuteronomistic History is first *described* as a tract of political propaganda, is it any wonder that its theological features are reductively *explained* as the ideological window dressing of a self-interested social elite?[10]

---

[6] Fowl, *Scripture*, 29. As a measure of its resonance within the contemporary debate, I note the citation of this same passage also in Wilson, *Sense*, 65, n. 14.

[7] Cf. Childs, *Biblical Theology of the Old and New Testaments*, 83–85.

[8] See Childs, 'Reclaiming', 10: 'This means that proper interpretation does not consist of an initial stance of seeking a purely objective or neutral reading ... but ... from the start, the Christian reader receives a particular point of standing ...'. Wolters has a similar point in view when he discusses the validity of 'top-down relationships' among various exegetical levels in his 'Criticism', 108–109. However, by working with the idea of exegetical 'levels' he reinforces the notion that theological interpretation represents a particular discrete operation upon a text rather than an entire manner of textual engagement.

[9] Childs, 'Reading'.

[10] Frick, 'History'. In this case unexamined sociological assumptions lead to the odd conclusion that those responsible for the Deuteronomistic History had no real interest in socio-economic justice or regard for the poor, passages like 1 Kgs. 21 notwithstanding.

How can theological interpretation build successfully upon such a tendentious foundation?

Theological interpretation cannot be thought of as a discrete operation conducted after all the exegesis is done, a closing platitude at the end of a section in a commentary, or a free-floating theme without any demonstrably necessary connection to the text. Neither can theological interpretation be pursued by initially employing only the language, methods and concepts of the social sciences, expecting that a robust theological interpretation can then be built directly on such differently conceived (and sometimes antagonistic) findings. What is needed instead is a way of approaching the biblical text that takes theological concerns seriously throughout the entirety of the interpretive process. This idea does not mean that other kinds of investigations (e.g., historical, sociological, etc.) lack explanatory merit or cannot lead to important insights into the biblical text. The point is not to reject methodological pluralism but rather to grant theological interpretation a full place at the hermeneutical table.

Such an idea would also not entail ruling out the consideration of other descriptive and explanatory modes as part of theological interpretation itself (self-critique is important for every method), but it would require at times a methodological forbearance in the way such modes are deployed so as not to compromise the ability of theological description and explanation to operate with their own freedom and integrity.[11] For example, in the previous case regarding the Deuteronomistic History, how much is already assumed about the nature of self-interest? Must a valid sociological approach assume that only one type of self-interest exists, namely the will to power? Might not a theological appropriation of such sociological work need to adopt a more cautious posture at precisely this point, in light of the reality (acknowledged by numerous religious traditions) that human beings possess various kinds of 'self-interest', which sometimes even conflict with each other?[12]

It is especially the idea that theological interpretation requires a particular quality of attention 'all the way down', a qualitatively different kind of engagement with the biblical text, that has increasingly led interpreters to consider how use of the imagination can instruct and guide the process of theological reflection. However, sometimes the kind of imagination advocated in response is conceived in such a way that the text becomes a launching pad for any kind of interpretive 'what-if'. Imagination can easily be construed as liberation *from*

---

[11] E.g., Albright, *Stone Age*, 390: 'Here the historian has no right to deny what he cannot disprove. He has a perfect right to unveil clear examples of charlatanry, or credulity, or of folklore, but in the presence of authentic mysteries his duty is to stop and not attempt to cross the threshold into a world where he has no right of citizenship.'

[12] Cf. Taylor, *Agency*, 15–44.

the text.[13] Moreover, imagination is sometimes presented as so non-discursive and non-analytical that the possibility of any concrete theological content is replaced by an inchoate and ultimately uninhabitable 'story world'. What is needed for the purpose of theological interpretation is a way of employing the imagination that will promote a critical attentiveness *toward* Scripture rather than away from it.[14]

In light of this analysis of the current situation, a restatement of the diagnostic question is now in order: *how can imagination provide for the kind of critical attentiveness to the biblical text that counts as theological?* What follows is an effort to sketch a role for the imagination in the theological interpretation of Scripture by using this reformulated question as the crucial criterion.[15]

The Vulnerable Imagination

In the view taken here, it will be held that although recent work on the imagination does offer a number of useful insights for theological interpretation, worrisome difficulties are also apparent on closer examination. These difficulties are all the more in need of attention because they have not been sufficiently acknowledged in the discussion up to this point. The positive uses of the imagination for theological interpretation can only be identified with the potential pitfalls clearly in view.

What follows is not by any means intended to be an exhaustive list of strengths and weaknesses. Instead, the hope is that an articulation of even an initial and partial list will be of benefit to the current conversation. In the first section, six problems relating to the use of the imagination for the theological interpretation of Scripture will be outlined. Then, in a second section, four constructive proposals will be made about particular ways the imagination can

---

[13] Notoriously, at the 1993 Re-Imagining Conference in Minneapolis. For the conference papers, see Dimon, *Church*. For astute criticism of this continuing event, see Hailson, 'Re-Imagining' and 'Re-Imagining Revisited'.

[14] I perceive common ground between what I am calling 'critical attentiveness' and J. Webster's description, in his contribution to this volume, of the 'holy attentiveness' necessary in order for the church to read Scripture rightly.

[15] I am purposefully avoiding offering a definition of 'the imagination' at this point in order to proceed inductively rather than deductively. The goal of the following discussion is to offer a treatment of imagination ruled by Christian interpretive practices rather than by philosophical distinctions. Specialists will note that both the so-called 'reproductive' as well as 'productive' aspects of the imagination play a role here. No effort will be made on purpose to distinguish them from each other in advance. For a good overview of definitional matters, see Perdue, *Collapse*, 263–98; for a more technical constructive proposal, see Green, *Imagining*.

work in favour of theological interpretation, understood here as a characteristic mode of critical textual attentiveness (as identified above). The two-part structure of this argument should not be taken as implying that the later constructive proposals necessarily avoid all of the problems mentioned first. In what follows, constructive proposals constitute desiderata rather than accomplishments.

Imagination as cipher

In English, the semantic distinction between 'imaginative' and 'imaginary' can be taken as providing prima facie evidence of a problem intrinsic to the concept of the imagination and the history of its use. The term 'imaginary' is primarily used in reference to that which is unreal and insubstantial, even delusional. By contrast, the term 'imaginative' signals a more intuitive kind of perception, a different 'take' on what is considered ordinary reality, something which is not untrue but not necessarily true in the obvious sense either. The dilemma of the imagination, then, is a matter of the imagination's location in the shadowy border country between the familiar territory of the real and the never-never land of illusion.

The rationalist critique of the imagination has therefore traditionally emphasized epistemological questions: how can the imaginative be recognized as true? How can it be desirable if false? In response, the standard line in defence of the imagination has been to subvert the pretensions of rationality to serve as sole arbiter of reality by exposing the disguisedly imaginative character of ordinary reason, while simultaneously providing examples of truths incapable of being identified and expressed within a purely rationalistic worldview. In other words, defence of the imagination has typically involved showing at once both its similarity to and its difference from reason, both reason's deep indebtedness to the imagination and reason's tragic lack of it.

The idea that reason and imagination ultimately overlap tends to make intuitive sense to those who approach epistemological questions from the standpoint of a religious background or theological commitment. On the whole, religious people readily recognize rationalism as reductive of reality and they frequently (but certainly not always!) possess the right mixture of self-examination, humility and honesty to admit that not all their own reasons are, strictly speaking, rational ones (e.g., Rom. 7:15). Yet orthodox Christianity, to speak more confessionally, has also possessed from its beginnings a firm commitment to historical and epistemological truth (e.g., 1 Cor. 15:14; 2 Pet. 1:16).

George Ramsey expresses the view increasingly common to many scholars regarding the imagination and Scripture when he writes:

Irrespective of their rootage in historical events or of their 'historical accuracy', biblical stories cast up images which capture our imagination, illumine our contemporary situation, clarify what it means to live in the presence of God, and serve us as paradigms for the structuring of individual and corporate lifestyles.[16]

It is difficult, however, to see any substantial difference between this view of Scripture and, say, the 'cleverly devised myths' attributed to 2 Peter's opponents. Therefore, the theological objection to narrative treatments of Scripture in which a reality external to the text is rejected, 'bracketed' or simply overlooked remains formidable. Such a realization suggests in turn that a Christian view of the imagination will be unable to divorce itself from questions of reality and truth if it is to be considered proper and compelling on theological grounds.

Yet this kind of challenge to the imagination is obviously external to it rather than internal, a challenge posed by a theological appraisal of history. A more subtle internal challenge to the imagination exists in what literary critic James Engnell has termed its 'terrible inner vulnerability to deception and weaknesses'.[17] This vulnerability arises from the moral ambiguity of the imagination on its own terms, its ability to conduce to either goodness or badness depending upon the purpose to which it is put. As a human faculty, the imagination lacks internal self-correcting criteria. This failing is signalled in contemporary appeals to the imagination within theological and biblical studies by the term's reinforcement with various modifiers: the 'religious imagination',[18] the 'theological imagination',[19] 'Christian imagination',[20] the 'exegetical imagination',[21] the 'paschal imagination',[22] the 'eschatological imagination',[23] 'baptized imagination',[24] as well as others.

The proliferation of modifiers raises a further question: how much of the conceptual work being attributed to the imagination is actually done by the imagination itself and how much by the various kinds of modifiers being used in reference to it? In other words, to take the example of the category 'baptized imagination', how much of what is being attributed to the helpfulness of this

---

[16] Ramsey, *Quest*, 124.

[17] Engnell, *Imagination*, 293. The phrase is used in his discussion of Keats, who among all the Romantic poets was the one most concerned about the problematic character of the imagination.

[18] E.g., Green, *Imagining*.

[19] E.g., Walker-Jones, 'Imagination'. Cf. Kaufman, *Imagination*.

[20] E.g., Ryken, *Imagination*.

[21] E.g., Davis, *Imagination*, 243–67. Cf. Fishbane, *Imagination*.

[22] Schneiders, 'Imagination'.

[23] E.g., Alison, *Abel*; cf. Hays, 'Conversion', and Braaten, 'Recovery'.

[24] E.g., Scorgie, 'Hermeneutics'.

particular term relates to the notion of the imagination and how much to the theological concept of baptism? The worry is that current appeals to the imagination may in fact provide less than they offer; otherwise, why would they require such conceptual reinforcement? Similarly, is there anything special about the category 'imagination' that would be lost if a seemingly synonymous term were used instead (e.g., 'originality', 'creativity' or 'inventiveness')? How much actual content does the term 'imagination' possess in contemporary appeals and how much is it a cipher standing for something else?

Even if 'imagination' is shown to have an indispensable and non-substitutable content, it should be recognized that there is a strongly rhetorical aspect to its present invocation – and if appeals to the imagination are in fact rhetorical as well as substantive, then the question must also be posed as to why these appeals currently possess such considerable rhetorical force.

Cultural accommodation

While talk of the imagination may have been truly counter-cultural when scientific positivism was at its height,[25] in the present postmodern climate a focus on the imagination may actually serve to blur the necessary critical distance between church and culture, contributing to the undue cultural accommodation of the gospel.

Describing the contemporary intellectual scene, the classicist Paul Veyne writes,

> The idea that it is impossible to rely on the authority of truth is what distinguishes modern philosophy from its counterfeits. Yes, imagination is fashionable; irrationalism is more in vogue than reason ... and the unsaid improvises.[26]

No retrograde rationalist, Veyne is quite convinced by the postmodern analysis of the human condition but at the same time feels forced to concede the current popularity and mood of intellectual correctness concerning the imagination's self-evident superiority to rationalistic accounts of truth.

It is, in fact, in the present revival of imagination, irrationalism and mystery that some of postmodernism's closest resemblances to Romantic hermeneutics become evident.[27] Isaiah Berlin once described the insight that:

---

[25] See the telling deconstruction of W.F. Albright as 'scientist', in Long, *Planting*, 141–45. The accompanying photograph of Albright posing as a scientist in the midst of investigating ancient artefacts (p. 144) seems as obviously staged today as it no doubt appeared 'natural' in 1955.

[26] Veyne, *Greeks*, 125.

[27] Avis, *God*, 30.

... [the historical] task of integrating disparate data and interpretations of events, movements, situations, and synthesizing such heterogeneous material into a coherent picture, demands gifts very different from those required for rational methods of investigation or formulation and verification of specific hypotheses: above all, the gift of breathing life into the dead bones in the burial ground of the past, of a creative imagination.[28]

Yet Berlin was not referring to himself or one of his contemporaries but to Herder.

Critiques of Romantic hermeneutics may therefore apply with just as much force to fashionably 'postmodern' readings. Both Romantic and postmodern hermeneutics privilege reader over text. For this reason, appeals to the imagination within biblical studies should not proceed innocently of past philosophical debates or unaware of how current emphases within theology may mirror wider cultural trends unwittingly in the absence of sufficient critique and challenge.

Anti-intellectualism

From another vantage point, something of the present attractiveness of the imagination may also lie in its very lack of intrinsic criteria, rules and methodology. A character in Don DeLillo's novel *White Noise* relates the popularity of automobile crashes in Hollywood movies to the desire in contemporary US society for 'something elemental, something fiery and loud and head-on.' He continues insightfully, 'It's a conservative wish-fulfillment, a yearning for naïveté.' We want to be artless again. We want to reverse the flow of experience, of worldliness and its responsibilities.'[29] With these remarks DeLillo identifies a cultural mutiny against method.

It needs to be acknowledged that a similar reaction may drive some of the recent shift in emphasis within biblical studies from critical methods to imaginative treatments. David Jasper warns of some works of narrative theology: 'On the one hand many of them use the idea of "story" as an easy way out of giving serious attention to the problems of the New Testament ... On the other hand, many fail to perceive the extremely difficult relationship between "narrative" – the telling of a story – and theology.'[30] By its very nature, the work of biblical interpretation demands precision, consumes considerable time (often with significant personal sacrifice) and is subject to communal approval. Any reason to adopt a more immediate, impressionistic and

---

[28] Berlin, *Vico*, xxvi. Cited in Engnell, *Imagination*, 224.
[29] DeLillo, *White Noise*, 218.
[30] Jasper, *New Testament*, 43; cf. also Cunneen, 'Bible'.

subjective approach to the task could be sure of receiving a decent welcome by those wearied from past efforts or awed by the prospect of beginning the daunting labour.

In fact, 'criticism' in general has often been miscast and put into the role of opposing the imagination more or less by definition. The poet Wallace Stevens once gave the following comparison between the function of the literary imagination and the experience of listening to music:

> When we hear the music of one of the great narrative musicians, as it tells its tale, it is like finding our way through the dark not by the aid of any sense but by an instinct which makes it possible for us to move quickly when the music moves quickly, slowly when the music moves slowly. It is a speed that carries us on and through every winding, once more to the world outside the music at its conclusion ... When it is over, we are aware that we have had an experience very much like the story just as if we had participated in what took place.[31]

The idea of allowing literature to wash over the reader, enabling him or her to relive the experience it describes, may initially sound appealing. Yet Stevens excludes without mention the possibility that a critical awareness of music might actually deepen one's understanding of it and thereby intensify its impact. Just how much of the music can one actually appreciate when listening naïvely? Is it not true that one cannot even *hear* certain aspects of music before learning what to listen for?[32]

Similarly intuitive readings of Scripture privilege subjective experience, taking individual encounters with the text beyond the range of inter-subjective accountability. It is crucial to see, however, that even for individuals the practice of naïve reading involves a fatal lapse, amounting to what Alan Jacobs calls a 'universal ethical failure'.[33] Jacobs cites the description in Solzhenitsyn's novel *The First Circle* of what happens when the State Counselor first begins to read forbidden books:

> It turned out that you have to know how to read. It is not just a matter of letting your eyes run down the pages. Since Innokenty, from youth on, had been shielded from erroneous or outcast books, and had read only the clearly established classics, he had grown used to believing every word he read, giving himself completely to the author's will. Now, reading writers whose opinions contradicted one another, he was

---

[31] Stevens, *Angel*, 70. Cited in Fischer, *Rainbow*, 19–20.

[32] A brief example may help: it is fully possible to listen to Handel's *Concerto Grosso* 7 and appreciate its sprightly beauty without any kind of critical awareness, but one does not hear or appreciate its intrinsic wit unless one understands that the idea of a one-note fugue subject is itself an amusing one.

[33] Jacobs, *Theology*, 107.

unable for a while to rebel, but could only submit to one author, then to another, then to a third.[34]

Rather than merely failing on pragmatic grounds, the State Counselor's lack of critical distance is faulted by Jacobs as exemplifying a hermeneutics in which what is read can only be authoritarian and readers are tragically passive. As Jacobs puts it: 'Innokenty's interpretive humility is a false humility.'[35]

For this reason, efforts simply to repristinate naïve readings are morally lacking and theologically unsatisfactory, as are versions of the call for a 'second naïveté' that do not allow for a fully robust critical encounter with the text even while they recover a sense of aesthetic enjoyment in the text's playful surfaces.[36] The employment of criticism within biblical studies can be thought of as analogous to disciplines like music theory or art history, which aim to deepen appreciation for their subjects precisely by teaching students *how* to listen and see in more sensitive and knowledgeable ways.[37]

Even though such a perspective rules out naïve efforts to recapture a Christian past, it should be noted that it also voices a traditional Christian affirmation about the nature of Scripture. One of the Desert Fathers, Abba Nesteros, is remembered by John Cassian as telling how the reading of Scripture deepens over time:

> As our mind is increasingly renewed by this study, the face of the Scriptures also begins to be renewed. It is as though the beauty of a more sacred understanding keeps pace with our progress. The Scriptures accommodate themselves to the capacity of human perception; what appears to be earthly to the carnal seems divine to the spiritual.[38]

---

[34] Solzhenitsyn, *First Circle*, 344.

[35] Jacobs, *Theology*, 107. However, Jacobs qualifies a similar point earlier on (p. 24) when he allows that sometimes it is neither appropriate nor charitable to respond to a work 'according to a rigid criterion of studious application', drawing an analogy between a 'well-crafted literary work' and a 'well-cooked meal'. The response to both should be simple gratitude and not criticism, he maintains. But this analogy elides the difference between the reality of the reader's appreciation and the way in which that appreciation is best expressed. One can notice how food has been prepared without necessarily making a comment about it (especially an uncharitable observation) to one's host.

[36] Cf. Ricœur, *Symbolism*, 350–51: 'We can … aim at a second naïveté in and through criticism. In short, it is by *interpreting* that we can *hear* again' (his italics).

[37] Cf. the discussion of the relationships between imagination, creativity and discipline in Hauerwas, 'Keeping'.

[38] Cassian, *Conferences* 14.11. Cited in Casey, *Reading*, 52.

Not all of Scripture's treasures are immediately viewable; study is required. As with music or art, the proper mindset for biblical interpretation is one that has been conformed to the object of its study – and renewing the mind takes time.

Elitism

By stressing the nature of biblical interpretation as a product of intuition and personal encounter, the appeal to imagination may also eventuate in the idea of interpretation as the irreplicable, uniquely personal tour de force of particularly gifted individuals. It is this aspect of the imagination that has traditionally led to its connection with the notion of the 'genius'.[39]

Brevard Childs is remembered as having responded to a student's question about how to become a better exegete by saying, 'Become a more profound person.'[40] To those who do not know him, Childs's comment might sound like a personal put-down. Instead, it was a characteristically humble reminder to everyone in the class that a truly profound interpretation of Scripture embraces a number of existential factors that cannot be reduced to matters of methodology or even instruction. This Childsian reminder voices a long-overdue corrective to narrow forms of historical criticism that would rule out such factors, except as necessary evils.

Yet to make such personal intangibles the exclusive or even primary key to scriptural interpretation would be a great mistake, something Childs himself understands very well as a long-time advocate of a 'learned clergy'. Without sufficient emphasis on methods, training, study (especially the history of interpretation) and communal accountability, the successful interpretation of Scripture devolves into the inimitable achievement of a spiritual titan, and the practice of interpretation turns decidedly elitist. By contrast, interpretive methods, when employed successfully, actually have a democratizing tendency by making more transparent the grounds and procedures for exegetical claims.[41] The average pastor confronting the task of preaching to the average congregation is in very great need of just this kind of help.[42]

---

[39] See, e.g., Warnock on 'Imagination and the Idea of Genius' in her *Imagination*, 22–44; cf. 102–105.

[40] I witnessed such an encounter when I served as one of Childs's teaching assistants in the academic year 1995–96, but it also may have happened more than once. See also his similar remark in 'Foreword', xvi.

[41] On this view, the problem with critical methods as they have been employed within biblical studies is more their inadequate transparency than their use as such. As much as methods can have a democratizing force when used well, when perceived as idiosyncratic and unrelievedly complex, they easily take on elitist and gnostic qualities.

[42] It should be noted that a contemporary obsession with genius also seems to exist in US society at large. For insightful cultural analysis on this topic, see Barber, 'Genius'.

Ultimately, a virtuoso approach to scriptural interpretation contradicts the traditional Protestant view of the perspicuity of Scripture.[43] Furthermore, it discourages those who do not consider themselves geniuses from seeking suffi-cient hermeneutical instruction and guidance.

A virtuoso approach also removes Scripture from the community and makes it the property of individuals. A constructive use of the imagination in theological interpretation will require a strongly social basis, since individual Christians are ordinarily dependent on the church for sustenance and support. Moreover, imaginative insights will need to remain subject *in some way* to ecclesial approval and censure (1 Jn. 4:1).[44]

Experiential limitations

Another problem to mention concerns the imagination's functional bound-aries. Part of what makes the imagination such an attractive faculty is that it allows for a transcendence of the limits to one's own personal experience so as to entertain other as-of-yet unexperienced experiences, other realities, other worlds.[45] Yet it must be acknowledged that one still participates in such imagi-native worlds on the basis of some kind of analogy with what one has in fact experienced oneself.

A great risk of reductionism arises at precisely this point, namely that the person doing the imagining will domesticate the unexperienced or the unknown in favour of the reality he or she already knows and understands. For example, there do not seem to be any theoretical limits to what one *could* imag-ine of life after death, but in actuality most imaginative treatments of it tend to be rather like life before death, only a bit different. Similarly, there may be real-ities so extreme that they are best left alone as simply incommensurate with one's own reality.

Ought one try to depict the gas chambers at Auschwitz imaginatively? Such a suggestion is unseemly precisely because it is difficult to see how the result would not involve the trivialization of its subject to some degree, and in this case *any* degree of trivialization is unacceptable. Perhaps certain things are, and should remain, 'un-imaginable'. This concern is particularly acute with regard to film because the nature of the medium itself inclines toward filling in for the imagination as much as possible.[46] For example, in Cecil B. DeMille's 1956 movie *The Ten Commandments*, what is the impact on the viewer of recreating

---

[43] See Wilson, *Sense*, 24.

[44] For a suggestive account of social embodiment as a criterion of right interpretation, see Hays, *Vision*, 304–306.

[45] For a helpful elaboration of this point, see Hart, 'Imagination', 316–17.

[46] See Lewis, 'On Stories' (pp. 3–20 in *On Stories*), 16, on 'death in the camera'.

the miraculous events of the biblical book of Exodus? No matter how impressive a particular 'special effect' in the film may be, does it not, by virtue of its being a 'special effect', substitute for the biblical text more than illuminate it? Special effects by definition manipulate perception and emotion. By showing the crossing of the Red Sea as this kind of an 'effect', does not the film finally inhibit the imagination more than liberate it?[47] Also, is there not a further theological danger precisely in restricting biblical revelation exclusively to the 'extraordinary mode'?[48]

In a slightly different context, Ellen Davis refers to demythologizing interpretive moves as 'translating away the wonder'.[49] The challenge relating to the role of experience in theological interpretation is to use the imagination tactfully and strategically in ways that create or explore new textual possibilities, rather than translating away such possibilities by seeking to depict too much.

Enlightenment framework

Finally, it must be firmly acknowledged that the modern concept of the imagination was an Enlightenment invention.[50] Thus, there is not a little irony in the way that some contemporary commentators have emphasized use of the imagination as a means of breaking with the Enlightenment legacy.[51] In reality, by focusing on the imagination a postmodern approach works with 'the same dichotomy between rational discourse and imagistic thinking [as in modernity], but ... reverses modernity's valuation', according to Paul Avis. He summarizes: 'Postmodernity privileges image over discourse, *eidos* over *logos*.'[52] The very idea of a gulf between the two, however, plays into the same basic Enlightenment framework that some proponents of the imagination claim they are seeking to challenge.

---

[47] This danger does not apply equally to all kinds of visual representations. To my mind, Spiegelman's *Maus* succeeds surprisingly well in overcoming the problems being discussed by depicting the Holocaust using cartoon animation as his artistic medium. Perhaps the more fully the art form becomes representational, the greater its potential for reductionism. 'Illustration' is the term often used for representational art that conforms the artistic subject to the viewer's expectations instead of transforming them, as great art does.

[48] Cf. the defence of creation theology within the Old Testament in Murphy, *Tree*, 276.

[49] Davis, *Imagination*, 251.

[50] Engnell, *Imagination*, 3 and *passim*. This is not to say that there was no such thing as the imagination earlier in history, only that what is recognized today as the imagination was first identified as a distinct mental faculty in the eighteenth century. On the 'heart' as a possible biblical precursor, see Green, *Imagining*, 109–10.

[51] Brueggemann, *Texts*.

[52] Avis, *God*, 23.

Once more, the most troubling consequence of this situation from a theological perspective is how it refocuses biblical interpretation on human experience – either the experience of the interpreter, the experience of the interpreted (author), or both. As much as the imagination can be used to recognize, challenge and broaden the limits of one's own experience, the phenomenal (to use the Kantian term) still never disappears from view, human experience itself becomes the subject of interpretation rather than divine revelation, and anthropology trumps theology. In the end, perhaps this dilemma cannot be fully solved; the theological problems confronting a persuasive account of revelation are exceptionally thorny. Still, it should not be overlooked that without some recourse to revelation or, say, the action of the Holy Spirit, an emphasis on imagination becomes, in effect, a backdoor into liberal Protestantism and its characteristically reductionistic view of Scripture.[53] Within the biblical traditions, the externality and objectivity of the divine word stands as a permanent check against such a move (e.g., Jer. 23:28–29).

However, this is not to argue that a view of the imagination and a reliance upon the agency of the Spirit cannot coexist in some kind of tensive relationship. One fruitful way of describing such 'creative tension' is to draw upon the theological notion of divine accommodation, so that 'God's revelation is conveyed or articulated not with clarity, precision and literalness, but in the obscure and opaque figures of metaphor, symbol and myth'.[54] On this view, a theologically satisfactory account of the imagination must include how *God* communicates to human beings through their imaginative faculties and not just how human beings think imaginatively about God, the world and themselves. Scripture would then be read as not only an imaginative human vision of God but also as God's 'imaginative' accommodation to the human capacity for understanding and obedience. The logical extension of such an idea would be that revelation itself is poetic in nature,[55] with God in the role of 'author' or 'poet'.[56] Thus, it could be claimed, the imaginative, figurative language of Scripture is perfectly formulated to communicate God's will and purpose while preserving 'through its combination of disclosure and concealment' God's 'transcendence and mystery'.[57]

This way of thinking provides an important theological alternative to questions that frequently appear to be within the exclusive domain of historicism. For example, how is the genre of the parable to be explained? In exclusively socio-historical terms? Or like this:

---

[53] For the classic critique, see Barth, 'World'. Cf. Childs, *Crisis*, 102.

[54] Avis, *God*, 50.

[55] Avis, *God*, 51.

[56] Avis, *God*, 65. Cf. Bayer, *Gott*.

[57] Avis, *God*, 51. On the relation between imaginative interpretation and the notion of concealment in Scripture, see Burrows, 'Taste', esp. 176–78.

Thus Jesus did not teach in parables simply because he was a first-century rabbi preaching to first-century peasants and fishermen, but because his gospel was addressed to the whole person in its depth and integrity – to the heart as well as to the head, to children to whom the kingdom of heaven belonged as well as to the intelligentsia of scribes and Pharisees, to the alienated and outcast as well as to the aristocracy of the Sadducees.[58]

As in this example, perhaps biblical genres and literary characteristics can themselves be interpreted as an integral part of the biblical message. This possibility would serve as a profoundly theological impetus to read the biblical witnesses for their form as well as for their content. If the literary form of biblical revelation can be said to have been intended by a 'poetic' God, then an aesthetic response to Scripture is crucial for discerning the fullness of its meaning.[59] Here the study of what might be called biblical poetics is revealed to be peculiarly well suited to convey the theological meaning of the biblical text.[60]

As Coleridge insightfully perceived, although the metaphorical figures within Scripture certainly are not to be treated as identical with God, they nevertheless mysteriously participate in God's reality and are thus 'consubstantial with the truths of which they are the conductors'.[61] To elaborate on this idea, Coleridge brilliantly applied a biblical figure to the idea of biblical figures:

---

[58] Avis, *God*, 66.

[59] Avis, *God*, 67. The frequent objection that a 'merely' aesthetic response to Scripture represents a kind of theological voyeurism, an avoidance of Scripture's moral claim, must be taken seriously. See Webster, Ch. 14 in this volume, esp. his final section. Yet while aesthetic response *may* be detached from morality, such detachment is not necessarily the case, as recent work in 'transformational aesthetics' has demonstrated compellingly. See Scarry, *Beauty*, and de Gruchy, *Christianity*. As both these authors describe, a sense for beauty can also de-centre the self and lead to the rejection of superficial realities. Wonder is not a barrier to moral action but is, in several ways, its precondition. The classic expression of this view is found in Book Fourteen of Wordsworth's poem, 'The Prelude': 'To fear and love, / To love as prime and chief, for there fear ends, / Be this ascribed; to early intercourse, / In presence of sublime or beautiful forms …' (62–65).

[60] Coming to the same conclusion, but for different reasons, is Alter, *Art*, 22; 176–77. Alter attributes the peculiar character of biblical prose to the change in human consciousness brought about by monotheism. This means he sees a literary connection between biblical poetics and biblical theology but grounds this connection in history. While the biblical guild has severely criticized the historical claims he makes or implies, it has also left largely unexamined his fascinating linkage between poetics and theology; see the review articles in *JSOT* 27 (1983) and 29 (1984).

[61] Coleridge, *Aids*, 171; cited in Engnell, *Imagination*, 364.

> These [i.e., the text's figures] are [like] the *wheels* which Ezekiel beheld, when the hand of the Lord was upon him, and he saw the visions of God as he sate among the captives by the river of Chebar. *Whithersoever the Spirit was to go, the wheels went, and thither was their spirit to go:— for the spirit of the living creature was in the wheels also.*[62]

For Coleridge, the symbols and metaphors of biblical language are the very wheels of the chariot of the Spirit of God.

Again, the ultimate question becomes whether a particular use of the imagination leads toward the biblical text or away from it, because the *form* of the text serves as a crucial criterion for a determination of its content. The real potential for the imagination in theological interpretation will only be seen clearly once it is recognized that the form of the biblical text is itself theologically meaningful and must therefore be susceptible of literary investigation for theological reasons. As Karl Barth put it: 'The biblical texts must be investigated for their own sake to the extent that the revelation which they attest does not stand or occur, and is not to be sought, behind or above them but in them.'[63] What is needed, therefore, is not a concept that will discipline the imagination by providing the best critical norm for its use, but the right practices of critical attentiveness in which the imagination can play a distinctive role. It is through imaginative practices of critical attentiveness, rightly framed, that theological interpreters can regain the biblical text for the church.

Toward a Poetics of the Theological Imagination

Mindful of the problems that have been discussed, there now follow four constructive proposals about concrete contributions the imagination can and does make helpfully in the theological interpretation of Scripture. The modifying adjectives found in the next four subheadings represent not different kinds of imagination, but certain of its uses that can be said to have particular relevance and promise for the theological task. In each case, an effort is made to view imagination as a mode of critical attentiveness to the biblical text.

Exegetical imagination

Although the term 'poetics' has sometimes been used as a way of talking about particular conventions or 'rules' that govern the shape and dynamics of particular narratives or narrative types, here the claim will be more modest – not that there are necessarily definable 'rules' governing biblical literature, but only that this particular body of literature possesses certain characteristic features which

---

[62] Coleridge, *Aids*, 171 (his italics).
[63] Barth, *Dogmatics* I/2, 494.

can be fairly described as sharing a family resemblance and thus help to guide (but not determine!) the reader's comprehension.[64] In this way poetics can serve as a bridge between text and interpretation.[65] One important use of the imagination in the theological interpretation of Scripture can therefore be characterized as the effort to discern and describe the poetical cues of the biblical text exegetically.

In other words, rather than beginning with a notion of imagination that pursues liberation from the literary constraints of the text, the imagination can be understood as a means of getting even closer to the text than is ordinarily the case. Thus Robert Alter writes of the kind of 'scrutiny' that 'cannot be based merely on an imaginative impression of the story but must be undertaken through minute critical attention to the biblical writer's articulations of narrative form'.[66] Obviously, much could be said about the particular ways in which the imagination could be used to gain a closer scrutiny of biblical texts. Here both the interpretive traditions of Judaism and Christianity are remarkably rich and suggestive, and the ongoing reconsideration of this material for contemporary exegetical practice is to be welcomed. An expanding body of contemporary literary scholarship on the Bible also exists, which in many instances brings features of the biblical narrative into sharper focus through the identification and application of literary devices and techniques.[67] However, there still appears to be much uncertainty about how best to use the results of this literary work for theological exegesis and for preaching.

In the hope of offering a few concrete suggestions, it will be instructive to compare two attempts to use the imagination in a sermon on biblical narrative. The first comes from a sermon by Paul Scott Wilson, which he includes in his recent book *God Sense* as 'theological imagination of the sort that is needed for preaching, taken from a sermon on Genesis 3'.[68] An excerpt will convey the style and substance of his effort:

---

[64] See, however, the criticism of 'poetics' as an overly formalistic category by Gunn, 'Narrative', esp. 231, 236. Gunn is concerned that a literary orientation towards 'poetics' obscures the need for sufficient self-critique and will serve to encourage 'my own disposition to read to suit my own interest'. The extent to which poetics are 'in' the text or 'in' the mind of the reader is an important question to keep open, but it would be a mistake to dismiss the possibility of any textual characteristics existing independently of the reader. Genres may be dependent on being recognized by readers in order to be identified, but literary works are still crafted according to particular genres prior to being read.

[65] Berlin, *Poetics*, 82.

[66] Alter, *Art*, 12.

[67] For an excellent historical overview and analysis of this scholarship, see Gunn, 'Narrative'.

[68] Wilson, *Sense*, 76.

On the way out of Eden, Eve must have had a conversation with God, 'O God, I know we brought this upon ourselves. But is there no way we could stay, not for ourselves but for the sake of our children?' We don't know exactly what she said, but we know something of how God answered. God said, 'Eve, it breaks my heart that you have to leave. This is what I planned for you and Adam and your descendants. But Eve, when your teeth bit the fruit, your feet stood still, but you had already left, because when you bit the fruit, you lost your innocence. Now you know good and evil. When you lose your innocence, Eden does not exist anymore.' Eve pondered God's words in her heart. 'Well, God,' Eve said, 'I can stand leaving, if I must. I can stand facing hardship, if I must. I can stand almost anything, if I can only know that I am not leaving you.' In spite of messing up her own life, Eve knew what she needed, and she needed God. She needed God to walk with her and Adam out into the world, not to forsake them as they had forsaken God. She needed to have God answer in the middle of the night when she was anxious about her children. She needed God to be in charge of the world – to know that God would still heed her cries. [69]

In this treatment Wilson's use of the imagination seems to consist mostly in supplementing the biblical account with a highly sentimental dialogue between Eve and God. The main point offered is orthodox enough: God provides ongoing care and support to humankind in spite of human sin. However, the sentimental language (e.g., 'in the middle of the night when she was anxious about her children') has no genuine relation to the biblical narrative and is introduced only to force an emotional effect, much in the same way a Spielberg film manipulates the emotional reactions of its audience.

Curious, however, is the way this heavy-handed sentimentalizing consistently goes hand in hand with a rationalizing move. Note the 'must have had' of the first sentence. Why 'must' Eve have had a conversation with God? The implication is that since Eve was a person of faith, and faith experience is unchanging, it is therefore unthinkable that in distress she would not have spoken in this way to God in prayer. Thus Wilson's interpretation is partly dependent upon an implied claim about a normative style of piety.

However, this 'must' also serves as an implied apology for the 'imaginative' dialogue to follow. Because a conversation 'must' have happened in some form, it is therefore permissible to imagine its particular features. At this point, then, the hypothetical assertion based on transhistorical religious experience bleeds over into an implicit historicist claim ('we don't know exactly what she said, but …'). When 'must' this conversation have happened (since it does not happen in the text)? The underlying presumption is that this encounter really took place in space and time and that an authoritative theological conclusion can be drawn from its history-like reconstruction.

---

[69] Wilson, *Sense*, 76–77.

Suddenly the 'imaginative' aspect of this textual treatment looks remarkably thin. Its prevailing rationalism is revealed again in its symbolic approach to Eden ('When you lose your innocence, Eden does not exist anymore'). Aware that a fundamentalistic insistence on the geographical reality of the primeval garden beggars modern belief, Wilson treats Eden as a state of mind. The move betrays an anxiety about the historicity of the narrative and stands in significant tension with the sermon's earlier implicit insistence upon the narrative's history-likeness. In this respect rationalistic questions dominate the background of the sermon and subvert its explicit intention to be imaginative. This failure of imaginative nerve is then compounded by the sermon's consistent moralizing tone. Note how Eve is made to say: 'I know we brought this upon ourselves.' There is no room for epistemological uncertainty or moral ambiguity in this account. Eve knows full well that she and Adam have done wrong. God's justice is so entirely defensible as to be depicted as pat, even trite ('Eve knew what she needed, and she needed God').

In various ways, then, Wilson's sermon trades on the notion of the imagination, yet in reality offers a heavy-handed, didactic and sentimental account that detracts from the artistry of the text rather than inspiring listeners to hear the text more closely.[70] In the end, one might well argue that this particular sermon offers exactly the kind of psychological treatment of sin that the biblical text itself purposefully and firmly avoids.

The point of subjecting Wilson's sermon to analysis is not to be overly critical of Wilson, for he has written a fine book that will undoubtedly foster the increased retrieval of patristic traditions within contemporary homiletics. It is just that this particular sermon's tepid and counter-productive way of using the imagination appears to be rife in much contemporary preaching: the addition

---

[70] Another contributing factor to the weakness of this sermon has to do with its use of language. I do not wish to single out Wilson unfairly for the colloquial style in evidence here (e.g., 'In spite of messing up her own life …'). Its employment seems rampant in contemporary preaching, so far as I can tell. While the intentional use of colloquialism may have an important rhetorical function on occasion, surely imaginative preaching should display a more formal discourse than this, exhibiting a more sensitive use of rhetorical figures as well as an obvious care for and enjoyment in words and language. There is always the danger of style replacing substance, of course, but could not one have the goal of combining both, of a truly *poetic* style of preaching? The primary objection to such a homiletical proposal is likely to be framed in terms of the need for an effective sermon to communicate well, and this is necessarily a consideration. The opposite danger, however, is to accommodate to the devaluation of language so evident in contemporary hypercapitalism, in which the cheapened lingo of jingles and sound bites becomes the only widely recognized and socially acceptable terminology. To my mind, one of the most important challenges facing contemporary preaching has become finding a way of speaking that reinvests language with the meaning it has all but lost (cf. Brueggemann, *Finally*).

of details extraneous to the text (especially with an eye toward their psychological or sentimental effect), which then purport to explain the text's 'real' story. In Wilson's sermon 'story' is separable from and in fact preferred to 'text'.

However, a much better model is also available, one in which extra details are also playfully added at times but always in the service of hearing the biblical text better precisely as text. In this model, the text *is* the story, as demonstrated by selections from Father Mapple's sermon on Jonah in Herman Melville's masterwork *Moby-Dick*:[71]

> With this sin of disobedience in him, Jonah still further flouts at God, by seeking to flee from Him. He thinks that a ship made by men, will carry him into countries where God does not reign, but only the Captains of this earth. He skulks about the wharves of Joppa, and seeks a ship that's bound for Tarshish. There lurks, perhaps, a hitherto unheeded meaning here. By all accounts Tarshish could have been no other city than the modern Cadiz. That's the opinion of learned men. And where is Cadiz, shipmates? Cadiz is in Spain; as far by water, from Joppa, as Jonah could possibly have sailed in those ancient days, when the Atlantic was an almost unknown sea. Because Joppa, the modern Jaffa, shipmates, is on the most easterly coast of the Mediterranean, the Syrian; and Tarshish or Cadiz more than two thousand miles to the westward from that, just outside the Straits of Gibraltar. See ye not then, shipmates, that Jonah sought to flee world-wide from God?[72]

Without relinquishing the lyrical quality of his sermonic prose, Melville offers a fine example of how to use historical criticism in the service of theological meaning! It is also important to see, however, that the precipitating factor for a consideration of historical issues is the mention of Tarshish in the text itself, to which the historical discussion returns when it is concluded. Melville, schooled in the Puritan hermeneutics of New England, exhibits what is in fact the working practice of centuries of ecclesial exegesis by assuming that anything mentioned by the text must be intentionally placed there to convey a theological point. Note the use of the deictic 'here' with reference to the biblical text ('... a hitherto unheeded meaning here'). For Melville's preacher, theological meaning is sought and found within the text.[73] Thus, fixing the geographical

---

[71] Melville, 'Sermon'. I am aware that it may seem slightly odd to use a fictional sermon rather than a real one, but the fictionality of the sermon is not really related to my interest in it. Moreover, Melville appears to have modelled this sermon quite closely on the sermons of Edward Thompson Taylor, the well-known pastor of the Seamen's Bethel Church in Boston. For a fascinating account of Taylor's influence on Melville, as well as on Emerson and Whitman, see Reynolds, *Beneath*, 15–30.

[72] Melville, 'Sermon', 44.

[73] This is the case whether or not Melville ultimately uses the sermon ironically within the context of the book as a whole. For an example of the ironic interpretation, see Holstein, 'Inversion'. In order to make his case, Holstein characterizes the sermon as

location of Tarshish ultimately serves to reinforce the same connection implied in the biblical text itself at Jonah 1:3, 'to Tarshish, away from the presence of the Lord'.[74]

At the same time, matters that a reader might reasonably expect to find in the biblical narrative, but which the text nevertheless passes over in silence, also contribute to the theological reading developed in Melville's sermon:

> Miserable man! Oh! most contemptible and worthy of all scorn; with slouched hat and guilty eye, skulking from his God; prowling among the shipping like a vile burglar hastening to cross the seas. So disordered, self-condemning is his look, that had there been policemen in those days, Jonah, on the mere suspicion of something wrong, had been arrested ere he touched a deck. How plainly he's a fugitive! no baggage, not a hat-box, valise, or carpet-bag, – no friends accompany him to the wharf with their adieux.[75]

In this case it is the *omission* – especially obvious to Father Mapple's seafaring audience! – of any reports in the text about Jonah stowing his luggage or taking farewell of his friends that informs the retelling of the biblical story and shapes it theologically. The crucial aspect of this reading of the 'gaps', however, is that it is also used to return the reader/hearer, with increased sensitivity, to the explicit wording of the text. Some things are indeed conspicuous by their absence. In effect, Melville invokes human experience in order to call attention to how the narrative unfolds *differently* from one's usual expectations.

---

an intentional example of unfaithfulness by Melville, a telling subversion of the biblical text. However, greater attention to the history of Christian interpretation of Jonah would force Holstein to qualify his position. Some of what he characterizes as foreign to the Old Testament text would be very much at home in Christian interpretation of it, suggesting that Mapple is intended as an example of faithfulness after all. For a brief but persuasive treatment of Mapple's sermon as non-ironic, see Steward, 'Vision', 256.

[74] I note again the lyrical language of this sermon. It cannot be said often enough that preaching poetically is not (necessarily) about using hard words in ways that make it difficult for people to understand what is being said. Preaching poetically means primarily to shade each word with meaning (e.g., 'flouts', 'skulks', 'lurks') and to match the seriousness of the subject matter with a style that has enough weight and polish to carry the sense of the subject matter with conviction (e.g., 'See ye not then, shipmates, that Jonah sought to flee world-wide from God?'). In Wilson's characterization of the loss of paradise as Eve's having 'messed up' (see above), the language is so out of proportion to the subject matter that the effect is trivializing. I do not mean to fault Wilson for not being a Melville; very few preachers can rival Melville's way with words. I am convinced, however, that most of us (myself very much included) should work harder on the stylistic aspects of sermons than we do.

[75] Melville, 'Sermon', 44.

Acknowledging that the text fails to fulfil those expectations helps one to see the text more fully as it is.

In this sermon, the text is the target, not a launching pad. Even with all its interpretive freedom and its readiness to embellish, Melville's sermon is relentless in seeking cues from the biblical text at each interpretive turn in the retelling:

> 'I'll sail with ye', – he says, – 'the passage money, how much is that? – I'll pay now.' For it is particularly written, shipmates, as if it were a thing not to be overlooked in this history, 'that he paid the fare thereof' ere the craft did sail. And taken with the context, this is full of meaning.[76]

Melville's sermon is even more 'psychological' than Wilson's version of Eve's departure from Eden, but where Wilson replaces the story of the text for another story behind it, Melville's treatment illuminates the text itself as the story that counts.

Exegetical use of the imagination does not necessarily avoid improvisation or embellishment, but it does preserve a clear sense of the difference between text and commentary, always directing the reader/hearer, equipped with a new angle of vision, once more back to the text.

Historical imagination

Melville's sermon already nicely demonstrates that historical criticism can contribute successfully to homiletical purpose. The idea that historical information can be used imaginatively is likely to be relatively uncontroversial, however. More disputed is the question of how much the imagination plays a role in historical work itself.[77]

When history was still thought to involve a degree of sympathy with the objects of one's study, use of the imagination in historical reconstruction was held to be a commendable means of inspiration. Here is Gibbon on the origin of his great work:

> ... at the distance of twenty-five years I can neither forget nor express the strong emotions which agitated my mind as I first approached and entered the Eternal City. After a sleepless night I trod, with lofty step, the ruins of the Forum; each memorable spot where Romulus stood, or Tully spoke, or Caesar fell, was at once present to my eye; and the several days of intoxication were lost or enjoyed before I could descend to cool and minute investigation.... It was at Rome, on the 15th of October, 1764, as

---

[76] Melville, 'Sermon', 45.

[77] Now see the interesting treatment of imaginative historical reconstruction as a type of figural interpretation in Wright, 'Inhabiting', 514–16.

> I sat musing among the ruins of the Capitol, while the barefooted friars were singing
> Vespers in the temple of Jupiter, that the idea of writing the decline and fall of the
> city first started to my mind.[78]

Even Gibbon, as dispassionate a historian as any (e.g., 'cool and minute investigation'), forged history at the imagination's fire.

Only with the heyday of history as a positivistic science in the first half of the twentieth century was a role for the imagination ruled absolutely out, but in fact this development was contested almost as soon as it became established.[79] Thus, calls to accord a greater role to the imagination within biblical studies are nothing new.[80] Now, however, the discussion has been radicalized by a deeper sense of the subtle indebtedness of *all* historical work to the imagination. In fact, after the work of Hayden White and others, it is difficult to think of any biblical scholars who would seriously dispute the need for, or even the inevitability of, imaginative probes and constructs in historical investigation.[81] Increasingly the problem is rather to state how history amounts to something more or other than what the imagination does. The current debate, then, turns on the question of whether the imagination might actually be able to *replace* historical work in the task of characterizing the delineaments of the biblical text and thereby make for more fruitful theological interpretation.

Thus, some literary approaches to the Bible 'bracket' or even reject the notion of historical truth altogether. In his description of literary method Kenneth Gros Louis asserts:

> The text to us is not sacred, and whether the events it describes are historical is not
> relevant to our purposes.... Our approach is essentially ahistorical; the text is taken
> as received, and the truth of an action or an idea or a motive, for literary criticism,
> depends on its rightness or appropriateness in context. Is it true, we ask, not in the
> real world but within the fictive world that has been created by the narrative?[82]

---

[78] Gibbon, *Autobiography*, 122; cited in Warnock, *Imagination*, 147–48. Cf. Bowersock, *Imagination*.

[79] See Collingwood, *Idea*, 231–49.

[80] E.g., Cadman, *Imagination*; Farrer, *Glass*. Cf. Eslinger's very brief but interesting account of the imagination as a persistent topic throughout the more than one-hundred-year history of Yale's Beecher Lectures in his *Narrative*, 213–23.

[81] White, *Metahistory* and *Tropics*. Cf. Hart, 'Imagination', 325–26.

[82] Gros Louis, 'Considerations', 14. Gros Louis is bracketing historical truth rather than rejecting it, as the rest of his exposition makes clear despite his very strong rhetoric in this instance. He means to say that concern for historical truth, while it may be appropriate in other approaches to the Bible, does not properly enter into literary analysis as a discipline. On this point, however, I still disagree with Gros Louis, as the following discussion will make clear.

For the moment, one simply notes the implicit either/or of Gros Louis's position, with its dichotomy between the 'real world' and the 'fictive world'.

Within biblical studies, Luke Timothy Johnson adopts a similar methodological stance. Although Johnson grants the need of the *reader* for historical background in order to preserve the 'otherness of the text', he denies the need of *theology* for historical criticism: 'There is no intrinsic reason why historical reconstruction of the past should have any impact on theology.'[83] Johnson is so unwilling to have theology beholden in any way to historical reconstruction that he equates a sense for history's importance with secularism, pure and simple. Yet this move is ultimately to deny theology the ability to make a historical claim as such.[84] Although in contrast to Gros Louis the biblical text is fully sacred for Johnson, historical fact is similarly discounted.

Henry Jansen provides a helpful response to the assertion that a literary approach makes the idea of historical 'facts' unnecessary or misguided.[85] As he shows quite convincingly, some works of literature and poetry actually draw upon a sense of 'what happened' and rely upon their readers' knowledge of it in order to achieve their full *literary* effect.[86] The extent to which literary works do this must be gauged on a case-by-case basis, Jansen maintains, resisting broad generalizations about 'all literature' as imprecise and misleading. His argument proceeds, therefore, on literary rather than theological grounds. The often-assumed dichotomy of poetry *or* historical facts is not necessarily an either/or after all, he concludes: 'to say that poetic utterances do more than convey information is not to say that poetic utterances cannot convey information as well'.[87] In reality, poetry and facts often exist in a literary mixture.

Jansen's careful analysis of these questions leads to a more nuanced literary view of the Bible able to embrace both its narrative claim to offer a 'story world' as well as its historical claim to witness to particular events in space and time.[88] By virtue of its ostensive references and history-like character, most of

---

[83] Johnson, 'Imagining', 7. Johnson's quote begs the question, of course, of what he means by 'intrinsic', which is unclear even within the context of his original article.

[84] In principle, theology can make a theological claim without necessarily recognizing any validity to history's jurisdiction of the past, but theology cannot make a historical claim without implying the validity of that claim's basis in history.

[85] Jansen, 'Poetics'.

[86] Jansen, 'Poetics', 28–29. His examples are Shakespeare's *Richard III* and Siegfried Sassoon's poem 'Blighters'.

[87] Jansen, 'Poetics', 32. Cf. the similar conclusions, expressed rather differently, in Schneiders, 'Imagination', 63, and Hartt, 'Investments', 119–22.

[88] For further discussion and a similar conclusion, see Ryken and Longman, 'Introduction', esp. 25–29; cf. in the same volume Greidanus, 'Value', esp. 513–14. See also, from other hermeneutical perspectives but reaching similar literary conclusions, Schneiders, 'Imagination', 62–63, and Hartt, 'Investments', 125–27.

the Bible functions as historical 'witness' as well as literary 'world' (with the possible exception of books like Song of Songs, Jonah and Job, which were already recognized by the rabbis as *not* requiring a particular historical context for the determination of their meaning, and perhaps the gospel parables as well).[89] The role of historical criticism therefore remains especially important for theological interpretation as a means of confronting the moralism, both liberal and conservative, that casually insists on the superiority of modern cultural truisms without investigating the thick historical situatedness of Scripture.[90]

Theological interpretation requires a supple treatment of the interaction between literary and historical claims, in which both kinds of approaches, the literary and the historical, maintain their own integrity but also cohere within a common reading. 'Narrative' and 'story' can function helpfully as modes of theological description and explanation but not with a concomitant loss of all historical grounding, *not if the literary form of Scripture itself is truly to be honoured.* Historical methods consistently continue to offer the best reminder of the biblical text's strangeness and uncapturability. Historical use of the imagination can therefore contribute much to theological interpretation, so long as it resists any moves unfairly reductionistic of human beings and their religious faith.

Analogical imagination

For a scriptural interpretation to convey meaning forcefully, it seems that a tight analogy of some sort must be perceived between the situation of the text and the situation of the reader/hearer. The history of premodern interpretation is filled with examples in which a startlingly fitting sense of analogy suddenly turned the interpreter into the interpreted; the question at hand is how to achieve the same result after the advent of historical critical awareness. When biblical texts are not thought to be interpreted with sufficient skill today, often the lack of such an analogy is the particular deficiency at issue. The fascinating predominance of Psalm 46 ('Therefore we will not fear, though the earth should change, though the mountains shake ...') in public events commemorating the disastrous events of September 11, 2001, suggests that this kind of interpretive analogy still has tremendous resonance when it can be established.

The significance of the issue is highlighted by the famous Leipzig dispute between J.S. Bach and J.A. Ernesti, insightfully explored by Paul Minear.[91] In

---

[89] This formulation is qualified as a 'possible exception' because, while the portions of Scripture mentioned probably can be readily understood without much historical background, even here one might well argue that additional historical information could still deepen an interpreter's appreciation and understanding – and should this possibility be ruled out, even if it remains only a theoretical one?

[90] See Davis, *Imagination*, 260–61.

[91] Minear, 'Bach'.

1743, the philologist and biblical scholar Ernesti became rector of the St Thomas School, and thus Bach's superior. They quarrelled over student discipline and the music budget, but their disagreements ran much deeper. As Minear details, in these two men two very different approaches to the Bible collided. The crucial difference between the two was not only that one approached the biblical text philologically and the other did so musically, but also that the primary goal of the one was to hear the text in all its difference from received tradition (Ernesti) and the overriding intention of the other was to relate the truth of the text to the lived reality of the present-day worshiper (Bach).[92] Ernesti's goal was not in itself a bad one, perhaps being even necessary after the domestication of Scripture brought about by seventeenth-century Protestant orthodoxy.[93] Bach's quite different aim, however, was to provide replicable musical moments in which the reader/hearer would be grasped by the certain knowledge that the biblical story was not only true but in fact told the truth of his or her own particular experience.

Bach used his music so as to free the 'stories told in the Gospel out of remoteness into a highly actual relation to the audience, comparable to Nathan's address to David, "Thou art the man" (2 Sam. 12:7 [KJV])…. The decisive task of the cantatas consists not in narration or dramatic presentation of the events, but in an always new relation of this event to … the present.'[94] Bach was not any less committed than Ernesti to the primacy of the biblical text, word for word, as his cantatas and passions make quite clear. His extraordinary artistry consisted of writing musical 'analogies' with the goal of bringing text and worshiper together, even while preserving the verbal text as text. The result combines great interpretive freedom with simultaneous textual fidelity. In Bach's version of the analogical imagination the text absorbs the worshiper rather than the worshiper absorbing the text.

One of the chief problems confronting the theological interpretation of Scripture, as it is currently practised in academic circles anyway, is the failure to consider the analogical contexts in which particular texts will resonate. Good preachers grow accustomed to thinking about how their scriptural interpretations will be received by various individuals in their congregations and take such knowledge into account as they craft their sermons. However, in

---

[92] Minear, 'Bach', 28.

[93] Minear, 'Bach', 33. It is a telling indication of the current confusion within evangelical scholarship that an effort is now being made to claim Ernesti as an ally; see Sailhamer, 'Ernesti'. This turn of events might be compared to a tale in which chickens defend the leadership skills of a fox, saying by way of explanation that he knows a thing or two about how a hen house is guarded.

[94] Werthemann, *Bedeutung*, 31; cited and translated by Minear, 'Bach', 28. Cf. Werthemann, *Bach*.

academic biblical interpretation, especially in biblical commentaries, this kind of imaginative work is rarely done at all.

A pressing need exists for interpretive work that will envision the circumstances in which a particular biblical text may obtain renewed currency, meet fresh approval or resistance, and be heard with an urgent directness. Taking up such work as an explicit task would also increase awareness within biblical studies of the danger posed when an interpreter assumes that a biblical text will confront everyone in just the same way as it confronts him or her personally. Of course, the possibility of certain analogies cannot be overdetermined either – no one can ever fully predict how Scripture will be heard, nor should one even try to do so. Yet the greater problem in the theological interpretation of Scripture today is one caused by too little attention to analogies of reception and by the refusal to acknowledge implicit analogies openly. Charting such possibilities will not necessarily restrict an interpretive work's potential audience (as authors and publishers sometimes fear). The universality of Bach's musical analogies arises precisely from their explicit particularity.

Analogical use of the imagination can thus serve a crucial role in bringing the theological interpretation of Scripture into contemporary focus. The establishment of such analogies must be an explicit part of the task of theological interpretation and not simply left up to the reader/hearer to develop independently.[95]

Doctrinal imagination

Of all the possible ways in which the imagination can be used in the theological interpretation of Scripture, the idea of 'doctrinal' imagination will probably occasion the most surprise. An imaginative approach to Scripture is frequently construed as being in opposition to any kind of doctrinal or systematic interpretive grid. So, for example, Walter Brueggemann resists the idea that an interpretive approach to Scripture could be closely related to systematic theology: 'Focus on the … story requires us to be, to some extent, free of systematic perspective, and especially of systematic theology.'[96] Yet Brueggemann appears not to consider that traditional theological treatments of biblical texts can be just as 'angular' as the biblical texts themselves, challenging interpretive

---

[95] For a good example of explicit reflection on the role of analogy in biblical interpretation, see Hays, *Vision*, 298–304.

[96] Brueggemann, *Texts*, 58. Brueggemann also charges systematic theology with imposing 'Hellenistic modes of rationality' upon the text, resulting in 'a violation of what is most characteristically Jewish' in it. While in some ways I am sympathetic with Brueggemann's point, I do not believe that such a broad distinction between the 'Jewish' and the 'Hellenistic' can be sustained.

assumptions and spurring counter-cultural imagination in exactly the same way he advocates for Scripture on its own.

Moreover, seminarians and pastors are now in acute need of assistance precisely in moving between the biblical text and the church's theological tradition. They are uncertain about how to make such connections for themselves and even more unsure about how to present such connections to their congregants in ways that will be found comprehensible and compelling.

Are there any models from the tradition for combining attentiveness to the biblical text with the tradition of systematic theology through the application of imaginative skill? One remarkable example is provided by Martin Luther's 'Hymn of the Holy Christian Church':

1. To me she's dear, the worthy maid,
And I cannot forget her;
Praise, honor, virtue of her are said;
Then all I love her better.
I seek her good,
And if I should
Right evil fare,
I do not care,
She'll make up for it to me,
With love and truth that will not tire,
Which she will ever show me;
And do all my desire.

2. She wears of purest gold a crown
Twelve stars their rays are twining;
Her raiment, glorious as the sun,
And bright from far is shining
Her feet the moon
Are set upon.
She is the bride
With the Lord to bide.
Sore travail is upon her;
She bringeth forth a noble Son
Whom all the world must honor,
Their king, the only one.

3. That makes the dragon rage and roar,
He will the child upswallow;
His raging comes to nothing more;
No jot of gain will follow.
The infant high
Up to the sky

Away is heft,
And he is left
On earth, all mad with murder.
The mother now alone is she,
But God will watchful guard her,
And the right Father be.[97]

What Luther has done is to draft a sly paraphrase of Revelation 12. It is sly because its connection to Scripture and theology is not immediately clear. Literary critic Walter Jens describes how the poem moves from a disguised retelling of the text to a theological redescription of present reality.[98] The first stanza could easily be taken for a simple secular love song between a young man and a young woman, but the second stanza refers to the figures with increasingly fantastic language, prompting the reader/hearer to question their true identities. Only in the third stanza do the cosmic dimensions of the hymn's theological framework become fully clear, but still in a way that retains the charm of the hymn's initial presentation. Here Luther does theology by *extending* the biblical text, by elaborating its own metaphors and symbols. For those familiar with Scripture, at some point during the hymn there will be the surprise of recognition and a renewed apprehension of this particular biblical text's meaning. In fact, by at first obscuring the source of his extended poetic metaphor, Luther ensures the biblical text's fresh consideration.

The point is not that doctrinal language should cease to be rigorous, traditional and possessed of the subtle distinctions at home in any significant body of knowledge. People in the pew may complain now and then about theology being lifeless, but this criticism has two main causes. First, the 'theology' they are likely to get from the pulpit all too often consists of watered down slogans and sloppy generalizations. Church people are routinely exposed to an uncreative, repetitive handling of the biblical text that all too easily conspires with a natural human tendency to avoid the hard challenges presented by a close encounter with the gospel. In reality, when believers have the opportunity to gain exposure to substantive theology for a change, they tend to notice the difference, appreciate it and remark, 'Why have we never heard this before?'

The second cause is that over time, as a consequence of the prior problem, many church people develop low expectations concerning what theology is and what it has to offer them. They internalize and then insist on the slogans they have heard as representing the truth of the gospel, even though, when pressed, they are actually unsure of what such slogans mean. In this way,

---

[97] Jenny, *Lieder*, 111–13, 292 also cited in Jens, 'Phantasie', 9–10. This English translation is found in MacDonald, 'Hymns', 292–94.

[98] Jens, 'Phantasie', 11.

Christians become 'dis-enchanted' in their very belief, a response only reinforced by a global commercial culture antagonistic to any objects of 'enchant-
ment' other than money and material goods. Thus Christians collaborate in the
domestication of the gospel, which, precisely because it is domesticated, then
possesses little resonance for them.[99]

The proper response from the side of those concerned about theology
should not be a program of demythologization, in which the effort is made to
exchange traditional theological language for new words and concepts – but
rather a program of 're-enchantment', in which traditional metaphors and
symbols can be conveyed creatively in bold and original ways.[100] People in the
pews need creative *uses* of the church's traditional teaching about the Trinity
much more than they need a new conceptual explanation of the Trinity. There
will always be an ongoing need for theology to reinterpret and reframe its
inherited body of knowledge in order to ensure that it remains true and precise
for the present generation of the faithful. Some of this substantive work of reinterpretation transpires in the pulpit as well as in the study. However, the truly
urgent need at present is for a new creativity in using doctrine rather than a new
content for it. Instead of the replacement of religion by poetry once envisioned
by Matthew Arnold, the crucial role for the imagination is to enhance the
movement between Scripture and doctrine through art.[101]

Few have seen more clearly art's potential to be used as a new way of speaking to a modern world about faith than the Inklings, that group comprising
C.S. Lewis, J.R.R. Tolkien, Charles Williams and Owen Barfield, among
others. As much as they can be said to have possessed a common project, it
involved the expression of their Christian faith through fiction, fantasy and
myth. Lewis once said of how he came to write the *Narnia Chronicles*:

> I thought I saw how stories of this kind could steal past a certain inhibition which
> had paralysed much of my own religion in childhood. Why did one find it so hard to
> feel as one was told one ought to feel about God or about the sufferings of Christ? I
> thought the chief reason was that one was told one ought to. An obligation to feel
> can freeze feelings. And reverence itself did harm. The whole subject was associated
> with lowered voices; almost as if it were something medical. But supposing that by
> casting all these things into an imaginary world, stripping them of their stained-glass
> and Sunday School associations, one could make them for the first time appear in
> their real potency? Could one not thus steal past those watchful dragons? I thought
> one could.[102]

---

[99] Cf. Heerden, 'Imagination'.

[100] For more on this idea, see Schoberth, 'Spiel'.

[101] For a similar position, although with a somewhat different topic in view, see
Wright, 'Experiment'. For a recent treatment of Arnold's theological views, see
Caperon, 'Worlds'.

[102] Lewis, *Stories*, 45–48; esp. 47.

If anything, today's dragons are only more vigilant; skirting them successfully requires a kind of cunning not ordinarily associated with theological exposition. To be effective, the intramural language of the church as well as its extramural speech (that is, both dogmatics and apologetics) will require unusual framings, strange formulations and odd juxtapositions. Both faith and the imagination have in common the insistence that there is more to reality than what is apparent at first glance.[103]

If the gospel is to be heard today, it must be proclaimed in ways that challenge or subvert the 'common sense' of the present age, *especially* the 'common sense' of Christians. This is not to advocate an exclusively didactic purpose for Christian literature,[104] and certainly not to elevate ironic style over orthodox substance, but it is to say that fiction, fantasy and play have much to teach theology about slipping the modern bonds of sense and convention in order to convey a fuller understanding of the world.[105] Examples are actually quite numerous in modern society, which is perhaps something of a confirmation of the position being taken. One thinks of Charles M. Schultz's 'Peanuts' cartoons[106] or the animated television program 'The Simpsons',[107] contemporary writers John Updike[108] and Frederick Buechner,[109] the Christian rock group Jars of Clay[110] and Garrison Keillor's weekly radio programme 'Prairie Home Companion',[111] just to name a few. As different as they are from each other, all of these people and groups have in common that they successfully skirt Lewis's watchful dragons, regularly managing to say remarkably Christian things (often ironically, sometimes almost unintentionally) to a bored and jaded society.[112]

The idea of a need for such hermeneutical manoeuvring is not a new one, although it has become radicalized in modernity. Søren Kierkegaard developed his 'indirect method of communication' precisely in response to this

---

[103] Cf. Schoberth, 'Spiel', 87–88; Hauerwas, 'Keeping'.

[104] Lewis rejected this possibility in his own work; see his *Experiment*, 84–86. Lewis insisted that writing must be guided by aesthetic rather than didactic considerations and he favoured myth over allegory, in part because he was too good a literary critic not to know that literary works inevitably mean more than their authors intend. Cf. Lewis, *Stories*, 127–41; esp. 139–41. On the other hand, some allegories can be quite artistic in their own right and also mean more than their authors intend (e.g., Bunyan's *Pilgrim's Progress*).

[105] For a recent pedagogical probe in this direction, see Bechtel, 'Teaching'.

[106] See Short, *Gospel*.

[107] See Pinsky, *Gospel*.

[108] See Yerkes, *Updike*. Cf. Crowley, 'Updike'.

[109] See McCoy and McCoy, *Buechner*. Cf. Woelfel, 'Buechner'.

[110] See Balmer, 'Hymns'.

[111] See Heim, 'Keillor'.

[112] Cf. Rahner, 'Future'.

distinctively modern hermeneutical situation.[113] But can this kind of 'indirect method' be applied specifically to the interpretation of Scripture? Yes; a classic example is Kierkegaard's own *Fear and Trembling*, whose 'Prelude' still seduces and shocks its readers into a fresh theological encounter with Genesis 22 by peeling away the accumulation of domesticated interpretations through a succession of imaginative retellings.[114]

In the future, if the theological interpretation of Scripture is to find a receptive audience – if it is to touch hearts as well as minds – it will need to be just as indirect, every bit as imaginative, and similarly sly.[115]

---

[113] Kierkegaard, *Point*.

[114] Kierkegaard, *Fear*, 26–29. Kierkegaard's entire theological project is very much at issue here. At the meeting of the Scripture and Hermeneutics Seminar, C. Stephen Evans helpfully noted how Kierkegaard also worked imaginatively with biblical exegesis in his *Practice*, esp. 40–53, where he attempts to depict the reactions of various members of the crowd to Jesus' words 'Come here now all you who labour and are burdened'.

[115] I would like to thank E.F. Davis and C.K. Rowe for reading this essay prior to its initial oral presentation and offering helpful suggestions. I would also like to express my deep gratitude to Craig Bartholomew and all of the participants in the seminar for their warm welcome and for our stimulating conversations together.

Bibliography

Albright, W.F., *From the Stone Age to Christianity: Monotheism and the Historical Process* (Garden City, NY: Doubleday, 2nd edn, 1957)

Alison, J., *Raising Abel: The Recovery of the Eschatological Imagination* (New York: Crossroad, 1996)

Alter, R., *The Art of Biblical Narrative* (New York: Basic Books, 1981)

Avis, P., *God and the Creative Imagination: Metaphor, Symbol and Myth in Religion and Theology* (London and New York: Routledge, 1999)

Balmer, R.H., 'Hymns on MTV', *CT* 43 (1999), 32–39

Barber, M., 'Our Genius Problem', *The Atlantic Monthly* (Dec. 2002), 65–72

Barr, J., *The Concept of Biblical Theology: An Old Testament Perspective* (Minneapolis: Fortress Press, 1999)

Barth, K., *Church Dogmatics* III/1: *The Doctrine of Creation* (ed. G.W. Bromiley and T.F. Torrance; Edinburgh: T. & T. Clark, 1958)

—, *Church Dogmatics* I/2: *Doctrine of the Word of God* (ed. G.W. Bromiley and T.F. Torrance; Edinburgh: T. & T. Clark, 1956)

—, 'The Strange New World Within the Bible', in *The Word of God and the Word of Man* (trans. D. Horton; New York: Harper Torchbooks, 1956)

Bartholomew, C., C.S. Evans, M. Healy and M. Rae (eds.), *'Behind' the Text: History and Biblical Interpretation* (SHS 4; Carlisle: Paternoster; Grand Rapids: Zondervan, 2003)

Bartholomew, C., C. Greene and K. Möller (eds.), *Renewing Biblical Interpretation* (SHS 1; Carlisle: Paternoster; Grand Rapids: Zondervan, 2000)

Bayer, O., *Gott als Autor: Zu einer poietologischen Theologie* (Tübingen: J.C.B. Mohr [Paul Siebeck], 1999)

Bechtel, C.M., 'Teaching the "Strange New World" of the Bible', *Int* 56 (2001), 368–77

Berlin, A., *Poetics and Interpretation of Biblical Narrative* (Sheffield: Almond Press, 1983)

Berlin, I., *Vico and Herder: Two Studies in the History of Ideas* (New York: Viking, 1976)

Bowersock, G.W. (ed.), *Gibbon's Historical Imagination: Presented at the Stanford Humanities Center, May 8, 1987, on the Occasion of the 250th Anniversary of Edward Gibbon's Birth* (Stanford, CA: Stanford Humanities Center, 1988)

Braaten, C.E., 'The Recovery of the Apocalyptic Imagination', in *The Last Things: Biblical and Theological Perspectives on Eschatology* (ed. C.E. Braaten and R.W. Jenson; Grand Rapids: Eerdmans, 2002), 14–32

Brueggemann, W., *Texts under Negotiation: The Bible and Postmodern Imagination* (Minneapolis: Fortress Press, 1993)

—, *Finally Comes the Poet: Daring Speech for Proclamation* (Minneapolis: Fortress Press, 1989)

Burrows, M.S., '"To Taste with the Heart": Allegory, Poetics, and the Deep Reading of Scripture', *Int* 56 (2001), 168–80

Cadman, S.P., *Imagination and Religion* (New York: Macmillan, 1926)

Caperon, J., '"Between Two Worlds": The Religion of Matthew Arnold', *MTh* 104 (2001), 352–57

Casey, M., *Sacred Reading: The Ancient Art of* Lectio Divina (Liguori, Missouri: Liguori / Triumph, 1996)

Cassian, J., *Conferences* (SC 54; Paris: Cerf, 1959)

Childs, B.S., 'Foreword', in *Renewing Biblical Interpretation* (ed. C. Bartholomew, C. Greene and K. Möller; SHS 1; Carlisle: Paternoster; Grand Rapids: Zondervan, 2000), xv–xvii

—, 'Retrospective Reading of the Prophets', *ZAW* 108 (1996), 362–77

—, 'On Reclaiming the Bible for Christian Theology', in *Reclaiming the Bible for the Church* (ed. C.E. Braaten and R.W. Jenson; Grand Rapids: Eerdmans, 1995), 1–17

—, *Biblical Theology of the Old and New Testaments: Theological Reflection on the Christian Bible* (Minneapolis: Fortress Press, 1992)

—, *Biblical Theology in Crisis* (Philadelphia: Westminster Press, 1970)

Coleridge, S.T., *Aids to Reflection* (London: William Pickering, 1836)

Collingwood, R.G., *The Idea of History* (Oxford: Clarendon Press, 1946)

Crowley, S.M., 'John Updike and Kierkegaard's Negative Way: Irony and Indirect Communication in *A Month of Sundays*', *Soundings* 68 (1985), 212–28

Cunneen, J., 'The Bible: Imagination as Liberation', *Religion and Intellectual Life* 6 (1989), 157–60

Davis, E.F., *The Imagination Shaped: Old Testament Preaching in the Anglican Tradition* (Valley Forge, PA: Trinity Press International, 1995)

DeLillo, D., *White Noise* (New York: Viking, 2001)

Dimon, K.E. (ed.), *Church and Society* 84 (1994)

Engnell, J., *The Creative Imagination: Enlightenment to Romanticism* (Cambridge, MA and London: Harvard University Press, 1981)

Eslinger, R.L., *Narrative and Imagination: Preaching the Worlds That Shape Us* (Minneapolis: Fortress Press, 1995)

Farrer, A., *The Glass of Vision* (Westminster: Dacre, 1948)

Fischer, K.R., *The Inner Rainbow: The Imagination in Christian Life* (New York and Ramsey, NJ: Paulist Press, 1983)

Fishbane, M., *The Exegetical Imagination: On Jewish Thought and Theology* (Cambridge, MA and London: Harvard University Press, 1998)

Fowl, S.E., *Engaging Scripture* (Oxford: Basil Blackwell, 1998)

Frick, F.S., '*Cui bono?* – History in the Service of Political Nationalism: The Deuteronomistic History as Political Propaganda', *Semeia* 66 (1995), 79–92

Gibbon, E., *Gibbon's Autobiography* (ed. M.M. Reese; London: Routledge and K. Paul, 1971)

Green, G., *Imagining God: Theology and the Religious Imagination* (Grand Rapids and Cambridge: Eerdmans, 1989)

Greidanus, S., 'The Value of a Literary Approach for Preaching', in *A Complete Literary Guide to the Bible* (ed. L. Ryken and T. Longman III; Grand Rapids: Zondervan, 1993), 509–19

Gros Louis, K.R.R., 'Some Methodological Considerations', in *Literary Interpretations of Biblical Narratives*, II (ed. K.R.R. Gros Louis; Nashville: Abingdon Press, 1982), 13–24

Gruchy, J. de, *Christianity, Art and Transformation* (Cambridge: Cambridge University Press, 2001)

Gunn, D.M., 'Hebrew Narrative', in *Text and Context: Essays by Members of the Society for Old Testament Study* (ed. A.D.H. Mayes; Oxford: Oxford University Press, 2000), 223–52

Hailson, D.F.G., 'Re-Imagining: Relishing Eve's Rebellion', *CRJ* 20 (1998), 48–49

—, 'Re-Imagining Revisited', *Touchstone* 10 (1997), 24–29

Hart, T., 'Imagination and Responsible Reading', in *Renewing Biblical Interpretation* (ed. C. Bartholomew, C. Greene and K. Möller; SHS 1; Carlisle: Paternoster; Grand Rapids: Zondervan, 2000), 307–34

Hartt, J., 'Theological Investments in Story: Some Comments on Recent Developments and Some Proposals', *JAAR* 52 (1984), 117–30

Hauerwas, S., 'On Keeping Theological Ethics Imaginative', in *Against the Nations: War and Survival in a Liberal Society* (Minneapolis: Seabury / Winston, 1985), 51–60

Hays, R.B., 'The Conversion of the Imagination: Scripture and Eschatology in First Corinthians', *NTS* 45 (1999), 391–412

—, *The Moral Vision of the New Testament: Cross, Community, New Creation* (San Francisco: HarperSanFrancisco, 1996)

Heerden, W. van, 'Imagination and the Interpretation of the Old Testament', *OTE* 7 (1994), 343–59

Heim, D., 'Garrison Keillor and Culture Protestantism', *ChrCent* 104 (June 3–10, 1987), 517–19

Holstein, J.A., 'Melville's Inversion of Jonah in *Moby-Dick*', *Iliff Review* 42 (1985), 13–20

Jacobs, A., *A Theology of Reading: The Hermeneutics of Love* (Boulder, CO and Oxford: Westview Press, 2001)

Jansen, H., 'Poetics and the Bible: Facts and Biblical Hermeneutics', *NZST* 41 (1999), 22–38

Jasper, D., *The New Testament and the Literary Imagination* (London: Macmillan, 1987)

Imaginative Readings of Scripture and Theological Interpretation 445

Jeanrond, W., 'After Hermeneutics: The Relationship between Theology and Biblical Studies', in *The Open Text* (ed. F. Watson; London: SCM Press, 1993), 85–102

Jenny, M. (ed.), *Luthers geistliche Lieder und Kirchengesänge* (Archiv zur Weimarer Ausgabe der Werke Martin Luthers 4; Cologne: Böhlau, 1985)

Jens, W., 'Die Phantasie und die Bibel', in *Religion und Phantasie: Von der Imaginationskraft des Glaubens* (ed. W.H. Ritter; Biblisch-theologische Schwerpunkte 19; Göttingen: Vandenhoeck & Ruprecht, 2000), 7–14

Johnson, L.T., 'Imagining the World Scripture Imagines', *MTh* 14 (1998), 165–80; also in *Theology and Scriptural Imagination* (ed. L.G. Jones and J.J. Buckley; Directions in Modern Theology; Oxford: Basil Blackwell, 1998), 3–18 (I cite from the latter)

Kaufman, G.D., *The Theological Imagination: Constructing the Concept of God* (Philadelphia: Westminster Press, 1981)

Kierkegaard, S., *Practice in Christianity* (ed. H.V. Hong and E.H. Hong; Princeton, NJ: Princeton University Press, 1991)

—, *Fear and Trembling* (ed. W. Lowrie; Princeton, NJ: Princeton University Press, 1968)

—, *The Point of View for My Work as an Author* (ed. B. Nelson; New York: Harper Torchbooks, 1962)

Lewis, C.S., *On Stories and Other Essays on Literature* (ed. W. Hooper; San Diego and New York: Harcourt; London: Harvest, 1982)

—, *An Experiment in Criticism* (Cambridge: Cambridge University Press, 1961)

Long, B.O., *Planting and Reaping Albright: Politics, Ideology, and Interpreting the Bible* (University Park, PA: Pennsylvania State Press, 1997)

MacDonald, G., 'The Hymns', in *Luther's Works,* Vol. 53: *Liturgy and Hymns* (ed. U.S. Leupold; Philadelphia: Fortress Press, 1965), 188–309

McCoy, M.C., and C.S. McCoy, *Frederick Buechner: Novelist / Theologian of the Lost and Found* (San Francisco: HarperSanFrancisco, 1988)

Melville, H., 'The Sermon', in *Moby-Dick, or, The Whale* (Berkeley and Los Angeles: University of California Press; London: Arion, 1979), 42–51

Minear, P.S., 'J.S. Bach and J.A. Ernesti', in *Our Common History as Christians: Essays in Honor of Albert C. Outler* (ed. J. Deschner, L.T. Howe and K. Penzel; New York: Oxford University Press, 1975), 131–55; a revised form of this essay appears as 'The Musician Versus the Grammarian: An Early Storm Warning', in *The Bible and the Historian: Breaking the Silence About God in Biblical Studies* (Nashville: Abingdon Press, 2002), 25–36 (I cite from the latter)

Murphy, R.E., *The Tree of Life: An Exploration of Biblical Wisdom Literature* (Grand Rapids and Cambridge: Eerdmans, 3rd edn, 2002)

Perdue, L.G., *The Collapse of History: Reconstructing Old Testament Theology* (OBT; Minneapolis: Fortress Press, 1994)

Stephen B. Chapman

Pinsky, M.I., *The Gospel According to the Simpsons* (Louisville, KY: Westminster John Knox Press, 2001)

Rahner, K., 'The Future of the Religious Book', *Theological Investigations* (trans. D. Bourke; 14 vols.; New York: Seabury / Crossroad, 1977), 8:251–56

Ramsey, G.W., *The Quest for the Historical Israel: Reconstructing Israel's Early History* (Atlanta: John Knox Press, 1981)

Reynolds, D.S., *Beneath the American Renaissance: The Subversive Imagination in the Age of Emerson and Melville* (Cambridge, MA and London: Harvard University Press, 1988)

Ricœur, P., *The Symbolism of Evil* (trans. E. Buchanan; New York: Harper & Row, 1967)

Ritter, W.H. (ed.), *Religion und Phantasie: Von der Imaginationskraft des Glaubens* (Biblisch-theologische Schwerpunkte 19; Göttingen: Vandenhoeck & Ruprecht, 2000)

Ryken, L. (ed.), *The Christian Imagination: Essays on Literature and the Arts* (Grand Rapids: Baker, 1981)

Ryken, L., and T. Longman III, 'Introduction', in *A Complete Literary Guide to the Bible* (ed. L. Ryken and T. Longman III; Grand Rapids: Zondervan, 1993), 15–39

Ryken, L., and T. Longman III (ed.), *A Complete Literary Guide to the Bible* (Grand Rapids: Zondervan, 1993)

Sailhamer, J.H., 'Johann August Ernesti: The Role of History in Biblical Interpretation', *JETS* 44 (2001), 193–206

Scarry, E., *On Beauty and Being Just* (Princeton, NJ: Princeton University Press, 1999)

Schneiders, S., 'The Paschal Imagination: Objectivity and Subjectivity in New Testament Interpretation', *TS* 43 (1982), 52–68

Schoberth, W., 'Das Spiel der Begriffe – oder: wie phantasievoll muß die Dogmatik sein?', in *Religion und Phantasie: Von der Imaginationskraft des Glaubens* (ed. W.H. Ritter; Biblisch-theologische Schwerpunkte 19; Göttingen: Vandenhoeck & Ruprecht, 2000), 63–88

Scorgie, G.A., 'Hermeneutics and the Meditative Use of Scripture: The Case for a Baptized Imagination', *JETS* 44 (2001), 271–84

Short, R.L., *The Gospel According to Peanuts* (Richmond: John Knox Press, 1965)

Solzhenitsyn, A., *The First Circle* (trans. T.H. Whitney; New York: Harper & Row, 1968)

Spiegelman, A., *Maus: A Survivor's Tale* (New York: Pantheon, 1986–91)

Stevens, W., *The Necessary Angel: Essays on Reality and the Imagination* (New York: Vintage, 1951)

Steward, R., 'The Vision of Evil in Hawthorne and Melville', in *The Tragic Vision and the Christian Faith* (ed. N.A. Scott, Jr; New York: Association Press, 1957), 238–63

Taylor, C., *Human Agency and Language: Philosophical Papers 1* (Cambridge: Cambridge University Press, 1985)

Veyne, P., *Did the Greeks Believe in Their Myths? An Essay on the Constitutive Imagination* (trans. P. Wissing; Chicago and London: University of Chicago Press, 1988)

Walker-Jones, A.W., 'The Role of Theological Imagination in Biblical Theology', *HBT* 11 (1989), 73–97

Warnock, M., *Imagination and Time* (Oxford and Cambridge, MA: Basil Blackwell, 1994)

Werthemann, H., *Johann Sebastian Bach: Prediger in Tönen* (Karlsruhe: Evangelische Akademie Baden, 1985)

—, *Die Bedeutung der alttestamentlichen Historien in Johann Sebastian Bachs Kantaten* (Tübingen: Mohr Siebeck, 1960)

White, H.V., *Tropics of Discourse: Essays in Cultural Criticism* (Baltimore: The Johns Hopkins University Press, 1978)

—, *Metahistory: The Historical Imagination in Nineteenth-Century Europe* (Baltimore and London: The Johns Hopkins University Press, 1973)

Wilson, P.S., *God Sense: Reading the Bible for Preaching* (Nashville: Abingdon Press, 2001)

Woelfel, J.W., 'Frederick Buechner: The Novelist as Theologian', *ThTo* 40 (1983), 273–91

Wolters, A., 'Confessional Criticism and the Night Visions of Zechariah', in *Renewing Biblical Interpretation* (ed. C. Bartholomew, C. Greene and K. Möller; SHS 1; Carlisle: Paternoster; Grand Rapids: Zondervan, 2000), 90–117

Wright, S.I., 'Inhabiting the Story: The Use of the Bible in the Interpretation of History', in *'Behind' the Text: History and Biblical Interpretation* (ed. C. Bartholomew, C.S. Evans, M. Healy and M. Rae; SHS 4; Carlisle: Paternoster; Grand Rapids: Zondervan, 2003), 492–519

—, 'An Experiment in Biblical Criticism: Aesthetic Encounter in Reading and Preaching Scripture', in *Renewing Biblical Interpretation* (ed. C. Bartholomew, C. Greene and K. Möller; SHS 1; Carlisle: Paternoster; Grand Rapids: Zondervan, 2000), 240–67

Yerkes, J. (ed.), *John Updike and Religion: The Sense of the Sacred and the Motions of Grace* (Grand Rapids: Eerdmans, 1999)

17

Biblical Theology and Preaching
Charles H.H. Scobie

Introduction

Years ago, *Punch* published a cartoon showing a young Church of England curate (presumably a recent graduate of theological college) holding forth in the pulpit of a small rural church. A few parishioners, some with straw coming out of their ears, sit in the pews looking up with vacant expressions on their faces. According to the caption, the curate, in the midst of his sermon, is exclaiming, 'Aha! But you will say to me – Sabellianism!' The cartoon suggests (to put it mildly) a failure in communication: the curate is not enabling the congregation to hear the word of God speaking to them in the context of their daily lives.

Hopefully the situation in churches today is not always as serious as this, yet there seems to be an increasing suspicion among lay people about what goes on in preaching. Among preachers, there seems to be an unease regarding what to do with the Bible and how to appropriate the Bible as a whole (especially the OT) in Christian preaching.

The recent resurgence of interest in 'biblical theology' may offer help in finding a way through the present impasse. Unfortunately, as Goldsworthy points out, 'much of the literature on preaching either ignores biblical theology completely or makes only a passing reference to it';[1] moreover, biblical theology is still a largely neglected subject in mainline denominational seminaries.[2]

This chapter will look briefly at the nature of preaching and then seek to relate what takes place in preaching to recent hermeneutical discussion and to the current 'crisis in biblical interpretation'. A short critique will be offered of the paradigm that has dominated biblical studies until recently – that is, the historical critical method. Drawing on more recent trends in biblical studies, we

---

[1] Goldsworthy, *Preaching the Whole Bible*, 7.

[2] Cf. Goldsworthy, 'Biblical Theology', 280: 'Biblical theology should be a core subject in all ministerial training.'

will then offer a sketch of a canonical biblical theology capable of occupying an intermediate position between the historical study of Scripture and its appropriation by theology and homiletics. The kind of contribution such a biblical theology can make to preaching will be illustrated by some examples. Finally, we will offer some suggestions as to areas in which further work is needed if biblical theology is to play a key role in the hermeneutical process and contribute to sermons that truly connect both with the Bible and with the hearers in the pew.

The Practice of Preaching

Virtually all discussions of preaching take it as a given that the role of preachers is not to put forward their own ideas and opinions, but in some way to mediate a God-given message.[3] Presupposed is a confessional position to the effect that, for the community of faith, the Scriptures of the Old and New Testaments are 'the supreme rule of faith and life'. Most theologies of preaching therefore assume something akin to Karl Barth's distinction of the three forms of the word of God. 1) The *revealed word* was spoken by God 'in many and various ways' through prophets and apostles, and supremely in Jesus, the Son of God (Heb. 1:1, 2) who is the Word made flesh (Jn. 1:14). 2) The *written word* in the Old and New Testaments witnesses to the revealed Word. The precise sense in which the Bible can be said to be 'the word of God', however, will depend on one's understanding of the inspiration and authority of Scripture. 3) The *proclaimed word* is the way God speaks to the church today, through preaching, based on the written word of Scripture.

Preaching thus involves three essential elements:

1) *The reading of the word.* There is the closest possible connection between the reading of Scripture and the proclamation of the word in the sermon. Acts 2 gives an account of the first Christian sermon delivered by Peter on the Day of Pentecost – a sermon that provides a model for later Christian proclamation. As in all of the earliest Christian preaching, the 'text' comes from the Hebrew Scriptures; Peter quotes in full Joel 2:28–32a; Pss.16:8–11; 16:10; 110:1. Today, preaching is normally preceded by Scripture lessons from the Old and New Testaments. Increasingly, not only Roman Catholic and Anglican churches, but also all of the mainline Protestant denominations, follow a lectionary that provides Old Testament, Epistle and Gospel readings, as well as a Psalm selection.

---

[3] Cf. Ferguson, *Biblical Hermeneutics*, 116–19.

2) *The preaching of the word.* By definition, preaching involves the spoken proclamation of a message and, hence, a proclaimer. In Acts 2, Peter stands up, raises his voice and addresses the crowd (Acts 2:14). 'How are they to hear without a preacher?' asks Paul (Rom. 10:14, RSV). The position of preacher is one of both authority and responsibility. In worship the sermon frequently has a central position; it is usually delivered from a pulpit which may, symbolically, be set at a higher level than the congregation. The preacher's responsibility is twofold: firstly, to interpret Scripture and determine its meaning for the contemporary situation, and secondly, to communicate this to the congregation. In Acts 2 Peter connects the situation of his hearers with the words of Scripture: 'This is what was spoken through the prophet Joel ...' (Acts 2:16). He then goes on to interpret both the scriptural texts and the present experience of his hearers in the light of the Christ event. Discussion of biblical interpretation usually revolves around the 'text' and the 'reader(s)'; in the case of preaching, however, the interpretation of Scripture is mediated to 'hearers' by a preacher. The preacher thus has a dual role as both 'interpreter' and 'proclaimer'.[4]

3) *The hearing of the word.* Proclamation cannot occur without *hearers* of the proclaimed message. Of course, the hearers in their turn interpret what the preacher says, and different hearers may well interpret the sermon differently. The matter is complicated by the fact that many, if not all, of the hearers may also be readers. What is clear is that a sermon aims to elicit a response from the hearers. When the crowd heard Peter's Pentecost sermon 'they were cut to the heart' and asked, 'What should we do?' (Acts 2:37). Sermons should aim to change not just people's minds but people's lives; preachers are to 'serve as catalysts for change in the lives of [their] listeners as they discern the significance for themselves of the meaning of the text'.[5]

A considerable amount of the content of Scripture is kerygmatic in nature – that is, it originated in a verbally proclaimed message. Deuteronomy is 'preached law' (von Rad); the prophets proclaimed 'the word of the LORD'; Jesus' ministry was focused in his proclamation of the kingdom of God; Acts gives a major role to evangelistic preaching in the origins and spread of the faith; Paul's letters presuppose an original preached message – 'faith comes from what is heard, and what is heard comes by the preaching of Christ' (Rom. 10:17, RSV); Timothy is exhorted to 'preach the word' (2 Tim. 4:2, RSV). This kerygmatic material is 'inscripturated' in the Bible; in preaching it is, as it were, 'reconstituted' as verbal proclamation.

---

[4] See Osborne, *Hermeneutical Spiral*, 325.
[5] Freeman, 'Biblical Criticism'. 315.

Preaching and Hermeneutics

From the above it is clear that preaching is a form of biblical interpretation; in practice it is one of the commonest and most important forms. Osborne claims that 'the true goal of hermeneutics is not the commentary but the sermon'.[6] Wolters characterizes the goal of biblical interpretation as 'confessional discernment' which 'focuses in hearing what God has to say to his people', and contends that 'for most readers of the Bible, both today and in ages past, this is the most important level of interpretation, the *raison d'être* of all other aspects of hermeneutical inquiry'.[7] As such, therefore, preaching is inevitably embroiled in the current 'crisis in biblical interpretation'. What happens in preaching runs counter to the mindset that characterizes much of society at the start of the new millennium, often characterized broadly as 'postmodernism'. Claims that a text has meaning that can be interpreted and communicated today are viewed with deep suspicion. Critics point to conflicting interpretations relating to topics of current concern (e.g., abortion, homosexual practice, the war in Iraq) advanced by Christian preachers, each of whom claims to offer the authoritative interpretation.[8] 'Don't preach at me' is a common attitude; people should be free to make up their own minds. These are but surface indications of a widespread crisis that ultimately has to be analysed and addressed at a deeper theological and philosophical level.[9]

There is a universal consensus that the preacher's task is to relate Scripture to the present situation of the hearers, though this may be expressed in a variety of ways. Whereas biblical studies is concerned with what Scripture 'meant', theology and hence homiletics are concerned with what Scripture 'means'.[10] Alternatively, biblical studies may be thought of as concerned with the 'meaning' of a text, theology and homiletics with its 'significance' (Hirsch).[11] Picking up on Hirsch's categories, Krabbendam argues that 'the biblical text has a *single meaning* determined by the will of the author as expressed in the text' but that it also has 'a *manifold significance* that is squarely based upon the meaning of the text and can be formulated by means of universal principles and patterns to be gleaned from it with a view to any public'.[12] Osborne distinguishes the

---

[6] Osborne, *Hermeneutical Spiral*, 339.

[7] Wolters, 'Confessional Criticism', 103; cf. Freeman, 'Biblical Criticism', 307.

[8] On this problem see Vanhoozer's discussion of 'The Conflict of Interpretations', in *Meaning*, 292–303.

[9] See Bartholomew, et al. (eds.), *Renewing Biblical Interpretation*, esp. ch. 1.

[10] This oft-quoted distinction was made by K. Stendahl in *IDB* 1:419.

[11] On this distinction see Osborne, *Hermeneutical Spiral*, 393–95; Vanhoozer, *Meaning*, 260–63, 421–24.

[12] Krabbendam, 'Hermeneutics', 213.

unchanging 'content' of the biblical revelation from the ever-changing 'form' in which it must be presented to new audiences.[13] Hanson speaks of preaching revolving round 'two poles' – one is the biblical text, the other the contemporary life of the community of faith.[14] Others speak of the preacher's task as 'contextualizing' the message embedded in the original context. Hermeneutical discussion influenced by the work of Gadamer distinguishes 'the horizon of the text' and 'the horizon of the interpreter'; what takes place in genuine interpretation is a 'fusion of horizons'. Preaching is, in fact, usually concerned with both horizons: thus a sermon frequently begins with 'exposition', a verse by verse analysis of what the passage meant in its original historical setting, then proceeds to 'application', perhaps following a central turning point in the sermon signalled by a question such as, 'Now what has all this to do with us today?' Thus in the terminology employed by Adam, 'The task of *internal hermeneutics* (i.e., biblical theology) needs to be addressed first, and only then the task of *external hermeneutics* (the meaning of the text today)'.[15]

Today it is widely recognized and generally accepted that *both* the original text *and* the modern interpreter are conditioned by a particular historical and cultural setting. This poses the most acute problems in biblical interpretation for Christian theology and Christian ethics, and not least for Christian preaching. Few women, even in conservative churches, feel bound to wear hats in church on the basis of 1 Corinthians 11:2–16; but if texts such as this reflect first-century custom, then in each individual case the interpreter must seek to distinguish the 'cultural' from the 'supracultural'. Where a text is bound up with its historical context, interpretation must then involve first a 'decontextualization' that identifies underlying theological and ethical principles, followed by 'recontextualization' that translates these principles into a form meaningful to modern readers/hearers.[16]

Precisely here is the crux of the hermeneutical problem. When the horizons are fused, which horizon predominates?[17] If preachers simply repeat the message of Scripture in its own words, they run the risk of espousing a proof-texting fundamentalism that fails to address the real needs and concerns of their hearers. If they seek above all else to preach sermons that are 'relevant', they

---

[13] Osborne, *Hermeneutical Spiral*, ch.15.

[14] Hanson, 'Responsibility', 45.

[15] Adam, 'Preaching', 107.

[16] On this complex but all-important issue see, e.g., the discussion of 'normativity and cultural conditioning' in Hagner, 'Biblical Theology', 138–39; the detailed suggestions for guidelines to follow in Osborne, *Hermeneutical Spiral*, 326–38, 343–58; and the discussion in Sanchez, 'Contextualization', 299–304, which employs social science concepts in the attempt to distinguish supracultural and cultural elements of a biblical text.

[17] Cf. the critique of Gadamer in Vanhoozer, *Meaning*, 390, 409.

run the risk of capitulating to the latest fads and fashions and of conforming to the spirit of the age.[18] The latter temptation is no doubt a real one for many clergy who face pressure to be 'popular preachers' – to say nothing of the fact that their jobs and salaries are often more or less dependent on their hearers. Words of comfort and assurance may be appreciated; 'prophetic' sermons that 'rock the boat' by challenging hearers to deeper and costlier commitment may be met with indifference if not hostility. The challenge for the preacher is to provide what may be termed 'communication without compromise'.

Three Stages in Biblical Interpretation

How is the preacher to get from what a Scriptural text 'meant' in its original historical setting to what it 'means' for those who hear the sermon today? In probing what is meant by the 'meaning' of a text, in the past century or so literary criticism and hermeneutical theory have focused in turn on: a) the author, b) the text, and c) the readers. Each of these approaches, it may be argued, has some validity, and together they suggest the three basic stages of biblical interpretation that must be followed by the preacher in constructing the sermon.

The first stage is to determine *what the text meant in its original historical context*. At this point preachers must declare themselves as 'hermeneutical realists'. Utilizing the vast resources of modern historical scholarship it is possible, with a reasonable degree of certainty, to recover what the author was saying, by means of the text, to his original readers. This is where biblical interpretation must start, and this stage is an essential one to safeguard against arbitrary or subjective interpretations in the course of the move from the text to the modern application.

This, it should be noted, does not mean seeking to look *through* the text to what is today frequently referred to as 'the world behind the text'. Historical criticism has frequently used the text in order to reconstruct the history that allegedly lies behind it; this procedure, though claimed as 'objective' and 'historical', is in effect often highly speculative and dependent upon flawed presuppositions. Rather, it involves looking *at* the text and seeking to discern the message that the author sought to convey to the readers in the original historical situation. As Wells puts it, 'the interpreter's task is not to find and interpret the events behind the text but rather to find what the author is telling the readers by means of the text'.[19] Vanhoozer defines the author as 'communicative

---

[18] Cf. Sanchez's analysis of 'approaches that risk failing to do justice to the modern context' and 'approaches that risk failing to do justice to the biblical text' (Sanchez, 'Contextualization', 295–97).

[19] Wells, 'Figural Representation', 112.

agent' and argues that 'to enquire into what the text means is to ask what the author has done in, with, and through the text'.[20]

The second stage is to determine *what the text means in its canonical context*. As adherents of 'the New Criticism' emphasized, once a text is committed to writing it floats free of its original historical moorings and can be read and studied in and of itself. The focus shifted to what is called 'the world within the text'.

Although each book of the Bible had its own original historical context, the various books acquired a new context over the course of time as they were gradually brought together to form the canon of the OT and finally, with the addition of the NT books, the canon of Christian holy Scripture. Preaching must not be based on a haphazard, atomistic exegesis. Recalling the old tag that 'a text, taken out of context, can easily become a pretext', every passage that is the subject of a sermon must be seen 'in context' – this means not just in the context of the book of the Bible of which it is a part, but also in the context of canonical Scripture as a whole. This does not mean denying or ignoring the meaning of the text in its original historical context, but it does involve going beyond that and discerning deeper dimensions of meaning that only become apparent when the text is read in the context of the entire canon. This is where a key role must be played by *biblical theology* in the sense of the discipline that studies the Bible as a theological whole.

Some recognize the necessity of this stage in the interpretive process without designating it 'biblical theology'. Thus Greidanus, who identifies ten stages from text to sermon, calls his sixth stage 'canonical interpretation' or 'redemptive historical interpretation'. This stage involves asking the question, 'What does this passage mean in the context of God's all-encompassing story from creation to new creation?'[21] In Wolters' scheme of nine levels of biblical interpretation, the eighth is 'redemptive-historical analysis', where the interpreter 'looks at a passage from the standpoint of its place within the grand narrative of the Christian canon'.[22] 'Biblical theology', however, is a wider and more satisfactory term for the discipline which 'involves the quest for the big picture, or the overview, of biblical revelation'.[23]

The third stage of the interpretive process to be followed by preachers is to determine *what the text means for the hearers of the sermon*. In the latter part of the twentieth century the focus was no longer on the author nor on the text.

---

[20] Vanhoozer, *Meaning*, 218.

[21] Greidanus, *Preaching Christ*, 288. Greidanus reserves the designation 'biblical theology' for the study of 'longitudinal themes' that can be traced from the OT to the NT (266–68).

[22] Wolters, 'Confessional Criticism', 102.

[23] Goldsworthy, *Preaching the Whole Bible*, 22.

Rather, it shifted to the reader, or to what is termed 'the world in front of the text'. Various forms of reader-response criticism developed, stressing that texts have meaning only in so far as they are read and interpreted by a reader. In its extreme form, this view sees meaning as not in any way residing in the text but rather being entirely created by the reader. A theology of preaching will be attentive to the idea of 'reader-response', for an effective sermon must take full account of the horizon of the hearers as well as the horizon of the text. On any given Sunday, thousands and thousands of preachers around the world who follow the lectionary will preach from the same text; no two sermons, however, ought to be the same, for in each case the audience is different.

Today it is generally agreed that there can be no neutral, impartial interpretation of a text; all readers inevitably bring with them some form of 'preunderstanding', and in fact interpretation requires this. Different 'interpretive communities' approach the Bible with different preunderstandings and different sets of questions, and there is nothing wrong with this.[24] The Bible can be read for many reasons: as a source for the history of the Ancient Near East, in order to appreciate its matchless poetry, for the light it sheds on symbolism employed in Western art, and so on. However, from the viewpoint of Christian theology and hence of the preacher, the appropriate interpretive community is the Christian church – since it is the church that recognizes the Scriptures as canonical and finds in them the supreme rule of faith and life. Scripture embodies the self-communication of God through his word. The most appropriate interpretation is therefore that which, as it were, 'tunes in on this wavelength'. Theologically, the link between the Bible and the interpretive community is provided by the work of the Holy Spirit: all Scripture is Spirit inspired (2 Pet. 1:21; cf. 2 Tim. 3:16), and the text is heard as the word of God addressed to the readers/hearers through 'the inner testimony of the Holy Spirit' (*testimonium spiritus sancti internum*).[25] As Ferguson puts it, 'It is not so much the preacher's learning, oratorical skill, or pleasing personality which makes the sermon effective (although these qualities are not unimportant); it is rather the Spirit of God using the words of the preacher to "make real" to the hearers the truth of the scriptural message'.[26] Preaching takes place in the context of worship and should be preceded by prayer for Spirit-bestowed guidance and illumination of both preacher and congregation.

This, however, does not imply an extreme form of reader-response criticism whereby the community in fact determines the meaning of the text. Although the community of faith approaches the text via their preunderstanding, they must nevertheless be prepared to modify and expand their

---

[24] See Fish, *Is There a Text?* on the whole notion of 'interpretive communities'.

[25] See the discussion in Osborne, *Hermeneutical Spiral*, 340–41.

[26] Ferguson, *Biblical Hermeneutics*, 116.

understanding on the basis of the message of the text mediated by the preacher. As Hanson puts it, 'An openness to be addressed by the text, to be challenged, to be called into question, is essential in all interpretation, and especially when one believes that the texts being interpreted are expressions of the will of God.'[27]

The Scriptural Basis of Preaching: Historical Criticism

Preaching is grounded in Scripture. Ideally, therefore, in approaching the horizon of the text preachers should employ all of the tools made available by modern biblical scholarship.[28] Of course, in practice busy preachers seldom have time to apply these methods for themselves. For the text itself the preacher will rely on a few modern translations, while the fruits of modern scholarship in other areas will usually be mediated (either directly, or via 'preaching guides') by standard reference works and especially by *biblical commentaries* on the passage on which the sermon is to be based.

For the past two centuries, the type of biblical scholarship that underlies most commentaries has been dominated and shaped by what is broadly termed 'the historical-critical method'.[29] It has long been a complaint on the part of preachers, however, that critical commentaries provide them with everything they need to know except the most important thing – the *theology* of the text which will provide the basis for the transition from the horizon of the text to the horizon of the readers. As Adam laments, 'If it is hard to find commentaries that discuss theology, it is even more difficult to find any that discuss biblical theology.'[30]

The unease with which preachers have long viewed the historical-critical approach has been underscored, and in many ways validated, by recent recognition of the flaws and limitations of this method of biblical study.

1) The claim (whether explicit or implicit) of historical criticism to represent *an unbiased, neutral, scientific, value-free approach to Scripture* is today widely rejected. As noted above, contemporary hermeneutical theory recognizes that all approaches to a text are governed by presuppositions, and this is no

---

[27] Hanson, 'Responsibility', 44.

[28] For an appreciation of the various historical critical disciplines as a resource for preachers see Freeman, 'Biblical Criticism'.

[29] Here it is only possible to speak in broad terms; 'historical criticism' in fact covers a spectrum of approaches and methods. For an overview see Krentz, *Historical-Critical Method*.

[30] Adam, 'Preaching', 109.

less true for historical criticism. This approach was born during the Enlightenment as a method of throwing off the shackles of a dogmatic interpretation of Scripture controlled by the church. Thus, it was believed, 'the rediscovered Jesus of history could replace the dogmatically encrusted Christ of faith. The historically established essence of Christianity could free our faith from the accretions of tradition'.[31] In reality, this approach smuggled in a whole new series of presuppositions which involved the elimination of much of what is most typical of the biblical account: the presence and activity of God in nature and in history, the possibility of miracles, the possibility of predictive prophecy – in fact, any form of the supernatural.

2) Typical of most historical-critical scholarship is an attitude of *detachment* from the believing community and from any kind of discussion of what Scripture 'means'. Thus Wrede, in his influential 1897 monograph, 'Über Aufgabe und Methode der sogennanten neutestamentlichen Theologie' bluntly declared, 'Like every other real science, New Testament Theology has its goal simply in itself, and is totally indifferent to all dogma and systematic theology'.[32] Yet for preachers it is the theology of the text that is of prime importance as they seek to mediate the message of the text to their hearers.

3) A third feature of the historical approach has been *the dissolving of the canon of Scripture*. If the aim of biblical scholars is to reconstruct the history of the religion of Israel and of the early church, then contemporary non-canonical historical sources are just as important as canonical ones. Wrede sounded the death knell of the canon (or so he thought). 'No New Testament writing,' he declared, 'was born with the predicate "canonical" attached',[33] and thus for NT scholarship the limits of the canon are totally irrelevant. Yet it is precisely the bringing together of the books of the Bible into the canon that identifies them as 'the Holy Scriptures', the inspired and authoritative Scripture of the Christian church that forms the basis of preaching.

Even this brief critique of the historical-critical method is sufficient to highlight its severe limitations when it comes to interpreting the Bible as Holy Scripture in preaching. Obviously a historical approach is required at stage one of interpretation (determining what the text meant in its original historical context).

---

[31] Davis, 'Theological Career', 274.

[32] Translation in Morgan, *Nature*, 69. Against this, however, note the article by Paul D. Hanson in which he urges 'The Responsibility of Biblical Theology to Communities of Faith'.

[33] Morgan, *Nature*, 70. On the pervasive influence of Wrede on modern biblical studies see Fowl, 'Conceptual Structure', 226–32.

Historical criticism as currently practised, however, needs to become much more aware and much more critical of its own presuppositions.

It is at stage two of interpretation (determining what the text means in its canonical context) that historical criticism really fails the preacher; and it is here that biblical theology has a vital role to play. Though originally hailed as the key to the interpretation of Scripture in modern times, historical criticism has in fact led inevitably to the current impasse in biblical interpretation as far as the preacher is concerned. The development of what was termed 'biblical theology' from the time of Gabler onwards, as a historical not a theological discipline, as concerned with what Scripture 'meant' but not at all with what it 'means', resulted, I have argued elsewhere,[34] first in the *division* of biblical theology (into OT theology and NT theology), then in its *decline* (in the face of the History of Religions), and finally in its near *demise* (for the best part of a century virtually no true biblical theologies were produced).[35] Much valuable work has been done and continues to be done on the individual 'theologies' of Deuteronomy and the Priestly source, of Paul and John, and so on, but these tend to be highly compartmentalized with the emphasis overwhelmingly on the overall *diversity* of the biblical witness.

Without denying the importance of studying the Scriptures in their original historical context (using appropriate historical methods), nevertheless what is required as a key intermediate step between such historical study and the interpretation of the Bible as the word of God by theologians and by preachers today (stage three) is what is most accurately termed 'biblical theology'.[36]

The Scriptural Basis of Preaching: Biblical Theology

Unfortunately the term 'biblical theology' is ambiguous and is often used very loosely, sometimes as little more than a synonym for 'biblical studies'. At best it most often refers to OT theology and NT theology (practised as two quite separate disciplines); in practice, biblical theology is more often applied to more compartmentalized studies – for example, Deuteronomic theology or Pauline theology. While such studies are of course quite legitimate and indeed very important, they do not constitute 'biblical theology' in the strict sense of the term as the discipline that must undergird theology and preaching.

---

[34] Scobie, *Ways*, 6.

[35] Cf. L. Houlden's comments ('Bible') on how modern biblical scholarship has resulted in the disintegration and dismemberment of Scripture thought of as a unitary whole.

[36] Cf. Osborne's view that 'biblical theology provides a bridge to systematic theology and the contextualization of Scripture' (*Hermeneutical Spiral*, 263–70).

If 'biblical theology' is to be truly 'theology', then it must go beyond a purely historical, descriptive approach and aim at 'a reinvigoration of theological interpretation of Scripture'.[37] If it is to be truly 'biblical', it must be concerned with the whole Bible, taken together, as the canonical Scriptures of the Christian church. As Goldsworthy argues, 'by definition, a theology of either the Old or the New Testament is not really a biblical theology'.[38] We concur with the definition offered by Rosner:

> Biblical theology may be defined as theological interpretation of Scripture in and for the church. It proceeds with historical and literary sensitivity and seeks to analyse and synthesize the Bible's teaching about God and his relations to the world on its own terms, maintaining sight of the Bible's overarching narrative and Christocentric focus.[39]

When preachers read from Psalm, Old Testament, Epistle and Gospel, then launch into a sermon, it is on these selections from the canonical Scriptures recognized by the church that the sermon must be based. A biblical theology that lives up to its name must therefore be in essence a *canonical theology* – a theology that takes the whole canon seriously.

This means in the first instance that a biblical theology must be limited to the canon of Christian Scripture. This is precisely what distinguishes it from the History of Religion. Christian believers do not deny that truth can be found in many places (e.g., in the writings of the church fathers, of the Reformers or of modern theologians, or for that matter in literature, art or in creation), but all other sources of Christian truth must be tested at the bar of the word of God in Scripture. Revelation did not cease with the closing of the canon, but since then revelation takes the form of applying to new situations, under the guidance of the Holy Spirit, the norms of belief and conduct found in Scripture.

Secondly, a canonical biblical theology must encompass the whole of canonical Scripture and must thus overcome the separation of the Testaments in critical scholarship. Biblical theology must tackle head-on the question of the relationship between Old and New Testaments in Christian interpretation. The relationship in a sermon between Psalm and Old Testament lessons on the one hand, and Epistle and Gospel readings on the other, must be based on a well-thought-out interpretative framework for understanding the relationship between the Testaments.

Thirdly, a canonical biblical theology will avoid as far as possible any 'canon within the canon' – that is, the privileging of some parts of Scripture or some authors at the expense of others. Historically this has been a common

---

[37] Fowl, 'Conceptual Structure', 235.

[38] Goldsworthy, *Preaching*, 63.

[39] Rosner, 'Biblical Theology', 10.

procedure in order to find unity within the biblical revelation – as, for example, Luther's preference for those books that 'show Christ', the liberal focus on the historical Jesus, or Bultmann's privileging of Paul and John. Preachers (especially those who do not accept the discipline of a lectionary) face a strong temptation to keep coming back to a relatively small selection of favourite passages. Biblical theology, however, must seek to do justice to the whole range of the biblical material.[40] For example, the so-called 'biblical theology movement' of the mid-twentieth century placed a premium on 'salvation history' or 'redemptive history' (*Heilsgeschichte*), and some biblical theologians today continue to see this as the key to the unity of Scripture. While this is a major theme of Scripture, it does not exhaust the full scope of the biblical revelation and does not recognize a range of biblical themes such as creation, blessing, Wisdom, the Land, and so on. A full-fledged biblical theology must recognize God as the Lord of creation as well as the Lord of history.[41]

Fourthly, a canonical biblical theology will be based primarily on the final form of the canonical text. In this endeavour it can find an ally in 'the literary turn' that characterized much of biblical studies in the closing decades of the twentieth century. The literary criticism of the Bible covers a wide range of approaches, many of which have no interest in theological interpretation. Most types of literary criticism, however, share a concern with biblical theology for the final form of the text. And those approaches, for example, which deal with genre and structure, can make a significant contribution to biblical theology (whether this is their intention or not). Indeed some literary critics have been more appreciative of the unity, or perhaps better the continuity, of Scripture than have some biblical scholars.[42]

Fifthly, a canonical biblical theology will recognize the presence of different layers of meaning in Scripture. Historical criticism tends to hold that there is only one level of meaning – that intended by the original author in the original historical situation.[43] A full-fledged biblical theology will always respect the historical meaning of a passage, but it will also recognize that when a text is read, not in isolation (which is essentially what historical criticism does) but within the context of the canon, in juxtaposition with other texts, it may take on a 'fuller sense'.[44] Old Testament texts, for example, may have a historical

---

[40] Cf. the titles of Goldsworthy's book, *Preaching the Whole Bible as Christian Scripture* ,and of Clowney's essay, 'Preaching Christ From All the Scriptures'.

[41] For a fuller discussion see Scobie, *Ways*, 100–101, and chs. 2 and 3.

[42] Cf. the work of Northrup Frye, esp. *Great Code*.

[43] See esp. the strong challenge to this position by Steinmetz, 'Superiority'.

[44] Vanhoozer emphasizes that this takes place at the level of the canon: 'The canon is a complete and completed communicative act, structured by a divine authorial intention. *The divine intention does not contravene the intention of the human author but rather supervenes on it.*' Thus, for example, when the NT identifies the Suffering Servant of

meaning, but within the total context of the canon Old Testament persons or events may function as types or prefigurings of Christ.[45]

Sixthly, some scholars emphasize that this type of biblical theology essentially summarizes the teaching of Scripture, still employing scriptural language and terminology. It must be emphasized, however, that no claim is being made that such a biblical theology is a purely descriptive discipline, solely concerned with what the Bible 'meant'. Biblical theologians also have their presuppositions, which have to be continually tested. As a stage in the process of biblical interpretation, biblical theology is concerned with both what the text 'meant' and with what it 'means'.[46]

Finally, what is proposed here involves more than 'intertextuality' in the sense of reading a passage in the light of related passages elsewhere in Scripture, and more than tracing individual themes through the Bible – extremely valuable though such studies may be, not least for the preacher who wants to preach on an individual topic. Biblical theology, if it is truly to serve as a bridge to theology and ethics and hence to homiletics, must shed light on the overall structure of biblical thought and identify its overarching unity; it must therefore be structured in accordance with the overall structure of Scripture itself. It is critical that such a structure arise from within the biblical material, and not be imposed from the outside. On the other hand it does not necessarily require the selection of one 'centre' to which all else must be related; at best biblical theology should identify a cluster of major themes to which minor themes may be related.[47]

It will be observed that the type of biblical theology sketched here in some respects resembles pre-critical approaches. The aim of identifying the overarching unity of Scripture, despite its manifest diversity, is at least as old as Irenaeus (one of the earliest biblical theologians), who employed the concept of the divine *oikonomia* as a key to co-ordinating the divine self-revelation in the Scriptures. The church fathers and medieval exegetes recognized different levels of meaning in Scripture so that, despite the excesses of allegorization, in some respects they were closer to understanding how Scripture can be the word of God for believers than modern exegetes, who rely solely on the

---

Isaiah 53 with Christ, 'the canon does not change or contradict the meaning of Isaiah 53 but supervenes on it and specifies its referent' (Vanhoozer, *Meaning*, 265).

[45] See the discussion by Wells of the role of 'figural representation' in constructing 'a biblical theology of the whole canon'. Wells argues that 'intertextual figural interpretation is not a method of interpretation brought to the text but a method of composition within the text' ('Figural Representation', 114).

[46] Cf. Hagner, 'Biblical Theology', 138.

[47] I have discussed the question of the structure of biblical theology in *Ways*, 81–102. Cf. also Osborne's remarks on 'The Problem of a Unifying Center' in *Hermeneutical Spiral*, 282–84.

historical-critical method.[48] Interpreting Scripture in terms of an overarching unity which finds its centre in the Christ event echoes Reformation hermeneutical principles including *scriptura sui ipsius interpres* ('Scripture is its own interpreter'). It must be emphasized, however, that the type of biblical theology outlined here is far from a reversion to a pre-critical position. It recognizes the necessity of a sound historical approach and it builds on the huge amount of work done by historical scholars in illuminating the meaning of the biblical text. However, in light of the current crisis of interpretation, it seeks to advance towards a post-critical hermeneutical methodology that seeks to recover some valid earlier insights, though applying them in a new situation.

Biblical Theology and Preaching

Biblical theology should play a key role in preaching as the preacher seeks to move from what a text meant in its original historical setting to what it means for those who hear the sermon today. Given that sermons are usually based on an individual text or short passage of Scripture, it is essential to place the text in its true context and, as Adam argues,

> to place a text in context we must identify its *literary context* in the book, its *theological context* in the writings of the author, and the *historical context* of the book. Then to place a text in the context of the whole biblical revelation will involve understanding its *context in OT or NT theology*, its *context in God's progressive revelation* within each period of salvation history, and its *context in biblical theology.*[49]

For example, the Gospel for the fourth Sunday after Epiphany, Year A is Matthew's version of the Beatitudes (Mt. 5:1–12).[50] The danger of treating this passage in isolation is that it may be read as a list of 'entrance qualifications' for the kingdom: those who attain to the qualities listed will be rewarded by the promised blessings. It is essential, therefore, that the passage be read in the context of the Gospel as a whole: the Beatitudes are addressed to the disciples (Mt. 5:1) and more generally to all who have responded to Jesus' proclamation and inauguration of the kingdom. Indeed, interpretation of the passage should be set in the context of a complete biblical theology of blessing that would go back to the OT roots of the *'ashrê* formula ('Blessed are ...'). There is continuity in the theology of blessing, but there is also discontinuity since Jesus' Beatitudes in some ways turn the OT idea of blessing upside down.

Luke's version of four Beatitudes plus four woes (Lk. 6:20–26) is part of the Gospel for the sixth Sunday after Epiphany, Year C, where it is aligned with

---

[48] See esp. Steinmetz, 'Superiority'.

[49] Adam, 'Preaching', 107.

[50] References are to the widely used Revised Common Lectionary (1992).

Psalm 1 and Jeremiah 17:5–10. The danger of Psalm 1, with its double refer-ence to 'law' in connection with the righteous, is that this could open the door for an approach (still not unknown today) that sees the OT as a religion of law: those who obey God's Torah will be rewarded by his blessing, and vice versa. In the context of a sound biblical theology, however, interpretation of the psalm would begin with the recognition that in the OT, as in the NT, God is first and foremost a God of grace. God took the initiative, redeemed his people from slavery and offered them a covenant relationship in which Torah consti-tutes the guidelines for a life lived in glad and willing response to God's grace. Incidentally this is clearer in Micah 6:1–8, the OT reading paired with Mat-thew's Beatitudes: this passage details what God has done for Israel before spec-ifying 'what the LORD requires of you'.

'Topical' sermons, which begin with a contemporary issue or problem, are particularly difficult and demanding. There is a real danger that preachers will bring their own particular political, social or ethical viewpoint to the topic and then look for a text, or handful of texts, on which to hang their opinions. As far as is possible within the bounds of a sermon, preachers must make a real attempt to examine all of the key biblical passages on the topic, or at least a cross-section of them. 'To do this the preacher needs biblical theology, which can place each relevant text in its theological context in the light of the whole Bible.'[51]

For example, a sermon on 'healing' would of course cite Jesus' healings and point to a passage such as James 5:13–16, which encourages prayers for healing. But a well-rounded biblical theology of healing would also point to passages in both the OT (2 Sam. 12:15–19) and NT (2 Cor. 12:7–10) where prayers for healing did not result in a cure, and would seek to reconcile these apparent contradictions. To give another example, a sermon on capital punishment could not possibly be based on individual texts, but could only be tackled in the context of a comprehensive understanding of biblical ethics (something which must stand in a close relationship to biblical theology). Thus OT passages that prescribe the death penalty for a whole range of offences would have to be bal-anced against the narratives of God's treatment of Cain, Moses and David (all murderers), as well as related to the attitude of Jesus revealed in John 7:53 – 8:11.

Biblical theology will play a particularly important role in preaching from the OT. The great majority of Christian sermons are probably preached from NT texts (even use of a lectionary does not guarantee that the sermon will be based on, or even refer to, the OT selection). Greidanus has boldly argued the case for 'preaching Christ from the Old Testament'.[52] Goldsworthy reminds us

---

[51] Adam, 'Preaching', 109. He adds a warning that 'inexperienced preachers should not preach topical sermons'.

[52] See Greidanus, *Preaching*, 33–67.

that 'Jesus is the goal and fulfillment of the whole Old Testament, and, as the embodiment of the truth of God, he is the interpretative key to the Bible'.[53] The temptation to tackle difficult OT texts by allegorizing is perhaps not as great today as it once was, but the temptation is strong to moralize or to preach on OT characters as examples (which most of them were not!). Only a comprehensive biblical theology will show how not just a few isolated 'messianic proof texts', but indeed the whole OT, is to be seen as part of a progressive revelation in which God, the Creator and Ruler of all, in his dealings with his people prepares the way for the Christ event which forms the centre of Scripture.[54] The OT *proclaims* what God has done in creation and in history, but again and again it also holds out the *promise* of a future action of God on behalf of his people and of his world. The shape of the OT canon, with the prophetic books at the end, gives it an open-ended character. The NT proclaims the *fulfilment* of the promise in the Christ event, though it also looks towards a future and final *consummation*. This basic structure of biblical theology provides a hermeneutical key to the relationship between the Testaments,[55] a relationship in which the categories of progressive revelation, salvation history, promise-fulfilment, typology[56] and continuity–contrast all have a role to play. Preaching from the OT must operate within this theological framework and must always point towards the Christ event as the centre and high point of the biblical revelation.

Limitations of space forbid all but a few illustrations of how biblical theology can impact and inform preaching. In an extended discussion of 'The Practical Application of Biblical Theology to Preaching' Goldsworthy suggests how one might approach preaching from each of the major literary genres of the Bible.[57]

Conclusion

Christian preaching is surely one of the most difficult and demanding tasks required of any member of the community of faith today. As a form of biblical interpretation it raises profound and challenging hermeneutical questions.

---

[53] Goldsworthy, *Preaching*, 33.

[54] See Clowney, 'Preaching', 166.

[55] For a helpful recent discussion of the main hermeneutical categories relating Old and New Testaments, from the viewpoint of preaching, see Greidanus, *Preaching*, 227–77.

[56] On typology as a valid component in biblical theology see Clowney, 'Preaching', 174–83; Greidanus, *Preaching*, 249–61.

[57] Goldsworthy, *Preaching*, 140–244.

Unfortunately, the abundant literature on preaching tends to focus on the preparation, construction and delivery of sermons, on providing 'twenty steps to effective preaching'. It is seldom that such works recognize and tackle the fundamental hermeneutical problems and the challenges they pose in the postmodern context.

Conversely, however, the vigorous contemporary debate over hermeneutics, while of necessity academic (in a good sense) in nature, is always in danger of becoming academic (in a pejorative sense) and failing to take sufficient account of the actual contexts in which biblical interpretation takes place – preaching being a prime example.

In short, homiletics needs to focus more on hermeneutics, and hermeneutics needs to focus more on homiletics. More lines of communication need to be opened up and dialogue encouraged. In this dialogue, a canonical biblical theology has an important role to play – though more needs to be done to determine the relationship between a historical approach to Scripture and biblical theology on the one hand, and between biblical theology and determining the significance of the text for modern hearers on the other hand.

Bibliography

Adam, P.J.H., 'Preaching and Biblical Theology', in *New Dictionary of Biblical Theology* (ed. T.D. Alexander and B.S. Rosner; Downers Grove, IL: InterVarsity Press, 2000), 104–12

Bartholomew, C., C. Greene and K. Möller (eds.), *Renewing Biblical Interpretation* (SHS 1; Carlisle: Paternoster; Grand Rapids: Zondervan, 2000)

Clowney, E.P., 'Preaching Christ From All the Scriptures', in *The Preacher and Preaching: Reviving the Art in the Twentieth Century* (ed. S.T. Logan; Phillipsburg: Presbyterian and Reformed Publishing, 1986), 163–91

Corley, B., S. Lemke and G. Lovejoy (eds.), *Biblical Hermeneutics: A Comprehensive Introduction to Interpreting Scripture* (Nashville: Broadman, 1996)

Davis, C., 'The Theological Career of Historical Criticism of the Bible', *CC* 32 (1982), 267–84

Ferguson, D.S., *Biblical Hermeneutics: An Introduction* (London: SCM Press, 1986)

Fish, S.E., *Is There a Text in This Class? The Authority of Interpretive Communities* (Cambridge: Harvard University Press, 1980)

Fowl, S.E., 'The Conceptual Structure of New Testament Theology', in *Biblical Theology: Retrospect and Prospect* (ed. S.J. Hafemann; Leicester: Apollos; Downers Grove, IL: InterVarsity Press, 2002), 225–36

Freeman, H., 'Biblical Criticism and Biblical Preaching', in *Biblical Hermeneutics: A Comprehensive Introduction to Interpreting Scripture* (ed. B. Corley, S. Lemke and G. Lovejoy; Nashville: Broadman, 1996), 307–17

Frye, N., *The Great Code: The Bible and Literature* (Toronto: Academie, 1981)

Goldsworthy, G., *Preaching the Whole Bible as Christian Scripture* (Grand Rapids: Eerdmans, 2000)

—, 'Biblical Theology as the Heartbeat of Effective Ministry', in *Biblical Theology: Retrospect and Prospect* (ed. S.J. Hafemann; Leicester: Apollos; Downers Grove, IL: InterVarsity Press, 2002), 280–86

Greidanus, S., *Preaching Christ from the Old Testament: A Contemporary Hermeneutical Method* (Grand Rapids: Eerdmans, 1999)

Hafemann, S.J. (ed.), *Biblical Theology: Retrospect and Prospect* (Leicester: Apollos; Downers Grove, IL: InterVarsity Press, 2002)

Hagner, D.A., 'Biblical Theology and Preaching', *ExpTim* 96 (1985), 137–41

Hanson, P., 'The Responsibility of Biblical Theology to Communities of Faith', *ThTo* 37 (1980), 39–50

Houlden, L., 'Is the Bible Still There?', *Theol* 89 (1986), 87–89

Krabbendam, H., 'Hermeneutics and Preaching', in *The Preacher and Preaching: Reviving the Art in the Twentieth Century* (ed. S.T. Logan; Phillipsburg: Presbyterian and Reformed Publishing, 1986), 212–45

Krentz, E., *The Historical-Critical Method* (Philadelphia: Fortress Press, 1975)

Logan, S.T. (ed.), *The Preacher and Preaching: Reviving the Art in the Twentieth Century* (Phillipsburg: Presbyterian and Reformed Publishing, 1986)

Morgan, R., *The Nature of New Testament Theology* (London: SCM Press, 1973)

Osborne, G.R., *The Hermeneutical Spiral: A Comprehensive Introduction to Biblical Interpretation* (Downers Grove, IL: InterVarsity Press, 1991)

Rosner, B.S., 'Biblical Theology', in *New Dictionary of Biblical Theology* (ed. T.D. Alexander and B.S. Rosner; Downers Grove, IL: InterVarsity Press, 2000), 3–11

Sanchez, D., 'Contextualization in the Hermeneutical Process', in *Biblical Hermeneutics: A Comprehensive Introduction to Interpreting Scripture* (ed. B. Corley, S. Lemke and G. Lovejoy; Nashville: Broadman, 1996), 293–306

Scobie, C.H.H., *The Ways of our God: An Approach to Biblical Theology* (Grand Rapids: Eerdmans, 2003)

Steinmetz, D.C., 'The Superiority of Pre-Critical Exegesis', *ThTo* 37 (1980), 27–38

Vanhoozer, K.J., *Is There a Meaning in This Text?* (Grand Rapids: Zondervan, 1998)

Wells, M.J., 'Figural Representation and Canonical Unity', in *Biblical Theology: Retrospect and Prospect* (ed. S.J. Hafemann; Leicester: Apollos; Downers Grove, IL: InterVarsity Press, 2002), 111–25

Wolters, A., 'Confessional Criticism and the Night Visions of Zechariah', in *Renewing Biblical Interpretation* (ed. C. Bartholomew, C. Greene and K. Möller; SHS 1; Carlisle: Paternoster; Grand Rapids: Zondervan, 2000), 90–117

University of Gloucestershire

In 1997 when Craig Bartholomew began to propose, with colleagues, a ten-year project on Scripture and Hermeneutics, it seemed to be an ambitious idea. Indeed, it was ambitious! To engage busy scholars from a variety of disciplines, based in various countries, in extra writing and draw them together for a few days of concentrated debate and exploration was a visionary proposal.

However, from the beginning the Cheltenham and Gloucester College of Higher Education (University of Gloucestershire since 2001) supported the plan. We gladly recognize the outstanding leadership given to the Seminar by Craig Bartholomew, and are pleased that he is continuing in this role as part of his work at Redeemer University College, Ancaster, Canada. Our links with Redeemer University College are not new, having held the 2000 Scripture and Hermeneutics Consultation there, but we look forward to developing further our relationship with Redeemer University College.

The publication of volume 5, *Out of Egypt: Biblical Theology and Biblical Interpretation* is a significant landmark. Biblical theology is vital to the life of Christian scholars and the wider church and we gratefully acknowledge the hard work of the contributors and editors. Also, volume 5 indicates the continuing validity of the Scripture and Hermeneutics Seminar and signals its capacity to continue with the publication of the planned three further volumes in 2005–7.

Throughout the life of the Seminar, we have been pleased to work in partnership with the British and Foreign Bible Society and more recently Baylor University. The University looks forward to participating fully in the future work of the Seminar.

Dr Fred Hughes
School of Humanities
University of Gloucestershire
Francis Close Hall
Swindon Road, Cheltenham, Gloucestershire GL50 4AZ
UK

www.glos.ac.uk/humanities/content.asp?rid=14

The British and Foreign Bible Society

Two hundred years on from the founding of the British and Foreign Bible Society, the task of encouraging the translation, distribution and use of the Bible remains undiminished. It is as vital for this generation's human flourishing as it was for our nineteenth-century forebears. Much of Bible Society's current work is predicated on the notion that a credible church needs a credible Bible and a credible Bible needs a credible church. Some recent research commissioned by Bible Society (the Biblos Project, 2003/4, at Exeter University) into the attitudes of young people towards the Bible shows that they are indifferent to it rather than hostile, not sure how it fits with twenty-first century culture. If the church is to present the Bible confidently to a doubtful world then the hermeneutical task becomes all the more urgent. Ideas have legs! It will only be a matter of time before the scholarship generated by the Scripture and Hermeneutics Project begins to impact the use of the Bible in the church and beyond with the necessary greater confidence born of deeper understanding.

In sponsoring the seminars and published volumes and helping to grow a unique interdisciplinary network of scholars from all over the world, Bible Society believes that it is making a valuable contribution to the Academy and to the church that will have an impact far beyond the life of the project. Education is one of the four cultural drivers that we are seeking to use to make the Bible heard. The Scripture and Hermeneutics Project is one of four Higher Education initiatives that are not only using education as a channel but are affecting the very way in which the academic world works with the Bible. This is our dual intention.

Volume 5, *Out of Egypt : Biblical Theology and Biblical Interpretation*, promises to be a rich resource flowing out of the serious discussions between the eminent contributors committed to applying their understandings derived from their work in biblical theology to hermeneutical issues. As with the other volumes, Bible Society is pleased to commend this one as we continue to be convinced of the importance of this work and our support for such a constructive partnership, to which we now welcome Redeemer University College in Ancaster, Ontario, Canada as one of the sponsoring partners.

Ann Holt
Partnerships and Development Executive
British and Foreign Bible Society
Stonehill Green
Westlea
Swindon
Wiltshire, SN5 7DG
UK

Baylor University

Baylor University is honoured to be able to join with the British and Foreign Bible Society, the University of Gloucestershire and Redeemer University College in supporting the Scripture and Hermeneutics Seminar as a North American partner. As a university community with 157 years of commitment to Christian higher education, we are deeply interested in the kinds of issues the Seminar pursues. As the largest Baptist university in the world, we have a particular interest in the themes of the present volume – biblical theology and its relation to biblical interpretation – since Baptists have always believed that the Bible is central for Christians, not just for theology but for the whole of Christian intellectual life and indeed for Christian existence in its entirety.

It is fitting and proper that this inquiry into biblical theology and biblical interpretation be interdisciplinary in character. Interdisciplinary scholarship is an increasingly necessary and highly productive feature of academic life generally, and it is particularly important when the goal is to produce theology and biblical interpretation that will support the life of the church. A Christian university such as Baylor places particular value on such work, and we strive to make Baylor a place where it is encouraged. We relish occasions during which Christian philosophers can talk with biblical scholars, theologians, missiologists, social scientists and other intellectuals concerned about the vitality of Christian faith in the contemporary world.

We congratulate the editors and contributors to the present volume on the vigour and quality of their exchange of views. This volume makes evident that biblical theology should not be identified with the so-called biblical theology movement, widely thought to have met its demise in the early sixties of the last century. Rather, biblical theology is an enterprise that has always been and should always be central to the intellectual life of Christian scholars. We look forward to working with the Seminar in the years ahead and to hosting a future Consultation here on the campus at Baylor University.

David Lyle Jeffrey, Distinguished Professor of Literature and
Humanities and Provost
C. Stephen Evans, University Professor of Philosophy and Humanities
Baylor University
One Bear Place
P.O. Box 97404
Waco, Texas 76798–7404, USA

Redeemer University College

Redeemer University College is honoured to have become the Canadian home to the Scripture and Hermeneutics Project since the Rev Dr Craig Bartholomew, Director of the Scripture and Hermeneutics Project, took up our endowed chair as the H. Evan Runner Professor of Philosophy and Professor of Religion and Theology. We are glad to serve with Baylor University as the North American representatives for this important international project. Redeemer University College has been associated with this project from an early date and hosted the Consultation of 2000. This scholarly undertaking is of one piece with the mission of Redeemer.

Redeemer University College – a Reformed Christian university – is young but is deeply rooted in a very old tradition of Christian scholarship. Like the Church Father, Irenaeus, in the second century, and John Calvin in the sixteenth century, we emphasize the unity of the biblical story, that the Old and New Testaments are one unified account of God's revelation. Like Hilary of Poitiers in the fourth century, we value the imagination to retell the biblical story in engagement with the newest intellectual developments in our culture. For this reason, we are deeply grateful for the Scripture and Hermeneutics Project. We recognize in it the spirit of the Church Fathers who, standing firmly on the creeds of the church, were not afraid to interact vigorously with the best minds of their culture. We applaud the publication of this fifth volume on biblical theology and hermeneutics which we cheer as carrying forward that essential project of cultural engagement.

Jacob P. Ellens, PhD,
Vice-President (Academic)
Redeemer University College
Ancaster
Ontario
Canada

Scripture Index

Names Index

Subject Index